Competition Law and Policy in the EU and UK

Competition Law and Policy in the EU and UK provides a clear guide to the general policies behind and the main provisions of EU and UK competition law, including topics such as private enforcement, anti-competitive agreements, cartels, mergers, and market investigations.

The book's contents are tailored to cover all major topics in competition law, and the authors' clear and accessible writing style offers an engaging and easy to follow overview of the subject for course use. New features to help clarify topics and reinforce key points include:

- **chapter overviews and summaries** highlight the key points to take away from each chapter to structure student learning;
- **discussion questions** facilitate self-testing and seminar discussions of the major issues covered in each chapter, to help reinforce understanding of these topics;
- **further reading** lists additional resources in order to guide research and develop subject knowledge.

The fifth edition of this textbook has been revised and updated to take into account all developments and changes in the law, presenting and contextualising the impact of key cases, and providing a useful glossary of competition terminology that will be invaluable to those studying this subject.

Barry J Rodger is a Professor at the Law School, University of Strathclyde.

Angus MacCulloch is a Senior Lecturer in Law at the Law School, Lancaster University.

Competition Law and Policy in the EU and UK

FIFTH EDITION

Barry J Rodger and Angus MacCulloch

Routledge
Taylor & Francis Group

LONDON AND NEW YORK

First published 2015
by Routledge
2 Park Square, Milton Park, Abingdon, Oxon, OX14 4RN

and by Routledge
711 Third Avenue, New York, NY 10017

Routledge is an imprint of the Taylor & Francis Group, an informa business

British Library Cataloguing in Publication Data
A catalogue record for this book is available from the British Library

Library of Congress Cataloging-in-Publication Data
A catalog record has been requested for this book

ISBN: 978-0-415-52456-8 (hbk)
ISBN: 978-0-415-53883-1 (pbk)
ISBN: 978-1-315-84853-2 (ebk)

Typeset in Times
by RefineCatch Limited, Bungay, Suffolk

MIX
Paper from
responsible sources
FSC
www.fsc.org   FSC® C013056

Printed and bound in Great Britain by
TJ International Ltd, Padstow, Cornwall

Contents

Acknowledgements

Thanks are due to all those who inspired, facilitated and helped on previous editions. In relation to the new edition, we both would specifically like to thank Liam Maclean for his excellent and assiduous work as a research assistant on various chapters. Barry would also like to thank his wife Susan, whose insight in refurbishing the study at home allowed him to spend several weeks cocooned there, finally undertaking the research and writing to update his contribution to the textbook. Angus would like to thank his family for their support during the final stress of 'the crunch'.

Table of Cases

Table of UK Legislation and International Legislation

Table of Statutory Instruments

Table of Decisions, Directives, Regulations, Treaties and Conventions

Directives

Regulations

Treaties

Preface

Competition law has changed considerably in the EU and UK in the sixteen years since the first edition of this student textbook. Even in the five years since the fourth edition, in addition to extensive new enforcement practice, 'soft law' and case law, we have witnessed further radical legislative and institutional reforms at both the EU and UK levels. As a result of these reforms, and because of changes in the structure of the book, which were inspired by developments in practice and our desire for the book to remain a focused 'one-stop shop' for undergraduate students taking a competition law course, this fifth edition is radically different in structure and content from the fourth edition. At the EU level, the ratification of the Treaty of Lisbon resulted in a new EU Treaty structure with the main competition rules on anti-competitive agreements and abuse of a dominant position now located, unchanged, in Articles 101 and 102 of the Treaty on the Functioning of the European Union ('TFEU'). In addition, following the Treaty of Lisbon, the 'Community' is now referred to as the 'Union' or 'EU', and the title of the book has changed accordingly. Throughout the text we have sought to use the new Treaty numbering and nomenclature (TFEU as opposed to EC Treaty, EU as opposed to Community), except where there are historical quotations from case law or academic literature. In the UK, the Enterprise and Regulatory Reform Act 2013 ('ERRA13') has made some minor revisions to substantive aspects of UK competition law, but has overhauled the institutional structure by introducing the unitary competition authority, the Competition and Markets Authority ('CMA'), to assume the competition law enforcement tasks previously undertaken by both the Office of Fair Trading and the Competition Commission as of 1 April 2014. At the time of writing, we are in a transitional phase between the two eras, but we will refer to the CMA throughout the text except in relation to examples of earlier enforcement practice (involving the OFT and/or the Competition Commission) and where there are historical quotations from case law or academic literature. Moreover, further reform of UK competition law, in relation to aspects of 'private enforcement', will occur when the Consumer Rights Bill is passed by Parliament.

The chapter structure has been radically altered in this edition. In order to ensure that the book provides focused reading on the key, core competition institutions, laws and practices, we decided that it was appropriate to jettison the old Chapter 8 (Overview: policy developments and practical implications), which was under-utilised by students and lecturers. The material has been subsumed within the appropriate chapters. Moreover, we noted that in many institutions there are specialist in-depth courses dealing with the multifarious, vexed and complicated ways in which competition law may apply to the relationship between States and markets, notably through the State aid rules, and we consider that these issues merit separate and fuller treatment than could be offered in a short chapter. Accordingly, the chapter on State aid and State regulation has been excised from this edition, which focuses on the application of the competition rules to undertakings operating on markets (although this indeed can extend to economic activities by public undertakings, as discussed in Chapter 3). Nonetheless, there is brief discussion of the interaction between State intervention on markets in relation to the application of Articles 101 and 102 TFEU in Chapters 4 and 6. Just as the fourth edition introduced a new chapter focusing on cartels (now Chapter 7), to reflect prioritisation of public enforcement in this area, this fifth edition introduces a completely new Chapter 3, on private enforcement, an area where there has been considerable case law and which is the focus of policy and legislative developments by the competition authorities at both the EU and UK levels. Furthermore, the unique system of market investigations in the UK, subject to important institutional reform by the ERRA13, has been given its own chapter (Chapter 5). Although historically known by the misnomer of 'monopoly' investigations, this set of provisions really has little in common with the prohibitions on the abuse of dominance discussed in Chapter 4, and merited separate treatment. As in previous editions, each chapter concludes with discussion points and considerable (updated) further reading for students seeking to explore aspects of the material in each chapter in greater depth. In order to enhance student experience and learning, each chapter has also been supplemented with an initial overview of the topic and a summary of the key points at the end of the chapter to lead into the discussion issues. We hope and trust that the significant structural and textual changes to this edition will ensure that it is an excellent, focused and helpful companion for the lecturers and students on a typical undergraduate competition law course. It should also act as a basic primer for PG students and practitioners.

Another innovation for this edition is our commitment to support the text in the dynamic competition law environment. Where there are significant legal developments that we consider worthy of note, we will use Angus's blog, 'Who's Competing?' <whoscompeting.wordpress.com>, to update readers on those developments, and we will indicate where in relation to the text those developments should be considered.

Chapter 1

Introduction to Competition Policy and Practice

Chapter Contents

Overview

- Competition law concerns intervention in a market where there is 'market failure': through either the action of a monopolist, an anti-competitive agreement, or a merger.
- All the concerns of competition law stem from the neoclassical economic model of monopoly (which we refer to as the 'pure competition objective') which indicates that a monopolist can exploit its position to earn a supra-competitive profit at the expense of consumer welfare. A profit-maximising monopolist would reduce output to increase prices, and also reduce allocative and productive efficiency. Such behaviour would create a deadweight loss for the whole economy.
- Competition policy may feature a range of policy objectives which can be employed alongside the core economic concern of consumer welfare. These include: concentration of economic power, wealth distribution, consumer protection, regional policy, and market integration.
- All competition regimes have their own historical and social context which shapes them. Each regime can only be understood in that context as policy develops over time, affected by the changing economic and political climate within each jurisdiction.

Competition Law Background

Competition law concerns intervention in the marketplace when there is some problem with the competitive process or when there is 'market failure'. This broad generalisation needs to be clarified in two respects.

Firstly, public authority intervention has traditionally been the dominant mode of competition law enforcement. However, although competition law has generally been enforced administratively by national or European Union regulatory authorities intervening in markets, there has been a more recent development, towards private enforcement of competition laws through regular court processes.[1] Nonetheless, it is difficult to equate competition law with other areas of law, such as the law of contract or delict/tort, which rely almost exclusively on adjudication by normal court processes. Administrative enforcement of competition law is currently still the norm, although we have to be aware of developments in private enforcement of competition law 'rights' in the courts, particularly following the 'modernisation' of European Union law[2] and recent reforms of UK competition law.

Secondly, the broad definition does not really clarify exactly what kinds of ills competition law seeks to remedy. In order to explain and understand the role of competition law more fully, one should assess what is meant by a failure in competition or the competitive process. This must also be considered in its appropriate context. We must ask whether all systems of competition law consider the same types of conduct or market result to be a 'market failure' and anti-competitive. The basic answer is no; this will become apparent on closer analysis of the respective roles that economics and politics play in competition law, as well as the different concerns of the principal legal systems to be considered.

It is possible at this introductory stage to outline broadly the types of issues that competition law will be concerned with, although the policies and specific rules adopted in various legal

---

1   See, further, in Chapter 2. US antitrust law is particularly distinctive in that it relies more heavily on private enforcement in the courts.
2   Hereinafter referred to as the EU or the Union. References in pre-Lisbon Treaty material may still refer to the European Community or the Community.

systems may differ. The following are the key issues concerning competition law which will be addressed in this book.

Monopoly

In strict economic terms, a monopoly is a market in which one company or business controls 100% of the market.[3] In practice, this situation is very rare. However, competition law is also interested in businesses with smaller, but still significant, market shares which enable such businesses to have power or influence over the market. For instance, the term adopted in EU law and the Competition Act 1998 is that of an 'undertaking' with a 'dominant position',[4] whereas s 2 of the Sherman Act 1890 in the USA applies to 'every person who shall monopolise, or attempt to monopolise' trade or commerce. The general concern in these situations is that the 'monopolist' will exploit its power over the market and act anti-competitively.[5]

Cartels

This is a non-technical term for various forms of co-operation between companies, which may be prohibited by competition law. In everyday use, 'cartel' signifies a group of conspirators pooling their production resources. Readers may be aware of the OPEC oil cartel as an example of such behaviour. The 'cartel' phenomenon is usually dealt with under competition law provisions regarding anti-competitive agreements, although looser collaborations[6] are also considered under this broad heading.[7] The main concern, in relation to competition, is that a group of producers will conspire or agree to act together and, in effect, will collectively carry the same threat to competition as a monopolist. In recent years, supported by the moral argument that cartelisation be equated with other behaviour where companies are effectively 'ripping off' consumers by fixing high prices, competition authorities worldwide have focused their enforcement on major cartels and have imposed very considerable fines.

Mergers

This covers the situation where two companies, and their respective shareholders, have agreed on some form of union between them. It also includes hostile takeovers, where the takeover by a 'predator' company has been resisted by the 'target' company. It should be emphasised, however, that competition law is not concerned with shareholder welfare or interests. There are a wide variety of types of merger that may provoke different concerns, but there is a general consensus that the principal focus of competition law should be on the effect that the merger has on competition in the market. The basic concern is that two or more companies can achieve a position akin to that of a monopolist by formally merging their companies. It should be noted here that, probably to a greater extent than with either monopoly or cartel control, mergers may directly impact on politically sensitive 'public interest' issues, such as the resultant loss of jobs and, accordingly, competition law merger controls may not focus solely on the competitive impact of any merger.

---

3   We shall return to the complex issue of the determination of what constitutes a particular market in Chapter 4.

4   See, further, in this chapter and also the detailed consideration of Art 102 under EU law and the Chapter II prohibition under UK law in Chapter 6.

5   The economic concern with monopolies will be addressed more fully in this chapter. The idea of what constitutes exploitation or anti-competitive behaviour will also be addressed in outline in this chapter and further reference should also be made to consideration of the particular EU and UK rules in Chapter 6.

6   See, further, Chapter 7.

7   See, further, Chapters 7 and 8.

The objective(s) of competition law

Monopoly, cartels and mergers are the three principal issues of interest for most competition law systems. The concern with the potential anti-competitive market consequences of a monopoly situation is the unifying link between the three issues. In other words, the primary concern with cartels and mergers between competitors is that they will in effect achieve a monopoly position, dominate the market and exploit their position as an anti-competitive monopolist would be expected to do.[8] We consider the 'pure competition' objective in competition law to be this concern with monopoly and neoclassical economic theory's prediction of the negative consequences of a monopolistic market.

However, things are not as simple as they may seem. First, virtually no competition law system bans monopolies outright. Such an outcome would seem to be the logical consequence of reliance on the pure competition objective. As very few companies have a true monopoly position, reliance on this pure competition objective is not realistic. Rather, the debate has focused on the situations under which a powerful market player's behaviour may be declared anti-competitive and unlawful. A key factor in many jurisdictions, in particular in the USA, is whether or not a powerful market player's behaviour is efficient; this is certainly not the same as the pure competition objective. Cartels tend to be prohibited, particularly where they fix prices between competitors, even where the companies combined do not have monopoly power. In addition, some restrictions placed upon a retailer by a producer of goods may be caught by some competition law systems even though they do not seek to create a traditional type of monopoly. These are known as vertical restraints. Merger control can appear to reflect the pure competition objective in that a merger may be blocked when it threatens to create a greater degree of concentration in the market. Nonetheless, similar to the position with a single powerful market player, pro-efficiency arguments in favour of the merger may counterbalance such concerns. Furthermore, there are also a range of other objectives that may be embodied in the legal rules.[9] To conclude, the core concern with competition as an objective exists within all systems of competition law, through analysis of the degree of concentration in markets, but it will also be applied in tandem with other policy objectives. The potential for economic analysis and political input into competition controls shall be examined in more detail later in this chapter.

Practical examples

Understanding these basic problem issues is assisted by a consideration of practical examples, and readers may note that competition-related issues are reported daily in the press, particularly in the *Financial Times*. Readers should be aware that competition law has directly affected the pricing and availability of goods and services, such as petrol, milk, cheese, electrical and electronic goods, ice cream, bananas, beer, contraceptive sheaths, cigarettes, breakfast cereals, perfume, tampons, estate agents, air travel, travel agents, banking services, Coca-Cola, whisky, cars, CDs and DVDs, TV rights for football, replica football strips, children's board games, video games and vitamins. Competition law and policy, therefore, have a direct impact upon all our daily lives.

Monopoly

This concept could be more readily associated with the pre-privatisation nationalised industries, such as British Gas and British Telecom. Although competition has been introduced in both

---

8   The economic analysis of monopoly will be discussed shortly in this chapter.
9   See, further, below in this chapter.

industries, both remain in a particularly strong position in their markets.[10] In recent years there have also been allegations that British Airways has used its strong market position unfairly to competitors' detriment. For instance, BA was fined by the European Commission in respect of its unlawful incentive scheme for travel agents.[11] Microsoft has been the subject of antitrust law litigation in the USA and was fined €497m by the European Commission in relation to its Windows operation system, and required to provide vital interoperability information to its competitors.[12] On a more localised level, UK competition law authorities have in the past monitored the behaviour of Stagecoach Holdings plc in various local areas, particularly in regard to allegations of price-cutting to force out actual and potential competitors.[13] The Competition Appeal Tribunal (CAT) in the UK also held that refusal to allow access by a rival local firm of funeral directors to a crematorium constituted an abuse of a dominant position.[14]

Cartels

The most obvious historical examples, in a UK context, concern agreements to fix prices of two products: books and drugs. The Net Book Agreement (NBA) raised particular controversy in 1995. The NBA was a long-standing agreement by book publishers to set prices for their titles for up to six months after their publication. This agreement had been approved by the UK competition authorities under the restrictive trade practices legislation. Although its approval would appear to be contrary to anti-cartel type laws, the approval highlights the different interests and policies that can operate under competition law in different periods. In this case, the cultural argument was that price-fixing under the NBA allowed a wide range of books to be stocked by small as well as by large shops, thus encouraging new writers. In 1995, certain publishers withdrew from the NBA, and the NBA was subsequently declared unlawful by both the UK[15] and EU authorities. Similar arguments and developments were noted in relation to the resale price maintenance agreement for non-prescription drugs, which Asda breached in 1996 to sell cut-price branded drugs.

Over the last ten years EU competition law enforcement has focused on cartels, which increase prices considerably for consumers across the European market. The European Commission has fined companies involved in cartels in a number of industries, particularly those with homogeneous products, in which there is no difference between the products of different suppliers, where price fixing is easier to maintain. For example, it began an investigation, in May 1999, into eight distinct cartels concerning market sharing and price-fixing agreements in vitamin markets. On 21 November 2001,[16] the Commission found that thirteen companies had participated in these cartels between September 1989 and February 1999 with the aim of eliminating competition. As a result, eight of the companies were fined a total of €855.22m. Hoffmann-La Roche and BASF were subject to particular criticism for their roles and individually fined €462m and €296.16m, respectively. The same companies were also subject to antitrust investigation in

---

10 Regulation of the privatised utilities forms a distinct set of regulatory controls which will not be dealt with in this book. See, generally, Ogus, A, *Regulation: Legal Form and Economic Theory* (1994) Oxford: Clarendon. See, also, Robinson, C, *Utility Regulation in Competitive Markets: Problems and Progress* (2007) London: Edward Elgar.

11 Commission Decision 2000/74/EC *Virgin/British Airways* [2000] OJ L30/1. Confirmed on appeal by the CFI in Case T-219/99 [2003] ECR II-5917, and subsequently by the ECJ in Case C-95/04 P [2007] ECR I-2331.

12 Commission Decision 2007/53/EC *Microsoft* [2007] OJ L32/23. Because of Microsoft's failure to comply with the 2004 Decision, the penalties increased to €1.4bn; see Commission Press Release IP/08/318, Antitrust: Commission imposes €899 million penalty on Microsoft for noncompliance with March 2004 Decision, 27 February 2008.

13 See discussion of this tactic, known as 'predatory pricing', in Chapter 6.

14 *Burgess and Sons v OFT* [2005] CAT 25.

15 This illustrates the change in emphasis on different policy goals within the same framework of competition rules over a period of 30 years.

16 IP/01/1625.

the US, resulting in fines for the companies, and individual fines and imprisonment for several senior-level directors involved in the cartel.

The case also serves to illustrate the use of a key tool in competition law enforcement by the European Commission (and the US antitrust authorities), namely by encouraging whistle-blowing by the offer of leniency in relation to fines for infringements of competition law.[17] In the vitamins case, Aventis (formerly Rhône-Poulenc) was granted full immunity with regard to its participation in two of the eight cartels because it was the first company to co-operate with the Commission and it provided decisive evidence relating to those two cartels. By encouraging whistle-blowing, the Commission can destabilise ongoing cartels and potentially become a more effective and efficient enforcer. However, the Commission cannot offer immunity from civil proceedings instigated by private parties as a result of the cartel activity; there is still litigation ongoing in relation to the vitamins cartel in various jurisdictions, including the UK. High-profile examples of the combined impact of the Commission's fining and leniency policies to police cartels were the fine of over €900m imposed in February 2007 on a number of companies involved in a European-wide cartel in relation to lifts and elevators[18] and the fine of €1.38bn imposed in 2008 on the Car Glass cartel;[19] both followed leniency applications by one of the companies involved.

In the late 1970s, there was prominent coverage of an alleged cartel in the airline industry. Sir Freddie Laker began operating a cheap rate, cost-cutting service between the UK and the US, a forerunner to today's budget airlines. Several years later, his company was forced out of business and he claimed that this was as a result of a conspiracy among other carriers, including British Airways, to collectively drop their fares. Litigation ensued in both the English and American courts.[20] Interestingly, British Airways was fined considerable sums more recently by both the US and UK competition authorities for its part in a cartel relating to fuel surcharges for consumers.[21] Given that Laker Airways was the forerunner to Richard Branson's Virgin Airways, it was somewhat ironic that the latter used the OFT leniency programme to confess, gain immunity from fines and ensure that BA was considered the blameworthy party in a cartel in which both were involved. Another example of UK cartel enforcement arose in September 2009, when 103 construction firms in the UK were fined £129.2m for their roles in a bid-rigging cartel in the UK construction industry.[22]

Vertical restraints are not strictly a cartel-type problem, but such agreements between companies have been subject to scrutiny by competition authorities and debate by competition practitioners and academics. A clear early example arose under Community law in relation to the marketing of Johnny Walker Red Label whisky in the 1970s. Distillers plc, who produced Johnny Walker, wanted to sell Red Label in France and, in order to protect distributors there, imposed an export ban on its UK distributors. This ban was declared contrary to the competition rules by the EU authorities,[23] and reflected a particular EU interest in maintaining the free flow of trade across Member State borders.[24] As a result, Distillers decided that Johnny Walker Red Label would no

---

17 See Commission Notice, [2006] OJ C298/1, replacing its earlier Leniency Notice of 2002.

18 Commission Decision, 21 February 2007, *PO/Elevators and Escalators* [2008] OJ C75/19. See Commission press release IP/07/209, 21 February 2007. Although, one of the companies' fines was reduced on appeal; see Cases T-141, 142, 145 and 146/07 *General Technic-Otis and Others v European Commission*, [2011] ECR II- 4977. A further appeal by another one of the infringing companies was, however, unsuccessful; see Case C-494/11P *Otis Luxembourg Sàrl v European Commission* [2012] ECR I-0000.

19 Commission Decision, 12 November 2008, *Car Glass* [2009] OJ C173/13. See Commission press release IP/08/1685, 12 November 2008.

20 *British Airways Board v Laker Airways Ltd* [1985] AC 58; and *Laker Airways v Pan American World Airways* [1984] ECC 296, District of Columbia.

21 See OFT Press Release 33/12, 'British Airways to pay £58.5m Penalty in OFT Fuel Surcharge Decision', 19 April 2012.

22 See OFT Press Releases 114/09, 22 September 2009, and 135/09, 20 November 2009. Many of these fines were subsequently reduced on appeal by the CAT.

23 Case 30/78 *Distillers Co Ltd v Commission* [1980] ECR 2229.

24 See, further, below in this chapter, regarding Community competition law objectives, and Chapter 4, on vertical restraints.

longer be sold in the UK, in order to protect Distillers' overseas distributors. This highlighted the dramatic effect that competition laws can produce. A more recent example was the condemnation by the Commission of the practice of 'freezer exclusivity' in Ireland, which restricted the access of potential competitors to the market for the supply of 'impulse' ice cream.[25] Generally, EU competition law now tends to focus less on vertical restraints, although price-fixing in the form of resale price maintenance is still condemned in the EU. There have been a number of examples of such practices being prohibited in the UK by the OFT; for instance in relation to price fixing of replica football shirts by the manufacturer Umbro, and a number of retailers, and an agreement between the UK retailers Argos and Littlewoods and toy manufacturer Hasbro to fix the prices of toys and games.[26] Ironically, the latter case involved the board game 'Monopoly'.

Mergers

Examples of competition law authorities' interest in mergers are numerous, and can range in scale from the very localised to the global. In the late 1980s, controversy arose, for a variety of reasons, during the protracted takeover by Guinness plc of Distillers plc, Guinness and Distillers being two major UK drinks companies. The UK merger controls played a significant, though ultimately limited, role in the process and eventually led to the takeover being permitted, subject to conditions. The affair also highlighted the potential conflict between a pure competition policy and other policy reasons for prohibiting mergers and takeovers.[27]

The 'old' UK system of merger control was also seen working during the late 1990s when the proposed takeover by BSkyB of Manchester United was blocked controversially following the recommendation of the Competition Commission (CC) that it would be against the public interest by limiting competition and exacerbating the unequal share of wealth in English football.[28]

In 2003 the Competition Commission (CC) investigated the proposed takeover of the supermarket chain Safeway by a number of other supermarket chains, including Asda, Morrisons, Sainsbury's and Tesco. Following advice on the proposed acquisition from the OFT, the Secretary of State accepted the conclusions of the CC report and, on 26 September 2003, prohibited the proposed acquisition by Asda, Sainsbury's or Tesco.[29] The proposed acquisition by Morrisons was given conditional clearance, with the proviso that it could successfully negotiate undertakings, relating to the divestment of 53 stores, with the OFT. Without such a divestment, the CC concluded that the acquisition would operate against the public interest. The three prohibited acquisitions were expected by the CC to operate against the public interest at both a national and local level, which, it was decided, could not be remedied by any divestiture. Another example of a highly politicised merger case arose in 2011, with the consideration whether News Corp, the owner of *The Sun* and *The Times* newspapers, should be permitted to gain full control of BSkyB, and therefore Sky News. While there were competition issues in the merger, the main issue of concern was media concentration and plurality.[30] The merger proposal was eventually dropped when News Corp became embroiled in the *News of the World* phone hacking scandal.

---

25 Commission Decision 98/531/EC *Van Den Bergh Foods* [1998] OJ L246/1, approved on appeal by the Court of First Instance in Case T-65/98 *Van Den Bergh Foods Ltd v Commission* [2003] ECR II-4653.

26 See Chapter 7 below. The OFT Decision was ultimately upheld by the Court of Appeal although the fines had been reduced, *Argos, Littlewoods and JJB v OFT* [2006] EWCA Civ 1318 on appeal from [2004] CAT 24, [2005] CAT 13, [2004] CAT 17 and [2005] CAT 22.

27 In this instance, there was a strong, but insufficient, 'pro-regional policy' lobby that sought to prevent the takeover on the basis that indigenous control of a major Scottish-based company would be lost from Scotland.

28 See *British Sky Broadcasting Group plc and Manchester United plc: A Report on the Proposed Merger*, Cm 4305, 1999 and DTI Press Release, P/99/309, 9 April 1999.

29 *Safeway plc and Asda Group Ltd (owned by Wal-Mart Stores Inc); Wm Morrison Supermarkets plc; J Sainsbury plc; and Tesco plc – A Report on the Mergers in Contemplation*, Cm 5950, 18 August 2003.

30 See the OFT Report to the Secretary of State for Media, Culture and Sport concerning the anticipated acquisition of News Corporation of British Sky Broadcasting Group plc, 11 February 2011.

The UK authorities are often concerned with the competitive effects in localised markets, as exemplified by the Commission's report in February 2006 into the acquisition of six multiplex cinemas in the UK by Vue Entertainment Holdings (Ltd) ('Vue'). The Commission concluded that Vue would be required to sell one of two cinemas in Basingstoke, one it already owned and one it had acquired, to avoid the higher prices and reduced choice for consumers in that area as a result of the merger.[31] Another example of the application of the Enterprise Act merger control provisions involved the joint venture between Stagecoach, with its megabus brand, and Scottish Citylink. In October 2006, the Commission considered that this was likely to lead to a substantial lessening of competition on the 'Saltire Cross' routes (Glasgow–Aberdeen and Edinburgh– Inverness routes, which cross at Perth). The Commission considered that the removal of competition between megabus and Scottish Citylink could lead to higher fares and reduced service levels, and the sale of certain services was required.[32]

In contrast, EU merger controls often involve major international business mergers. For instance, the EU authorities were involved in extensive and well-publicised negotiations concerning the proposed merger involving Boeing and McDonnell Douglas.[33] Subsequently, the Directorate General for Competition (DG Comp) controversially blocked the proposed conglomerate merger between General Electric and Honeywell, which provoked tension with the US antitrust authorities that had earlier approved the deal.[34]

Economics of Competition Law and Terminology

In order fully to appreciate the objectives of competition law and, indeed, the debate on the aims and objectives of competition law across differing legal systems, it is vital to be aware of the economic background to competition policy. It is important to understand the significant role that both economics and politics play in the formation of competition policy. For competition law students, it is sufficient to gain a basic appreciation of economic theory in relation to market structures, but some form of understanding is a necessity, given that it forms the basis of competition policy. This section will give an introduction to some economics-based concepts, which have a bearing on competition policy, and a brief account of developments that challenge the application of basic economic theory to competition law.

Neoclassical economic theory plays a crucial role in competition policy, and is based on the presumption that society, or consumer welfare, to use a more technical term, is better off when a state of perfect competition exists in a market. Perfect competition under economic theory has certain prerequisites. There must be identical products;[35] there must be an infinite number of buyers and sellers; there must be free entry and exit from the market; and full information must be available to all buyers and sellers, allowing them to make rational decisions. Much like the concept of a total monopoly discussed above, the perfect competition model is abstract and unlikely to arise in practice due to the improbability of all these conditions existing simultaneously. The reader could, nonetheless, consider the degree of competition between individual fruit sellers within a large fruit market to reflect the main ideas in the theory. The theory is based on

---

31 Competition Commission, *Vue Entertainment Holdings (UK) Ltd and A3 Cinema Ltd*, 24 February 2006.
32 Competition Commission, *Stagecoach and Scottish Citylink*, 23 October 2006.
33 See Case IV/M877, Commission Decision 1997/816/EC *Boeing/McDonnell Douglas* [1997] OJ L336/16.
34 See Commission Press Release, IP/01/939, 3 July 2001; Case IV/M2220, Commission Decision 2004/134/EC *GE/Honeywell* [2004] OJ L48/1; and Case T-210/01 *GE v Commission* [2005] ECR I-5575. For discussion, see Burnside, A, 'GE, Honey, I Sunk the Merger' [2002] ECLR 107 and Killick, J, 'The *GE/Honeywell* Judgment – in Reality Another Merger Defeat for the Commission' [2007] ECLR 52.
35 The technical term is 'homogeneous'.

the prediction of different market outcomes, from perfect competition at one end of the spectrum to monopoly at the other.

The theory predicts that perfectly competitive markets will result in both allocative efficiency and productive efficiency.[36] Allocative efficiency is achieved when resources are allocated in accordance with consumer demand. This arises under perfect competition because the producer is a 'price-taker', the price of the product being determined by aggregate industry output and consumer demand through the law of supply and demand. The individual company has a minimal effect on aggregate output and, hence, is a price-taker. On the other hand, where a monopolist controls the output of the market, the monopolist can manipulate output, thereby determining the price. The monopolist is a 'price-maker'. Perfect competition, according to the theory, results in the most efficient allocation of resources – 'allocative efficiency'. Alternatively, it is predicted that a monopolist will create a scarcity of the product in order to make excess or monopoly profits, and resources are thus misallocated. In addition, the theory predicts there will be productive inefficiency on the part of the monopolist because there will be neither the incentive nor the competitive pressure to keep down production costs as would exist under perfectly competitive conditions.

The graph in Figure 1.1 illustrates the neoclassical economic model which predicts certain outcomes in markets characterised by perfect competition and monopoly respectively. An

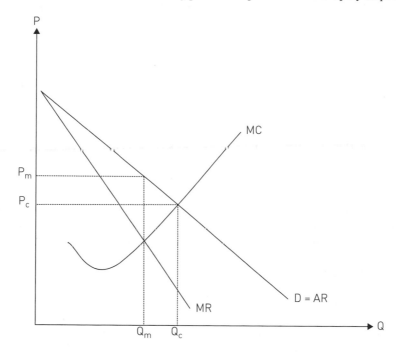

Figure 1.1 Perfect competition/monopoly

36 See economic textbooks for a general description: Scherer, FM and Ross, D, *Industrial Market Structure & Economic Performance*, 3rd edn (1990) Boston: Houghton Mifflin; and Livesey, F, *A Textbook of Core Economics*, 4th edn (1995) London: Longman. For more specific reading on antitrust economics, see Bishop, S and Walker, M, *The Economics of EC Competition Law: Concepts, Application and Measurement*, 3rd edn (2010) W Greens; Niels, G, Jenkins, H and Kavanagh, J, *Economics for Competition Lawyers* (2011) Oxford: Oxford University Press and Wils, W, *The Optimal Enforcement of EC Antitrust Law: A Study in Law and Economics* (2002) The Hague: Kluwer Law International.

understanding of this basic dichotomy is vital to understanding competition law, and a graphical representation provides a relatively simple explanation. Understanding the model of perfect competition requires awareness of the constituent elements within the graph. The two axes (labelled P and Q) represent Price and Quantity respectively. The other elements are explained in relation to these two core factors. The downward-sloping line (labelled D=AR) is the industry demand curve. This indicates the amount of a product consumers will demand at various prices. As demand for a product is low when prices are high, and increases as prices decrease, the demand curve is always downward-sloping. The upward-sloping curved line (labelled MC) is the marginal cost curve. The marginal cost curve represents the cost to industry of producing an extra unit of production. The curve is usually U-shaped, as smaller numbers of units are often relatively costly to produce, with the marginal cost then falling away and eventually rising again as production increases. In a competitive industry it is rational for a firm to continue to increase production until the quantity Q_c is reached. Until that point, each extra unit of production commands a price greater than its marginal cost – and that unit of production is therefore profitable. If a firm expands production beyond Q_c it will find that the extra marginal cost does not generate a profitable sale as the price drops (due to the increase in production) and the marginal cost of production exceeds the return from that sale. In a competitive market, production will reach an equilibrium at Q_c, the point at which the marginal cost curve intersects the industry demand curve (MC intersects D), resulting in a competitive market price close to the marginal cost of production, P_c.

The static model of perfect competition focuses on two important types of efficiency; these are allocative and productive efficiency. Allocative efficiency occurs in a competitive market as the price approaches marginal cost. Only at this point is there a match between the price consumers are willing to pay for a product and the cost of production. At any other point resources are misallocated, either through consumers paying too much, or through producers' costs exceeding the market price. The best allocation of resources always happens at the competitive equilibrium. Productive efficiency also occurs in a competitive market. Productive efficiency occurs when products are produced at the lowest possible cost. This is encouraged in competitive markets as producers are encouraged to maximise profits by reducing their production costs as the price approaches marginal cost. A producer who cannot produce at the lowest possible cost will be forced to exit the market as more efficient producers take their business.

A different equilibrium is reached in a market dominated by a monopolist. To understand why this is the case in a monopoly, another element in Figure 1.1 is important. The other downward-sloping line (labelled MR) is the marginal revenue curve. This line indicates the extra revenue the monopolist earns when he sells one more unit of product. For each extra unit of product a monopolist produces and sells, the monopolist will earn extra revenue. However, as the monopolist produces more, and therefore moves down the demand curve, it will command a lower price for all the units that it sells (including all the units produced before the extra unit). Because of this compounding effect, the marginal revenue curve always lies below the industry demand curve. A rational monopolist will seek to maximise its profitability and will expand its production to the point where marginal revenue meets marginal cost (MR intersects MC). Any further production would be unprofitable. This results in lower levels of production than we would expect in a perfectly competitive market (Q_m as opposed to Q_c) and a higher price (P_m as opposed to P_c). Figure 1.2 illustrates the cost to the economy associated with monopoly. The lightly hatched area is the deadweight welfare loss. This is the cost to the economy of the market not operating as efficiently as it would in perfect competition. Another feature of monopoly is a distributive concern; the monopolist will make a supra-competitive profit. The amount of that supra-competitive profit is illustrated in Figure 1.2 in the dark hatched area where the monopoly price (P_m) exceeds the average cost of production (AC). This supra-competitive profit is sometimes known as a 'monopoly rent', or can be described as a reduction of 'consumer surplus'. In a monopoly market, both productive and allocative efficiency are reduced from the equivalent

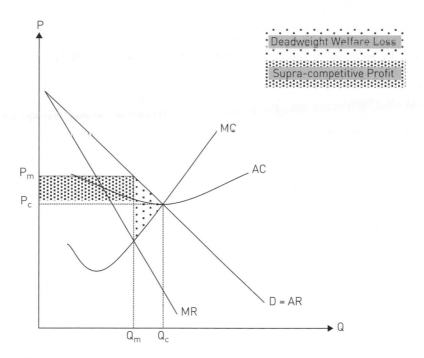

Figure 1.2 Impact of monopoly

position in a competitive market. There is no incentive for a monopolist to produce at as low a cost as possible, potentially resulting in 'χ-inefficiency' within the market

What must be remembered is that the models of perfect competition and monopoly are best used as tools to provide us with an understanding of how markets would operate under such theoretical conditions. They are useful as a point of reference when considering real market conditions. Indeed, real market conditions reflect a range of competitive structures between perfect competition and monopoly. The theory is a useful starting point when identifying a core concern in competition policy – maximising consumer welfare through competition, or what we might term 'the pure competition objective'. The concern with monopolies, as alluded to earlier, also explains the attention that competition law pays to cartels and mergers. However, because the theoretical true monopoly situation is likely to be very rare in practice, competition policy has generally tended to use the tenets of the theory in relation to high degrees of concentration in a particular market. Another way of describing this is that competition law is concerned with concentrated markets – that is, when there are few competitors. Thus, a company with a high market share may be able to act in a similar way to a monopolist, through the exercise of their 'market power', without achieving true monopoly. Furthermore, a high degree of concentration may lead to the problem of oligopoly,[37] where the limited number of market competitors may facilitate collusion, whether intentionally or tacitly.

A further argument is that the models may not necessarily be accurate. The theory suggests that perfect competition caters best for society's needs through satisfying consumer demand, but it is difficult to prove empirically. Firstly, the ideal state of perfect competition is in reality an unattainable goal. Secondly, although the theory predicts that monopolists will be inefficient in

---

37 This will be discussed briefly towards the end of this chapter.

their production, as there is no pressure of competition, this has not been proven conclusively. Indeed, it may be argued that powerful firms are in that position simply because they are more efficient and responsive to consumer demand. Thirdly, although competition policy may be shaped on the basis of this theory and termed a pro-competition policy, its influence has waned, particularly in the US. Certain scholars in the US adopted the concept of 'workable competition' as a means to counter the argument that the theoretical model could not work in practice. In effect, this means that competition law should adopt rules that are not abstract, but which attempt to ensure an appropriate and adequate level of competition. This is, of course, a generalisation of the 'workable competition' school, and it also begs the question as to what level of competition is appropriate.[38] This issue has stimulated a great deal of debate, notably in the US, where a particular approach to competition policy based on the analysis of the efficiency of conduct has been especially prominent. In effect, this approach seeks to assess company behaviour and is based not strictly on analysis of the effects of market power, but rather on whether the particular behaviour is efficient. This will be outlined further in this chapter, but this different economic view of the function of competition law as an alternative to the traditional theory is noteworthy.

Traditional economic theory is static in that it predicts the effect of competitive markets but does not consider competition as a process. For instance, the theory is generally considered to be laissez-faire in that it allows competitive forces to have a free role. The pure competition objective has, thus, been taken to connote 'let the free market operate'. However, competition law looks to intervene when markets do not perform according to the competitive ideal. The paradox inherent in this simplistic outline of competition law objectives is clear. Competition law should seek to encourage the free play of competitive forces in the market on a neutral basis – Darwinian-style survival of the fittest. Yet, in certain conditions, competition law will seek to interfere with these forces, for example, where there may be 'detrimental behaviour', such as a cartel agreement or a monopolist exploiting its position in some way. Accordingly, neoclassical economic theory predicts the best outcome if there are many competitors. But what should happen if, in the 'process of competition', one competitor wins fairly, and then makes excess profits out of the unwitting consumer? This highlights that the theory may not be pro-competitive, in that it may not encourage companies to compete, and also that different policy goals are likely to exist in any system in order to help to determine when the law should intervene.

It is interesting to note here the confusion of competition objectives with support for a pro-competitive free market stance, which would advocate minimal market intervention. One extreme of this latter stance is termed 'creative destruction' and is related to the Austrian school of economics. This group of economists regarded competition as a process rather than a desirable end, and believed, particularly, that innovation would result from non-intervention in the competitive process. Similar ideas have been expressed through the Chicago school in the US and in UK competition policy, particularly during the 1980s.

The influence of the Chicago school has waned in the US since its heyday in the 1980s and 90s. In the post-Chicago era there has been a move to look at markets in a more dynamic way. Rather than simply focusing on measuring consumer welfare solely in the terms of efficiency, some have argued, notably Averrit & Lande, that consumer welfare should be widened as a concept given that consumers do not only desire efficient markets, but also benefit from innovation and choice in markets.[39] Another new approach uses 'behavioural economics' to move anti-trust thinking on from the perhaps flawed presumptions in static neoclassical models in order to focus on how real-world markets work.[40]

---

38 See Easterbrook, FH, 'Workable antitrust policy' (1986) 84 Michigan L Rev 1696.
39 See Averitt, NW and Lande, RH, 'Using the "Consumer Choice" Approach to Antitrust Law' (2007) 74 Antitrust LJ 175.
40 See Reeves, AP and Stucke, ME, 'Behavioural Antitrust' (2010) 86 Indiana LJ 1527.

To sum up, neoclassical theory is a guide – albeit an imperfect one – to basic analysis of competition law problems. It can be criticised as being too abstract, and alternative modern economic theories have sought to marginalise its basic concerns. In addition, competition law is not solely about the fulfilment of economic ideals. These economic ideals would not relate directly to each individual rule; economic theory is combined with other political and social goals to form competition policy. Indeed, an interesting debate concerns the role of economics in competition law. The next section outlines the problems of relying solely on economic theory, which it is suggested can be distinguished from economic analysis. General economic theory has problems in dealing with real-world market situations, but economic analysis of particular markets and predicted outcomes is useful for competition law enforcers. Economic analysis can be used to aid enforcement of existing competition laws and policies, but we should be wary of uncritically accepting economic theory as a pure science to guide competition policy. The politics of competition law and the legal context in which it is applied, should not, and cannot, be ignored.

Politics of Competition Law

It is clear that in all developed competition law systems, competition policy does not seek solely to fulfil the competition objective of competitive markets, with cartels outlawed, no monopolistic companies and mergers between competing companies prohibited. For instance, in the EU one must note the important link between competition law and industrial policy. There have been instances when the EU authorities have approved what appeared to be highly anti-competitive agreements – market-sharing or price-fixing cartels. These have been justified on various grounds; for instance, that these were 'crisis cartels' and were allowed in order to protect the continuing existence of an industry within the EU. Similar trends can be identified in EU merger policy. There has been a debate as to whether Europe-wide alliances should be encouraged to foster pan-European businesses more able to compete in the global market. It could also be argued that US antitrust's more lenient approach to 'monopolistic' abuses, compared to the more interventionist European Commission line, is consistent with the very different socio-political background in the US, sometimes expressed as the 'American dream' of an individual's entrepreneurial route to success and wealth. Also, among the variety of interests that have been relevant considerations in UK merger policy, regional policy was at one stage a particularly important factor.

Accordingly, a discussion of the political goals and policy objectives forming the basis of a system of competition laws is necessary. Furthermore, these objectives are linked to the interpretation given to the concepts used in competition law. Terms are, therefore, only given meaning or content in the context of the particular competition law system.

Subsidiary questions, here, concern whether we have a scientific understanding of markets, what ideal competition is and the extent to which we can define the role of competition law. As discussed above, there are economic theories defining and delimiting what is termed perfect competition, monopoly or oligopoly, but the fundamental flaws or deficiencies in these theories limit their applicability in real-world situations, although they are extremely useful reference points.

The limitations are exemplified by the work of the late Robert Bork, an influential American economist and antitrust lawyer associated with the Chicago school and renowned for his important contribution to economic theory and competition policy in his book, *The Antitrust Paradox: A Policy at War with Itself*.[41] In this book he advocates that one economic theory should be at the core of antitrust policy – the efficiency of a monopolist's behaviour or the enhanced efficiencies

---

41 Bork, R, *The Antitrust Paradox: A Policy at War with Itself* (1993) Oxford: Maxwell Macmillan.

derived from a merger. Nonetheless, it is clear that his work is based on his own beliefs as to the success of markets and the limited scope for intervention in markets by competition authorities. It has been suggested by John Flynn[42] that all scientific models, whether political, economic or other, must be aware of the 'ought assumptions' that underlie them. Furthermore, these 'ought assumptions' form the basis of key terms, such as consumer welfare, as defined by various economic and competition policy scholars. In other words, they seek to implement ideological beliefs through supposedly scientific economic models, but antitrust/competition law has to be clear and specific about its socioeconomic and political goals.[43]

Looking, for instance, at the US, we can see that historically there have been two dominant schools of antitrust thinking in the last 60 years, namely those associated with the Harvard and Chicago schools. The models of competitive analysis associated with each school[44] are, in essence, related to the academics' fundamental beliefs as to what is meant by the competitive process and the role of the State via the law in that process. In other words, what ends does competition law serve? This academic debate in the US has been referred to as the 'battle for the soul of antitrust'.

Importantly, this is also part of the free market/government interference dichotomy[45] as to what legitimate role the State should play in interfering to correct perceived market failures. However, again we fall back on the as-yet-unresolved issue of what constitute the legitimate competition policy goals upon which the role of the State is dependent. For instance, is the aim of competition law to protect the public interest, and how is this to be defined and quantified?[46] This leads to a discussion of the various potential aims and objectives that competition policy may wish to include.

Competition Policy Objectives

The pure competition objective or ideal based on neoclassical economics has already been outlined. However, in practice there are a number of different economic, social and political objectives which may also form part of any particular competition policy. It is often the extent to which these other policies should and do play a role that causes greatest debate among practitioners, competition administrators and academics. Some of these other policies may be termed 'extra-competition' policies or 'non-competition law proper' policies, and it has often been suggested that competition law should not be concerned with them; however, this argument often comes from those, particularly academics associated with the Chicago school, who consider that efficiency should be the only criterion of legality, ignoring the inherent political bias of that preference. Also, as this introduction suggests, competition law or policy is not fixed, but is dependent, to a great extent, upon the particular temporal, political and social emphases of the legal system in which it operates. It can, therefore, be justifiably stated that, in applying the core economic thesis that informs competition law, any set of appropriate principles and policies may play a part in a coherent competition law system. It has been recognised that the fundamental rationale for the introduction of a set of competition policies has been to promote the economy of a given country and the wellbeing of both its consumers and its industries generally. The appropriate balance must be sought between industry and the consumer, but this illustrates that the incorporation of any set of extra-competition policy objectives will be to further national interest,

42 In Flynn, J, 'Legal reasoning, antitrust policy and the social sciences of economics' (1985) 62 *Antitrust Bulletin* 713.
43 Helm, D, *The Economic Borders of The State* (1999) Oxford, New York: OUP, pp 1–45, uses corresponding terminology of underlying value assumptions and suggests that political arguments about economic policy tend to start with ideology and progress to search for an economic rationale.
44 To be discussed, briefly, later in this chapter.
45 Discussed by Helm, above, n 43.
46 For instance, the public interest test which existed in UK competition law under s 84 of the Fair Trading Act 1973.

irrespective of the outcome predicted by economic theory. The following are examples of political, social and economic objectives that may form part of competition policy.

Consumer welfare

Consumer welfare is now arguably the central economic rationale at the heart of contemporary competition/antitrust policy in most legal systems. It is generally accepted as being the main goal of EU competition and US antitrust law. Nonetheless, while the concept is referred to in many policy documents it is not well defined, and there is a suspicion that while different authorities may use the same terminology, their understanding of its meaning and impact may be different. If competition policy sought merely to encourage efficiency through competition that ensured that society, as a whole, was wealthier, this would be characterised as a 'total welfare' standard. Under that standard, any behaviour that increases the total welfare of society should be encouraged, and there would be no concern with the distribution of the wealth – as long as wealth was created. A consumer welfare standard is more nuanced as it seeks to ensure that the wealth created does not simply stay in the hands of those who make economic choices on the marketplace, usually the producers, but stresses that the consumer must also benefit from the efficiency-enhancing behaviour. The debate surrounding the consumer welfare standard involves two main issues of contention. First, what sacrifice of total welfare is acceptable when encouraging consumer welfare, and second, what are the efficiencies that consumers desire and which should be considered? An example of the first concern is the worry that a narrow focus on direct short-term consumer welfare may lead to reduced incentives for producers to invest in innovation and efficient production. Those investments may not enhance consumer welfare in the short term but they may well result in greater overall efficiency and benefits for the consumer in the longer term. As such, a narrow view of consumer welfare sees little difference between consumer and total welfare. Such a view is characteristic of the Chicago school, and is epitomised by Robert Bork's statement that consumer welfare 'is merely another term for the wealth of the nation'.[47] This is very close to the total welfare standard in that it allows behaviour to continue where the total efficiency gain exceeds the loss of welfare to the consumer. This non-interventionist stance presumes that the operation of the market will ensure that the consumer will eventually see the benefit of efficiencies and there is little need for the law to intervene. In the narrow view there is less concern with 'equity' in the market as is presumes that the increase in societal wealth will trickle down through the marketplace[48] or that 'equity' goals would be better served through other means – for example, redistribution through taxation. A wider view of consumer welfare, associated with 'post-Chicago' scholars such as Brodley,[49] suggests that efficiencies should show direct benefits to consumers in either price or quality in the long run. It is not suggested that consumers should always see short-term benefits from all behaviour by producers, but that where behaviour does not directly benefit consumers it must be necessary for production or innovation efficiencies, and that there must be a clear mechanism, usually continuing competitive rivalry among producers, for the consumer to see benefits in a reasonable time frame. The second area of contention regards the mechanisms through which consumer welfare is expressed. Traditionally the expectation was that consumer welfare would always be expressed in lower prices. But this assumption is now being challenged. There is an increasing acceptance that consumers are not only concerned with competition on price, but that they also desire other forms of 'efficiency'

---

47 Bork, RH, *The Anti-trust Paradox: A Policy at War with Itself* (1978) NY: Basic Books, p 90.
48 See, for example, Elzinga, KG, 'The Goals of Antitrust: Other than Competition and Efficiency, What Else Counts?' (1977) 125 Uni of Penn LRev 1191.
49 See, Bodley, JF, 'The Economic Goals of Antitrust: Efficiency, Consumer Welfare and Technological Progress' (1987) 62 NY Uni LRev1020.

such as innovation, variety, quality and safety.[50] The difficulty with such a multifactorial concept of 'efficiency' is finding a reliable way to measure and balance the potentially conflicting desires it contains and to include them in a workable definition of consumer welfare.

While it appears that a global competition/antitrust orthodoxy is beginning to emerge behind consumer welfare as being competition policy's primary goal, there is still no consensus as to its proper interpretation. In particular, that means that notwithstanding the similar sounding rhetoric coming from both sides of the Atlantic, there is still real scope for disagreement between agencies on the impact of consumer welfare on the implementation of competition policy in context in specific areas. While the US courts have explicitly adopted the consumer welfare standard[51] it is not a phrase that has apparently been accepted by the European Courts, although often used in argument before the Court and more regularly in Commission policy documents.

Prevention of the concentration of economic power

This is a political ideal is based on the idea that economic corporations should not become more powerful and influential than elected democratic governments. This was a particularly influential idea at the time of the introduction of the first US antitrust statute at the end of the nineteenth century[52] and in Europe following the Second World War.[53]

Regulation of excessive profits and fairer distribution of wealth

This goal is essentially derived from the neoclassical theory's concern with monopolies. The general idea was fairly topical in 1997, with discussion in the UK surrounding the introduction of windfall taxation of the regulated utilities, and was a traditional concern of anti-monopoly laws, particularly evident during the 1970s in the UK. However, this concern has been more generally less well regarded in recent times, partly because of the advanced debate on incentives to new market entrants created by excessive profits and the ongoing criticism that redistribution of wealth should not be a concern of competition law. However, it was prominent in the CC's criticism of the proposed BSkyB/Manchester United merger concerning the potential worsening of the distribution of wealth in English football.[54] More generally, the post-1997 Labour Government introduced a high-profile 'Rip-Off Britain' campaign, which resulted in subsequent referrals to the CC concerning perceived excessive pricing in supermarkets and of new cars in the UK.[55] Similarly, in the *Banking* report in 2002, the CC was highly critical of the excessive prices charged to small- and medium-sized enterprises by major banks. Nonetheless, in 2007 in *Attheraces Ltd v British Horseracing Board*, the Court of Appeal rejected an excessive pricing claim and rejected the idea that competition law should regulate prices and redistribute wealth.[56] The notion of regulation of excessive prices and/or profits was again on the political agenda in the UK in 2013 in the light of a continued rise in consumer energy tariffs by the 'big six' energy providers in the UK.

50 See, for example, Averitt, NW and Lande, RH, 'Using the "Consumer Choice" Approach to Antitrust Law' (2007) 74 Antitrust LJ 175.
51 In cases such as, *Reiter v Sonotone Corp* 422 US 330 (1979) and *Nat'l Collegiate Athletic Ass'n v Bd of Regents of Uni of Oklahoma* 468 US 85 (1984). For a discussion of the confusion surrounding the US adoption of the standard, see Orbach, BY, 'The Antitrust Consumer Welfare Paradox' (2010) 7(1) J of Comp Law & Econ 133.
52 Sherman Act 1890.
53 See Amato, G, *Antitrust and the Bounds of Power* (1999) Oxford: Hart.
54 See *British Sky Broadcasting Group plc and Manchester United plc: A Report on the Proposed Merger*, Cm 4305, 1999 and DTI Press Release, P/99/309, 9 April 1999.
55 *Supermarkets: A Report on the Supply of Groceries from Multiple Stores in the United Kingdom*, Cm 4842, 2000 and *New Cars: A Report on the Supply of New Motor Cars within the UK*, Cm 4660, 2000.
56 [2007] EWCA Civ 38, CA.

Protection of consumers

Competition laws invariably need to balance the competing demands of industry and the consumer.[57] In most legal systems, however, specific regard is had to furthering the interests of consumers as goal in its own right. The historical link between consumer policy and competition policy was highlighted in the UK by the existence of one body, the OFT, which supervised both areas and championed the interests of consumers. The Competition and Markets Authority ('CMA') in the UK, which replaced the OFT and Competition Commission as of 1 April 2014, will similarly under take the role of consumer champion in a competition law context.[58] The link is also illustrated in the EU by the role of the Consumer Liaison Officer within the DG Comp. The importance of the consumer was further demonstrated by the introduction, under the Enterprise Act 2002,[59] of a system where super-complaints can be made by designated consumer bodies. The emphasis on the impact on consumers and the requirement to consider customer benefits in designing appropriate remedies, together with the innovation of the consumer super-complaints procedure which has kick-started a number of market investigations, demonstrates that consumer protection has been a key focus of the market investigation provisions of the Enterprise Act. Furthermore, the Consumer Rights Bill, when enacted, will ensure more effective redress for consumers under competition law.

Regional policy

This may seem to be a strange component of competition policy, but it can be understood given that competition law is part of an overall policy to promote the national, or regional, economy. Thus, regional policy formed a clear part of UK competition policy under the Fair Trading Act (FTA) 1973. Furthermore, regional policy constituted an overriding consideration in the analysis of a series of mergers, which might have proven detrimental to the Scottish economy and which were ultimately prohibited under this regional policy criterion.[60]

Creation of unified markets and prevention of artificial barriers to trade

This is a political objective peculiarly related to EU competition policy, and is known as the policy of 'market integration'. It is derived from the overall aim of integrating the markets of Member States to create a European internal market.[61] Historically, it was crucial to the development of European competition policy but, arguably, is now of diminishing significance.

Small is beautiful

This is indirectly related to the pure competition policy objective in that competition policy may seek to foster the ability of smaller companies to compete with established, powerful companies. This appears to have been one of the rationales which lay behind the adoption of the Sherman Act in the US. One way that this competition can be achieved is by responding more leniently to forms of co-operation between smaller firms, for example the sharing of technology. Competition authorities may also adopt the concept of 'countervailing power', based on the need for strength

---

57 See, for instance, the conditions for gaining an exemption under Art 81(3) in Community law.
58 For further detail on the CMA, see www.gov.uk/government/organisations/competition-and-markets-authority.
59 Section 11. In addition, ss 22 and 33 of the 2002 Act allow the OFT to decide against referring mergers if relevant 'customer benefits' outweigh the substantial lessening of competition concerned. Section 30 outlines the relevant customer benefits to be considered, such as lower prices, higher quality or greater choice of goods or services.
60 See Rodger, BJ, 'Reinforcing the Scottish "Ring-fence": A Critique of UK Mergers Policy vis à vis the Scottish Economy' [1996] 2 ECLR 104.
61 This will be assessed in fuller detail later in this chapter.

on one side of the market in order to counteract strength on the other side, the general consensus being that this may ultimately benefit the consumer. The promotion of small- and medium-sized enterprises (SMEs) has been a particular goal of the EU authorities, on the basis that such companies may start to compete across national frontiers and, hence, indirectly support the market integration policy.

Balancing objectives

These are some of the individual objectives that may form part of competition law and policy. Once we have identified the particular objectives that form part of a particular system's competition policy, one of the difficulties for competition law enforcement lies in assessing the priorities and trade-offs among the various objectives in a concrete case.[62] These political objectives inevitably affect the types of competition rules employed by the particular system. We will see, for instance, in the EU context how important the principle of market integration has been. Indeed, it has appeared, at times, to have overridden many other objectives, such as efficiency.

During different periods in a competition law system's development there will be changes in the emphasis given to the various policy objectives. For instance, the last decade has witnessed many developments under both EU and UK law to emphasise the importance of the consumer in competition law, both substantively, through the increasing importance of consumer welfare, and procedurally. Changes in preoccupations are also evidenced by a brief consideration of the situation in the US, where an initial fear of big business was obvious when antitrust law was introduced at the end of the nineteenth century but is no longer seen today. In the UK, collusive practices were encouraged in the post-war era, but some are now criminalised. The marked change in approach is illustrated by the Net Book Agreement, which was prohibited in the 1990s after over 30 years in existence.

EU competition law in practice reflects many of the above comments. There are a number of policy objectives that may be identified in EU competition law and the emphasis given to each may vary over time. These objectives inevitably affect the interpretation of specific legal provisions.

The inclusion of political objectives or extra-competition policies raises two further issues, as it suggests the necessity of some degree of discretion within the rules to accommodate flexibility. Firstly, their inclusion may have repercussions on the type of remedies that will be available under the competition rules. Should the remedies be public or private remedies and should they be retroactive and punitive, or prospective? Secondly, the flexible nature of the administrative intervention in advancing those political objectives has led to calls for greater certainty and predictability in the enforcement of competition law. Indeed, criticism over the inclusion of extra-competition policies is essentially due to the unpredictability of administrative intervention in the market. Accordingly, there is a clear link between the substantive content of competition law and its enforcement. It should also be noted that, particularly under UK competition law, there has been a recent move to 'depoliticise' competition law, for instance, by discarding the focus on the public interest test, enforcing the law through fines and enhancing the availability of private rights of redress through court processes. More generally, there have also been developments at the EU and UK level seeking to further facilitate and encourage private enforcement of competition law. This will lead competition law further away from the traditional policy-oriented administrative enforcement framework.

---

62 This is often the matter that is debated most strongly.

US Antitrust Law and Policy

In this book we shall be focusing on the competition law and policy of the EU and the UK. However, some reference will be made to US antitrust law and policy, due to its influence on the competition policy of other jurisdictions. The US was the first jurisdiction to introduce a coherent competition system, known as 'antitrust', and it produces a vast amount of academic literature on the topic. The substantive provisions of US law are notable for their brevity. Essentially, legislative provision is made in three statutes: the Sherman Act 1890, the Clayton Act 1914 and the Federal Trade Commission Act 1914. The Sherman Act is the most important. The core provisions of the Sherman Act are in ss 1 and 2, and there has been intense debate throughout the history of the Sherman Act as to the role of antitrust policy, and the ensuing implications for the interpretation of those provisions.

The history and traditions of US antitrust law form an essential backdrop to the continuing debate over its role and purpose. It has been argued that 'American antitrust law is not only "law" but also a socio-political statement about our society'.[63] The political consensus reflected in the law during the early years of antitrust, and for a considerable period thereafter, was that high concentration of industry lessened competition. This mainstream antitrust tradition was also sceptical of the notion that the competitive process adequately controls market power.

The Harvard school of antitrust law and economics had its origins in the 1930s and shared many of the above-mentioned concerns of classic US antitrust. In particular, Harvard school economists placed great emphasis on market structure as the root of market failure and, particularly, on poor performance, primarily in the form of high profits, as a result of excessive concentration of market power, which is detrimental to the consumer. Parallel to the academic prominence achieved by the Harvard school, the US Supreme Court, in the 1960s and 1970s, appeared to adopt a similar concern for increasing market concentration.

The Chicago school of antitrust law and economic analysis began its development in the 1950s, partly in reaction to the Harvard school, and is particularly associated with the work of Robert Bork. The Chicago school tends to focus on two 'truths'. The first is that the Chicago school are 'efficiency advocates'. The goal of markets is the efficient allocation of resources, and the only concern of antitrust, therefore, is to intervene to prevent the inefficient allocation of resources. The second 'truth' is that there is very little scope for antitrust law and, consequently, for government intervention in the functioning of markets. This is a logical consequence of the Chicago school's presumption as to the efficiency of firms and the functioning of markets. The Chicago school's aim would appear to be to 'keep government out' and to seek the least disruptive way to correct market failures. Following the inauguration of President Reagan, in 1981, the Chicago school approach was adopted by the US Government with Reagan's promise to curtail the Government's role in the market. During this period, as a result of adherence to Chicago school inspired policies, government enforcement of antitrust was at a low ebb. However, it should be noted that the Supreme Court never fully embraced the concept that efficiency was the only concern. The Chicago school also encouraged a black letter approach to competition law, based on the importance of legal certainty and predictability.

Although the Chicago school's beliefs are still important in the US, there has been constant debate and criticism of the Chicago school's approach. In addition, there has been a recent rise in the prominence of a new school of industrial economics, in response to the Chicago school, which seeks to analyse strategic behaviour affecting competition, emphasising in-depth analysis

---

63 Sullivan, T, *The Political Economy of the Sherman Act: The First One Hundred Years* (1991) Oxford: OUP, p 3; but it has also been referred to as 'humbug based on economic ignorance': Wendel Holmes, O, 'Privilege, Malice and Intent' (1894) 8 Harv L Rev 1.

of the particular market involved.[64] Behavioural economics is also having an increasing influence on contemporary antitrust thinking. This new school of thinking does not presume that market players are always 'rational' profit maximisers, sometimes known as 'Homo economicus'. It treats them as human beings who tend to act in more unexpected ways. It seeks to use the lessons learnt from disciplines like psychology to further our understanding of how markets work in reality.[65] Nonetheless, there is still a sense that, generally, US antitrust embodies an optimism about how markets work, and that the 'hope for monopoly' is a driver of competition, as allowing monopolies, with limitations, may create incentives to innovate. Despite differences in approach on the two sides of the Atlantic, it is clear that the focus of EU and UK competition law and its reform has been greatly inspired by a number of fundamental aspects of US antitrust law and its enforcement, namely: the prominence of private enforcement, notably involving consumers in class actions; the dramatic increase in fines imposed on cartels; and the adoption of antitrust leniency programmes for cartel 'whistle-blowers'.

Development of EU Competition Law

The earliest European competition controls were introduced by the Treaty of Paris 1951, which established the European Coal and Steel Community. However, these were specialised rules pertaining only to limited markets, and shall not be considered further in this text. The main European competition provisions were introduced in the Treaty of Rome 1957. This established the European Economic Community (EEC). Following the adoption of the Treaty of Lisbon in 2009, the EEC is now known as the European Union.[66] EU law is a separate supranational legal order which applies throughout the whole of the Union. Accordingly, both governments and private citizens, including companies that operate within the EU, are required to comply with the legal rules established by EU law.

It is useful to be aware of the Treaty background, in addition to the specific provisions on competition law, partly because of what is known as the teleological system of interpretation used in EU law. This means that, in interpreting any particular or specific provision of the Treaty or EU law, regard should be had to the spirit of the Treaty as well as to its wording. The following is a brief review of the introductory Articles of the two Treaties that constitute the EU: the Treaty of European Union (TEU) and the Treaty on the Functioning of the European Union (TFEU).

Article 1 TEU establishes the European Union and Art 3(3) TEU sets out one of the central tasks for the Union as follows:

> The Union shall establish an internal market. It shall work for the sustainable development of Europe based on balanced economic growth and price stablility, a highly competitive social market economy, aiming at full employment and social progress, and a high level of protection and improvement of the quality of the environment. It shall promote scientific and technological advance.

Protocol No 27 to the TFEU, which has equal status to the Treaty, sets out that the internal market, which is referred to in Art 3 TEU, 'includes a system ensuring that competition is not distorted'.

---

64 For an interesting discussion on the relationship between the Harvard and Chicago schools in the development of US antitrust, see Kovacic, WE, 'The Intellectual DNA of Modern US Competition Law for Dominant Firm Conduct: The Chicago/Harvard Double Helix' [2007] Columbia Bus LRev 1.

65 See, for example, Reeves, AP, and Stucke, ME, 'Behavioural Antitrust' (2011) 86(4) Indiana LJ 1527.

66 The EEC was originally formed with six Members and the EU has now grown to have 27 Member States. For further detail on the background to the European Union and European Community law, see, for example: Craig, P and de Búrca, G, *EU Law: Text, Cases and Materials*, 5th edn (2011) Oxford: OUP; and Steiner, J and Woods, L *EU Law*, 10th edn (2009) Oxford: OUP.

It is interesting to note that, following intervention by the French Government, the Lisbon Treaty removed the reference to undistorted competition from the objectives of the then EC Treaty, Article 3(g) EC, and relegated it to a legally binding protocol. While this has little legal significance in practice, it was clearly a political gesture which challenged the centrality of competition in the EU internal market.

One of the objectives of the establishment of what is now the European Union was to increase harmony and integration across Europe. From the beginning of the European project, economic unity has been a core tenant of this objective. Indeed, the Common Market, known since 1992 as the Internal Market, was intended to create interdependence between the States of Europe. It was considered that, in order to make the Common Market operate successfully, it would be necessary to ensure that more or less equivalent competitive opportunities existed throughout this 'integrated market'. Accordingly, competition rules were included in the Treaty to assist in the creation of a unified competitive environment, and partly in an attempt to prevent private companies from re-erecting trade barriers dismantled by the Member States.

Articles 101 and 102 TFEU are the principal substantive rules dealing with anti-competitive agreements and the dominant market players respectively. Article 106 TFEU contains specialised provisions relating to undertakings where there is some form of state regulation or involvement. Merger control was introduced in 1990, through Regulation 4064/89. The current Merger Regulation, Regulation 139/2004,[67] provides a specific set of Community merger control provisions.

Initially Regulation 17/62 introduced a set of measures for enforcement of the competition rules, affording the European Commission responsibility for investigating and fining companies for breaches. Regulation 17/62 was superseded by Regulation 1/2003, which revised the powers available to the Commission and provided for a decentralised network involving National Competition Authorities (NCAs) and national courts to assist the Commission in its regulatory tasks.[68] Accordingly, after 1 May 2004, the Office of Fair Trading (OFT) was a member of the European Competition Network (ECN), the network of national competition authorities applying Arts 101 and 102 TFEU alongside the Commission.[69] The Competition and Markets Authority took over that role on 1 April 2014. The modernised enforcement regime introduced by Regulation 1/2003 also includes private enforcement of competition law in the national courts, albeit with limited success to date.

Development of UK Competition Law

Current competition law in the UK is essentially statute-based. It was a notable feature of the development of the common law that it abstained from competition issues. Indeed, the common law's interaction with economic issues has tended to reflect the philosophy of Adam Smith, the famous Scottish economist, an advocate of the free market and laissez-faire in the early nineteenth century. Attempts to develop methods of dealing with competition problems in three common law areas have met with little success.

Criminal law

The criminal law is not generally considered to be the best venue in which to pursue anti-competitive behaviour, although breach of the former UK restrictive trade practices legislation,

---

67 Regulation 139/2004/EC on the control of concentrations between undertakings [2004] OJ L24/1.
68 Regulation 1/2003/EC on the implementation of the rules on competition laid down in Arts 81 and 82 of the Treaty, [2003] OJ L1/1.
69 See Competition Act 1998 and Other Enactments (Amendment) Regulations 2004, SI 2004/1261, para 3; OFT Guidance, Modernisation, OFT 442.

which was repealed by the Competition Act 1998, constituted a contempt of court, with the possibility of fines and imprisonment for senior managers.[70] There also existed the possibility of prosecuting those involved in price-fixing or bid-rigging for conspiracy to defraud.[71] Breach of EU competition law may lead to 'administrative' fines of up to 10% of a company's annual turnover. Similarly, breach of either prohibition under the Competition Act 1998 may result in a fine imposed by the CMA; the fine may not exceed 10% of the relevant turnover of the undertaking in the last financial year. There is debate as to whether these fines should be considered penal in nature.[72] It is worth noting that the Competition Act 1998 includes particular provision, in s 72, in respect of bodies corporate and partnerships for offences committed under the Act, such as destroying or falsifying documents to be attributed to individual officers, directors or partners. In addition, following EU law, a number of classes of individuals (for example, opera singers) can be considered to be 'undertakings' for competition law purposes and can face the full range of penalties. Furthermore, the Enterprise Act 2002 introduced a criminal offence, punishable by a fine or imprisonment, for individuals involved in cartels in an attempt to increase the deterrent effect of the law.[73] However, this offence led to only two successful prosecutions and, after trenchant criticism from some quarters, was reformed by the Enterprise and Regulatory Reform Act 2013.[74]

Delict/tort

The law of delict or tort is also of limited application to competition matters, being intended to regulate personal and property interests. However, there are various forms of competition-related delictual or tortious action, under both UK legal systems, which may be collectively termed the 'economic delicts'.[75] The most relevant, for this discussion, is the action based on conspiracy to injure. The classic example, in *Mogul Steamship Co Ltd v McGregor Gow and Co*,[76] highlights the limitations of this action. A shipping conference regulated freight in the China tea trade. Mogul joined the trade and managed to transport tea at lower rates. The reaction of its competitors was to drop their rates to such a level that Mogul went out of business. In competition law terms, this is a classic predatory pricing case, and Mogul sued for conspiracy to injure. There was a clear intention to restrain trade, but the action would only succeed if the conspiracy was to fulfil an improper purpose. Although there was abundant evidence of a cartel, there was no liability, as the protection of legitimate trade interests was not deemed to be an improper purpose, even if it restricted competition.

In the UK legal system, before the enactment of the 1998 Act, the most important competition action under delict/tort was that of passing off. The basic premise is that it is not permissible to confuse the public into thinking one company's goods are, in fact, those of another company. This allows an action to be brought if the public associates particular goods, or the way they are marketed, with one company and another company misrepresents their goods in such a way as to confuse the public and seeks to benefit from the goodwill of the other.[77] Passing off is one area of the present law that may be considered as falling under the general principle against unfair

---

70 *Re Supply of Ready Mixed Concrete (No 2), Director General of Fair Trading v Pioneer Concrete UK Ltd and Another* [1995] 1 All ER 135.
71 The usefulness of such prosecutions was challenged by the ruling of the House of Lords in *R v GG plc* [2008] UKHL 17.
72 As in the US, where the principal method of enforcement is through private actions for 'treble damages' in which the aggrieved litigant will be awarded three times the amount of their alleged loss as a result of the anti-competitive action.
73 See Pt 6, ss 188–202 of the Enterprise Act 2002. Section 188 created a criminal offence for those who agree with others to make or implement an agreement as outlined in s 188(2), such as price-fixing.
74 See Pt 4, s 47 of the Enterprise and Regulatory Reform Act 2013. Section 47 removed the need for dishonesty requirement from the offence under s 188 of the 2002 Act, and introduced new defences. See Chapter 7 for further discussion.
75 See Thomson, J, *Delictual Liability*, 4th edn (2011) Edinburgh: Tottel; Murphy, J, *Street on Torts*, 13th edn (2012) Oxford: OUP; and Carty, H, *An Analysis of Economic Torts*, 2nd edn (2010) Oxford: OUP.
76 [1892] AC 25.
77 See, for example, *Erven Warnink BV v J Townend and Sons (Hull) Ltd (No 1)* [1979] AC 731; *Haig and Co Ltd v Forth Blending Ltd* 1954 SC 35; and *Scottish Milk Marketing Board v Dryborough and Co Ltd* 1985 SLT 253. Also, note the related remedies under s 56(2) of the Trade Marks Act 1994 in respect of the proprietor of a 'well-known' trade mark.

competition, an area of law which is more developed in, for example, the German legal system.[78] It should be noted that the Competition Act 1998 and Enterprise Act 2002, discussed more fully in Chapter 2, facilitate claims being brought before the courts or the Competition Appeal Tribunal for breach of the prohibitions in the 1998 Act. These claims will be determined on normal principles of delictual/tortious liability as breaches of a statutory duty. Similar claims can also be made on the basis of a breach of the EU prohibitions.

Restraint of trade

The third area of common law involvement in competition law is through the contract-based remedy of unreasonable restraint of trade. This is a fairly limited doctrine which allows a party to escape a contract that unreasonably restrains their ability to trade. The remedy relies on two tests: firstly, reasonableness as between the parties; and, secondly, reasonableness in the public interest. The doctrine was given importance in *Esso Petroleum Co Ltd v Harper's Garage (Stourport) Ltd*[79] where purchasing agreements, which required the purchase of petrol exclusively from Esso, were considered. Although the effect is limited,[80] the restraint of trade doctrine still has vitality. In particular, restraint of trade actions have been taken by individuals claiming that long-term agreements have been in restraint of trade due to the inequality of bargaining power between the parties. Notable in this context have been claims by various recording artists, for instance, George Michael's claim against Sony.[81] That action failed, although it was noted that agreements of lesser duration involving Holly Johnson and the Stone Roses were held to be invalid in earlier litigation. In practice, it appears that parties often make alternative claims under Art 101 TFEU or the 1998 Act Chapter I prohibition or the common law restraint of trade doctrine in order to seek to avoid their contractual obligations.[82]

Statutory development

As noted above, competition policy objectives can change. This can be observed in the changing attitudes towards differing competition concerns, such as cartelisation and pricing, which are reflected in the statutory developments and their enforcement. It should also be stressed at this stage that the content and enforcement of UK competition law has altered dramatically in a short space of time.

The first competition-related statute was the Profiteering Act 1919, which was aimed at excessive pricing following the First World War. The 1944 White Paper on Employment Policy led to the Monopolies and Restrictive Trade Practices (Inquiry and Control) Act 1948. A major concern of the administrative body established by the 1948 Act, the Monopolies and Restrictive Practices Commission, was with the activities of trade associations, which were prevalent in the UK. Following upon the Monopolies and Restrictive Practices Commission's 1956 report, *Collective Discrimination*,[83] the Restrictive Trade Practices Act 1956 was introduced, later extended by the Resale Prices Act 1964. The only other major statutory development before 1973 was the Monopolies and Mergers Act 1965, which introduced merger controls for the first time.

---

78 See, for example, Willimsky, S, 'Aspects of Unfair Competition Law in Germany' [1996] ECLR 315.
79 [1968] AC 269.
80 See *Texaco Ltd v Mulberry Filling Station Ltd* [1972] 1 All ER 513.
81 *Panayiotou and Others v Sony Music Entertainment (UK) Ltd* [1994] 1 All ER 755. See, also, the earlier case of *Schroeder Music Publishing Co Ltd v Macauley* [1974] 3 All ER 616.
82 See *Days Medical Aids Ltd v Pihsiang Machinery Manufacturing Co* [2004] EWHC 44 (Comm) where it was considered that the common law doctrine did not have a different objective from Art 81 EC and indeed the court would be precluded from applying it to the extent that it was inconsistent with the application of Art 81 EC.
83 Monopolies and Restrictive Trade Practices Commission, *Collective Discrimination: A Report on Exclusive Dealing, Collective Boycotts, Aggregated Rebates and Other Discriminatory Trade Practices 1955–56*, Cmnd 9504, 1956.

The UK entered the EEC in 1973 and, in that year, the Fair Trading Act 1973 was enacted and came into force. This statute was not a response to membership of the EEC, but was a consolidating piece of legislation adding a major new feature to the UK competition law regime. This was the creation of the post of the Director General of Fair Trading (DGFT), who would be assisted in the task of overseeing competition law enforcement in the UK by the Office of Fair Trading (OFT). The 1973 Act covered monopolies, in the loosest possible sense, and mergers. Further consolidating legislation was introduced in 1976, regulating anti-competitive agreements: the Restrictive Trade Practices Act 1976, the Restrictive Practices Court Act 1976 and the Resale Prices Act 1976. The only competition legislation introduced by successive Conservative Governments from 1979 to 1997 was the Competition Act 1980. This Act extended the powers of the DGFT to regulate 'anti-competitive practices' and also introduced a measure, latterly of limited significance, providing for efficiency audits of nationalised industries.

From the late 1980s, there was continuous debate on whether UK competition law should be reformed to mirror the then EC competition law provisions.[84] In 1996, the outgoing Conservative Government published a consultation document[85] followed by a draft Competition Bill.[86] This would have introduced an Art 101 TFEU-type provision in place of the 1976 Acts and added newer enforcement powers for the DGFT under the FTA 1973 and Competition Act 1980. The Labour Government, following the 1997 election, introduced the Competition Bill, subsequently passed as the Competition Act 1998. This radically altered UK competition law by repealing the 1976 Acts and the Competition Act 1980. In their place, the Competition Act 1998 introduced, as of 1 March 2000, new controls known as the Chapter I and Chapter II prohibitions, essentially modelled on the EU prohibitions. The FTA 1973 was retained at that stage, subject to certain modifications.

It appeared at that stage that major competition law reform in the UK occurred on a 25-year cycle. However, in 2001, the Government proposed further radical changes to the UK competition law structure.[87] The Enterprise Act 2002 was subsequently introduced and further reformed UK competition law, repealing the monopoly and merger provisions of the FTA 1973 and making the following changes, *inter alia*: transfer of the functions of the DGFT to a new corporate body, the OFT; reform of merger control and the replacement of the public interest test with a new competition test; introduction of a market investigation scheme to replace the FTA 1973 'monopoly' provisions; enhanced rights for consumer bodies to complain ('super-complaints'); creation of a specialist competition tribunal, the Competition Appeal Tribunal (CAT); and the creation of a criminal offence for involvement in cartels.[88] As of 1 May 2004, a number of important changes were made to domestic competition law to mirror the changes introduced following modernisation of EU competition law, including notably the abolition of the notification system originally introduced under the Competition Act 1998.[89]

Further, albeit less fundamental, reforms of UK competition took place in 2013. The Enterprise and Regulatory Reform Act 2013 received Royal Assent on 25 April 2013 and its competition provisions came into force in April 2014. The 2013 Act made radical changes to the

---

84 *Opening Markets: New Policy on Restrictive Trade Practices*, Cm 727, 1989, following the earlier Green Paper, *Review of Restrictive Trade Practices Policy*, Cm 331, 1988; *Abuse of Market Power*, Cm 2100, 1992; House of Commons Trade and Industry Committee, Fifth Report, HC 249-I, 1995; see, also, *Government Observations on the Fifth Report from the Trade and Industry Committee (Session 1994–95) on UK Policy on Monopolies*, HC 748, 19 July 1995.

85 Department of Trade and Industry, *Tackling Cartels and the Abuse of Market Power: Implementing the Government's Policy for Competition Law Reform, a Consultation Document*, March 1996, London: DTI.

86 Department of Trade and Industry, *Tackling Cartels and the Abuse of Market Power: A Draft Bill, An Explanatory Document*, August 1996, London: DTI.

87 HM Treasury and DTI, *Productivity in the UK: Enterprise and the Productivity Challenge*, June 2001, and *Productivity and Enterprise: A World Class Competition Regime*, Cm 5233, 31 July 2001.

88 The Enterprise Act introduced the first specific competition law offence but there have been common law prosecutions, for instance *R v GG plc* [2008] UKHL 17.

89 See, generally, the Competition Act 1998 and Other Enactments (Amendment) Regulations 2004, SI 2004/1261.

UK's criminal cartel offence, with the aim of making it easier to secure convictions. The Act also merged the UK's two traditional competition authorities into a new, single regulator – the Competition and Markets Authority – as well as making a variety of other procedural reforms aimed at making the competition regime more streamlined and efficient.[90] Measures to engender greater private enforcement at a UK level are also imminent; the draft Consumer Rights Bill seeks to enhance the role of the CAT by allowing it to hear stand-alone actions and grant injunctions, introduce a limited 'opt-out' collective action, and promote the greater use of ADR in competition law disputes by introducing an 'opt-out' collective settlement scheme.[91]

Comparison of Competition Law Objectives under EU and UK Law and Policy

EU competition policy objectives

Market integration is a general aim of the EU, and played a crucial role in the development of EU competition policy. It is generally accepted that market integration was the unifying aim of EU competition policy; however, it is difficult to discern which other policy objectives have been pursued alongside it. Nonetheless, certain objectives have become clear in the jurisprudence of the Commission and Court in applying EU competition law, such as: the diffusion of economic power; the protection of the economic freedom of market participants, specifically of small- and medium-sized firms; and the assurance that economic resources are efficiently allocated. More generally, and in contrast to the US, the social value of 'fairness' has also been incorporated. The EU's refusal to adopt the Chicago school approach, based solely on efficiency, can be linked to these broad objectives.

Furthermore, Art 173 TFEU gives legal basis to the link between competition law and industrial policy. Similar links exist with other tangential policy objectives pursued by the Commission. Competition law does not exist in a vacuum and this is clearly recognised by the Commission. Indeed, it is instructive each year to examine the *Annual Report on European Competition Policy*, compiled by the Commission, to gain an insight into the Commission's views on the objectives of competition law. The *XXVIth Report* (1996) was particularly informative and stated that:

> (1) . . . competition policy interacts with most other broadly based policies such as the development of the internal market, the policy on growth and competitiveness, the policy on cohesion, research and development policy, environmental policy and consumer protection.
>
> (2) Competition policy is thus both a Commission policy in its own right and an integral part of a large number of Union policies and with them seeks to achieve the Community objectives set out in Art 2 of the Treaty.[92]

In particular, that report identified a positive link between competition policy and employment policy. In addition, it stressed that before Community competition policy could function fully, it should be required to 'take account of globalisation' and 'help to develop the full potential of the internal market'.

During the process of reforming the Merger Regulation, the Commission highlighted the potential for an increased role for efficiency arguments.[93] In addition, the importance of the

---

90 Department for Business, Innovation and Skills, 'Enterprise and Regulatory Reform Act 2013: A guide', June 2013, London: BIS.
91 Department for Business, Innovation and Skills, 'Draft Consumer Rights Bill: Government Response to Consultations on Consumer Rights', June 2013, London: BIS.
92 *European Community Competition Policy – 1996*, 1997, Brussels: OOPEC.
93 *XXXIInd Report on Competition Policy 2002*, p 4: 'A further objective of the . . . proposal is to take greater account of the efficiencies that can result from mergers.'

interests of consumers has also been stressed as a key factor in EU competition policy generally,[94] bolstered by the appointment of a Consumer Liaison Officer within DG Comp. Market integration is no longer the predominant principle in EU competition policy. In any event, from analysis of EU jurisprudence, it is apparent that market integration has not been an issue in all, or even most, cases involving the application of the competition rules, notwithstanding its persuasive effect in early cases such as the *Johnny Walker Red Label* case.[95] The Commission has focused its current enforcement effort on international cartels affecting the EU market and consumers, such as the vitamins and the escalators and lifts cartels, both discussed above. It is instructive to read an excerpt from the foreword to the Report on Competition Policy 2010 by the European Commission, as it provides a flavour of the current EU competition law agenda:

> It is clear from the early annual Reports that the contribution and support of competition towards other policy objectives has gone well beyond being used as a crisis resolution instrument. As the EU exits from the current crisis in the face of fierce global competition, a major challenge for competition policy in the coming years will be to support as effectively as possible the Europe 2020 Strategy for smart, inclusive and sustainable growth.
>
> Competition policy is well placed to make such a contribution as it is a key driver for making markets work better through an efficient allocation of resources and increased productivity and innovation. It therefore underpins the competitiveness of the EU economy, which is more important than ever to maintain economic and financial stability. Competition policy and competition-enhancing reforms must thus form an integral part of the economic governance.
>
> Competition rules also recognise the need to enable Member States to promote the Union's objectives of economic, social and territorial cohesion. The regional aid guidelines facilitate the realisation of the territorial cohesion of the Union by promoting the development of poorer regions. The different state aid rules also allow for training aid and the promotion of the access of disadvantaged and disabled workers to employment
>
> Another essential area where competition policy has evolved to take into account a long term challenge to the Union is the protection of the environment and the promotion of sustainable growth. Through both its antitrust enforcement activities in the energy sector which enhances liquidity and security of supply in the internal market and its adoption of environmental state aid guidelines, which facilitate aid to address market failures in this area, the Commission has ensured that competition policy supports the shift towards a more sustainable economy.[96]

UK Competition Policy Objectives

This section aims to give a brief background to the history of UK competition law and the approach adopted by the UK authorities involved. At no time have the objectives of UK competition law been clearly stated and defined. However, general indications about competition policy and law in action in the past can be derived from the reports of the DGFT, policy statements by the Secretary of State and various policy review documents. More recently, the OFT has adopted a more transparent approach, notable through its publication of an Annual plan, preceded by a period of consultation on a draft. The UK legislative materials provide a useful example of how competition

---

94 Ibid, p 12: 'One of the main purposes of European Competition Policy is to promote the interests of consumers, that is, to ensure that consumers benefit from the wealth generated by the European economy . . . the Commission thus takes the interest of the consumers into account in all aspects of its competition policy.'

95 Case 30/78 *Distillers v Commission* [1980] ECR 2229. For a contemporary case with a clear 'market integration' influence, see Case C-439/09, *Pierre Fabre Dermo-Cosmétique SAS v Président de l'Autorité de la concurrence* [2011] ECR I-9419.

96 European Commission, 'Report on Competition Policy 2010', SEC(2011) 690 final, paras 29–32.

law objectives can change, even within the context of the same domestic setting. Under the FTA 1973, conformity of market structure and conduct with the public interest test comprised the basic benchmark, but this broad test comprised a variety of vague economic and socio-political concerns. Its flexibility allowed markets to be investigated without the requirement for blame and, consequently, a variety of factors that may have led to market failure could be assessed. The utilitarian model of public interest assessment was central to a statutory framework, which concentrated on market failure and not necessarily on some form of reproachable behaviour. The public interest test was certainly not based on the need for certainty and predictability.

There was debate in the UK regarding the suitability of the public interest test and its concern with non-competition issues. The tension was noted by Sir Geoffrey Howe, as the Minister for Trade and Consumer Affairs, after the 1973 Act was passed, in relation to merger control:

> If a merger seemed likely to cause significant redundancies or to be incompatible with the Government's regional policies, the case for full investigation would be strengthened . . . What I have deliberately not attempted to do is to say what weight is to be attributed, for all time, to any particular aspect. Our national priorities change. The Government's powers must be sufficiently flexible to reflect these changing priorities.[97]

Subsequently, in July 1984, the then Secretary of State for Trade and Industry, now Lord Tebbit, issued a statement now known as the 'Tebbit Doctrine'. He stated, in relation to merger control, that the merger referral policy would be based 'primarily on competition grounds'. Although retained when the Competition Act 1998 was introduced, the FTA 1973 and its public interest test have now largely been consigned to historical interest, since the coming into force of the Enterprise Act 2002. The 2002 Act sought to depoliticise UK competition law by in effect removing the Secretary of State's role in merger control, and also by replacing the public interest test with a competition-based test for market and merger investigations.[98] Of course, as will be discussed in Chapter 8, the Secretary of State retains a residual role in certain mergers which are deemed to be of public interest, where for instance there is a national security consideration; the merger is a newspaper or media merger; or following the 'economic crisis' in 2007/08 where a merger may affect the maintenance of the stability of the UK financial system, as exemplified by the approval of the Lloyds/HBOS merger.[99]

The Competition Act 1998 has already clearly become the predominant statute in UK competition law and policy. It is suggested that there were two principal objectives behind this legislation. The first was to harmonise domestic controls with those under Arts 101 and 102 TFEU, partly in order to avoid the imposition of a double compliance burden on UK business. The second, perhaps paradoxical, object has been to increase the deterrent effect of UK competition law by providing enhanced investigatory and fining powers. The Enterprise Act 2002, with the introduction of criminal sanctions and a specialist competition court (CAT), was also clearly designed to enhance the deterrent effect of the new prohibition-based system in the UK, while the subsequent reforms introduced as of 1 May 2004 reflect the harmonisation objective. In addition, many of the reforms introduced by the 2002 Act made promotion of the consumer interest an explicit objective of the system, both substantively and institutionally. The OFT's Annual Report for 2012/13 emphasised that the OFT is saving consumers £136m per year through its competition law enforcement activities. Furthermore, as mentioned above, the Consumer Rights Bill (cl 88 and Sch 8) will, if enacted, significantly change the landscape of private enforcement in the

97 'Government policy on mergers' (1973) 13 (1 November) Trade and Industry 230, p 235.
98 Enterprise Act 2002, Pts 3 and 4, more fully discussed in Chapter 8.
99 OFT, 'Anticipated acquisition by Lloyds TSB plc of HBOS plc – Report to the Secretary of State for Business Enterprise and Regulatory Reform', 24 October 2008.

UK. Potentially the most significant reform is the introduction of an opt-out representative collective redress mechanism for consumers to sue for damages for competition law infringements.[100]

Key Points

- Competition law will intervene in markets where there is 'market failure'. This failure can occur through a number of market features or mechanisms; notably, monopoly, cartels or mergers.
- The concern about monopoly or market power is the unifying theme of most competition law. Neoclassical economic predictions of the consequences of monopoly inform this 'pure competition' objective.
- The concept that defines the contemporary competition policy orthodoxy is 'Consumer Welfare'. Consumers benefit from efficient markets, but they also want innovation, choice, quality and safety.
- Several schools of economic thought have had influence over competition law thinking throughout its development.
- Political goals and other policy objectives have influence over the development of competition law. Individual jurisdictions will therefore develop different approaches to market challenges.
- The development of US, EU and UK competition policy has been influenced by the competition problems that each jurisdiction has faced and their very different political and social landscapes.

Discussion

Robert Bork, *The Antitrust Paradox: A Policy at War with Itself* (1993)
Oxford: Maxwell Macmillan

Antitrust policy cannot be made rational until we are able to give a firm answer to one question: what is the point of the law – what are its goals?

Discuss the possible goals of antitrust/competition law and, in particular, the development of EU and UK competition law and policy objectives.

Further Reading

Competition policy general
Amato, G, *Antitrust and the Bounds of Power* (1997) Oxford: Hart.
Stucke, ME, 'Is Competition Always Good?' (2013) 1(1) J Antitrust Enforcement 162–197.
Willimsky, S, 'The Concept(s) of Competition' [1997] 1 ECLR 54.

The consumer and competition policy
Ahdar, 'Consumers, Redistribution of Income and the Purpose of Competition Law' [2002] ECLR 341.
Averitt, NW and Lande, RH, 'Using the "Consumer Choice" Approach to Antitrust Law' (2007) Antitrust Law Journal 175.
Marsden, P and Whelan, P, ' "Consumer Detriment" and its Application in EC and UK Competition Law' [2007] ECLR 569.

---

100 For a fuller discussion of the proposed reforms, see Wisking, S, Dietzel, K and Herron, M, 'The Rise and Rise of Private Enforcement in the United Kingdom – Government Announces Far-reaching Overhaul of the Competition Law Private Actions Regime' [2013] 6 GCLR 78–77.

EU competition policy development

Frazer, T, 'Competition Policy after 1992: The Next Step' (1990) 53 MLR 609.

Gerber, D, *Law and Competition in Twentieth Century Europe* (1998) Oxford: Clarendon.

Lianos, I, 'Some Reflections on the Question of the Goals of EU Competition Law' Chapter 1 in
I Lianos and D Geradin, eds, *Handbook on European Competition Law: Substantive Aspects*
(2013) Edward Elgar Publishing.

Townley, C, 'Which Goals Count in Article 101 TFEU? Public Policy and its discontents' [2011]
ECLR 441.

Weitbrecht, A, 'From Freiburg to Chicago and Beyond – The First 50 Years of European
Competition Law' [2008] ECLR 81.

UK competition policy development

Maher, I, 'Juridification, Codification and Sanction in UK Competition Law' (2000) 63 MLR 544.

Rodger, BJ (ed), *Ten Years of UK Competition Law Reform* (2010) Dundee: DUP.

US background

Baker, DI, 'An Enduring Antitrust Divide Across the Atlantic Over Whether to Incarcerate
Conspirators and When to Restrain Abusive Monopolists' [2009] 5(1) European Competition
Journal 145–200.

Bork, R, 'Introduction: The Crisis in Antitrust', in *The Antitrust Paradox: A Policy at War with Itself*
(1993) Oxford: Maxwell Macmillan.

Fox, E, 'The New American Competition Policy – from Antitrust to Pro-efficiency' [1981] ECLR
439.

Kovacic, WE, 'The Intellectual DNA of Modern US Competition Law for Dominant Firm Conduct:
The Chicago/Harvard Double Helix' [2007] Columbia Business Law Review 1.

Pitofsky, R, 'The Political Content of Antitrust' [1979] 127 UPLR 1051.

Reeves, AP and Stucke, MF, 'Behavioural Antitrust' (2011) 06(4) Indiana Law Journal 1527.

Stucke, ME 'Reconsidering Competition law and the Goals of Competition Law' (2011) 81
Mississippi Law Journal 107.

Sullivan, L, 'Antitrust, Microeconomics and Politics: Reflections on Some Recent Relationships'
[1980] 68 Calif LR 1.

Chapter 2

Enforcement of EU and UK Competition Law

Chapter Contents

Overview

- The European Commission, through DG Comp, is at the apex of the EU competition law enforcement system. But, under Regulation 1/2003, the Commission enforces the EU prohibitions alongside Member States' NCAs, as part of the European Competition Network (ECN).
- Regulation 1/2003 affords the Commission extensive powers to investigate and sanction infringements of the rules. It can carry out dawn raids and impose significant fines on business. It also uses informal mechanisms such as settlements and commitments.
- The Commission's decision-making processes must be in line with due process requirements and are subject to review by the General Court and Court of Justice.
- The central enforcement role in the UK lies with the Competition and Markets Authority, which has assumed the tasks previously undertaken by the Office of Fair Trading. The CMA has a range of powers, remedies and sanctions which are closely modelled on those available to the European Commission, and its decisions are subject to appeal first to the Competition Appeal Tribunal and then the civil appeal courts.
- Competition law has responded to the globalisation of markets and anti-competitive behaviour by developing mechanisms for developing shared experiences and best practices in competition law policy and practice.

Introduction

This chapter deals with the ways in which the main prohibitions under EU and UK competition law are administered and enforced. The chapter will review the administrative enforcement framework in each system, the public authorities involved in enforcement, and outline the relevant rules for investigation, decision-making and judicial review. The starting point is the European Competition Network (ECN) and the EU framework of enforcement led by the Commission. In particular, we shall address the EU competition law enforcement system in relation to Arts 101 and 102 TFEU set out in Regulation 1/2003.[1] In the UK context, the enforcement system has developed through the Competition Act 1998, the Enterprise Act 2002 and the Enterprise and Regulatory Reform Act 2013. The new unitary enforcement authority in the UK, as of April 2014, is the Competition and Markets Authority (CMA), which is entrusted with enforcing the Competition Act 1998 prohibitions and Articles 101 and 102 TFEU, as the UK's National Competition Authority in the ECN. The CMA's investigative and fining powers for both the UK and EU prohibitions are identical. Markets, and hence the application of competition rules in relation to market behaviour, are not necessarily confined to the territorial boundaries of either the EU or the UK – particularly given the increasing tendency towards market globalisation. The potential for the extraterritorial application of the competition rules will be considered, together with steps towards international co-operation in competition law enforcement, at the end of this chapter. The enforcement structure for market and merger investigations under the Enterprise Act 2002 will be considered in Chapters 5 and 8 respectively. This chapter focuses on the public enforcement mechanisms for the EU and UK prohibitions, and in Chapter 3 there will be detailed consideration of private enforcement of competition law, including developments to facilitate private competition litigation at both EU and UK levels to ensure adequate respect for rights damaged by competition law infringements and further enhance competition law deterrence.

---

1   Regulation 1/2003/EC on the implementation of the rules on competition laid down in Arts 81 and 82 of the Treaty, [2003] OJ L1/1.

EU Enforcement Framework

Outline

The EU enforcement system has undergone significant reform since its inception in 1962. While the majority of this text will focus on the framework under Regulation 1/2003, it is still necessary to have a basic understanding of the original regime, under Regulation 17/62,[2] to appreciate the reasons for, and importance of, the reform. The European Commission ('the Commission'), based in Brussels, has an important central role in the enforcement of EU competition law, but it is also assisted by a network of National Competition Authorities (NCAs) across the EU. There are also two EU courts, which are important in the development of EU competition law. First, applications for the review of Commission Decisions may be made to the General Court (GC), and thereafter a further appeal on a point of law may be made to the Court of Justice of the EU (CJEU). The CJEU may also deal with Art 267 TFEU references for preliminary rulings, which are received from domestic courts and tribunals seeking authoritative rulings on matters of EU competition law to assist them in resolving competition law disputes before them. The practical issues involved in private competition law actions before domestic courts within the EU are discussed more fully in Chapter 3, but it must be remembered that the Art 267 TFEU reference procedure means that those cases can be an important mechanism for the development of EU-wide competition law.

The former regime under Regulation 17

From 1962 until 2004 the Commission was, for all intents and purposes, solely entrusted with enforcement of the EU competition rules. This was known as centralised enforcement. This task was carried out within the Commission by the Directorate General for Competition (DG Comp, formerly Directorate General IV 'DGIV'). Regulation 17 set up the framework for the enforcement of Arts 101 and 102 TFEU and contained provisions for investigation procedures, the Commission's conduct of infringement proceedings, general rules for hearings, while also giving the Commission power to take other decisions. The Commission had the central enforcement role under Regulation 17, but its powers were subject to certain limitations. Procedural fairness and other general principles of EU law, such as a right to a hearing, proportionality and fundamental freedoms, had to be ensured, particularly in the exercise of its fining powers. The Commission's role was central to the system as the Commission retained sole control over a number of important powers, particularly the power to grant exemptions from the Art 101 TFEU prohibition under Art 101(3) TFEU. In the early years of the EU competition regime, the central role of the Commission was useful as the Commission gained valuable experience of the way in which European business was conducted. The parties to potentially anti-competitive agreements would have to notify their agreements to the Commission and seek an exemption. The Commission used the notification process to gain insight and experience, and then used its decision-making powers to shape future developments; however, the centralised notification procedure also had other effects. Because of the importance of the power of exemption, the NCAs and the domestic courts found it very difficult to enforce the competition rules effectively; often domestic courts would have to stop their proceedings and await a Commission ruling. The procedure also created a heavy administrative burden for the Commission, which spent a great deal of its time and resources dealing with a large number of relatively benign agreements rather than focusing on more serious, and more covert, competition infringements. In the late 1990s it became abundantly clear that the administrative arrangements that had served the embryonic EU well in the 1960s were increasingly unable to deal with the pressures of a much larger and more integrated

---

2   Regulation 17/62/EEC First Regulation implementing Arts 85 and 86 of the Treaty, [1959–62] OJ sp ed 87.

EU of a then total of 15 Member States. With the certainty of further enlargement into Central and Eastern Europe, it was evident that reform was necessary.

The Commission began a process of consultation, which led to the Regulation 1/2003 'modernisation' reform, by publishing its *White Paper on Modernisation of the Rules Implementing Articles 85 and 86 of the EC Treaty*.[3] The White Paper highlighted the problems with the Regulation 17 regime and suggested various options which the Commission might have been able to adopt. It also sparked an enormous amount of debate.[4] The Commission's preferred option was to move towards a 'directly applicable' system whereby it would give up its sole power to grant exceptions under Art 101(3) TFEU. This would allow NCAs and national courts, alongside the Commission, to apply Art 101 in a comprehensive manner.[5] After further consultation on the issue, the Commission put forward proposals for a new governing regulation, to replace Regulation 17, based on the 'directly applicable' model.[6] The debate in Council, leading up to the adoption of Regulation 1/2003, was heated, with several Member States having concerns about various aspects of the new regime.[7] While the main focus of the debate was on the direct application of Art 101(3) TFEU, the Regulation also updated various aspects of the enforcement regime, and introduced several innovations that were not part of Regulation 17, including the introduction of structural remedies and sectoral investigations. The Regulation was eventually adopted by Council in December 2002 and came into force on 1 May 2004.[8] The Commission also adopted a number of other procedural Regulations and Notices in order to facilitate the operation of the new system.[9]

It is not coincidental that Regulation 1/2003 came into force on the same day that the EU enlarged to 25 Member States. The ongoing expansion of the EU, and the role of the NCAs within the EU competition regime, creates a unique set of problems, in particular as a consequence of many EU accession states moving, within a relatively short timescale, from planned economies to a liberalised market economy model. Notwithstanding these challenges, most accession states were prepared for their role within the ECN, as they had existing NCAs with experience of operating prohibitions that were based on the EU prohibitions.[10]

---

3 Commission Programme No 99/027, [1999] OJ C132/01.

4 See, for example, Forrester, I, 'Modernisation of EC Competition Law' (2000) 23 Fordham Int LJ 1032; Ehlermann, CD, 'The Modernisation of EC Antitrust Policy: A Legal and Cultural Revolution' (2000) 37 CML Rev 537; Rodger, BJ, 'The Commission White Paper on Modernisation of the Rules Implementing Articles 81 and 82 of the EC Treaty' (1999) 26 EL Rev 653; Wesseling, R, 'The Commission White Paper on Modernisation of EC Antitrust Law: Unspoken Consequences and Incomplete Treatment of Alternative Options' [1999] ECLR 420; and, Odudu, O, *The Boundaries of EC Competition Law* (2006) Oxford: OUP.

5 See Todino, M, 'Modernisation from the Perspective of National Competition Authorities: Impact of the Reform on Decentralised Application of EC Competition Law' [2001] ECLR 349.

6 Proposal for a Council Regulation on the implementation of the rules on competition laid down in Articles 81 and 82 of the Treaty, COM(2000) 582. See, also, Jones, T, 'Regulation 17: The Impact of the Current Application of Article 81 and 82 by the National Competition Authorities on the European Commission's Proposals for Reform' [2001] ECLR 405.

7 In particular a debate concerning whether Art 101(3) TFEU was capable of having direct effect; see, Odudu, O, 'Article 81(3), Discretion and Direct Effect' [2002] ECLR 17.

8 Regulation 1/2003/EC, [2003] OJ L1/1. See, also, Riley, A, 'EC Antitrust Modernisation: The Commission Does Very Nicely – Thank You!' Part 1 [2003] ECLR 604; Part 2 [2003] ECLR 657. Cf Pijetlovic, K, 'Reform of EC Antitrust Enforcement: Criticism of the New System is Highly Exaggerated' [2004] ECLR 356.

9 The original 2004 Regulations and Notices were: Regulation 773/2004/EC relating to the conduct of proceedings by the Commission pursuant to Arts 81 and 82 of the EC Treaty, [2004] OJ L123/18, Commission Notice on co-operation within the Network of Competition Authorities, [2004] OJ C101/43, Commission Notice on the co-operation between the Commission and the courts of the EU Member States in the application of Arts 81 and 82 EC, [2004] OJ C101/54, Commission Notice on the handling of complaints by the Commission under Arts 81 and 82 of the EC Treaty, [2004] OJ C101/65, Commission Notice on informal guidance relating to novel questions concerning Arts 81 and 82 of the EC Treaty that arise in individual cases (guidance letters), [2004] OJ C101/78, Commission Notice, Guidelines on the effect on trade concept contained in Arts 81 and 82 of the Treaty, [2004] OJ C101/81, Commission Notice, Guidelines on the application of Art 81(3) of the Treaty, [2004] OJ C101/97, and Commission Notice on the rules for access to the Commission file in cases pursuant to Articles 81 and 82 of the EC Treaty, Articles 53, 54 and 57 of the EEA Agreement and Council Regulation (EC) No 139/2004, [2005] OJ C325/7.

10 For example, Poland.

Decentralised EU competition enforcement

The institution of a decentralised network of National Competition Authorities enforcing EU competition law is at the core of Regulation 1/2003. Enforcement by the Commission alone was no longer plausible and the difficulties encountered in facilitating widespread recourse to national courts, as discussed in Chapter 3, required a more radical solution. The solution was to institute a system of NCAs enforcing EU competition law in each Member State on a decentralised basis. Most Member States had a body which could fulfil the NCA role, and several Member States had already adopted rules enabling their NCAs to apply EU competition law.[11] In 1997 the Commission Notice on Co-operation between National Competition Authorities and the Commission, on handling competition cases, was published.[12] The crucial feature of the Notice was the provisions on the allocation of competencies for applying EU competition law both between the Commission and the Member States and between the Member States themselves. The Notice also provided advice to NCAs as to how they should proceed in enforcing the EU competition rules. Although the intention was to reduce the workload of the Commission, the impact of the Notice in practice was minimal. The value of the Notice was particularly limited by the absence of a provision by all Member States affording their NCAs the competence to apply Arts 101 and 102 TFEU. Nonetheless, the Notice did set the platform for the more detailed provisions subsequently introduced in Regulation 1/2003.

Probably the most important aspect of Regulation 1/2003 was the provision for an increased level of co-operation between all the authorities involved in the enforcement of EU competition law.[13] This operates through the network of competition authorities, known as the 'European Competition Network' (ECN), incorporating the Commission and all the NCAs. The direct applicability of Art 101(3) TFEU means that many of the barriers to the enforcement of EU competition law by domestic authorities have been removed, but it is still vital that the Commission plays a central role to co-ordinate the enforcement activities of the separate NCAs and to assist, when required, the national courts. The Commission's role will now focus on co-ordinating and developing policy, rather than on day-to-day enforcement;[14] however, it will still play the lead role in enforcing the most serious infringements. Article 11 of Regulation 1/2003 establishes the principle of close co-operation between the Commission and NCAs to enable the system of parallel competences within the ECN to function smoothly. It sets out the basic information exchange and consultation mechanisms, and is supplemented by the Network Notice.[15] Article 13 of the Regulation seeks to ensure effective case allocation and to avoid duplication of effort by allowing an NCA or the Commission to suspend or terminate proceedings where a case is being, or has been, dealt with by another authority.[16] The Network Notice sets out that most cases should be dealt with by a single 'well-placed' authority. The Notice envisages three possibilities: enforcement by a single NCA; enforcement by several NCAs acting in parallel; or enforcement by the Commission. Cases will normally remain with the authority that begins the proceedings, either of its own initiative or as the result of a complaint,[17] but some proceedings will need to be

---

11 See, for further discussion of the limited UK provision, Kerse, CS, 'Enforcing Community Competition Policy under Articles 88 and 89 of the EC Treaty – New Powers for UK Competition Authorities' [1997] ECLR 17.

12 [1997] OJ C313/3.

13 See Dekeyser, K and Jaspers, M, 'A New Era of ECN Cooperation, Achievements and Challenges with Special Focus on Work in the Leniency Field' (2007) 30(1) *World Competition* 3.

14 As Dekeyser and Jaspers *supra* note, between 1 May 2004 and 31 December 2006, 670 cases were pursued under the EU competition rules, and the Commission was involved in investigation in less than 25% of cases. For a more up-to-date account of the ECN mechanisms in practice, see Wils, WJ, 'Ten Years of Regulation 1/2003 – A Retrospective' *Journal of European Competition Law and Practice* (2013) 4(4) 293–301 in which it is noted that by end December 2012, the NCAs had adopted 88% of all decisions enforcing Arts 101 and 102.

15 Commission Notice on co-operation within the Network of Competition Authorities, [2004] OJ C101/43.

16 For a detailed discussion, see Brammer, S, 'Concurrent Jurisdiction under Regulation 1/2003 and the Issue of Case Allocation' (2005) 42(5) CMLRev 1383.

17 Commission Notice on the handling of complaints by the Commission under Articles 81 and 82 of the EC Treaty, [2004] OJ C101/65.

reallocated. Where reallocation is required, the proceedings will preferably go to 'a single well-placed' authority.[18] There are three key factors in determining which authority is most appropriate, and they are as follows: (a) the area in which the anti-competitive practice has substantial, actual or foreseeable effects, is implemented, or originated; (b) which authority is most able to effectively bring the infringement to an end and impose an appropriate sanction; and (c) which authority can gather the evidence required to prove the infringement.[19] The Commission will usually be best placed to deal with a practice that has effects in more than three Member States[20] or the Community interest requires a decision to develop competition policy.[21] To ensure this division of work operates effectively, Regulation 1/2003 provides, in Art 11, for the exchange of information between all the authorities. This seeks to ensure that where related practices are being examined by more than one authority, this should be identified quickly. When a case has been allocated to an authority, any other authorities that have received similar complaints are empowered by Art 13 of Regulation 1/2003 to reject those complaints and terminate their investigations.

To assist in the cross-border investigation of possible infringements, Regulation 1/2003 also provides, under Art 12, for the exchange of information between NCAs. In addition to the exchange of existing material, an authority can ask another authority, under Art 22, to assist it in gathering material. The information that can be exchanged includes confidential information gathered by an authority for the purpose of applying the EU prohibitions. The power to exchange information does not always include information that has been gathered in relation to proceedings under national law, if the application of national law leads to an outcome different from that of the EU prohibitions, or where sanctions could be imposed on individuals.[22] This will obviously include material gathered in the UK in relation to a potential prosecution of the cartel offence under s 188 of the Enterprise Act 2002. There are several provisions that seek to ensure consistency and uniformity in the application of EU law within the ECN. Article 11 of Regulation 1/2003 sets out situations in which the NCAs must inform the Commission of their activities. Article 11(3) requires the NCAs to inform the Commission as soon as they commence an investigation. They are also required to inform the Commission, at least 30 days in advance, of any decision being made. The information passed to the Commission may then be shared with other NCAs. These procedures ensure that the Commission should be aware of the ongoing investigations across the ECN and will be able to intervene to ensure consistency. Article 14 of Regulation 1/2003, on the other hand, consolidates the existing role of the Advisory Committee on Restrictive Practices and Dominant Positions (ACRPDP), which is made up of representatives from the NCAs, by requiring the Commission to consult with it prior to taking decisions.

The final way in which the central role of the Commission in the ECN is retained is through the operation of Art 11(6) of Regulation 1/2003. If, after being informed of the initiation of an investigation by one or more NCAs under Art 11(3) or (4), the Commission decides that the Community interest would benefit from action by the Commission, the Commission can 'call in' the investigation under Art 11(6). When the Commission initiates proceedings it has the effect of relieving any NCA from dealing with that case and reserving all future action in the case to the Commission. This has the dual effect of ensuring that the Commission retains the central 'policy-making' role, and allows the Commission to act decisively if there is a concern that NCAs may not deal consistently with anti-competitive practice.[23]

---

18 Network Notice, para 7.
19 Network Notice, para 8.
20 Network Notice, para 14.
21 Network Notice, para 15. The Network Notice was adopted in the Pre-Lisbon era and therefore refers to the 'Community interest' rather than the Union interest.
22 Network Notice, para 28.
23 Network Notice, para 54.

When investigating an infringement of EU law, the NCA must rely upon the powers granted to it within domestic law as neither Regulation 1/2003 nor the Network Notice sought to harmonise domestic rules on enforcement procedures and powers of the various NCAs. The ability to exchange information and engage in dialogue within the ECN has facilitated a certain degree of convergence already,[24] particularly in relation to leniency, where virtually all Member States now have some form of leniency programme. To facilitate co-ordination, the ECN has developed a Model Leniency Programme.[25]

Enforcement of EU law in the UK

Prior to the adoption of Regulation 1/2003, the Office of Fair Trading (the then NCA within the UK) was not empowered to enforce EU law within the UK; only the domestic provisions that were based on EU law were within its competence. The Enterprise Act 2002 contained a number of provisions that gave the Government powers to adapt the competition regime to fit in with the final shape of the modernised EU regime. In order to participate in the ECN, a number of measures were adopted in early 2004 and the OFT published new guidance setting out its role and responsibilities.

The UK now designates the CMA[26] as the authority that will exercise the relevant powers and functions of a Member State NCA under Regulation 1/2003. Section 25 of the 1998 Act provides the necessary powers to the CMA to enable it to carry out the necessary investigations under both the Competition Act 1998 prohibitions and Arts 101 and 102 TFEU. The CMA can also impose fines for breaches of the EU prohibitions, and the Guidance on Fines allows the CMA to take into account anti-competitive effects in other Member States when determining a penalty.[27] Sections 46 and 47 of the 1998 Act give the Competition Appeal Tribunal (CAT) the role of hearing appeals from CMA decisions regarding the EU prohibitions. The UK and EU prohibitions have been applied together on a number of occasions – for example, *Airline passenger fuel surcharges for long-haul flights*[28] and *Reckitt Benckiser.*[29]

Relationship between EU and national law

An important question concerns the relationship between national, or domestic, competition rules and EU competition law. Of course, the UK provisions under the Competition Act 1998 are modelled on the EU provisions, and there are measures to ensure consistency in ss 10 and 60; therefore, disharmony is less likely. How, then, is the general potential dilemma of the dual application of domestic and EU competition rules resolved? The EU establishes an independent legal order capable of affecting Member States' governments and of conferring rights on individuals in certain instances. The basic rule regarding the relationship between the EU legal system and national laws is that of the supremacy of EU law. Directly applicable EU rules, such as competition law, take precedence over national law. This principle of supremacy of EU law, or the doctrine of 'precedence', was established by the seminal CJEU judgments in *Van Gend en Loos*[30] and *Costa v*

---

24 See ECN Working Group on Cooperation Issues, 'Results of the questionnaire on the reform of the Member States national competition laws after EC Regulation No 1/2003', as of 18 May 2007, at http://ec.europa.eu/comm/competition/ecn/index_en.html, which demonstrates the increasing degree of convergence in Member States' procedural and remedial rules.

25 The ECN Model Leniency Programme (revised in November 2012), See, Commission Press Release, 'Competition: European Competition Network refines its Model Leniency Programme', MEMO/12/887, 22 November 2012, and further discussion in Chapter 7.

26 And any other UK regulator mentioned in s 54(1) of the 1998 Act.

27 The CMA will continue the follow the OFT's 2012 Guidance on Fines: OFT 423, 'OFT's guidance as to the appropriate amount of a penalty', September 2012, para 2.10.

28 OFT Decision No CA98/01/2012, 19 April 2012.

29 OFT Decision No CA98/02/2011, *Abuse of a dominant position by Reckitt Benckiser Healthcare (UK) Ltd and Reckitt Benckiser Group plc*, 12 April 2011.

30 Case 26/62 [1963] ECR 1.

ENEL,[31] and is given effect in the UK by ss 2(1) and 3(1) of the European Communities Act 1972.[32] Accordingly, when a conflict exists with UK domestic competition law, it follows that EU competition law is treated as supreme, and any conflicting provisions of UK law cannot be relied upon.

The respective roles for the application of national and EU competition laws were laid down in *Walt Wilhelm v Bundeskartellamt*,[33] a case that involved a company that was allegedly involved in a price-fixing cartel in the aniline dyes industry. Parallel proceedings were commenced in Germany, under German law, and by the European Commission under the EU competition rules. The German court sought a preliminary reference asking the Court if the company could be subject to penalties under national rules in respect of the same conduct that could be penalised under EU law. The Court confirmed that this was possible but that, in imposing the penalties, the national authorities must bear in mind the penalties that may be imposed by the EU authorities. The Court also confirmed the following points: (a) any conflicts between EU and domestic law are to be resolved by the principle of supremacy of EU law; (b) if an NCA decision is incompatible with a Commission decision, the national authority needs to take proper account of the Commission decision; and (c) if, during the national proceedings, it appears possible that the Commission may adopt a conflicting decision, then it is for the national authority to take the appropriate measures to avoid such a conflict. However, the NCAs can still apply national rules, even where the same issues are under investigation by the Commission, provided that the national decision does not prejudice the full and uniform application of EU law. For instance, the NCAs cannot condemn agreements that fall within an Art 101(3) TFEU block exemption. The rule in *Walt Wilhelm* has been described as a procedural precedence rule that concentrated on the status of administrative decisions, providing that national authorities should have regard to EU decisions that are issued or expected. The potential for delay and confusion caused by the rule has been mitigated to an extent through the mechanisms for co-ordination and communication within the ECN.

Regulation 1/2003[34] seeks to avoid potential problems arising from the procedural precedence rule. Article 3(1) provides that, where there is an effect on interstate trade, national courts and authorities shall, in applying domestic competition law rules, also apply Arts 101 and 102 TFEU.[35] This seeks to ensure a clearer substantive rule of precedence in the application of EU law and national law. Nonetheless, Art 3(3) limits the scope of the rule as follows:

> Without prejudice to general principles and other provisions of Community law, paragraphs 1 and 2 do not apply when the competition authorities and the courts of Member States apply national merger control laws nor do they preclude the application of provisions of national law that predominately pursue an objective different from that pursued by Articles 81 and 82 of the Treaty.

The first part of this provision is straightforward; the second is more complicated, and allows scope for the application of laws which are, for example, based on cultural or environmental policy even where they are in conflict with EU competition law.

Under Regulation 1/2003, NCAs may apply either or both national and EU competition law. Nonetheless, the difficulties under the *Walt Wilhelm* rule are minimal, mainly due to the distinct trend towards the harmonisation of substantive national competition rules with EU law and the convergence of procedural rules. This has not stemmed from any form of 'hard' harmonisation or

---

31 Case 6/64 [1964] ECR 585.
32 The European Communities Act 1972, s 2(1) provides: 'All such rights, powers, liabilities, obligations and restrictions from time to time created under . . . Treaties . . . are without further enactment . . . to be treated as law in the UK.' Section 3(1) provides that if there is any question as to the meaning or effect of the Treaty, such a question of law will go to the Court or be dealt with in accordance with the principles laid down by it.
33 Case 14/68 [1969] ECR 1. See, also, Cases 46/87 and 227/88 *Hoechst v Commission* [1989] ECR 2859.
34 [2003] OJ L1/1.
35 Art 3(2) notes that agreements, etc, which comply with Art 81, are not to be prohibited by domestic law, whereas domestic competition law may apply stricter standards to that which constitutes unilateral abusive conduct.

legislative intervention by the EU, but has been based on four principal developments. Firstly, EU expansion has proceeded on the basis that accession countries adopt market-based competition laws framed on the EU model. A clear example of this exists in relation to the four Visegrad countries: Poland, Hungary and the Czech and Slovak Republics, each of which introduced competition laws in 1990–91, modelled on the EU rules. Secondly, certain Member States (for example, Italy and the Netherlands), which previously had little or no national competition law provision, have adopted legislation based on the EU model. Thirdly, other Member States have amended their existing competition law systems to be modelled on or complement the EU rules. The UK Competition Act 1998 is a classic example of this trend, introducing competition prohibitions modelled on Arts 101 and 102 TFEU, with a general requirement to interpret the prohibitions consistently with EU law. Finally, co-operation and dialogue within the ECN has led to procedural convergence with NCAs assimilating the investigative and fining powers accorded to the Commission under Regulation 1/2003.

The European Commission

The Commission's main task under Art 17 TEU is to 'promote the general interest of the Union' and it has been described as the 'guardian of the Treaties'. It represents the EU's interests and seeks to ensure that the provisions of EU law are applied. Accordingly, the Commission has general supervisory powers under the TEU and TFEU, and more specific powers, under Regulation 1/2003, in relation to enforcement of Arts 101 and 102 TFEU. Figure 2.1 provides an outline illustration of the enforcement framework. The Commission has a number of members, presently one from each Member State with 28 in total, called Commissioners, one of whom is allocated responsibility for competition policy.[36] The Commissioner for competition policy in the 2nd Barroso Commission was Vice President Joaquín Almunia. The staff of the Commission is divided into a number of departments, each with a specialist portfolio of responsibilities. These departments are known as 'Directorates General', shortened to DG for ease of reference, each headed by a Director General. There are a number of DGs, which cover the full range of EU policies from Agriculture to Trade. Competition policy and enforcement is allocated to the DG for Competition and the current Director General is Alexander Italianer. The Commission also has a separate Legal Service.

EU competition law enforcement is complex and the Commission has to be careful how it allocates its limited resources. Therefore, the number of formal decisions taken has been relatively small, and those have generally concerned important points of principle in the development of EU competition policy or particularly serious transgressions of the rules. For many years the Commission has been keen to encourage the enforcement of EU competition law before the national courts and through the NCAs. This push towards the decentralisation of competition enforcement has been a priority of the Commission for some time,[37] and has come to fruition under Regulation 1/2003. The Commission will focus its efforts on its overall supervisory role, ensuring that enforcement within the network of NCAs is consistent and follows broader EU policies.[38] The Commission will also handle cases which, because of their nature, are better suited to direct enforcement at the EU level, such as secret pan-European cartels.

---

36 The number of Commissioners may reduce after the 2nd Barroso Commission, in October 2014, in line with Art 17(5) TEU.
37 The Commission's early attempts can be seen in the Commission Co-operation Notices, [1993] OJ C39/6 and [1997] OJ C313/3.
38 See Brammer, S, 'Concurrent Jurisdiction under Regulation 1/2003 and the Issue of Case Allocation' (2005) 42(5) CMLRev 1383; and Dekeyser, K and Jaspers, M, 'A New Era of ECN Cooperation, Achievements and Challenges with Special Focus on Work in the Leniency Field' (2007) 30(1) *World Competition* 3. For a more recent discussion and overview, see Wils, WJ, 'Ten Years of Regulation 1/2003 – A Retrospective' (2013) 4(4) *Journal of European Competition Law and Practice* 293–301.

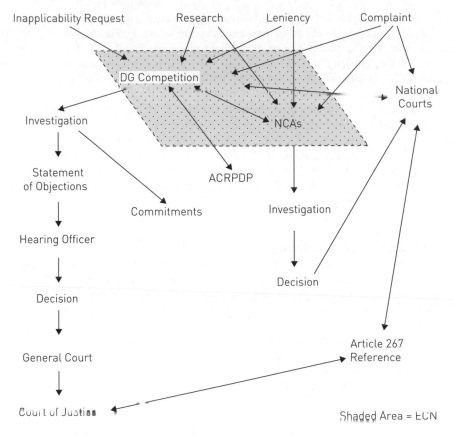

Figure 2.1 The EU System

The Commission, alongside the NCAs, has wide powers to carry out investigations into possible infringements of the competition rules and it also has the power to impose fines or, in some cases, a structural remedy. Some of the Commission's powers have been criticised as being unfair, as the Commission is involved in all stages of investigation, effectively acting as police, prosecutor and judge. In order to deflect some of that criticism, the Commission has taken a number of procedural steps to protect the rights of the defence during Commission proceedings. The enforcement process by the Commission can be divided into three broad phases:

1   initiation of proceedings and investigation;
2   decision-making; and
3   judicial review.

Initiation and investigation

This refers to the fact-finding stage of the enforcement process. There are three main ways in which the Commission can gather initial information about potential competition problems:

1   its own research, for example, sectoral surveys of particular markets;[39]
2   complaints; and
3   information from those who may be involved in infringing behaviour.

The latter two methods raise certain issues which need to be addressed before analysing the Commission's investigative powers.

Complaints

The Commission receives numerous complaints that EU competition rules have been infringed, most frequently from competitors or customers of the company that is the subject of the complaint. There is a specific form, Form C, which is provided by the Commission and upon which complaints can be made, although its use is not obligatory. Any natural or legal person who can show a legitimate interest is entitled to lodge a complaint.[40] Any communications to the Commission are privileged for defamation purposes.[41] The Commission has no obligation to act positively on a complaint. The Court has made it clear that the Commission can reject complaints on the basis that there is no 'Community interest' in pursuing the matter.[42] The Commission may also reject a complaint on the basis that an NCA is already dealing with the matter.[43] The ability to reject a complaint on this latter ground is designed to avoid the duplication of investigations across the enforcement network. The judgment in *Guerin* held that when a complaint is rejected by the Commission, complainants can have that decision reviewed.[44] It is intended that the NCAs will deal with most of the day-to-day enforcement activity and the majority of complaints, with the Commission only becoming involved in important cases or those that span a number of Member States. In 2004, the OFT referred a complaint by Which? to the Commission relating to alleged price discrimination in Apple's iTunes service, as the latter operated in more than three Member States and the Commission would be in a better position to consider the online exploitation of music across Europe.[45] The Commission gives guidance on the appropriate body to approach with a complaint in its Notice on the handling of complaints by the Commission.[46]

Information from those who may be infringing

Although Regulation 1/2003 has brought to an end the individual exemption procedure under Art 101(3) TFEU, there are still a number of situations in which companies may wish to bring their potentially anti-competitive agreements or practices to the attention of the Commission.

The first situation in which a company might approach the Commission is where it is seeking a 'finding of inapplicability'. The Commission can, under Art 10 of Regulation 1/2003, adopt a decision that an agreement or practice: does not breach the prohibition in Art 101(1); fulfils the conditions within Art 101(3); or does not fall within the prohibition in Art 102 TFEU. Such a decision would be of obvious benefit to the parties concerned, as it would ensure that they could proceed with that course of conduct without fear of interference from the Commission or the NCAs, and they would also be able to defend any competition challenge in the national courts. It

---

39 See, for example: Communication from the Commission – Inquiry pursuant to Article 17 of Regulation (EC) No 1/2003 into the European gas and electricity sectors (Final Report), COM(2006) 851 final; and, the Communication from the Commission on the Pharmaceutical Sector Inquiry Report, 8 July 2009.
40 Regulation 1/2003/EC, Art 7(2).
41 See *Hasselblad (GB) Ltd v Orbinson* [1985] QB 475.
42 See Case T-24/90 *Automec v Commission II* [1992] ECR II-2223. This is another example of the pre-Lisbon phrase 'Community interest' still having relevance even though the European Community no longer exists.
43 Regulation 1/2003/EC, Art 13(1).
44 Case C-282/95P *Guerin Automobiles v Commission* [1997] ECR I-1503.
45 OFT Press Release, 'OFT refers iTunes complaint to EC', 3 December 2004.
46 Commission Notice on the handling of complaints by the Commission under Arts 81 and 82 of the EC Treaty, [2004] OJ C101/65.

is, however, unlikely that the Commission will adopt many such decisions, and in most cases it is much more likely to proceed informally. The Commission has published a Notice on informal guidance relating to novel questions,[47] which makes it clear that it will only issue such guidance in very limited circumstances. The status of informal Commission communications has proved controversial in the past, particularly in relation to Commission 'comfort letters' under Art 101(3) TFEU.[48] Informal clearance is not formally binding on the Commission, but it will not normally act inconsistently with its own advice. Nor is informal guidance binding on the NCAs or national courts, although they should bear any such guidance in mind when taking their own decisions.[49]

The other, increasingly important, instance when companies may approach the Commission with evidence of infringing behaviour is where a cartel member brings evidence of the existence of a cartel to the Commission in order to seek leniency. Leniency programmes are becoming an important part of a competition authority's enforcement armoury. The idea behind the emergence of leniency programmes is that cartels are inherently unstable, with each member of the cartel constantly balancing the benefits of solidarity with the other cartel members against the benefits of withdrawing co-operation. By offering leniency to cartel members, who inform the authority of the existence of a cartel, the authority hopes to increase significantly the benefits of withdrawing from the cartel, and therefore increase the likelihood that a cartel will break up. If the offer of leniency also encourages the breakaway cartel member to provide useful information to the authority, it also means that the authority can take enforcement action against the other cartel participants.[50] In the US system this is known as the 'race to the courtroom door'.[51] The Commission adopted a leniency programme in 1996,[52] but the current policy was adopted in 2006.[53] Under the Commission programme a 'whistle-blower' who seeks leniency can be granted immunity from Commission fines if it is the first to provide sufficient evidence to allow the Commission to carry out a targeted inspection or find an infringement.[54] Any undertaking that comes forward after an investigation has begun and co-operates with the investigation may be granted a reduction in any fines subsequently imposed by the Commission.[55]

Investigatory powers

During the course of an investigation, the Commission has wide powers to collect information, even from third parties. The full extent of those powers can be witnessed when a 'dawn raid' is carried out simultaneously on multiple businesses across the EU, in co-ordination with similar raids by the authorities in the US and Asia, in relation to alleged infringements of Art 101 TFEU. The information-gathering powers are contained in Arts 17–22 of Regulation 1/2003.[56] The

---

47 Commission Notice on informal guidance relating to novel questions concerning Arts 81 and 82 of the EC Treaty that arise in individual cases (guidance letters), [2004] OJ C101/78.

48 See Case 71/74 *FRUBO v Commission* [1975] ECR 563.

49 See the 'Perfumes' cases, for example, Case 99/79 *Lancome v Etos* [1980] ECR 2511, and *Inntrepreneur Estates Ltd v Mason* [1993] 2 CMLR 293.

50 For fuller discussion of leniency programmes at the EC and UK levels, respectively, see Chapter 5.

51 For a useful discussion of the US leniency programme, see Harding, C and Joshua, J, *Regulating Cartels in Europe*, 2nd edn (2010) Oxford: OUP, Chapter VIII, and Miller, NH, 'Strategic Leniency and Cartel Enforcement' (2009) 99 *American Economic Review* 750–768.

52 [1996] OJ C207/4.

53 Commission Notice on immunity from fines and reduction of fines in cartel cases, [2006] OJ C298/17. See, generally, Wils, W, 'Leniency in Antitrust Enforcement: Theory and Practice' (2007) 30(1) *World Competition* 25, and Sandhu, JS, 'The European Commission's Leniency Policy: A Success?' [2007] ECLR 148.

54 Paras 8–13.

55 Paras 23–26. Further fine reductions are also available through the Commission's settlement procedure, see Commission Notice on the conduct of settlement procedures in view of the adoption of Decisions pursuant to Arts 7 and 23 of Council Regulation (EC) No 1/2003 in cartel cases, [2008] OJ C167/1. See further discussion of the leniency and settlement processes in Chapter 7.

56 The Commission's powers of investigation under the Merger Regulation are contained in Regulation 139/2004/EC, [2004] OJ L24/1, Arts 11–13.

principal powers are contained in Arts 18, 19 and 20. Article 17 provides for inquiries where there may be a competition problem in a sector of the economy. Article 22 allows the Commission to request authorities of Member States to carry out investigations into alleged breaches of the competition rules.

Article 18: requests for information

Article 18 sets out two separate procedures by which the Commission can make requests for information. The first procedure, in para 2, provides for the Commission to make a 'simple request' for information. This is the less invasive of the two procedures. There is no penalty for a failure to provide information, but there are penalties, under Art 23, for supplying incorrect or misleading information. This procedure is often used where information is sought from under-takings that are not the subject of a competition investigation. The request itself will set out the information that is requested, the legal basis for the request, the deadline for the provision of the information and an indication of the possible penalties that could be imposed. The procedure for a mandatory request for information is set out in Art 18(3). In respect of a mandatory request, the Commission uses the vehicle of a Decision to require the undertaking to produce the information. The Decision resembles the format of a simple request under Art 18(2), but will also set out the penalty that will be imposed if the undertaking fails to provide the information within the time limit set. Article 24 allows the Commission to impose a periodic penalty of up to 5% of daily turnover on a continuing basis for each day of failure to provide the information. The Art 23 penalties for supplying incorrect or misleading information also apply.

Article 19: taking of statements

This power was introduced by Regulation 1/2003. Under the Regulation 17 regime the Commission could not take oral statements and could only formally deal with documentary evidence. Article 19 of Regulation 1/2003 allows the Commission to interview persons, who consent to be interviewed, in order to gather information. While this power will not necessarily be used in contested investigations, as there is no provision for compulsion, it will be useful in non-contested investigations where information can be gathered orally from the competitors or customers of an undertaking that is alleged to have infringed the competition rules or, in leniency cases, where a member of a cartel co-operates with a Commission investigation. The Commission's Leniency Notice includes provision for corporate statements to be made orally.[57] This is done to limit the potential for leniency statements being the subject of legal discovery for use in litigation in the US or elsewhere.

Article 20: inspections

Article 20 empowers the Commission to carry out inspections, which are more commonly known as 'dawn raids'. To authorise an inspection, the Commission must adopt a Decision, after consulting the relevant NCAs, setting out the subject matter of the inspection, the nature of the inspection, the date of the inspection, and the possible penalties under Arts 23 and 24 of Regulation 1/2003. Officials who undertake the inspection are required to produce written authorisation, setting out the above information, at the beginning of the inspection. The Commission co-operates closely with the NCAs in the exercise of its powers, and in many cases the initial information that has led to the need for an inspection may have come to the Commission via the NCAs. Article 20(6) requires the officials of the NCA to assist the Commission within their territory, including acquiring judicial authority if that is required. During an inspection the Commission has a wide range of powers, including:

---

57 Commission Notice on Immunity from fines and reduction of fines in cartel cases, [2006] OJ C298/1, paras 31–35.

- entering any premises, land, and means of transport;
- examining the books and other records related to the business, irrespective of the medium on which they are stored;
- taking, or obtaining in any form, copies of, or extracts from, such books or records;
- sealing any business premises and books or records for the period and to the extent necessary for the inspection; and
- asking any representative or member of staff of the undertaking for explanations of facts or for documents relating to the subject matter and purpose of the inspection and thereafter recording the answers.

In addition to the power in Art 20 to inspect business premises, Art 21 gives the Commission the power to inspect other premises, if a reasonable suspicion exists that books or other records related to a serious violation of Arts 101 or 102 TFEU are being kept in those premises. This includes the homes of the directors or managers of the undertakings concerned. An order for such an inspection must also be made by Decision, which must set out the reasons why such a suspicion exists. Before an Art 21 inspection takes place, an application must be made for the appropriate judicial authority, for instance, a search warrant, within the relevant Member State.

In cases such as *Hoechst*,[58] the Court has shown that it is concerned with the rights of the undertaking which is the subject of an inspection, but it also indicated that such undertakings receive relatively limited protection. The judgments of the European Court of Human Rights in *Colas Est*[59] and the Court of Justice in *Roquette Freres*[60] indicate that the matter is still controversial. The lesser extent of protection afforded to business premises by Art 8 of the European Convention on Human Rights explains the stricter test which must be met for an inspection of premises other than business premises in Art 21 of Regulation 1/2003. In its Decision, the Commission must set out sufficient detail in relation to the subject matter of the investigation to allow the target to assess sufficiently the scope of their duty to co-operate.[61] The Commission must also have sufficient reason to suspect the existence of an infringement in relation to the whole of the subject matter of its investigation; it cannot use the inspections as part of a 'fishing expedition'.[62]

An inspection will often take several days to complete. Should the inspection take more than one day, the Commission will 'seal' any spaces where they have not yet completed their work, with forensic tape, to ensure that the undertaking cannot interfere with the material while the Commission officials are not present. In 2008, E.On Energie were fined €38m when a Commission seal was interfered with during an inspection.[63]

Special types of information

In most mature legal systems there exists some form of protection for certain kinds of documents, or information, and those documents, or information, are granted privileged status. This means that they need not be disclosed and cannot be relied upon by the other party in a dispute. The two main types of information that need not be divulged to the Commission are those covered by professional legal privilege and by the privilege against self-incrimination.

---

58 Cases 46/87 and 227/88 *Hoechst v Commission* [1989] ECR 2859; [1991] 4 CMLR 410.
59 *Ste Colas Est v France* App no 37971/97 (ECtHR, 16 April 2002).
60 Case C-94/00 *Roquette Freres SA v Director General de la Concurrence, de la Consommation et de la Repression des Fraudes* [2002] ECR I-9001; [2003] 4 CMLR 1.
61 See Case T-15/09 *Nexans France SAS v European Commission* [2013] ECR II-0000.
62 The Commission inspection Decision in *Nexans*, ibid, was partially annulled on the basis that it did not have reasonable suspicion of an infringement for all the products set out in the Decision.
63 See Case C 89/11 P *E.ON Energie v Commission* [2012] ECR I-0000. An €8m fine was also imposed in 2011, Commission Press Release IP/11/632, 'Antitrust: Commission fines Suez Environnement and Lyonnaise des Eaux €8 million for the breach of a seal during an inspection', 24 May 2011.

Professional legal privilege

The existence of this doctrine under competition law enforcement was confirmed in *A, M & S Europe Ltd v Commission*.[64] In that case, which was undertaken under the investigation powers of Regulation 17, the Commission sought to carry out an inspection, but documentation was withheld by the company. The Commission had demanded disclosure of certain documents in an inquiry into an alleged zinc suppliers' cartel. A, M & S Europe Ltd had withheld the documents on the basis of the professional legal privilege, which was attached to certain documents and correspondence between the company and its legal advisers. The Commission fined A, M & S for its failure to produce the documents. A, M & S sought a review of the Commission Decision before the European Court. The Court confirmed the existence of the doctrine of professional legal privilege, subject to three limitations:

1   it only covers documents between lawyer and client and related to the purpose of the defence;
2   it only applies to communications between a client and an independent lawyer. Advice and documents prepared by in-house lawyers are not covered; and
3   it extends only to independent lawyers based in the EU.

The latter two limitations have been criticised. The exclusion of in-house lawyers makes little sense in legal systems where such lawyers have the same status as independent lawyers, and this exclusion may also prejudice the ability of companies to organise an effective competition law compliance programme. The exclusion of in-house lawyers from the privilege was confirmed by the Court in *Akzo Nobel Chemicals v Commission*.[65] The restriction to EU-based lawyers is discriminatory, but the restriction still applies. Nonetheless, the CFI in *Akzo Nobel*[66] relaxed the first limitation by extending the potential scope of the privilege to company documents or memoranda drawn up exclusively for the purpose of seeking legal advice from an external lawyer in exercise of the rights of the defence. In practice, should the Commission demand information for which privilege is claimed, the recourse available is to seek review of that demand by the GC.[67] These principles apply equally to information required under Art 18 or 20 of Regulation 1/2003.

Self-incrimination

The increasing impact of 'human rights' on competition investigations is exemplified by the growing importance of the privilege against self-incrimination in competition proceedings. The privilege was initially developed in the criminal law field but its use has now spread, through the operation of Art 6 of the ECHR, to other fields including competition law.[68] In *Orkem*,[69] *Solvay*[70] and *Société Générale*[71] the Court set out that the Commission is entitled to compel, under Art 18 of Regulation 1/2003, an undertaking to provide all necessary information and to disclose to the Commission such documents in its possession, even if they may be used to establish the existence of anti-competitive conduct. An undertaking required to produce information can rely on the privilege only where the undertaking would be compelled to provide answers that might involve an admission of an infringement. The Court's judgments in these cases were

---

64   Case 155/79 [1982] ECR 1575.
65   Case C-550/07 P *Akzo Nobel Chemicals & Akcros Chemicals v Commission* [2010] ECR I-8301.
66   Cases T-125 & 253/03 *Akzo Nobel Chemicals v Commisssion* [2007] ECR II-3523.
67   The detailed procedure for sealing documents in dispute for review by the GC was set out in *Akzo Nobel*, ibid.
68   Even though Art 23(5) of Regulation 1/2003 states that fines imposed under that Regulation 'shall not be of a criminal law nature'.
69   Case 374/87 *Orkem v Commission* [1989] ECR 3283.
70   Case 27/88 *Solvay v Commission* [1989] ECR 3355.
71   Case T-34/93 *Société Générale v Commission* [1995] ECR II-545.

thrown into doubt by a number of important decisions by the European Court of Human Rights (ECtHR), most notably *Funke v France*,[72] but the CJEU confirmed the position it adopted in *Orkem* in *Mannesmannröhren-Werke AG v Commission*.[73] There has been an interesting debate whether the CJEU's position on this matter is sustainable.[74] There is also the wider issue of whether companies that are the subject of competition investigations can benefit from 'human rights', such as the privilege against self-incrimination, or whether they should have different rights to represent their different status.[75]

Decision-making

Once the Commission has gathered sufficient information, using any of the methods mentioned, it will then decide which decision-making process is most appropriate. If the competition rules have not been breached, the Commission will take no further action. If a finding of inapplicability has been sought, and it is considered that there is a Community interest, the Commission will proceed to adopt the appropriate decision. Should the Commission consider that the competition rules have been breached, the Commission will initiate infringement proceedings. At an earlier stage, most commonly upon receipt of a serious complaint, the Commission may exercise its powers to adopt interim measures.

Interim measures

Article 8 of Regulation 1/2003 provides the Commission with power to take interim measures where necessary. The power to take interim measures is subject to certain limitations, the most important of which is that the measures must be necessary due to the urgency of the situation. The urgency must arise 'due to the risk of serious and irreparable damage to competition'.[76] For the Commission to act there must be a reasonably strong *prima facie* case, though it is not necessary to establish an infringement with certainty [77] Another significant limitation is that the Commission must adhere to the essential procedural requirements within the Regulation. Accordingly, unlike certain interlocutory court orders, interim measures will not be awarded *ex parte* and interested undertakings will be given the opportunity to be heard. The Commission has rarely granted interim measures; the most noteworthy example in the UK context is *BBI/Boosey and Hawkes: Interim Measures*,[78] in which the Commission took action in respect of a refusal, by a company, to supply brass band instruments to an existing customer who was also going to produce similar instruments in competition with it. A Commission Decision to adopt interim measures is subject to review by the GC.

---

72 [1993] 1 CMLR 897; (1993) 16 EHRR 297. See, also, *Saunders v UK* (1997) 23 EHRR 313.
73 Case T-112/98 [2001] ECR II-729.
74 See, for example, Van Overbeek, WBJ, 'The Right to Remain Silent in Competition Investigations: The *Funke* Decision of the Court of Human Rights Makes Revision of the ECJ's Case Law Necessary' [1994] 3 ECLR 127; Riley, A, 'Saunders and the Power to Obtain Information in Community and United Kingdom Competition Law' [2000] ECLR 264; Riley, A, 'The ECHR Implications of the Investigation Provisions of the Draft Competition Regulation' (2002) 51 ICLQ 55; Wils, W, 'Self-incrimination in EC Antitrust Enforcement: A Legal and Economic Analysis' (2003) 26 W Comp 567; and MacCulloch, A, 'The Privilege against Self-incrimination in Competition Investigations: Theoretical Foundations and Practical Implications' (2006) 26(2) *Legal Studies* 211. For an overview of due process and human rights issues in competition law, see Andreangeli, A, *EU Competition Enforcement And Human Rights* (2008) Cheltenham: Edward Elgar.
75 See Harding, C and Joshua, J, *Regulating Cartels in Europe*, 2nd edn (2010) Oxford: OUP, Chapter 7, and MacCulloch, A, 'The Privilege against Self-incrimination in Competition Investigations: Theoretical Foundations and Practical Implications' (2006) 26(2) *Legal Studies* 211.
76 For the Court's view on the interim measures under Regulation 17, see Case 792/79R *Camera Care v Commission* [1980] ECR 119.
77 Case T-44/90 *La Cinq v Commission* [1992] ECR II-1.
78 [1987] OJ L286/36.

Infringement proceedings

Infringement proceedings are brought under Art 7 of Regulation 1/2003 and commence with the Commission issuing a document called the 'Statement of Objections' to the undertakings involved in the alleged breaches. The Statement of Objections must contain a statement of the facts, a legal assessment of the position and, if the Commission intends to impose a fine, must state the alleged period of infringement. When adopting its final decision the Commission cannot rely on matters not included in the Statement of Objections or matters that are discovered after it has been issued. The parties involved, and any interested third parties, must be given a hearing,[79] although representations are also made to the Commission in writing. The Hearing Officer conducts the hearing[80] and their remit is to ensure that the parties receive a fair hearing and that the rights of the defence are respected.[81] After the hearing, in consultation with the Advisory Committee on Restrictive Practices and Dominant Positions,[82] the Commission may adopt a formal Decision.[83] Notwithstanding the increased role of the Hearing Officer, there are ongoing concerns that the decision-making process does not fully respect the due process rights of the undertakings suspected of an infringement. With the greater status of the EU Charter of Fundamental Rights and the EU's accession to the European Convention of Human Rights, it is likely that the Commission's decision-making processes will be subject to further challenge and scrutiny.

Article 7 of Regulation 1/2003 sets out that an infringement decision can require the undertakings concerned to bring any breach of the competition rules to an end. The Commission may also impose any proportionate behavioural or structural remedies that are necessary to bring the infringement to an end. Structural remedies will only be adopted, under Art 7, where there is 'no equally effective behavioural remedy or where any equally effective behavioural remedy would be more burdensome for the undertaking concerned than the structural remedy'. Regulation 1/2003 also contains a power, in Article 9, for the Commission to accept binding commitments from a party to address the Commission's competition concerns instead of proceeding to a formal decision requiring the infringement to be brought to an end.

Commitments

The ability to accept binding commitments was a new enforcement mechanism formally introduced by Regulation 1/2003, intended to ensure the effective enforcement of the EU competition rules by delivering a quicker and more efficient solution to the competition problems identified by the Commission without requiring a formal finding of an infringement. It would allow undertakings to participate in the procedure by proposing solutions that they considered to be most appropriate to deal with the competition concerns of the Commission. This was an important additional competition law enforcement tool but the scope and the nature of the commitment remedy and process were examined by the CJEU in *Commission v Alrosa Co Ltd*.[84] Alrosa and De Beers were both active in the world market for rough diamonds. As part of a long-standing commercial arrangement, in 2002 the parties entered into a supply agreement whereby Alrosa undertook to sell De Beers rough diamonds produced in Russia to the value of $800m a year and De Beers undertook to buy those diamonds from Alrosa.

---

79 See Regulation 1/2003, Art 27. See, also, Commission Regulation 773/2004/EC relating to the conduct of proceedings by the Commission pursuant to Arts 81 and 82 of the EC Treaty, [2004] OJ L123/18.
80 Commission Regulation 773/2004/EC, [2004] OJ L123/18, Art 14.
81 See, more generally, Commission Decision (2001/462/EC, ECSC) on the terms of reference of hearing officers in certain competition procedures, [2001] OJ L162/21, replacing Commission Decision (94/810/ECSC, EEC), [1994] OJ L330/67. See, also, House of Lords Select Committee on the European Union, Session 1999–2000, 19th Report, *Strengthening the Role of the Hearing Officer in EC Competition Cases*, HL Paper 125, HMSO, 21 November 2000.
82 Regulation 1/2003, Art 14. A body staffed by officials from each of the Member States' NCAs, whose task is to advise the Commission on competition law and policy issues.
83 It is assisted in this process by the Legal Service of the Commission.
84 Case C-441/07 P, [2010] ECR I-5949.

De Beers offered unilateral commitments to progressively reduce their purchase of rough diamonds from Alrosa. These were accepted by the Commission, which, after providing Alrosa with a copy and receiving comments, adopted a decision to make the commitments binding.[85] Alrosa appealed that decision to the GC, which annulled the decision,[86] on the basis that the Commission had breached the principle of proportionality in accepting commitments that were more onerous than necessary to address the competition problem. The CJEU set aside the GC's judgment. In assessing the application of the proportionality principle, the CJEU stressed the consensual nature of commitment proceedings, in comparison with the adversarial context of Article 7 decisions. Accordingly, in relation to commitments, the proportionality test did not require the Commission to seek less onerous or more moderate solutions.[87] In recent years, commitments have been increasingly used as a tool to address allegedly anti-competitive abusive behaviour by dominant companies under Article 102 TFEU. This is evidenced by the commitments accepted by the Commission in relation to: the sale of e-books in Europe;[88] ensuring browser choice with Microsoft windows;[89] and requiring Google to provide a comparable display of specialised search rivals.[90] These examples demonstrate that the commitments remedy can ensure a swift and effective resolution of alleged abusive behaviour in complex, technological new economy markets where an infringement might be difficult to prove. The process has similarities with the concept of plea-bargaining, and arguably can allow powerful companies too much scope to negotiate a suitable remedy. A commitment decision does not finally establish an infringement, and this may make any potential 'follow-on' private enforcement by aggrieved parties more problematic.[91] Although commitments do not require the Commission to establish an infringement of Article 101 or 102 TFEU, Regulation 1/2003 gives the Commission power to fine any undertaking for failure to comply with a commitment.[92] This was exemplified by the fine of €561m imposed on Microsoft for its failure to offer users a browser choice screen enabling them effectively to select their preferred web browser.[93]

Fines

The most common type of behavioural remedy imposed is a fine. Article 23 of Regulation 1/2003 allows the Commission to impose fines of up to 10% of an undertaking's total turnover in the preceding year. Periodic penalty payments can also be imposed under Art 24 for continued infringements. The largest fines imposed have tended to be for price-fixing agreements and agreements that divide up the internal market in the EU.[94] The Commission enjoys a wide discretion in imposing fines and generally takes into account such factors as the gravity of the behaviour, its duration, the size of the market in question and the likely deterrent effect of a fine. To improve transparency, the Commission published its first Notice on the setting of fines in 1998.[95] According

---

85 Commission Decision COMP/B-2/38.381- *De Beers*, 22 February 2006.
86 Case T-170/06 *Alrosa v Commission* [2007] ECR II-2601.
87 For further discussion, see Kellerbauer, M, 'Playground Instead of Playpen: The Court of Justice of the European Union's Alrosa Judgment on art 9 of Regulation 1/2003' [2011] ECLR 1.
88 Commission Press Release IP/12/1367, 'Antitrust: Commission accepts legally binding commitments from Simon & Schuster, Harper Collins, Hachette, Holtzbrinck and Apple for sale of e-books', 13 December 2012 and Commission Press Release IP/13/746, 'Antitrust: Commission accepts legally binding commitments from Penguin in e-books market', 25 July 2013.
89 Commission Press Release IP/13/196, 'Antitrust: Commission fines Microsoft for non-compliance with browser choice commitments', 6 March 2013.
90 Commission Press Release IP/14/116, 'Antitrust: Commission obtains from Google comparable display of specialised search rivals', 5 February 2014.
91 See further discussion in Chapter 3.
92 See Art 23(2)(c), Regulation 1/2003.
93 Commission Press Release IP/13/96, n 89. See Aleixo, M, 'An Inaugural Fine: Microsoft's Failure to Comply with Commitments (case COMP/39530)' [2013] 9 ECLR 466–479.
94 The largest fine imposed under Art 101 TFEU was €1.71bn, and the largest fine under Art 102 TFEU was €1.06bn. See Commission Press Release IP/13/1208, 'Antitrust: Commission fines banks €1.71 billion for participating in cartels in the interest rate derivatives industry', 4 December 2013, and Commission Press Release IP/09/745, 'Antitrust: Commission imposes fine of €1.06 bn on Intel for abuse of dominant position; orders Intel to cease illegal practices', 13 May 2009.
95 Guidelines on Method of Setting Fines, [1998] OJ C9/3. See, also, Spink, PM, 'Enforcing EC Competition Law: Fixing the Quantum of Fines' [1999] JBL 219.

to that Notice the basic amount of the fine was to be set according to the gravity and duration of the infringement, with infringements categorised into several levels of gravity. Minor infringements, usually vertical in nature and affecting a limited market, received fines of up to €1m. Serious infringements, usually horizontal or vertical infringements or abuses with more effect over a larger area, received fines of up to €20m. Very serious infringements, usually horizontal price-fixing or market-sharing or serious abuses of near-monopoly positions, could be fined in excess of €20m. The duration of the infringement was also important, with infringements of a medium duration, of more than one year, receiving a 50% uplift on the fine. In relation to infringements of long duration, of more than five years, an uplift of 10% would be applied for each year the infringement continued. On top of this 'basic' amount there are certain aggravating factors which, if present, could result in a fine being increased further. Aggravating circumstances included, for example, refusals to co-operate or being the 'leader' of the infringement. In contrast with the aggravating circumstances just described, there could be attenuating circumstances resulting in the reduction of the basic fine.

The 1998 Notice was revised in 2006 in three principal ways to enhance deterrence.[96] Firstly, the fine will be based on a percentage, of up to 30%, of the yearly sales in the relevant sector for each company participating in the infringement, multiplied by the years of participation. Secondly, the Commission may impose an additional 'entry fee' of 15% to 25% of yearly relevant sales for seriously illegal conduct, including cartels. Thirdly, the guidance on aggravating factors was amended to deal more harshly with repeat offenders, known as 'recidivists'; they face increases in fines of up to 100% for each prior infringement.[97] There has been a dramatic increase in the overall fines imposed by the Commission, particularly in relation to cartels, following the 2006 Notice. The two most impressive years for cartel fines were 2007 and 2010 with total fines of €3,333,802,700 and €2,868,459,674 respectively. The largest annual aggregate cartel fine pre-2006 was €683,029,000 in 2005.[98]

Another, increasingly important, factor in the setting of the level of fines is the operation of the Commission's cartel leniency programme. 'Whistle-blowers' who have participated in secret cartels can secure either partial or total immunity from fines by disclosing the existence of the cartel to the Commission.[99] The first undertaking that brings sufficient information to the Commission to allow it to carry out a targeted inspection or find an infringement will normally receive complete immunity from any subsequent Commission fines. Any other undertakings that go on to provide the Commission with information and continue to co-operate may receive a reduction in any subsequent fines.[100]

The Commission also has a direct settlement process whereby infringing parties may be granted a fine rebate of 10% conditional upon acceptance, within a set deadline, of the commission of the infringement, admission of liability, and the level of fine. The faster and simplified procedure envisaged will, it is hoped, lead to a more efficient use of enforcement resources and fewer judicial challenges to fining decisions.[101] The expedited procedure will operate only in relation to cartel cases, and there are clearly implications in such a system for third party rights, due process and 'fair trial' objections, and for follow-on private enforcement actions.

---

96 Guideline on the method of setting fines imposed pursuant to Article 23(2) of Regulation 1/2003, [2006] OJ C210/2.
97 See Nordlander, K, 'The Commission's Policy on Recidivism: Legal Certainty for Repeat Offenders' (2005) CompLRev 55. See also Case C-413/08 P *Lafarge v Commission* [2010] ECR I-5361, at paras 65–67.
98 For the full breakdown on aggregate cartel fines 2003–12, see Chapter 7.
99 Commission Notice on immunity from fines and reduction of fines in cartel cases, [2006] OJ C298/17. See, also, the discussion of the leniency programme above.
100 For fuller discussion of leniency programmes in the EU and UK, see Chapter 5.
101 Commission Regulation 622/2008/EC, [2008] OJ L171/3, Commission Notice on settlement procedures, [2008] OJ C167/1.

Rights of the defence

The development of the rights of the defence in EU competition law enforcement has been a feature of the Court's jurisprudence. An important starting point would be to note the decision of the European Human Rights Commission (EHRC) in *Stenuit*.[102] In that case, the EHRC considered that competition law proceedings, which may lead to the imposition of a fine, are of such a nature that Art 6 of the European Convention for the Protection of Human Rights and Fundamental Freedoms is applicable to them. The EU is not yet a signatory to the European Convention;[103] however, it is clear from the Treaty and Court jurisprudence that the principle in Art 6, providing for a fair and public hearing within a reasonable time by an independent and impartial tribunal, is to be respected. When the EU becomes a signatory to the Convention its procedures will be directly challengeable before the ECtHR. In the EU context, administrative decisions by the Commission are not contrary to Art 6 ECHR because of the existence of a full and independent review, involving due process, before an independent tribunal, the GC or CJEU.[104] Nonetheless, the Court has continually insisted that the Commission is obliged to give a fair hearing in terms of its procedure and administration. In response to this, the Commission has taken several steps, including the introduction of the Hearing Officer,[105] to clarify and enhance the Commission's hearings procedure with a view to improving the rights of the defence. Even the role of the Hearing Officer has been criticised, as it is thought that Officers may become entrenched in proceedings where they have been running for a lengthy period of time.[106] While some useful steps have been taken, it is clear that further developments may be triggered by increased scrutiny from the ECtHR.[107] In addition to the issues of legal professional privilege and self-incrimination, the greatest focus has been on the issue of access to the Commission file by parties involved in the decision-making process.

Access to the file

The Commission, under Art 27(2) of Regulation 1/2003, is bound to disclose all documents upon which it relies to substantiate its allegations to the undertakings accused of infringing the competition rules. In addition, according to the case law in *Hercules*[108] and *Hoechst*,[109] this requirement of disclosure extends equally to exculpatory documents held by the Commission. These are documents that tend to clear the undertaking under investigation of the allegations made by the Commission. In the first instance, the Commission decides which documents must be disclosed, and will then forward them to the undertakings concerned. Deciding which documents must be disclosed is not straightforward, and the Commission has produced guidance in a Notice.[110] Deciding which documents to disclose is a difficult task to combine with the Commission's duty of confidentiality to those who provide it with information. No access will be given to confidential information or the internal documents of the Commission. There exists a general duty of confidentiality under the Treaty, although the extent of the duty is unclear where there is a conflict

---

102 (1992) 14 EHRR 509.
103 The EU is going through a process to become a signatory to the Convention – it was expected to conclude in 2014.
104 For a discussion on this, see the House of Lords Select Committee on the European Union, 19th Report, *Strengthening the Role of the Hearing Officer in EC Competition Cases*, 21 November 2000, HL Paper 125, paras 55–56 and 75–78, and Andreangeli, A, *EU Competition Enforcement And Human Rights* (2008) Cheltenham: Edward Elgar.
105 Commission Regulation 773/2004/EC, [2004] OJ L123/18, Art 14.
106 House of Lords Select Committee on the European Union, 19th Report, *Strengthening the Role of the Hearing Officer in EC Competition Cases*, 21 November 2000, HL Paper 125, and also Levitt, M, 'Commission Hearings and the Role of the Hearing Officers: Suggestions for Reform' [1998] ECLR 404.
107 For a discussion of the potential problems under Art 6 ECHR see, Andreangeli, A, 'Toward an EU Competition Court: "Article-6-proofing" Antitrust Proceedings before the Commission?' (2007) 30(4) *World Competition* 595.
108 Case T-7/89 *SA Hercules Chemicals NV v Commission* [1991] ECR 1171.
109 Cases 46/87 and 227/88 *Hoechst AG v Commission* [1989] ECR 2859.
110 Commission Notice on the rules for access to the Commission file in cases pursuant to Arts 81 and 82 of the EC Treaty, Arts 53, 54 and 57 of the EEA Agreement and Council Regulation (EC) No 139/2004, [2005] OJ C325/7.

with the principle of access to the file. More specifically, Art 28 of Regulation 1/2003 places a duty on the Commission not to disclose information which falls within the heading of professional secrecy,[111] and the Notice sets out that 'business secrets' are also non-communicable. The breadth of the concept of professional secrecy is unclear, but in practice the protection of business secrets is more crucial. It has been established by the Court, in *AKZO v Commission*,[112] that business secrets may never be divulged by the Commission. If there is a dispute as to whether information or documentation falls within this category, the Commission will take a decision subject to review by the GC.

There have been a significant number of legal challenges to Commission Decisions on access to the file issues. For instance, judgments in the *Soda Ash*[113] cases annulled, on procedural grounds, Commission Decisions in five related cases. Two of the cases involved a failure by the Commission to respect the rights of the defence in relation to access to the file. These cases were a major setback for the Commission, and the most significant judicial pronouncement on the exercise of the right of access to the file and the rights of the defence generally. Importantly, the CFI confirmed that the right of access to the file is a fundamental right of the defence, and not a self-imposed requirement by the Commission. Parties are entitled to see all documents relating to the case. The three protected categories of information are retained: professional secrets, business secrets and other confidential information. The third category would protect information which would breach the requested anonymity of an informant, and also sensitive commercial information that is not technically a business secret. Determination of what constitutes a business secret will be made on a case-by-case basis and will cover information relating to the commercial interests of its owner, such as internal price calculations, market strategy plans and know-how. Access to the file helps to ensure that the right to be heard is protected, but the *Soda Ash* cases demonstrated the difficulties involved when access to documentation, relating to competitors, held by the Commission is requested. The Commission has to carry out a sensitive balancing act in conducting the procedure due to the conflict between the rights of the defence and the duty of confidentiality.

Review of Commission decision-making

The appellate bodies involved in EU competition law are the General Court and the Court of Justice.

General Court (GC)

The GC was established in 1989 as the Court of First Instance (CFI)[114] in order to reduce the increasing workload of the Court of Justice. It was reformed and renamed as the General Court in 2009 by the Lisbon Treaty. The remit of the GC is currently limited,[115] but as it includes the review of the Commission's competition Decisions, its workload is substantial and significant. The GC reviews Commission Decisions, under Art 263 TFEU, on points of fact and law. The broad scope that the GC has adopted in its review role equates, in effect, to a near appeal; however, it is in reality a form of judicial review. This scope is apparent from judgments of the GC, which can be lengthy and highly detailed, explaining the arguments of the parties on every point raised, before the GC

---

111 See, also, Art 339 TFEU.
112 Case 53/85 *AKZO Chemie BV v Commission* [1986] ECR 1965.
113 Cases T-30–32/91 *Solvay SA v Commission* [1995] ECR II-1775, II-1821, II-1825, and T-36 and 37/91 *Imperial Chemical Industries plc v Commission* [1995] ECR II-1847 and II-1901.
114 As provided for by the Single European Act 1986.
115 While it currently has a limited remit, the Treaties provide that the powers of the GC may be substantially increased by the Council.

sets out its own findings. The level of scrutiny given to Commission Decisions has been questioned as the GC does appear to leave the Commission a certain level of discretion, particularly where it is making decisions based on 'complex economic appraisals'. The GC will confine its role to 'checking whether the relevant rules on procedure and on stating reasons have been complied with, whether the facts have been accurately stated and whether there has been any manifest error of assessment or a misuse of powers'.[116] There are questions whether this limited form of review is compliant with the requirements of due process under Art 6 ECHR, which arguably demands a full appeal on the merits.[117] In the majority of cases where large fines are imposed there will be, in practice, automatic recourse to the 'appeal' process. If either party is not satisfied with the findings of the GC, a further appeal may be made to the Court of Justice on a point of law. A party may apply for an expedited procedure before the GC, where special urgency can be shown to exist.

Court of Justice of the EU (the Court, or CJEU)

The task of the Court under Art 19 TEU is to 'ensure that in the interpretation and application of the Treaties the law is observed'. The Court is the ultimate authority on EU law issues, including competition law. The Court is renowned for its creative techniques of interpretation, partly due to the need to 'fill the gaps' in the EU Treaties. It has been criticised for this judicial activism, which has been obvious in the development of competition law principles from the limited text of the Treaty. In addition to the Court's judgments, there are the opinions of the Advocates General. An Advocate General is an official with the same status as a Court judge, but their task is to prepare a review of the facts and legal analysis of the issues, together with recommendations for the Court. The Advocate General's opinion is delivered in advance of the Court's final deliberations and is important because it is of persuasive effect in both the instant case and later cases, and also because it gives a wider picture of EU competition law development. The opinions tend to look more comprehensively at the background of the case and related developments, and, also, tend to make a comparative assessment of national Member State laws. This contrasts with the shorter and more precise judgments of the Court, which can give less indication of their rationale or the developments leading to their partic ular legal analysis. The trend has changed in recent years with longer judgments in competition law cases, particularly where the CJEU is dealing with a technical appeal from the GC.

Article 263 TFEU

Article 263 TFEU provides for review of the legality of any act by an EU institution. Accordingly, the legality of a Commission Decision taken in competition proceedings may be reviewed under this procedure, which allows for annulment of the act. There are three requirements which need to be satisfied for an act to be annulled:

1   Who may seek review?
    Article 263(2) TFEU states that the act must be of 'direct and individual concern' to the party seeking its annulment. This would obviously apply to a party that is the subject of a Commission Decision. It has also been held to apply to a complainant who was unhappy with a Commission's Decision[118] and, in appropriate circumstances, a non-complainant may also qualify under this head.[119]

---

116 Case T-201/04, *Microsoft v Commission* [2007] ECR II-3601, para 87.
117 See Andreangeli, n 107.
118 Case 26/76 *Metro v Commission* [1977] ECR 1875.
119 For fuller analysis of the issue of 'direct and individual concern', see Nordberg, C, 'Judicial Remedies for Private Parties under the State Aid Procedure' [1997] LIEI 35, 54–59, which is of general interest regarding *locus standi* for competitors. See, also, de Sousa e Alvim, M, 'The Fundamental Right to an Effective Judicial Protection of Individuals in the European Union's Competition Law, Quid Juris?' [2013] 6(4) GCLR 151–154.

2   What constitutes an 'act'?
     This term covers more than the formal decisions such as infringement decisions, taken by the Commission. A wide view was taken in the *IBM* case,[120] which held that an act capable of affecting the interests of an applicant, by bringing about a change in their legal position, could be challenged. On the particular facts of that case the action was unsuccessful, as an 'act' did not include issuing a Statement of Objections, as this was held to constitute merely a procedural step in the process. In subsequent case law,[121] letters rejecting complaints have been held to constitute 'acts' and it is also possible that informal guidance could be construed as an act. The Court of First Instance held in *Alrosa v Commission* that although commitments under Art 9 of Regulation 1/2003 were proposed by an undertaking, the decision by the Commission to make those commitments binding was subject to review by the Court.[122] However, an act does not extend to decisions taken by the Commission on whether, and to what extent, it will allow access to its files by undertakings under investigation.

3   What we the grounds for review?
     The following are the grounds for review available when seeking annulment of a Commission act: lack of competence/authority; infringement of an essential procedural requirement; infringement of the Treaty or any rule of law relating to its application; or misuse of powers. These grounds are alternatives, although they overlap to a certain extent. Annulment may be sought for, for instance: failure to give a party a hearing; inadequate reasoning in a decision; a decision based on inadequate evidence; or erroneous application of the competition rules. An action for annulment is often combined with an action seeking review of a decision by the Commission to fine. Article 261 TFEU provides the Court with unlimited powers to annul, vary or increase fines imposed by the Commission.

Article 265 TFEU

This provides for an appeal against a failure by a Community institution to act. In competition law proceedings, this may be appropriate for a complainant that considers that the Commission has not dealt with its complaint properly, for instance, by taking action against the alleged infringements. There are limitations on the availability of this review mechanism.[123]

Article 267 TFEU

Article 267 TFEU provides for a system of 'preliminary rulings' to be given by the Court. This means that national courts can request an authoritative opinion from the Court concerning the application and interpretation of an issue of EU law. The rulings are designed to ensure the uniform application of EU law throughout the legal systems of the various Member States. A national court may refer an issue to the Court where a ruling is necessary to enable the national court to give judgment, and must do so where there is no right of further appeal. The Court does not decide the dispute between the parties, but provides an interpretative 'preliminary ruling' which provides guidance on the interpretation of the point of EU law which is at issue. The Art 267 procedure is increasingly important for the development of EU competition law given the role of NCAs and private enforcement at the national level under Regulation 1/2003. The review of infringement actions instigated by the NCAs will occur before the domestic courts, which may then use Art 267 rulings to ensure the application of EU law by the NCA is consistent with the

---

120 Case 60/81 [1983] ECR 3283. See also Cases T-125/03 and T-253/03 *Akzo Nobel Chemicals v Commission* [2007] ECR II-479.
121 Case 142/84 *BAT v Commission* [1986] ECR 1899.
122 Case T-170/06, [2007] ECR II-2601.
123 Case 15/71 *Mackprang v Commission* [1971] ECR 997.

Court's. Recourse may also be made to the Art 267 procedure when a domestic court is dealing with a private dispute between parties which involves EU competition law.[124]

Ancillary enforcement issues

Articles 103–105 TFEU

Article 103 TFEU enables implementing Regulations, such as Regulation 1/2003, to be introduced. Article 104 TFEU provides that national authorities retain the power to apply the rules in Arts 101 and 102 TFEU until appropriate provisions have been adopted under Art 103 and are in force. Article 105 allows the Commission to act and to authorise Member States to act on its behalf where the appropriate implementing Regulations have not been introduced under Art 83.

Exclusions from Regulation 1/2003

Regulation 1/2003 does not apply to merger control, which has its own separate Regulation, Regulation 139/2004, containing both the substantive and procedural rules for reviewing merger activity.[125] There is also specific provision under Art 109 TFEU, which regulates the procedure in respect of state aid.[126] Regulation 1/2003 has limited application to various market sectors, such as transport, agriculture, telecommunications and various energy markets, in relation to which particular Treaty provisions exist with specialised enforcement regimes.[127]

Administrative Enforcement in the UK

Introduction

This section is concerned with the principal bodies involved in the same general stages of administrative enforcement – initiation, decision and review – of EU and UK competition law within the UK. Several introductory comments are necessary nonetheless. The UK framework is particularly interesting, given the remarkable changes introduced within the last 15 years by the Competition Act 1998, Enterprise Act 2002, Regulation 1/2003 and the Enterprise and Regulatory Reform Act 2013. The 1998 Act introduced new enforcement authorities and abolished other bodies, such as the Restrictive Practices Court. It also varied the functions performed by the competition authorities and the powers available to them. Although the Competition Act prohibitions can also be enforced by consumers or other interested parties through normal court processes, it is important to note that an essentially administrative enforcement framework has been retained. The Enterprise Act 2002, largely replacing the Fair Trading Act 1973, continued an administrative enforcement scheme in respect of UK market and merger investigations, discussed in Chapters 5 and 8 respectively. It also made other important changes in respect of UK enforcement: transfer of functions from the Director General of Fair Trading (DGFT) to the OFT;[128] provision of a role for the CAT in private damages claims; introduction of a fast-track super-complaints procedure for consumer

---

124 See, for a comprehensive analysis of all competition law-related preliminary rulings, Rodger, B (ed), *Article 234 and Competition Law: An Analysis* (2008) The Hague: Kluwer Law International. See also Ibanez Colomo, P, 'The Law on Abuses of Dominance and the System of Judicial Remedies' (2013) 32(1) *Yearbook of European Law* 389–431.

125 Regulation 139/2004/EC on the control of concentrations between undertakings, [2004] OJ L24/1.

126 Regulation 659/1999/EC lays down detailed rules for the application of Art 88 of the EC Treaty, [1999] OJ L83/1. Detailed coverage of the state aid regime is outside the coverage of this book; see de Cecco, F, *State Aid and the European Economic Constitution* (2012) Oxford: Hart Publishing.

127 See Whish, R and Bailey, D, *Competition Law*, 7th edn (2012) Oxford: OUP, Chapter 23 for further detail on these issues, which are outside the scope of this book.

128 Section 2.

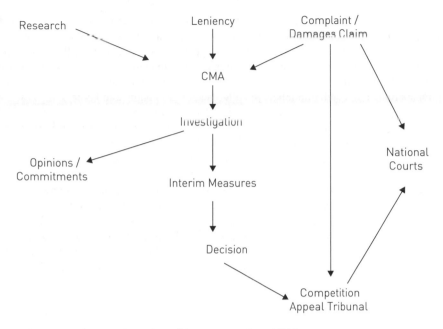

Figure 2.2 Competition Act 1998 and the Chapter I and II prohibitions

organisations;[129] and creation of a criminal offence for involvement in cartel activity.[130] From 2004 to 2014, the OFT, as the NCA for the UK, had a duty to apply both domestic prohibitions and the EU rules in Arts 101 and 102 TFEU, often simultaneously. Following the implementation of Regulation 1/2003, and in order to ensure harmony between the enforcement of Arts 101 and 102 and the domestic prohibitions under the 1998 Act, a number of amendments were made to UK Law and OFT practice[131] – for instance, the extension of the appeals process to the appeal tribunal, CAT, in relation to OFT decisions on Arts 101 and 102 TFEU, and the alignment of calculation of fines with Commission practice.[132] The OFT's role in the enforcement process has now been taken over by the CMA, following the Enterprise and Regulatory Reform Act 2013. The same processes, powers and decision-making competences are provided in relation to both the domestic and EU prohibitions, and, accordingly, CMA enforcement of both will be examined together. Figure 2.2 illustrates the enforcement mechanism in relation to the domestic and EU prohibitions. Thereafter, there will be a brief discussion of the institutions and processes involved in the prosecution of the cartel offence under s 188 of the Enterprise Act 2002.

Competition and Markets Authority (CMA)

As of 1 April 2014, the CMA took over the previous competition law responsibilities of both the OFT and the Competition Commission. In this chapter, we are focusing on the administrative

---

129 Section 11.
130 Section 188.
131 See the Competition Act 1998 and Other Enactments (Amendment) Regulations 2004, SI 2004/1261; the Competition Act 1998 (Determination of Turnover for Penalties) (Amendment) Order 2004, SI 2004/1259; the Competition Act 1998 (Land Agreements Exclusion and Revocation) Order 2004, SI 2004/1260; the Competition Act 1998 (Office of Fair Trading's Rules) Order 2004, SI 2004/2751.
132 'OFT's guidance as to the appropriate amount of a penalty', OFT 423. It should be noted that the Commission subsequently revised their equivalent Notice and practice in 2006, as discussed above.

enforcement of the EU and UK prohibitions, and in that context it is the OFT's roles and functions which have been transferred to the CMA. After outlining the structure of the CMA, we will focus on its role in enforcing the prohibitions. It appears that in undertaking this task, at least for the foreseeable future, the CMA has adopted and will utilise the vast majority of the Guidance documents that the OFT published to ensure that its enforcement policies and practices are clear and transparent. There will continue to be reference in this chapter, and others, to OFT decision-making practice. The previous OFT practice in relation to the prohibitions helps us to understand the ongoing application of the competition provisions in the UK and thereby inform how they may be used in future CMA enforcement activity, despite the institutional change.

The institution of the CMA was intended to be a process of 'evolution rather than revolution', and the administrative model of enforcement, mirroring the European Commission system, was retained. A far more radical proposed prosecutorial model of enforcement was rejected during the consultation phase leading up to the ERR Act 2013. In other words, the CMA investigates and takes final decisions, on infringements and sanctions, which are subject to appeal. Under a prosecutorial model the CMA would have prosecuted alleged infringements before a court or tribunal, which would then adjudicate on the existence of an alleged infringement. It is clear that the CMA is seeking to both build on the existing work and successes of the Office of Fair Trading and Competition Commission, while revising specific policies and establishing its own vision, values, strategy and prioritisation principles to ensure it is a leading competition and consumer agency.[133] Investigations into alleged infringements of the prohibitions will be undertaken by the Enforcement Directorate of the CMA, with the intention of improving the speed and robustness of the decision-making process by modifying certain rules and procedures followed by the OFT. The CMA consulted on its investigation procedures to produce an equivalent but revised set of Rules[134] and Guidance[135] setting out the procedural rules the CMA will follow in the application and enforcement of Chapters I and II of the 1998 Act and Arts 101 and 102, as required by ss 51(3) and 52 of the 1998 Act. Section 52 of the 1998 Act required publication of advice and information on the Act and the OFT published a wide range of guidelines on various aspects of the legislation to help companies and their advisers. Given that the substantive rules and maximum penalties for infringement of either set of prohibitions remained unchanged, aside from the minor changes to the Procedural Rules and Guidance to reflect the changes introduced by Enterprise and Regulatory Reform Act 2013 (ERRA13) and developments in OFT practice, the CMA has effectively adopted, at least for the short term and subject to review, the existing OFT guidance on most aspects related to substantive assessment, and the investigation and enforcement regime.[136] In particular, the ERRA13 made the following changes to the enforcement system: the power for the CMA to interview individuals;[137] a lower threshold for the CMA to impose interim measures; the introduction of introducing new statutory factors to be taken into account in fixing a penalty; and the introduction of a power for the CMA to make rules on the settlement of investigations under the 1998 Act.

Investigation and decision-making process

It is evident from enforcement practice under the 1998 Act that complaints by competitors or customers have played an important role in the detection of anti-competitive behaviour, and this

---

133 See generally www.gov.uk/cma, and in particular CMA 13, 'Vision Values and Strategy for the CMA', CMA16, 'Prioritisation principles' and CMA15, 'Annual Plan 2014/2015'.
134 CA98 Rules.
135 CMA8, Guidance on the CMA's investigation procedures in Competition Act 1998 Cases, March 2014.
136 CMA12con, 'Proposed approach to the treatment of existing Office of Fair Trading and Competition Commission guidance', September 2013; in particular see Annexe A. These documents need to be read subject to the changes introduced by the ERRA13 (for example, reading references to the OFT as referring to the CMA).
137 Section 39 of the ERRA13 introduces a new s 26A of the CA98, providing the CMA with power to require individuals who have a 'connection with a relevant undertaking . . . to answer questions with respect to any matter relevant to the investigation'.

is likely to continue. The introduction of a leniency programme for whistle-blowers, following developments in the US and EU, enhances the deterrent effect of the legislation[138] and plays a key role in uncovering secret cartels. The CMA decides which cases to investigate on the basis of its published Prioritisation Principles.[139] The CMA has considerable powers to enable officials to investigate potential infringements of the domestic and EU prohibitions once a formal investigation has been opened,[140] including: entering premises to inspect and copy documents; using force to enter premises upon authority of a warrant; and allowing CMA officials to be accompanied on raids by other professional support personnel, such as IT experts. The ERRA13 also introduced the power for the CMA to interview individuals. To support these powers, a penalty may be imposed on any person for failure to comply with any requirement imposed in relation to the CMA's exercise of its powers, without reasonable excuse,[141] and it is a criminal offence to provide false or misleading information to the CMA,[142] or to destroy, falsify or conceal documents under s 43 of the CA 98. The CMA has the power to make decisions on an interim basis to protect the public interest or to prevent a competitor being damaged. Section 43 of the ERRA13 amends s 35(2)(a) of the CA98 by replacing the current test for the imposition of interim measures from 'preventing serious, irreparable damage' to 'preventing significant damage'. The CMA has various options in dealing with a case. It can close the investigation on the grounds of administrative priorities, or issue a no grounds for action decision. Following the adoption of Regulation 1/2003, the power to accept binding commitments was also introduced in relation to the domestic and EU prohibitions,[143] although the use of this remedy does not appear to have been as significant as at the EU level. Most importantly, the CMA can make a formal decision that the rules have been infringed and can order the parties in breach to cease the infringing conduct and impose penalties. Where the CMA forms the provisional view that there has been an infringement of either prohibition, it is required to issue a Statement of Objections, if it proposes to make an infringement decision against any undertaking which it considers to be responsible for the alleged infringement. The CMA must include in its Statement of Objections any action it proposes to take, such as the imposition of a financial penalty, for the alleged breach of the prohibitions. The CMA gives each addressee of a Statement of Objections an opportunity to inspect the investigation file,[144] and also gives those businesses an opportunity to discuss potential settlement of the case. Within the Enforcement Directorate, the Case Decision Group, which is independent of the investigation process, decides whether an infringement is established and the appropriate level of a penalty to be imposed. It issues an infringement decision to each business considered to have infringed the law. If there is insufficient evidence of an infringement, the CMA may alternatively publish a reasoned decision explaining why no further action will be taken. The Procedural Officer has the important role, within the Enforcement Division, of ensuring the rights of the defence are respected during the process, and will deal with any procedural complaints. Of course, this does not prejudice the normal rights of appeal from decisions of the CMA to the Competition Appeal Tribunal, as discussed later.

---

138 See Guidance as to the appropriate amount of a penalty, OFT 423, Pt III, which has been adopted by the CMA Board.
139 See CMA16, 'Prioritisation principles for the CMA', April 2014. Only a brief outline is provided here. Further detail on the process is set out in CMA8, above, n 135.
140 See ss 25–29 generally as amended by paras 10–14 of Sch 1 to the Competition Act 1998 and Other Enactments (Amendment) Regulations 2004, SI 2004/1261.
141 Section 40A of the 1998 Act.
142 Section 44 of the 1998 Act. CMA4, 'Administrative penalties: statement of policy on the CMA's approach', January 2014.
143 See para 18 of Sch 1 to the Competition Act 1998 and Other Enactments (Amendment) Regulations 2004, SI 2004/1261 and Sch 6A to the Competition Act 1998. See, also, 'Enforcement, incorporating the Office of Fair Trading's guidance as to the circumstances in which it may be appropriate to accept commitments', OFT 407.
144 See s 42 of the ERRA13 and Chapter 5 of CMA6, 'Transparency and disclosure: statement of the CMA's policy and approach', January 2014.

It is clear that the OFT was particularly active in its dealings with cartels.[145] This is an area of enforcement practice which has become increasingly significant and is likely to remain the focus of the CMA's enforcement activities in the coming years. Three aspects of the enforcement policy are particularly significant in this context: fines, the leniency policy and the settlement process.

Fines

The most important sanction, in practice, is the power to impose penalties under s 36 of the 1998 Act. Section 36(8) provides that no penalty may be imposed that exceeds 10% of the turnover of an undertaking, calculated in accordance with the Competition Act 1998 (Determination of Turnover for Penalties) Order 2000.[146] Section 44 of the ERRA13 introduced a new section 36(7A) to the CA98, setting out statutory provisions to which the CMA must have regard when fixing the level of a fine for an infringement as follows: (a) the seriousness of the infringement concerned, and (b) the desirability of deterring both the undertaking on which the penalty is imposed and others from infringing the domestic and EU prohibitions. These factors were already a central aspect of the Fines Guidance,[147] but a more significant statutory amendment requires the CAT under s 38 of the Competition Act 1998 to have regard to the CMA's Fines Guidance in reviewing and setting fines imposed.

There have been three different sets of Guidance published on the approach to be adopted in calculating financial penalties, with the most recent Guidance being adopted by the CMA. The first guidance published in 1998 related solely to the calculation of fines in relation to the domestic 1998 Act prohibitions. The Guidance was revised in 2004 to take account of the post-modernisation context in the EU in which NCAs would also have to apply the EU prohibitions now contained in Articles 101 and 102 TFEU. The Guidance therefore applied equally to fines for infringements of both sets of prohibitions. Although certainly not required by Regulation 1 or the Network Notice, the European Commission's model for calculation of penalties was generally followed by the revised 2004 Guidance. In order to bring UK fines into line with Commission practice, the 2004 Guidance ensured that the starting point for fines in relation to the domestic and EU prohibitions was a lump sum calculated with reference to the seriousness of the infringement and the relevant turnover. Ironically, as outlined above, the Commission's revised 2006 Guidance changed approach and now utilises a percentage of the relevant sales turnover as the starting point. The revised 2012 Guidance on the Appropriate Amount of a Penalty again sought to mirror broadly the Commission's Guidance and sets out a six-step approach for the CMA to use when calculating financial penalties:

1   The starting point is determined by the seriousness of the infringement, taking into account the effect on competitors and consumers. The starting point is calculated on the basis of a percentage of the relevant sales turnover (in relation to the goods or services subject to the infringing conduct), with a maximum starting point of 30% of the relevant sales turnover.

2   Thereafter, the CMA can make an adjustment, which will be related to the duration of the infringement. This allows the starting figure to be multiplied by the number of years during which the infringement has continued.

3   The CMA can adjust the figure at this stage in light of other further aggravating or mitigating factors. This stage allows a range of factors to be considered, such as the role of the undertaking, the involvement of senior managers, continued or repeated infringements,

---

145 See Chapter 7 for a fuller discussion.
146 SI 2000/309, as amended by the Competition Act 1998 (Determination of Turnover for Penalties) (Amendment) Order 2004, SI 2004/1259.
147 OFT 423 'OFT's guidance as to the appropriate amount of a penalty', September 2012.

genuine uncertainty as to the existence of an infringement, adequate steps taken to ensure compliance and co-operation with the CMA.

4   The CMA can adjust the level of fine for specific deterrence and proportionality, taking into account such factors as the business's size and financial position.

5   The OFT can make an adjustment to the figure to prevent the maximum penalty being exceeded and to avoid double jeopardy. The maximum turnover level was revised in 2004 to allow a maximum penalty of 10% of the worldwide turnover of an undertaking, as opposed to the UK turnover of the undertaking, for the previous business year. The OFT is also required to take into account any fine imposed by the European Commission, other NCA, or national court.

6   The fine may also then be adjusted to factor in the application of fine reductions under the leniency scheme and for settlements.

There have been a considerable number of cases in which fines have been imposed for breach of one of the prohibitions, although some of the examples discussed arose before the Guidance revisions in 2004 and 2012. The first financial penalty to be imposed concerned a breach of the Chapter II prohibition by Napp Pharmaceuticals, which charged both excessive and predatory prices for sustained-release morphine. The Competition Commission Appeal Tribunal (CCAT), now the Competition Appeal Tribunal (CAT), upheld the decision as to the infringement itself, but reduced the penalty imposed from £3.21m to £2.2m.[148] This case demonstrated that the CAT was then not bound by the Guidance on determining the appropriate amount of a penalty, although, as noted above, this has been revised following the ERRA13. In July 2001 it was found that Aberdeen Journals had abused a dominant position in the market for the supply of advertising space in local newspapers in the Aberdeen area,[149] and a penalty of £1,328,040 was imposed. Subsequently, the CAT upheld the decision against Aberdeen Journals, and confirmed the alleged conduct of predatory pricing. The CAT did, however, reduce the penalty imposed from the original £1,328,040 to £1,000,000.[150] In November 2003 the OFT decided that Argos, Littlewoods and Hasbro had been involved in price-fixing agreements, in relation to games and toys, in breach of the Chapter I prohibition.[151] Argos was accordingly fined £17.28m and Littlewoods £5.37m. Hasbro's fine of £15.59m was reduced to zero on the basis of its co-operation under the OFT leniency programme. In August 2003 the OFT fined ten businesses that had engaged in resale price maintenance in the market for replica football kits manufactured by Umbro, thereby infringing the Chapter I prohibition.[152] The OFT imposed a total of £18.6m in fines, the size of the fines varying between the businesses according to the OFT guidance, with some qualifying for reductions under the terms of the leniency programme. The fines included the following: JJB Sports – £8.373m; Umbro – £6.641m; Manchester United – £1.652m; the FA – £198,000 (reduced to £158,000); and Sports Connection – £27,000 (reduced to £20,000). In 2006, in one of a number of cases under UK competition law involving the construction industry, and the roofing trade in

---

148 CCAT Case No 1001/1/1/01 *Napp Pharmaceutical Holdings Ltd v DGFT*, 15 January 2002, paras 497–541.
149 DGFT Decision CA98/5/2001, Case CF/99/1200/E *Predation by Aberdeen Journals Ltd*, 16 July 2001. See, also, subsequent DGFT Decision CA98/14/2002, 16 September 2002.
150 *Aberdeen Journals v The Office of Fair Trading (formerly the Director General of Fair Trading)* [2002] CAT 6; [2003] CAT 11, paras 476–500.
151 OFT Decision CA98/8/2003, Case CP/0480–01 *Agreements between Hasbro UK Ltd, Argos Ltd and Littlewoods Ltd Fixing the Price of Hasbro Toys and Games*, 21 November 2003. On appeal, the CAT, in *Argos Ltd & Littlewoods Ltd v OFT*, upheld the OFT decision on liability ([2004] CAT 24) but reduced the fines to Argos to £15m, and to Littlewoods to £4.5m ([2005] CAT 13). See also *Argos Ltd/Littlewoods Ltd/JJB v OFT* [2006] EWCA Civ 1318, where the Court of Appeal upheld the CAT.
152 DGFT Decision CA98/06/2003, Case CP/0871/01 *Price-fixing of Replica Football Kit*, 1 August 2003. On appeal, the CAT reduced JJB's fine to £6.7m, Manchester United's fine to £1.5m, and Umbro's fine to £5.3m ([2005] CAT 22). See also *Argos Ltd/Littlewoods Ltd/JJB v OFT* [2006] EWCA Civ 1318, where the Court of Appeal upheld the CAT.

particular, the OFT fined 13 roofing contractors a total of £2.3m, reduced to £1.6m by leniency, for collusive tendering processes ('bid-rigging') to fix prices in relation to flat roofing and car park surfacing contracts.[153]

In recent years, we have seen a dramatic increase in the levels of fines imposed by the OFT under the 1998 Act. For instance, in 2007, the OFT imposed a then record fine of £121.5m on British Airways, in an early resolution agreement, for colluding with Virgin Atlantic in increasing prices payable for long-haul passenger fuel surcharges, although this was subsequently reduced in the final decision to £58.5m.[154] The Decision on *bid-rigging in the construction industry in England* was also notable,[155] with a collective fine of over £129m on 103 undertakings involved in a particular form of bid-rigging comprising cover pricing. These decisions, together with other cases, highlight the important role played by the new fining powers under the 1998 Act, in particular to seek to deter future infringements.[156] The fining powers and Guidance have been used most frequently in relation to anti-competitive agreements, although in 2011 Reckitt Benckisser were fined over £10m for abusive behaviour in withdrawing and de-listing its heartburn medicine, Gaviscon original liquid, from the NHS prescription list. The review of OFT fining decisions by the CAT and CA will be discussed in a following section, although in one appeal in the construction bid-rigging case, the CAT urged caution in selecting the parameters to compare fines with previous decisions, where it was claimed that fines were excessive in comparison with the fines imposed in *Replica Football Kit*.[157]

Leniency

The EU, UK and indeed virtually all competition authorities have followed the US DoJ Antitrust Division's lead by introducing a version of a leniency policy to encourage whistle-blowers to come forward and give information about cartels. It is now widely recognised that leniency can both destabilise existing cartels and deter the formation of future cartels.[158] The OFT introduced a leniency policy at the same time as the Chapter I and II prohibitions came into force, and the leniency policy has been modified most recently in July 2013[159] to combine the leniency process for corporate applicants, in relation to Chapter I/Art 101 TFEU, and individual applicants, in relation to the cartel offence. In relation to corporate infringements, there are three types of leniency available to undertakings. Type A, which guarantees complete corporate immunity from fines (i.e. a 100% fine reduction), is available to the first member of the cartel to come forward with relevant information relating to the infringement before the CMA have started an investigation of the cartel activity, provided that the information gives the CMA sufficient basis for taking forward a credible investigation. The business must also comply with the following five conditions: accept its participation in the cartel; provide the CMA with all the information, documents and evidence available to them regarding the cartel; maintain continuous and complete co-operation throughout the investigation; refrain from further participation in the cartel from the time of disclosure of the cartel activity (except as may be directed by CMA); and not have taken steps to coerce another business to take part in the cartel. Type B leniency, which provides discretionary corporate immunity from fines of up to 100%, is available, where the first applicant provides information that adds 'significant value' to the investigation, where an investigation has already commenced but a

153 *Collusive Tendering for flat roof and car park surfacing contracts in England and Scotland*, OFT Decision No. CA98/01/2006 (Joined Cases CE/3123–03 and CE/3645–03); OFT press release 34/06, 23 February 2006.
154 See http://www.oft.gov.uk/news-and-updates/press/2012/33–12.
155 See http://www.oft.gov.uk/OFTwork/competition-act-and-cartels/ca98/decisions/bid_rigging_construction.
156 See, for instance, the application of the minimum deterrence threshold (MDT) in the latter case, although its application was reviewed successfully in various appeals in that case, e.g. *GF Tomlinson Group Ltd and others v OFT* [2011] CAT 7.
157 Ibid.
158 See, for example, Leslie, C, 'Antitrust Amnesty, Game Theory and Cartel Stability' (2006) *Journal of Corporation Law* 453.
159 OFT 1495, 'Applications for leniency and no action in cartel cases', July 2013.

statement of objections has not been issued, subject to fulfilment of the same five conditions required for a Type A application. Type C leniency provides for corporate reductions in penalty of up to 50% if an applicant is a second or later applicant (or coercer) and provides information of 'significant added value' prior to the statement of objections, and all the same conditions are satisfied with the exception of the 'non-coercion' requirement. It should be noted that leniency-plus is also available under the CMA's leniency policy. Accordingly, an additional fine discount may be awarded in one market where an undertaking receives Type A or B leniency in a second market.

Although the specifics of the leniency policy have varied over the last 15 years, the general impact in uncovering secret cartels has been clearly evidenced by the enforcement practice in the UK, in relation to the Chapter I and Article 101 TFEU prohibitions. Hasbro was the first beneficiary to be granted leniency, in *Toys and Games*,[160] and the various levels of potential leniency available was demonstrated in *Replica Football Kit*.[161] Sportsetail were granted total immunity, whereas Umbro could not qualify for 100% immunity as it had compelled others to participate contrary to the required conditions. Accordingly, the most it could hope for was a 50% reduction, and it was awarded 40%, which it sought unsuccessfully to increase on appeal. The FA were also granted a 20% reduction in connection with their leniency application. Finally, demonstrating the benefits of a 'leniency-plus' component of a leniency programme, Sports Connection were granted full immunity in exchange for details about another infringement.[162] The impact of the leniency policy was also starkly demonstrated in *Airline Passenger Fuel Surcharges for Long Haul Passenger Flights*, where there were only two undertakings involved in the infringement and one of them, Virgin Atlantic Airways, was granted a 100% discount from fine by making a successful Type A leniency application.

Settlement

Settlement is a voluntary process whereby an undertaking admits an infringement of the prohibitions in exchange for an expedited process and a reduction in fine – akin effectively to a plea-bargaining process. As noted above, the European Commission introduced a settlements procedure to reinforce deterrence by helping the Commission deal more quickly with cartel cases, freeing up resources to open new investigations. Such a process may benefit suspect undertakings by reducing financial penalties and leading to a faster outcome and reduced costs, as a lengthy administrative procedure is avoided. In the UK, the OFT had operated an informal 'settlements' policy whereby certain cases were brought to a swift conclusion by a process known as 'early resolution agreements'. This was evidenced, for instance, in *Independent Schools*,[163] *Airline Passenger Fuel Surcharges for Long Haul Passenger Flights*,[164] *Dairy*[165] and *Tobacco*.[166] There have, however, been concerns regarding the transparency of this process and whether there is undue pressure on undertakings to settle, even in situations where the case against them is weak.[167] The settlement process has been formalised by the adoption of a specific Procedural Rule and

---

160 Above, n 151
161 Above, n 152.
162 Ibid, para 661.
163 The OFT imposed a reduced fine of £10,000 on each participant in the systematic exchange of information on future fees by a group of 50 independent fee-paying schools, in return for a voluntary admission by those parties and an *ex gratia* payment to fund a £3m educational trust See OFT press release 166/06, 23 November 2006.
164 OFT Decision CE/7691–06.
165 OFT Decision CA98/03/2011. Following a provisional finding of collusion between certain large supermarkets and dairy processors, in September 2007, a number of the parties admitted their participation in anti-competitive prices and agreed to pay fines of over £116m in total.
166 OFT Decision CA98/01/2010, all available at www.oft.gov.uk/OFTwork/competition-act-and-cartels/ca98/decisions.
167 See Stephan, A, 'OFT Dairy Price-fixing Case Leaves Sour Taste for Cooperating Parties in Settlements' [2010] 30(11) ECLR 14–16.

inclusion of details of the settlement process in the CMA's Procedural Guidance.[168] The CMA may consider settlement for any case, provided the evidential standard for giving notice of its proposed infringement decision is met, and the reward for a business which settles is a settlement discount, which will be capped at 20% for settlement pre-Statement of Objections and 10% for settlement post-Statement of Objections.

Concurrent powers

It should be noted that s 54 of the 1998 Act provides for the CMA to exercise its powers concurrently with a variety of utility regulators: Office of Gas and Electricity Markets (OFGEM), Office of Communications (OFCOM), Office of Water Services (OFWAT), Office of Rail Regulation (ORR), Monitor, and the Utility Regulator, Northern Ireland (NIAUR).[169] The consultation on competition reform identified a number of weaknesses in the concurrency regime involving the OFT and the sectoral regulators. The Competition Act 1998 (Concurrency) Regulations 2004 required regulators to agree among themselves which authority should deal with an investigation. There were provisions merely to enable (but not require) those authorities to send to each other information they receive that an antitrust behaviour may have taken place, but no provision to require the sharing of information once an investigation was underway. The new Competition Act 1998 (Concurrency) Regulations 2014[170] give the CMA the authority to decide that it or another authority will exercise the enforcement functions under the 1998 Act in a particular case. Following the initial allocation of a case, the CMA will also have power to take over a case, but only with the agreement of the regulator, after a Statement of Objections has been issued. The CMA will exercise its power, consistent with the Commission's power to take cases from NCAs, where it considers itself best placed to take a decision setting an important precedent, and to take an effective or timely decision. There will also be more rigorous requirements in relation to information-sharing between the CMA and regulators, as part of the United Kingdom Competition Network (UKCN), to make the system more effective.

Competition Appeal Tribunal (CAT)

The Enterprise Act 2002 established the CAT[171] to replace the CCAT. The CAT is administered by the Competition Service, which was created at the same time.[172] The CAT hears appeals against the CMA's decisions. Appeals are available against the substance of any decision taken by the CMA, as detailed in s 46(1), including the level of any penalties imposed. In relation to penalties, the CAT's primary task is to 'determine whether the overall figure for penalty was appropriate in the circumstances'.[173] The CAT stressed in *Napp*[174] that it would make this assessment based on a 'broad brush' approach, and then carry out a 'cross check' to assess if it was within the parameters of the Guidance. In *Replica Football Kit*, the CAT held that it had the power to increase the penalty,[175] albeit this power 'should not be exercised lightly'.[176] As noted

168 See Rule 9 and CMA8, Guidance on the CMA's investigation procedures in Competition Act 1998 cases, March 2014, at paras 14.1–14.33.
169 See, for a detailed consideration of this issue, Prosser, T, 'Competition, Regulators and Public Service', in Rodger, BJ and MacCulloch, A, *The UK Competition Act: A New Era for UK Competition Law* (2000) Oxford: Hart.
170 The Concurrency Regulations, SI 2014/536, under s 54 CA98, as amended by s 51 of the ERRA13. See CMA10, 'Regulated industries: guidance on concurrent application of competition law to regulated industries', March 2014. See Dunne, N, 'Recasting Competition Concurrency Under the Enterprise and Regulatory Reform Act 2013' (2014) 77(2) MLR 254–276.
171 Enterprise Act 2002, Pt 2, particularly s 12. For a detailed discussion of the development of the CAT, its various roles and its case law, see Bailey, D, 'Early Case-law of the Competition Appeal Tribunal', Ch 2 in, Rodger B, (ed), *Ten Years of UK Competition Law Reform* (2010) Dundee: DUP.
172 Ibid, s 13.
173 *Argos Ltd and Littlewoods Ltd v OFT and JJB Sports plc v OFT* [2006] EWCA Civ 1318, at para 194.
174 See *Napp*, above n 148, paras 497–503, and *Napp Pharamaceutical Holdings Ltd v DGFT* [2002] EWCA Civ 796.
175 [2005] CAT 22 at paras 208–235.
176 Ibid at para 218.

above, s 38 of the 1998 Act has been amended, by the ERRA13, to require the CAT to have regard to the CMA's Fines Guidance in setting appropriate penalties.

In the case of *Bettercare v DGFT*[177] the CAT made clear that whether an appealable decision has been taken is a matter of substance, based on the position adopted on the complaint and the stage the investigation has reached.[178] Accordingly, an appeal may be made to the CAT where the CMA has not formally issued a decision, but, for instance, advised a complainant informally that it will not proceed with a complaint because it does not appear that either prohibition has been infringed. The main party or parties against whom the CMA has made decisions can appeal, as can 'qualifying third parties' with a sufficient interest in the issue. The qualifying test is wider than the EU law test under Art 263 TFEU, and allows interested consumers and organisations representing such consumers to appeal directly to the CAT. Section 12, and Sch 2, of the 2002 Act make provision for the constitution of the CAT, including the appointment of its President who presides over the Tribunal. As set out in s 14 of the 2002 Act, a Tribunal dealing with an appeal consists of a Chairman, who is either the President or a member of the panel of Tribunal Chairmen, and two other appeal panel members. The CAT may confirm, set aside or vary the CMA's decision, or remit the matter to the CMA, or make any other decision that the CMA could have made. Detailed rules concerning the CAT procedure have been adopted as required under the legislation.[179] There is a right to an oral hearing, although oral hearings have tended to be short and structured, being conducted on the basis of the detailed skeleton arguments submitted to the CAT by counsel. There is a further right of appeal, under s 49 of the 1998 Act, on a point of law to the Court of Appeal in England and Wales, the Court of Session in Scotland and the High Court in Northern Ireland.[180] Accordingly, the CAT must determine in which jurisdiction it is sitting for the purposes of an appeal from the CMA, and this determines in which jurisdiction a subsequent appeal will be heard.[181] Rule 60 of the 2003 CAT Rules allows for the possibility of a reference to the CJEU for a preliminary ruling under Art 267 TFEU.[182] There have already been a number of judgments by the CAT in which they have resorted to the range of powers available to them under the Act.[183] For instance in *Napp Pharmaceuticals v DGFT*,[184] *Toys and Replica Kits*,[185] the fine was reduced; in *Aberdeen Journals v DGFT*,[186] the case was remitted to the DGFT after the first appeal hearing; in *Bettercare v DGFT*, the decision was set aside and the issue remitted for reconsideration;[187] the decision of the OFT was simply set aside in *The Racecourse Association and others v OFT*;[188] and in *Burgess v OFT*,[189] an appeal against a rejection of a complaint by the OFT, the CAT held that there had been an infringement of the Chapter II prohibition.[190] Subsequent appeal is on a point of law only. In undertaking its task, the Court of Appeal has expressed its deference to the specially created CAT as follows: 'it seems to us that it is right for the court to

---

177 *Bettercare v DGFT* [2002] CAT 6. See, also, *Freeserve.com v DGFT* [2002] CAT 8; *Claymore/Express Dairies v DGFT* [2003] CAT 3; and *Pernod Ricard SA and Campbell Distillers Ltd v OFT* [2004] CAT 10.
178 See the fuller discussion in Alese, F, 'The Office Burden: Making a Decision without a Decision for a Third Party' [2003] ECLR 616.
179 The Competition Appeal Tribunal Rules 2003, SI 2003/1372, applicable to proceedings commenced after 20 June 2003, replacing the 2000 Rules (SI 2000/261).
180 Note that the requirement for resolution of a point of law limits the potential availability of appeal. See, for instance, *Napp Pharmaceutical Holdings Ltd v DGFT (No 5)* [2002] EWCA Civ 796; [2002] 4 All ER 376.
181 See Rodger, B, 'Competition Law in a Scottish Forum' (2003) *Juridical Review* 247.
182 See Middleton, K, 'Harmonisation with Community Law: The Euro-clause', in Rodger and MacCulloch, above, n 169.
183 Under para 3(2) of Sch 8 to the 1998 Act. See CAT judgments on the CAT website at www.catribunal.org.uk.
184 [2001] CAT 1.
185 *Umbro and Others v OFT*, [2005] CAT 22 and *Argos Ltd & Littlewoods Ltd v OFT* [2005] CAT 13, respectively.
186 [2002] CAT 6.
187 [2002] CAT 7.
188 The appeals were allowed and the OFT Decision that the sale of certain rights infringed the Chapter I prohibition was set aside, [2005] CAT 29.
189 [2005] CAT 25.
190 See discussion in Chapter 4.

recognise that the Tribunal is an expert and specialised body, and that . . . the court should hesitate before interfering with the Tribunal's assessment.'[191]

In addition to its appellate role, ss 47A and 47B of the Competition Act, introduced by ss 18 and 19 of the Enterprise Act, provide for the CAT to hear claims for monetary awards in respect of established infringements of the Chapter I and II prohibitions and Arts 101 and 102 TFEU,[192] and for aggregated claims by consumer representative bodies.[193] The provisions in the Consumer Rights Bill seek to further expand the role of the CAT in private enforcement.[194] Furthermore, the CAT is responsible for reviewing decisions by the CMA, and the Secretary of State, in relation to merger and market investigation inquiries under the Enterprise Act,[195] as discussed in Chapters 5 and 8 respectively.

Cartel offence investigations and director disqualification

In addition to the 'administrative' sanctions available to the CMA against 'undertakings', businesses which infringe the domestic or EU prohibitions, there are also specific sanctions targeted at individuals who are involved directly in the anti-competitive behaviour; for instance, a marketing director involved in cartel meetings. These sanctions are considered in more detail in Chapter 7, but we give a brief outline here.

When the cartel offence was introduced in ss 188 and 189 of the Enterprise Act 2002, the rationale put forward was largely based on the deterrence of cartel conduct.[196] The offence criminalised individuals who 'make or implement' horizontal cartel arrangements within the UK.[197] The aim was to enhance the deterrent effect by increasing personal incentives to comply, and to increase the destabilising impact on cartels by the possibility of immunity from prosecution for individuals who 'whistle-blow' on a cartel. In addition, s 204 of the Enterprise Act empowers the CMA to seek a competition disqualification order, which will disqualify a director of a company that breaches any of the competition law prohibitions. Both these measures should enhance the likelihood that organisations will institute and maintain effective competition law compliance programmes.

There have been only two successful prosecutions under the UK cartel offence. Three men pleaded guilty, in 2008, to charges in relation to international bid-rigging in the marine hoses cartel and were initially sentenced to two-and-a-half to three years' imprisonment and another man pled guilty in 2004 in relation to a cartel in galvanized steel tanks.[198] Generally, criminal penalties can improve the deterrent effect by affecting the individuals who decide that an undertaking should participate in unlawful behaviour. While fines imposed on an undertaking will simply affect its profit and loss account, the real threat of the imprisonment or director disqualification of company decision-makers is expected to have a more immediate impact. The existence of criminal law sanctions for competition violations in a number of Member States raises questions regarding the relationship between domestic criminal prosecutions and the enforcement of the EU prohibitions. A prosecution may be brought by the CMA under s 188 of the

---

191 *Argos*, above n 173, at para 165.
192 See, for instance, *HealthCare at Home Ltd v Genzyme Ltd* [2006] CAT 29, and a number of cases before the CAT in relation to the Vitamins cartel.
193 For instance, *The Consumers' Association v JJB Sports plc* (Case No 1078/7/9/07), a follow-on consumer representative action under these provisions before the CAT in relation to *Replica Kit*, although this case was settled out of court in January 2008 following an agreement by JJB to pay consumers who were unlawfully overcharged £20 each (see CAT Order of 14 January 2008).
194 See discussion in Chapter 3.
195 In relation to the former, see for instance *IBA Health Ltd v OFT* [2003] CAT 28, discussed more fully in Chapter 8.
196 See MacCulloch, A, 'The Cartel Offence and the Criminalisation of UK Competition Law' [2003] JBL 615.
197 Enterprise Act 2002, s 188(1). See CMA9, 'Cartel Offence Prosecution Guidance', March 2014.
198 See OFT Press Release 72/08, 11 June 2008 and 'former MD pleads guilty in UK industry price-fixing case', *Financial Times*, 17 June 2014. The sentences in Morine Hores were reduced somewhat on appeal see *R v Whittle & Ors* [2008] EWCA Crim 2560.

Enterprise Act 2002, with regard to cartel activity which may also be the subject of an investigation under Art 101 TFEU by the CMA, another NCA or the European Commission. While the ECN has systems to ensure that only one NCA deals with an Art 101 investigation, there is no similar procedure to decide whether an NCA investigation should be suspended to allow a domestic criminal investigation to go ahead. It is relatively clear that a criminal prosecution must precede an Art 101 infringement decision, in order to avoid prejudicing the criminal trial. While it is clear that the criminal case should proceed first, that does not mean that the Art 101 infringement investigation is suspended; it should proceed as normal.[199] This was exemplified in the charge and conviction under the cartel offence in respect of the supply in the UK of galvanised steel tanks for water storage, while there was an ongoing civil investigation into the alleged cartel.[200] The potential for procedural conflicts and appeals against conviction on the basis of procedural irregularities makes this area an obvious minefield for the investigating authorities. The collapse of the OFT prosecution of the 'BA Four' in 2010,[201] when the OFT failed to disclose potentially exculpatory evidence to the defence, was indicative of the difficulties that face the case teams within the CMA, who will have very limited experience of handling criminal investigations and prosecutions. It was also suggested that the Commission might find itself increasingly marginalised if the NCAs used their criminal powers regularly, and effectively suspend the application of Art 101 TFEU in important cartel cases,[202] although this fear has not been realised in practice.

Globalisation and Extraterritoriality

Extraterritoriality

Extraterritoriality concerns the extent to which competition laws can be applied and enforced outside the specific territory of their competence. For instance, can UK competition law be applied to an agreement between companies based in America, or can EU law be applied in respect of a merger between a Japanese company and an American company? The reason for the significance of extraterritoriality in competition law is the potential for effects on international trade, or another economic area, as a result of competition violations. This potential for multi-jurisdictional issues to arise has increased due to the enhanced globalisation of markets. For instance, there may be a production cartel based in State A which artificially increases the supply price of the product to State or economic area B, thereby affecting the latter state's economic interests. As a result, State B may decide to apply its competition laws to the participating companies and impose fines. This issue is controversial as it implies a breach of territorial sovereignty of State A. On the other hand, many systems of competition law that are applicable to anti-competitive actions, which are harmful within a state or which affect the economy of a state, make no provision for conduct that produces effects only outside that state's territory. An example of this would be the grant of a competition law exemption to an export cartel. The potential impact of extraterritorial enforcement of US antitrust law can be seen in the UK's intervention in *Hoffmann-La Roche v Empagran*[203] before the US Supreme Court. In that case, a number of organisations that had suffered losses through the activities of the Vitamins cartel in Australia,

---

199 While it has always been presumed that a criminal prosecution must come first it should be noted that in the investigation into BA's fuel surcharge the Art 101 case was settled while the criminal investigation was still ongoing – see OFT Press Release, 'British Airways to pay record £121.5m penalty in price fixing investigation', 113/07, 1 August 2007.
200 OFT Press Release 04/14, 'Man faces charge in criminal cartel investigation', 27 January 2014.
201 OFT Press Release 47/10, 'OFT withdraws criminal proceedings against current and former BA executives', 10 May 2010.
202 See Riley, A, 'EC Antitrust Modernisation: The Commission Does Very Nicely Thank You!' Pt 1 [2003] ECLR 604; Pt 2 [2003] ECLR 657.
203 *F Hoffmann-La Roche Ltd, Hoffmann-La Roche Inc, Roche Vitamins Inc, BASF AG, BASF Corp, Rhône-Poulenc Animal Nutrition Inc, Rhône-Poulenc Inc v Empagran SA* 124 S Ct 2359 (2004).

Ecuador, Panama and Ukraine were seeking damages before the US courts. The UK Government intervened, as *amicus curiae*, to argue that an extension of the US's jurisdiction to this extent would be damaging to global competition enforcement.[204]

Subject matter jurisdiction

The basic problem that faces the enforcement of competition law outwith the territory of a state arises from the commonly accepted principle of public international law that there are limits to a state's jurisdictional competence. The starting point is to differentiate between subject matter jurisdiction and enforcement jurisdiction. A state may consider that it has subject matter jurisdiction to apply its rules to conduct, or more often to the economic effects of conduct, irrespective of the precise locus of the conduct. The principal reason this issue has arisen in competition law is because the economic effects of market conduct are often easily separable from the conduct itself. Accordingly, it is perhaps understandable that difficulties arise and that states may consider their competition laws applicable to economic effects produced within their state, which derive from conduct or activity that originated elsewhere. However, this becomes particularly contentious if the state seeks to go further and exercise enforcement jurisdiction, enforcing its competition rules by normal means, such as serving court papers or demanding evidence from a company. Enforcement of competition laws abroad may cause conflict with the state in which enforcement is sought.

Under international law, subject matter jurisdiction may be based on nationality or territorial grounds. Under the territoriality principle, jurisdiction may exist if the act originated abroad but was completed within the jurisdiction. A straightforward example would be the refusal to supply goods or services. However, it is less clear whether the territoriality principle can be applied where there are only economic effects produced within the territory. Often, the anti-competitive behaviour, such as predatory or excessive pricing, will be within the jurisdiction, or at least one party to an agreement will be based within the territory. Should this not be the case, one possibility for competition authorities would be to invoke the 'economic entity' doctrine. Using this approach, enforcement may be sought against a parent company outwith the jurisdiction on the basis of the actions of a subsidiary company within the jurisdiction, where the conduct or activity was controlled or directed by the parent company. The main controversy arises where the actions take place outside the jurisdiction but produce economic effects in a market within the jurisdiction. A clear example of this would be a price-fixing cartel based in another jurisdiction. One possible solution to this controversial problem is to adopt the effects doctrine derived from the famous *Alcoa*[205] decision in the US, which confirmed that liability can exist for breach of the antitrust rules for conduct outside the borders of the US that produces consequences within it. Regarding the UK, there is little or no mention of extraterritorial enforcement within the competition law provisions. The main reason has been a strict adherence to traditional international law principles which are opposed to concepts such as the effects doctrine. The Competition Act makes no reference to extraterritorial application and the prohibition of anti-competitive agreements only applies to those 'implemented within the United Kingdom'.[206]

EU competition law and extraterritoriality

EU law applies if there is an effect on interstate trade. Beyond this basic rule, it is unclear whether an effects doctrine may be applied by the Commission. The economic entity doctrine was

---

204 See the UK's *amicus* brief at http://www.berr.gov.uk/bbf/competition/international/ukbriefs/page33060.html.
205 *United States v Aluminium Co of America (Alcoa)* 148 F 2d 416 (1945), 2 Circ. Cf *Hoffmann-La Roche Ltd v Empagram SA* 124 S Ct 2359 (2004).
206 For the limits of the new Chapter I and II prohibitions, see ss 2 and 18, respectively.

approved by the Court in early case law.[207] The *Dyestuffs* case involved illegal price-fixing within the EU, where the price-fixing was principally carried out by non-EU-based undertakings through EU-based subsidiaries. The anti-competitive conduct was attributed to the parent company as the subsidiaries were effectively under its control. The application of the economic entity doctrine has been criticised as ignoring the separate legal personality of the companies, but it has been relied on extensively by the Commission.[208]

Application of the doctrine is dependent on the existence and exercise of control by the parent company, such as its representation on the subsidiary board. Although the doctrine allows EU competition law to be enforced against companies beyond the EU, enforcement is ensured, practically, by serving documentation on the subsidiary. An alternative approach would be the adoption by the Commission of the effects doctrine. However, its application is still unclear as a result of the Court's judgment in *Wood Pulp*.[209] The *Wood Pulp* case involved allegations of price-fixing between wood pulp producers throughout the world, including various non-EU-based producers. The Commission claimed that EU competition law applied where the conduct produced effects within the Union. The Court avoided the controversial issue of the applicability of the economic effects doctrine by stating, based on the facts, that the agreement had indeed been implemented within the EU. It remains unclear what constitutes implementation, and also whether purely economic effects within the EU would be considered sufficient. A possible scenario could, for instance, involve a refusal to supply within the EU by a cartel boycotting the EU market. As far as enforcement is concerned, the Court has considered that the Commission is competent to serve documents, and indeed necessary for enforcement to be pursued, on a non-EU company.[210] On a practical level, the main difficulty in enforcing any Commission decision and/ or penalty may be overcome by seizing that company's assets in the EU.

Extraterritorial application of EU law was particularly high-profile following the Commission's involvement in the mergers between US companies, for example, McDonnell Douglas and Boeing, and GE and Honeywell, and the controversial CFI ruling in *Gencor Ltd v Commission*.[211] In that case, parent companies Gencor and Lonrho agreed to merge the activities of their platinum mining subsidiary companies in South Africa. The South African authorities did not object to the merger, but the Commission blocked the merger on the basis of collective dominance theory.[212] A key issue in *Gencor* concerned the territorial reach of the Merger Regulation.[213] The starting point was that the Regulation applies to all mergers with a Community dimension, and there was a Community dimension in the case in this instance. Sales within the EU constituted substantial operations in the EU,[214] and were deemed to satisfy the implementation test set out in *Wood Pulp*. The most controversial aspect of the case was the CFI's view that the 'application of the Merger Regulation is justified under public international law when it is foreseeable that a proposed concentration will have an immediate and substantial effect in the Community'.[215] This appears to endorse the widely criticised effects doctrine, although the impact of the judgment is arguably restricted to merger control. The Commission Decision to prohibit the proposed merger of two

207 Case 48/69 *ICI v Commission (Dyestuffs)* [1972] ECR 619.
208 For example, Case 7/73 *Commercial Solvents v Commission* [1974] ECR 223.
209 Cases C-89, 104, 114, 116, 117 and 125–29/85 *A Ahlstrom Oy v Commission* [1988] ECR 5193.
210 Case 52/69 *Geigy v Commission* [1972] ECR 787. However, see Feibig, A, 'International Law Limits on the Extra-territorial Application of the European Merger Control Regulation and Suggestions for Reform' [1998] 6 ECLR 323.
211 Case T-102/96 [1999] ECR II-753.
212 For further discussion of collective dominance, see Chapters 4 and 8.
213 See Fox, E, 'The Merger Regulation and its Territorial Reach: *Gencor Ltd v Commission*' [1999] ECLR 334; Porter Elliott, G, 'The Gencor Judgment: Collective Dominance, Remedies and Extraterritoriality under the Merger Regulation' (1999) 24 EL Rev 639.
214 *Per* the 11th recital to the Merger Regulation. This is another aspect of the continued reference to the 'Community' in the application of EU competition law.
215 [1988] ECR 5193, para 90.

American undertakings involved in aero-engines, avionics and other aircraft components and systems, General Electric Co and Honeywell Inc, also resulted in tension between the US and EU competition authorities, the former having earlier approved the merger.[216]

Resistance to extraterritorial application

Disputes can arise between different legal systems due to the controversial nature of the extraterritorial application and enforcement of competition laws. For example, in the mid-1980s, Laker Airways sued certain UK-based airline companies for breach of US antitrust law, and that litigation involved sensitive considerations of the possibility of UK courts preventing the US courts from enforcing US antitrust laws against the UK-based companies.[217] A number of countries have passed blocking statutes to prevent the extraterritorial application of US antitrust law, in some instances as a direct response to the *Alcoa* decision. This demonstrates how the extraterritoriality issue clearly relates to political and nationalistic considerations, evidenced by the introduction of the Protection of Trading Interests Act 1980 in the UK. This legislation is not limited to the possible extraterritorial enforcement of US antitrust laws, but may be more broadly applicable in relation to possible harm to commercial interests in the UK. The Act gives the Secretary of State powers to prohibit UK firms from complying with foreign laws and/or complying with any requirement to submit information to any foreign authority beyond the territorial jurisdiction of the foreign authority.[218] Sections 5 and 6 of the Protection of Trading Interests Act 1980 provide that multiple damages awards are not enforceable in the UK, and that an action may be brought in the UK to 'claw back' the excess awarded in a foreign multiple damages action when compared to a domestic single damage action.

International Co-operation and Global Competition Rules

Enforcement jurisdiction, as noted, may lead to possible conflicts where authorities seek to serve court papers or order the production of documents. However, as markets become more global and the larger companies operate on a worldwide scale, information regarding a company's operations beyond the particular territory of the enforcement authority is becoming even more important. Partly as a result of globalisation, and in an attempt to ensure more effective enforcement of competition law generally, there have been various developments to seek to ensure some form of co-operation between national and supranational agencies. Efforts to improve co-operation have developed on both a multilateral and a bilateral basis. The United Nations Conference on Trade and Development (UNCTAD) and the Organisation for Economic Cooperation and Development (OECD) are active in this area, and there are suggestions that competition enforcement should be brought within the auspices of the World Trade Organization (WTO). Bilaterally, there has been increased international co-operation in competition law enforcement between a number of states.[219] There have also been important developments involving the EU. The EU entered a co-operation Agreement with the US in 1991. The Agreement was successfully challenged before the Court of Justice by the French

---

216 Commission Decision 2004/134/EC *General Electric/Honeywell*, [2004] OJ L48/1. See Zanettin, B, *Cooperation between Antitrust Agencies at the International Level* (2000) Oxford: Hart, for discussion on the impact of the Commission prohibition on US/EU antitrust relations. See, also, Burnside, A, 'GE, Honey, I Sunk the Merger' [2002] ECLR 107. The Commission's decision was upheld by the CFI in Case T-209/01 *Honeywell International Inc v Commission* [2005] ECR I-5527 and Case T-210/01 *General Electric Co v Commission* [2005] ECLR I-5575. See Howarth, D, 'The Court of First Instance in GE/Honeywell' [2006] ECLR 485.

217 See *Midland Bank plc v Laker Airways plc* [1986] 1 All ER 526; and *British Airways v Laker Airlines* [1984] 3 All ER 39.

218 Protection of Trading Interests Act 1980, ss 1–3.

219 See, for instance, Galloway, J, 'Moving Towards a Template for Bilateral Antitrust Agreements' (2005) 28(4) *World Competition* 589.

Government on the basis that the Commission was acting *ultra vires*. In April 1995, this was remedied with retroactive effect by a Decision of the Council and Commission.[220] The Agreement is significant in that it provides for notification, consultation, information-sharing, and co-operation and co-ordination in enforcement; although the Agreement makes clear that it should be interpreted in conformity with the respective substantive rules of the US and European Union, and that the competition authorities remain bound by their own internal rules on confidentiality.[221] There has been a substantial body of practice developed under the Agreement, and the Commission publishes an annual report on its operation. In 1999, the Community and Canada also finalised a co-operation agreement due to the increase in the number of cases being investigated by the authorities of both jurisdictions.[222] The European Economic Area (EEA) Agreement provides a clear system of collaboration between the Commission and the European Free Trade Association (EFTA) Surveillance Authority in the enforcement of EU and EEA competition rules. Furthermore, the European Competition Network is probably the best example of co-operation and co-working involving a number of competition authorities, albeit in the application of the same set of substantive rules.[223]

There have been developments within the WTO framework with a view to establishing, in the longer term, an international antitrust code.[224] At present, a global code or competition authority seems highly unlikely. Nonetheless, there was an important report, in 2001, by the International Competition Policy Advisory Committee (ICPAC) of the antitrust division of the US Department of Justice.[225] It focused on the issues of multi-jurisdictional mergers and international co-operation, particularly in relation to cartels, and the interface between trade and competition rules. The report considered that the WTO was not the appropriate forum for advancing global competition issues and it proposed a global competition initiative as a new venue for the exchange of ideas and progress towards common solutions for competition law and policy problems. The search for a worldwide competition culture has been developed through the International Competition Network (ICN), launched in 2001 as a project-orientated, consensus-based informal network of antitrust agencies from developed and developing countries. The ICN does not seek to introduce any form of global competition law but, instead, gradual convergence through understanding of best practice in the area of competition law enforcement. The ICN's mission statement is:

> to advocate the adoption of superior standards and procedures in competition policy around the world, formulate proposals for procedural and substantive convergence, and seek to facilitate effective international cooperation to the benefit of member agencies, consumers and economies worldwide.[226]

There are, as of January 2014, 118 member agencies of the ICN worldwide. The ICN has an annual conference and has constituted working groups on: advocacy; agency effectiveness;

---

220 Agreement Between the Government of the United States of America and the European Communities Regarding the Application of their Competition Laws, [1995] OJ L95/47, as corrected by [1995] OJ L131/38.

221 The Community and the US entered into an agreement on the application of 'positive comity' principles to strengthen further existing co-operation under the 1995 Agreement. The main objective, further to Art V of the 1995 Agreement, is to provide that either party, whose interests are adversely affected by anti-competitive activities occurring in whole or in substantial part in the territory of one of the parties, may request the other party to take action in the form of investigating and remedying the anti-competitive activities. See, in particular, Arts I and III, [1998] OJ L173/28. More recently there has been increased focus on best practices, on the basis that these achieve a greater degree of procedural convergence, thus lessening the risk of conflicting decisions.

222 [1999] OJ L175/50. See, also, Agreement between the EC and the Government of Japan concerning co-operation on Anti-Competitive Activities, [2003] OJ L183/12.

223 See, for instance, Canebley, C and Rosenthal, M, 'Co-operation between Antitrust Authorities In and Outside the EU: What Does it Mean for Multinational Corporations?' Part I [2005] ECLR 106; Part II [2005] ECLR 178.

224 See Koczarowska, A, 'International Competition Law in the Context of Global Capitalism' [2000] 2 ECLR 117.

225 At www.usdoj.gov/atr/icpac/finalreport.htm, 20 April 2001.

226 See www.internationalcompetitionnetwork.org.

cartels; mergers; and unilateral conduct. During its first decade it has established itself as the primary forum for competition law policy-makers and officials to meet, discuss, learn, share ideas and develop best practices across a range of key competition law areas, and it will be interesting to assess its development and role during its second decade.[227]

Key Points

● The European Commission, through DG Comp, plays a central role in the system for enforcement of Articles 101 and 102 TFEU. Under Regulation 1/2003 the Commission enforces those prohibitions alongside, and in co-operation with, Member States National Competition Authorities (NCAs), as part of the European Competition Network (ECN).

● Regulation 1/2003 affords the Commission extensive powers to investigate and sanction infringements of the rules. Its decision-making powers must be in line with due process requirements and are subject to review by the General Court and Court of Justice.

● The central enforcement role in the UK lies with the Competition and Markets Authority (CMA). The CMA has a range of powers, remedies and sanctions which are closely modelled on those available to the European Commission, and its decisions are subject to appeal first to the Competition Appeal Tribunal and then to the civil appeal courts.

● Competition law has responded to the globalisation of markets by developing the International Competition Network (ICN); a global forum for developing shared experiences and best practices in competition law policy and practice.

Discussion

1 What changes did Regulation 1/2003 introduce to the enforcement of EU competition law?

2 What alternatives exist to the formal infringement decision-making process for the European Commission?

3 What mechanisms exist for case allocation within the ECN?

4 How has UK competition law been transformed by the Competition Act 1998 and Enterprise Act 2002?

5 What powers does the CMA have to enforce the EU and UK prohibitions, and can the decisions of the CMA be reviewed?

6 Why is globalisation a problem for competition law? How has international co-operation been facilitated and to what extent are global competition initiatives likely to be successful?

Further Reading

Commission Enforcement, Regulation 1/2003, and the ECN

Brammer, S, 'Concurrent Jurisdiction under Regulation 1/2003 and the Issue of Case Allocation' (2005) 42(5) CML Rev 1383.

Branki, S-P, 'The First Cases under the Commission's Cartel-settlement Procedure: Problems Solved?' [2011] 4 ECLR 165–169.

Dekeyser, K and Jaspers, M, 'A New Era of ECN Co-operation' (2007) 30(1) World Competition 3.

Kellerbauer, M, 'Playground Instead of Playpen: The Court of Justice of the European Union's Alrosa Judgment on Art 9 of Regulation 1/2003' [2011] 1 ECLR 1–8.

Ortega Gonzalez, A, 'The Cartel Settlement Procedure in Practice' [2011] 4 ECLR 170–177.

---

227 See Hollman, HM and Kovacic, WE, 'The International Competition Network: Its Past, Current and Future Role' 20 Minn J Int'l L (2011) 274–323.

Wesseling, R, 'The Commission White Paper on Modernisation of EC Antitrust Law: Unspoken Consequences and Incomplete Treatment of Alternative Options' [1999] ECLR 420.

Wils, WJ, 'Ten Years of Regulation 1/2003 – A Retrospective' *Journal of European Competition Law and Practice* (2013) 4(4) 293–301.

UK competition law reform: the Competition Act 1998, Enterprise Act 2002 and Enterprise and Regulatory Reform Act 2013

Freeman, P, 'The Competition and Markets Authority: Can the Whole be Greater than the Sum of its Parts?' (2013) JAE 4–23.

Rodger, B (ed) *Ten Years of UK Competition Law Reform* (2010) Dundee, DUP.

Rodger, BJ and MacCulloch, A, *The UK Competition Act: A New Era for UK Competition Law* (2000) Oxford: Hart.

Wilks, S, *In the Public Interest: Competition Policy and the Monopolies and Mergers Commission* (1999) Manchester: MUP.

Wilks, S, 'Institutional Reform and the Enforcement of Competition Policy in the UK' (2011) Comp L J 1.

Globalisation

Canenbley, C and Rosenthal, M, 'Co-operation between Antitrust Authorities In and Outside the EU: What Does it Mean for Multinational Corporations?' Part 1 [2005] ECLR 106; Part 2 [2005] ECLR 178.

Gerber, D, *Global Competition: Law, Markets and Globalization* (2010) Oxford: OUP.

Hollman, HM and Kovacic, WE, 'The International Competition Network: Its Past, Current and Future Role' 20 Minn J Int'l L (2011) 274–323.

Maher, I, 'Competition Law in the International Domain: Networks as a New Form of Governance' [2002] *Journal of Law and Society* 111.

Shaheln, H, 'Designing Competition Laws in New Jurisdictions: Three Models to Follow', Ch 2 in Whish, R and Townley, C (eds), *New Competition Jurisdictions, Shaping Policies and Building Institutions* (2010) Edward Elgar Publishing.

Von Meibom, W and Geiger, A, 'A World Competition Law as an Ultima Ratio' [2002] ECLR 445.

Chapter 3

Private Enforcement

Chapter Contents

Overview

- Private enforcement is where a party (whether a consumer or competitor) seeks to rely on their rights, or another party's obligations, under competition law in the course of litigation; a particular example of this is where consumers who have been adversely affected by a price-fixing cartel law seek compensatory redress directly from those who committed the infringement.
- Private enforcement actions can either 'follow-on' from a decision of a competition authority or be 'stand-alone' actions; they can use competition as a 'sword' to claim redress or a 'shield' to defend a claim made by another party. A variety of remedies may be available, dependent on the context in which competition law is being relied upon.
- Traditionally there has been a very strong private antitrust enforcement tradition in the US because of a number of institutional and cultural factors, notably opt-out class actions. Conversely, private enforcement has been less prominent in the EU, although there have been attempts to facilitate and encourage it, leading to fairly recent reform proposals and legislation. In particular, there have been significant and ongoing reforms to engender greater resort to private enforcement in the UK, particularly before the specialist competition tribunal, the CAT.

Introduction

As discussed in Chapter 1, competition law seeks to regulate the market behaviour of businesses, for instance, by prohibiting the abuse of monopoly power and the operation of cartels. Chapter 2 provided a detailed review of the institutions, structures and processes in respect of the public enforcement of both the EU and UK competition law prohibitions (contained in Arts 101 and 102 TFEU and the Competition Act 1998 Chapters 1 and 2 prohibitions respectively). This was a crucial starting point because EU and UK competition law have traditionally been enforced virtually exclusively by administrative bodies: the European Commission and the OFT/CMA. However, the fines imposed by those competition authorities do not compensate directly any of the victims of competition law infringements. The historical primacy of public/administrative enforcement in Europe is in stark contrast with US competition law ('antitrust law') where private enforcement plays a more central role. The availability of a well-developed system of class actions has ensured that private enforcement is extremely effective in the US and can result in end-consumers being compensated for their losses. The US system also emphasises the importance of consumer rights, and the possibility of substantial damages awards enhances the deterrent impact of the antitrust laws. Accordingly private enforcement of competition law can: first, ensure that rights are respected by providing a means of redress for any damage caused by a competition law infringement, either to another business forced out of a market by abusive behaviour or an end-consumer paying excessive prices for a product as a result of a price-fixing cartel; and, second, bolster or even replace (where the competition authority has insufficient resources or does not prioritise sanctions of particular competition law infringements) public enforcement action, in order to enhance or at least ensure the deterrent effect of the competition rules. Accordingly, the European Commission and various Member States, including the UK, have recognised that private enforcement should be encouraged and facilitated.

This chapter will outline various ongoing developments and policy initiatives in this area and the background to US private antitrust enforcement before considering key aspects of private enforcement of competition law. It will then consider EU developments leading to the adaption, in April 2014, of the EU'S antitrust damages Directive and Recommendation on Collective

Redress. The statutory and institutional context for private enforcement will then be addressed, before the current institutions and mechanisms are compared with those in the US and the proposed reforms in the Consumer Rights Bill are outlined. A brief review of the EU and UK developments in private enforcement concludes the chapter.

Background to US Private Antitrust Enforcement

Historically, a range of institutional factors and mechanisms have combined to ensure that private enforcement of US antitrust law is effective;[1] namely, the wider litigation culture, the significant period of development of antitrust law and economics and, in particular, the specific characteristics of US civil procedure.[2] The important procedural mechanisms are:

1   The rules on discovery

These are fairly wide-ranging, and essentially allow a claimant to ask the court to require the defendant in an antitrust damages claim to produce a significant amount of documentation held by it which might allow the claimant(s) to prove their case against the defendant.

2   The funding of actions

US civil procedure allows for contingency fees to be charged by lawyers. No win, no fee contingency fees appeal to potential claimants because of the absence of the risk of having to pay considerable legal fees should a claim be unsuccessful. They also incentivise lawyers, who, in the event of success, take a percentage of the overall damages award or agreed settlement sum; this is generally 30% of the antitrust damages awarded. This can lead to very profitable work for lawyers, where antitrust settlements can be upwards of $1bn in some cases.[3]

3   The availability of class actions

Consumers are often directly affected by antitrust infringements, in particular, cartels which fix the prices of products or services. However, in such situations, individual consumer losses, and correspondingly the incentive to go to court, may be quite low. US law provides for a class action mechanism which allows individual claims to be combined together simply and effectively in what is known as an opt-out class action procedure. A lawyer simply requires to raise an action using a single lead claimant and requests the court to certify the action as being appropriate for a class action on the basis that there is sufficient 'commonality' between all the potential individual claims. Once an action is certified by the court, all potential claimants within the scope of the claim are automatically parties to the claim unless they specifically opt-out. This procedure overcomes potential consumer apathy and again incentivises lawyers to raise mass claims where the awards and legal rewards (fees) are considerably higher than in individual low-value claims.

4   The existence of treble damages actions

Damages actions in most areas of the law, and generally in relation to competition claims in the legal systems of the EU, are based on the principle of compensation. This means damages claims purely compensate claimants for any loss or damage actually suffered as a result of the wrongful behaviour of the defendant; generally, multiple, penal or exemplary

---

1   See, for instance, Foer, AE and Cuneo, JW (eds), *The International Handbook on Private Enforcement of Competition Law* (2010) Edward Elgar In association with the American Antitrust Institute; Jones, CA, *Private Enforcement of Competition Law in the EU, UK and USA* (1999) Oxford: OUP; Lande, RH and Davis, JP, 'Benefits from Private Antitrust Enforcement: An Analysis of Forty Cases' (2008) 42 *University of San Francisco Law Review* 879.
2   See Foer and Cuneo, ibid, Part II.
3   See Lande and Davis, n 1.

damages awards are prohibited. Under US antitrust law, the position is entirely different. The damages calculator has been specifically amended to provide that antitrust claimants are entitled to sue for three times their actual losses suffered as a result of the antitrust law infringement.[4] The availability of treble damages encourages claimants and lawyers to pursue antitrust infringements and seek compensation. The increased damage awards also contribute towards deterring potentially infringing conduct.

Partly as a result of these mechanisms and incentives, private antitrust enforcement is a well-developed and mature system of litigation in the US. A recent example highlights the complementary role of these various incentivising mechanisms. Following the announcement of an investigation into the BA/Virgin passenger fuel surcharge price-fixing cartel by the US and UK authorities, sparked by leniency applications by Virgin Atlantic, a class action was raised in the federal courts in the US. Lawyers raised an action using a lead claimant and asked the courts to require BA to deliver all passenger records for the period of the infringement, and the action was certified as a class action for all those parties by the court. A settlement on the basis of a considerable pay-out was agreed, and the lawyers, incentivised by this possibility, received a large contingency fee payment and any passenger who had paid excess flight charges during the period could claim a refund from the settlement fund. While this may be viewed as a positive development in punishing an infringement and compensating victims, the debate in the European Union has often been critical of these procedural mechanisms, dubbed as a 'toxic cocktail' leading to 'ambulance-chasing' lawyers and 'innocent' defendants effectively being 'blackmailed' into settling claims for vast sums.

Key Aspects of Private Enforcement in the EU

This section will address three crucial and often inter-related aspects to the debate on the development of private enforcement in an EU context: the remedies available, the use of follow-on or stand-alone actions and the availability of consumer collective redress mechanisms.

Remedies

There are a range of remedies potentially available to a party who claims to have suffered as a result of an alleged competition law infringement. The Commission's focus in this area has been on damages actions,[5] yet it is clear that EU and domestic competition law are relied upon by parties in both sword (claimant relying on competition law) and shield (defendant relying on competition law) situations, including nullity actions, and therefore it is important to seek an understanding of how competition law rights are exercised in all contexts, not just damages actions.[6] In some circumstances, a party may simply seek a declaration that a particular competition rule has been infringed. This may be important, for instance, in allowing that party to renege on purported contractual commitments where the contract is null and void in contravention of the competition rules. Historically, particularly in the UK, competition law was pleaded and relied on most often by parties as a defence to an action; this became known as a 'Euro-defence' in the period before the UK adopted its own competition law prohibitions. A counter-claim based on an alleged abuse of a dominant position was particularly popular (though not very successful) as a defence to claims for royalty payments in respect of intellectual property licensing agreements. The use of competition

---

4   See the Clayton Act, but note the impact of the Antitrust Criminal Penalty Enhancement and Reform Act 2004 which de-trebles damages awards in relation to successful antitrust immunity applicants – see discussion of leniency in Chapter x.
5   See Milutonivic, V, *The Right to Damages' Under EU Competition Law* (2010) Kluwer Law International.
6   Komninos, AP, 'Private Enforcement in the EU with Emphasis on Damages Actions', Chapter 4 in Lianos, I and Geradin, D (eds), *Handbook on European Competition Law* (vol 2) (2012) Edward Elgar.

law as a defence is still common in contractual disputes throughout Europe. Another potential remedy available to claimants is the use of an injunction (or interdict in Scotland) to stop behaviour that infringes competition law.[7] This would be particularly suitable for businesses which might be vulnerable to a forced exit from a market because of alleged abusive, exclusionary behaviour by a dominant undertaking.[8] In particular, if court processes allow for a swift, expedited procedure to enable the alleged infringement to be ended at least on a temporary basis, this would provide a better alternative than the slower process of public enforcement by a competition authority which would follow a complaint.[9] Interlocutory injunctions are available in the courts of England and Wales, and the equivalent interim interdict in the Scottish courts, although it is not always easy to persuade courts that such interim remedies are appropriate and necessary. Finally, there is the damages remedy for losses suffered as a result of a competition law infringement. Such losses can arise in a myriad of ways: in the form of loss of profit or investment caused to a rival competitor by anti-competitive abuse behaviour by a dominant undertaking; claims by end-consumers who have overpaid for a product or service purchased directly from a price-fixing cartel; direct purchaser claims for cartel overcharge/surcharges where those direct purchasers have then passed on some of the overcharge, or where indirect purchasers have paid more for a product than the hypothetical competitive price as a result of the increased price of inputs to that product caused by a cartel. Classic examples of the problematic situation involving direct and indirect purchasers were the Vitamins and Lysine cartels, discussed in Chapter 7, as the cartel products were subsequently inputs into a wide range of products which were sold on at inflated prices. The standard requirements in damages actions to prove causation and quantification of damages can always be problematic, but in competition law claims there are additional potential complications: how the calculation of losses suffered by parties at different levels of the supply chain should take into account whether and to what extent overcharges have been passed on by suppliers, or to customers.[10]

Follow-on and stand-alone actions

Follow-on actions 'follow on' from prior public authority enforcement decisions, for example, a damages action which is raised against a party or parties who against whom there has been a Commission cartel infringement decision based on Article 101 TFEU. As discussed in Chapter 2, the Commission (and the CMA in the UK) has extensive investigative powers which, allied to the leniency programme, ensures that it can uncover cartels across the European Union. By contrast, that would be virtually impossible for a business or other private party which merely had a suspicion that it may have been harmed by a secret cartel. Accordingly, cartel damages actions are nearly always follow-on actions, facilitated by a provision in Regulation 1/2003 which makes prior Commission infringement decisions binding subsequently on national courts.[11] There are similar provisions in many Member States in relation to the evidential value or binding nature of prior infringement decisions by their NCAs.[12] The Commission's Draft Directive, proposed an EU-wide rule on the binding effect of prior infringement decisions by any NCA (or a review court). In follow-on actions, the claimant's chances of success are greatly aided where there is no requirement to prove the infringement. However, Art 9 of the Directive, as approved by the EP on 17 April 2014, only provides for the binding effect of NCA decisions of that Member State, and the persuasive effect of others.

7 This would normally arise in stand-alone actions, discussed below.
8 See Chapter 4.
9 Unless of course the authority could be persuaded that the matter was one of urgency and that interim measures were necessary, as discussed in Chapter 2.
10 See Petrucci, C, 'The Issues of the Passing-on Defence and Indirect Purchasers' Standing in European Competition Law' [2008] ECLR 33, and note also the Directive, discussed below.
11 Art 16 of Regulation 1/2003.
12 See, for example, in the UK under its follow-on mechanism, discussed below. Note also the Directive.

Stand-alone actions are independent of, and usually in the absence of, enforcement action by a competition authority. This would arise either because the competition authority will not deal with a complaint in accordance with its prioritisation principles, or because the victim needs to take immediate court action to bring a halt to the alleged anti-competitive behaviour. Stand-alone actions are most commonly associated with allegations based on the abuse of a dominant position under Art 102 TFEU. The distinction between follow-on and stand-alone cases can become somewhat blurred. In the UK, litigation preceded by a CMA decision may be raised in the normal courts outside the designated follow-on mechanism. The term 'follow-on' can be used in a narrow sense to refer to actions raised against parties named in infringement decisions by the relevant authorities. In other cases the defendants are not directly named in the infringement decision, but are related companies, perhaps the parent company in a corporate group. In a wider sense these could be seen as follow-on claims, but because the defendants are not the specific addressees of the decision, they could also be seen as stand-alone claims.[13]

The US experience demonstrates that follow-on actions were vital in the development of private enforcement. In the 1960s, 75% of all individual actions followed on from government-led actions. The availability of follow-on actions ensures that private claimants can get a 'free ride' on a public enforcement action. An American study[14] in the 1980s revealed how important public enforcement of the antitrust laws was to the early development of private antitrust enforcement in the US. There is more recent evidence that although follow-on actions still play an important role in US antitrust enforcement, stand-alone actions now play a more significant role. Lande and Davis's study of 40 recent private settlements of $50m or more demonstrated that almost half of the violations were uncovered by private parties, as opposed to government enforcement.[15] Nonetheless, in the context of the significantly more mature US private antitrust system, that study demonstrated that the experience developed in follow-on actions was essential to the subsequent development of a culture of stand-alone damages litigation.

Consumer collective redress mechanisms

Discussion of the availability of consumer collective redress mechanisms is important for a number of reasons. First, because of the historical and contemporary focus on the 'consumer' at the heart of competition/antitrust law, as outlined in Chapter 1; whether from a neo-classical economic model of perfect competition and monopoly, the Chicago school influence on US antitrust, its (limited) concept of the 'consumer welfare', or the consumer-interest model which has predominated in the European debate in recent years. Second, because it chimes with more recent debates generally in legal practice about 'access to justice'. Third, because it was developed by the Commission as a central theme in the debate surrounding encouraging and facilitating private enforcement in the EU.[16] Finally, and related to this third aspect, the influence of class actions in the US antitrust enforcement system in which private enforcement has played a considerably more significant role than in the EU over the last 30 years. On the one hand, the US system demonstrates the potential for consumer redress for competition law infringements, but on the

---

13 See, for instance, *Cooper Tire & Rubber Co v Shell Chemicals UK Ltd* [2010] EWCA Civ 864, CA. See also more recently, *Nokia Corporation v AU Optonics Corporation and* others [2012] EWHC 732 (Ch) and *Toshiba Carrier UK Ltd and others v KME Yorkshire Ltd and others* [2011] EWHC 2665 (Ch).

14 Known as the 'Georgetown Study'. Kauper, TE and Snyder, A, 'Private Antitrust Cases that Follow on Government Cases' in White, L (ed), *Private Antitrust Litigation: New Evidence, New Learning* (1988) Cambridge, MA: MIT Press, pp 329–370.

15 Lande and Davis, above n 1.

16 See the Commission website at http://ec.europa.eu/competition/antitrust/actionsdamages/index.html, as discussed further below. See Andreangeli, A, 'Collective Redress in EU Competition Law: An Open Question with Many Possible Solutions' (2012) 3 *World Competition* 529–558; See Hodges, C, 'The European Approach to Justice and Redress' (2011) 53 *Supreme Court Law Review* (2d) 301–346.

other, the EU (and UK) debate on reform has been burdened with a fear of the over-zealous litigant and the establishment of an excessive and costly private enforcement system of which 'class actions' form a central feature.[17]

A consumer can be defined as 'an end-purchaser acting outwith their trade or profession'. Considerable academic study and literature in this field, led by the work of Rachel Mulheron,[18] and other empirical work, has highlighted major gaps in redress for consumers in relation to competition law infringements.[19] Obviously consumers can simply raise actions individually in respect of any competition law infringements that have affected them. This is more likely to be in a follow-on action and for the remedy of damages. However, given that an individual consumer is likely to be seeking a very minimal sum, it may be difficult to encourage that person to seek redress, due to the potential costs involved in litigation. There are traditional legal mechanisms, not necessarily associated with consumer redress, for grouping actions which may in some way be related. One method here may be, where permitted, for parties to assign their claims either to a particular litigant or a third party. However, some form of collective redress mechanism is generally accepted as necessary:

> Collective redress is a procedural mechanism that allows, for reasons of procedural economy and/or efficiency of enforcement, many similar legal claims to be bundled into a single court action. Collective redress facilitates access to justice in particular in cases where the individual damage is so low that potential claimants would not think it worth pursuing an individual claim. It also strengthens the negotiating power of potential claimants and contributes to the efficient administration of justice, by avoiding numerous proceedings concerning claims resulting from the same infringement of law.[20]

The key choice in determining an appropriate collective redress model is whether to allow opt-in or opt-out forms of action. Under an opt-in model, the claimants must take action to be included in the class, whereas in the opt-out system claimants, who have the same interest, are automatically included in the class by default unless they expressly exclude themselves. This model can reduce the costs of both the defendant and court. The opt-in system is limited in that:

> [r]equiring the individuals affirmatively to request inclusion in the lawsuit would result in freezing out the claims of people – especially small claims held by small people – who for one reason or another, ignorance, timidity, unfamiliarity with business or legal matters, will simply not take the affirmative step. . . . In [such] circumstances . . . it seems fair for the silent to be considered as part of the class.[21]

Opt-in models have been criticised as being ineffective, with very low take-up rates, and accordingly a major part of the debate in the EU, borrowing heavily from the US class action tradition, has been whether an opt-out mechanism should be adopted. A further subdivision of the type of

---

17 See Heffernan, L, 'Comparative Common Law Approaches to Multi Party Litigation; The American Class Action Procedure' (2002) 25 DULJ 102. For criticism of the 'irrational' approach to class actions in Europe, see Schnell, G, 'Class Action Madness in Europe – a Call for a More Balanced Debate' [2007] ECLR 617–619.

18 For some of the work undertaken in this field by Rachael Mulheron, see 'Recent Milestones in Class Actions Reform in England: A Critique and a Proposal' (2011) 127 *Law Quarterly Rev* 288–315; 'The Impetus for Class Actions Reform in England Arising From the Competition Law Sector' in Wrbka, S et al (eds), *Collective Actions: Enhancing Access to Justice and Reconciling Multilayer Interests?* (2012) Cambridge: CUP, ch 15, 385–412.

19 *Reform of Collective Redress in England and Wales: A Perspective of Need* (Report submitted to the Civil Justice Council of England and Wales, February 2008).

20 Communication From The Commission, 'Towards a European Horizontal Framework for Collective Redress', COM(2013) 401 final, para 1.2.

21 Kaplan, B, 'Continuing Work of the Civil Committee: 1966 Amendments of the Federal Rules of Civil Procedure' (I), *81 Harvard Law Review*, 356, 397–398.

collective redress available is whether the mechanism provides for some form of representative action, whether in relation to an opt-out or an opt-in scheme. Recent proposals at the EU and UK level on collective redress mechanisms will be discussed further below.

Developments in EU Private Enforcement

Although it has been stressed that public enforcement of EU competition law is the norm, the basic EU doctrine of direct effect ensures that certain EU Treaty rules create rights and obligations which can be enforced in the domestic courts. In an early Article 267 TFEU ruling, the Court confirmed that the doctrine applied to the TFEU competition rules.[22] Furthermore there have been a number of important developments over the last 20 years to encourage private enforcement of competition law, such as the Commission Notice on Co-operation with the National Courts in 1993,[23] the European Court's *Crehan* and *Manfredi* rulings,[24] and the introduction of Regulation 1/2003.[25] The 1993 Notice was ostensibly published to establish communication between national courts and the Commission, to assist the former in dealing with competition law issues arising in litigation. It also set out to the potential benefits to parties of going to court to obtain effective and 'personalised' remedies as opposed to simply complaining to the Commission (or NCAs) about alleged anti-competitive behaviour. Regulation 1/2003 sets out the context in which EU competition law is to be enforced in a more decentralised manner, both by the NCAs as discussed in Chapter 2, and by parties seeking to exercise their rights before national courts. The move towards private enforcement was exemplified by the *Manfredi* and *Crehan* litigation in the Italian and English courts

The *Crehan* ruling took on particular significance.[26] It was one of five joined cases concerning the validity of provisions, known as beer ties, whereby the tenant of a public house was required by the terms of his lease to purchase all or most of the beer required for sale in such premises from the landlord or a brewer nominated by him at the prices prescribed by the supplier. Mr Crehan, who ran two pubs, the Cock Inn and the Phoenix, complained that the brewer had sold beer to publicans not subject to a beer tie, at substantially lower prices than those charged to tenants who were tied. He sought, in effect, to recover the difference between the prices paid and those which would have been payable if he had not been subject to the tie. The basis of Mr Crehan's claim was that either the tie, or the events leading up to its imposition, constituted infringements of Article 101 TFEU as agreements restricting competition. The landlord maintained that, even if this was the case, the tenant was not entitled to recover damages from his landlord because the provisions of Article 101 TFEU were not enacted for the benefit of parties to the prohibited agreement – co-contractors. The matter was referred to the CJEU by the English Court of Appeal under the preliminary ruling procedure. The ruling shed light on the extent to which EU law requires the effective harmonisation of national remedies to ensure consistent treatment of EU competition law.[27] The Court held that there should not be any absolute bar to an action brought by a party to a contract in breach of the competition rules. Nonetheless, in the absence of EU rules governing the matter, it was for each legal system to determine how the rights derived from EU law were to be safeguarded:

---

22 See Case 127/73 *BRT v SABAM* [1974] ECR 51.
23 [1993] OJ C39/6.
24 Case C-295/04 *Manfredi v Lloyd Adriatico Assicurazioni SpA* [2006] ECR I-6619.
25 Note also the developments in various Member States, exemplified by the provisions for private enforcement in the UK through the Competition Act 1998, the Enterprise Act 2002 and the important reforms contained in the Consumer Rights Bill currently passing through Parliament (cl 82 and Sch 7).
26 Case C-453/99 *Courage v Crehan* [2001] I-6297. See Komninos, A, 'New Prospects for Private Enforcement of EC Competition Law: *Courage v Crehan* and the Community Right to Damages' [2002] 39 CMLRev 447; Andreangeli, A, '*Courage Ltd v Crehan* and the Enforcement of Article 81 before National Courts' [2004] ECLR 758.
27 See also now Case C-295/04 *Manfredi v Lloyd Adriatico Assicurazioni SpA* [2006] ECR I-6619.

provided that such rules are not less favourable than those governing similar domestic actions (principle of equivalence) and that they do not render practically impossible or excessively difficult the exercise of rights conferred by [EU] law (principle of effectiveness).[28]

The Court recognised that the legal systems of most Member States applied the principle that a litigant should not profit from his own unlawful conduct. Accordingly, it concluded that EU law did not 'preclude national law from denying a party who is found to bear *significant responsibility for the distortion of competition* the right to obtain damages from the other contracting party'.[29] In particular, it is for the national court to ascertain whether one party was in a 'markedly weaker position than the other party, such as seriously to compromise or even eliminate his freedom to negotiate the terms of the contract'[30] and therefore bears a significant responsibility for the distortion of competition. The ruling was perhaps a disappointment to observers who may have hoped that the Court would be more proactive and provide a harmonised system of remedies for breach of the competition law provisions. Nonetheless, it is arguable, in hindsight, that the publicity associated with the ruling was an important catalyst in the Commission's subsequent process of facilitating effective private enforcement of EU competition law. The case returned to the High Court, Chancery Division where a complex myriad of facts was presented in court; from the complicated structure of the UK beer and pub industry, which had been the subject of previous UK and EU competition law investigations, to evidence about the hardened drinkers of Staines. As Park J remarked:

> Staines seems to have been quite a heavy drinking area and I heard evidence about the habits of regular drinkers there . . . I listened with a mixture of apprehension, admiration and alarm to accounts of the volumes which they consumed nightly.[31]

The nearby Angel pub sold pints of beer 40p cheaper than Mr Crehan's pubs, and regulars would apparently drink seven to ten pints there before heading to the Cock Inn or Phoenix, where they wouldn't need to drink as much. Ultimately Park J rejected Mr Crehan's claim on the basis of industry evidence that the UK beer market was competitive, despite earlier indications to the contrary by the European Commission. The case was appealed to the Court of Appeal, which in a unanimous single judgment, allowed the appeal and awarded Crehan damages of £131,336. The case was subsequently appealed to the House of Lords. Disappointingly, the House of Lords did not rule on the key remedy issue or on the appropriate quantification of damages, but focused on the issue of the national court's duty of sincere co-operation in overruling the Court of Appeal.[32] Accordingly, as determined earlier by Park J, Mr Crehan was not entitled to damages, and the first final damages award in a competition law case was not made in the UK until much later, in 2012.

The Commission's Reform Package

The enforcement landscape has been changing, albeit slowly, since the Commission began to encourage private enforcement in the early 1990s, partly to enhance the deterrence and effectiveness of EU competition law and alleviate its own resource limitations. The Ashurst Report and subsequent Green and White Papers on 'Damages actions for breach of the EC Antitrust Rules'[33]

---

28 *Crehan*, n 26 [29].
29 Ibid, [31]
30 Ibid, [33].
31 *Crehan v Inntrepreneur CPC* [2003] EWHC 1510 (Ch), [249].
32 See *Crehan v Inntrepreneur CPC* [2003] EWHC 1510 (Ch); *Crehan v Inntrepreneur CPC* [2004] EWCA Civ 637, [2004] ECC 28, CA; *Crehan v Inntrepreneur Pub Co (CPC)*, 19 July 2006, [2007] 1 AC 333, HL.
33 Ashurst, 'Study on the conditions of claims for Damages in case of Infringement of EC Competition Rules', 31 August 2004, available at http://ec.europa.eu/competition/antitrust/actionsdamages/index.html.

demonstrated the Commission's intention to consider mechanisms to facilitate private competition law enforcement across the EU, to allow for a new wave of litigation following the 2002 Leniency notice and the so-called European cartel enforcement revolution.[34] It is arguable that with the Commission Consultation on 'Towards a Coherent European Approach to Collective Redress'[35] and recent 2013 Commission Communication[36] and Recommendation on Collective Redress,[37] the emphasis has shifted to ensuring effective consumer redress. The public consultation entitled 'Towards a coherent European approach to collective redress'[38] aimed to identify common legal principles on collective redress and to examine how they could be adapted to fit into the legal orders of the 28 EU Member States. In this period there was also a Collective Redress Study produced for DG for Internal Policies,[39] which proposed the following as the key legal objectives of an antitrust collective redress mechanism:

(i)   to discourage unmeritorious actions, while guaranteeing that those who have actually suffered harm obtain and adequate and fair compensation;
(ii) to ensure a fair trial by providing legal certainty and consistency;
(iii) to lower the financial and organisational hurdles that consumers and small businesses face.[40]

It proceeded to consider that an opt-out mechanism should be exceptionally permitted, partly due to the low participation in opt-in models.

The 2013 Commission Communication noted that business stakeholders opposed the 'opt-out' model, and consumer organisations viewed it as desirable in delivering effective justice. The Commission, however, considered that the opt-out model curtailed claimant freedom in making informed decisions, and, rather bizarrely, that it might be inconsistent with the central aim of collective redress on the basis that the parties were not identified, and accordingly an award could not be distributed to them. The outcome of the Commission's consultation was probably inevitable, given the popular rhetoric in relation to the toxic cocktail of mechanisms supporting the US antitrust class action system.[41] The Commission, endorsing harmonisation at the lowest common level, recommended that Member States should have collective redress mechanisms in place to ensure effective access to justice, but the general rule is that these should be based on the opt-in model, with exceptional resort to an opt-out model justified on the basis of the sound administration of justice.[42] Furthermore, the Recommendation provides that Member States should not permit contingency fees and that punitive damages are to be prohibited.

---

34 For a detailed discussion of this issue, see Riley, A, 'Beyond Leniency: Enhancing Enforcement in EC Antitrust Law' (2005) 28(3) *World Competition* 377–400.
35 At http://ec.europa.eu/competition/consultations/2011_collective_redress/index_en.html.
36 Communication, Strasbourg, 11.6.2013 COM(2013) 401 final.
37 Commission Recommendation of 11 June 2013 on common principles for injunctive and compensatory collective redress mechanisms in the Member States concerning violations of rights granted under Union Law [2013] OJ L 201/60–65.
38 See generally http://ec.europa.eu/consumers/redress_cons/collective_redress_en.htm#comrec.
39 See DG for Internal Policies, Policy Department, Economic and Scientific Policy, Collective Redress in Antitrust Study 2012, available at http://www.europarl.europa.eu/document/activities/cont/201206/20120613ATT46782/20120613ATT46782EN.pdf.
40 Ibid, p 12.
41 Among many statements to this effect by EU leaders, European Commission DG SANCO, MEMO/08/741, 2009, p 4 ('The US-style class action is not envisaged. EU legal systems are very different from the US legal system which is the result of a "toxic cocktail"—a combination of several elements (punitive damages, contingency fees, opt-out, pre-trial discovery procedures) . . . This combination of elements – "toxic cocktail" – should *not* be introduced in Europe. Different effective safeguards including, loser pays principles, the judge's discretion to exclude unmeritorious claims, and accredited associations which are authorised to take cases on behalf of consumers, are built into existing national collective redress schemes in Europe.').
42 Commission Recommendation, above n 37 at para 21.

In June 2013, the Commission also proposed a Draft Directive to harmonise aspects of private litigation across the EU.[43] The Antitrust Damages Directive will, *inter alia:* provide easier access to evidence through minimum disclosure rules;[44] effectively limit access to leniency documentation;[45] provide for decisions of all NCAs to constitute proof of infringement before their own Member State civil courts;[46] establish clear limitation periods;[47] give protection to successful leniency immunity applicants, with limitation of their joint and several liability to compensate infringements;[48] establish rules on the passing-on of overcharges;[49] and introduce a rule on presumption of harm.[50] Although weaker than the proposal the Directive contains significant measures aimed at facilitating the task of potential claimants in proving their competition law claims. The greatest controversy related to the protection of leniency applicants' documentation from access by claimants through court disclosure processes. This issue has already been the subject of Court of Justice judgments in *Pfleiderer*[51] and *Donau Chemie*,[52] where the Court emphasised the need for individual national courts to balance the interests of claimants and immunity recipients when deciding on disclosure applications. The Draft Directive overrules the existing CJEU rulings and arguably goes too far in protecting the leniency applicant. The Commission has emphasised the central role for the leniency scheme in uncovering cartels and the danger that fewer leniency applicants may come forward due to the risk that they would have to disclose all leniency documentation in a subsequent private enforcement claim.

UK Private Enforcement

Introduction

In the UK, competition law enforcement has traditionally been the virtually exclusive dominion of administrative authorities, formerly the Office of Fair Trading,[53] and after 1 April 2014 the Competition and Markets Authority. In addition to ongoing developments under EU law,[54] the Competition Act 1998 system of UK competition law was underpinned by the intention that the Chapter I and Chapter II prohibitions (equivalent to Arts 101 and 102 TFEU) would be enforced by private party litigants before the courts. Moreover, the Enterprise Act 2002 subsequently made provision *inter alia* for follow-on actions before a specialist Competition Appeal Tribunal ('CAT').

Statutory developments

The Competition Act 1998 ('1998 Act') put in place a system based on the rules set out in Arts 101 and 102 TFEU, known as the Chapter I and Chapter II prohibitions.[55] The Act placed the Office of Fair Trading ('OFT') at the apex of the enforcement system with similar powers and

---

43 Gamble, R, 'Whether Neap or Spring, the Tide Turns for Private Enforcement: The EU Proposal for a Directive on Damages Examined' [2013] 34(12) ECLR 611–620.
44 Proposal for a Directive on certain rules governing actions for damages under national law for infringements of the competition law provisions of the Member States and of the European Union, COM(2013) 404 final, Art 5. The Directive was adopted by the European Parliament in April 2014.
45 Ibid, Arts 6–7.
46 Ibid, Art 9.
47 Ibid, Art 10.
48 Ibid, Art 11.
49 Ibid, Arts 12–15.
50 Ibid, Art 17.
51 Case C-390/09 *Pfleiderer AG v Bundeskartellamt* [2001] ECR I-5161.
52 Case C-536/11 *Bundeswettbewerbsbehörde v Donau Chemie AG* [2013] ECR I-0000.
53 Note that this is a relatively simplistic outline, and in fact the Office of Fair Trading in its current statutory corporate guise was created under s 2 of the Enterprise Act 2002. Note that under the Enterprise and Regulatory Reform Act 2013, the functions of the OFT and the Competition Commission have been brought together in a combined Competition and Markets Authority ('CMA').
54 See http://ec.europa.eu/competition/antitrust/actionsdamages/index.html.
55 Sections 2 and 18 of the Act respectively. For a historical discussion of the issue, see MacCulloch, chapter 5 in Rodger, B and MacCulloch, A (eds), *The UK Competition Act: A New Era for UK Competition Law* (2000) Oxford: Hart Publishing. See also Rodger, Chapter 3 in Rodger, B (ed), *Ten Years of UK Competition Law Reform* (2010) Dundee: DUP.

sanctions to the European Commission.[56] Those powers are now exercised by the CMA. It was clearly intended that the 1998 Act prohibitions should be enforceable by means of private law actions through normal court processes. The Enterprise Act 2002 ('2002 Act') made further provision for encouraging private actions in relation to breaches of the 1998 Act prohibitions. Under s 47A of the 1998 Act,[57] the Competition Appeal Tribunal ('CAT')[58] could award damages and other monetary awards where there has already been a finding by the relevant authorities of an infringement of the Chapters I and II prohibitions, or Arts 101 or 102 TFEU.

Section 19 of the 2002 Act added s 47B to the 1998 Act, allowing damages claims to be brought before the CAT by a specified body on behalf of two or more consumers who have claims in respect of the same infringement[59] – a form of 'consumer representative action'. The representative body requires the consent of the individuals to pursue their claims: effectively an opt-in representative action. Section 47B was inserted to support an underlying aim of the Enterprise Act to reinforce the links between competition law and consumers. The only specified body to date is Which? (formerly the Consumers' Association),[60] and there has only been one high-profile s 47B claim: *Consumers' Association v JJB Sports plc*,[61] in relation to *Football Shirts*.[62] The claim was for compensatory damages and also contained an interesting claim for exemplary or restitutionary damages of 25% of the relevant turnover of the defendant. Ultimately, this action, following a day of mediation, with only 144 consumers becoming party to the action, was settled on the basis of compensation up to a maximum of £20 per individual consumer,[63] and the action was withdrawn. At least in this case it was relatively straightforward for claimants to prove purchase by production of the relevant football shirts, which changed regularly. This case was positive in demonstrating that some consumers could obtain reimbursement of their 'overcharge', but also negative, as the numbers were so limited. Although, as a postscript, it should be noted that the defendant, JJB Sports, offered a gesture of goodwill, by offering a free England away shirt and a mug in return for production of a shirt of the relevant period and upon agreement not to pursue JJB further. Apparently around 12,000 consumers took up this offer, and the follow-on action therefore had a positive indirect effect. Another downside in relation to this dispute was the difficulties encountered by the Consumers' Association in recovering their costs.

The ability to bring a claim before the CAT does not affect the right to commence ordinary civil proceedings, as made clear by s 47B(10) of the 1998 Act, in respect of any infringement. Accordingly, follow-on actions may, but are not required to, be brought before the CAT.[64] Stand-alone actions and non-monetary claims cannot yet be raised before the CAT[65] and, given that claims against multiple parties often combine stand-alone and follow-on elements, such claims lie outside the CAT's jurisdiction and must be raised before the High Court.[66] Another rationale for a claim being raised before the High Court relates to the fact that a CAT action cannot be

---

56 See Whish, R, 'The Role of the OFT in UK Competition Law' chapter 1 in Rodger (ed) (2010) ibid.
57 As introduced by s 18 of the Enterprise Act.
58 For a fuller discussion of the CAT, its role, functions and case-load, see Bailey, D, 'The Early Case Law of the Competition Appeal Tribunal', chapter 2 in Rodger (ed) (n 55).
59 Section 47B(1) and (4). Subss (9)-(10) make provision regarding the specification of a body by the Secretary of State.
60 Pursuant to Specified Body (Consumer Claims) Order 2005, SI 2005/2365.
61 Case no 1078/7/9/07. See further below regarding the BIS proposals for reform and the provisions in Sch 7 to the Consumer Rights Bill, and also above regarding the EU consultation process on collective redress generally.
62 As *Replica Football Kit* had become known in the CAT follow-on case. See discussion of the case and its background by Rodger, chapter 13, in B Rodger (ed) *Landmark Cases in Competition Law: Around The World in Fourteen Stories* (2012) Kluwer Law International.
63 If receipts had been retained, see http://www.which.co.uk/news/2008/01/jjb-to-pay-fans-over-football-shirt-rip-off-128985.jsp.
64 As subsequently demonstrated, for example, in *Devenish Nutrition Ltd v Sanofi-Aventis SA (France)* [2007] EWHC 2394, (Ch) and [2008] EWCA Civ 1086 (CA).
65 See further below re the BIS consultation on private actions in competition law, 2012.
66 See, for instance, *Cooper Tire & Rubber Co v Shell Chemicals UK Ltd* [2010] EWCA Civ 864, CA. See also, more recently, *Nokia Corporation v AU Optonics Corporation and* others [2012] EWHC 732 (Ch) and *Toshiba Carrier UK Ltd and others v KME Yorkshire Ltd and others* [2011] EWHC 2665 (Ch).

raised until all public enforcement appeal processes have been finalised.[67] The restrictions on the jurisdiction of the CAT and the advantage of being able to proceed immediately with a follow on action before the High Court were exemplified by *National Grid*,[68] a follow-on claim seeking damages in the sum of £249m. It was clear that proceedings were raised in the High Court because a number of parties to the Commission *Switchgear* decision had appealed, and the claimants ran the risk of an 'Italian torpedo' from a negative declaratory action being raised in an alternative jurisdiction if they waited until appeal proceedings had been completed and an action could be raised before the CAT.

To facilitate follow-on litigation, it was considered necessary to provide for the binding nature of prior NCA enforcement decisions. The 1998 Act facilitated claims by providing, in s 58, that the findings of fact by the OFT, which are relevant to an issue arising in a court action, are binding on the parties, if that decision in which the findings of fact were made is no longer subject to appeal.[69] Section 58A of the 1998 Act provides that in any action for damages for an infringe-ment of the 1998 Act prohibitions or Arts 101 or 102 TFEU, a court will be bound by a decision of the OFT or CAT that any of the prohibitions have been infringed,[70] if the requisite appeal process has taken place or the period for appeal lapsed.[71] Nonetheless, despite this supporting provision, there have been difficulties in determining the scope of the effect of a prior binding infringement decision.[72] A problematic issue concerns the precise nature of the competition authority's findings and the consequences of those findings. These may involve factually compli-cated determinations by the CAT, as evidenced by *Enron Coal Services ltd (in Liquidation) v EWS Ltd*. This was a follow-on claim to an ORR decision that EWS had infringed the Chapter II prohibition and Art 102. The claimant sought various remedies including damages for lost profits. It was stressed throughout the proceedings that establishing liability was not an issue for the CAT under the follow-on procedure.[73] This case, involving a regulator's Decision of over 400 pages, demonstrates the difficulties in ascertaining exactly what support the enforcement authority deci-sion provides for subsequent claims.[74] An advantage of claims raised before the CAT is that they leave a 'footprint', even where the case settles before any judicial determination of the issues arising. There is also anecdotal evidence from practitioners indicates that there has been a consid-erable increase in competition claims raised at the High Court in recent years, with a number of disputes related to prior infringement decisions, particularly those by the European Commission. In that sense, although there is an increasing level of 'follow-on' litigation before the High Court one must always be aware of the 'hidden story' of competition litigation settlements which means that the visible litigation practice is effectively the 'tip of the iceberg'.

---

67 *Emerson III* [2008] CAT 8 involving claims against parties who had appealed to the General Court.
68 *National Grid Electricity Transmission Plc v ABB Ltd* [2009] EWHC 1326 (Ch).
69 See the discussion by the Court of Appeal in *Enron Coal Services Ltd (in Liquidation) v English, Welsh and Scottish Railway Ltd* [2011] EWCA Civ 2.
70 Section 58A(2).
71 Section 58A(3). See also Art 16 of Regulation 1/2003 in relation to Commission decisions. See the discussion in *Enron Coal Services Ltd (in Liquidation) v English, Welsh and Scottish Railway Ltd* [2011] EWCA Civ 2.
72 See *Enron Coal Services Ltd (in Liquidation) v English, Welsh and Scottish Railway Ltd* [2009] CAT 7 and on appeal to the Court of Appeal, [2009] EWCA Civ 647, and also the subsequent Court of Appeal ruling in the same case [2011] EWCA Civ 2. See also *Emerson Electric Co v Morgan Crucible Co PLc* [2011] CAT 4.
73 It is concerned with causation and quantum only.
74 This was reinforced by the subsequent CA decision in the case in relation to the issue of binding questions of fact. See the discussion in *Enron Coal Services Ltd (in Liquidation) v English, Welsh and Scottish Railway Ltd* [2011] EWCA Civ 2 and Woodgate, T and Filippi, I, 'The Decision That Binds: Follow-on Actions for Competition Damages After Enron' [2012] ECLR 175–178. See also *Emerson Electric Co v Morgan Crucible Co plc* [2011] CAT 4 particularly at para 59. Upheld by the Court of Appeal at [2012] EWCA Civ 1559.

Case law developments

Empirical research has demonstrated a slow but significant increase in the rate of cases through the 1970s, 80s and 90s. Nonetheless, the relatively frequent airing of competition law issues during the earlier period in particular may come as a surprise. Litigants started to use the competition law provisions fairly early following the UK's accession to the EEC, although the resort to the competition law provisions as a Euro-defence, particularly by defendants in IPR infringement cases, is fairly notable. There has been an increase in case law judgments, and the anecdotal evidence is that there has been a considerable increase in private litigation over the past ten years, with the majority of cases settling.[75] There is considerable ongoing litigation in the High Court in relation to a number of major international cartels.[76] The award of over £33k (plus interest) in lost profit and, perhaps more significantly, an additional award of £60k for exemplary damages in *2 Travel Group PLC (in Liquidation) v Cardiff City Transport Services Ltd*[77] was the first successful final award of damages by the CAT. It was followed by a subsequent £1.6m damages award in March 2013 in *Albion Water v Dwr Cymru Cyfyngedig*.[78] There is some evidence of an increase in the number of claims being raised before the CAT, and it has delivered some important judgments to date; although these have tended to be procedural skirmishes related to time-bar, costs and jurisdiction. It appears the consumer representative claim provision is clearly not an appropriate mechanism to incentivise 'class actions'. It may be that the profile associated with the very recent, successful damages awards in *2 Travel Group PLC (in Liquidation) v Cardiff City Transport Services Ltd and Albion Water v Dwr Cymru Cyfyngedig* may increase awareness of the possibility to seek redress for aggrieved parties, and thereby encourage follow-on claims, particularly before the CAT. Collective redress may also be facilitated by the proposals made by BIS in 2013 and subsequently included in Sch 7 to the draft Consumer Rights Bill, as discussed below.

Review of UK institutions and mechanisms

The UK now has a well-established specialist court and follow-on action mechanism, albeit one that will be subject to further reform. In comparison with the key features of the US civil procedural system, the UK is generally well placed to incentivise competition law damages claims.

1. Discovery

    In England and Wales the Civil Procedure Rules require a party to disclose all documents which are relevant to the litigation, including those that harm your own case or support the opposing party.[79] Although it is clear that disclosure is considerably broader than across most legal systems in continental Europe, there are clear limits on pre-trial disclosure.

2. Funding

    The available funding mechanisms and costs rules can clearly act as a major incentive or disincentive to claimants and/or lawyers in relation to competition law claims.[80] Conditional fee agreements ('CFAs') involving a fee uplift (success fee) to the winning legal team, recoverable from the loser, have been available for years in England and

---

75 See Rodger, B, 'Private Enforcement of Competition Law, The Hidden Story: Competition Litigation Settlements in the UK 2000–2005' [2008] ECLR 96.

76 Rodger, B, 'Why Not Court? A Study of Follow-on Actions in the UK' (2013) 1(1) *Journal of Antitrust Enforcement* 104–131.

77 *2 Travel Group PLC (in Liquidation) v Cardiff City Transport Services Ltd* [2012] CAT 19. See Veljanovski, C, 'CAT Awards Triple Damages, Well Not Really – Cardiff Bus, and the Dislocation between Liability and Damages for Exclusionary Abuse' [2012] ECLR 47–49.

78 [2013] CAT 6.

79 Civil Procedure Rules Part 31; in particular Part 31.6(b).

80 See Riley, A and Peysner, J, 'Damages in EC Antitrust Actions: Who Pays the Piper?' (2006) EL Rev 748; Peysner, J, 'Costs and Funding in Private Third Party Competition Damages Actions' [2006] Comp L Rev 97.

Wales,[81] but it is recognised that contingency fees would create greater incentives for lawyers than CFA's, and accordingly s 45 of the Legal Aid, Sentencing and Punishment of Offenders Act 2012 generally allows damages-based agreements in civil cases. Under Scots law, the Taylor Review into the Expenses and Funding of Civil Litigation in Scotland published its Report in September 2013 and proposed various reforms, including the introduction of damages based agreements in relation to monetary claims.[82]

3. Collective redress

There is currently limited scope for collective redress in the UK courts.[83] In England and Wales, there is the possibility of bringing a test case, consolidation and single trial of multiple actions, a GLO (group litigation order), or a representative action; however, the Civil Justice Council issued a report outlining the limitations of each of these options and recommended the introduction of a new collective procedure, allowing particular cases to proceed on an opt-in or opt-out basis.[84] The difficulties of bringing collective actions under existing mechanisms was demonstrated by *Emerald Supplies Ltd v British Airways Plc*.[85] The limited opt-in representative action before the CAT was discussed above and is subject to proposed reform which would introduce an opt-out collective mechanism.

4. Damages

Although the European Court considered in *Manfredi*[86] that national systems could provide for exemplary damages, the *Devenish*[87] ruling emphasised that the UK courts should adopt a strictly compensatory approach and that there will be little scope for restitutionary, exemplary or other forms of multiple damages awards. Nonetheless, the CAT has awarded, in addition to an award of over £33k (plus interest) in lost profit, £60k for exemplary damages in *2 Travel Group PLC (in Liquidation) v Cardiff City Transport Services Ltd*.[88] Until that ruling, here had only been an interim damages award by the CAT in *Healthcare at Home*, and different approaches adopted at first instance and the Court of Appeal in *Crehan* to quantification of damages. However, *Travel Group PLC (in Liquidation) v Cardiff City Transport Services Ltd* was the first successful, final award of damages as quantified by the CAT (including an exemplary damages award) which was followed in 2013 by a damages award in *Albion Water v Dwr Cymru Cyfyngedig*.

BIS and further reform – the draft Consumer Rights Bill

In 2012, the Department for Business, Innovation and Skills in the UK ('BIS') consulted on proposals to reinforce the system of private enforcement in the UK through important reforms included in cl 80 and Sch 8 of the Consumer Rights Bill which will significantly change the landscape of private enforcement in the UK.[89] There are important litigation strategy reasons why

---

81 Similar arrangements, known as speculative fees, are available in Scotland.
82 See Review of Expenses and Funding of Civil Litigation in Scotland, Report by Sh P James A Taylor, September 2013, available at http://scotland.gov.uk/About/Review/taylor-review/Report, particularly chapter 9 in relation to damages-based agreements.
83 In Scotland, note the following developments: Ervine, C, *A Class of their Own: Why Scotland needs a class action procedure* (2003) Edinburgh; Scottish Consumer Council and *Report of the Scottish Civil Courts Review: Volume 2* (2009) Edinburgh: Scottish Civil Courts Review 48.
84 'Improving Access to Justice Through Collective Actions' Developing a More Efficient and Effective Procedure for Collective Actions, Final Report, Nov 2008, Civil Justice Council. The ongoing Civil Courts Review in Scotland is also considering ways of enhancing collective redress.
85 [2009] EWHC 741 (Ch).
86 *Manfredi*, n 24.
87 *Devenish*, n 64.
88 *2 Travel Group PLC (in Liquidation) v Cardiff City Transport Services Ltd* [2012] CAT 19; Veljanovski, C, 'CAT Awards Triple Damages, Well Not Really – Cardiff Bus, and the Dislocation between Liability and Damages for Exclusionary Abuse' [2012] ECLR 47–49.
89 See BIS 12/742, 'Private Actions in Competition Law: A Consultation on Options For Reform', April 2012, and BIS 14/556, 'Consumer Rights Bill: Statement on Policy Reform and Responses to Pre-Legislative Scrutiny', January 2014.

follow-on claims are not raised before the CAT, and parties can always raise any competition law actions before the High Court. The proposed changes, when enacted, will enhance the role of the specialist court, the CAT by extending its competence to hear stand-alone actions as well as follow-on actions, and allow parties to seek injunctions as well as monetary awards. Potentially the most significant reform is the introduction of an opt-out representative collective redress mechanism.[90] Nonetheless, the BIS 2013 proposals recommended the prohibition of damages-based lawyers' fee agreements for collective opt-out cases before the CAT,[91] and provisions in the Consumer Rights Bill make such fee arrangements in opt-out collective proceedings unenforceable;[92] this may disincentivise lawyers from acting in such cases. More innovative in this context, is the proposed introduction of a collective mass settlement regime and also provision to enable the competition authorities to certify a voluntary redress scheme.[93]

Key Points

- The advanced state of private antitrust litigation in the US is based on a number of important institutional mechanisms which facilitate private damages claims.
- Several steps have been taken in the EU to encourage parties to sue in respect of competition law infringements. While progress has been slow, there is evidence of an increase in litigation across the EU.
- The European Commission has introduced a package of measures to ensure greater progress across the EU, including the Antitrust Damages Directive and a Commission Recommendation on Collective Redress.
- Private enforcement practice will continue at variable levels across different Member States.
- The Competition Act 1998 marked the start of the transformation in the UK beginning the facilitation of private enforcement. There has been a slow increase in resort to the legal remedies in competition cases, and a greater number of law firms and practitioners are involved in the practice of competition law.
- Proposed reforms in the UK Consumer Rights Bill, notably the introduction of an opt-out collective proceedings mechanism, will further develop a claimant friendly environment in the UK.

Discussion

1. Why is private enforcement necessary if competition authorities have been established specifically for the purpose of the public enforcement of the rules?
2. Why is antitrust litigation such an important feature of US antitrust enforcement?
3. To what extent has the EU harmonised the national processes, institutions and rules for private enforcement?
4. What are the differences between a follow-on and a stand-alone action?
5. Should collective redress for consumer compensation be the primary focus of the development of the rules to facilitate private enforcement?
6. Should opt-out collective redress mechanisms for competition law claims be introduced in the EU/UK?

---

90 For a fuller discussion of the proposed reform, see Wisking, S, Dietzel, K and Herron, M, 'The Rise and Rise of Private Enforcement in the United Kingdom – Government Announces Far-Reaching Overhaul of the Competition Law Private Actions Regime' [2013] 6 GCLR 78–77.
91 BIS 'Private Actions', above n 89, paras 5.62–5.63.
92 Section 47(C)(7) to be inserted into the Competition Act 1998.
93 BIS, 'Consumer Rights', above n 89, paras 6.20–6.26.

Further Reading

US background

Foer, SAE and Cuneo, JW (eds), *The International Handbook on Private Enforcement of Competition Law* (2010) Edward Elgar In association with the American Antitrust Institute.

Jones, CA, *Private Enforcement of Competition Law in the EU, UK and USA* (1999) Oxford: OUP.

Lande, RH and Davis, JP, 'Benefits from Private Antitrust Enforcement: An Analysis of Forty Cases' (2008) 42 *University of San Francisco Law Review* 879.

EU general

Gamble, R, 'Whether Neap or Spring, the Tide Turns for Private Enforcement: The EU Proposal for a Directive on Damages Examined' [2013] 34(12) ECLR 611–620.

Komninos, AP, 'Private Enforcement in the EU with Emphasis on Damages Actions', chapter 4 in Lianos, I and Geradin, D (eds), *Handbook on European Competition Law* (vol 2) (2012) Edward Elgar.

Rodger, B (ed), *Competition Law Comparative Private Enforcement and Collective Redress Across the EU* (2014) Kluwer law International.

Wils, 'Should Private Antitrust Enforcement be Encouraged in Europe?' [2003] *World Competition* 26/3 473–488.

UK general

Rodger, B, 'Private Enforcement of Competition Law, The Hidden Story: Competition Litigation Settlements in the UK 2000–2005' [2008] ECLR 96.

Rodger, B, 'UK Competition Law and Developments in Private Litigation', chapter 3 in Rodger, B (ed), *Ten Years of UK Competition Law Reform* (2010) Dundee: DUP.

Rodger, B, 'Why Not Court? A Study of Follow-on Actions in the UK' (2012) *Journal of Antitrust Enforcement* 1–28.

Collective redress

Andreangeli, A, 'Collective Redress in EU Competition Law: An Open Question with Many Possible Solutions' (2012) *World Competition* 3 529–558.

Heffernan, L, 'Comparative Common Law Approaches to Multi Party Litigation; The American Class Action Procedure' (2002) 25 DULJ 102.

Hodges, C, 'The European Approach to Justice and Redress' (2011) 53 *Supreme Court Law Review* (2d) 301–346.

Schnell, G, 'Class Action Madness in Europe – a Call for a More Balanced Debate' [2007] ECLR 617–619.

Chapter 4

The Control of Abuse of Dominance

Overview

- Art 102 TFEU prohibits the 'abuse' of a 'dominant position' within the European Union so far as it may affect trade between Member States. It is not unlawful simply to have a dominant position; some form of behaviour recognised as an abuse must also be present.
- Only the actions of 'undertakings', all natural or legal persons carrying on some form of commercial activity in the goods or services sectors, may be caught by the prohibition.
- For an undertaking to be considered dominant in a market, the relevant market has to be ascertained. The relevant market defines the range of products in competition with those of the undertaking in question.
- An undertaking will be considered to be dominant in a market if it has market power, usually evidenced by a high market share and significant barriers to entry, making it difficult for potential competitors to enter the market.
- More than one undertaking, particularly in oligopolistic markets, may hold a collective dominant position, if they have sufficient economic links between them.
- There are two main categories of abusive behaviour. First, exploitative abuse, where a dominant undertaking can maximise profits by reducing output and increasing the prices, thereby exploiting its customers. Second, exclusionary abuses, where the behaviour of the dominant undertaking actually or potentially forecloses the market to existing competitors or new entrants.
- The Chapter II prohibition, under s 18 of the Competition Act 1998, replicates the Art 102 prohibition for abuse of a dominant position within the UK. Consistency of interpretation with EU law is ensured by s 60 of the Act.

Introduction

In the introductory chapter of this book, it was made clear that one of the central concerns of the economics of competition was the control of market power. It is therefore unsurprising that all competition law regimes have measures that seek to control the exercise and maintenance of such power. In this chapter we shall discuss the ways in which the EU, through Art 102 TFEU, and the UK, through the Chapter II prohibition, seek to deal with the abuse of market power, or dominance, as it is known in the prohibitions.

Article 102 TFEU

The essence of the internal market within the European Union is the freedom of movement of goods, services, labour and capital. Competition law is vital as the four freedoms will only be fully attained if businesses within the EU can compete freely. A principal objective of EU competition law is to prevent businesses from reducing competition by distorting or dividing up markets within the EU. The objective of the EU's competition provisions is set out in Protocol No 27 to the TFEU on the Internal Market and Competition.[1] The internal market includes 'a system ensuring that competition is not distorted'. The first substantive provision in the TFEU that we shall discuss is Art 102 TFEU. It is designed to deal with the activities of businesses, 'undertakings' in European

---

1   The content of the Protocol was formerly, before the Lisbon Reform Treaty, found in Art 3(1)(g) of the EC Treaty. Following intervention by the French Government, the reference to 'free and undistorted competition' was removed from the Art 3 objectives of the Treaty and relegated to a legally binding protocol annexed to the Treaty. The CJEU made it clear in Case C-52/09 *Konkurrensverket v TeliaSonera Sverige AB* [2011] ECR I-527 [20] that the revised context does not change the legal importance of the concept of 'free and undistorted' competition.

legal terminology, that have a powerful market position related to the economists' concept of monopoly. The actions of a business that has market power can have serious effects on the operation of a market. Article 102 is directed at the activities of a powerful single business which is not subject to effective competition. An undertaking in a dominant position may use its market power in several ways: to exploit consumers by restricting output and increasing prices; to perpetuate its own position, perhaps through unfair discounting; or to extend its position into another market, perhaps by tying the sale of one product to another. For that reason, Art 102 prohibits the 'abuse' of a 'dominant position' within the EU so far as it may affect trade between Member States. It is not illegal under EU competition law simply to have a dominant position; some form of behaviour recognised as an abuse must also be present. Chapter 2 outlined the enforcement process and potential sanctions for breach of the prohibition, notably fines of up to 10% of worldwide turnover. It also highlighted the increasing use of the commitments remedy to deal with alleged abuses of a dominant position.

The European Commission, beginning in December 2005, undertook a large-scale review of the operation of a number of aspects of Art 102.[2] This review can be seen as the final element in a wide reform of much of EU competition law. The Art 102 review focused on the handling of exclusionary abuses within the prohibition. The review led to an interesting debate about the purpose and future shape of the Art 102 prohibition and its relationship to economic theory. The review was completed with the publication in February 2009 of the Commission's 'Guidance on its enforcement priorities in applying Art 82 (EC) to abusive exclusionary conduct by dominant undertakings'.[3] That document set out the methodology the Commission intends to utilise in relation to Art 102 investigations, but it should be noted that the Guidance only outlines Commission practice and the CJEU remains the final arbiter as to the correct interpretation of the Treaty provisions and its case law is authoritative. The impact of the Guidance will be discussed more fully throughout this chapter.

When examining the application of Art 102 in practice, it is better to consider the interpretation of the constituent parts of the prohibition in reverse order: 'undertakings', 'effect on trade between Member States', 'dominant position' and, finally, 'abuse'.

Undertakings and the Effect on Trade Between Member States

Only 'undertakings', within the terms of EU law, are controlled by the competition provisions of the Treaty. The definition used is the same for both Arts 101 and 102 TFEU.[4] The Court and the Commission have interpreted the term very broadly, maximising the scope of the competition rules. All natural or legal persons carrying on some form of commercial activity in the goods or services sectors will be included.[5] Commercial activity includes those activities which are not designed to be profit-making.[6] For instance, it was held, in proceedings before a Scottish court, that a statutory body, the Keeper of the Registers of Scotland, which is also an officer of the Crown, constituted an undertaking for the purposes of Art 102.[7] The interaction between the State and the competition rules, as seen in *FENIN*[8] and *AOK Bundesverband*,[9] is a very sensitive, and

2   DG Competition discussion paper on the application of Art 82 of the Treaty to exclusionary abuses, Brussels, December 2005.
3   [2009] OJ, C45/7. For discussion of the Guidance see Akman, P, 'The European Commission's Guidance on Article 102TFEU: From Inferno to Paradiso?' (2010) 73(4) MLR 605.
4   See, also, the discussion of the concept of 'undertaking', within Art 101 TFEU, in Chapter 6.
5   E.g. opera singers in Commission Decision 78/516/EEC *RAI/UNITEL*. [1978] OJ L157/39; [1978] 3 CMLR 306.
6   Commission Decision 82/1283/EEC *ANSEAU-NAVENA* [1982] OJ L167/39; [1982] 1 CMLR 221. See also Case C-49/07 *MOTOE v Greece* [2008] ECR I-4863.
7   *Miller & Bryce v Keeper of the Registers of Scotland* 1997 SLT 1000 (OH).
8   Case T-319/99 *FENIN v Commission* [2003] ECR II-357; [2003] 5 CMLR 1.
9   Cases C-264, 306, 354 and 355/01 *AOK Bundesverband v Ichthyol-Gesellschaft Cordes, Hermani & Co* [2004] ECR I-2493.

highly politicised, issue.[10] Both these cases involved the State's provision of health services, and the question of whether the bodies managing that health service provision were undertakings within the competition rules. The Court has consistently held that where a body entrusted with the management of statutory health provision pursues an exclusively social objective it does not engage in economic activity and is therefore not considered to be an 'undertaking'. As the UK looks to be moving towards a more 'market'-based Health Service, it appears likely that competition law is set to become more important in that sector. Legally distinct companies, when they are not independent from each other, may be considered as one undertaking for the purposes of EU competition law. This is the case in a parent/subsidiary situation. Although legally separate, the subsidiary may be controlled by the parent company. This is known as the 'economic entity' doctrine.[11] Accordingly, when dealing with connected companies it is important to examine the economic and managerial independence of the companies in question.[12] The attribution of a subsidiary company's responsibility for a competition violation to a parent, a particularly significant issue in practice, remains a contentious issue. The key issue is whether the parent company exercises decisive influence over the subsidiary company; there is a rebuttable presumption that this is the case where the parent has a 100% shareholding in that subsidiary.[13]

The prerequisite that there should be an effect on trade between Member States acts as a jurisdictional test to demarcate the boundary between the application of EU and national competition law. The interpretation of this concept, therefore, is politically important. The relationship between EU and domestic competition law is now governed by Art 3 of Reg 1/2003.[14] Article 3(1) provides that, where there is an effect on inter-state trade, national courts and authorities shall, in applying domestic competition law rules, also apply Arts 101 and 102. Article 3(2) provides that domestic competition law may apply stricter standards to that which constitutes unilateral abusive conduct. These rules seek to ensure a clearer substantive rule of precedence in the application of EU law and national law. Not surprisingly, the EU Courts have given the inter-state trade concept a broad interpretation. The general test, which applies to cases under Arts 102 and 101 TFEU, was laid down in *Societe Technique Miniere*.[15]

> it must be possible to foresee with a sufficient degree of probability on the basis of a set of objective factors of law or fact that the agreement in question may have an influence, direct or indirect, actual or potential, on the pattern of trade between Member States.

The effect on trade test, therefore, covers any conduct which could affect the way in which trade patterns operate across the EU.[16] In addition to this general test, because of the importance of market structure, there is a structural test peculiar to Art 102. Where market power is concentrated in one undertaking, it can have damaging effects on competition. An undertaking's economic power can discourage other undertakings from entering the market. The economic models of competition require new market entrants to control the power of existing undertakings. The ability of a dominant undertaking to use market power to exclude competitors, or potential competitors, is therefore of particular concern. The structural test operates where there is an

---

10 See, also, Montana, L and Jellis, J, 'The Concept of Undertaking in EC Competition Law and its Application to Public Bodies: Can You Buy Your Way into Article 82?' (2003) 2 Comp LJ 110. See also Case C-49/07 *MOTOE v Greece* [2008] ECR I-4863.
11 Case 22/71 *Beguelin Import v GL Import Export* [1971] ECR 949. See, also, the recent discussion in the English courts in *Provimi Limited v Aventis Animal Nutrition SA* [2003] ECC 29.
12 Case T-102/92 *Viho v Commission* [1995] ECR II-17. On appeal Case C-73/95P [1996] ECR I-5457.
13 See, for instance, Case C-97/08 P, *Akzo Nobel NV v Commission of the European Communities* [2009] ECR I-8237.
14 Regulation 1/2003/EC, OJ 2003, L1/1.
15 Case 56/65 *Société Technique Minière v Maschinenbau Ulm GmbH* [1966] ECR 235. See also the Commission 'Guidelines on the effect on trade concept contained in Articles 81 and 82 of the Treaty', [2004] OJ C101/81.
16 See, also, Case C-359/01P *British Sugar v Commission* [2004] ECR I-4933.

alteration in the structure of competition within the market.[17] The test will usually be fulfilled even where the dominant undertaking only operates in one national market, as the strength of that undertaking will tend to reinforce the division of markets along national lines. The strengthening of such a division will have an effect on trade between Member States.[18]

Dominant Position

The use of economic analysis in the application of Art 102 is very important. A finding of dominance will be based on economic factors, although there are legal guidelines laid down by the Court and the Commission. In practice, three main areas have to be examined before dominance[19] can be established. These are: the definition of the relevant market; the establishment of market power; and, the consideration of possible barriers to entry. Only once all three of these areas have been examined will any finding be reliable.

The relevant market

The first, and potentially most vital, step in ascertaining whether an undertaking is dominant is to define exactly which market the undertaking is competing in. That market is known as the 'relevant market' – a concept which is of key importance to all competition law rules, but particularly in relation to the abusive conduct prohibition. Without delineating the products or services that are in competition, it is impossible to gauge how much power an undertaking has over its competitors and consumers. Determination of the relevant market has three aspects: product market, geographical market and temporal market.

The Commission has produced a Notice on the definition of the relevant market. The Notice sets out the methods the Commission employs in market definition. The Commission's aim is to increase the transparency of its decision-making process. It is particularly interesting in that the Notice explains the practical steps the Commission takes when it examines a market.[20]

The relevant product market

Before it is possible to say that an undertaking is dominant in a market, it has to be ascertained what constitutes that market, and that is done by defining the range of products in competition with those of the undertaking in question. Only an undertaking's position in relation to actual or potential competitors will give a true indication of its dominance. The importance of market definition was emphasised in *Continental Can v Commission*,[21] where the Commission's decision was annulled by the Court because of the Commission's failure to properly demarcate the relevant market. The definition of a market can be very controversial. If the product market is drawn narrowly, with relatively few competing products, it is much more likely that the undertaking will be found to be dominant. The legal test, as set out by the Court, is that of interchangeability.[22] The Commission, in its Notice, relies on SSNIP tests, otherwise known as the 'hypothetical monopolist' test. It is worth looking at both tests in turn as they are different in methodology, although they may produce similar results.

---

17 Cases 6 & 7/73 *Commercial Solvents v Commission* [1974] ECR 223.
18 See Case T-30/91 *Solvay v Commission (Soda Ash)* [1995] ECR II-1775. See Commission 'Guidance on the effect on trade concept', [2004] OJ C101/81, paras 93–99.
19 In more general terms, it is sometimes known as 'market power'.
20 Commission Notice on the definition of the relevant market for the purposes of Community competition law, [1997] OJ, C372/3. See Baker, S and Wu, L, 'Applying the Market Definition Guidelines of the European Commission' [1998] 5 ECLR 273.
21 Case 6/72 *Continental Can v Commission* [1973] ECR 215.
22 Sometimes referred to as 'substitutability'.

The Commission's practice is based on discovering the level of demand substitution in a market; that is, the ease with which customers will switch their allegiance to other products when faced with price increases. SSNIP is an acronym for a 'Small, but Significant, Non-transitory Increase in Price'. The test operates by applying a hypothetical permanent increase in price to a product; usually the price increase will be in the range of 5–10%. Initially this hypothetical increase is applied to the products produced by the undertaking in question. If there is evidence that customers would switch to purchasing other products when faced with such a price increase, the original product and the substitute products are considered to be in the same market. This calculus is reset and repeated using the expanded group of products until there are no further products that would be considered as substitutes. If one undertaking produced all such products it could be said that the undertaking would not be subject to competition from other products and would, therefore, be a 'hypothetical monopolist'.[23] Although this is a hypothetical test, the Commission must still gather hard evidence to support its arguments that substitution would occur in this way. It therefore gathers evidence from a great many sources, and that evidence includes evidence of substitution in the recent past, econometric studies, views of customers and competitors, customer preference, and marketing studies. The use of this test gives Commission practice a solid economic grounding, but is not free of potential difficulties. One problem is the application of such a test where there is a paucity of economic evidence, particularly in very small or new markets. In that case it is very difficult to gather sufficient evidence to make useful findings. Another problem is known as the 'cellophane fallacy'. This is not directly related to cellophane as a product, but to the US case in which the fallacy was discussed.[24] It relates to the situation in which a dominant undertaking has already been able to increase prices to a monopolistic level. In most markets there will be some level of competition in the market and a rational dominant undertaking will only raise its prices above the competitive level until the point where the existence of remaining competitors would make any further rises unprofitable. At that point any increase in price might result in demand substitution for products which would not have been considered as substitutes at the lower hypothetical 'competitive' price. Application of the SSNIP test to this elevated price may lead to the assumption that the products were effective substitutes, whereas they would not have been at the 'competitive' price. Accordingly, in markets where competition is already severely limited, the SSNIP test may give erroneous results. It is, therefore, vital that the Commission handles the available economic data sensitively.

While Commission practice is important, it is not the authoritative legal test; for that, we must look to the judgments of the EU Courts.[25] However, while it has not adopted the terminology of the Notice, it is clear that the Court is generally supportive of the practice adopted by the Commission. The Court's traditional test is also based on substitution, or interchangeability. In *Continental Can* the Court considered that an examination must be made of products that are 'particularly apt to satisfy an inelastic need and are only to a limited extent interchangeable with other products'.[26] At its simplest level the test requires an examination of the products which a consumer will regard as interchangeable with the product in question: demand-side interchangeability or substitution. This raises very similar questions to those posed by the Commission under the SSNIP test. To help to define the market, the Court has set out a number of areas to be considered.

---

23 See Crocioni, P, 'The Hypothetical Monopolist Test' [2002] ECLR 354.
24 *United States v EI du Pont de Nemours & Co* 118 F Supp 41 (D Del 1953); aff'd 351 US 377 (US Sup Ct 1956).
25 While the Court's tests may be legally authoritative, they have been economically criticised: see Azevedo, JP and Walker, M, 'Dominance: Meaning and Measurement' [2002] ECLR 363.
26 [1973] ECR 215, para 14. 'Inelastic' is an economic term describing a type of demand. For a simple explanation of cross-elasticity, and other economic terms, see Glossary.

Cross-elasticity of demand

The economic test of cross-elasticity of demand is, in effect, the same test as applied by the Commission under its Notice. Where cross-elasticity is high, any increase in the price of a product will cause significant shifts by consumers to other products. If demand is 'elastic' it means that customers switch readily, whereas if demand is 'inelastic' they will not shift to other products until there is a relatively high price increase. Cross-elasticity may be valuable in that it gives an objective determination of the actual operation of the market. Such economic analysis has been found to be of value[27] but, as with all statistical analysis, great care must be taken to ensure that the results are a true reflection of the market.

Physical characteristics

The physical characteristics of a product will obviously be vital to a decision as to whether products are interchangeable. If products are physically similar and have similar functions, the consumer is more likely to see them as being interchangeable. Even where products have broadly similar characteristics, it may be possible to find ways in which particular characteristics place them in separate markets. A classic example of such a distinction was seen in *United Brands*.[28] The Commission argued that the market for bananas was separate from the market for fresh fruit generally. The Commission concentrated on the year-round availability of bananas, their appearance, softness and seedlessness, which meant that they satisfied the particular needs of the very young, the old and the sick. On the basis of this and other arguments the Court accepted that bananas should be differentiated from other fresh fruit. The Court's reasoning on this point has been challenged, but it illustrates the way in which minor differences between products can affect the consideration of the market in which they are competing with other similar goods. A more contemporary example is *AstraZeneca v Commission*,[29] where evidence showed that proton pump inhibitors (PPIs), used to treat a range of gastrointestinal disorders, were not in the same market as antihistamines, even though they could be used to treat the same conditions, as PPIs had superior efficacy and commanded a price premium.

Price

The price of a product can affect the relevant market. Take, for example, the market for domestic vehicles. It is unlikely that a Ferrari 458 and a Mazda MX-5 would be considered to be competing in the same market. Even though they fulfil the same function, two-seater sports cars, they do not compete. It is unlikely that a consumer would consider them interchangeable. The significance of the price premium commanded by PPIs in *AstraZeneca* also indicates that significant price differentials can be indicative of a separate market.

Intended use

The intended use of the product is a very important consideration. A product may have a number of different uses, each of which may form a different market. In *Michelin*,[30] the Court examined the market for car tyres. Because of the differing nature of demand, the Court found that the original-equipment tyres, to be fitted to new vehicles during manufacture, and replacement tyres, to be fitted during repairs, were in separate markets. Manufacturers ordered original-equipment tyres in bulk, while replacement tyres were ordered as and when required.

---

27 See, for example, Case 27/76 *United Brands Continental BV v Commission* [1978] ECR 207.
28 See Case 27/76 *United Brands Continental BV v Commission* [1978] ECR 207.
29 Case T-321/05 *AstraZeneca AB v Commission* [2010] ECR II-2805. See also Veljanovski, C, 'Markets Without Substitutes: Substitution Versus Constraints as the Key to Market Definition' [2010] 31(3) ECLR 122.
30 Case 322/81 *Nederlandsche Banden-Industrie Michelin NV v Commission* [1983] ECR 3461.

Another way in which the intended use criterion can narrow a market was seen in *Commercial Solvents*.[31] A subsidiary of Commercial Solvents supplied Zoja with nitropropane, which Zoja processed into an anti-TB drug. When Commercial Solvents ceased supplies of the raw material, Zoja claimed Commercial Solvents was in a dominant position. Commercial Solvents argued that other chemicals could be used to produce the drug, and that those chemicals should be considered as part of the overall market of materials for producing the drug. The Court disagreed, and focused on the fact that the process in Zoja's plant relied on supplies of nitropropane; no other raw material could be used. Therefore, the way in which Zoja utilised the product limited the market.

Supply-side interchangeability

So far, we have considered a number of demand-based factors, concentrating on consumer perception, but the supply side can also affect the relevant product market. A product may not be directly interchangeable with any others, but this may not mean that it is the only product to be considered. The Commission Notice on market definition indicates this calculation is also an important part of its practice, but only in situations where supply-side substitutability is equivalent to demand substitution in terms of effectiveness and immediacy. If other suppliers, currently manufacturing other products, can 'switch production to the relevant products and market them in the short term without incurring significant additional costs',[32] they should also be considered as part of the market. This possible alternative supply, known as potential competition, is likely to exert a competitive pressure on the current supplier. In the Notice, the example of paper production is used. While different grades of paper may not be substitutable by the consumer, it may be relatively easy for a paper manufacturer to alter production to produce different grades. In *Continental Can*,[33] the Court annulled the Commission's decision on the basis that it had not properly considered whether the producers of other types of can, largely cylindrical cans, could enter the market for meat and fish cans. However, it is arguable that the supply-side substitutability issue is not about the determination of the relevant market as such, but allows for a fuller consideration of any competitive constraints to market power.

The relevant geographical market

It is also important to determine the geographical extent of the relevant market. Before evaluating dominance, it is important to ensure that the same conditions of competition exist across the whole market.[34] There may be legal, technical or practical reasons why a product only competes within a limited area of the EU. Accordingly, the assessment of market power can only take place in the geographical area where competition can be realistically expected. The general test was laid down in *United Brands* where the Court limited the geographical market to 'an area where the objective conditions of competition applying to the product in question must be the same for all traders'. In the market for bananas, the UK, France and Italy were excluded from consideration, as the conditions of competition were different in those states because of their long-term relationships with former colonies that produce bananas.

Geographical markets may also be limited by transport restrictions on the product. If the unit transport cost of the product is high it is less likely that the product will have an EU-wide market. This is particularly important for products which are difficult or relatively expensive to transport over long distances, for instance, dangerous chemicals, low-value bulk commodities, or for some types of fresh food, such as bread.

---

31 See Cases 6 and 7/73 *Commercial Solvents v Commission* [1974] ECR 223.
32 Commission Notice on market definition, OJ 1997, C372/5, para 20.
33 See Case 6/72 *Continental Can v Commission* [1973] ECR 215.
34 In Commission practice, the geographical market is addressed alongside the product market using the SSNIP test.

The temporal market

A market may vary over time. This can be due to seasonal variations in production. The seasonal nature of fruit production was raised in *United Brands*.[35] External factors may also affect the market, altering the conditions of competition. If those factors are temporary in nature the period in which they affected the nature of competition will be considered separately.[36]

Dominance

Once the relevant market has been determined it is then possible to calculate if an undertaking is dominant. The traditional definition of dominance was laid down by the Court in *United Brands*:

> The dominant position thus referred to [by Art 102] relates to a position of economic strength enjoyed by an undertaking which enables it to prevent effective competition being maintained on the relevant market by affording it the power to behave to an appreciable extent independently of its competitors, customers and ultimately of its consumers.[37]

The dominance test has two main elements. Firstly, the allusion to the ability to act independently refers to an economic view of market power: the fact that the undertaking's actions are not constrained by effective competition. The dominant undertaking is no longer a 'price-taker'.[38] Secondly, the reference to the prevention of effective competition refers to a dominant undertaking's ability to prevent potential competitors from entering the market. This is referred to as exclusionary conduct, and it enables an undertaking to protect its dominant position. The difference between these two elements is more important in the discussion of types of abusive conduct. The tools used to investigate whether an undertaking is dominant are the same in both situations.

For the purposes of this text we shall split that investigation into two separate sections, market power and barriers to entry, although in practice both are usually considered together. There is an ongoing policy debate as to what should properly be termed as a barrier to entry, and for that reason it warrants separate discussion. The debate over the importance of barriers to entry has largely been conducted in the US and its impact has been limited in the EU. In EU cases there has been very little reference to the conceptual problems but, in practice, problems concerning barriers to entry are addressed in a number of cases. Before we go on to deal with that debate, the somewhat less controversial area of market power will be discussed.

Market power

One of the first steps in investigating dominance is to establish the market share held by the undertaking in question. The market share will not in itself establish an undertaking's dominance but it will be evidence of its power on the market. It is only the ability to maintain that power over time which will constitute dominance. That is why barriers to entry, which give an insight into potential long-term power, are very important. A market share percentage only gives a snapshot of the relative strengths of undertakings at a particular moment. If market shares have changed considerably over a period of time, it suggests that there may be effective competition on the market.

---

35 See Case 27/76 *United Brands Continental BV v Commission* [1978] ECR 207. As the Court defined the market narrowly, it did not rely on the seasonal nature of the market in its judgment.
36 This was the case during the 1970s oil crisis. See Commission Decision 77/327/EEC *ABG*, OJ 1977, L117/1; [1977] 2 CMLR D1. On appeal Case 77/77 *Benzine Petroleum Handelmaatschappij BV v Commission* [1978] ECR 1513.
37 Case 27/76 *United Brands Continental BV v Commission* [1978] ECR 207, para 38.
38 For an argument that the concept of dominance should rely exclusively on the constraining effect of competitors, see Azevedo, JP and Walker, M, 'Dominance: Meaning and Measurement' [2002] ECLR 363.

The Court has relied heavily – some would say too heavily – on market shares. By analysing the Court's judgments and statements by the Commission it is possible to suggest some rules of thumb. Market shares nearing 100% are very rare in practice, although some undertakings have come close to that mark.[39] Although it may be tempting to think so, very high market shares will not always indicate the existence of a dominant position; however, the higher the market share, the easier it will be to find good evidence of restricted competition within a market. The existence of market shares approaching 75% may lead to an undertaking being deemed so powerful as to have the special responsibilities of 'super-dominance' placed upon them.[40] Although the EU Courts have not used the term 'super-dominance', it has been adopted by the Commission,[41] and the Courts have approved the Commission's thinking.[42] It is now clear that undertakings with such high market shares have an increased responsibility not to adopt behaviour that will further disrupt the already weak competitive process in their markets. This issue was discussed in the CFI in *Microsoft*, where it found that:

> the Commission was correct to find . . . that when Microsoft had responded to the letter of 15 September 1998 it had not taken sufficiently into account its special responsibility not to hinder effective and undistorted competition in the common market. The Commission was also correct to state . . . that that particular responsibility derived from Microsoft's 'quasi-monopoly' on the client PC operating systems market.[43]

The Court, however, made it clear in *TeliaSonera* that the 'degree' of dominance is not usually important in relation to the lawfulness of conduct, but may be relevant to the extent of its effects.[44] Where market shares are slightly lower, perhaps below 70%, there is no question of super-dominance, but a finding of dominance is still a distinct possibility. In *Hoffmann-La Roche*, the Court took the view that very large market shares will give rise to a presumption of dominance, unless there are exceptional circumstances.[45] The reference to 'exceptional circumstances' takes account of potential competition from outside the existing market. Large market shares held for a period of time will give rise to a stronger presumption. A market share of 50% was considered to be very large in *AKZO*.[46]

Market shares below 50% can still be indicators of market power. When shares are between 35 and 50%, it is important to compare the undertaking's market share with the share of its nearest rivals. If an undertaking has a 40% share and its rivals all have small shares of the remaining market, that undertaking will still have considerable power in the market. In *United Brands*, the undertaking in question, UBC, had a market share between 41% and 45%, but its closest rival held only 16% of the market. It was, therefore, apparent that UBC had a position of considerable strength. If UBC had a competitor with a 35% market share, the findings in that case might have been very different. An undertaking with similar market power would have been in a position to exert competitive pressure on UBC. The lowest market share that the GC has confirmed as supporting a dominant position was 39.7% in *British Airways v Commission*.[47] In the Commission

---

39 In Case T-6/89 *BPB and British Gypsum v Commission* [1993] ECR II-389, it was established that the undertakings had a 96–98% market share of the plasterboard market in the UK, and a 92–100% share in Ireland.

40 The figure of 75% was used by the Commission in its DG Competition discussion paper on the application of Art 82 of the Treaty to exclusionary abuses, Brussels, December 2005, at para 92.

41 See the comments of the Competition Commissioner with regard to the *Microsoft* decision and judgment in Commission Press Release, IP/04/382, and SPEECH/07/539 respectively.

42 See Case T-228/97 *Irish Sugar plc v Commission* [1999] ECR II-2969; Case C-396/96 *Compagnie Maritime Belge Transports SA v Commission* [2000] ECR I-1365; and Case T-201/04 *Microsoft v Commission* [2007] ECR II-3601.

43 Case T-201/04 *Microsoft v Commission* [2007] ECR II-3601, at para 775.

44 Case C-52/09 *Konkurrensverket v TeliaSonera Sverige AB* [2011] ECR II-0000, at paras 78–82.

45 Case 85/76 *Hoffmann-La Roche v Commission* [1979] ECR 461, 463.

46 Case C-62/86 *AKZO Chemie BV v Commission* [1991] ECR I-3359, para 60.

47 Case T-219/99, [2003] ECR II-5917. The finding of dominance was not raised on appeal in Case C-95/04 P *British Airways v Commission* [2007] 4 CMLR 22.

Guidance on Art 102, which focuses mostly on abuse, the Commission stresses that dominance is not likely if an undertaking's market share is below 40%.[48]

As an undertaking enjoys a larger market share, it is more likely that it will be found to have a dominant position in a market. When an undertaking has a smaller market share, an increasing number of other factors will need to be used as evidence to support a finding of dominance. Temporary power on a market does not become dominance until there is an element of permanence. A strong undertaking must be in a position to protect its market share effectively before it will be truly dominant.

Barriers to entry

There is great debate over what should be included within the term 'barrier to entry'. The debate occurs in both law and economics. For the purposes of this text we will concentrate on the legal implications of the debate, but the economic arguments will be noted where relevant. A commonly accepted view is that a barrier to entry is any cost which is higher for a new entrant to the market than for an existing market player.[49] Any such cost is important because where there are few barriers to entry, an undertaking with market power cannot easily protect itself from new entrants to a market, should it act inefficiently, either through charging a supra-competitive price or by stifling innovation. Accordingly, potential entrants to markets with few entry barriers will exert competitive pressures on existing market players, and there will be little need for competition law to intervene and control undertakings with market power. Such a market is sometimes described as being 'contestable'. Where barriers to entry exist, undertakings with market power are, on the other hand, more likely to be considered to hold a dominant position, and will be in a better position to exert an anti-competitive influence on the market.

Barriers to entry play an important role in the indication of the existence of dominance of an undertaking in a market; therefore, any decision as to what is included in the term 'barriers to entry' is vital to the way in which Art 102 works in practice. The debate over what is included in the definition centres around two schools of thought. One school perceives many purported barriers to entry as entirely natural, being related to efficiency. That school of thought would argue that a true barrier to entry is a cost to new entrants which was not applicable to the existing market operators when they entered the market.[50] This strict view of barriers to entry discounts many potentially massive costs that face new entrants, as those costs were also faced by the operators who currently hold positions of market power. Under this type of analysis, the only real barriers to entry are legal provisions that restrict entry to the market. The narrow view of barriers concentrates on the perceived ability of the market to rectify any inefficiency without intervention by the law.

The other school of thought that is linked, for instance, with the Commission approach, views barriers to entry as being much wider, and including any factor which would tend to discourage new entrants from entering the market. This is a more pragmatic view which focuses on the actual difficulties faced by potential entrants. This view has been challenged on the basis that it penalises, through the increased likeliness of a finding of dominance, those undertakings that entered a market early and made large investments to become efficient. They paid the costs of entry and through that investment reached a position of strength. The position is often referred to as a 'first

---

48 Commission Guidance on the Commission's enforcement priorities in applying Art 82 of the EC Treaty to abusive exclusionary conduct by dominant undertakings, [2009] OJ, C45/7, para 14.
49 See Stigler, GJ, *The Organization of Industry* (1968) Chicago: Chicago UP.
50 See the work of the Chicago school of antitrust economics and, in particular, Bork, R, *The Antitrust Paradox: A Policy at War with Itself* (1978) New York: Basic Books, and Posner, RA, *Antitrust Law: An Economic Perspective* (1976) Chicago: Chicago UP.

mover' or 'strategic' advantage. Should potential entrants not be forced to do the same? In any jurisdiction the decision to prefer a particular school will largely depend on policy or political views as to the need for intervention in markets. Another important factor in determining what constitutes a barrier to entry is the timescale which is used for reference purposes. The Commission uses short to medium timescales for its calculations and, therefore, might intervene more readily than a regulator that utilises a long-term reference period. For these reasons, distinctions can be observed in the practice in the EU, the UK and the US, partly reflecting the EU's caution and conservatism and the US's optimism about how real markets operate, and their contestability.

In the EU, the Court and the Commission have followed a policy closer to the broader definition of barriers to entry, as set out above. In their reasoning they have suggested many factors as being potential barriers to entry or, as they are sometimes referred to, factors indicating dominance.

Legal provisions

Statutory or regulatory powers granted by national legislation can act as barriers to entry. One example is intellectual property rights that protect the exclusivity of the right holder. Such rights can effectively grant a monopoly which can be protected through the national courts.[51] Dominance can also arise through government licensing restrictions which impede entry to a market.[52]

Technological advantage

The possession of existing technology, and potential access to future technology, is also relevant.[53] This is one of the areas in which the divergence between the two schools of thought is clearly seen. Advocates of the narrow view of barriers to entry would argue that a new entrant would face the same research costs as the existing market operators faced and, therefore, that any purported technological advantage is not a true barrier to entry but merely evidence of the efficiency of the incumbent undertaking. As the Court has indicated that it may accept technological advantage as a potential barrier, it has indicated its support for the broader view.

Financial resources

A leading undertaking that has easy access to large amounts of capital, often termed as 'having deep pockets', will be able to utilise its capital to protect itself from new entrants. Access to capital is one of the major difficulties for all small- and medium-sized enterprises (SMEs). The sheer size of the leading undertakings, and their international links, were considered by the Court in *Continental Can*[54] and *United Brands*.[55]

Economies of scale

Some markets, particularly those that demand complex manufacturing processes, require an operation to be on a large scale before high levels of efficiency are reached. Where there are economies of scale it can be very difficult for new entrants; to be as efficient as existing undertakings they must enter the market with a high level of output. If there was a market with one major supplier, but the efficient scale of operation was 60% of the existing market, it would be very difficult for a new entrant to compete. If the new entrant operates below the 60% scale, they would be less efficient. If they operate at the 60% scale, there would be overcapacity in the market.[56]

---

51 See Case T-30/89 *Hilti AG v Commission* [1991] ECR II-1439; and Case T51/89 *Tetra Pak v Commission* [1990] ECR II-309.
52 Case 311/84 *Tele-Marketing v CLT* [1985] ECR 3261; [1986] 2 CMLR 558.
53 See Case 85/76 *Hoffmann-La Roche v Commission* [1979] ECR 461.
54 See Case 6/72 *Continental Can v Commission* [1973] ECR 215.
55 See Case 27/76 *United Brands Continental BV v Commission* [1978] ECR 207.
56 Similar problems were discussed in Case T-6/89 *BPB and British Gypsum v Commission* [1993] ECR II-389.

Vertical integration

An undertaking is vertically integrated when it controls upstream and downstream production facilities. Integration allows an undertaking a much higher level of control over the way in which a product reaches the market. A good example of vertical integration was seen in *United Brands*.[57] For bananas to reach the European market, there are many stages in the production process: growing, picking, shipping, ripening and distribution. United Brands (UBC) was highly vertically integrated, controlling its own research and development, plantations, refrigerated ships, ripening stores and distribution system. As UBC had complete control over the product, it had the advantage of commercial stability. A new entrant would be forced to invest heavily or rely on others to provide those services.

Product differentiation

Product differentiation can be a barrier to entry. It occurs when consumers perceive, due to advertising or brand loyalty, homogeneous products as being different. Consequently, the consumer will not consider the new entrant's product as interchangeable, making it difficult for the entrant to break into the market. Again, this phenomenon could be observed in *United Brands*. Some of UBC's bananas were marketed under the 'Chiquita' brand, the bananas having a small blue sticker attached to them. The branded bananas sold at a premium of around 10%. Despite this, the Court found that there was no real difference in quality between the unbranded and branded product. The consumer was willing to pay 10% more for the branded product, as they perceived it as being of a higher quality. A new entrant would not only be competing against the product but also against the consumers', sometimes erroneous, perceptions. The importance and value of branding emphasises the level of product differentiation in many markets. Nonetheless, it has been argued that the importance of brands can facilitate entry by allowing new entrants to adopt a 'niche marketing' strategy, whereby they do not directly compete with the incumbent, but rather differentiate their products into separate 'niche' markets.[58]

Conduct

One of the most controversial barriers to entry adopted by the Court has been the conduct of the undertaking in question. The Court adopted this reasoning in *AKZO*.[59] Conduct is normally considered when the alleged abuse is examined, but in *AKZO* an exclusionary abuse, one designed to discourage new entrants, was seen as a barrier to entry that indicated dominance. This approach can be seen as somewhat circular. Conduct will not normally be considered abusive until an undertaking is in a position of dominance. However, if conduct can indicate dominance, through being a barrier to entry, it could greatly increase the likelihood of such a finding. Such an argument has logical flaws but the reasons for its adoption are straightforward. If an undertaking has a history of reacting to new entrants with exclusionary conduct, it will discourage potential entrants from attempting entry. They will be well aware of the likely response of that undertaking.

Criticism

The Court and the Commission have reacted to criticism about their broad definition of dominance by emphasising that a finding of dominance is not, in itself, a finding of wrongdoing.[60] There are no penalties for simply being dominant. As long as the dominant undertaking does not abuse its position, it will not come under the scrutiny of the competition authorities.

---

57 See Case 27/76 *United Brands Continental BV v Commission* [1978] ECR 207.
58 See Paterson, L, 'The Power of the Puppy – Does Advertising Deter Entry?' [1997] ECLR 337.
59 Case C-62/86 *AKZO Chemie BV v Commission* [1991] ECR I-3359.
60 Case 322/81 *Michelin v Commission* [1983] ECR 3461.

Such an assertion is of little comfort to undertakings that have achieved a position of market power, particularly if they have market shares of around 40% or more. Undertakings will have to be very careful to ensure that their actions do not attract an accusation of abuse, particularly where their market shares are very high. The cost of compliance programmes and the potential cost of defending such an accusation may lead to a 'chilling effect'; where undertakings act in a manner that may be less efficient, but less likely to fall foul of the competition provisions. In addition, the Court has often reiterated that what is acceptable competitive behaviour, for instance in terms of pricing, by a non-dominant undertaking may be abusive when engaged in by a dominant undertaking; accordingly, the assessment of dominance can have an important impact on an undertaking's overall competitive strategy. It is questionable whether the broad definition of dominance used in the EU truly encourages efficient competition within the Internal Market. Nonetheless, the different context in which barriers to entry are considered under US antitrust law means that we should not be over-reliant on the criticisms levelled at the broader definition by some commentators.[61] It appears, from an examination of recent enforcement trends, that there is a greater enforcement focus on undertakings with a position of super-dominance in a market and that such undertakings should be aware of, and particularly sensitive to, the potential application of the competition rules.[62]

Collective Dominance

One of the most hotly debated issues in the 1990s was the attempt by the Commission to control oligopolistic markets using Art 102 TFEU. An oligopolistic market is one that has few suppliers, none of which have market dominance, but all of which are relatively large. A small number of undertakings exercise collective market power. Although all oligopolistic markets will be different, they will tend to have similar features. There will usually be a small number of sizeable undertakings operating in a market with homogeneous products. The market may also be characterised by limited price competition and parallel behaviour. It is because of this tendency toward limited competition and parallelism that the competition authorities are interested in finding ways to regulate such markets. An example of an oligopolistic market is the groceries market in which a small number of supermarkets sell nearly all the UK's groceries. It is now very common to see markets becoming oligopolistic in Europe as competition drives out weaker competitors, and mergers lead to increased market concentration.

Although oligopolistic markets do not raise the same problems as monopolies, they can have similar effects. Often, oligopolists do not compete strongly on price, and there is little incentive to compete in other ways. This is because of what is known as 'oligopolistic interdependence'. For example, in a market with three equally strong undertakings, known as a tight oligopoly, no one undertaking would be dominant. In a truly competitive situation, a price cut by one undertaking should result in an increase in profit. Customers would switch to the lower-priced good. However, in a tight oligopoly, such a cut would result in a swift response from the other undertakings. They would quickly be aware of the price change and would intelligently respond with a similar cut. As there are few competitors, it is easy to keep track of the actions of rivals. The reaction of the competitors would quickly negate any rise in market share. As all the undertakings would be charging at the same level, market shares would remain at similar levels as before the

---

61 For an insightful examination of the contextual differences between the EC and US systems see Amato, G, *Antitrust and the Bounds of Power* (1997) Oxford: Hart.

62 This issue is highlighted by the Commission's enforcement action against Microsoft, Case COMP/37792; Intel, Case COMP/37990; and, Google, Case COMP/ 39740. See also Case C-52/09 *Konkurrensverket v TeliaSonera Sverige AB* [2011] ECR II-0000.

price cut. The end result of a price cut would be a similar market share, but lower levels of income as the unit price would have dropped. A unilateral price cut, therefore, would bring little benefit.

Similarly, there will be little benefit from a unilateral price increase. If one undertaking were to increase its prices, its customers would soon switch to purchase from the undertaking's rivals whose prices remain at the original level. Such an increase would simply result in a loss of custom. As unilateral price changes appear to have little merit, it follows that price competition tends to stagnate. Although the undertakings may try to compete in other ways, through service or product differentiation, the competitive process is very limited, with no benefits passing on to the customer or the economy.

When oligopolists become aware of this situation they become very sensitive to each other's actions, and are aware that they have limited opportunities to independently increase their profit levels. At this stage 'game theory' and practice suggest that an even more worrying development may occur. When the oligopolists become sensitive to the situation they are in, it becomes apparent that together they can maximise their profits by gradually increasing their prices. If they do this simultaneously, they will not lose any market share, but will receive a higher unit price. They can act, in effect, as a single 'monopolistic' entity. At this stage, they realise that they are interdependent and can work together to maximise profits. The difficulty competition law has with this type of market is that there is little need for formal organisation of such a scheme; it can occur through 'tacit co-ordination' – a natural operation of such a market. Most of the regulatory tools used in competition law are aimed at dealing with market behaviour rather than market structure itself.

While the theory of oligopolistic interdependence can help to explain apparent parallelism in oligopolistic markets, it does not satisfactorily explain how the simultaneous action comes about. Traditional theory suggests that a price rise will result in customer desertion and, therefore, it is unlikely that an undertaking would be willing to risk such desertion without some form of guarantee that its competitors would follow. There are several possible explanations. First, a branch of economics known as 'game theory' has attempted to explain business behaviour by examining the way in which business decisions are taken as part of a game of strategy. This theory is interesting in that it helps to explain why such interdependent behaviour might come about, but not how it occurs in practice. The second possible explanation relies on the existence of a 'price leader'. The price leader is an undertaking in the market that traditionally signals price rises to other undertakings, which then habitually follow the signalling undertaking because it has a good eye for changes on the market. If that price leader becomes aware of its position, it will be able to increase prices gradually in the knowledge that the others will follow and that, hence, profits will be maximised. The other undertakings will be aware that a failure to follow could result in a destructive price war, which would be harmful for all. As oligopolistic markets differ greatly, no single theory can hope to explain all the potential scenarios, but the explanations above may help to describe some of the problems that are likely to be encountered.

To control the competitive problems in oligopolistic markets, the Commission extended its ability to regulate under Art 102 by developing the concept of collective dominance. It argued that such a concept was envisaged by the drafters of the Treaty, wherein it states, in Art 102, that 'Any abuse by *one or more undertakings* of a dominant position' will be prohibited. Some view this as a reference to the possibility of more than one undertaking being collectively dominant. The Commission tried to raise the possibility of collective dominance in *Hoffmann-La Roche*,[63] but the Court rejected it on the basis that dominance requires unilateral action. The Court relaxed its position in *Ahmed Saeed*,[64] where it held that Arts 101 and 102 could be applied to the same situation.

---

63 See Case 85/76 *Hoffmann-La Roche v Commission* [1979] ECR 461.
64 Case 66/86 *Ahmed Saeed Flugreisen v Zentrale zur Bekämpfung Unlauteren Wettbewerbs* [1989] ECR 803.

It was not until the CFI dealt with *Italian Flat Glass*[65] that the position of collective dominance was clarified. Three Italian undertakings, in the automotive and non-automotive flat glass markets, had aggregate market shares of 79% and 95%, respectively. The Commission found that the three undertakings had formed a cartel contrary to Art 101, but also found that there was a collective dominant position as the undertakings 'present themselves on the market as a single entity and not as individuals'.[66] The Commission based this Decision on the existence of a tight oligopoly, the long-term stability of market shares, the interdependence of the three undertakings, and the structural links between them. When it came to consider collective dominance, the CFI adopted the interpretation of Art 102 suggested above, allowing for collective dominance, and stated:

> There is nothing, in principle, to prevent two or more independent economic entities from being, on a specific market, united by such economic links that, by virtue of that fact, together they hold a dominant position vis à vis the other operators on the same market.[67]

The actual Decision of the Commission was overturned as it had 'recycled' the facts found under Art 101 and had not detailed the necessary findings on the nature of the market. However, the concept of collective dominance as set out by the CFI in *Italian Flat Glass* was approved by the Court of Justice in *Almelo*.[68]

The Commission went on to use the CFI's findings in *Flat Glass* in its *Cewal* Decision.[69] The Commission decided that the shipping conference, Cewal, had abused its collective dominant position. Shipping conferences are organisations of shipping companies that plan schedules and pricing levels for particular shipping routes. Shipping conferences were exempted from the prohibition in Art 81 by Council Regulation 4056/86.[70] Cewal controlled 90% of the market, and had abused its position by using 'fighting ships' against its main competitor.

On appeal before the Court of Justice,[71] the nature of the 'economic links' required for a finding of collective dominance was clarified. Although there was strong evidence of linkage through the conference agreement, the Court did not find it necessary to limit its discussion to such formal arrangements. It noted that:

> The existence of a collective dominant position may therefore flow from the nature and terms of an agreement, from the way in which it is implemented and, consequently, from the links or factors which give rise to a connection between undertakings which result from it. Nevertheless, the existence of an agreement or of other links in law is not indispensable to a finding of a collective dominant position; such a finding may be based on other connecting factors and would depend on an economic assessment and, in particular, on an assessment of the structure of the market in question.[72]

This suggested that it may be possible to show that there are 'links' between undertakings and that those links stem entirely from the structure of the market. Links stemming from market structure would obviously be useful in dealing with undertakings in oligopolistic markets. The

---

65 Cases T-68, 77 and 78/89 *Società Italiana Vetro v Commission* [1992] ECR II-1403.
66 Commission Decision 89/93/EEC, OJ 1989, L33/44.
67 [1992] ECR II-1403, para 358.
68 Case C-393/92 *Municipality of Almelo v Energiebedrijf Ijsselmij NV* [1994] ECR I-1477, an Art 234 reference.
69 Commission Decision 93/82/EEC, OJ 1993, L34/20; [1995] 5 CMLR 198.
70 [1986] OJ L378/4.
71 Case C-395/96 *Compagnie Maritime Belge Transports SA v Commission of the European Communities* [2000] ECR I-1365.
72 Ibid, para 45.

CFI elaborated on this issue in *Gencor*,[73] stating that 'there is no reason whatsoever in legal or economic terms to exclude from the notion of economic links the relationship of interdependence existing between the parties to a tight oligopoly'.[74] Nonetheless, the Court, in *Airtours*,[75] clarified that the Commission must satisfy the following three issues in order to establish collective dominance:

i   each member of the dominant oligopoly must have the ability to know how the other members are behaving, in order to monitor whether or not the oligopolists are adopting the common policy;

ii   there must be an incentive for oligopolists not to depart from the common policy on the market; and

iii   the foreseeable reaction of current and future competitors, as well as of consumers, would not jeopardise the results expected from the common policy.[76]

It must be noted that both *Gencor* and *Airtours* discussed the creation of a collective dominant position within the terms of the Merger Regulation. The same 'dominance'-based terminology, used in Art 102, was also used in the substantive test in the 1989 Merger Regulation, but the control of mergers does raise a somewhat different set of issues compared to Art 102 cases.[77] Although the Merger Regulation appraisal criteria were revised in 2004, these cases bring the control of oligopolistic markets more securely within the terms of Art 102, subject to satisfaction of the *Airtours* conditions, as demonstrated in *Laurent Piau v Commission*.[78]

Abuse

Article 102 TFEU gives several examples of abusive conduct. The list is purely indicative, leaving the Court a wide discretion when interpreting the basic prohibition. The list includes:

i   directly or indirectly imposing unfair purchase or selling prices or other unfair trading conditions;

ii   limiting production, market or technical development, to the prejudice of consumers;

iii   applying dissimilar conditions to equivalent transactions with other trading parties, thereby placing them at a competitive disadvantage; and

iv   making the conclusion of contracts subject to acceptance by the other parties of supplementary obligations that, by their nature or according to commercial usage, have no connection with the subject of such contracts.

The Court, using teleological interpretation of of the Treaty, has given the concept of abuse a very wide scope. The test used is objective, although intent may be a factor in the determination of the level of fine, and there is no requirement that there be a causal link between the existence of dominance and the abuse itself.

---

73   Case T-102/96 *Gencor Ltd v Commission* [1999] ECR II-753.
74   Ibid, para 276.
75   Case T-342/99 *Airtours v Commission* [2002] ECR II-2585.
76   Ibid, para 62.
77   Under the Merger Regulation the issue concerns whether a concentrated market may, in the future, be oligopolistic, whereas under Art 102 the Commission or an NCA must establish collective dominance in existing markets. For the discussion of collective dominance under the Merger Regulation, see Chapter 8. See, also, Haupt, H, 'Collective Dominance Under Article 82 EC and EC Merger Control in the Light of the *Airtours* Judgment' [2003] ECLR 434.
78   Case T-193/02 [2005] ECR II-209.

There are two main categories of abusive behaviour, although some types of behaviour contain elements of both. First, exploitative abuse, which most closely follows the neoclassical economic models concerned with monopolies. The concern is that a monopolist will be in a position to maximise profits by reducing output and increasing the price of its product above a competitive level. By ensuring such a price increase, the monopolist will exploit its customers. Sometimes this form of exploitative behaviour is, rather confusingly, known as pro-competitive. This is because price rises would, in the absence of barriers to entry, encourage new entrants to enter and compete on the market. If there are barriers to entry, the dominant undertaking will not be constrained effectively and may be in a position to continue to charge a supra-competitive price.

The second form of abusive conduct is exclusionary abuse, sometimes referred to as abuse that forecloses a market. Exclusionary abuse is where a dominant undertaking adopts behaviour which would be considered perfectly legitimate if the undertaking had no market power, but may cause serious concerns when a position of market dominance is held. The Court has held that an undertaking in a dominant position has 'a special responsibility not to allow its conduct to impair undistorted competition on the Common Market'.[79] As an undertaking's level of dominance increases, its responsibility to the rest of the market becomes more onerous, and it is more likely that its behaviour will be considered abusive.[80] Therefore, any form of conduct by a dominant undertaking that threatens the competitive structure of the market might be considered abusive. Exclusionary abuses, that actually or potentially foreclose the market to existing competitors or new entrants, have been the subject of EU enforcement action more frequently than exploitative abuses. This may be because exclusionary abuses are often easier to prove and can also be seen as more likely to harm the competitive process itself. Exclusionary abuses tend to bolster the undertaking's dominant position, making it more difficult for entrants to challenge the undertaking's market strength. An undertaking that indulges in exclusionary abuses may also find it easier to charge higher prices or find there is less need to be innovative as there is less chance of effective competition developing in the market.

Not all types of abuse can be easily categorised. Some abuses can fall into both categories. An example is discriminatory pricing; by way of illustration, consider the scenario of a dominant undertaking offering different prices to different consumers. This strategy may be adopted in order to exploit some consumers who find it difficult to get supplies elsewhere, or lower prices could be charged if there was a concern that customers might be tempted to obtain supplies from a competitor. While the Court has never found it necessary to state explicitly whether a particular abuse falls into either category, it is easier to discuss the different forms of abuse separately.

Exploitative Abuses

Excessive prices

The classic form of exploitative abuse is the charging of a monopoly price or 'monopoly rent'. An undertaking which is unconstrained by competitive pressures no longer takes a price from the market but can maximise profits by reducing output and charging a higher monopolistic price.[81] The difficulty is deciding exactly at what point a price becomes excessive or unfair.

In *General Motors v Commission*,[82] the Court confirmed that it is an abuse to charge an excessive price. It suggested that prices would be excessive where they do not reflect the

---

79 Case 322/81 *Michelin v Commission* [1983] ECR 3461, para 10. The concept of 'special responsibility' was reinvigorated by the CFI in cases like Case T-201/04 *Microsoft v Commission* [2007] ECR II-3601.
80 See the discussion of super-dominance above.
81 This process is explained more fully in Chapter 1.
82 Case 26/75 [1975] ECR 1367.

'economic value' of the goods. In that case the Court decided that the prices were not excessive. No real indication was given as to exactly how the 'economic value' of a product could be calculated other than by reference to a hypothetical competitive market. In *United Brands*,[83] the Commission used various factors to support its finding of excessive pricing in continental Europe. It compared prices between Member States of branded and unbranded bananas, and between different brands of banana. After these comparisons were made, the prices charged on the relevant market appeared to be unjustifiably high. The Court quashed the Commission's findings as it had failed to examine UBC's costs before coming to its Decision.

In subsequent cases there have been two main approaches taken to excessive prices. The first is to examine prices in markets across Europe to determine if one price is *prima facie* excessive. This approach has its limitations in that different markets have very different cost structures. The variations in taxation, marketing strategy and consumer behaviour may result in different price levels without there being any hint of exploitation. The Court has recognised this by treating evidence pointing to excessive prices as raising a presumption of abuse that can be rebutted by evidence of differences among the markets on which the comparison was based.[84] The second approach has a 'cost plus' basis. The Court's assertion about the need to examine costs in *United Brands* suggests that a certain level of profit may be excessive. So far, the Court has made no statement about what level above cost constitutes a reasonable profit.

Many commentators consider direct intervention in market pricing decisions as a step too far for competition law, and that the operation of the market alone should control prices. If high prices are charged, new entrants should be encouraged to enter the market by the prospect of good returns, and the fear that intervention is an inefficient tool ill-suited to control prices effectively. The difficulties in proving excessive pricing are reflected in Commission policy. It has not made a decision based on excessive pricing since *United Brands*, and all subsequent cases have been considered by the Court under the Art 267 TFEU reference procedure. The amount of information that would need to be gathered before an excessive price could be proved constitutes a major hurdle to effective enforcement. Nonetheless, it should be noted that the first case under the Chapter II prohibition of the UK's Competition Act 1998, discussed later in this chapter, involved excessive pricing by a dominant undertaking, Napp Pharmaceuticals Ltd.[85] While the OFT was successful in showing excessive pricing in *Napp*, the difficult nature of establishing what is excessive was illustrated in *Attheraces Ltd v The British Horse Racing Board Ltd*.[86] The Court of Appeal, considering an appeal against a finding of excessive pricing, rejected the High Court's use of a 'cost+' approach. Two of the reasons given for allowing the appeal were the difficulty in establishing which costs to take into account in a cost+ calculation and, more importantly, the fact that 'economic value' of the product to the purchaser was not only related to the costs of the producer, but also the value that the purchaser could expect to gain from exploiting the product on downstream markets.

Unfair conditions

One of the only cases in which unfair conditions have been considered as an abuse in themselves is *BRT v SABAM*.[87] SABAM, a performing rights society, was found to have abused its dominant position by imposing on its members obligations which were not absolutely necessary for the attainment of its object. This unfairly restricted the members' freedom to exercise their copyright

---

83 See Case 27/76 *United Brands Continental BV v Commission* [1978] ECR 207.
84 Case 110/88 *Lucazeau v SACEM* [1989] ECR 2811.
85 DGFT Decision CA98/2/2001 *Napp Pharmaceutical Holdings*, 30 March 2001. On appeal *Napp Pharmaceutical Holdings v DGFT* [2002] CAT 1.
86 *Attheraces Ltd v The British Horseracing Board Ltd* [2007] EWCA Civ 38, [2007] UKCLR 309.
87 Case 127/73 [1974] ECR 313.

as they wished. Many other abuses, where additional unfair conditions are imposed by a dominant undertaking, are considered to be exclusionary rather than exploitative.

The quiet life

The final type of exploitative abuse is predicted by the neoclassical economic models. Accordingly, a monopolist will not be subject to competitive pressure forcing it to innovate and it can enjoy a 'quiet life'. It is sometimes also known as 'x-inefficiency'. The Court has adopted this form of reasoning in its judgments. In *Porto di Genova*,[88] the Court held that a port operator's refusal to utilise modern technology in its unloading operations constituted an abuse. The use of older methods meant that the unloading of vessels took much longer, and was consequently more expensive. Another example of the complexity of proving the quiet life was seen in the binding commitments secured by the Commission from ENI who were alleged to have systematically under-invested in their dominant long-distance gas pipelines as any increase in capacity would have threatened profits in other parts of their business.[89]

As can be observed from the cases mentioned above, the difficulty in proving exploitative abuse stems from the subjective decisions involved. How excessive, unfair or inefficient must a practice be before an abuse is proved? The inherent uncertainty in such a question discourages both the Commission and individual claimants or pursuers from bringing actions. This may be one of the reasons why most of the cases coming before the Commission and the courts have concentrated on exclusionary abuses.

Exclusionary Abuses

The majority of abuses dealt with under Art 102 TFEU are exclusionary. While this type of abuse is not expressly predicted by the neoclassical economic model of monopoly, discussed in Chapter 1, it is very important in practice. Exclusionary, or anti-competitive, abuses are harmful to competition in that they allow dominant undertakings to protect their market power, usually by discouraging or making it more difficult for new entrants to challenge them on the market. Such abuses are harmful in that they distort the process of competition itself by actually or potentially foreclosing a market to competitors. As we have already discussed, easy entry and exit from markets are important. By discouraging or stopping entry, a dominant undertaking will be able to perpetuate its market power. Furthermore, it will be in a better position to exploit its customers. It is also important that a dominant undertaking should not be able to drive out existing weaker competitors by using methods other than normal competition on the merits.

The Court has shown willingness to consider many forms of conduct as exclusionary, even when they are economically beneficial to the undertaking itself. The concept of abuse in such situations is an objective one. The Court often concentrates on the effect of a practice on the structure of the market itself, not necessarily on the benefits to the dominant undertaking or on proof of consumer harm. The Court explained its approach in *Michelin*:[90]

> Article 102 covers practices which are likely to affect the structure of the market where, as a direct result of the presence of the undertaking in question, competition has already been weakened and which, through recourse to methods different from those governing normal

---

88 Case C-179/90 *Merci Convenzionali Porto di Genova SpA v Siderurgica Gabrielli* [1991] ECR I-5889.
89 Commission Decision of 29 September 2010, *ENI* (Case COMP/39.315), [2010] OJ C352/8.
90 Case 322/81 [1983] ECR 3461, para 70.

competition in products or services based on traders' performance, have the effect of hindering the maintenance or development of the level of competition still existing on the market.

How far the methods of the dominant undertaking have to differ 'from those governing normal competition' is a controversial question. What is normal in competitive situations is a perplexing question in itself. The Court has taken a broad pro-competitive approach, condemning methods of competition that in practice could be exclusionary but which many critics would argue were 'normal' in competitive situations. A controversial example of this broad approach was seen in the Commission's decision in *British Midland v Aer Lingus*.[91] British Midland was attempting to enter the market for the Dublin to Heathrow air route. The Commission required Aer Lingus, the dominant operator, to allow British Midland to 'interline' with it. This meant that British Midland was allowed to use the Aer Lingus computer system to sell its tickets for the same route. The effect was that Aer Lingus was to assist a competitor in entering the market. Although interlining is common on established air routes, arguably it is unusual to interline with a new competitor. The broad approach can partially be explained by examining the objectives of the EU Treaties. Protocol 27 on the internal market and competition sets out that the internal market includes a system 'ensuring that competition is not distorted'.[92] Thus, the structure of competition itself is one of the main planks upon which the whole EU system is built. An example of the way in which Art 102 TFEU focuses on the structure of the market can be seen in *Microsoft v Commission*.[93] The CFI confirmed the Commission's Decision, which required Microsoft to provide interoperability information, which permits network clients and servers to communicate with each other, to allow competitors to develop products that would compete with its own work group server operating system. The absence of proper interoperability reinforced Microsoft's position and risked the elimination of competition on the secondary market.

The main policy document in relation to exclusionary abuses under EU law is the European Commission's 2009 'Guidance on the Commission's enforcement priorities in applying Article 82 of the EC Treaty to abusive exclusionary conduct by dominant undertakings'.[94] This is a unique document in that it does not try to set out what is lawful or unlawful, but rather it explains what the Commission sees as being the worst types of abuse, which it should prioritise in its enforcement efforts. The Guidance is seen as being a key part of the Commission's drive to give its enforcement practice a greater economic focus. The Commission's focus is on exclusionary conduct by dominant undertakings that might foreclose their competitors and thereby have an adverse impact on consumer welfare. The concentration on foreclosure and consumer welfare is a distinct departure from the jurisprudence of the Court, which has never required either for a finding of infringement. 'Anti-competitive foreclosure' is described as being the situation where 'effective access of actual or potential competitors to supplies or markets is hampered or eliminated'.[95] The Commission will examine the following factors when considering if there has been anti-competitive foreclosure and an impact on consumer welfare: the position of the dominant undertaking; the conditions on the relevant market; the position of the dominant undertaking's competitors; the position of the customers or input suppliers; the extent of the allegedly abusive conduct; possible evidence of actual foreclosure; and direct evidence of any exclusionary strategy. The Guidance also explicitly recognises, for the first time, that the

---

91 Commission Decision 92/213/EEC, [1992] OJ L96/34.
92 Before the Lisbon Reform Treaty this passage was found in Art 3(1)(g) EC. The Court, in Case C-52/09 *Teliasonera*, confirmed that the transfer of the text to Protocol 27 did not reduce its importance.
93 Case T-201/04 *Microsoft v Commission* [2007] 5 CMLR 11.
94 [2009] OJ C45/7.
95 Guidance, at para 19.

Commission may not challenge behaviour which is 'objectively necessary', or in situations where the conduct produces substantial efficiencies that outweigh any anti-competitive effects on consumers.[96] This firmly establishes an 'efficiency defence' in Commission practice.

The status and legal effect of the Commission Guidance is a matter of contention. The guidance itself states that it 'is not intended to constitute a statement of the law and is without prejudice to the interpretation of Article 82 [102] by the Court of Justice'.[97] The Commission itself should be bound by its own Guidance, but in situations where Commission Decisions have been challenged on the basis of economic arguments similar to those outlined in the Guidance, the EU courts have tended to only require proof of the older more formalistic legal tests in order to support the finding of an infringement. An undertaking that considers that the Commission has not followed its own Guidance may find it very difficult to challenge that Decision before the EU courts.[98] Essentially, the approach adopted by the Commission in the Guidance is accepted by the EU courts as an appropriate way to examine Art 102 cases, but the Court does not require that approach, and the depth of economic analysis represented, to support all findings of abuse.

As there are a number of different forms of exclusionary abuse the best approach is to examine a number of broad types of behaviour that have been found to be abusive. Although the situations examined below are by no means an exhaustive list, they do give a good indication of the types of behaviour that the Court and the Commission are likely to consider as anti-competitive, and therefore condemn.

Export bans

Any attempt by a dominant undertaking to impose export bans on its purchasers will be considered abusive. Obviously, this forms part of the EU's attempt to stop undertakings re-erecting trade barriers which have been dismantled at state level. Export bans distort both trade flows across the EU and intra-brand competition (competition between same brand products). If such bans were put in place, a dominant undertaking would be able to segregate national markets. In *United Brands*, a clause prohibiting the resale of green bananas[99] was considered to be an export ban and was condemned because it would grant national distributors protection from parallel imports. Export bans may also be dealt with under Art 101 TFEU, even when they appear to be unilaterally imposed.[100] The importance of the internal market in EU competition law was reaffirmed in *GlaxoSmithKline* in 2008, where the Court of Justice made it clear that to protect 'the integration of national markets' the competition rules would not allow a dominant undertaking 'to defend its own commercial interests' by not selling its products into particular national markets.[101]

Pricing strategies

Article 102 limits the pricing strategies of undertakings where those undertakings are considered to be dominant.[102] The most important cases in this area have considered discounting, rebates and

---

96 Guidance, at para 28.
97 Guidance, at para 3. The impact of Guidance on national courts and NCAs is discussed by AG Kokott in Case C-226/11 *Expedia*, 6 September 2012.
98 See, for example, the CJEU's rejection of the need for economic evidence to support the finding of an infringement in Case C-549/10P *Tomra Systems & Others v Commission* [2012] ECR I-0000.
99 Unripe, 'green' bananas are much easier to transport long distances.
100 See Commission Decision 96/478/EEC *Adalat*, [1996] OJ L201/1. On appeal, see Case T-41/96 *Bayer v Commission* [2000] ECR II-3383, and Cases C-2 and 3/01 P *BAI and Commission v Bayer* [2004] ECR I-23.
101 Case C-468 to 478/06 *Sot Lélos Sia EE and Others v GlaxoSmithKline AEVE* [2008] ECR I-7139, at para 68.
102 For a critique of this area of law, see Ridyard, D, 'Exclusionary Pricing and Price Discrimination Abuses Under Article 82 – an Economic Analysis' [2002] ECLR 286.

predatory pricing. While many of these practices will lower prices for the customer in the short term, it may be possible for the dominant seller to benefit eventually by reducing the level of competition they face on the market in the longer term. These pricing strategies can therefore be exclusionary, as they tend to foreclose markets by reducing current or future competition. New entrants may be discouraged by the dominant undertaking's pricing policy. Prices may be lowered to drive out an existing competitor or make it difficult for the new entrant to obtain a foothold in the market.

Discounts, rebates and price discrimination

The use of discounts and rebates, and other forms of price discrimination – where different prices are paid by different customers – can be problematic when an undertaking is in a dominant position. Discounts can be used to tie a customer to a particular supplier. The customer may be aware that if they were to take supplies from a competitor they would lose their discount with the dominant supplier. A new supplier would have to charge prices low enough to compensate their new customers for the loss of those discounts. The impact of such discounts is sometimes known as a 'suction' or 'loyalty-inducing' effect. One particularly damaging form of discount is known as a 'loyalty rebate'. These rebates are given to a customer who takes a certain percentage of their total requirements from a supplier. For example, they may receive a 10% discount if they buy 75% of their requirements from the supplier and a 15% discount if they purchase 90% of their requirements. Such a discounting structure may be useful for an entrant firm, but as dominant undertakings are the major supplier on a market, they can act anti-competitively. The discount tends to tie customers to the dominant undertaking and makes it very difficult for other undertakings to increase their market share.

The jurisprudence of the Court has found that a great many discounts and rebates to be abusive. In the classic cases the Court has tended to focus on the form of the discount or rebate without examining their effect in any detail. For example, *Hoffmann-La Roche*[103] concerned the adoption of loyalty rebates alongside some other abusive discounts. The loyalty rebate was connected to a so-called 'English clause', which allowed customers to obtain supplies from other undertakings where they were charging a lower price if the customers informed La Roche of the lower price. While this may appear to be pro-competitive, it meant that La Roche was given full information about its competitors' pricing policies by its customers, allowing La Roche to react and maintain its market share. This was also found to be abusive. It did not matter that the use of loyalty rebates was at the request of customers; the effects on potential competitors were obvious. Hoffmann-La Roche also used 'across the board' rebates. These rebates awarded a discount where a customer purchased all of the supplier's range of products. This type of rebate would tend to foreclose the market in that it would discourage customers from dealing with different suppliers for different products.

Another abusive discounting practice was considered in *Michelin*.[104] The Court found that annual discounts awarded by Michelin, on the basis of sales targets set for dealers, amounted to an abuse, as the dealers could not deal with another supplier without fear of heavy economic loss. The discounts were awarded on an informal basis, for short time periods, and the rates varied enormously between dealerships. It was considered that the ad hoc nature of the rebates, and the lack of certainty faced by dealers, tended to increase the tying effect.

In *Irish Sugar* the Commission appeared to take a stronger view, which was supported by the Court, on targeted discounts suggesting that such discounts will always be unlawful as they are 'clearly aimed at tying customers closely to the dominant company'.[105] In *British Airways v*

---

103 See Case 85/76 *Hoffmann-La Roche v Commission* [1979] ECR 461.
104 Case 322/81 *Michelin v Commission* [1983] ECR 3461.
105 Commission Decision 1997/624/EC, OJ 1997, L258/1, para 152. On appeal Case T-228/97 *Irish Sugar plc v Commission* [1999] ECR II-2969, para 191.

Commission,[106] the Commission's fine of €6.8m, imposed on British Airways for offering commission bonuses to travel agents who exceeded BA sales targets, was confirmed. BA's 'performance reward scheme' was found to be 'fidelity building' because of its progressive nature, with the potential for exponential changes in the levels of bonus payable based on marginal changes in sales.[107]

Although the Court has challenged a number of different types of discount, not all such discounts or rebates are abusive. If the discounts are objectively based on savings made by the producer, they will be justifiable.[108] If, for example, a manufacturer can reduce costs by making volume sales, enabling larger manufacturing runs, those savings can be reflected in discounted pricing. However, any such discounts must be fixed objectively and be open to all customers. The *Irish Sugar* case suggests there may be an overlap between the case law on discounts and the abuse of predatory pricing, in that prices could be considered as predatory where they discriminate between different customers without any objective justification. The controversy surrounding the Commission's *Michelin II* Decision[109] indicates a number of the diverging views in this area. The Commission's Decision found that Michelin had abused its dominant position through the operation of a complex discount system. Following the publication of that Decision, a number of commentators challenged the Commission's findings on the basis that insufficient economic analysis had been undertaken and that the Commission's approach did not take account of the complex economic reality of pricing strategy in modern economies.[110] On appeal, before the Court of First Instance (CFI), Michelin argued that the Commission had not undertaken sufficient economic analysis of the actual effects of the complex discount system, but its argument was rejected by the Court. The Court stressed that once it was established that the discounting practice adopted by the dominant undertaking was 'loyalty-inducing', it was not necessary to show that the discounting practice actually had anti-competitive effects on the market. All the Commission was required to establish was that 'the purpose of the discount systems was to tie the dealers to [Michelin]' as this tended to make it 'more difficult for . . . competitors to enter the relevant market'.[111] The rebates in *Michelin* were particularly damaging as: they were non-transparent, many of the factors affording Michelin a degree of discretion; they covered a lengthy period of up to 13 months, where a vendor would be required to sell at loss for a long period before it was able to claim the rebate that would bring it into profit; and they covered all sales during the reference period, not only those sales that were beyond the targets set.[112] Similar discounts implemented by Intel were a significant element of the infringement which resulted in the imposition of a record fine of €1.06bn in 2009.[113] The Court of Justice confirmed its adherence to this more 'formalistic' approach in 2012 in *Tomra Systems*, where it held that there was no need to show 'negative prices', i.e. prices below cost, as a prerequisite to a finding of abuse.[114]

---

106 Case T-219/99, [2003] ECR II-5917, on appeal, C-95/04 P, [2007] ECR I-2331.
107 See, in particular, paras 271–275.
108 Case 102/77 *Hoffmann-La Roche v Centrafarm* [1978] ECR 1139; and Case 85/76 *Hoffmann-La Roche v Commission* [1979] ECR 461.
109 Commission Decision 2002/405/EC *Michelin* [2002] OJ, L143/1, on appeal, Case T-203/01 *Michelin v Commission* [2003] ECR II-4071.
110 See Ridyard, D, 'Exclusionary Pricing and Price Discrimination Abuses Under Article 82 – an Economic Analysis' [2002] ECLR 286, and the less-tempered Sher, B, 'Price Discounts and Michelin 2: What Goes Around, Comes Around' [2002] ECLR 482.
111 Case T-203/01 *Michelin v Commission* [2004] 4 CMLR 18, particularly paras 235–246.
112 For a fuller discussion see, Roques, C, 'CFI Judgment, Case T-203/01, *Manufacture Francaise des Pneumatiques Michelin v Commission*' [2004] ECLR 688.
113 See Commission Decision (COMP/C-3/37.990) *Intel*, 13 May 2009. See also Commission Press Release, 'Antitrust: Commission imposes fine of €1.06 bn on Intel for abuse of dominant position; orders Intel to cease illegal practices', IP/09/745, 13 May 2009. The judgment of the General Court was confirmed on appeal in Case T-286/09, [2014] ECR II-0000.
114 Case C-549/10P Tomra Systems and others v Commission [2012] ECR I-0000, at para 73. The reasoning in Tomra was relied on by the GC in Intel, ibid, when the Cout again approved a traditional formulatic approach.

The Commission Guidance takes a more economically focussed approach than that adopted to date by the EU courts. The Commission Guidance on Art 102 TFEU sets out its enforcement priorities;[115] i.e. those circumstances in which it is most likely to consider infringement proceedings as being required.

The Guidance on pricing abuses concentrates on whether the discount or rebate would hamper competition from an 'as efficient' competitor.[116] The main tool the Commission will seek to use to establish whether an 'as efficient' competitor could compete is to establish if the dominant undertaking is engaging in below costs pricing through the operation of the scheme. The cost benchmarks that the Commission use through the Guidance are Average Avoidable Cost (AAC) or Long-Run Average Incremental Cost (LRAIC). AAC is the lower benchmark, as it includes all variable costs, but only those fixed costs incurred during the reference period.[117] If a dominant undertaking is selling below AAC they must be doing so at a loss as they cannot recover all of their fixed costs and some of their variable costs. An equally efficient competitor could not compete without also suffering a loss. LRAIC is often a slightly higher figure as it includes product-specific fixed costs.[118] It might be more appropriate to use the LRAIC figure where variable costs of production are low, but there are important fixed costs in relation to product research or development that must be recovered over the lifespan of the product. An example of such a product might be one in the information economy where R&D costs are high in developing a software product, but digital distribution means that production and marketing costs are relatively low. If the Commission discovers, using these benchmarks, that the dominant undertaking's sale price, including the discount or rebate, is above cost, it will assume that an equally efficient competitor could compete on the merits in the market and that there will be no adverse impact on competition or on consumers. The Court of Justice preliminary ruling in *Post Danmark*,[119] while reiterating the 'special responsibility' of dominant undertakings, and that not all forms of price competition are legitimate, emphasised the contemporary significance of the 'as efficient competitor' concept and the continued practical importance of cost-based tests under Art 102. The exclusion of less efficient competitors was not anti-competitive and, accordingly, a pricing policy whereby a charge to a particular customer was less than ATC (but above average incremental costs) was not necessarily abusive conduct. It should, however, be noted that in Intel[120] the GC rejected the necessity to rely on the 'as efficent competitor test' in relation to exclusivity discounts.

Predatory pricing

This type of abuse is characterised by a selective price reduction which is intended to harm a competitor. The reduction will usually be to levels at or below cost. Because of its economic strength, the dominant undertaking will be able to sustain its losses for a limited time, but its weaker competitor, with access to fewer resources, will be driven from the market.

The Court of Justice first upheld the proposition that not all such price competition is legitimate in *AKZO*.[121] The Court set out a formula to calculate whether pricing is 'predatory'. If prices are below Average Variable Costs (AVC – costs which vary according to the quantities produced), predatory pricing is presumed. If prices are between AVC and Average Total Costs (ATC – variable costs plus fixed costs), pricing will be predatory where it is shown to be part of a plan

---

115 Guidance on the Commission's enforcement priorities in applying Art 82 of the EC Treaty to abusive exclusionary conduct by dominant undertakings, [2009] OJ C45/7.
116 Guidance, ibid, paras 23–27.
117 The Guidance, at n 2, defines AAC as, 'the average of the costs that could have been avoided if the company had not produced a discrete amount of (extra) output, in this case the amount allegedly the subject of abusive conduct'.
118 The Guidance, at n 2, defines LRAIC as, 'the average of all the (variable and fixed) costs that a company incurs to produce a particular product'.
119 Case C-209/10 *Post Danmark A/S v Konkurrenceradet* [2012] ECR I-0000.
120 Above, n 113.
121 Case C-62/86 *AKZO Chemie BV v Commission* [1991] ECR I-3359.

to eliminate competition. This test can be difficult to apply, for two main reasons. Firstly, the assessment of what costs should be considered in either category is very controversial. Even if it is possible to categorise costs, the information can be difficult to gather, and may change rapidly. Secondly, it can be very difficult to prove the intentions of the dominant undertaking in the grey area between average variable costs and average total costs. In a competitive situation, most firms will be trying to 'eliminate' their competitors. That is the nature of competition. *AKZO* was the first case to use a cost-based approach to challenge 'illegitimate' price competition by a dominant undertaking which could foreclose a market. That approach is now adopted in relation to a range of different types of abuse under Art 102 TFEU.

Predatory pricing policy was developed in a novel way in *Tetra Pak II*.[122] In the Court's consideration of liquid food packaging, it decided that Tetra Pak was dominant in the aseptic packaging market and had been involved in abusive predatory pricing in the non-aseptic packaging market, in which it was not dominant. This was a novel extension of the doctrine, but only appears possible where there are associative links between the dominant market and the market in which the predatory behaviour took place. In the *Tetra Pak II* case, the markets were separate but closely related.

In *Irish Sugar*,[123] the Commission appeared to take a rather different approach to predation. It concentrated on the selectivity of Irish Sugar's price cuts rather than on the relation of prices to costs. Irish Sugar was cutting prices, in the border region, to protect the sugar market in the Republic of Ireland from competition from imports from Northern Ireland. Although this point was not directly addressed by the CFI, the Decision indicates that where price cuts are targeted at customers who might seek supplies from a competitor, this may be enough to found a finding of predatory pricing unless all customers are offered the favourable terms.[124] Similarly, in *Compagnie Maritime Belge*,[125] the practice of scheduling low-cost 'fighting ships' against competitors' vessels was considered predatory even where prices were above cost. It should be noted that in these cases the dominant undertakings were both in arguably 'super-dominant' positions. Although these cases were characterised as regarding 'predatory pricing', they are indistinguishable from discount cases in many ways. The current approach adopted by the Commission avoids this categorisation problem by treating most pricing abuses in a similar way.

The Commission's policy has been criticised as being confusing for undertakings that will have to decide what type of price competition is legitimate. Case law had suggested that meeting, but not beating, competition would be acceptable. Nonetheless, in *France Télécom v Commission*[126] the CFI made it clear that dominant undertakings had no 'absolute right' to align their prices with those of a competitor, especially where they are potentially abusive, being below cost. It also rejected the argument that a price below cost would not be predatory unless it was possible for the dominant undertaking to recoup its losses. Accordingly, it is potentially difficult to establish when an undertaking's behaviour crosses the line. This uncertainty arguably chills potential competition. However, it is clear that there are no abuses *per se* in this context, and in assessing the foreclosing effect of pricing strategies, the Commission, when prioritising its enforcement resources, had predominantly focused on the activities of super-dominant undertakings where the exclusionary impact is more self-evident.

The Commission Guidance foresees actions where the dominant undertaking 'sacrifices' by deliberately incurring losses in the short term to foreclose actual or potential competition.

---

122 Case C-333/94P *Tetra Pak International SA v Commission* [1996] ECR I-5951.
123 Commission Decision 1997/624/EC, OJ 1997, L258/1. On appeal Case T-228/97 *Irish Sugar plc v Commission* [1999] ECR II-2969.
124 See Andrews, P, 'Is Meeting Competition a Defence to Predatory Pricing? – the *Irish Sugar* Decision Suggests a New Approach' [1998] ECLR 49.
125 Case C-395/96 *Compagnie Maritime Belge Transports SA v Commission of the European Communities* [2000] ECR I-1365.
126 Case T-340/03 *France Télécom v Commission* [2007] ECR II-107. On appeal Case C-202/07 P, [2009] ECR I-2369. See, also, Gal, MS, 'Below-cost Price Alignment: Meeting or Beating Competition? The France Telecom case' [2007] ECLR 382.

Sacrifice occurs when, 'by charging a lower price for all or a particular part of its output over the relevant time period, or by expanding its output over the relevant time period, the dominant undertaking incurred or is incurring losses that could have been avoided'.[127] The benchmark adopted to assess whether losses are incurred is pricing below Average Avoidable Cost (AAC). This is similar to AVC, but may include some fixed costs if they were specifically related to the expansion of output. The AAC test is the normal gauge of sacrifice, but the Commission still state that predation may be indicated by direct evidence of a predatory strategy on the part of the dominant undertaking.[128] The Commission will then seek to show that the pricing strategy would foreclose the market for an 'as efficient' competitor. The Commission does not need to show that competitors have exited the market; a dominant undertaking may well prefer to 'discipline' an existing competitor so that it remains in the market but follows the dominant undertaking's pricing and refrains from vigorous competition in the future.[129]

Margin squeeze

Margin squeezes can occur where a vertically integrated dominant firm controls the input to a downstream market, and also directly operates downstream. It therefore is the main supplier to its own downstream competitors. Figure 4.1, an example of a vertically integrated market, allows us to understand the problem of margin squeeze.

A vertically integrated firm in this type of market sets the 'wholesale' price it charges its downstream competitors for the input product and also sets its own 'retail' price on the downstream

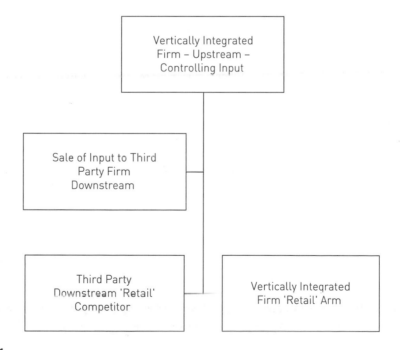

Figure 4.1

---

127 Guidance, above, n 115, at para 64.
128 Guidance, ibid, at para 66.
129 Guidance, ibid, at para 69.

market. It is possible for a dominant input provider to charge its third-party downstream rivals an input price equivalent to its own retail price on the downstream market. This would ensure that the downstream 'retail' business is protected from price competition from third-party rivals. The margin in which the third-party 'retail' competitor can profit on the basis of the input price is therefore squeezed

The most obvious practical examples of this type of situation can be observed in liberalised utility markets such as telecoms. Let us assume that a former state monopoly telecoms provider now operates in a liberalised market, but still has control of the network infrastructure. A third-party competitor, competing to offer telecoms services to customers, needs to purchase access to the network to provide their services. If the margin between the dominant network owner's wholesale access price and their own retail service price is narrow there is little room for any such third party to effectively compete on the retail market. European telecoms markets have provided a number of examples of cases where wholesale input prices have been the same as, or more than, the dominant undertakings retail prices, severely limiting the potential for competition on the downstream market.

In *Deutsche Telekom*[130] and *TeliaSonera*[131] the Court of Justice clarified its position on margin squeeze cases. Following these judgments, the key to abuse within a margin squeeze is the 'spread' between the wholesale and the retail price. The Court does not see it as necessary to prove that either price is too low or too high, only that the margin itself is being squeezed. If an 'as efficient' competitor could not compete effectively, by being forced to operate at a loss or at reduced profitability, on the basis of the input price charged there may be an abuse. The Court made it clear that proof of an anti-competitive effect is not necessary for the finding of an infringement, but that margin squeeze can result in entry to the market being more difficult or growth in products or services being stifled.[132] A counter-intuitive result of the Court's position is that the only response available to the dominant undertaking may be to raise their retail price to increase the spread.

The Commission Guidance on margin squeeze predates both *Deutsche Telekom* and *TeliaSonera* and treats margin squeeze as being analogous to a ('constructive') refusal to supply.[133] AG Mazák introduced a number of elements from refusal to supply cases in his opinion in *TeliaSonera*,[134] but the Court did not follow that line of reasoning. It appears therefore that the Commission's Guidance has been overtaken by the Court's jurisprudence, and margin squeeze should now be treated as 'stand-alone' abuse. It can apply in all cases where there a dominant undertaking decides to deal with downstream competitors. In that situation they must accept their 'special responsibility' to the market because of their dominance upstream. Ironically, this means that the rules on margin squeeze (a form of constructive refusal to supply) appear stricter than the rules applicable to an actual refusal to supply.

Tying and bundling

An undertaking can be dominant in one market and abuse its dominance in another. With tie-ins or bundling, a dominant undertaking attempts to extend, or leverage, its market power from the market in which it is dominant to another market. This usually involves a requirement for customers to obtain supplies of a secondary product when purchasing the product in which the undertaking has a dominant position. In this way, dominance over the market of the primary

---

130 Case C-280/08 P *Deutsche Telekom AG v Commission* [2010] ECR I-9555.
131 Case C-52/09 *Konkurrensverket v TeliaSonera Sverige AB* [2011] ECR I-527.
132 Case C-280/08 P *Deutsche Telekom AG v Commission* [2010] ECR I-9555, paras 251–254.
133 A fuller discussion of refusal to supply appears below.
134 AG Opinion in Case C-52/09 *Konkurrensverket v TeliaSonera Sverige AB* [2011] ECR I-527, paras 11–30.

product is extended into another market. If a customer wants to buy the dominant product, it must also purchase the 'bundle' of products. The customer may have been able to obtain the secondary product on better terms elsewhere, or it may not want to purchase it at all. In that sense, the abuse is exploitative, but it is also exclusionary in that it forecloses the secondary market. Other suppliers of the secondary product will struggle to find outlets for their versions of the product, as most customers will have been forced to obtain bundled supplies from the dominant undertaking.

A simple example of a traditional tying arrangement was evident in *Napier Brown/British Sugar*.[135] A sugar processor forced customers to buy bulk sugar at delivered prices, that is, the price including delivery costs. The purchase of haulage services was, therefore, bundled with the purchase of the sugar. Other haulage undertakings would have found it very difficult to break into the market.

The Court's approach to tying arrangements was further explained in *Hilti*.[136] A manufacturer of nail guns refused to supply cartridge strips containing the charge which fired the nails, and over which it had intellectual property (IP) rights, without customers also purchasing the corresponding nails. Suppliers of Hilti-compatible nails complained about the tie. In its Decision, the Commission concentrated on two particular consequences of the abuse: the extension of monopoly power into a new market, and the foreclosure of competitors. Hilti was protected from competition in the market for Hilti-compatible cartridge strips, as it had registered design rights. It was attempting to extend its power over that market into the market for Hilti-compatible nails, where it was much more vulnerable to competition. By extending that power Hilti was, in effect, seeking to exclude potential competitors from the secondary market in Hilti-compatible nails. All purchasers of Hilti-compatible nails would have already been required to obtain supplies with the cartridge strips and would not need to buy nails from any competing source. Therefore, no viable competition would be able to develop on the market. Hilti's attempts to justify the tie were dismissed. The controversy surrounding tying arrangements was rekindled by the Commission's Decision in the *Microsoft* case, which was confirmed by the CFI.[137] In that Decision the Commission required that Microsoft, which was found to be dominant in the PC client operating systems market, offer an unbundled version of its operating system without Windows Media Player to PC manufacturers. Microsoft was also challenged with regard to similar practices in the US.[138]

The Commission Guidance explains that they will only act where the tying and tied products are on separate markets and the tying practice is likely to lead to foreclosure.[139] The risk of foreclosure is considered to be greater where the tie or bundling is costly or difficult to reverse; this is particularly the case where a 'technical tie' exists making the products dependent upon each other or limiting the ability to resell the individual components.[140]

Mergers

Article 102 TFEU has, in the past, been used to control mergers. In *Continental Can*,[141] the Court held that it was an abuse for a dominant undertaking to strengthen its position in a market by merging with a competitor. Now, mergers are controlled by a more sophisticated system, under

135 Commission Decision 88/518/EEC, [1988] OJ L284/41; [1990] 4 CMLR 196. See, also, Case C359/01P *British Sugar v Commission* [2004] ECR I-4933.
136 Case C-53/92P *Hilti AG v Commission* [1994] ECR I-666; [1994] 1 CMLR 590.
137 Commission Decision 2007/53/EC *Microsoft* [2007] OJ L32/23, Case T-201/04, *Microsoft v Commission* [2007] 5 CMLR 11.
138 For further discussion see, Ridyard, D, 'Tying and Bundling – Cause for Complaint?' [2005] ECLR 316.
139 Commission Guidance, above, n 115, para 50.
140 Commission Guidance, ibid, paras 52–58.
141 See Case 6/72 *Continental Can v Commission* [1973] ECR 215.

Regulation 139/2004,[142] but the judgment in the *Continental Can* case does show the Court's concern to maintain a competitive structure within a market.

Refusal to supply

The treatment of refusals to supply is a particularly controversial area – due, in no small part, to competition law's interaction with other long-standing legal principles in the law of contract and intellectual property. Most legal systems have shied away from insisting that an undertaking be forced to contract when it does not see it to be in its best interests to do so. However, under EU law the basic rule is that a refusal to supply by a dominant undertaking must be objectively justified. The justification must not be based solely on the undertaking's commercial interests but on more general concerns.[143] In *ABG*,[144] a refusal to supply was justified on the basis of a global shortage of the goods in question, and in *Leyland DAF v Automotive Products*,[145] the English Court of Appeal considered that an undertaking's failure to pay for previous contract goods constituted sufficient justification.

There are three broad categories in which Art 102 TFEU has intervened, although it is sometimes difficult in practice to place a particular set of facts clearly in one class to the exclusion of others. The broad categories are as follows:

i   where a refusal to supply a customer, on an existing market, is used to damage or deter a competitor (usually known as a refusal to deal);

ii   where there is a refusal to allow a customer access to an 'essential facility'; or

iii where there is a refusal to grant a licence of IP rights.

Refusal to deal

The first category covers the most obvious threat to competition raised by a refusal to supply: a direct refusal to supply an existing customer where that refusal can be linked to an attempt to eliminate an actual or potential competitor. The central issue within the refusal to deal cases is, arguably, the general principle under Art 102 that a dominant undertaking has a special responsibility not to 'impair undistorted competition', as outlined in *Michelin*.[146] When a dominant undertaking has embarked on a commercial relationship with an actual or potential competitor, it must ensure that it acts in such a way as not to further damage the, already weak, competitive process by refusing to deal without objective justification. A clear example of an attempt to eliminate a competitor was seen in *Commercial Solvents*.[147] Commercial Solvents was the dominant supplier of a bulk chemical used in the production of pharmaceuticals. Another undertaking had purchased supplies of the chemical for manufacturing purposes but was refused further supplies when Commercial Solvents decided to expand into the market for the finished product. The Court held the refusal to be an abuse. By refusing to supply the raw material, Commercial Solvents had, in effect, removed its main competitor. In subsequent cases, such as *United Brands*,[148] refusals to supply that did not seek to eliminate, but which were likely to adversely affect competitors, have

---

142 [2004] OJ L24/1.

143 Commission Decision 87/500/EEC *BBI/Boosey & Hawkes (Interim Measures)* [1987] OJ L286/36; [1988] 4 CMLR 67.

144 Commission Decision 77/327/EEC *ABG*, [1977] OJ L117/1. On appeal Case 77/77 *Benzine Petroleum Handelmaatschappij BV v Commission* [1978] ECR 1513.

145 [1994] 1 BCLC 245.

146 Case 322/81, [1983] ECR 3461, para 10. The 'special responsibility' concept has seen resurgence in the CJEU's jurisprudence in contemporary cases like Case T-201/04 *Microsoft v Commission* [2005] ECR II-1491.

147 See Cases 6 and 7/73 *Commercial Solvents v Commission* [1974] ECR 223.

148 See Case 27/76 *United Brands Continental BV v Commission* [1978] ECR 207.

fallen foul of Art 102. In *United Brands*, the mere fact that a distributor had been involved in a competitor's promotional campaign did not justify the refusal to supply that distributor.

An overzealous reaction to a new competitor may also be seen as abusive. In *BBI/Boosey & Hawkes*,[149] an established manufacturer of brass band instruments refused to supply one of its existing distributors after that distributor started producing competing instruments. The Commission was of the opinion that a dominant undertaking can take steps to defend itself when faced by new competition, but those steps must be proportionate to the threat. In this case, the new competitor's level of production was such that an outright refusal to supply was disproportionate. Obviously, it will be difficult for a dominant undertaking to decide how to react to new competition in these circumstances. The interpretation of the proportionality doctrine can be very difficult. Two distinct types of refusal to deal can be indentified from the cases. The first, described as 'primary line injury', is where the competitor who would be damaged or deterred is on the same level of the market as the undertaking refusing to deal, as in *United Brands* and *BBI*. The second, described as 'secondary line injury', is where the competitor is at a different level of the market from the undertaking refusing to deal, as in the secondary, finished product, market in *Commercial Solvents*.

A refusal to supply an entirely new customer may also be classified as a refusal to deal. This would be the case when a supplier already provides such supplies or services to other customers but refused to extend supplies to a potential new customer. Once the dominant supplier has created a market in the product, an unjustified refusal to deal with a new customer may be abusive where it could damage or deter an actual or potential competitor. An example of such circumstances can be seen in *Sea Containers v Stena Sealink – interim measures*,[150] where Sea Containers sought access to Holyhead Port, which was owned and used by Sealink, but also by other ferry operators.

New markets and essential facilities

The next controversial area is the refusal to supply a new customer where supply would open up a new market where there has been no previous competition. This is particularly problematic when the supply of the goods or service would allow the new customer to compete with the dominant undertaking in a secondary market where there is no existing competition. The development of the law in this area has been complex and confusing. Many of the early cases, which developed some of the key concepts, may now be better understood as unique decisions, falling on their own facts, or as 'refusal to deal' cases, as discussed above. In light of their developmental importance, however, we shall discuss them in this section. It was only after more recent cases, such as *Oscar Bronner*,[151] that it became possible to draw distinctions more clearly between the different situations.

Most of the cases in this area have dealt with the refusal to supply a service. In a number of early cases the Court went some way towards holding that a dominant undertaking acts abusively if it fails to help a new competitor enter the market, but did little to indicate in which circumstances this would be required. An example is *London-European/Sabena*,[152] where Sabena was held to be abusing its position by refusing London-European access to its computerised reservation system. London-European wished to introduce an air service, in competition with Sabena, between London and Brussels. To compete effectively, London European needed access to Sabena's reservation system. The Commission decided that access to the system was essential for any competition to develop and, therefore, refusal of access to the service was an abuse. A similar

---

149 Commission Decision 87/500/EEC, [1987] OJ L286/36; [1988] 4 CMLR 67.
150 Commission Decision 94/19/EC *Sea Containers v Stena Sealink – interim measures* [1994] OJ L15/8.
151 Case C-7/97 *Oscar Bronner GmbH and Co KG v Mediaprint Zeitschriftenverlag GmbH and Co KG* [1998] ECR I-7791.
152 Commission Decision 88/589/EEC [1988] OJ L317/47; [1989] 4 CMLR 662.

decision was seen in *British Midland/Aer Lingus*.[153] This was the starting point for a number of cases where competitors have been granted access to what has become known as an 'essential facility', particularly where competition would not be possible without access. The inception of the 'essential facility' concept can be traced back to a number of US antitrust cases, notably *Terminal Railroad*[154] and *Associated Press*;[155] however, its place in US antitrust is still highly controversial, there being little agreement on its proper meaning.[156] Nevertheless, it became clear that the Commission, under Art 102, was keen to develop a European version of the doctrine.

In *Sealink/B & I – Holyhead: Interim Measures*,[157] the nature of an essential facility was demonstrated. Sealink owned the port of Holyhead and operated ferry services from it. The port was deemed to be an essential facility and Sealink was forced to grant B & I, a competing ferry operator, access on a non-discriminatory basis. Ports, such as the one at Holyhead, are good examples of the kind of facility to which access is vital to allow competition to develop, but the case itself is not a very good example of the doctrine in operation. Sealink had already granted B & I access to the facility; the dispute was focused on discriminatory access rather than refusal to grant access at all. It is, therefore, possible to read this decision as falling within the 'refusal to deal' category above, where Sealink had failed to fulfil its 'special responsibility' to an existing customer by discriminating without objective justification. While there is still debate over the proper understanding of the decision in *Sealink/B & I*, it was clearly the first step in the process, which led to a fuller exposition of an essential facility doctrine in Art 102.[158]

The Court clarified its position on a new competitor's access to an essential facility in *Oscar Bronner*.[159] The publisher of an Austrian daily newspaper, Bronner, sought access to a dominant rival's newspaper home-delivery system. The Court set out the conditions upon which the essential facilities doctrine could be invoked as follows:

i   the facility must be indispensable to carrying on the entrant's business, in that there are no potential substitutes;

ii   there must be technical, legal, or economic obstacles which make it impossible or un reasonably difficult to replicate the facility; and

iii the refusal must not be objectively justified.

The Court was of the view that there were no such obstacles to Bronner, alone or in co-operation with other publishers, in setting up an alternative distribution system. It was also made clear that it was not enough to argue that the alternative service would not be economically viable given the low circulation of Bronner's newspaper.[160] The Court's clarification in *Bronner* has, in effect, significantly reduced the potential scope of the essential facilities doctrine to situations in which it would be very difficult to replicate the indispensable facility. By bringing the relevant cases together it is now possible to set out a three-stage test for the use of the essential facility doctrine:

---

153 Commission Decision 92/213/EEC *British Midland/Aer Lingus* [1992] OJ L96/34.
154 *United States v Terminal RR Ass'n*, 224 US 383 (1912).
155 *Associated Press v United States*, 326 US 1 (1945).
156 The classic discussion of the early US cases can be found in Areeda, P, 'Essential Facilities: An Epithet in Need of Limiting Principles' (1989) 58 Antitrust LJ 841. The leading US cases are now *Aspen Skiing* 472 US 585 (1985) and *Trinko* 540 US 398 (2004).
157 [1992] 5 CMLR 255.
158 See, for example, Ridyard, D, 'Essential Facilities and the Obligation to Supply Competitors under the UK and EC Competition Law' [1996] ECLR 438. See also Müller, U and Rodenhausen, A, 'The Rise and Fall of the Essential Facility Doctrine' [2008] ECLR 310.
159 Case C-7/97 *Oscar Bronner GmbH and Co KG v Mediaprint Zeitungs und Zeitschriftenverlag GmbH and Co KG* [1998] ECR I-7791.
160 See Bergman, MA, 'The *Bronner* Case – a Turning Point for the Essential Facilities Doctrine' [2000] ECLR 59.

i   the facility must be indispensable to carrying on the entrant's business; there must be
      no potential substitutes and it must be impossible or unreasonably difficult to replicate;
ii   the refusal would exclude any effective competition on a neighbouring market; and
iii the refusal must not be objectively justified.

These cases can be distinguished from 'refusal to deal' cases in that the owner/creator of the
facility has not already allowed other competitors access, and therefore has not already allowed
a market for the facility to develop, arguably, they are not now required to create such a market
through their 'special responsibility' as a dominant undertaking unless these very specific conditions are met.[161]

This judgment in *Bronner* was a significant restriction compared to some of the more hyster-
ical predictions which followed the Court's judgment in the *Magill* case,[162] which itself was
further complicated by the introduction of intellectual property issues. There was also academic
argument that the essential facilities doctrine in *Bronner* was very different from the IP doctrine
developed in *Magill*, but following the *IMS* case[163] it is clear that *Bronner* and *Magill* are closely
related, and that the existence of an IP right simply adds a further complication to the essential
facility problem.

Intellectual property rights

The coexistence of IP rights and competition law has always been problematic. Intellectual property rights encourage innovation by rewarding the innovator with exclusivity, but that may in turn
become statutory dominance, which may be abused. Article 102 TFEU makes an attempt to
balance the various goals. It has always been held that the ownership of an IP right was not, in
itself, an abuse but that the use of such a right may amount to one.[164] One area where abuses have
been found is in relation to the refusal to grant licences of IP rights. One of the most important
cases concerned the licensing of copyright in TV listings. Magill, an Irish company, wished to
publish a weekly TV guide listing all the programmes which could be viewed in the Republic of
Ireland. Those programmes included those broadcast by RTE, the national Irish station, the BBC
and ITV. All three broadcasters published weekly guides of their own programmes and licensed
newspapers to publish daily listings. The broadcasters all refused to grant Magill a licence to
publish a weekly listing. This refusal meant that no comprehensive guide existed and consumers
were forced to purchase three separate weekly guides. The Commission held that the broadcasters
had abused their dominant positions by preventing a new product, the comprehensive guide, from
reaching the market[165] and using their copyright in the listings beyond the purpose for which the
right was granted. On appeal, the Court concentrated on the fact that the broadcasters were
denying consumers a product for which there was demand.[166] In addition, they were attempting
to reserve a secondary market – TV guides being a secondary market to broadcasting – for
themselves by denying others the basic information required.

---

161 This is difficult to reconcile with cases like Commission Decision 92/213/EEC *British Midland/Aer Lingus* [1992] OJ,
      L96/34, but perhaps if the Commission revisited them in light of *Bronner* they would be decided differently.
162 Commission Decision 89/205/EEC *Magill TV Guide/ITP, BBC & RTE* [1989] OJ L78/43, and Cases C-241 & 242/91P *RTE
      and Others v Commission* [1995] ECR I-743.
163 Case C-418/01 *IMS Health GmbH v NDC Health GmbH* [2004] ECR I-5039.
164 Case 24/67 *Parke, Davis & Co v Probel* [1968] ECR 55.
165 Commission Decision 89/205/EEC *Magill TV Guide/ITP, BBC & RTE* [1989] OJ L78/43; [1989] 4 CMLR 757.
166 Cases C-241 and 242/91P *RTE and Others v Commission* [1995] ECR I-743. For further consideration of the area, see Case
      T-504/93 *Tierce Ladbroke v Commission* [1997] ECR II-923.

Two subsequent disputes, *IMS*[167] and *Microsoft*,[168] illustrate the potential conflicts between Art 102 and IP law. The *IMS* and *Microsoft* cases both involve IP licensing, albeit in different ways. In *IMS*, a dispute before the German courts that was the subject of a preliminary ruling, an undertaking which had developed a system of 1,860 geographical areas, known as 'bricks', which segmented the German market for pharmaceuticals and enabled the undertaking to produce usage statistics, challenged the argument that its failure to license potential competitors to use the 'brick' system was abusive. In the *Microsoft* Decision, the Commission, confirmed on appeal by the CFI, required the dominant work group server operating system supplier, Microsoft, to disclose complete and accurate interface documentation to allow non-Microsoft work group servers to be fully interoperable with Windows PCs and servers. To the extent that such a disclosure requires the licensing of IP rights, Microsoft should receive reasonable remuneration. Both the decisions of the Court of Justice, in *IMS*, and the Court of First Instance, in *Microsoft*, are heavily dependent on the reasoning in *Bronner*. It appears, therefore, that cases involving refusal to license IP will be treated as similar to essential facility cases. This is presumably because the existence of the IP right means that the right holder always has the right to refuse to supply, as that right is implicit within the grant of an IP right, unless there are very strong competition reasons for requiring the licence. As the right holder has an implicit justification for refusing to license, these cases cannot fall into the 'refusal to deal' category discussed above, and are treated differently to other essential facility cases. The Courts have effectively combined the three elements of the essential facility test in *Bronner*, with the 'new product' requirement, which is unique to IP, from *Magill*. The test, as set out in *Microsoft*,[169] is as follows:

i   the refusal relates to a product or service indispensable to the exercise of a particular activity on a neighbouring market;
ii   the refusal is of such a kind as to exclude any effective competition on that neighbouring market;
iii the refusal prevents the appearance of a new product for which there is potential consumer demand; and
iv   the refusal is not objectively justified.

The *Micosoft* judgment also went some way to explaining how a number of the controversial elements of the test should be applied.[170] It made it clear that in relation to the second criteria it is only necessary to show that the refusal is 'is liable to, or is likely to, eliminate all effective competition on the market'.[171] The most controversial element of the *Magill/IMS* test has always been the 'new product' criteria. This essentially delimits the protection an IP right receives. The holder can refuse to license the IP right where the competitor will simply replicate the right holder's provision, but how new does a new product need to be? The CFI in *Microsoft* made it clear that problems may arise 'where there is a limitation not only of production or markets, but

---

167 Commission Decision 2002/165/EC *NDC Health/IMS Health: Interim Measures* [2002] OJ L59/18, subsequently withdrawn; Commission Decision 2003/174/EC, [2003] OJ L268/69; and Case C-418/01 *IMS Health GmbH v NDC Health GmbH* [2004] ECR I-5039.
168 Commission Decision 2007/53/EC *Microsoft* [2007] OJ L32/23. On appeal, Case T-201/04 *Microsoft v Commission* [2007] ECR II-3601.
169 At paras 331–334.
170 The *IMS* and *Microsoft* cases have generated an enormous amount of literature. A few of the more balanced examples are: Killick, J, '*IMS* and *Microsoft* Judged in the Cold Light of *IMS*' (2004) 1(2) CompLRev 23; Ahlborn, C and Evans, DS, 'The *Microsoft* Judgment and its Implications for Competition Policy towards Dominant Firms in Europe', (2009) 75(3) Antitrust LJ 887, and Andreangeli, A, 'Interoperability as an "Essential Facility" in the *Microsoft* Case – Encouraging Competition or Stifling Innovation?' (2009) 34(4) ELRev 58.
171 At para 563.

also of technical development'.[172] It is now clear that those seeking supply must show that the refusal denies them the opportunity to supply a new product or market, or to innovate in the way they provide products or services.

The Microsoft case may have helped to clarify some of the legal questions surrounding competition law's relationship with IP law, but it has not lead to any reduction in the potential for complex new questions to arise. The Commission have undertaken a number of investigations into high-tech and new-economy markets.[173] It is highly likely that knowledge-based industries, which are characterised by high sunk costs, low manufacturing costs, network effects and IP rights, will be a significant challenge for competition law, which has largely developed in the context of more traditional physical manufacturing markets, in the future. New-economy markets often feature a cyclical process of 'competition for the market' in which one product will 'win' the market for one generation of the product cycle and assume a dominant position. Competition on the market may then appear very limited until the next generation of products again enter a robust period of competition to establish the next winner or 'killer app' in a constantly iterating process. Competition law has traditionally seen competition as rather more static ('competition on the market') and has not yet established useful models of this 'dynamic' ('competition for the market') process of competition. The Commission has, largely through negotiation with undertakings, been grappling with these problems, but so far the Court has had little opportunity to develop the law in this area.[174]

State Intervention in the Market and Article 102 TFEU

Most EU Member States have 'mixed economies', in that the State may intervene in industries that are considered 'essential' to the national economy. State intervention, however, does not sit well with a literal interpretation of Protocol No 27 to the TFEU on the internal market and competition, which sets out that the 'EU includes a system ensuring that competition is not distorted'. The involvement of Member States in their national economy will inevitably distort competition to some extent.[175] The intervention of Member States will also be a particular problem as this could lead to markets being organised within national boundaries, thereby hampering the operation of the internal market. However, as market regulation, intervention or involvement is so well recognised, and even protected to a degree by Art 345 TFEU,[176] it is not directly challenged. Although there is no direct challenge to state regulation, there have been ways in which the Commission has used the Treaty to ensure that competition is distorted to the least extent possible.

The main limit on the behaviour of states within EU law is enshrined in Art 4(3) TEU. Article 4(3) obliges Member States to abstain from adopting measures that could jeopardise the attainment of the objectives of the Union. The Commission can enforce this obligation through

---

172 At para 647.
173 See, for instance: Commission Press Release, 'Antitrust: European Commission welcomes Apple's announcement to equalise prices for music downloads from iTunes in Europe', IP/08/22, 9 January 2008; Commission Press Release, 'Antitrust: Commission probes allegations of antitrust violations by Google' IP/10/1624, 30 November 2010; and Commission Press Release, 'Antitrust: Commission sends Statement of Objections to Microsoft on non-compliance with browser choice commitments', IP/12/1149, 24 October 2012.
174 For discussion of the issues in this area see, Messina, M, 'Article 82 and the New Economy: Need for Modernisation?' (2006) 2(2) CompLRev 73, and Graham, C and Smith, F, *Competition, Regulation and the New Economy* (2004) Oxford: Hart Publishing. See also forthcoming judgment by the General Court in relation to Case T-286/09 *Intel*.
175 For a comprehensive discussion of many of these issues, see Szyszczack, E, *The Regulation of the State in Competitive Markets in the EU* (2007) Oxford: Hart.
176 Art 345 TFEU provides that nothing in the Treaties shall prejudice the ownership of property. This has been taken to cover the purchase of property, or industries, by states themselves.

Art 258 TFEU where the actions of Member States threaten to distort competition. This general power is expressed more clearly in Art 106(1) TFEU, in relation to 'public undertakings and undertakings to which Member States grant special or exclusive rights'. Member States are required to 'neither enact nor maintain in force any measure contrary to the rules contained in the Treaties'. This provision is unusual in that it relies, for its effect, on other Articles of the Treaties. Despite referring specifically to Arts 18 and 101 to 109 TFEU, Art 106(1) also applies to all the other provisions of the Treaties. Article 106(1) also gives a special defence to undertakings that have been granted 'special or exclusive rights' from challenge under the competition rules.

Article 106(2) deals with situations in which undertakings are 'entrusted with the operation of services of general economic interest or having the character of a revenue-producing monopoly'. It is clear from this provision that such undertakings are subject to the competition rules, but only so far as the rules do not obstruct the 'particular tasks assigned to them'. This creates another potential defence for undertakings involved in some sectors of the economy where they are assigned a particular role by the State. The Commission has published a Communication on 'A Quality Framework for Services of General Interest in Europe'.[177]

Article 102 TFEU has been applied most frequently in relation to state measures. Its application is usually in conjunction with Art 106(1) TFEU, which deals with public undertakings[178] or undertakings granted special or exclusive rights.[179] It is obvious how the granting of special or exclusive rights to an undertaking may bring it within the concept of dominance under Art 102. While it was considered that EU law did not challenge the grant of such rights,[180] it was assumed initially that they were designed to deal with state measures that required undertakings with such rights to act in an abusive manner. This view was challenged in a number of cases in the early 1990s.

In *Höffner & Elser v Macrotron*[181] the Court considered the grant of exclusive rights in the employment procurement market to a public undertaking, the Federal Employment Office. The Court of Justice decided that the grant of an exclusive right would breach Arts 102 and 106(1) TFEU if the existence of that right would inevitably lead to an abuse under Art 102. This would be the outcome if the agency which was granted special rights could not satisfy demand while other competitors were barred from the market. The Court appeared to go further in *Porto di Genova*[182] when it suggested that there would be a breach not only where the undertaking in question cannot avoid abusing its dominant position, but also 'when such rights are liable to create a situation in which that undertaking is induced to commit such abuses'. However, in *Carra and Others*,[183] a case with similar facts to *Höffner*, the Court set out three cumulative criteria in order to establish a breach. Those criteria are:

i the public placement offices are manifestly unable to satisfy demand on the market for all types of activity;

ii the actual placement of employees by private companies is rendered impossible by the maintenance in force of statutory provisions; and

iii the placement activities in question could extend to the nationals, or the territory, of other Member States.

---

177 Communication from the Commission on A Quality Framework for Services of General Interest in Europe, COM(2011) 900 final.
178 Undertakings owned or controlled by the State.
179 'Exclusive rights' are defined in Art 2(f) of Directive 2006/111/EC on the Transparency of Financial Relations Between Member States and Public Undertakings As Well As On Financial Transparency Within Certain Undertakings, [2006] OJ L318/17.
180 Case 155/73 *Sacchi* [1974] ECR 409.
181 Case C-41/90 [1991] ECR I-1979.
182 Case C-179/90 *Merci Convenzionali Porto di Genova v Siderurgica Gabrielli SpA* [1991] ECR I-5889.
183 Case C-258/98 *Giovanni Carra and Others* [2000] ECR I-4217.

Therefore, where there is a necessary link between the grant of the right and the existence of an abuse the grant of the right can be challenged under Arts 106(1) and 102.

A second type of application of Arts 106(1) and 102 is evident in relation to the nature of special or exclusive rights granted by the Member State. This application of the provision allows the grant of such a right to be challenged but this time on a somewhat different basis. In *RTT v GB-Inno*,[184] the Court held that the extension of the monopoly on the public telephone market into the secondary market for the approval of equipment was a breach of Art 106(1). The Court so held on two grounds: firstly, the extension would have been an abuse of a dominant position as RTT could use its monopoly power to eliminate competitors from a secondary market; and secondly, Art 106(1) prohibits Member States from putting such undertakings 'in a position which the said undertakings could not themselves attain by their own conduct without infringing Art [102]'.

The reasoning in *RTT* was explained further by the Court in *Corbeau*,[185] in relation to the inclusion of express courier services within the Belgian postal monopoly. The Court interpreted Art 106(1) alongside Art 106(2), and was of the opinion that the reservation of the secondary market was inherently abusive and contrary to Art 106.[186]

State regulation and undertakings

Article 106(2) TEFU contains provisions that relate directly to undertakings that are 'entrusted with the operation of services of general economic interest or having the character of revenue producing monopolies'. The Article states that the competition rules apply to those undertakings but only in so far as 'the application of such rules does not obstruct the performance, in law or in fact, of the particular task assigned to them'. There is also the general proviso that trade should not be affected in a manner which is contrary to the interests of the EU. This is, in effect, a defence against the application of the competition rules in favour of undertakings given special responsibilities by the State. It is important that the undertaking has been 'entrusted' with the operation of the service by a Member State.[187]

As it is a defence, or derogation, from the competition rules, the Court has construed Art 106(2) TFEU very narrowly.[188] Before the defence is available the Court requires the anti-competitive behaviour to be necessary for the performance of the tasks assigned, not that it merely facilitates the performance of those tasks. That issue was considered by the Court in *Corbeau*.[189] Corbeau had set up an alternative express postal service in Liège and was prosecuted under Belgian law for breach of the postal monopoly system and he claimed, in his defence, that Belgian law was contrary to Art 106. The Court considered whether the reservation of the postal services to the national postal monopoly was necessary for the performance of its tasks. It would appear that the defence will only be available when a service of general economic importance is threatened by competitors who can 'cherry-pick' the profitable sectors of the business without bearing the costs involved in operating the general service. Competition will be allowed to operate in as many areas as possible unless the general service is threatened.[190]

---

184 Case C-18/88 [1991] ECR I-5941.
185 Case C-320/91 [1993] ECR I-2533.
186 See, also, Case C-260/89 *ERT v DEP* [1991] ECR I-2925.
187 Commission Decision 85/77/EEC, *Uniform Eurocheques* [1985] OJ L35/43.
188 Case 127/73 *BRT v SABAM* [1974] ECR 313. See, also, Case T-128/98 *Aéroports de Paris v Commission* [2000] ECR II-3929.
189 Case C-320/91 [1993] ECR I-2533.
190 See, also, Case C-340/99 *TNT Traco SpA v Poste Italiane SpA* [2001] ECR I-4109.

Control of Abuse of Dominance in the UK

Introduction

The remainder of this chapter shall focus on the Competition Act 1998 Chapter II prohibition and key aspects of the enforcement practice and case law under that prohibition in the UK. However, to understand the current legislative framework, one has to gain an outline appreciation of the nature of the Fair Trading Act (FTA) 1973 and the reform proposals that led to the 1998 Act, including the Chapter II prohibition.

Prior to 1998, the Fair Trading Act 1973 was the most important provision in UK anti-monopoly laws, although there was continued debate regarding its reform and/or replacement by new rules. Broadly speaking, the 1973 Act established an investigative system to look at 'monopolies' and at markets where there was some form of 'market failure', but there was no provision for deterrent effect, no prohibition of conduct as such, and no effective sanctions, as the 1973 Act merely required a consideration of the public interest impact of the 'monopoly' market.

The Conservative Government finally decided, in 1996, to introduce legislation to reform UK competition law and published a DTI consultation document followed by an explanatory document and draft Bill.[191] In 1997, the Labour Government, almost immediately upon election, published a new explanatory document and draft Bill, which formed the basis of the Competition Act 1998.[192] The Competition Act 1998 provided a new prohibition on the abuse of a dominant position based on the then Art 82 EC. However, at this stage, the FTA 1973 was retained due to the perceived advantages of flexibility and pragmatism under its provisions for control of structural and complex monopolies. One of the principal reasons was its suitability for dealing with problems in oligopolistic markets. This was later repealed and superseded by the set of provisions in part IV of the Enterprise Act 2002 on market investigations, as discussed in Chapter 5.

The Competition Act 1998 – the Chapter II prohibition

Part I of the Act introduces two new prohibitions based on Arts 101 and 102. These are known respectively as the Chapter I and Chapter II prohibitions. The Chapter II prohibition is in respect of abuse, by an undertaking or undertakings, of a dominant position in the UK. The Chapter II prohibition is contained in s 18 of the Act, which contains virtually identical provisions to those contained in Art 102 TFEU. Section 18(1) provides that 'any conduct on the part of one or more undertakings which amounts to the abuse of a dominant position in a market is prohibited if it may affect trade within the United Kingdom'. The only difference is that s 18 refers to a dominant position and the effect on trade within the UK. With the exception of debates on the introduction of a predatory pricing provision for the newspaper industry, there was little technical debate in Parliament during progress of the Competition Bill. The key statutory provision, s 18, like Art 102, is fairly succinct and the absence of any definition of key concepts is notable.[193] This absence was remedied to a certain extent by the publication, after consultation, of a wide range of guidelines on the application of the prohibition, and these have more recently been adopted by the CMA. Furthermore, consistency of interpretation with EU law, Art 102 in this context, is ensured by s 60 of the Act. Section 60 provides that the determination of any questions in relation to the

---

191 Department of Trade and Industry, *Tackling Cartels and the Abuse of Market Power: Implementing the Government's Policy for Competition Law Reform, a Consultation Document*, March 1996, London: DTI; and *Tackling Cartels and the Abuse of Market Power: A Draft Bill, an Explanatory Document*, August 1996, London: DTI.

192 Department of Trade and Industry, *A Prohibition Approach to Anti-Competitive Agreements and Abuse of a Dominant Position: Draft Bill*, August 1997, London: DTI. The subsequent Bill, which had its first reading in the House of Lords on 15 October 1997, was amended in certain respects from the original draft Bill.

193 See interpretation section, s 59 of the Competition Act 1998.

prohibitions should be consistent with the treatment of corresponding questions arising under EU law. This provision clearly ensures that EU case law on what constitutes an abuse of a dominant position will be followed to the extent that it is relevant in a national context. It is also clear from UK enforcement practice, notably from judgments by the Competition Appeal Tribunal, that EU case law is routinely relied on as underpinning the interpretation of the domestic prohibition.

Enforcement

Chapter III makes provision for the investigation and enforcement of the Chapter I and II prohibitions, and the EU prohibitions in Arts 101 and 102 TFEU. As noted in Chapter 2, the key role of enforcing and applying the two sets of prohibitions in the UK is undertaken by the CMA. Section 25 of the 2002 Act provides that the CMA may conduct an investigation upon reasonable suspicion that any of those prohibitions has been infringed. The powers of investigation provided under ss 26–29 are similar to those powers afforded to the Commission under Arts 18–21 of Regulation 1/2003.[194] Similarly, the CMA is required under s 31 to give persons affected by a proposed decision on whether the prohibition has been infringed an opportunity to make representations.[195] The CMA may make interim measures under s 35, and is empowered to require conduct in breach of the prohibition to be modified or terminated.[196] Section 36 provides for the imposition of a fine of up to 10% of the worldwide turnover of an undertaking whose conduct infringes the Chapter II prohibition. There is a detailed discussion in Chapter 2 on the fining policy and practice under the 1998 Act to date. Where conduct infringing the prohibition is of 'minor significance', there is immunity from the imposition of any fines under s 40.

The Competition Appeal Tribunal (CAT), established by s 12 and Sch 2 to the Enterprise Act 2002, acts as an appeals tribunal in relation to decisions made, primarily by the CMA, in respect of the Chapter II prohibition, the mechanism for appeals being regulated by Sch 8 to the 1998 Act. Third parties with a sufficient interest may also appeal. The CAT has already made a significant contribution to the interpretation and application of the Chapter II prohibition, and its judgments are available on the CAT website.[197] Appeals against CAT judgments may be made, on a point of law, to the Court of Appeal, Court of Session or Court of Appeal in Northern Ireland in respect of England and Wales, Scotland and Northern Ireland, respectively.

Consistency with EU law

Section 60(1) of the 1998 Act provides that:

> The purpose of this section is to ensure that so far as is possible (having regard to any relevant differences between the provisions concerned), questions arising under this Part in relation to competition within the United Kingdom are dealt with in a manner which is consistent with the treatment of corresponding questions arising in EU law in relation to competition within the European Union.

The basic rule, stemming from the overall objective of introducing a set of rules harmonised with EU law and minimising the risk of a double burden on UK business, is that the Chapter II

---

194 See Guidance on the CMA's investigation procedures in Competition Act 1998 Cases, CMA8, March 2014. Sections 42–44 of the 1998 Act create certain offences in relation to the obstruction of the information gathering tasks under these provisions.
195 See Chapter 2.
196 Under s 33. Section 34 provides that this may be enforced by a court order.
197 At www.catribunal.org.uk. See Bailey, D 'The Early Case Law of the Competition Appeal Tribunal' Chapter 2 in Rodger, B (ed), *Ten Years of UK Competition Law Reform* (2010) Dundee: DUP.

prohibition should be interpreted consistently with the interpretation of Art 102 TFEU.[198] Section 60(2) provides that a court (which includes any court or tribunal for these purposes) must act with a view to ensuring that its decisions are consistent with the jurisprudence of the Court of Justice. Furthermore, courts are to have regard to any relevant decision or statement of the Commission.[199] The requirement of consistency applies equally to decisions by the CMA in relation to the prohibitions. Section 60 contains the important proviso that consistency should be achieved, 'in so far as is possible (having regard to any relevant differences between the provisions concerned)'. This permits departure from EU law principles, but the scope of the proviso is rather limited.[200] It was introduced primarily to avoid the application of EU principles designed to further particular EU objectives which would be irrelevant for domestic purposes, primarily the attainment of the internal market. It should be noted, in the context of the Chapter II prohibition, that the application of Art 102 has not been greatly influenced by the integration imperative although there has been case law in relation to abuses, such as prohibiting imports[201] and discriminatory refusals to supply on the basis of nationality.[202] The CAT's treatment and application of EU jurisprudence in appeals under the Chapter II prohibition has generally been thorough and impressive. In its judgments on key issues, such as relevant market, dominance and abuse, following submissions from the parties, the Tribunal sets out its findings by commencing with an outline of the relevant law, derived primarily from EU Court pronouncements. These outlines provide readers with an excellent summarised account of the development of EU juris-prudence.[203] As discussed below, there were numerous examples of the interpretation and appli-cation of the Chapter II prohibition in the light of the s 60 requirement for consistency with EU law in the relatively recent aftermath of the introduction of the 1998 Act prohibitions. However, more recently, as public enforcement of the Chapter II prohibition has been relatively limited, opportunity to consider the application of the prohibition by the CAT has been restricted and most of the recent case law has involved private enforcement in the civil courts by parties seeking remedies in reliance on the prohibition.

Practice and case law to date

The following subsections will look at the application of the Chapter II prohibition in the UK (often in parallel with Art 102 TFEU) by focusing on CAT judgments, other public enforcement practice, and case-law of the civil courts in dealing with claims (or defences) based on an abuse of dominance.

To date, there have been a number of decisions taken under the Chapter II prohibition, and these are available on the public register of decisions available on the OFT and CMA websites.[204] This decision-making transparency facilitates understanding of practice under the prohibition. This includes decisions by other regulators and also decisions, following an investigation, finding

---

198 See Middleton, K, 'Harmonisation with Community Law: The Euro Clause', Chapter 2 in Rodger, BJ and MacCulloch, A (eds), *The UK Competition Act: A New Era for UK Competition Law* (2000) Oxford: Hart, and Rayment, B, 'The Consistency Principle: Section 60 of the Competition Act 1998' Chapter 4 in Rodger, B (ed), *Ten Years of UK Competition Law Reform* (2010) Dundee: DUP.

199 Competition Act 1998, s 60(3). This will extend to Commission Decisions and Notices published indicating Commission practice.

200 See, for example, *Pernod Ricard v Office of Fair Trading* [2004] CAT 10, where s 60 was held to apply to issues of procedural fairness. See Bailey, D, 'The Impact of Pernod v OFT on Section 60 and the Enforcement of UK Competition Law' [2004] Comp Law 153.

201 See Case 226/84 *British Leyland v Commission* [1986] ECR 3263.

202 See, generally, Sufrin, B, 'The Chapter II Prohibition', Chapter 6 in Rodger and MacCulloch, above, n 197.

203 *Napp Pharmaceutical Holdings Ltd v DGFT* [2002] CAT 1, [2002] ECC 13.

204 At www.oft.gov.uk and www.gov.uk/government/organisations/competition-and-markets-authority.

that there has been no infringement of the prohibition.[205] While there have been infringement findings by regulators, particularly in relation to abusive behaviour by English Welsh and Scottish Railways ('EWS') by the Rail Regulator,[206] the dearth of infringement decisions and frequency of non-infringement decisions by the various sectoral regulators,[207] particularly by OFCOM in relation to various pricing practices by BT, is notable. The OFT, the predecessor to the CMA, also made numerous non-infringement decisions,[208] but at least in the early years of the prohibition it also made several prominent infringement decisions, as discussed below. In this section, we will focus on key examples of the jurisprudence of the CAT.[209] An appeal can be made against an infringement or a non-infringement decision, and although not all decisions are appealed, it is evident that many of the early infringement decisions were. More recent practice has also involved appeals against non-infringement decisions. The CAT has dealt with many cases, but only one Chapter II case has gone to the Court of Appeal: the *Albion Water/Dwr Cymru* saga, discussed further below.[210]

The Tribunal has dealt with a number of issues pertaining to the application of the Chapter II prohibition, including the general role of EU jurisprudence: identifying what constitutes an undertaking; the determination of the relevant market; the establishment of dominance; and, also, what constitutes an abuse, as illustrated in the following cases.

Napp Pharmaceuticals Ltd v DGFT

The first infringement decision was taken against *Napp*;[211] the DGFT imposed a fine of £3.21m. Napp had a persistently high market share, well in excess of 90% in the market for sustained release morphine tablets and capsules in the UK. The abusive behaviour adopted by Napp included predatory discounting of drugs sold to hospitals. Discounts in excess of 90% were made available in some circumstances, particularly where there was a potential competitor. The DGFT followed the case law of the EU Courts, in particular *AKZO*, when discussing predation.[212] Napp was also found to be charging excessive prices to community customers, where Napp charged a 40% premium above its nearest rival while still maintaining a 90%-plus market share. The price to community customers was ten times that charged to hospitals. It was considered that this price was well in excess of that which would be expected in normal competitive conditions. It is interesting that there was a finding of excessive pricing in this first infringement Decision under the Act, as the European Commission has struggled to support findings of excessive pricing since the 1970s.[213] The Tribunal confirmed the finding of abuse, based on excessive prices, but paid greater attention to the predatory pricing abuse, setting out the principles established in

---

205 See, for instance, Rodger, B, 'Early steps to a mature competition law system: case law developments in the first eighteen months of the Competition Act 1998' [2002] ECLR 52.

206 ORR Decision, *English Welsh and Scottish Railway Limited*, 17 November 2006. This was followed by an ultimately unsuccessful claim for damages against EWS before the CAT under s 47A of the 1998 Act (see Chapter 3), in *Enron Coal Services Ltd in Liquidation v EWS* [2009] CAT 36, aff'd on appeal [2011] EWCA Civ 2.

207 See for instance ORR Decision, *DB Schenker Rail (UK) Ltd*, 2 August 2010.

208 See, for instance, OFT Decision CA98/07/2003; Case CP/1761/02 *EI Du Pont de Nemours & Company and Op Graphics (Holography) Ltd*, 9 September 2003, in which the OFT did not consider there was an abuse in relation to a complaint concerning a refusal to supply by a dominant company. See also OFT Decision CA98/05/2004; Case CP/0361–01, *First Edinburgh/Lothian*, 29 April 2004 where fare reductions did not constitute abusive predatory pricing; and OFT Decision, Case CE/9322/10 *Alleged abuse of a dominant position by IDEXX Laboratories Limited*, November 2011 (OFT1387).

209 See Bailey, D, 'The Early Case Law of the Competition Appeal Tribunal', Chapter 2 in Rodger, B (ed), *Ten Years of UK Competition Law Reform* (2010) Dundee: DUP.

210 [2008] EWCA Civ. 536.

211 *Napp Pharmaceutical Holdings Ltd and Subsidiaries (Napp)*, Decision CA98/2/2001, 30 March 2001. On appeal *Napp Pharmaceutical Holdings Ltd v DGFT* [2002] CAT 1. See, also, OFT Decision CA98/05/2004; Case CP/0361–01 *First Edinburgh/Lothian*, 29 April 2004 in relation to alleged predatory pricing in commercial bus services in Greater Edinburgh.

212 Case C-62/86 *Commission v AKZO* [1991] ECR I-3359, although it was interesting that the DGFT did not rely on the more recent decision in Case T-228/97 *Irish Sugar plc v Commission* [1999] ECR II-2969.

213 See, for example, Case 26/75 *General Motors Continental NV v Commission* [1975] ECR 1367.

AKZO, Tetra Pak II,[214] *Compagnie Maritime Belge*[215] and *Irish Sugar.*[216] The Tribunal stressed that the 'special responsibility' of a dominant undertaking was particularly onerous where, as with Napp's high and persistent market shares, the company enjoyed a position of 'dominance approaching monopoly' or 'super-dominance'. In line with *Tetra Pak II* and *AKZO*, Napp's pricing at below cost was presumed to be an abuse. Moreover, the principles set out in *Compagnie Maritime Belge* and *Irish Sugar* demonstrate that selective discounting by a super-dominant undertaking, without any objective justification which tends to eliminate competition, is an abuse. This judgment clearly applied EU jurisprudence widening the net of predatory pricing beyond below cost pricing, at least where super-dominance is involved, in accordance with s 60 of the Act.[217] Nonetheless, the CAT reduced the fine payable by Napp to £2.2m.

Aberdeen Journals Ltd v DGFT

In the second formal Decision that the Chapter II prohibition had been infringed, a penalty of over £1.3m was imposed on Aberdeen Journals Ltd for breach of the Chapter II prohibition in respect of predation, by incurring losses for selling advertising space in an attempt to expel its only local rival.[218] Following its first hearing in Scotland, the Tribunal set aside the original Decision on the basis that the treatment of the relevant product market was inadequate, and remitted the matter to the DGFT. A second Decision against Aberdeen Journals, on an almost identical basis to the first Decision, was also appealed to the Tribunal. The relevant market issue was particularly complicated as in essence the allegation was that Aberdeen Journals was using its free weekly journal as a fighting title to protect its sister paper, the daily paid-for *Evening Express*, from the new entrant, *The Independent*, by reducing its advertising prices. In order for Aberdeen Journals to be considered as dominant, its two titles would have to be deemed to be in the same relevant market. This was the focus of considerable debate between the parties, particularly on the issue of whether the two titles were complementary or substitutes for the purposes of advertisers. Ultimately, the Tribunal determined, on the basis of, *inter alia*, Aberdeen Journals' commercial strategy and the characteristics of the products, that the products were in potential competition for the business of local advertisers. The abuse issue was complicated even though the Tribunal relied on the EU jurisprudence on predatory pricing. The Tribunal considered that pricing below average variable cost by Aberdeen Journals was prohibited as predatory pricing. However, the Tribunal recognised that there were difficulties, both on the facts of the case and in guidance from the EU case law, in determining the precise approach to quantifying costs for the purpose of ascertaining the existence of predatory pricing. In any event, the Tribunal stressed that the cost-based predatory pricing rules were not to be applied mechanistically and that, as the Act sought to prevent dominant companies from strengthening their position by ways that were different from those under normal competitive conditions, the Chapter II prohibition applied to Aberdeen Journals' predatory pricing strategy. Despite confirming the infringement finding, the CAT reduced the fine imposed on Aberdeen Journals to £1m.

BetterCare II

In this case[219] the Tribunal decided that a Northern Irish health and social services trust (N & W) was engaged in economic activities, and, therefore, constituted an undertaking for the purposes

---

214 Case T-83/91 *Tetra Pak International v Commission* [1994] ECR II-755; and Case C-333/94P *Tetra Pak International v Commission* [1996] ECR I-5951.
215 Case T-24–26, 28/93 *Compagnie Maritime Belge Transport NV v Commission* [1996] ECR II-1201; [1997] 4 CMLR 273.
216 Case T-228/97 *Irish Sugar plc v Commission* [1999] ECR II-2969; [1999] 5 CMLR 1300.
217 See Kon, S and Turnbull, S, 'Pricing and the Dominant Firm: Implications of the Competition Commission Appeal Tribunal's Judgment in the *Napp* case' [2003] ECLR 70.
218 [2003] CAT 11.
219 Case 1006/2/1/01 *BetterCare Group Ltd v DGFT* [2002] CAT 7.

of the Chapter II prohibition, in running its statutory residential homes and engaging in the contracting out of social care to independent providers. BetterCare had appealed against an OFT Decision that the prohibition had not been infringed following BetterCare's complaint that N & W was abusing its dominant position as the sole purchaser of residential and nursing care home services from BetterCare by offering unreasonably low contract prices. The Tribunal considered a wide range of EU jurisprudence[220] on the controversial issue of when a public body constitutes an undertaking for these purposes. The Tribunal concluded that N & W's purchasing activities satisfied the test of whether the body was 'engaging in economic activities'. Subsequently, the OFT decided that N & W's conduct was not abusive as it did not set the prices in any event.[221] More generally, the OFT issued a policy note advising that it was unlikely to take enforcement action against public bodies engaged in the purchasing and provision of goods and services for non-economic purposes. This approach was largely justified by the Court of Justice's subsequent judgment in *AOK Bundesverband*, which provided further clarification of when a public body constitutes an undertaking for the purposes of competition law enforcement.[222]

Genzyme Ltd v OFT

In *Genzyme*, the DGFT, in March 2003, decided that Genzyme had abused its dominant position in the market for the supply of drugs in the UK for the treatment of Gaucher disease, a rare inherited disorder, and that Genzyme had breached the Chapter II prohibition.[223] Genzyme had a dominant position in the supply of the drug, Cerezyme, which it supplied to the NHS. Genzyme had abused its position by making the NHS pay a price for the drug where the price included home delivery of the drug and homecare service. This practice resulted in a margin squeeze for other potential homecare service providers, thereby preventing competition and reducing choice for consumers and the NHS. This was considered to be a serious infringement of the prohibition and Genzyme was fined £6.8m. Genzyme appealed to the CAT, which upheld the earlier finding that without any objective justification Genzyme had adopted a pricing policy which effectively resulted in a margin squeeze and foreclosed competition in the downstream market for provision of healthcare services.[224] Nonetheless, the CAT reduced the fine imposed on Genzyme to £3m.[225]

Burgess v OFT

This case involved an alleged abuse of a dominant position by the refusal by Austins, a firm of funeral directors in Hertfordshire, which also owned and ran the Harwood Park crematorium in Stevenage, to allow access to Burgess, another firm of funeral directors in Hertfordshire, to the crematorium. Burgess complained to the OFT in January 2002, and a long procedure ensued, including three failed applications by Burgess for interim measures, before the OFT finally adopted its Decision to reject the substance of the complaint on 29 June 2004. Burgess appealed to the CAT, which delivered its judgment on 6 July 2005.[226] The Tribunal set aside the OFT's

---

220 See discussion earlier in this chapter regarding the issue of 'undertakings' under Art 102 TFEU.
221 OFT Decision CA98/09/2003, Case CE/1836–02 *Bettercare Group Ltd/North & West Belfast Health & Social Services Trust*, 18 December 2003.
222 Policy note 1/2004, 'The Competition Act 1998 and public bodies', January 2004, OFT 443. See Case T-319/99 *FENIN v Commission* [2003] ECR II-357; on appeal Case C-205/03 P, [2006] ECR I-06295. See Cases C-264/01, C306/01, C-354/01 and C-355/01 *AOK Bundesverband* [2004] ECR I-2493.
223 DGFT Decision CA98/3/03, Case CP/0488–01 *Exclusionary Behaviour by Genzyme Ltd*, 27 March 2003.
224 *Genzyme Ltd v OFT* [2004] CAT 4. The CAT delivered a subsequent judgment in relation to the appropriate remedy, including a draft direction, [2005] CAT 32.
225 In a subsequent follow-on action (which ultimately settled out of court), the CAT awarded interim damages, pending quantification of actual losses to the claimant, of £2m (*Healthcare at Home v Genzyme Ltd* [2006] CAT 29).
226 *Burgess and Sons v OFT* [2005] CAT 25.

Decision on a number of grounds including its analysis of the relevant geographic market and abuse issues. Furthermore, the Tribunal adopted its own decision on the issues of dominance and abuse, first considering that Austins/Harwood Park had a dominant position in at least the Stevenage/Knebworth area in the supply of crematoria and funeral directing services. In relation to abuse, the Tribunal referred to *Genzyme* and reiterated the previous jurisprudence of the EU Courts in relation to refusal to supply, notably *Hoffmann-La Roche, Michelin, Commercial Solvents* and, in particular, *Oscar Bronner*,[227] to distil the key propositions to be applied in this area.[228] The Tribunal was clearly satisfied that the refusal to allow access constituted 'recourse to methods different from those which condition normal competition', and that the protection or strengthening of Austins' dominant position for funeral directing services which resulted from the elimination, or serious weakening of, Burgess was not the result of competition on the merits. Furthermore, even if Harwood Park was not dominant in relation to crematoria services, the Tribunal applied the *Tetra Pak II* 'associative links' doctrine[229] to hold that Austins' actions would also constitute an abuse of its dominant position in the related funeral directing services market. It is instructive to quote the Tribunal's discussion of the scope of the abuse concept and the justifications for competition law intervention in the competitive process:

> We accept therefore that the OFT is correct, up to a point, in submitting that the aim of the Chapter II prohibition is not to protect competitors, but to protect competition. On the other hand, where effective competition is already weak through the presence of a dominant firm, there are circumstances in which competition can be protected and fostered only by imposing on the dominant firm a special responsibility under the Chapter II prohibition not to behave in certain ways vis-à-vis its remaining competitors, particularly where barriers to entry are high. In such circumstances the enforcement of the Chapter II prohibition may in a sense 'protect' a competitor, by shielding the competitor from the otherwise abusive conduct of the dominant firm. However, that is the necessary consequence of taking action in order to protect effective competition. In a case such as the present, intervention under the Chapter II prohibition should not therefore be seen, as the OFT seemed to suggest, as merely 'protecting a competitor', but from the point of view of the wider interest of preserving effective competition for the ultimate benefit of consumers. While Burgess is not entitled to be protected against normal market forces, it is in our view entitled under the Act not to be eliminated as an efficient operator in the market by the abusive practices of a dominant firm.[230]

Albion Water Ltd v Water Services Regulation Authority (Dwr Cymru/Shotton Paper)

This was an incredibly lengthy legal saga with a decision by the water regulator followed by numerous rulings by the CAT, an appeal to the Court of Appeal, and subsequently various stages of a successful follow-on damages action, again before the CAT.[231] The dispute arose out of a complaint by Albion Water Limited ('Albion') against Dwr Cymru Cyfyngedig ('Dwr Cymru')

---

227 Case 85/76 *Hoffmann-La Roche v Commission* [1979] ECR 461; Case 322/81 *Michelin v Commission* [1983] ECR 3461; Cases 6 and 7/73 *Commercial Solvents v Commission* [1974] ECR 223; and Case C-7/97 *Oscar Bronner v Mediaprint* [1998] ECR I-7791.
228 *Burgess and Sons v OFT* [2005] CAT 25, at para 311.
229 Case T-83/91 *Tetra Pak v Commission* [1994] ECR II-755, and Case C-333/94 P *Tetra Pak v Commission* [1996] ECR I-5951.
230 *Burgess and Sons v OFT* [2005] CAT 25, at para 312. It should be noted that Burgess raised a claim for damages against Austins before the CAT under s 47A of the 1998 Act, which settled in 2008.
231 See, *inter alia*, [2006] CAT 23, [2006] CAT 36, [2008] EWCA Civ 536, [2008] CAT 31 and [2013] CAT 6.

under the 1998 Act Chapter II prohibition in relation to the price quoted by Dwr Cymru for the common carriage of water across the relevant part of its network, claiming that the price constituted a margin squeeze and was discriminatory. Albion complained to the Authority, which, under the Water Act 2003, was the specialist regulator for the water industry and given powers to apply the 1998 Act. The Authority, in 2004, rejected the complaint, but on appeal, the CAT found that Dwr Cymru was dominant[232] and that it had abused that position by imposing a margin squeeze.[233] An appeal to the Court of Appeal by Dwr Cymru was rejected[234] and subsequently the CAT also held that the access price Dwr Cymru proposed to charge Albion for common carriage through its water pipe network was an excessive and unfair price which was abusive.[235] Following this outcome in the lengthy public enforcement process, Albion raised a claim for damages against Dwr Cymru in reliance on the CAT's Chapter II infringement findings. In 2013, it was awarded over £1.8m (plus interest) in damages as a result of the high and abusive price it paid to Dwr Cymru, leading to lost profits under one contract and the lost chance to win another potentially lucrative contract.[236]

Other public enforcement practice

As stressed above, not all competition authority decisions on the Chapter II prohibition have been appealed to the CAT and some of these merit brief consideration here. First, to demonstrate the importance of establishing all the prerequisites of an abuse of dominance, the OFT non-infringement decision in *Flybe* is notable.[237] Following a complaint from Air Southwest in 2009, the OFT opened an investigation under Chapter II of the Competition Act 1998 and/or Art 102 TFEU into alleged predatory entry by Flybe on the Newquay to London Gatwick route, in competition with Air Southwest's operations on its Plymouth to Newquay to Gatwick route. The OFT concluded that it had no grounds to take action against Flybe on the basis: that the OFT considered that Flybe was not dominant on the relevant market covering the Newquay to London Gatwick route; and that the absence of sufficient evidence that its intentions were predatory and not part of a normal and robust competitive strategy.

Since 2003, there have been only three Chapter II infringement decisions by UK competition authorities,[238] and none of these have been appealed to the CAT. The first was the 2006 decision by the ORR that English Welsh & Scottish Railways (EWS) had infringed the Chapter II prohibition and Art 102 in the market for the haulage of coal by rail in Great Britain by, *inter alia*, concluding contracts with industrial users of coal, the terms of which excluded competitors from the market, and discriminating against Enron Coal Services Ltd. The ORR applied a 35% discount to the penalty, taking into account EWS's co-operation, and imposed a fine of £4.1m.[239] This dispute did reach the CAT in a claim for damages, under s 47A of the 1998 Act, which was ultimately unsuccessful as the claimant failed to satisfy the requirements of causation.[240] The next infringement decision was in 2009 against Cardiff Bus. Following a complaint made by 2 Travel Group plc (2 Travel) that in response to its entry into the Cardiff bus market with a new no-frills bus service, Cardiff Bus introduced a similar service on the same routes and at similar times of day at a loss. Those 'fighting' services were withdrawn shortly after 2 Travel's exit from the

---

232 [2006] CAT 36.
233 Ibid.
234 [2008] EWCA Civ 536.
235 [2008] CAT 31. See also the CAT's final ruling on remedies in [2009] CAT 12.
236 [2013] CAT 6.
237 OFT Decision, Case MPINF-PSWA001 *Alleged abuse of a dominant position by Flybe Ltd*, OFT1286, 5 November 2010.
238 For these purposes, we are not including the infringement findings by the CAT as discussed above in *Burgess* and *Albion Water*.
239 See ORR Decision, *English Welsh and Scottish Railway Limited*, 17 November 2006.
240 *Enron Coal Services Ltd in Liquidation v EWS* [2009] CAT 36, aff'd on appeal [2011] EWCA Civ 2.

market. A full market analysis demonstrated that Cardiff Bus had a dominant position in the relevant markets. The OFT considered that there was an exclusionary intent on the part of Cardiff Bus and that its conduct over a ten-month period did not constitute 'normal competition on the merits', but was predatory and an abuse of its dominant position. However, s 40 of the 1998 Act provides limited immunity from financial penalties for conduct of minor significance in relation to infringements of the Chapter II prohibition where the annual turnover of the undertaking does not exceed £50 million. In this case Cardiff Bus benefited from immunity and no fine was imposed.[241] Cardiff Bus did not appeal but the case came before the CAT indirectly in a subsequent claim for damages by the liquidator of the complainant, 2 Travel. The CAT's award of damages, including an award of exemplary damages, was the first final damages award by the CAT although the sum awarded was considerably lower than the claim as a result of the CAT's detailed findings on causation and quantum of loss.[242] In 2011, The OFT found that Reckitt Benckiser had abused its dominant position, under the Chapter II prohibition and Art 102, in the market for the NHS supply antacid heartburn medicines by withdrawing and de-listing Gaviscon Original Liquid. Reckitt Benckiser had agreed to pay a penalty of £10.2m under an early resolution agreement,[243] and did not appeal the infringement finding to the CAT. It is interesting to note that the allegations were originally brought to the attention of the OFT following an investigation by BBC's *Newsnight* programme. There have been no subsequent infringement decisions involving the Chapter II prohibition (or Art 102) in the UK. One of the concerns behind the institutional reforms introduced by the ERRA13 was the perceived intransigence of the sectoral regulators in enforcing the 1998 Act prohibitions, but the impression given in this early phase of the CMA's existence is that it will continue to focus on, and prioritise, its enforcement activities in relation to cartels rather than abusive behaviour.

Chapter II before the courts

There have been a number of private court disputes in which the prohibition has been raised by one of the parties.[244] The first judgment on the substance of the Chapter II prohibition was delivered eight months after its introduction, on 2 November 2000, by Lawrence Collins J in the High Court, Chancery Division, in *Claritas (UK) Ltd v The Post Office and Postal Preference Service Ltd*.[245] This judgment was in the context of an action for an interim injunction to restrain the despatch of consumer preference questionnaires using the Royal Mail brand and logo throughout the UK by the Royal Mail. The Post Office owned 30% of Postal Preference Service Ltd (PPS), and Claritas, a company involved in procuring, supplying and analysing consumer information for a fee for businesses, claimed that this amounted to an abuse of the Royal Mail's dominant position. The key question was whether, at this interim stage, there was a serious issue to be tried. Different strands of EU jurisprudence were analysed. Firstly, the possibility of an abuse based on refusal to license IP rights was rejected as Claritas would not be excluded from the market because it could not use the Royal Mail logo.[246] Secondly, the application of the essential facilities doctrine was deemed inappropriate as Claritas retained full access to the postal

241 OFT Decision CA98/01/2008, Case CE/5281/04. *Abuse of a dominant position by Cardiff Bus*, 18 November 2008.
242 [2012] CAT 19. See discussion in Chapter 3.
243 See Chapter 2.
244 See Robertson, A, 'Litigating under the Competition Act 1998: The Early Case Law' [2002] Comp Law 335; Rodger, B, 'Competition Law Litigation in the UK Courts – A Study of All Cases to 2004' [2006] ECLR Parts I, II and III at 241, 279 and 341 and 'Competition Law Litigation in the UK Courts: A Study of All Cases 2009–2012' (2013) *Global Competition Litigation Review*, 6 (2) 55–67.
245 [2001] UKCLR 2. This was followed by the DGFT Decision in relation to the same dispute, *Consignia plc and Post Preference Service Ltd*, Decision CS 98/4/2001, 15 June 2001.
246 See Case T-68/89 *Radio Telefis Eireann v Commission* [1991] ECR II-485.

facilities. Finally, in any event, given that the alleged abuse was not in a market in which the Post Office was dominant, Claritas had failed to demonstrate that this situation fell within the scope of the *Tetra Pak II* requirement for close links between the dominant market and abuse market.[247] Although the application was dismissed, this early resort to the prohibition in private litigation demonstrated an awareness of the possibilities under the Act for aggrieved competitors. It is interesting to note the way that Lawrence Collins J applied the s 60 'consistency with Community law' requirement seamlessly applying EU jurisprudence to the Chapter II prohibition as the Act intended.

In *Attheraces Ltd v British Horseracing Board*, the claimant, which supplied websites, TV channels, and other media relating to British horse racing, alleged that the defendant, which had a central role in the organisation and promoting of British horse racing and which kept a computerised database of pre-race data, including the date and place of the race meeting, name of the race, list of horses entered, etc., had abused a dominant position and thereby infringed both Art 82 EC and the Chapter 2 prohibition. BHB effectively held a monopoly in the provision of the pre-race data and it was held in the High Court that it had abused its dominant position by excessive, unfair and discriminatory pricing.[248] It was held, following the Court's jurisprudence on refusal to supply, that the pre-race date constituted an 'essential facility', essential to ATR's business, and that a constructive refusal to supply was caught by the prohibitions. Referring to court case-law on excessive and discriminatory pricing, the price was excessive in comparison to the cost to BHB plus a reasonable return, and discriminatory in being markedly higher than the sum normally charged to other broadcasters. On appeal, this ruling was overturned by the Court of Appeal, which was sceptical about Art 82 EC/Chapter II becoming a general provision for the regulation of prices.[249] The Court stated that exceeding cost was a necessary but not a sufficient test for abuse of dominance, there was little evidence that competition on the market was being distorted by BHB's demands and that the value to ATR of the pre-race data was relevant in determining whether the price was excessive. Furthermore, differential pricing was not necessarily abusive, and prices essentially were dependent on market forces. Accordingly, BHB's pricing strategy was not abusive and the Court of Appeal clearly advocated a restrained approach to court involvement in claims of excessive or discriminatory pricing.

The two most significant subsequent cases have both involved abusive behaviour by airport operators.[250] In *Purple Parking Ltd v Heathrow Airport Ltd*,[251] Mann J in the High Court held that the defendant airport operator had abused its dominant position by changing existing arrangements to effectively exclude 'meet and greet' car park operators from the airport terminal forecourts while maintaining its own 'meet and greet' operations there. Mann J undertook a comprehensive analysis of the existing EU (and UK) jurisprudence on the essential facilities doctrine and margin squeeze abuse. However, the defendant's 'pigeon-hole' approach whereby a claim should fit within the category of essential facilities or fail was not accepted by Mann J:

> a court is entitled to look at conduct, and ask the overall question of whether there is an abuse by reference to various ways of committing that abuse, and is not forced to find one single appropriate label to that abuse . . . and apply some test only applicable to that form.[252]

---

247 Case C-333/94P [1996] ECR I-5951.
248 [2005] EWHC 3015 (Ch) Ch D.
249 [2007] EWCA Civ 38, CA.
250 See also *Arriva Scotland West Ltd v Glasgow Airport Ltd* [2011] CSOH 69.
251 [2011] EWHC 987 (Ch).
252 Ibid at para 102.

The claimant's claim was based on an allegation of the application of dissimilar conditions to equivalent transactions, resulting in anti-competitive behaviour, and this was upheld on the basis of the effect on consumers. It was stressed that commercial justification did not constitute an objective justification for abusive behaviour, and the objective justification arguments based on security and congestion were rejected on the facts; it was clear that the airport operator was motivated by an anti-competitive intent. In *Arriva The Shires Ltd v London Luton Airport Operations Ltd*,[253] ATS had a concession agreement with the operator of Luton Airport ('Luton Operations') to carry passengers (over 1 million a year) on the 757 bus service from the airport direct to London Victoria. Following a tender process, the concession was awarded to a rival bus operator. ATS claimed that Luton Operations was dominant in the market for granting rights to operate bus services and that they had abused it in two ways: 1) the tender procedure in awarding the new concession was unfair, and 2) through the abusive terms contained in the award of the new concession to the rival bus operator. The first part of the claim was unsuccessful as the tender process was fair, but the seven-year exclusive period awarded to the successful tender bid operator was deemed to be abusive. The analysis and application of the abuse and objective justification in this judgment merits further analysis. It was noted that exclusionary abuses fall into two categories, where the dominant under-taking: a) competes on the downstream market and is acting to foreclose that market to its own advantage;[254] or b) distorts competition on the upstream market between itself and its competitors by entering contracts with customers to buy exclusively from the dominant undertaking.[255] This case clearly did not fall within the second category but Rose J rejected the defendant's assertion that to fall within the first category, the dominant undertaking had to derive a competitive advantage or commercial benefit through the exclusionary conduct; for instance, by using its dominance in one market to improve its own position in a downstream market.[256] Clearly, Luton Operations were not active on the downstream bus services market, but in any event they gained important commercial and financial advantages from the concession which gave them a percentage of revenue earned by the bus operator. Rose J also held that the grant of an exclusive right to the bus route for a lengthy period of seven years affected competition on that downstream market and was anti competitive. This reasoning is analogous with European Commission decisions in relation to the grant of media rights to broadcast football matches over an extended period.[257] As in *Purple Parking*, it was stressed that the objective justification defence was not available simply where a business decision was commercially rational; prohibited abusive conduct normally invariably furthers the business interests of the dominant undertaking.[258] Both these cases demonstrate a robust approach to abusive conduct and a restrictive approach to defences based on the objective justifica-tion for dominant undertakings' business decisions. Nonetheless, in practice claimants have often struggled to satisfy all the elements required for a successful abuse of dominance claim.[259]

Key Points

- Article 102 TFEU prohibits the abuse of a dominant position that affects trade between Member States. The relevant market is identified in order to determine if an undertaking has

---

253 [2014] EWHC 64 (Ch).
254 See *Commercial Solvents v Commission* [1974] ECR 223. This is also the type of abuse involved in *Purple Parking*.
255 See, for instance, Case C-549/10 P *Tomra Systems ASA v Commission* [2012] ECR I-0000.
256 See, for example, Case T-128/98 *Aeroports de Paris v Commission* [2000] ECR II-3939, and *SEL-Imperial Ltd v The British Standards Institution* [2010] EWHC 854 (Ch).
257 See Commission Decision, Case COMP/38173, *Joint Selling of the Media Rights to the FA Premier League*, 22 March 2006.
258 *ATS*, above, n 252, para 133.
259 See, for instance: *PIK Facilities Ltd v Watson's Ayr Park Ltd* (2005) CSOH 32; *Chester City Council v Arriva plc* [2007] EWHC 1373 (Ch); and, *BHB Enterprises Ltd v Victor Chandler International Ltd* [2006] EWHC 1074 (Ch).

sufficient power to be considered as a dominant undertaking on that market. However, a dominant position alone is not prohibited, and some form of abusive behaviour is required.

● A wide range of types of market behaviour can be deemed as abusive and the test for determining what constitutes abusive behaviour is very general and open-ended. Although we should be wary of pigeonholing, the competition authorities and courts have focused on certain types of conduct as abusive where it excludes or forecloses actual or potential competition from the market. In particular, there has been considerable focus on certain pricing strategies: discounts and rebates, predatory pricing and margin squeezes; and, refusals to supply a product/service, IPR or essential facility.

● The European Commission has published Guidance on its Enforcement Priorities under Art 102. This is an important document to guide businesses and their advisers and focuses on the concept of the 'as efficient competitor' cost-basis for identifying many types of abusive behaviour. Notwithstanding the Commission guidance the case law and principles established by the Court of Justice remain of primary authoritative value.

● The UK introduced the Chapter II prohibition, modelled on Art 102, in s18 of the Competition Act 1998 which came into force on 1 March 2000. Section 60 of the 1998 Act requires the prohibition to be interpreted by UK competition authorities and courts in a way that is consistent with the interpretation of Art 102 TFEU. The Chapter II prohibition extends the prohibition on abuse of dominance to local markets which would not satisfy the EU law effect on inter-state trade criterion.

Discussion

1   Why is the identification of the relevant market crucial for laws dealing with market power or monopoly?

2   Is dominance prohibited? When does the concept of super-dominance apply and what difference, if any, does it make?

3   To what extent do Art 102 TFEU and the Chapter II prohibition restrict the ability of companies to compete effectively, in particular in relation to their competitive pricing strategies? Can and should dominant companies be allowed to meet and beat competitors' prices?

4   To what extent do you agree with the proposition that the development of the law in relation to refusals to supply/essential facilities, particularly in the *Microsoft* judgment, stifles incentives to innovate?

5   Given that Art 102 TFEU applies throughout the EU and in certain circumstances is enforced by the UK's NCA, the CMA, what scope is there for the application of the Chapter II prohibition?

Further Reading

Article 102 TFEU

General

Azevedo, JP and Walker, M, 'Dominance: Meaning and Measurement' [2002] ECLR 363.

Colomo, PI, 'The Law on Abuses of Dominance and the System of Judicial Remedies' (2013) *Yearbook of European Law* 32(1) 389–431.

Gormsen, L, 'Article 82 EC, Where are We Coming from and Where are We Going?' (2005) 2(2) CompLRev 5.

Nazzini, R, *The Foundations of European Union Competition Law: The Objective and Principles of Article 102*, (2011) Oxford: OUP.

Veljanovski, C, 'Markets Without Substitutes: Substitution Versus Constraints as the Key to Market Definition' [2010] 31(3) ECLR 122.

Witt, A, 'The Commission's Guidance Paper on Abusive Exclusionary Conduct- More Radical Than it Appears?' (2010) 35 EL Rev 214.

Pricing strategies

Gal, MS, 'Below-Cost Price Alignment: Meeting or Beating Competition? The *France Telecom* Case' [2007] ECLR 382.

Jones, A and Lovdahl Gormsen, L, 'Abuse of Dominance: Exclusionary Pricing Abuses', Chapter 10 in Lianos and Geradin, *Handbook on European Competition Law, Vol 1* (2013) Edward Elgar.

Mateus, AM, 'Predatory Pricing: A Proposed Structured Rule of Reason' (2011) 7(2) Euro CJ 243–267.

Ridyard, D, 'Exclusionary Pricing and Price Discrimination Abuses under Article 82 – An Economic Analysis' [2002] ECLR 286.

Refusal to supply/essential facilities

Ahlborn, C and Evans, DS, 'The *Microsoft* Judgment and its Implications for Competition Policy towards Dominant Firms in Europe' (2009) 75(3) Antitrust LJ 887.

Andreangeli, A, 'Interoperability as an "Essential Facility" in the *Microsoft* Case – Encouraging Competition or Stifling Innovation?' (2009) 34(4) ELRev 58.

Bergman, M, 'The Bronner Case – A Turning Point for the Essential Facilities Doctrine' [2000] ECLR 59.

Hou, L, 'The Essential Facilities Doctrine – What was Wrong in Microsoft?' (2012) 43(4) IIC 451–471.

Killick, J, 'IMS and Microsoft Judged in the Cold Light of IMS' (2004) 1(2) Comp LRev 23.

Müller, U and Rodenhausen, A, 'The Rise and Fall of the Essential Facility Doctrine' [2008] ECLR 310.

Chapter II prohibition

Kon, S and Turnbull, S, 'Pricing and the Dominant Firm: implications of the Competition Commission Appeal Tribunal's Judgment in the Napp Case' [2003] ECLR 70.

Nazzini, R, 'A Welfare-based Competition Policy under Structuralist Constraints: Abuse of Dominance and OFT Practice', Chapter 5 in Rodger, B (ed), *Ten Years of UK Competition Law Reform* (2010) Dundee: DUP.

Sufrin, B, 'The Chapter II Prohibition', in Rodger, BJ and MacCulloch, A (eds), *The UK Competition Act: A New Era for UK Competition Law* (2000) Oxford: Hart.

Chapter 5

Market Investigations

Overview

- The system for market investigations is set out in Part 4 of the Enterprise Act 2002. It is based on the traditional model of UK competition law, pre-dating the Competition Act 1998, allowing for comprehensive (and fairly lengthy) investigations into markets where they are not working effectively, with a view to ensuring better and more effective future competition in the interests of consumers.
- Following the Enterprise and Regulatory Reform Act 2013, the two main phases of a market investigation are both undertaken by the Competition and Markets Authority. The CMA Board may make a market investigation reference and the subsequent market investigation, report and remedies phase will be undertaken by a CMA Panel group.
- Market investigations do not lead to fines or follow-on damages actions. The remedies which can be imposed may be either structural or behavioural to ensure more effective competition in the relevant market for the future.
- There is the possibility of judicial review by the Competition Appeal Tribunal of any aspect of the decision-making process in relation to market investigations.

Introduction

This chapter will provide a detailed consideration of the market investigations scheme in the United Kingdom. This is a unique set of rules which have evolved in the UK to play a significant role alongside the 'classic' or traditional competition law prohibitions of the type exemplified by the Chapter I and II prohibitions and Arts 101 and 102 TFEU. Although the provisions have been considerably modified by the Enterprise Act 2002 and the Enterprise and Regulatory Reform Act 2013, the market investigations scheme embodies the traditional UK approach to competition law.[1] Essentially, market investigations do not determine whether behaviour is legal or illegal; the process does not focus on the attribution of blame nor impose sanctions for past conduct. The broad purpose of the market investigation system is to determine whether the process of competition is working effectively in markets as a whole. This is reflected in the approach to remedies which generally focus on ensuring better, more effective competition in markets for the future in the interests of consumers. Accordingly, there are no fines and no scope for private enforcement where parties seek remedies for an 'infringement'. The remedies which are imposed may be structural or behavioural and can result in considerable burdens for businesses. Moreover, the system has become more legalistic as a result of the availability of, and frequent resort to, judicial review of all aspects of the process before the Competition Appeal Tribunal. Most importantly, market investigations have had an impact on vast areas of everyday life and society in the United Kingdom, and continue to play a significant role in ensuring that consumers benefit from effective competition in markets. The chapter will outline the historical development of market investigations, then provide an overview of the institutions and processes. The CMA's role in undertaking market studies and market investigation references will precede a discussion of the market investigation and remedial process. There will be a discussion of examples of the experience in undertaking market investigations followed by consideration of judicial review by the Competition Appeal Tribunal.

---

1 See Wilks, SRM, *In the Public Interest: Competition Policy and the Monopolies and Mergers Commission* (1999) Manchester: MUP.

History

The roots of the market investigation system can be traced to the first general competition legislation in the UK: the Monopolies and Restrictive Practices (Inquiry and Control) Act 1948. Subsequently, in 1973, the Fair Trading Act contained a detailed set of provisions for monopoly investigations. These were renamed 'market investigations' and subject to a revised set of institutions, tests and processes set out in Part 4 of the Enterprise Act 2002. The institutional structure, together with other aspects of the market investigation system under the 2002 Act, was subsequently revised by the Enterprise and Regulatory Reform Act 2013.

During the late 1980s and 1990s there was considerable debate on reform of UK competition law, as outlined in Chapter 1.[2] Ultimately, when the Competition Act 1998 was introduced, the Restrictive Trade Practices Act 1976 was repealed, but the Fair Trading Act 1973, with its investigative system for mergers and 'monopoly' was retained. However, these investigative systems were replaced by the provisions in Parts 3 and 4 of the Enterprise Act 2002. A similar administrative enforcement framework as under the 1973 Act was retained for market investigations, although the DGFT's functions were transferred to the OFT. The role of the Secretary of State was considerably limited, and the role of the Competition Commission (CC) was enhanced by providing that it should determine the appropriate remedies. The OFT would decide whether to make a market investigation reference to the CC,[3] and after a period of investigation, the CC would compile a report and had a duty to take action to remedy any adverse effects on competition identified in its report. Despite considerable change in the statutory language adopted, the basic purpose of market investigations under the 2002 Act was broadly similar to that of 'monopoly investigations' under the 1973 Act. The term 'monopoly investigation' was a misnomer, as both single firm and complex monopoly situations could be referred;[4] the modern terminology of 'market investigations' would have been more appropriate, as virtually all such investigations looked at practices across a market, rather than the behaviour of an individual business.[5] The Enterprise and Regulatory Reform Act 2013 maintained the same set of substantive rules for market investigations, but introduced some revisions, notably in relation to the institutions involved. As discussed in Chapter 1, the 2013 Act introduced the unitary competition authority in the UK, the CMA, which as of 1 April 2014 assumed the tasks previously undertaken by both the OFT and the Competition Commission. This was driven primarily by arguments based on resources and efficiency on the basis of criticisms that the prior regime was too slow and involved duplication of tasks between the OFT and the CC. The CMA can avoid duplication in evidence-gathering, while maintaining separation between the two stages of decision-making. The tasks of the OFT and CC will be undertaken by the Markets and Mergers Directorate of the CMA Board and CMA panel groups respectively. Given the limited changes in substance, and to ensure continuity and consistency, the CMA has adopted the existing main guidance documents by the OFT and CC in relation to market investigations,[6] and published additional guidance on the operation of the provisions post-ERRA13.[7] There has been no practice to date under the new provisions, but in a later section we will look at market investigation practice

---

2   See, for instance, Whish, R, 'The Competition Act 1998 and the Prior Debate on Reform', in Rodger, BJ and MacCulloch, A, *The UK Competition Act: A New Era for UK Competition Law* (2000) Oxford: Hart.

3   The reporting panel of the Competition Commission assumed the functions of the Monopolies and Mergers Commission under the FTA 1973 from 1 April 1999.

4   Where a single firm had a market share of at least 25%, and complex monopoly situations (where a set of independent firms, with an aggregate market share of at least 25%, so conducted their affairs as to prevent, restrict or distort competition) See FTA s 6.

5   Though see further below re the *BAA* market investigation.

6   Market Studies: *Guidance on the OFT approach* (OFT519), *Market investigation references* (OFT511), and *Guidelines for market investigations* (CC3 (revised)).

7   January 2014 CMA3 *Market Studies and Market Investigations: Supplemental Guidance on the CMA's approach.*

under the Enterprise Act 2002 provisions, albeit in a different institutional context, and also, given the broad similarity with earlier legislation, to certain reports completed by the Monopolies and Mergers Commission (MMC) and CC under the 1973 Act.

Institutions and Processes

Initiation

Competition and Markets Authority

Information is gathered by the staff of the CMA Board, Markets and Mergers Directorate, using a variety of research methods. For market investigations, initial information may come from complaints by aggrieved competitors or as a result of inquiries by parliamentary committees. In addition, s 11(1) of the 2002 Act introduced a fast-track complaints procedure for 'super-complaints' submitted by designated consumer bodies about market factors which may be significantly harming consumers' interests; this has already proved to be a valuable source of information in initiating proceedings.[8] Designated consumer bodies (such as Which? or Citizens Advice) may make 'super complaints', whereupon the CMA has 90 days to respond publicly to the complaint, indicating what action it intends to take (such as launching a market study or referring the market for investigation by the Competition Commission) in relation to the complaint and its reasons for doing so. A number of markets have been referred for a market investigation following a super-complaint, for example, *Payment Protection Insurance*[9] and *Northern Ireland Banking*.[10]

Under s 5 of the 2002 Act the CMA has the function of acquiring information necessary for it to undertake its tasks. The CMA may undertake a study of a particular market to ascertain whether it is working well for consumers. This has become the established starting point for subsequent market investigation references. The CMA Board will decide whether to launch a market study, by issuing a market study notice where there is a concern that a particular market is not working well.[11] There have been a considerable number of market studies undertaken, for instance, those in relation to *UK airports*,[12] *Personal Current Accounts in the UK*[13] and *Home Building in the UK*.[14] A market study may lead to undertakings in lieu of a reference or a market investigation reference. For example, a market study into store card services led to a full market investigation and very critical report.[15] A market investigation reference is made by the CMA, certain sectoral regulators or, in limited circumstances, the Secretary of State, and is followed by a market investigation by a CMA Panel Group. The CMA has considerable investigatory powers under s 174 of the Act, including the following: to require the attendance of parties to give evidence; to require the production of specified documents; and to require the supply of specified information, including estimates and forecasts.

The Secretary of State

Following DTI proposals to reduce ministerial influence and involvement in UK competition law, [16] the Enterprise Act 2002 removed the Secretary of State's authority to make any 'monopoly' investigation references and confined the ministerial role to cases involving an exceptional public

---

8 OFT 514, *Super-Complaints: Guidance for Designated Consumer Bodies*.
9 OFT896, *Payment Protection Insurance*, October 2006.
10 OFT976, *Personal current account banking services in Northern Ireland*, May 2005.
11 Chapter 2 of *Market Studies: Guidance on the OFT approach* (OFT519).
12 OFT912, *BAA*, April 2007.
13 OFT1005, *Personal Current Accounts in the UK*, July 2008.
14 OFT1020, *Homebuilding in the UK*, September 2008.
15 See OFT Press Release, 47/04, 'OFT refers store cards to Competition Commission', 18 March 2004.
16 *Productivity and Enterprise: A World Class Competition Regime*, Cm 5233, 31 July 2001.

interest, those involving national security, as set out in Chapter 2 of Pt 4 of the Act. The ERRA 2013 significantly amended the process whereby the Secretary of State can intervene in market investigation cases. There are two types of public interest reference: a full public interest reference, meaning the CMA investigates the public interest issue and the competition issues concurrently; and a restricted public interest reference, meaning the CMA will investigate the competition issues but the Secretary of State considers the public interest issue. The Secretary of State may issue an intervention notice at any point between the publication of a market study notice and the decision whether or not to commence a market reference. An intervention notice may only be issued to the CMA if the Secretary of State considers that one or more public interest considerations are salient to the market study being undertaken.[17] National security is the only specified public interest consideration in relation to the markets regime; however, further categories may be specified through secondary legislation. In market studies where an intervention notice has been issued, the CMA does not have the power to make a market reference or publish its study report. Rather it must make its market study report directly to the Secretary of State within 12 months of the intervention notice being issued. At that stage, the Secretary of State will decide whether it is appropriate to make one of the two kinds of public interest references set out above. This reference decision will be published by the Secretary of State. The Secretary of State is also able to modify by order certain provisions of the EA02, for example, the time limits that apply to market studies, market investigations and the remedies implementation period. Following the ERRA 2013, Ministers also have a reserve power to make references under s 132 of the EA02 where, in addition to the normal criteria for making a market investigation reference a minister is 'not satisfied' with a CMA decision not to make a reference or has not done so within a reasonable period. For reasons of space, this complicated set of provisions will not be considered further in this chapter.

Investigation and reporting

In April 1999 the Competition Commission (CC) replaced the Monopolies and Mergers Commission (MMC) in undertaking market investigations, a task which was taken on by panels of Competition Commission members. Upon receiving a reference, usually four or five members, but a minimum of three, were to form an inquiry group. This role has been taken over by the CMA, in particular panel groups of the CMA panel. The ERRA13 makes detailed provision on the constitution of the CMA panel and panel groups to undertake market investigations, with each CMA group to consist of at least three members of the CMA panel.[18] Subject to slight modifications, the constitution and work of the CMA panel will be similar to that of its predecessor, the Competition Commission, and the main stages of inquiries are as follows:

1   gathering information, including the issue of questionnaires;
2   hearing witnesses;
3   verifying information;
4   providing a statement of issues;
5   considering responses to the statement of issues;
6   notifying parties of and publishing provisional findings;
7   notifying and considering possible remedies;
8   considering exclusions from disclosure; and
9   publishing reports.

---

17 Section 139(1) of the 2002 Act.
18 2013 Act Sch 4 Pt 3.

Enforcement

Prior to the Enterprise Act 2002, the CC could only make non-binding recommendations in its reports. The Enterprise Act 2002, in addition to reducing the significance of the Secretary of State's role, enhanced the role and range of tasks to be performed by the CC. The CC was afforded the power to receive undertakings from parties and to impose orders, as appropriate, following a report. The enforcement tasks now lie with the CMA panel group which has reported on the market investigation. The more drastic action of imposing an Order can be taken if undertakings are not agreed, if they are broken, or if the conduct is particularly serious. The powers provided are fairly exhaustive and include, for instance, publication or notification of prices, regulation of prices, prohibition of the acquisition of undertakings or assets, and the division of a business.

Review

There is provision in the 2002 Act for judicial review of any aspect of the market investigation process before the CAT[19] with the possibility of subsequent appeal to the Court of Appeal in England and Wales or Court of Session in Scotland.

A Market Investigation Reference

Under s 131 of the 2002 Act a market investigation reference may be made by the CMA where it has reasonable grounds for suspecting that any feature, or combination of features, of a UK market prevents, restricts or distorts competition. The reasonable grounds may be based on a market study, but this is not a pre-requisite. It is clear that the CMA has a discretion, rather than a duty, to make a reference.[20] Section 131(2) states that a market feature includes reference to market structures or any conduct of one or more parties supplying or acquiring goods or services in that market. In addition, the CMA will consider whether it would be more appropriate to deal with the competition issues under the 1998 Act.

Most references under the monopoly provisions of the 1973 Act concerned specified practices in a market and were not confined to a single company. Under the 1973 Act, the OFT, or Secretary of State for Trade and Industry, could refer a 'monopoly situation' to the CC for investigation. Scale or structural monopoly situations could be referred where at least 25% of the goods of any description were supplied in the UK by the same person. Complex or behavioural monopoly situations could be referred where at least 25% of the goods of any description were supplied to, or by, two or more persons who 'whether voluntarily or not, and whether by agreement or not' so conducted their respective affairs in any way to prevent, restrict or distort competition in the production or supply of those goods.[21] The complex monopoly provisions under the FTA 1973 were useful in providing for the possibility of oligopolistic markets being referred to the CC, allowing any problems or market failure in oligopolistic markets to be considered. A key factor in retaining the FTA 1973 'monopoly' provisions, alongside the 1998 Act prohibitions, was their effectiveness and adaptability when dealing with oligopoly issues. The 1973 Act provisions were repealed, but they have left a lasting legacy, both in the terminology of references under the Enterprise Act and the application of market investigations to industry-wide problems – such as the specified practices at the centre of the *Electrical Goods* report.[22] Similarly, market

---

19 Section 179 of the Enterprise Act 2002.
20 See OFT511, *Market investigation references*, July 2002.
21 Section 6(2) of the 1973 Act.
22 Monopolies and Mergers Commission, *Electrical Goods: A Report on the Supply in the UK of Washing Machines, Tumble Driers, Dishwashers and Cold Food Storage Equipment*, Cm 3676-I and II, 1997.

investigations have focused on industry-wide problems where the market is not working effectively, as opposed to the Chapter II prohibition which concentrates on the abuse of a dominant position. While most ordinary market investigation references relate to features across a particular market, normally involving a number of businesses, the *BAA* reference was relatively unusual in that it related to the ownership of several airports by one undertaking.[23]

There have been a considerable number of references in relation to a wide range of different markets over the last ten years, as outlined below. A reference may be avoided where an undertaking has been accepted in lieu of a reference under s 154 of the 2002 Act.[24] This is unlikely to be a regular practice because the requirement to negotiate as comprehensive a solution as is reasonable and practicable with a range of different undertakings across an industry is likely to be problematic. However, a reference will only be made where the CMA suspects that the adverse effects on competition are significant, taking into account any potential detriment to consumers in the form of higher prices, lower quality, less choice or less innovation. Factors indicating significance include the size of the market, the proportion of the market affected and the persistence of the anti-competitive feature.

The ERRA13 introduced a novel element to the UK's markets regime: cross-market references, although these references are likely to be relatively infrequent. These are references in respect of a specific feature, or features, of more than one market, which do not require the investigation of each of the affected markets in their totality.[25] The CMA must reasonably suspect that such a cross-market feature, or features, present in multiple markets prevents, restricts or distorts competition in connection with the supply or acquisition of goods or services in the UK, or a part of the UK. The CMA's functions may also be exercised by sectoral regulators with concurrent powers to make references under the Act.[26]

The EA02 reference test requires a 'prevention, restriction or distortion of competition' to be identified. The CMA must specify the goods or services in relation to which competition is adversely affected and this will require the relevant market to be defined. Thereafter, the CMA will consider a range of issues pertaining to market structure. Concentration is the obvious starting point, although in oligopolistic industries the CMA will look for a range of structural market features that are conducive to co-ordination, such as firm symmetries, market transparency and stable demand conditions. Other relevant market structure factors include entry conditions and barriers to entry, countervailing buyer power, and the existence of any regulations or government policies that impact upon competition. The CMA, as required under s 131(2), will also consider firms' conduct and, again with reference to oligopolistic markets, examine practices which facilitate or co-ordinate market activity, such as any history of pre-announcing prices. General industry custom and practice may also be relevant, as will the existence of networks of vertical agreements. Nonetheless, it should be stressed that at this stage the CMA merely identifies competition concerns that warrant fuller investigation.

Undertaking the Market Investigation

CMA Panel Groups have responsibility for reporting on market investigation references under the Act. One aspect of the monopoly controls under the FTA 1973, which was criticised in the

---

23 Competition Commission, 'BAA airports market investigation', 19 March 2009.
24 The term 'undertaking' used in this context is very different from the usage of the term in EU law or the 1998 Act. In the 2002 Act it is used to refer to commitments given by those on the market with regard to future conduct.
25 Section 131(2A) and (6) of the 2002 Act.
26 Further information on the concurrency regime is contained in CMA 10, *Regulated Industries: Guidance on concurrent application of competition law to regulated industries*, 12 March 2014.

past, was the apparent duplication of effort. Nonetheless, the system of reference and report by two separate authorities, OFT and CC, was maintained under the 2002 Act until the creation of the CMA by the ERRA13. If the CMA Board decides that a market investigation reference is to be made, it refers the matter to the CMA Chair, who is responsible for constituting the market reference group that will undertake the market investigation. In practice, these responsibilities will be delegated to the CMA Panel Chair (or one of the Deputy Panel Chairs). The market reference group appointed by the CMA Panel Chair is responsible for the conduct of a market investigation. The group must consist of at least three members selected from the CMA panel. The market reference group is required to decide whether there is an adverse effect on competition ('AEC') in the market(s) referred and, if so, whether and what remedial action is appropriate. A market investigation report must be completed within 18 months of the reference, subject to one possible extension of six months. The remedies implementation stage must be completed within six months of the market investigation report, although this may be extended by four months.

Upon receipt of a reference, the CMA Panel group will carry out detailed investigations of the market under reference, in a manner similar to the process undertaken over the years by Competition Commission groups, as follows:

1   evidence would be invited from all interested parties, including the main parties to the inquiry and third parties, such as competitors and consumer organisations;
2   information would be gained by a variety of means including letters and questionnaires, press notices, and advertisements, surveys and visits to the principal parties;
3   at an early stage, an issues statement would be published, identifying the key questions being addressed during the investigation;[27]
4   a series of oral hearings with the parties in attendance, normally in private, would be held in order to confirm factual evidence obtained and clarify issues arising in relation to the inquiry;
5   consultation with all interested parties in publishing provisional decisions. For instance, in relation to *Groceries*, the Commission identified disadvantages to consumers by a lack of competition in local markets due to an absence of effective competing retailers in some areas, and suggested various remedies including requiring grocery retailers to divest land holdings and proposed changes to the planning system;[28] and
6   if minded to take any form of remedial action, the group must agree on an adverse finding by a two-thirds majority, and must consult on its package of finalised remedies.

The competition test

One of the key reforms in the 2002 Act was the replacement of the substantive test for assessing 'monopolies' under the 1973 Act. The public interest test under s 84 of the 1973 Act was then recognised as the cornerstone of UK competition law. Over the years, there were repeated demands for reform of the public interest test as the basis for market and merger investigations. Nonetheless, reform to a competition-focused test was clearly less controversial in this area than in relation to merger control. The Commission practice concentrated on competition-related

---

27 See, for example, Competition Commission Press Release 57/07, '*BAA Airports* Market Investigation – Issues statement', 9 August 2007, where the Commission indicated that it was considering, *inter alia*, 'how common ownership could affect BAA's incentives both to invest in and develop its airports, and operate them'. See also, for example, Competition Commission Press Release 33/06, '*Groceries* – issues statement', 15 June 2006.
28 Competition Commission Press Release 61/07, '*Groceries Market* – Provisional Findings', 31 October 2007. See also, for example, Competition Commission Press Release 18/08, '*PPI* – Provisional Findings', 5 June 2008.

problems in markets and has continued, notwithstanding that the statutory requirements under Part 4 of the Enterprise Act 2002 were a novelty,

Under s 134(1) of the 2002 Act, the CMA is required to decide:

> whether any feature, or combination of features, of each relevant market prevents, restricts or distorts competition in connection with the supply or acquisition of goods or services in the United Kingdom or in a part of the United Kingdom.

This would constitute an 'adverse effect on competition' ('AEC') under s 134(2) and would require the CMA to decide what action should be taken to remedy, prevent or mitigate that effect or any detrimental effect on consumers which results. A detrimental effect on consumers may be constituted by higher prices, lower quality, less choice or less innovation in relation to the goods or services considered under s 134(1).[29] For instance, in *Store Cards*, the Competition Commission confirmed that there was an adverse effect in relation to the supply of consumer credit through store cards in the UK, indicating that annual percentage rates (APRs) were on average too high and that consumer detriment was estimated as at least £55m a year.[30] The CMA will approach the competition test in two stages – identifying the relevant market, and then assessing competition in that market and whether any market features adversely affect competition. Consideration of the relevant market issue follows the generally accepted approach, outlined in relation to Art 102 TFEU in Chapter 4, of the hypothetical monopolist (or SSNIP) test.

The second stage of the investigation and the CMA's assessment of competition is of greater interest. Many of the pertinent issues are already broadly familiar to competition lawyers and have previously been considered in reports under the 1973 Act. Moreover the tests at reference and assessment stages are identical. Accordingly, the CMA Panel group will focus first on market structure issues and how these affect intra-market rivalry between businesses. Thereafter the group will consider to what extent the conduct of players in a market might adversely affect competition. The Market Investigations Guidance highlights the problem of co-ordinated pricing or 'conscious parallelism' and the conditions that facilitate such co-ordinated effects.[31] Consideration of market structure and conduct alone may be insufficient to allow a determination of the effectiveness of competition. Therefore, the CMA may also examine the outcome of the competitive process as indicated by prices and the pattern of price changes over time, persistently high profits and international price comparisons.

Remedies

If the CMA decides that there is an adverse effect on competition, it has to decide what action should be taken. The CMA may exercise its order-making powers or accept undertakings from parties under ss 159 and 162 of the 2002 Act, respectively.

Under the 1973 Act the Secretary of State had power to make a wide range of orders. The exercise of these powers was demonstrated by the Orders following the report, *The Supply of Beer*.[32] The Orders had a significant effect on the brewing industry in the UK. In 2000, the Order introduced following the report into new car pricing had a dramatic impact on the price of many new cars in the UK.[33] Nonetheless, the preferred method of enforcement was through a process

---

29 Section 134(5).
30 Competition Commission, 'Store cards market investigation', 7 March 2006.
31 CC3, April 2013, paras 244–261.
32 The Supply of Beer (Tied Estate) Order 1989, SI 1989/2390, and the Supply of Beer (Loan Ties, Licensed Premises and Wholesale Prices) Order 1989, SI 1989/2258.
33 The Supply of New Cars Order 2000, SI 2000/2088.

of negotiation between businesses, which were the subject of an adverse report, and the OFT, leading to businesses giving undertakings as to their future conduct with those undertakings based on the findings and recommendations in the report. For example, following the *Ice Cream* report,[34] undertakings were subsequently accepted from BEW, Mars and Nestlé on outlet exclusivity, and from BEW on, *inter alia*, freezer exclusivity.[35] Reflecting the pragmatic, political and ultimately discretionary approach of the 1973 Act, the Secretary of State was not bound by the advice of the DGFT or the findings of a CC report which he could choose to ignore.[36]

Under the 2002 Act, and following the ERRA13, the reporting CMA Panel Group has the primary role in taking remedial action following a market investigation and has a duty, under s 138, to remedy any adverse effects on competition. In doing so, it is required to have regard to the need to achieve as comprehensive a solution as is reasonable and practicable to the adverse effect on competition and any detrimental effects on customers,[37] whilst ensuring any remedies are reasonable and proportionate.

Sections 159 and 161 EA02 empower the CMA to accept undertakings from market participants or to impose any orders listed in Sch 8. Schedule 8 entrusts the CMA with an extremely wide range of remedial powers to address any adverse effects on competition identified in a market investigation. The potential remedies available in this context include the following:

1   remedies designed to make a significant and direct change to the structure of a market by a requirement, for example, to divest a business or assets to a newcomer to the market or to an existing, perhaps smaller, competitor;

2   remedies designed to change the structure of a market less directly by reducing entry barriers or switching costs, for example, by requiring the licensing of know-how or intellectual property rights or by extending the compatibility of products through industry-wide technical standards;

3   recommendations for changes to regulations found to have adverse effects on competition or detrimental effects on customers, for example, by limiting entry to a market;

4   remedies directing firms (whether sellers or buyers) to discontinue certain behaviour (for example, giving advance notice of price changes) or to adopt certain behaviour (for example, more prominently displaying prices and other terms and conditions of sale);

5   remedies designed to restrain the way in which firms would otherwise behave, for example, the imposition of a price cap; and

6   monitoring remedies, for example, a requirement to provide information on prices or profits.

The CMA's decision as to whether to implement remedies by means of accepting undertakings or making an order will be determined on a case-by-case basis taking into account the scope of the CMA's order-making powers and practical issues such as the number of parties concerned and their willingness to negotiate and agree undertakings. The ERRA13 introduced statutory time limits for the implementation of remedies by the CMA and it must accept final undertakings or make a final order within six months of the date of publication of the market investigation report. This may be extended by a period of up to a further four months if, for instance, the remedies are

34 *The Supply of Impulse Ice Cream: A Report on the Supply in the UK of Ice Cream Purchased for Immediate Consumption*, Cm 4510, 2000.

35 DTI Press Release, P2000/509, 20 July 2000.

36 This power was demonstrated when the Secretary of State rejected the Commission's recommended structural remedy following the Commission's report into the *Supply of Raw Milk: A Report on the Supply in Great Britain of Raw Cows' Milk*, Cm 4286, 1999.

37 Section 134(6).

complex, such as where consumer testing of the detailed implementation of remedies is necessary, or where an additional consultation is required to address changes arising from earlier consulta tions. The CMA, in devising remedies, will consider the question of effectiveness, in particular whether they are likely to be implemented and complied with. As remedies are likely to be market-wide, in order to avoid delays in negotiating undertakings it may be more effective to impose a remedy by order. For instance, in *Store Cards*, the report addressed the necessary remedies, which included the requirement to provide full information on statements, to provide APR warnings on statements, and to display prominently a facility to pay outstanding balances by direct debit. Following a period of consultation after publication of a notice of intention to make an order, the Store Cards Market Investigation Order was introduced and came into force on 1 May 2007 to implement the remedies set out in the report.[38] The Final Report on remedies in relation to the *Groceries* Investigation contained a number of remedial measures, including a recommendation to include a "competition test" for planning authority decisions in relation to large grocery stores.[39] It should be noted that before any remedial action can follow, the decision that there is an adverse effect on competition must be supported by at least two-thirds of the members of the CMA panel group. In the early years of the post-2002 regime, Reports focused on increasing the provision of information to customers, making the process of switching easier and facilitating consumer choice. Arguably, in more recent years, certain market investigations have evidenced a more aggressive approach to the nature and scope of the remedy involved: in the *BAA Airports* investigation the divestment of three of BAA's airports were ordered; in the *Groceries* investigation the introduction of a 'competition test' in the planning regime that would limit expansion possibilities for incumbents with large local market shares was recommended; and, in the *PPI* investigation a ban on selling PPI at the point of sale of the associated credit was imposed. The CMA is required to monitor undertakings and orders following a market investigation report.[40]

Market Investigation Experience

There has been limited experience to date involving the CMA in the post-ERRA13 landscape, although the substantive provisions remain relatively unchanged. Accordingly, we will consider the market investigation practice by the Competition Commission under the Enterprise Act 2002, and it still remains instructive to review the practice of the CC under the 1973 Act as, despite the different statutory framework, it gives an idea of the likely approach to structural and conduct issues in industry-wide investigations. However, it should be noted that certain issues, such as predatory pricing and refusal to supply, the subject of various reports under the 1973 Act, would generally now be considered under the 1998 Act.[41] It also needs to be stressed that there is no system of precedent as such in relation to market investigations as market investigation outcomes are dependent on the particular market structures and circumstances which vary significantly from market to market. We will outline important issues in market investigations over the years and highlight current and ongoing investigations which demonstrate the continued vitality of these provisions.

---

38 Store Cards Market Investigation Order, 26 July 2006. Similarly, the Home Credit Market Investigation Order 2007, 13 September 2007, came into force on 4 October 2007, and implements the remedies set out in the earlier Commission Report. See also, the Northern Ireland PCA Banking Market Investigation Order 2008, 19 February 2008, which came into force on 22 February 2008.
39 Competition Commission, *Groceries Market: Final Report*, 30 April 2008.
40 CMA, 'Remedies: Guidance on the CMA's approach to the variation and termination of merger, monopoly and market undertakings and orders', 11 January 2014.
41 See, for example, Wilks, S, *In the Public Interest: Competition Policy and the Monopolies and Mergers Commission* (1999) Manchester: MUP.

Market structure

Relatively few reports under the 1973 Act found that the market conditions themselves operated against the public interest.[42] A major problem when criticising the structure of the market is the difficulty of devising the appropriate remedy. The only logical solution would appear to be divestiture, which has been criticised in political debate as too gross an interference in market processes. Nonetheless, this remedy has been utilised in the past, most notably in 1989 in *The Supply of Beer* report[43] which made recommendations on the maximum number of retail outlets each of the six big brewers could own.[44] More dramatically, in its 1999 report on the supply of raw milk in the UK, the Commission noted that Milk Marque had a scale monopoly with 49.6% market share. With a view to eliminating the market power of Milk Marque, the Commission recommended that Milk Marque should be divided into a number of independent quota-holding bodies.[45] Divestiture certainly appears to be in current vogue as an appropriate remedy. For instance, in 2009, the market investigation report in relation to BAA identified the common ownership by BAA of Edinburgh and Glasgow airports as giving rise to an AEC and the common ownership by BAA of Heathrow, Gatwick and Stansted as giving rise to a further AEC. In order to remedy the effect of these AECs, the CC decided that BAA should be required to sell one of its Scottish airports (either Glasgow or Edinburgh) and should be required to sell both Gatwick and Stansted airports. Following a lengthy process, involving judicial review by the CAT, the structural changes to the market have been ensured by the sale of all three airports by BAA.[46]

Oligopolistic pricing

The theory of oligopolistic interdependence suggests that, where there are few firms in a market, they may act collectively, and in parallel, without the necessity of collusion between or among them. The investigative and non-doctrinaire approach under the 1973 Act was particularly suitable for dealing with competitive problems associated with oligopoly. Anti-competitive activity was not punishable as such, but in seeking ways to improve competition it was recognised that many factors might contribute to oligopolistic market failure. In its general report on *Parallel Pricing*,[47] the Monopolies and Mergers Commission considered parallel pricing in the absence of parallel costs to be generally detrimental to consumer welfare. Later, after years of speculation concerning similar price movements in the UK petrol retail market, the Commission produced its report, *Supply of Petrol*.[48] To the surprise of many, the Commission did not find the parallel prices and price movements to be against the public interest, as they could be accounted for by the same international cost factors. On the other hand, in *White Salt*,[49] the Commission had earlier produced a classic example of a report on parallel pricing in an oligopoly. In fact, the market was a duopoly involving British Salt and ICI. The report demonstrated how parallel pricing could also lead to excessive pricing, at least for one producer. The Commission recommended that British Salt's

---

42 See, for example, *Roadside Advertising Services* (1980–81) HCP 365; and *Contraceptive Sheaths* (1974–75) HCP 394.
43 Cm 651, 1989.
44 The Secretary of State subsequently made two orders, although these did not replicate the recommendations: Supply of Beer (Tied Estate) Order 1989, SI 1989/2390 and Supply of Beer (Loan Ties, Licensed Premises and Wholesale Prices) Order 1989, SI 1989/2258. The Beer Orders were reviewed in 2000, following which, the Supply of Beer (Tied Estate) (Revocation) Order 2002, SI 2002/3204 repealed the 1989 Order and the Supply of Beer (Tied Estate) (Amendment) Order 1997. See, also, MMC report, *Domestic Gas Appliances* (1979–80) HCP 703, and the subsequent report, *Gas and British Gas plc*, Cm 2317, 1993, which also recommended divestiture as a possible remedy.
45 *Supply of Raw Milk: A Report on the Supply in Great Britain of Raw Cows' Milk*, Cm 4286, 1999.
46 See Competition Commission, 'BAA airports market investigation', 19 March 2009.
47 Cmnd 5330, 1973.
48 Cm 972, 1990.
49 Cmnd 9778, 1986.

prices should be regulated and ICI could, therefore, only charge parallel prices in the future if its efficiency improved. In 2002, in its *Banking* report,[50] the Commission noted that the similarity of pricing structure between the main clearing banks restricted competition. It is clear that oligopolistic markets and associated competition problems are likely to remain a major concern under the market investigation provisions of the Enterprise Act 2002. The 2014 Report in *Aggregates, Cement and Ready Mix Concrete* noted that higher prices cost customers at least £30m per year as a result of the limited competition between the three effective competitors on the market, and required divestiture to facilitate the entry of a new producer and other measures to limit the flow of information and data concerning cement production and price announcements.[51]

Conduct – excess or unfair prices or profits

There are various types of conduct that have been the focus of market investigations, including pricing policies within certain industries. In this context, defining excessive pricing was not necessary as the investigation system did not seek to punish and apportion blame. Nonetheless, the Commission has frequently criticised profit levels. For instance, in its report on *Valium and Librium*,[52] it recommended reduction in the prices of the two drugs to 25% and 40% of their existing level. In its report on *Ready Cooked Breakfast Cereal Foods*,[53] the Commission concluded that the prices charged were excessive and, as a result, Kellogg's gave an undertaking not to increase prices without government approval. In *White Salt*,[54] the Commission recommended that British Salt's prices should be controlled directly and any increases were to be related to rises in costs. These three reports reflect an attitude, more prevalent in the 1970s, that direct regulation of prices by competition authorities was appropriate. The suitability of this approach was doubted in the 1980s and early 1990s when there were fewer reports directly criticising pricing levels, and little evidence of the direct approach to price regulation in enforcement. Two reports by the Commission in the mid-1990s nonetheless indicated a willingness to consider and criticise prices that were unfair on consumers. These reports again demonstrate how market failure, excessive prices in these instances, may result from a variety of factors. In its report, *Video Games*,[55] the Commission concluded that Sega and Nintendo used their control over IP rights to set excessive prices for their games, while setting low prices for consoles to lock customers into their systems. In *Domestic Electrical Goods*,[56] the Commission was critical of high prices maintained by a system of recommended retail prices, and suggested various ways to increase competition in order to reduce prices of electrical goods for the consumer. In the late 1990s we also witnessed the campaign by the Labour Government after the 1997 election concerning 'Rip-Off Britain' with its focus on the effect of excessive pricing on UK consumers. This resulted in the reports on *Supermarkets*[57] and *New Cars*.[58] The supermarket report was largely uncritical, but the direct impact of competition law on the consumer was evidenced by the reduction of UK prices by a number of car manufacturers after the introduction of an Order following the *New Cars* report.[59]

50 *The Supply of Banking Services by Clearing Banks to Small and Medium-Sized Enterprises*, Cm 5319, 2002.
51 See Competition Commission Press Release, 'CC to create new cement producer', 14 January 2014.
52 Chlordiazepoxide and Diazepam (1972–73) HCP 197.
53 (1972–73) HCP 2.
54 Cmnd 9778, 1986.
55 Monopolies and Mergers Commission, *Video Games: A Report on the Supply of Video Games in the UK*, Cm 2781, 1995.
56 Cm 3676, 1997. The Restriction on Agreements and Conduct (Specified Domestic Electrical Goods) Order 1998, SI 1998/1271, came into force on 1 September 1998.
57 *Supermarkets: A Report on the Supply of Groceries from Multiple Stores in the United Kingdom*, Cm 4842, 2000.
58 *New Cars: A Report on the Supply of New Motor Cars Within the UK*, Cm 4660, 2000.
59 See DTI Press Release, P/2000/549, 1 August 2000. The Supply of New Cars Order 2000, SI 2000/2088.

Similarly in the *Banking* report in 2002, the CC was highly critical of the excessive prices charged to small- and medium-sized enterprises by major banks.[60]

Financial Services and Consumer Protection

There has been a considerable focus on financial services in the market investigations undertaken under the Enterprise Act 2002, with an emphasis on consumer protection and remedies aimed generally at reducing prices/interest rates by enhancing transparency and increasing consumer awareness. The first report under the Act was *Store Cards*,[61] in 2006, and another two early reports published related to financial services: *Home Credit*[62] and *Northern Irish Banking*.[63] In *Store Cards*, the Commission was critical of the excessive APRs on store cards and its remedies included warnings that cheaper credit may be available elsewhere, to provide fuller information on monthly statements, and a requirement to offer an option to pay by direct debit. In *Home Credit*, the Commission identified obstacles that restricted competition and raised prices; notably the advantageous position of existing lenders in knowing customer creditworthiness. Remedial measures included a requirement to share customer information, and, importantly, a requirement to provide clearer information on the cost of loans to allow consumers to shop around and compare offers. In *Northern Irish Banking*, the Commission found that competition in relation to personal current accounts (PCAs) in Northern Ireland was limited by banks' complicated charging structures, their failure to explain them adequately, and by customers' reluctance to switch banks. As a result, banks had to provide better and clearer information about their PCA services, charges and interest rates, and facilitate the switching process.

The CMA has a role in both competition and consumer protection. The emphasis on the impact on consumers, the requirement to consider customer benefits in designing appropriate remedies, and the innovation of the super-complaints procedure, which has kick-started a number of inquiries, demonstrate that consumer protection has been a key focus of the assessment in market investigations. For instance, its reports in *Store Cards*, *Home Credit* and *Northern Irish Banking* each focused on the direct financial impact on consumers resulting from the absence of effective competition, and the remedies were designed to enhance transparency and facilitate more informed consumer decision-making. Furthermore, following the *PPI* investigation a ban on selling PPI at the point of sale of the associated credit was imposed.[64]

Recent and ongoing practice

A number of recent and ongoing market investigations demonstrate the significant impact that the market investigation regime has on multiple facets of everyday life and, while being less heralded than a prohibition- and fine-based approach to illegal conduct, why it remains of important contemporary significance. In 2011, the Report on *Local Buses* concluded that in many areas of the UK bus operators face little or no competition, leading to passengers facing less frequent services and, in some cases, higher fares than where there is some form of rivalry.[65] Subsequently an Order was made to require local bus operators that manage bus stations to provide access to bus stations for rival operators on fair, reasonable and non-discriminatory terms,[66] with the intention that passengers would benefit from greater competition, and lower fares, in the future. The

---

60 *The Supply of Banking Services by Clearing Banks to Small and Medium-Sized Enterprises*, Cm 5319, 2002.
61 Competition Commission, 'Store cards market investigation', 7 March 2006.
62 Competition Commission, 'Home credit market investigation', 30 November 2006.
63 Competition Commission, 'Personal Current Account Banking Services in Northern Ireland market investigation', 15 May 2007.
64 Competition Commission, 'Market investigation into payment protection insurance', 29 January 2009.
65 Competition Commission, 'Local bus services market investigation', 20 December 2011.
66 The Local Bus Services Market Investigation (Access to Bus Stations) Order 2012.

report into *Pay TV Movies* demonstrates that not all market investigations lead to a critical report, as it was concluded that Sky's position in relation to the acquisition and distribution of movies, whereby it offers the first pay movies of all the big Hollywood studios, did not adversely affect competition in the pay-TV retail market as the availability of Sky Movies was not a sufficient factor in the choice of pay-TV provider by subscribers.[67] In the ongoing *Private Motor Insurance Market* investigation, on the other hand, there have been provisional findings in December 2013 in relation to this important £11bn market, that the complex chain for the settlement of non-fault claims increases the costs of replacement cars and repairs which in turn is passed on to the insurers of at-fault motorists. This results in higher motor insurance premiums for all drivers. The investigation is looking at ways to ensure that premiums are reduced for consumers by proposing a cap on charges passed to the insurer of an at-fault driver.[68] Following the financial crisis, and as a result of the ensuing economic recession, payday lending has become commonplace in the United Kingdom and subject to a widespread debate in the media about the allegedly exorbitant rates of interest charged in connection with this lending practice. This led to a market investigation reference in 2013 and provisional findings by the CMA in 2014 that borrowers may be paying too much for their loans due to lack of price competition.[69] Another significant investigation *Private Health Care*, examined concerns that many private hospitals face little competition in local areas across the UK which, because of high barriers to entry, led to higher prices for insured patients. Private hospital operators have significant market power in negotiations with private medical insurers and self-pay patients in many local areas. The final report requires divestiture of certain hospitals and other measures to limit incentives to referring clinicians and increase information to patients on fees and performance.[70] This investigation demonstrates the impact of the market investigation scheme in dealing with competition problems which affect consumer choice and prices, and the structural remedies which may be imposed as a result of an adverse finding.

Judicial Review by the CAT

Any decision by the CMA (sectoral regulator, or Secretary of State) in relation to market investigations under Pt 4 of the Act is subject to judicial review by the CAT and, thereafter, is subject to an appeal to the Court of Appeal in England and Wales or the Court of Session in Scotland. It is therefore possible, *inter alia,* to challenge a decision as to whether or not to refer a market for investigation or the findings or remedies as a result of a market investigation if the market is referred. However, s 179(4) provides that the CAT shall apply the same standard of review as a court in a judicial review application, meaning that the CAT does not conduct a full 'merits review' of the relevant decision.[71] There is evidence of increasing resort to the CAT for judicial review of various stages of the market investigation process, though with limited success to date. In 2005, the Association of Convenient Stores ('ACS') sought judicial review of the OFT's decision not to refer the groceries market for investigation by the Competition Commission. The ACS argued, *inter alia*, that the OFT had mistaken the level of certainty as to the existence of adverse effects on competition required for a reference decision. Before the CAT could determine the

---

67 Competition Commission, 'Movies on pay TV market investigation' 2 August 2012.
68 Competition Commission, 'Private Motor Insurance market investigation – Provisional findings report', 17 December 2013 and CMA 'Provisional decision on remedies', 12 June 2014.
69 Competition Commission, 'Payday lending market investigation – Terms of Reference', 27 June 2013 and CMA 'Provisional finding report', 11 June 2014.
70 See CMA, 'Private healthcare market investigation – final report', 2 April 2014.
71 See Bailey, D, 'The Early Case law of the Competition Appeal Tribunal', Chapter 2 in Rodger, B (ed), *Ten Years of UK Competition Law Reform* (2010) Dundee: DUP.

matter, however, the OFT indicated that it wished to withdraw its decision not to refer the market because it considered its decision was not fully reasoned. The CAT therefore quashed the OFT's decision and directed it to consider the issue again, whereupon the OFT decided to refer the market to the Competition Commission.[72] In relation to *PPI*, Barclays challenged the remedy of a prohibition on the marketing of PPI at the point of sale (POSP). The CAT concluded that the Commission had failed to take into account the loss of convenience that would flow from the imposition of the POSP; it was therefore not proportionate to include it in its proposed remedies package. This constituted a failure to take into account a relevant consideration, and the CAT quashed that part of the Report.[73] The matter was remitted and the Report and remedies package were subsequently published to identical effect but revised to take into account the loss of convenience issue. There was a similar outcome (both in terms of the CAT ruling and the subsequent Report revisions) following the appeal by Tesco in relation to *Groceries*, where the CAT held that there had been a failure to consider properly certain matters that were relevant to the recommendation that the competition test be imposed as part of a package of remedies to address the adverse effect on competition identified in the Report.[74] In relation to the *Airports* investigation, BAA unsuccessfully challenged the decision to require it to sell two of its three London airports on the basis of proportionality, as BAA had not demonstrated a failure to take account of relevant considerations when deciding upon the timescale for the divestments in question.[75] The CAT upheld the challenge on the grounds of apparent bias (one member of the panel had links to a group potentially interested in Gatwick airport) but this was subsequently overturned by the Court of Appeal.[76] In this long saga, a subsequent Report was issued in 2011 in relation to whether there had been a material change in circumstances since the earlier Report. The CAT rejected BAA's application for review of that later Report and BAA's subsequent appeal, principally in relation to proportionality, was rejected by the Court of Appeal.[77]

Key Points

- Market investigations have played a vital role under UK competition law, as a complement to the enforcement of the EU and UK prohibitions on abuse of dominance and anti-competitive agreements, in seeking to ensure markets are healthy and competitive and bring benefits to consumers in the form of greater choice, variety and lower prices.
- Market investigations do not determine the legality of conduct *ex post facto*, but the potential remedies are wide-ranging and can significantly impact on business strategy.
- The CMA Board take the decision to refer markets for investigation and *ad hoc* CMA panel groups then undertake the investigations; producing reports on any adverse effects on competition, and reasonable and practicable remedies to resolve those adverse effects.
- The CMA has followed the previous practice and Guidance of the Competition Commission in many aspects of market investigations.
- The possibility of judicial review of all aspects of the decision making process and outcomes is becoming increasingly important.

---

72 *Association of Convenience Stores v OFT* [2005] CAT 36.
73 *Barclays Bank plc v Competition Commission* [2009] CAT 27.
74 *Tesco v Competition Commission* [2009] CAT 9.
75 *BAA v Competition Commission* [2009] CAT 35.
76 [2010] EWCA Civ 1097.
77 [2012] EWCA Civ 1077.

Discussion

1   What role do market investigations play and why are they perceived to be an important additional tool for the enforcement of competition law in the UK?
2   To what extent has the ERRA 2013 changed the UK market investigation system?
3   What is the difference between a market study and a market investigation?
4   What remedies may be imposed following a market investigation?
5   What are the respective functions of the CMA and the CAT under Part 4 of the Enterprise Act 2002?

Further Reading

Ahlborn, A and Piccinin, D, 'Between Scylla and Charibidis: Market Investigations and the Consumer Interest', Chapter 7 in Rodger, B (ed), *Ten Years of UK Competition Law Reform* (2010) Dundee: DUP.

McElwee, M, 'The Reform of the UK's Markets Regime' (2013) 12(1) Comp LJ 98–111.

Morris, D, 'The Enterprise Act 2002: Aspects of the New Regime' [2002] Comp Law 318.

Sufrin, B and Furse, M, 'Market Investigations' [2002] Comp Law 244.

Chapter 6

Control of Anti-Competitive Agreements

Chapter Contents

Overview

- Article 101 TFEU captures a range of behaviour where some form of agreement has been reached between independent undertakings. The form of agreement is unimportant, as long as the undertakings have replaced competition with co-operation.
- Where an agreement has the 'object' of restricting competition, it is not necessary to prove it also has the effect of doing so. Where an agreement is not an 'object' agreement it is necessary to prove that the agreement has anti-competitive effects in its market context.
- Agreements that are caught by the Art 101(1) prohibition are automatically void under Art 101(2).
- Agreements that are caught by the Art 101(1) may escape the prohibition if they can be shown to meet the four criteria for exception set out in Art 101(3): they must improve the production or distribution of goods or promote technical or economic progress; they must ensure that consumers receive a fair share of the resulting benefits; they cannot contain indispensable restrictions; and they must not substantially eliminate competition. Block exemptions have been introduced to automatically exempt common classes of benign agreements, such as vertical agreements, from the prohibition.
- Article 101 only applies to agreements which have an effect on trade between Member States. If an agreement does not affect trade in this way it will be subject to domestic competition law. The criteria have been interpreted broadly and EU law will often apply to very localised agreements.
- UK competition law has been reformed to mirror the EU law prohibitions and ensure that agreements not subject to EU competition law are treated in the same way under s 2 of the Competition Act 1998. Agreements which would be exempt through the operation of an EU block exemption Regulation are also exempted from the UK prohibition under s 10 of the 1998 Act.

Introduction

In this chapter we examine situations where undertakings can alter competition on a market by entering into anti-competitive agreements. We shall discuss the ways in which the EU, through Art 101 TFEU, and the UK, through the Chapter I prohibition, seek to deal with anti-competitive agreements.

Background to Art 101 TFEU

The EU rules surrounding the control of agreements[1] have been influenced to a greater extent by the general goals of the EU, and in particular the market integration imperative, than the rules on

---

1   In this context, the term 'agreement' should be used loosely; its more technical meaning will be introduced later.

control of dominant undertakings. The neoclassical model of competition, discussed in Chapter 1, highlighted the problems which a monopoly can create. It is also possible for undertakings to reach that monopoly position by agreeing with their competitors that they should not compete. In effect, the parties to the agreement, forming what is known as a cartel, will have a monopoly position on what was previously a competitive market. Historically, the existence of cartels was common in European markets and, therefore, their removal was one of the key goals of early European competition policy.[2] The competition rules in relation to anti-competitive agreements were also very important in relation to securing the four freedoms of the EU internal market. The achievement of free movement of goods would have been hampered were undertakings in a position to erect barriers to cross-border free trade after the EU had removed the barriers maintained by Member States. Undertakings which had previously been protected from competition by those state barriers might have been tempted to try to defend their privileged position by entering into agreements with potential competitors in other Member States.

Throughout the development of case law under Art 101 TFEU, there have been observable tensions between the desire to promote market integration on the one hand and to improve economic efficiency on the other. In some cases, market integration appears to have been preferred over economic efficiency. Article 101 is designed to prohibit agreements that restrict competition. This is self-evident in blatant breaches of competition law involving horizontal price-fixing and market-sharing; however, beyond those examples there are a great many types of agreement which are less obviously problematic. As a broad example, an important distinction can be drawn between horizontal agreements, which are between businesses operating at the same level of the market,[3] and vertical agreements, which are between businesses operating on different levels of the market.[4] Horizontal agreements are much more likely to threaten competition, as they involve two parties who would normally compete with each other. In comparison, vertical agreements are less likely to raise direct competition concerns, as the parties do not directly compete with each other, but operate at different levels of the market; eg producer and distributor. Awareness of these issues, and the balancing of different goals, is key to understanding the development of competition policy in relation to anti-competitive agreements. It is also important to consider the bifurcated structure of the prohibition in Article 101 TFEU. The first paragraph lays down the prohibition and the third sets out an exception to the prohibition if certain criteria are met. Article 101(2) serves a rather different function; setting out the consequences if the prohibition is breached. Each of these paragraphs will be dealt with in turn.

Article 101(1) TFEU

Article 101(1) TFEU prohibits agreements, decisions of associations and concerted practices that may affect trade between Member States and which have as their object the prevention, restriction or distortion of competition. It also includes an indicative list of types of agreement which may be covered. The Court of Justice and the Commission have given the Article a very wide interpretation, encapsulating many types of collusive or cooperative behaviour. The simplest way to approach the detailed analysis of the prohibition is to break it down into its constituent parts.

---

2   For an historical examination of cartels in Europe, and their regulation, see Harding, C and Joshua, J, *Regulating Cartels in Europe*, 2nd edn (2010) Oxford: OUP.
3   For example, between two manufacturers of the same product.
4   For example, between a manufacturer and a distributor or retailer.

Agreements, decisions of associations and concerted practices

Each of the terms used in Art 101 has a separate emphasis but there is considerable overlap among them. It is, therefore, not crucial that a particular 'agreement' is identifiable, so long as it is demonstrable that some form of collusion, falling within the concept of 'agreement' or 'concerted practice', has occurred.

Agreements

The concept of agreement is not restricted to legally binding and enforceable agreements, as this would make evasion of the prohibition very simple. In one of its early judgments in this area, *ACF Chemifarma v Commission (Quinine)*,[5] the Court found that an unsigned 'gentlemen's agreement' fell within the prohibition. The modern definition was more fully developed in *Polypropylene*.[6] Here, the Commission investigation centred on a complex cartel involving 15 undertakings. The agreement took the form of several oral, non-binding, arrangements for which there were no enforceable sanctions. It was held that the various arrangements formed a single agreement infringing Art 101(1). Some of the undertakings concerned had not attended all of the meetings, or had deviated from the terms of the agreement, but they were still considered to be party to it. The concept of a single ongoing 'agreement' has proved to be very important in recent Commission practice,[7] which illustrates that the concept does not focus on a one-off event whereby an agreement is reached, but rather an ongoing and developing process where undertakings agree on a continuing course of conduct. It is also clear that any participation in the process may lead to a finding that an undertaking is part of the ongoing agreement, no matter how minor a role it may have played. The extent of an undertaking's involvement is only taken into account when deciding the level of fine to be imposed. The extent of the 'single continuing infringement' concept was tested in *BASF v Commission*,[8] where the Commission argued that a number of global choline chloride producers were part of a single agreement. The European cartelists challenged that characterisation by arguing that there was no connection between the European agreement and the global one. The Court held that the Commission has not proved the complementary nature of the agreements, and the finding was overturned. It is not enough that the same product and undertakings are involved, but there must be a clear 'overall plan' which brings the separate agreements or understandings together.

In one of the first competition cases to come before the Court, the parties tried to draw a distinction between horizontal and vertical agreements. A horizontal agreement exists between undertakings at the same level of the market, for example, an agreement between two manufacturers of a product. Vertical agreements exist between undertakings that operate at different levels of the market, for example, an agreement between a manufacturer and a distributor or retailer. In *Consten and Grundig*, the Commission found that an exclusive distribution agreement between Grundig, a German electronics manufacturer, and Consten, a French distributor, infringed Art 101(1) TFEU.[9] On appeal, the undertakings argued that vertical agreements such as this did not fall within the terms of the prohibition. The Court was not convinced by the argument, and came to the conclusion that Art 101 protected both inter-brand competition (between different

---

5   Cases 41, 44 and 45/69 [1970] ECR 661. In cartel cases the Commission Decision is known by the product at the centre of the cartel, in this case quinine. Although the product name will not appear in any case challenging the Commission Decision, the common name is often still used as shorthand to refer to the litigation as a whole.
6   Commission Decision 86/398/EEC, [1986] OJ L230/1. Upheld, on appeal, in Case T-7/89 *Hercules NV v Commission* [1991] ECR II-1711 and Case C-49/92P *Commission v Anic Partecipazioni SpA* [1999] ECR I-4125.
7   See, for example, Commission Decision 89/191/EEC *LdPE* [1989] OJ L74/21; Commission Decision 94/559/EC *PVC* [1994] OJ L239/14; Commission Decision 94/601/EC *Cartonboard* [1994] OJ L243; and Commission Decision 2001/418/EC *Amino Acids* [2001] OJ L152/24.
8   Case T-101/05 *BASF AG & UCB SA v Commission* [2007] ECR II-4949.
9   Commission Decision 64/556/EEC, [1964] OJ 2545.

brands of the same product) and intra-brand competition (between the same branded product sold by different retailers).[10] Under the terms of the vertical agreement in question, intra-brand competition would have been almost eliminated; however, inter-brand competition may have been increased. Without the guarantee of exclusivity, Consten may not have been willing to invest as much time and resource into the promotion of Grundig's products. By investing in promotion, Consten would have increased competition between Grundig products and other brands. Without exclusivity, other retailers selling Grundig profits would benefit from Consten's promotional efforts; these retailers are known as 'free-riders'.

Another interesting interpretation of the concept of an agreement concerns situations where there is apparently unilateral behaviour. The Court has been willing to infer the existence of an agreement where behaviour confers a benefit on another undertaking. In *Ford Werke v Commission*,[11] the refusal of Ford in Germany to supply right-hand drive cars to its German distributors was challenged on the basis that the refusal was designed to protect Ford's UK distributors from competition from distributors selling right-hand cars in Germany. Although the refusal appeared to be unilateral, it was held to be part of an agreement. The extent of this ability to impute apparently unilateral behaviour to an agreement was further discussed by the Court in *BAI and Commission v Bayer*.[12] The Court stated that for an agreement to be concluded by 'tacit acceptance' it is necessary that 'the manifestation of the wish of one of the contracting parties to achieve an anti-competitive goal constitute an invitation to the other party, to fulfil that goal jointly'.[13]

The Court of Justice has stressed that mere exchanges of information between competitors may be 'incompatible with the rules on competition if they reduce or remove the degree of uncertainty as to the operation of the market in question with the result that competition between undertakings is restricted'.[14] An exchange of information is more likely to be prohibited (as an object infringement) if it concerns the exchange of commercially sensitive data, particularly in relation to prices and quantities, in comparison with exchanges of more publicly available information which will be assessed on an effects basis by comparing the competitive situation which would have prevailed in the absence of the shared information.[15]

Concerted practices

The term 'concerted practice' in Art 101(1) TFEU has been given a particularly broad definition. In many cases, the Commission will merely state that co-operation between undertakings amounts to an agreement 'and/or' a concerted practice. The important point, when dealing with concerted practices, is the existence of some form of collusion between undertakings. There is no easy way to define exactly where an agreement stops and a concerted practice begins, although it is evidently a looser form of 'agreement', which involves some form of understanding or collaboration. The seminal definition was given by the Court in *ICI v Commission (Dyestuffs)*[16] as follows:

---

10 Cases 56 and 58/64 *Consten and Grundig v Commission* [1966] ECR 299.
11 Cases 25 and 26/84 [1985] ECR 2725.
12 Cases C-2 and 3/01 [2004] ECR I-23.
13 Cases C-2 and 3/01 *BAI and Commission v Bayer* [2004] ECR I-23, at para 102. The Court also made it clear, at para 141, that 'the mere fact that a measure adopted by a manufacturer, which has the object or effect of restricting competition, falls within the context of continuous business relations between the manufacturer and its wholesalers is not sufficient for a finding that such an agreement exists'. See also Case T-208/01 *Volkswagen v Commission* [2003] ECR II-5141; Case T-53/03 *BPB plc v Commission* [2008] ECR II-1333 and Case T-18/03 *CD-Contact Data GmbH v Commission* [2009] ECR II-1021.
14 See Case C-238/05 *ASNEF-EQUIFAX Servicios de Informacion sobre Solvencia y Credito SL v Asociacion de Usarios de Servicios Bancarios (AUSBANC)* [2006] ECR I-11125.
15 See the Commission Guidelines on the Applicability of Art 101 on the Treaty of the Functioning of the European Union to Horizontal Co-operation Agreements, [2011] OJ, C11/1, C33/20.
16 Case 48/69 *ICI v Commission* [1972] ECR 619.

a form of co-ordination between undertakings which, without having reached a stage where agreement properly so called has been concluded, knowingly substitutes practical co-operation between them for the risks of competition.[17]

The forms of practical co-operation that were alluded to in *Dyestuffs* were more fully explained by the Court in *Suiker Unie v Commission (Sugar)*.[18] The emphasis was placed upon mental consensus[19] between the co-operating undertakings. The Court stated that Art 101 precluded:

any direct or indirect contact between such operators, the object or effect whereof is either to influence the conduct on the market of an actual or potential competitor or to disclose to such a competitor the course of conduct which they themselves have decided to adopt or contemplate adopting on the market.[20]

It should be noted that the term 'concerted practice' has been left broadly defined. This is a necessity due to the lengths to which undertakings go to disguise their activities. Moreover, the form of the agreement or practice is less important than the economic effect it has on the market. A formalistic approach would not help the law attain its objectives. Despite this broad definition, the concept of a 'concerted practice' is not suited to dealing with oligopolistic behaviour.

One of the reasons for avoiding formalism when dealing with concerted practices is the difficulty in proving the existence of collusion. There may be a suspicion that some form of collusion exists when there are parallel price rises or similar forms of behaviour. However, the Commission must be able to prove the existence of a concerted practice before it makes a decision against the relevant undertakings. To prove the existence of a concerted practice, or an overall agreement, the Commission will usually seek to rely on so-called 'plus' evidence. This is evidence that indicates that the parallel behaviour has occurred as a result of some form of collusion rather than other market factors. An example of the sort of 'plus' evidence that might be sought is illustrated by the *Dyestuffs* case. An investigation was carried out into similar price rises for aniline dyes across the Common Market. In total, ten undertakings were investigated. It was discovered that there were identical percentage increases within two or three days across the industry on a number of occasions. On one occasion, instructions were telexed by different undertakings to subsidiary companies on the same evening at the following times: 5.05 pm, 5.09 pm, 5.38 pm, 5.57 pm, 6.55 pm and 7.45 pm. On another occasion the telexes of 'competitors' used the same wording. On the basis of this evidence, the Commission had little difficulty showing that there must have been collusion between the undertakings. Unfortunately, in many cases, such clear evidence will not always be available.

Decisions of associations of undertakings

This section of Art 101 TFEU deals with the organisation of undertakings through a trade or professional association. Such associations have the aim of representing and promoting the interests of their members. It is easy to understand how the decision of such an association may affect competition in a market. An obvious example of how an association's rules may affect the market was the subject of investigation in *COAPI*.[21] The Colegio de Agentes de la Propiedad is

---

17 Ibid, para 64.
18 Cases 40–48, 50, 54–56, 111 and 113–14/73 [1975] ECR 1663.
19 It is interesting to note the increasing focus on mental consensus in the Commission's and Court's jurisprudence surrounding both 'concerted practices' and 'agreements'. It is arguable that there is in practice no real distinction between the two terms.
20 [1975] ECR 1663, at para 174. See also Case C-8/08 *T-Mobile Netherlands BV v Raad van Bestuur van de Nederlandse Mededingingsautoriteit* [2009] ECR I-4529 and the UK cases of *Argos, Littlewoods and JJB v OFT* [2006] EWCA Civ 1318 on appeal from [2004] CAT 24, [2005] CAT 13, [2004] CAT 17, [2005] CAT 22 and *Apex Asphalt and Paving Co Ltd v OFT* [2005] CAT 4.
21 Commission Decision 95/188/EC, [1995] OJ L122/37; [1995] 5 CMLR 468.

an association of all the industrial property agents practising in Spain. Any property agent breaching the set scale of fees could be punished by fines, suspension or expulsion from the association. It was argued that the association was a body set up by statute, with special regulatory functions, but the Commission concentrated on the fact that it was an association of independent undertakings attempting to fix prices across a market. Even non-binding recommendations by an association may be caught by Art 101, as those recommendations are likely to affect the behaviour of association members.[22]

In some Member States, associations of undertakings may have special status in national law or a particular regulatory responsibility. If that is the case the competition rules still apply to the association of undertakings. In *Wouters* the Court examined the compatibility of the Dutch Bar rules with EU competition law.[23] It was argued that as the Dutch Bar was regulated by the State, it could not fall within the competition rules, but the Court held that where the decision is attributable to the association itself, rather than being directly attributable to the State,[24] the competition rules still apply.

Parallelism and oligopoly

Where there is evidence of parallel behaviour there is often the temptation immediately to categorise the behaviour as a concerted practice. While parallelism may be an indicator that undertakings are colluding, it would be premature for the Commission to conclude that a concerted practice exists. The burden is on the Commission to prove the existence of the concerted practice. This may be difficult, as parallelism may occur through the natural operation of an oligopolistic market. In such circumstances proof may be very difficult.

As discussed in the previous chapter, oligopolists become interdependent and tend to follow each other's behaviour very closely. In the *Dyestuffs* case, the 'oligopoly' defence was raised by the parties, claiming that their parallel behaviour was a natural result of the oligopolistic market structure, but the Commission was able to show evidence of collusion. In other cases, the oligopoly defence has proved more successful. In relation to the oligopoly defence economic evidence is vital. The Court has accepted that in oligopolistic markets undertakings must take into account the behaviour of their competitors, and in so doing they may appear to act in parallel with their competitors. However, the Court has added that parallel behaviour may constitute strong evidence of collusion where parallelism would not result from the normal operation of the market. The Court considered the difficulties faced in such situations in the *Wood Pulp* case.[25] In his opinion, Advocate General Darmon explained the potential for parallelism as follows:

> parallel conduct is not necessarily the result of prior concentration. It can be explained or even dictated by the very structure of certain markets . . . The first situation involves a concentrated oligopoly, in which undertakings are independent: each undertaking must take into account in its decisions the conduct of its rivals. Alignment on others' conduct constitutes a rational response, independently of any concentration. 'Price leadership' constitutes the second situation: undertakings align themselves on a 'price leader' on account of the latter's power on the market. Mention may also be made of the spontaneous alignment on a price leader which acts as barometer, either its decisions reflecting changes in market conditions or for reasons linked, for instance, to previous knowledge of that market.[26]

---

22 See Case 8/72 *Cementhandelaren v Commission* [1972] ECR 977.
23 Case C-309/99 *Wouters v Algemene Raad van de Nederlandse Orde van Advocaten* [2002] ECR I-1577.
24 See paras 66–70. Where the State grants regulatory powers to a professional organisation, defines the public-interest criteria and essential principles with which its rules must comply, and retains power to adopt decisions in the last resort, the rules remain state measures.
25 Cases C-89, 104, 114, 116, 117 and 125–29/85 *A Ahlstrom Oy v Commission* [1993] ECR I-1307.
26 Ibid, at para 177.

The Court instructed two independent economic experts to investigate the market for wood pulp to aid it in its judgment. The experts' analysis explained in some detail the workings of the market and the external pressures that had effects on pricing within the period of the alleged infringement. In its judgment the Court accepted the findings of the experts and concluded that concerted practices were not the only plausible explanation for the parallel price announcements on the wood pulp market. The experts had identified that the long term nature of purchasing requirements, the limited number of customers for each producer and the transparency of price information, particularly through a dynamic trade press, could account for parallel behaviour in the market. As the parallel behaviour could be explained by the operation of the market, and the Commission had produced no evidence of actual collusion, the Court annulled the majority of the Commission's Decision.

Much of the literature on oligopolistic markets refers to the phenomenon of parallel behaviour as 'tacit collusion' or 'tacit co-ordination'. This terminology might suggest that Art 101 TFEU may be an appropriate tool to control this form of 'collusion' alongside other concerted practices, but it has become clear, in cases such as *Wood Pulp*, that Art 101 should only be used in situations where 'active' collusion has been proved. It may still be possible to use Art 101 where there is no other plausible explanation for the parallelism. However, regarding proof, the Court has confirmed the use of economic analysis where other means of proof may be impracticable or impossible. The Commission has to overcome a difficult burden in terms of the economic evidence required. The problem with dealing with 'tacit collusion' under Art 101 is that the problem is structural, in that the structure of the market creates the conditions where tacit collusion may occur, rather than behavioural, where there is active collusion between undertakings. The main remedy under Art 101, the imposition of a fine, is behavioural in nature and therefore not well suited to dealing with a structural problem. Structural remedies are available under Regulation 1/2003 but are still underutilised by the Commission.[27]

Undertakings

The definition of an undertaking in Art 101 TFEU is very similar to that under Art 102 TFEU, that being any legal or natural person involved in a commercial enterprise. In the context of Art 101 the 'economic entity' doctrine is of importance. If legally separate bodies are linked, through ownership or management agreements, any form of 'agreement' between them will not be considered under Art 101 as the separate bodies will be deemed to be within the same undertaking.[28] The Court's jurisprudence on groups of companies is illustrated by *Viho Europe v Commission*.[29] Viho had challenged the restrictions imposed by Parker Pen on its national distributors which prohibited the distributors from supplying customers outside their respective national territories. The Court confirmed that the arrangements between Parker and its national distributors, which were also its subsidiaries, fell outside Art 101(1). The reason for this finding was that Parker owned 100% of the shares in the subsidiary companies and their sales and marketing activities were directed by an area management team appointed by the parent company. It would appear that both ownership and management are important when deciding if intra-group agreements are caught by Art 101. This use of the economic entity doctrine has been criticised as it encourages undertakings to vertically integrate their distribution systems to avoid the prohibition. If an undertaking owns or manages its own distributors, or assumes the financial and commercial risks linked to sales to third parties, it can impose whatever restrictions it considers necessary without the threat

---

27 Art 7, Regulation 1/2003/EC on the implementation of the rules on competition laid down in Arts 81 and 82 of the Treaty [2003] OJ L1/1.
28 See Case 22/71 *Beguelin Import v GL Import Export* [1971] ECR 949.
29 Case C-73/95P [1996] ECR I-5457.

of sanction under Art 101. A good example of the sort of finance and management links between parent and subsidiary companies which can lead to them being considered a single undertaking under the UK's Chapter I prohibition, was dealt with by the CAT in *Sepia Logistics Ltd & Precision Control Ltd v OFT*.[30] One man, Mr Sander, was on the board of both the parent and subsidiary companies and had personally guaranteed debts of both companies. All the shares of the parent company were in the ownership of Mr Sander's family, and the parent owned 80% of the shares in the subsidiary.

Effect on interstate trade

The requirement of an effect on interstate trade concerns the jurisdictional scope of the provision. The Court and the Commission have given the phrase a broad interpretation. Many agreements which at first sight appear to only affect one Member State have been held to come within the ambit of the EU rules. Article 3 of Regulation 1/2003 sets out the relationship between EU law and national law in the area of interstate trade.[31]

The Court laid out the basic test for the effect on interstate trade in *Société Technique Minière v Maschinenbau Ulm* as follows:[32]

> it must be possible to foresee with a sufficient degree of probability on the basis of an objective set of factors of law or fact that the agreement in question may have an influence, direct or indirect, actual or potential, on the pattern of trade between Member States.

This broad test has also been given a wide interpretation in the Commission Notice, Guidelines on the effect on trade concept contained in Arts 81 and 82 of the Treaty.[33] Where an agreement is between undertakings based in the same Member State, it may still be deemed to affect interstate trade. Agreements in one state may have the effect of compartmentalising the market and thus discouraging undertakings from other states from entering the market.[34] Very minor agreements may also affect interstate trade if the agreements are part of a larger network of agreements.[35] The importance of such networks can be seen when one considers complex distribution systems used in industries such as brewing. A brewer may have thousands of agreements with pubs, relating to the supply of beer. Each one of those agreements would have little impact on interstate trade but, taken as a network, the economic impact of the agreements may be significant.

Prevention, restriction or distortion of competition

The next section of the prohibition in Art 101(1) TFEU concerns the competitive impact of an agreement or concerted practice. Unless the Commission or the Court is satisfied that an agreement has as its 'object or effect the prevention, restriction or distortion of competition', it will not infringe Art 101. There has been great difficulty in discerning clearly what types of agreement should be of concern to competition law; in other words, when does an agreement distort, restrict or limit competition?[36]

---

30 [2007] CAT 13.
31 Regulation 1/2003/EC on the implementation of the rules on competition laid down in Arts 81 and 82 of the Treaty, [2003] OJ L1/1. National law may be applied alongside EU law where there is an effect on interstate trade but must not lead to the prohibition of agreements which are not prohibited by Art 101 TFEU.
32 Case 56/65 [1966] ECR 235.
33 [2004] OJ C101/81.
34 Case 8/72 *Cementhandelaren v Commission* [1972] ECR 977. See, also, Cases T-202, 204 & 207/98 *Tate & Lyle and Others v Commission* [2001] ECR II-2035. Cf Cases C-215 & 216/96 *Carlo Bagnasco and Others v Banco Polare di Navara and Others* [1999] ECR I-135.
35 Case C-234/89 *Delimitis v Henniger Bräu* [1991] ECR I-935.
36 See Lugard, HHP, 'Vertical Restraints under EC Competition Law: A Horizontal Approach' [1996] ECLR 166.

This area, the distortion, restriction or limitation of competition, has proved to be one of the most controversial in EU competition law. It is an area that highlights the conflict between the economic and political goals that exist within EU competition policy, particularly in relation to vertical restraints.[37] For that reason, this chapter will concentrate on the basic application of Art 101, giving examples of some of the common types of restrictive agreements. In the following chapter, there will be a more detailed discussion on the difficulties faced by the competition authorities in dealing with secret cartels.

Article 101 includes an indicative list of the types of agreement that will prevent, restrict or distort competition, although, as with Art 102, this list is not exhaustive. The Commission and the Court have given the terminology a wide interpretation. Some commentators have argued that the interpretation adopted is so wide that it bears little relation to competitive reality. One possible reason for this broad interpretation is the existence of Art 101(3) TFEU which allows for the prohibition to be inapplicable. The US antitrust regime, to which the EU rules are often compared, has no corresponding provision. Under the US Sherman Act provisions, the consideration of any economic benefits stemming from an agreement is made within the prohibition itself; the process is known as the 'rule of reason'. Another reason for differential treatment is historic as, in the early years of EU competition law's development, a broad interpretation of Art 101(1) meant that most potentially restrictive agreements required notification for exemption under Regulation 17/62. As the power to grant an exemption, at that time, rested solely with the Commission, the Commission was in the position to shape the development of the rules through its use of the Art 101(3) exemption procedure. If more flexibility had been built into Art 101(1) the national courts would have had a far greater role to play in the evolution of the rules. The Commission used its position to develop the rules and prevent the development of conflicting interpretations. Whatever reasons lay behind the broad interpretation of Art 101(1), when the EU system matured its wide scope caused several problems.[38]

The 'object' of restricting competition

A distinction has been made between agreements which have the object of restricting competition and those which have the effect of doing so. In *STM*,[39] the Court stated that the words should be read disjunctively and thus consideration should first be given to whether an agreement has the object of restricting competition. Only when it does not is it necessary to consider, in detail, the effects of the agreement. In *Polypropylene*,[40] there was considerable evidence of the cartel members' intention of co-operating across the market, but there was little evidence of any anti-competitive effects. Nonetheless, the Commission imposed a large fine that was upheld on appeal.[41] The Commission's Guidelines on Horizontal Co-operation Agreements sets out the approach to be adopted in relation to by object restrictions as follows:

> Restrictions of competition by object are those that by their very nature have the potential to restrict competition within the meaning of Article 101(1). It is not necessary to examine the actual or potential effects of an agreement on the market once its anti-competitive object has been established.[42]

---

37 See Hawk, B, 'System Failure: Vertical Restraints and EC Competition Law' (1995) 32 CML Rev 973.
38 A number of those problems, and the prospective solutions, were discussed in Chapter 2 and will be examined in detail later in this chapter.
39 Case 56/65 *STM v Maschinenbau Ulm* [1966] ECR 235.
40 Commission Decision 86/398/EEC, [1986] OJ L230/1; [1988] 4 CMLR 347.
41 Commission Decision 86/398/EEC, [1986] OJ L230/1; [1988] 4 CMLR 347. Upheld on appeal in, for example, Case C-49/920 *Hercules NV v Commission* [1991] ECR II-1711 and *Commission v Anic Partecipazioni SpA* [1999] ECR I-4125.
42 Guidelines on the applicability of Art 101 of the Treaty on the Functioning of the European Union to Horizontal Co-operation Agreements [2011] OJ C11/1, para 24; as amended by [2011] OJ C33/20.

Certain types of agreements are therefore deemed to be 'object' or 'per se' infringements of Art 101(1), whereas other possible infringements require a fuller examination of the economic context in which the possible infringements take place.[43] The simplification of the Commission's task, in that there is no need to consider an agreement's effects, has been largely welcomed but it does not obviate the need for any supporting evidence in all cases. In Pedro IV[44] and Ziegler[45] the Court indicated that it may have been necessary to adduce evidence that 'object' agreements had an appreciable effect on competition. However, in Expedia[46] the Court reaffirmed its traditional position that there was 'no need to take account of the concrete effects of an agreement' where its object was the restriction of competition.[47] This was the case as object agreements 'by their very nature' are 'injurious to the proper functioning of normal competition'.[48] The contemporary approach to object agreements, reflecting the Commission Guidelines, is epitomised by the Court of Justice ruling in Competition Authority v Beef Industry Development Society Ltd ('BIDS').[49] In that case, due to perceived overcapacity in the Irish beef-processing industry, processors formed BIDS, which purchased cattle from breeders, slaughtered and deboned them, and then sold the beef in Ireland and abroad. The processors sought to reduce overcapacity and set up arrangements whereby those remaining in the industry ('the stayers') would compensate those leaving the industry ('the goers'). The Court confirmed that where the object of an agreement, taking into account its wording and objectives, was to restrict, limit or distort competition, it was prohibited by Article 101(1) irrespective of any anti-competitive effects produced by the agreement.[50] In this case, the object of the agreement was to change appreciably the structure of the market by encouraging the withdrawal of competitors, thereby replacing a process of rivalry with a process of co-operation, blatantly conflicting with the purposes of Article 101(1).[51] Nonetheless, the Court in BIDS looked beyond the objectively 'hard-core' nature of the infringement, stressing that even by object restrictions had to be assessed in their economic context taking into account the nature of the particular industry and the rivalry involved.[52] The Court's approach has been criticised for causing uncertainty by blurring the lines between object and effect restrictions.[53]

Many of the types of agreement which have been considered to have the object of restricting competition are well-known horizontal cartel activities, such as price-fixing[54] or market-sharing.[55] However, other forms of behaviour, such as collective boycotts[56] and information exchanges,[57] have also been challenged. Due to the importance of market integration in EU competition law,

---

43 For an indicative list of 'object' agreements see, Commission Staff Working Document, 'Guidance on restrictions of competition "by object" for the purposes of defining which agreements may benefit from the De Minimis Notice', SWD (2014) 198 final. See also Cases T-374, 375, 384 and 388/94 European Night Services Ltd v Commission [1998] ECR II-3141, at para 136: 'account should be taken of the actual conditions in which it functions, in particular the economic context in which the undertakings operate, the products or services covered by the agreement and the actual structure of the market concerned . . . unless it is an agreement containing obvious restrictions of competition, such as price-fixing, market-sharing or the control of outlets.'
44 Case C-260/07 Pedro IV Servicios SL v Total España SA [2009] ECR I-02437.
45 Case T-199/08 Ziegler SA v European Commission [2011] ECR II-3507.
46 Case C-226/11 Expedia Inc v Autorité de la concurrence and Others [2012] ECR I-0000.
47 Ibid, para 35.
48 Ibid, para 36.
49 Case C-209/07, [2008] ECR I-8637.
50 Ibid, paras 18–21.
51 Ibid, paras. 24–37.
52 Ibid, para 17. See Andreangeli, A, 'Modernising the Approach to Article 101 TFEU in Respect to Horizontal Agreements: Has the Commission's Interpretation "Come of Age"?' (2011) Competition and Regulation 195; Odudu, O, 'Restriction of Competition by Object: What is the Beef?' (2008) 8 Competition Law Journal 11.
53 See Case C-32/11 Allianz Hungária Biztosító Zrt, v Gazdasági Versenyhivatal [2013] ECR I-000, and Nagy, CI, 'The Distinction Between Anti-competitive Obejct and Effect after Allianz: The End of Coherence in Competition Analysis?' (2013) 36 World Competition 541–564.
54 Cases 48, 49 and 51–57/69 ICI v Commission (Dyestuffs) [1972] ECR 619.
55 Case 41/69 Quinine, ACF Chemifarma v Commission [1970] ECR 661.
56 Case 71/74 FRUBO v Commission [1975] ECR 563; [1975] 2 CMLR 123.
57 Commission Decision 80/1334/EEC, [1980] OJ L383/19; Italian Cast Glass [1982] 2 CMLR 61. See, also, Cases T-202/98, T-204/98 and T-207/98 Tate & Lyle etc regarding meetings where parties revealed future price intentions, particularly para 73.

many forms of export restriction, in both vertical and horizontal agreements, have been taken to have the object of restriction of competition.[58] An excellent example of such a situation can be seen in the *Nintendo* Decision.[59] Prices for Nintendo games cartridges were lower in the UK than other Member States, and Nintendo and their UK distributor, THE Games, had taken steps to reduce the potential for parallel trade from the UK into continental Europe. Firstly, THE Games would only supply cartridges to retailers who sold directly to end-consumers. Secondly, any approaches from retailers outside the UK would initially be referred to the local distributor, as selling to retailers outside the UK was 'not a desirable practice'. Thirdly, THE Games would not sell to wholesalers in the UK, as they could sell on to UK retailers or retailers outside the UK, and lead to violations of one of the first two principles.[60] Even with these policies, Nintendo was still concerned that UK stocks were reaching the continental market, but THE Games assured it that 'we will try at all costs, to prevent product arriving in Europe'.[61] Because of this, and other practices designed to reduce parallel exports, Nintendo and its distributors were found to be in breach of Art 81 EC. This strict approach to restrictions of parallel imports being considered as 'object' restrictions was confirmed in *GlaxoSmithKline*.[62]

The *Polypropylene* case, mentioned above, is a good example of the way that a horizontal cartel can operate.[63] After its investigation, the Commission found strong evidence that 15 undertakings working in the polypropylene market had formed an agreement to restrict competition. It was discovered that there had been regular contact between the suppliers of polypropylene since 1977. These meetings were held on a EU-wide basis between senior management, referred to as the 'bosses' meetings, and technical managers, referred to as the 'experts' meetings. The bimonthly EU-wide meetings were supplemented by occasional national meetings.

In its legal assessment of the cartel, the Commission decided that the complex scheme of arrangements between the 15 suppliers formed a single continuing agreement. There was no need for the agreement to contain sanctions or to be in writing. There was also no need, when considering the cartel, to differentiate between the aspects which constituted an agreement and those which were merely concerted practices. Even where particular undertakings were not present at all the meetings, they were held to be involved via a reporting system whereby all the undertakings knew what was being proposed by the others. The important point was the consensus that was reached between the producers and the steps that were taken over a period of time to implement that consensus. The Commission did not consider it necessary to address in any detail the effects of the agreement as its object was obviously anti-competitive, but the Commission did outline a number of ways in which it believed the effects were manifested.

On appeal, the CFI upheld the Commission's findings.[64] It agreed that there was effectively a single 'agreement' operated over a period of time. It added that where some parts of the 'agreement' could be described as an agreement proper, others could be better categorised as concerted practices. Despite this, there was no need to distinguish between them, especially where the various schemes formed a single infringement of a complex nature. The argument that the cartel's activities did not affect competition was also dismissed by the CFI on the basis that the effects of

---

58 See Cases 56 and 58/64 *Consten and Grundig v Commission* [1966] ECR 299.
59 Commission Decision 2003/675/EC *Video Games/Nintendo* [2003] OJ L255/33.
60 Recital 102.
61 Recital 118.
62 Cases C-501, 513, 515 and 519/06 P *GlaxoSmithKline Services Unlimited v Commission* [2009] ECR I-9291.
63 Cartel control is discussed in more detail in Chapter 7. For an excellent account of the operation of cartels in Europe and their legal regulation, see Harding, C and Joshua, J, *Regulating Cartels in Europe*, 2nd edn (2010) Oxford: OUP.
64 See Case T-7/89 *Hercules NV v Commission* [1991] ECR II-1711. The appeal to the Court of Justice did not directly address this issue: Case C-51/92P [1999] ECR I-4235.

the agreement were not relevant as its object was clear. The relevant question was whether the agreement could have affected the market, and as the undertakings concerned represented nearly the whole market that question must be answered in the affirmative. The CFI's findings were upheld by the Court of Justice.[65]

The 'effect' of restricting competition

Where an agreement does not have the object of restricting competition, it is necessary to consider its effects. Even horizontal agreements between competitors may not have the object of restricting competition. In innovative or high technology industries it is common for undertakings to co-operate in the development of new technology or products. That co-operation will be designed to improve competition by bringing new products on to the market or to improve the technology used in existing production, thereby allowing for greater efficiency. Without spreading the risks involved in research and development the project may not be viable. Even if the research would have gone ahead, the co-operation may result in the development reaching the market more quickly. While the agreements in such situations may result in advantages, they may also have disadvantages. When the research work is complete should there also be co-operation in production and marketing of the new technology? At what stage should the co-operation cease? By allowing competitors to work together on the development programme, will co-operation blunt their desire to compete in other areas? These concerns mean that the particular agreement must be carefully considered to establish its potential effects on the market.[66]

When the effect of an agreement is considered, it is important to examine the market in its economic context. Without a full analysis of the market in question it will be impossible to discover if the agreement has prevented, restricted or distorted competition, or has the potential to do so. This was emphasised by the Court in *Brasserie de Haecht v Wilkin*:[67]

> It would be pointless to consider an agreement, decision or concerted practice by reason of its effect if those effects were to be taken distinct from the market in which they are seen to operate.[68]

The Court adopted similar reasoning in *Delimitis*.[69] In both these cases the agreements were between brewers and cafes. The agreements tied the cafe owners to purchase beer supplies from the brewer. A single agreement would be of limited impact; however, a network of similar agreements across a national market could have the effect of foreclosing competition. If large numbers of outlets were tied to brewers, potential competitors might find it difficult to enter the market and compete against existing brewers. Although the definition of the relevant market is more traditionally associated with Art 102 TFEU, in this type of Art 101 TFEU case it is also vital. Before deciding whether a network of agreements can foreclose a market it is important to define exactly which type of outlets are competing. For example, do cafes compete with off-licences and supermarkets? It is also apparent from the reasoning in *Delimitis* that not only must consideration be given to the effects of the agreement on the existing market, but also to the agreement's potential effects on the development of the market. The Court emphasised

---

65 See, for example, Case C-49/92P *Commission v Anic Partecipazioni SpA* [1999] ECR I-4125.
66 For the Commission's treatment of such agreements, see Commission Regulation No 1217/2010 on the application of Article 101(3) of the Treaty on the functioning of the European Union to categories of research and development agreements, [2010] OJ L355/36, and Commission Guidelines on the applicability of Article 101 of the Treaty on the Functioning of the European Union to horizontal co-operation agreements, [2011] OJ C11/1.
67 Case 23/67 [1967] ECR 407.
68 Ibid, at para 40.
69 See Case C-234/89 *Delimitis v Henniger Bräu* [1991] ECR I-935. For an application of these principles by the CFI, see Case T-25/99 *Roberts v Commission* [2001] ECR II-1881.

that the effects of the agreement, taken together with other contracts of the same type, may have an impact on the opportunities for other organisations to gain access to the market. This would in turn have an effect on the products offered to consumers. The Court decided that the demand structure for beer to be consumed on the premises, in particular in public houses and restaurants, was very different from the retail sector in that there was also a provision of services where beer was consumed on the premises. The differing nature of different sectors of the trade was also indicated by the different distribution systems. As this was a preliminary ruling under the Art 267 TFEU procedure, the Court indicated a number of factors which should be taken into account when examining the potential to foreclose the market through a network of agreements:[70]

1   the possibilities for a new competitor to penetrate the bundle of contracts by acquisition of an established operator or the establishment of new outlets;
2   the conditions of competition on the market, including the level of product saturation and customer loyalty.

When a market is difficult to enter, the national court should also examine the effects of the bundle of agreements in question to decide the extent to which the bundle of agreements contributes towards that effect. If the effect is insignificant, the agreements will not fall within the Art 101(1) prohibition.

The legality of exclusive purchasing commitments was considered by the CFI in *Van Den Bergh v Commission*.[71] This dispute concerned single-wrapped ice creams intended for immediate consumption, referred to as 'impulse ice cream'.[72] In the late 1980s and early 1990s, HB supplied its retailers with freezer cabinets free or at nominal rent. The freezer agreements could be terminated at any time with two months' notice on either side. HB owned and maintained the cabinets and they were to be used exclusively for products supplied by HB. At least 40% of all outlets in the relevant market only had freezer cabinets supplied by HB with its freezer exclusivity requirements. The CFI stressed that 'the contractual restrictions on retailers must be examined not just in a purely formal manner from the legal point of view, but also by taking into account the specific economic context in which the agreements in question operate'.[73] The CFI supported the view that the HB network had a 'considerably dissuasive effect on retailers' and 'operate *de facto* as a tie on sales outlets' such that 'the effect of the exclusivity clause in practice is to restrict the commercial freedom of retailers to choose the products they wish to sell in their sales outlets'.[74] Accordingly, the CFI rejected a purely formalistic approach which would rely on formal contractual periods of notice.

Market analysis is now very important in the consideration of the effect of an agreement, although in the early years of the EU competition system the Commission and the Court gave the 'effect' requirement a very broad interpretation, catching many agreements which appeared to be restrictions on conduct rather than on competition. The Commission subsequently used Regulation 17's exemption procedure to allow agreements which had positive benefits to proceed. This approach came under strain as the workload of the Directorate General for Competition

---

70 Case C-234/89 *Delimitis v Henniger Bräu* [1991] ECR I-935, paras 20–26. See, also, Case T-25/99 *Roberts v Commission* [2001] ECR II-1881 and *Crehan v Inntrepreneur Pub Co (CPC)* [2004] EWCA Civ 637 for consideration of the network of brewers and potential foreclosures in a UK context.
71 Case T-7/93 *Langnese-Iglo GmbH v Commission* [1995] ECR II-1533; Case C-279/95P *Langnese-Iglo GmbH v Commission* [1998] ECR I-5609; and Case T-65/98 *Van den Bergh Foods v Commission* [2003] ECR II-04653. See also *IMS v Ofcom* [2008] CAT 13.
72 The Commission found, at para 28, that HB's value share of the impulse ice cream market in Ireland was about 85% from June to September 1986.
73 At para 84.
74 At para 98.

increased. The Commission was no longer capable of giving each potentially restrictive agreement individual attention. Partly in order to relieve this problem, a number of block exemptions[75] were adopted to exempt classes of agreements from the prohibition. The block exemptions cover a number of common types of agreement, including vertical agreements[76] and technology transfer agreements.[77]

The Court also became involved in developing jurisprudence, which has gone some way to reducing the scope of Art 101(1). When considering a number of vertical agreements, the Court appeared to be willing not to prohibit agreements that contained restrictive clauses, if the clauses were pro-competitive when considered in context.[78] More particularly, in a series of cases, the Court has shown that it will analyse restrictions in agreements to examine whether they are 'necessary' for the agreement to be of commercial value; this is often referred to as the 'ancillary restraints' doctrine. One of the earliest examples was in *Remia*.[79] This case involved an agreement, for the sale of a business, which included a restrictive covenant. It is common for the sale price of a business to include an amount for the goodwill that the business has built up over time. The purchaser would not wish to pay for this goodwill if the vendor were able to open a competing business in the vicinity and entice customers away from the original business. A restriction is often placed in such contracts prohibiting the vendor from trading in the same type of business in that vicinity for a period of time. A restrictive covenant was examined in this case. Looking at the term, it is clear to see how competition might be affected. One potential competitor is barred from entering the market for a stipulated period, but, on the other hand, the whole agreement is pro-competitive, as without such a term a potential purchaser would be deterred from investing in the business. They would not want to pay for the goodwill. It would, therefore, be considerably more difficult to enter, or exit, the market. The Court found that the restrictive covenant was necessary as an ancillary restraint.[80] Without the restrictive term, the pro-competitive agreement would not go ahead. It did not, therefore, fall within Art 101(1).

On a number of occasions, the Court has used similar reasoning to find that agreements, which are pro-competitive but which contain potentially restrictive terms, do not fall within the prohibition so long as the restrictions are necessary for the agreement to work. Examples can be found in a variety of areas: the licensing of intellectual property rights, as in *Nungesser*;[81] the qualitative membership criteria in selective distribution systems, as in *Metro I*;[82] and the prescribed sales methods and limited territorial restrictions in franchising systems, as in *Pronuptia*.[83]

The conception of the 'ancillary restraints' doctrine within Art 101(1) is not universally supported. Strong arguments have been made in support of a more flexible 'rule of reason'

---

75 While the term 'block exemption' is somewhat erroneous in light of the abolition of the exemption process under Regulation 1/2003, it still forms a useful shorthand reference for the Regulations.
76 See Commission Regulation 330/2010 on the application of Art 101(3) of the Treaty on the Functioning of the European Union to categories of vertical agreements and concerted practices, [2010] OJ L102/1, and Commission Notice, Guidelines on Vertical Restraints, [2010] OJ C130/1.
77 See Regulation 316/2014/EU on the application of Art 101(3) of the TFEU to categories of technology transfer agreements, [2014] OJ L93/17, and Commission Notice, Guidelines on the application of Art 101 of the TFEU Treaty to technology transfer agreements, [2014] OJ C89/3.
78 See Case C-234/89 *Delimitis v Henniger Bräu* [1991] ECR I-935. For an implementation of the *Delimitis* principles in the UK, see *Passmore v Morland plc* [1999] 3 All ER 1005; [1999] 1 CMLR 1129 where the English Court of Appeal ruled that the validity of an agreement may change as the market conditions alter.
79 Case 42/84 *Remia and Nutricia v Commission* [1985] ECR 2545.
80 The CFI has gone some way to define what constitutes an ancillary restraint in Case T-112/99 *Métropole Télévision and Others v Commission* [2001] ECR II-2459. See, also, Commission Notice, Guidelines on the application of Art 81(3) of the Treaty, [2004] OJ C101/97, paras 28–31.
81 Case 258/78 *Nungesser v Commission* [1982] ECR 2015.
82 Case 26/76 *Metro v Commission* [1977] ECR 1875.
83 Case 161/84 *Pronuptia v Schillgalis* [1986] ECR 353.

approach similar to that adopted in the US.[84] In some cases it would appear that the Court is effectively balancing the pro-competitive and anti-competitive elements of a particular agreement. One of the leading cases that supports this reading is *Wouters*,[85] an Art 267 TFEU reference regarding the compatibility of Dutch rules that prevented members of the Bar operating in multi-disciplinary partnerships with accountants. The Court initially stated that the rules, which were a decision of an association of undertakings, were restrictive of competition; but it also stressed that account must be taken of the 'overall context' in which the decision was taken and its effects.[86] After completing its analysis the Court came to the view that the rules did not go beyond, 'what is necessary in order to ensure the proper practice of the legal profession'.[87] The manner in which the Court undertook its analysis seemed much closer to a balancing approach than in many other cases.[88] It should be noted that the Court has tended to restrict this form of reasoning to cases in which a balance has to be struck between the economic imperatives of competition and some other type of principle; for example the interests of good administration of justice or the special situation of sports.[89] The arguments surrounding the Court's approach to restrictions within vertical agreements, which have their own specific Regulation, are discussed in more detail later in this chapter.

Agreements of minor importance

A limit on the application of Art 101 is the *de minimis* principle. The *de minimis* principle covers agreements which, due to their limited significance, may not be caught by the prohibition. Such agreements do not fall within the prohibition as either they do not have an appreciable effect on competition or they do not affect interstate trade. This principle was first expounded by the Court in *Völk*[90] and has been formalised by the Commission in a series of Notices. The latest Notice on agreements of minor importance was published in 2014.[91] The Notice is based on a market share test and differentiates between horizontal and vertical agreements. Paragraph 8 of the Notice states that an agreement will not appreciably restrict competition if the aggregate market share of the participating undertakings does not exceed 10% of the relevant market for agreement between competition, or 15% of the relevant market for agreement between non-competition.[92] For mixed agreements, the 10% threshold is applicable. The market share threshold is reduced to 5% where a market is affected by networks of similar agreements.[93] In addition to the market share test, the Commission states that agreements between small- and medium-sized undertakings will rarely be capable of affecting trade between Member States.[94] Even where an agreement falls below the thresholds in the Notice, it may still be considered to be appreciable if it is an 'object' agreement,

84 See, for instance, Hawk, B, 'System Failure: Vertical Restraints and EC Competition Law' (1995) 32 CMLRev 973 and Callery, C, 'Should the European Union Embrace or Exorcise *Leegin*'s "Rule of Reason"?' [2011] ECLR 42.
85 Case C-309/99 *Wouters v Algemene Raad van de Nederlandse Orde van Advocaten* [2002] ECR I-1577.
86 At para 97.
87 At para 109.
88 For a discussion of many of these issues in the UK context see, *The Racecourse Assoc v OFT* [2005] CAT 29.
89 See, for instance, Case C-519/04 P, *Meca-Medina v Commission* [2006] ECR I-6991. See, for instance, Weatherill, SR, 'Anti-doping Revisited – the Demise of the Rule of "Purely Sporting Interest"?' [2006] ECLR 645.
90 Case 5/69 *Völk v Ets Vervaecke Sprl* [1969] ECR 295, [1969] CMLR 273.
91 Commission Notice on agreements of minor importance which do not appreciably restrict competition under Art 101(1) of the TFEU (*de minimis*), C (2014) 4136 final. See, also, Commission Notice, Guidelines on the effect on trade concept contained in Arts 81 and 82 of the Treaty, [2004] OJ C101/81.
92 The importance of this figure was reduced following the adoption of the original Vertical Agreements BER, Regulation 2790/1999/EC, [1999] OJ L336/21.
93 At para 10 of the Notice.
94 At para 4 of the Notice. Medium-sized undertakings are defined, in Commission Recommendation 2003/361/EC concerning the definition of micro-, small- and medium-sized enterprises, [2003] OJ L124/36, as undertakings with fewer than 250 employees and either an annual turnover of no more than €50m or a balance sheet not exceeding €43m.

or it contains one of the 'hard-core' restrictions set out in para 13, such as price-fixing, limitation of output or allocation of markets. This important caveat regarding the use of the *de minimis* Notice was set out by the Court in *Expedia*.[95] The Court determined that the Notice is binding only on the Commission in its enforcement of the competition rules. The NCAs are not bound by the Notice, as it is merely 'soft law' and their duty is to enforce the binding Treaty provisions. However, the NCAs, and presumably the national courts, may choose to take into account the Notice in their consideration of the appreciability of the effects of the agreement in its own particular context.

Within the Internal Market

The final part of the prohibition focuses on its territorial extent. Only agreements which restrict competition within the 'internal market' are prohibited. Questions have been raised as to the application of the EU rules to agreements between undertakings established outside the EU. The Commission has always been of the opinion that such application is possible under the Treaty. In *Dyestuffs*,[96] the Commission found against ICI on the basis that, even though it was at that time established outside the EU, it had put the concerted practice into effect through its subsidiaries in Europe.

The same question was considered in *Wood Pulp*.[97] The majority of wood pulp suppliers investigated by the Commission were then based outside the EU in North America and Scandinavia. Sales were made directly into the EU via subsidiaries, branches or agents. The Court's judgment concentrated on the 'implementation' of the agreement, decision or concerted practice within the internal market, but the Court added that it was immaterial that the implementation was carried out through persons operating within the territory. The exact meaning of implementation within the judgment is not entirely clear; however, the Court appeared willing to uphold the application of EU competition law against undertakings which had no physical presence in the territory of the EU.

Although *Wood Pulp* is still the leading judgment in this area the CFI adopted a different approach in *Gencor*.[98] Rather than discussing the 'implementation' of the agreement the CFI concentrated on whether there was an 'immediate and substantial effect in the Community'.[99] The concentration on 'effect' rather than 'implementation' would lead to a wider and much more flexible test.

Article 101(2) TFEU

Article 101(2) TFEU describes the consequence of breaching the prohibition contained in Art 101(1) TFEU. The agreement is automatically void. The sanction of nullity is not significant for agreements which involve market sharing or price-fixing, as it would be incredibly unusual if the parties to such an agreement were to seek its enforcement. In those circumstances, the parties would seek to deny the agreement and hope that they could avoid a fine or the civil consequences of being found in breach.

The sanction of nullity is more important when Art 101 is used as a 'Euro-defence' by a party that is already in breach of the contested agreement or wishes to escape its terms.

---

95 Case C-221/11 *Expedia Inc v Autorité de la concurrence and Others* [2011] ECR I-0000. See also the Commission Staff Working Document, 'Guidance on restrictions of competition "by object" for the purpose of defining which agreements may benefit from the De Minimis Notice', SWD (2014) 198 final.
96 Cases 48, 49, 51–57/69 *ICI v Commission* [1972] ECR 619.
97 See Cases C-89, 104, 114, 116, 117 and 125–27/85 *A Ahlstrom Oy v Commission* [1993] ECR I-1307.
98 Case T-102/96 *Gencor v Commission* [1999] II-ECR 753. Although this is a merger case, the principles are similar.
99 Ibid, at para 90.

The use of Art 101 as a defence is quite common in respect of agreements for the licensing of intellectual property rights or for other vertical restraints, such as distribution agreements.[100] One of the first competition cases to come before the UK courts involved, *inter alia*, an Art 101 Euro-defence, although the defendant in that case was not party to the relevant agreement. *Application des Gaz v Falks Veritas*[101] was a preliminary hearing in a copyright dispute. A French company, Application des Gaz, claimed copyright in a metal gas canister and sought to prevent an English company, Falks Veritas, from producing an identical can. The French company had already granted an exclusive right to production to another English company. After the coming into effect of the UK's accession to the EU, Falks Veritas sought to amend its defence to include an alleged breach of Art 101. It claimed that there was a concerted practice between the French company and its English licensees to discourage retailers from stocking the Falks Veritas product. The Court of Appeal did not consider the merits of the case in detail but accepted that the defence based on Art 101 appeared to be valid.

Another example of an Art 101 Euro-defence was considered by the English High Court in *Inntrepreneur Estates v Mason*.[102] Inntrepreneur, the landlord of a chain of pubs, sought to forfeit the lease granted to Mason after Mason fell into arrears with his rent. The landlord sought rent arrears and other sums due, a total of £38,000. The tenant claimed in his defence that because of the 'tie' in the lease requiring the tenant to purchase beers and other drinks directly from the landlord, the lease was an agreement falling within the prohibition under Art 101(1) and therefore null and void under Art 101(2). In the interlocutory appeal it was not contested that the argument based on Art 101 had a real prospect of success. The contentious issue concerned the effects of nullity. If the whole lease became void the claim would fail, but if Art 101(2) only affected the clause of the agreement which restricted competition, the 'tie', the rest of the lease would stand and the back rent would still be due. This question of severance was also considered by the European Court of Justice in *STM*.[103] The Court stated that the sanction of nullity only applied to those parts of the agreement that were subject to the prohibition. If it is possible to sever the offending parts, the rest of the agreement may stand. This coincides with the English case law on severance. In an earlier English intellectual property case involving Art 101, *Chemidus Wavin*,[104] the Court of Appeal decided that the offending term should be severed unless the contract would be so altered in character as not to be the contract into which the parties entered. Such an alteration would occur if a major term of the contract was removed and the removal dramatically changed the nature of the contract.

In *Passmore v Morland and Others*,[105] the English Court of Appeal addressed the question of when an agreement becomes void. Mr Passmore was, at the time of the dispute, the tenant of a pub which was tied to a small brewery. Because of the brewery's size the beer tie did not have an appreciable effect on competition. When the lease was originally granted the pub was owned by a much larger brewer that had transferred the lease to the current owner. It was argued that the lease was void when it was granted and was, therefore, still unenforceable. The Court of Appeal decided that the sanction of nullity is 'temporaneous or transient'[106] in effect, as is the prohibition. Even if the lease might have been void when it was granted it was not to be considered as still being void following the change in circumstances. It must, however, be noted that the Court of

---

100 See Odudu, O, 'Contract and Competition Law: the Euro-defence in the English Courts' in Leczykiewicz and Weatherill (eds), *The Involvement of EU Law in Private Law Relationships* (2011) Oxford: Hart, pp 395–415.
101 [1974] 1 Ch 381.
102 [1993] 2 CMLR 293.
103 Case 56/65 *STM v Maschinenbau Ulm* [1966] ECR 235.
104 *Chemidus Wavin v Société pour la Transformation et L'Exploitation des Resines Industrielles SA* [1978] 3 CMLR 514.
105 [1999] 3 All ER 1005; [1999] 1 CMLR 1129.
106 *Per* Chadwick LJ, at p 1014.

Justice has not expressed a view on this issue and the Court of Appeal did not consider it necessary to make a preliminary reference under Art 267 TFEU.[107]

Article 101(3) TFEU

Article 101(3) TFEU allows for the prohibition in Art 101(1) TFEU to be declared inapplicable if certain criteria are met. The importance of Art 101(3) stemmed from the wide interpretation adopted under Art 101(1). As a result, a large range of common agreements that fell within the prohibition could not be enforced without benefiting from the terms of Art 101(3). Under the original Regulation 17 regime, the Commission had the sole power to grant exemption under Art 101(3). This gave the Commission extensive and exclusive powers which it used to mould the shape of the competition system in the EU. It also gave the Commission the opportunity to promote other EU goals, such as market integration, within the competition sphere. The broad interpretation of Art 101(1) worked well for the Commission in the early years of competition enforcement, as it allowed the Commission to gather a large amount of information about the way in which agreements operated across the EU. As undertakings became more aware of the provisions, and the internal market became more integrated, the number of exemptions which were sought increased to such levels that the Commission had difficulty handling the workload.

The Commission took several steps to reduce the number of agreements notified for exemption. A number of block exemptions, which automatically exempted certain classes of agreement, were adopted. These allowed many common agreements, such as exclusive distribution agreements, to go ahead without Commission involvement. The Commission also sought to adopt more efficient procedures, including informal methods of closing cases. Even with these efforts the Commission's workload was still overwhelming and led to the more radical steps in the 1999 White Paper and ultimately the reforms introduced in Regulation 1/2003;[108] primarily the abolition of the notification requirement and the Commission's exclusive power to grant exemptions, with Art 101(3) becoming directly effective.

The Exception Rule

Under the pre-2004 Regulation 17 regime, if the parties to an agreement sought to benefit from the terms of Art 101(3) they needed to notify their agreement to the Commission. The Commission would then investigate the agreement, using information supplied by the parties, and decide whether it was appropriate to grant an exemption. An exemption was granted through a formal Commission decision. Because of the complexity of the procedure required, the Commission granted very few formal exemptions and a great many cases were closed informally. Because of the level of informality in the process, the detailed processes that led to exemption decisions were often somewhat opaque. In practice, the Commission tended to favour the exemption of particular classes of agreement, particularly those between parties without market power. The Commission also took into account a broad range of factors, including wider EU policies, when making a decision. For that reason the Court was not willing to interfere with the Commission's discretion, even where the Commission's reasoning was remarkably brief.[109]

---

107 See Maitland-Walker, J, 'Have English Courts Gone Too Far in Challenging the Effectiveness of EC Competition Law?' [1999] 1 ECLR 1. See, also, the discussion of *Gibbs Mew v Gemmell* [1998] EuLR 588 and Case C-453/99 *Courage Ltd v Bernard Crehan* [2001] ECR I-6297, in Chapter 2.
108 The reform process is outlined more fully in Chapter 2.
109 See Case 8/72 *Consten and Grundig v Commission* [1972] ECR 977.

Under Regulation 1/2003 there is no longer any notification procedure and the criteria for inapplicability in Art 101(3) can be applied directly by the National Competition Authorities (NCAs) and national courts, as well as by the Commission. However, the Commission's previous practice is still important as guidance on how these other authorities should approach their role under Art 101. The Commission also retains a pivotal position within the new enforcement system, being consulted by NCAs before decisions are taken and having the ability to appear before national courts as an *amicus*. The EU Courts also have an increased role under Art 101(3) through the Art 267 TFEU preliminary ruling procedure.

The four conditions for inapplicability

To benefit from the exception the agreement must satisfy the four conditions in Art 101(3). An agreement must:

1   improve the production or distribution of goods or promote technical or economic progress;
2   ensure that consumers receive a fair share of the resulting benefits;
3   not contain indispensable restrictions; and
4   not substantially eliminate competition.

To assist the NCAs and the courts in discharging their role under Regulation 1/2003, the Commission has produced Guidance on the application of Art 101(3).[110] The Guidelines follow, and expand on, the analytical framework developed by the Commission in its block exemption Regulations. The Guidelines state that once an agreement has been found to infringe Art 101(1) the role of Art 101(3) is to determine the pro-competitive benefits produced by that agreement and to assess whether these pro-competitive effects outweigh the agreement's anti-competitive effects.[111] In *Van Den Bergh*, the Commission and the CFI rejected HB's arguments for an exemption on the grounds that, *inter alia*, 'those arrangements did not present appreciable objective advantages of such a character as to compensate for the disadvantages caused to competition'.[112] It should be remembered that the Commission Notice is not binding. The Commission should follow its own Guidance, but only the Court's interpretation of the Treaty itself is binding law. The Court has generally accepted the Commission's approach but has indicated that Commission Guidance is not binding on NCAs and the domestic courts,[113] and that its Guidance cannot effectively 'narrow' the prohibitions as laid out by the Court.[114] Each of the Art 101(3) criteria will be examined in turn.

Benefit – efficiency gains

The benefit, usually through some form of efficiency gain, must be for the EU as a whole, not just the parties to the agreement. All efficiency claims must be substantiated in several ways: the nature of the efficiencies; the link between the agreement and the efficiency; the likelihood of and magnitude of the efficiency; and how and when the efficiency will be achieved.[115] In its practice under Regulation 17 the Commission was creative in using the other goals of the Community to demonstrate benefit

---

110   Commission Notice, Guidelines on the application of Art 81(3) of the Treaty, [2004] OJ C101/97.
111   At para 11.
112   Case T-65/98 *Van den Bergh Foods Ltd v Commission* [2003] ECR II-4653, [2004] 4 CMLR 1, para 140.
113   See, Case C-226/11 *Expedia Inc v Autorité de la concurrence and Others* [2012] ECR I-0000.
114   See Case C-549/10P *Tomra Systems & Others v Commission* [2012] ECR I-0000 in relation to the Art 102 TFEU Guidance.
115   Guidelines, at para 52.

where the beneficial effects, defined strictly, for competition, were limited. In *Metro*,[116] the Court accepted that the stabilisation of employment might improve production, and may therefore fall under Art 81(3). In *CECED* the Commission took into account environmental benefits that would be achieved through an agreement to restrict the manufacture or import of the least energy-efficient washing machines.[117] The Commission's approach to 'crisis cartels' is also instructive in this area.[118] Crisis cartels are cartels that may be permitted within an industry to allow for reorganisation during periods of economic difficulty. There is little reference to wider EU goals in the Commission Guidelines.[119]

No indispensable restrictions

This condition can be regarded as the Art 101(3) version of the proportionality test. An exemption will not be granted unless the restriction of competition is no less than is necessary to allow the agreement to go ahead. The Commission does not apply this test as rigorously as it does in other areas of EU law. The test has two elements: (i) the restrictive agreement must be reasonably necessary in order to achieve the efficiencies; and (ii) the individual restrictions of competition must also be reasonably necessary for the attainment of the efficiencies. The decisive factor is 'whether or not the restrictive agreement and individual restrictions make it possible to perform the activity in question more efficiently than would likely have been the case in the absence of the agreement or the restriction concerned'.[120] However, there are some forms of restriction which are very unlikely to be accepted, even if the restrictions make commercial sense in the particular agreement. This is especially the case with price-fixing, absolute territorial protection, and the other 'hard-core' restraints identified in block exemptions and the Commission Notices. Under the Regulation 17 regime the Commission often took the opportunity, post-notification, to suggest possible amendments which would have made the agreement more likely to be exempted. This will not be normal under Regulation 1/2003 and the parties to the agreement have a much more central role.

Fair share to consumers

The parties are unlikely to proceed with an agreement unless they benefit in some way from it. This criterion seeks to ensure that the benefits received by the parties to the agreement are ultimately passed on to the consumer. The reference to the consumer refers to 'the customers of the parties to the agreement and subsequent purchasers'.[121] The consumers who may receive a share of the benefit therefore range from manufacturers to high street shoppers. The main benefit is likely to be improved quality or a reduction in price. The Guidelines explain that:

> the pass-on of benefits must at least compensate consumers for any actual or likely negative impact caused to them by the restriction of competition . . . If such consumers are worse off following the agreement, the second condition of Article 81(3) is not fulfilled.[122]

---

116 See Case 26/76 *Metro v Commission* [1977] ECR 1875; [1978] 2 CMLR 1.
117 Commission Decision 2000/475/EC, [2000] OJ L187/47.
118 For example, Commission Decision 84/380/EEC *Synthetic Fibres* [1984] OJ L207/17 and Case C-209/07 *Competition Authority v BIDS* [2008] ECR I-8637.
119 But see for example Townley, C, *Article 81 EC and Public Policy* (2009) Oxford: Hart and 'Which Goals Count in Article 101 TFEU?: Public Policy and its Discontents' [2011] 9 ECLR 441–448; see also Van Rompuy, B, *Economic Efficiency: The Sole Concern of Modern Antitrust Policy? Non-efficiency Considerations under Article 101 TFEU* (2012) Kluwer Law.
120 Guidelines, at paras 73–74.
121 Guidelines, at para 84.
122 Guidelines, at para 85.

No substantial elimination of competition

The final condition is a catch-all provision which may stop agreements that would remove competition from a market. As the Guidelines put it, 'the protection of rivalry and the competitive process is given priority over potentially pro-competitive efficiency gains which could result from restrictive agreements'.[123] It is likely that agreements which substantially eliminate competition would have fallen at an earlier stage of the deliberations under Art 101(3), though, in some circumstances, this condition posed problems for the Commission under Regulation 17. This was the case where the Commission was inclined to grant an exemption but where it was difficult to show that some competition would remain on the market. The Commission considered this issue in *Synthetic Fibres*.[124] A crisis cartel was organised to reduce production levels in the fibres market. The cartel involved most of the market operators but it was argued that competition from other types of fibre would retain a level of competition. Many considered the Commission arguments not to be particularly convincing in this case. Under the modernised system it is unlikely that other national authorities will be given this type of latitude. The difficulties in sustaining a crisis cartel were also illustrated by the Irish Government's ultimately doomed attempt to support a planned reduction in capacity in the Irish beef processing industry from 2003 to 2011.[125]

Block Exemptions

The main Commission weapon, under Regulation 17, in the struggle to control its exemption workload was the adoption of Block Exemption Regulations. Block exemptions differed from individual exemptions in that they exempted a class of agreements automatically without formal intervention by and approval from the Commission. Even though the Commission's notification burden has been removed by Regulation 1/2003, the role of block exemptions remains vital. The Regulations create 'safe harbours' for the parties to common types of agreement. The parties know that if they bring their agreement within the terms of the block exemption it will be safe from challenge under Art 101 TFEU. Before the Commission may adopt a Block Exemption Regulation it must be given authority by Council.[126] Once a block exemption is in place a large number of common business agreements can be assured of validity without the parties having to individually assess their agreements under Art 101(1) and (3).

Block exemptions have been adopted for the following types of agreement: vertical agreements,[127] specialisation,[128] research and development,[129] motor vehicle distribution,[130] technology

123 Guidelines, at para 105.
124 Commission Decision 84/380/EEC, [1984] OJ L207/17.
125 See Case C-209/07 *Competition Authority v BIDS* [2008] ECR I-8637, and Irish Competition Authority, 'Notice on Agreements to Reduce Capacity', N/11/001, 16 June 2011.
126 For example, Regulation 19/65/EEC on application of Art 85(3) of the Treaty to certain categories of agreements and concerted practices, [1965] OJ Spec Ed 35.
127 Commission Regulation 330/2010/EU on the application of Art 101(3) of the Treaty on the Functioning of the European Union to categories of vertical agreements and concerted practices, [2010] OJ L102/1, and Commission Notice, Guidelines on Vertical Restraints, [2010] OJ C130/1.
128 Commission Regulation 1218/2010/EU on the application of Art 101(3) of the Treaty to categories of specialisation agreements, [2010] OJ, L335/43. See, also, Commission Guidelines on the applicability of Art 101 of the Treaty on the Functioning of the European Union to horizontal co-operation agreements, [2011] OJ C11/1.
129 Commission Regulation 1217/2010/EU on the application of Art 101(3) of the Treaty on the functioning of the European Union to categories of research and development agreements, [2010] OJ L335/36. See, also, Commission Guidelines on the applicability of Art 101 of the Treaty on the Functioning of the European Union to horizontal co-operation agreements, [2011] OJ C11/1.
130 Commission Regulation 461/2010/EU on the application of Art 101(3) of the Treaty on the Functioning of the European Union to categories of vertical agreements and concerted practices in the motor vehicle sector, [2010] OJ, L129/52.

transfer,[131] and insurance agreements.[132] The way in which the block exemptions operate has been largely overhauled since the mid-1990s. The details of the block exemptions are quite technical and therefore will not be discussed fully here. A more detailed discussion of the Vertical Agreements Regulation is contained later in this chapter. The format of all 'new-style' Regulations is basically similar. Although many of the Regulations are quite long, the central provisions are relatively short. The bulk of each Regulation deals with specialist areas which require more detailed consideration.

The first 'new-style' Block Exemption Regulation (BER) was introduced in 1999 with the adoption of the original Vertical Agreements Regulation.[133] The current Vertical Agreements Regulation[134] is discussed in detail below and carries on that approach. The Regulation creates an 'umbrella' exemption for all vertical agreements that are not covered by other block exemptions and where the seller or buyer under the agreement has a market share of less than 30%. A form of black list, of prohibited clauses, is retained in that the benefit of the exemption will be removed if the agreement contains any of the 'hard-core' restraints, such as maximum price-fixing or certain territorial restrictions. The new-style BERs are more flexible in that they do not concentrate on a clause by clause examination of each agreement. Following the adoption of the 1999 Vertical Agreements Regulation, a process of reform was undertaken in which the other BERs were transformed to reflect the new style.

The introduction of the new-style Regulations was the beginning of an overarching process in which the Commission recognised industry and commentators' concerns about the lack of flexibility in EU competition law, epitomised by the traditional block exemptions. The problems of formalism and flexibility were discussed at length in the consultation process which led to the adoption of the Vertical Agreements Regulation.[135] The use of market share thresholds to allow for increased flexibility was initially controversial. The calculation of market shares can be potentially complex problem but this approach has now been adopted in all BERs and the *De Minimis* Notice.[136]

The Commission's radical reforms in Regulation 1/2003,[137] as discussed in Chapter 2, also moved forward the discussion of BERs. The exception in Art 101(3) is now directly applicable and any agreement that falls within its terms is not prohibited without the need for notification. The position of block exemptions under such a system is interesting. The Commission intends to continue to utilise BERs under the directly applicable system to ensure that the legal certainty offered by those Regulations is retained. While the BERs will be useful for organisations planning agreements, it is clear that they are not be the only way that parties could seek clearance. Even if an agreement falls outside a BER it will still be possible to benefit from the exception in Art 101(3) as a matter of course if it can be shown to fulfil it terms. National courts may be willing to clear agreements that fall outside the terms of a BER but arguably fit within

131 Regulation 316/2014/EU on the application of Art 101(3) of the TFEU to categories of technology transfer agreements, [2014] OJ L93/17.
132 Commission Regulation 267/2010/EU on the application of Art 101(3) of the Treaty on the Functioning of the European Union to certain categories of agreements, decisions and concerted practices in the insurance sector, [2010] OJ L83/1–7.
133 Commission Regulation 2790/99/EC, [1999] OJ L336/21. See Whish, 'Regulation 2790/99: the Commission's "new style" block exemption for vertical agreements' (2000) 37 CMLRev 887.
134 Commission Regulation 330/2010/EU on the application of Art 101(3) of the Treaty on the Functioning of the European Union to categories of vertical agreements and concerted practices, [2010] OJ L102/1. See Commission Notice, Guidelines on Vertical Restraints, [2010] OJ C130/1 and Whish, R and Bailey, D, 'Regulation 330/2010: the Commission's New Block Exemption for Vertical Agreements' (2010) 47(6) CMLRev 1757–1791.
135 See, for example, the Green Paper on vertical restraints in EC competition policy C(96) 721 final, and the follow-up Commission communication, [1998] OJ, C365/3.
136 Commission Notice on agreements of minor importance which do not appreciably restrict competition under Art 101(1) of the TFEU (De Minimis Notice), C (2014) 4136 final.
137 Proposal for a Council Regulation on the implementation of the rules on competition laid down in Arts 81 and 82 of the Treaty, C(2000) 582, [2000] OJ C365/284.

Art 101(3); however, it is questionable whether the courts will be quick to approve agreements containing a BER's black list terms.

Article 101 TFEU and the National Courts

As Art 101 is directly effective it has an important impact on national courts.[138] Under Regulation 17 the concurrent jurisdiction of the national courts and the Commission resulted in several problems, especially where a dispute over an agreement came before the national courts and the agreement had been notified to the Commission. As the national courts could not apply Art 101(3) they had difficulty dealing with such cases. The majority of those problems have been resolved by the introduction of Regulation 1/2003 and the direct applicability of Art 101(3). However, some problems may still occur where the Commission or an NCA is investigating a potential breach of the prohibition and the matter also comes before the courts in a domestic dispute. The Commission issued guidance to the national courts as part of the 'modernisation package'.[139] The guidance states that where the Commission is dealing with a matter that comes before a national court the court should ensure that it does not adopt a decision that would conflict with the decision contemplated by the Commission. The national court may, therefore, wish to stay its proceedings until the Commission has reached its decision.[140] If a Commission decision has been adopted the courts cannot make a decision contrary to the Commission decision without referring a question to the Court under Art 267 TFEU.[141] While domestic litigation should now be less problematic, the *Masterfoods* and *Crehan* litigation indicate the problems which may be encountered.[142] As many of the questions concerning the uniform application of the law are common between Art 101 and 102 TFEU, these issues are dealt with more fully in Chapter 2.

State Intervention in the Market and Article 101 TFEU

The main limit on the behaviour of Member States within EU law is enshrined in Art 4(3) TEU. Article 4(3) obliges Member States to abstain from adopting measures which could jeopardise the attainment of the objectives of the Union. The Commission can enforce this obligation through Art 258 TFEU where the actions of Member States threaten to distort competition. In *Inno v ATAB*[143] the Court of Justice stated in very broad terms that Member States should not adopt measures which deprived the competition rules of their effect. The subsequent case law has largely been used to refine that judgment.

In several cases the Court of Justice has challenged the sanctioning of private cartels by a Member State. In *BNIC v Yves Aubert*,[144] the Court examined the extension of a price-fixing agreement set up by BNIC, a trade organisation for cognac producers, to the entire industry through a ministerial order. An action had been brought against Yves Aubert for undercutting the fixed price. The Court was of the view that the ministerial order extended the impact of the

---

138 See Odudu, O, 'Contract and Competition Law: The Euro-defence in the English Courts' in Leczykiewicz and Weatherill (eds), *The Involvement of EU Law in Private Law Relationships* (2011) Oxford: Hart, pp 395–415.
139 Commission Notice on the co-operation between the Commission and the courts of the EU Member States in the application of Arts 81 and 82 EC, [2004] OJ C101/54.
140 Ibid, at para 12.
141 Although the issue is potentially more problematic where it is not the same agreement and parties under scrutiny. See Case C-344/98 *Masterfoods Ltd v HB Ice Cream* [2000] ECR I-11369.
142 Ibid, and *Crehan v Inntrepreneur Pub Co (CPC)* [2006] UKHL 38, [2007] 1 AC 333, [2006] 4 All ER 465.
143 Case 13/77 [1977] ECR 2115.
144 Case 136/86 [1987] ECR 4789.

private agreement and constituted a breach of France's obligations under EU law. It seems obvious that the Court was able to challenge the state support of a blatant price-fixing agreement, but the use of Art 101 has been extended to less obvious situations. There is no need for the state measure to support an existing agreement, only the need, as in *Vlaamse Reisbureaus*,[145] that the state measure be related to an agreement between private undertakings. In that case, the state measure prohibited travel agents from passing on commissions to their clients.

In *Van Eycke*[146] the Court held that Member States could not 'deprive [their] own legislation of its official character by delegating to private traders responsibility for taking decisions affecting the economic sphere'. The danger with such delegation is that it may lead to traders disguising anti-competitive activity behind the veil of state regulation. As traders would represent only their own interests, rather than the interests of the state as a whole, traders should not be granted such powers. It can be seen that the grant of such powers would result in an organisation that would effectively operate as a cartel.

The operation of Art 101, in relation to state measures, is therefore dependent upon the activities of undertakings in the market. The acts of the state will not be challenged unless they come within one of the types of situation mentioned above.

Introduction to UK Controls on Anti-Competitive Agreements

The remainder of this chapter shall focus on the Competition Act 1998 Chapter I prohibition and key aspects of the enforcement practice and case law under that prohibition in the UK. The Competition Act 1998 repealed the restrictive trade practices legislation of 1976 and set out a new prohibition on anti-competitive agreements, the 'Chapter I prohibition', modelled on Art 101 TFEU. However, it is instructive to consider the structure and nature of the legislation it replaced in order to understand the rationale for reform and basis for introducing the new rules.

The 1976 Restrictive Trade Practices Legislation and Reform

The principal, pre-1998, legislation was the Restrictive Trade Practices Act (RTPA) 1976 which, together with the Resale Prices Act 1976, consolidated earlier UK legislation. After the enactment of the Fair Trading Act 1973, the Director General of Fair Trading (DGFT) was given the functions of the Registrar under the existing restrictive trade practices legislation, and those functions were continued when the RTPA 1976 was introduced. The formalistic style of the RTPA 1976 was one of the most significant aspects of the legislation, as the Act's provisions relied on the technical form of an agreement in order for an agreement to be registrable. This aspect was criticised and often led to very technical arguments as to which types of restrictions in agreements were covered by the legislation. If parties failed to register a registrable agreement it was rendered void. Registered agreements would come before the Restrictive Practices Court (RPC) to determine if the agreement was in the public interest. If the RPC found the relevant restrictions to be contrary to the public interest, it would make an appropriate declaration and those restrictions would be void.

---

145 Case 311/85 *Vereniging van Vlaamse Reisbureaus v Sociale Dienst* [1987] ECR 3801.
146 Case 267/86 [1988] ECR 4769. See also the related cases of Case C-35/96 *Commission v Italy* [1998] ECR I-3851 and Case T-513/93 *CNSD v Commission* [2000] ECR II-1807.

The 1976 Act was partially successful in dealing with restrictive trade practices. Nonetheless, the evidence that many cartels still operated without detection was one of the reasons for reform proposals which addressed the lack of sanctions and investigative powers under the legislation. The Conservative Government finally decided, in 1996, to introduce legislation to reform UK competition law[147] and published a consultation document followed by an explanatory document and draft Bill[148] which proposed the replacement of the 1976 Acts with a prohibition on anti-competitive agreements, based on Art 101. Following the 1997 election the Labour Government almost immediately published a new explanatory document and draft Bill, the latter forming the basis of the Competition Act 1998.[149]

The Competition Act 1998 – The Chapter I Prohibition

Part I of the Act introduced two new prohibitions based on Arts 101 and 102 TFEU. These are known as the Chapter I and Chapter II prohibitions. The Chapter I prohibition is in respect of agreements, decisions and concerted practices, between or by undertakings or associations of undertakings, which are implemented in the UK, and the object or effect of which is the prevention, restriction or distortion of competition in the UK. The Chapter I prohibition is in s 2 of the Act, which sets out virtually identical provisions to those in Art 101 TFEU. The principal difference is that s 2 refers to agreements, etc., which are implemented and affect trade in the UK. Consistency of interpretation with EU law, Art 101 in this context, is ensured by s 60 of the Act. This provides that the determination of any questions under the prohibitions should be consistent with the treatment of corresponding questions arising under EU law. This provision ensures that EU case law as to what types of agreement are caught by the Art 101 prohibition, will be followed to the extent that it is relevant in a national context.[150] It is also clear from UK enforcement practice and, notably, from the judgments of the Competition Appeal Tribunal, that EU case law is routinely relied on as underpinning the interpretation of the domestic prohibition.

Chapter III of the 1998 Act makes provision for the investigation and enforcement of the Chapter I and II prohibitions. As noted in Chapter 2, the key role of enforcing and applying the two sets of prohibitions in the UK is undertaken by the CMA. Section 25 of the 1998 Act provides that the CMA may conduct an investigation upon reasonable suspicion that the prohibition has been infringed. The powers of investigation provided under ss 26–29 are similar to those powers afforded to the Commission under Arts 18–21 of Regulation 1/2003.[151] Similarly, the CMA is required under s 31 to give persons affected by a proposed decision on whether the prohibition has been infringed an opportunity to make representations. The CMA may make interim measures under s 35, and is empowered to require conduct in breach of the prohibition to be modified or terminated.[152] Section 36 allows the imposition of a fine of up to 10% of the worldwide turnover of an

---

147 See for example, White Paper, *Opening Markets: New Policy on Restrictive Trade Practices* Cm 727, 1989.

148 Department of Trade and Industry, *Tackling Cartels and the Abuse of Market Power: Implementing the Government's Policy for Competition Law Reform, a Consultation Document*, March 1996, London: DTI and *Tackling Cartels and the Abuse of Market Power: A Draft Bill, an Explanatory Document*, August 1996, London: DTI. See, also, Robertson, A, 'The Reform of UK Competition Law – Again?' [1996] ECLR 210; and Rose, S, 'Tackling Cartels: The Green Paper Proposal for Implementing the Government's Policy on Restrictive Trade Practices' [1996] ECLR 384.

149 Department of Trade and Industry, *A Prohibition Approach to Anti-Competitive Agreements and Abuse of a Dominant Position: Draft Bill*, August 1997, London: DTI. The subsequent Bill, which had its first reading in the House of Lords on 15 October 1997, was amended in certain respects from the original draft Bill. See Peretz, G, 'Detection and Deterrence of Secret Cartels under the UK Competition Bill' [1998] ECLR 145.

150 See discussion in Chapter 4 at 'Consistency with EU law'.

151 Sections 42–44 of the 1998 Act create certain offences in relation to the obstruction of the OFT's information gathering tasks under these provisions.

152 Under s 33. Section 34 provides that this may be enforced by a court order.

undertaking whose conduct infringes the Chapter I prohibition. There is a detailed discussion, in Chapter 2, on the fining policy and practice under the 1998 Act, and also in Chapter 7 in relation to Cartels. 'Small agreements' are immune from the imposition of penalties for breach of the prohibition.[153] The CAT, established by s 12 and Sch 2 to the Enterprise Act 2002, acts as an appeals tribunal in relation to decisions taken in respect of the prohibition. The mechanism for appeals is regulated by Sch 8 to the 1998 Act. Third parties with a sufficient interest may also appeal. CAT judgments are available on its website.[154]

Further appeals against CAT judgments may be made on a point of law to the Court of Appeal, Court of Session in Scotland or Court of Appeal in Northern Ireland in respect of England and Wales, Scotland and Northern Ireland, respectively.

The operation of the prohibition

Harmonisation

Section 60(1) of the 1998 Act provides that:

> The purpose of this section is to ensure that so far as is possible (having regard to any relevant differences between the provisions concerned), questions arising under this Part in relation to competition within the United Kingdom are dealt with in a manner which is consistent with the treatment of corresponding questions arising in EU law in relation to competition within the European Union.

The introduction of the new Chapter I prohibition was intended to harmonise domestic law with EU law. Thus, s 2 replicated the Art 101 TFEU model and was reinforced by the requirement, under s 60, to interpret the prohibition consistently with EU law, subject to 'any relevant differences' between the national and EU provision.[155] This means that EU jurisprudence, on such issues as what constitutes an agreement or concerted practice, and the distinction between by object and by effect restrictions, is applied by the UK competition authorities (CMA and sectoral regulators) and the courts (including the CAT). Moreover, some business arrangements may benefit from the parallel exemption system in s 10, whereby certain forms of agreement, such as research and development agreements which fall within the relevant EU Block Exemption Regulation, are automatically exempted from the Chapter I prohibition. The position on vertical agreements under the prohibition is also aligned with EU law and the Vertical Agreements Block Exemption Regulation (VABER) as discussed below.

Agreements and concerted practices

Like Art 101(1) TFEU, s 2 prohibits certain agreements, decisions of associations and concerted practices; it also includes an indicative list of types of agreement which may be covered. Each of the terms used in Art 101 – agreements, decisions of associations and concerted practices – has a separate definition, but there is considerable overlap between them. It is, therefore, not crucial that an 'agreement' is identifiable, so long as it is demonstrable that some form of collusion, falling within the concept of 'concerted practice', has occurred.[156] The concept of agreement is not restricted to legally binding and enforceable agreements, as this would make evasion of the

---

153 Competition Act 1998 (Small Agreements and Conduct of Minor Significance) Regulations 2000, SI 2000/262.
154 At www.catribunal.org.uk.
155 See Rayment, B, 'The Consistency Principle: Section 60 of the Competition Act 1998', Chapter 4 in Rodger, B (ed), *Ten Years of UK Competition Law Reform* (2010) Dundee: DUP.
156 The European Court discussed the overlap between 'concerted practices' and 'agreements' in Case C-49/92P *Commission v Anic Partecipazioni SpA* [1999] ECR I-4125.

prohibition very simple. The term 'concerted practice' has been given a particularly broad definition. There is no simple way to define exactly where an agreement stops and a concerted practice begins, although a concerted practice is evidently a looser form of 'agreement' which involves some form of understanding or collaboration.[157] Article 101 also deals with the grouping of organisations through trade or professional associations.

Effect on competition and appreciability

Section 2 mirrors Art 101(1) TFEU by prohibiting agreements, etc., which 'have as their object or effect the prevention, restriction or distortion of competition'. What constitutes such an effect on competition has been at the core of the prolonged EU debate on vertical agreements, which are discussed in more detail below. Market analysis is now crucial when considering the effect of an agreement;[158] certain restrictions will be allowed as they are 'necessary' for the commercial agreement to proceed, although, in the early years of the EU competition system, the Commission and the Court gave the 'effect' requirement a very broad interpretation, catching many agreements that appeared to be restrictions on conduct rather than of competition.

The concept of the appreciability of the effect on competition is crucial in delimiting the scope of the prohibition; while no express criterion of appreciability was included in s 2, there is well-established EU jurisprudence on the concept.[159] When applying the principle of appreciability, the CMA may find that an agreement does not have an appreciable effect on competition even where EU thresholds are exceeded. However, appreciability is irrelevant where the agreement involves price-fixing or market sharing, imposes minimum resale prices, or forms part of a network of agreements with cumulative effects.

Extra-territoriality

Section 2(3) states that the prohibition only applies 'if the agreement, decision or practice is, or is intended to be, implemented, in the United Kingdom'. There is no equivalent explicit provision setting out a territorial limitation on the effect of the prohibition in Art 101. The form of words adopted in the provision replicates the European Court's test of 'implementation' as set out in *Wood Pulp* and maintains this test for the future.[160] However, the line between implementation and effects is not particularly clear and the adoption of the term specifically from EU jurisprudence suggests that UK competition authorities will be required by s 60 to follow the line of authorities about implementation.[161]

Voidness and private litigation

Section 2(4) provides that '[a]ny agreement or decision which is prohibited by subsection (1) is void'. The European Court has confirmed that it is only those elements of an agreement that are prohibited under Art 101 TFEU that are void.[162] Ultimately, it is a matter of the general law of contract applicable in England and Wales, Scotland and Northern Ireland as to whether or not the offending provisions are severable from the agreement and the remaining agreement is enforceable. There has been considerable case law, before the English courts, involving Art 101 and the question of remedies, particularly in relation to unjust enrichment arising out of void and illegal

---

157 See discussion above in relation to Art 101 TFEU. See, for instance, *Apex Asphalt and Paving Co Ltd v OFT* [2005] CAT 4, and *Argos, Littlewoods and JJB v OFT* [2006] EWCA Civ 1318 on appeal from [2004] CAT 24, [2005] CAT 13, [2004] CAT 17 and [2005] CAT 22.

158 See Case 234/89 *Delimitis v Henniger Bräu* [1991] ECR I-935. See now, also, Commission Notice, Guidelines on vertical restraints, [2010] OJ C130/1.

159 See Commission Notice on agreements of minor importance which do not appreciably restrict competition under Art 101(1) of the TEFU (De Minimis Notice) C (2014) 4136 final.

160 Cases C-89, 104, 114, 116, 117 and 125–29/85 *A Ahlstrom Oy v Commission* [1988] ECR 5193.

161 But, see, for instance, Case T-102/96 *Gencor v Commission* [1999] II-ECR 753.

162 Case 56/65 *STM v Maschinenbau Ulm* [1966] ECR 235.

contracts.[163] The Court of Justice made clear, in *Courage v Crehan*, that EU law requires appropriate remedies for breach of competition law to be made available by national courts; this issue is discussed more fully in Chapter 3. The development of remedies under EU law is important for the 1998 Act, given that the s 60 consistency requirement also applies to decisions as to 'the civil liability of an undertaking for harm caused by its infringement of EU law'.[164]

Exemption

When the 1998 Act was introduced, ss 12–16 of Chapter I made provision for a person to make notification in respect of conduct which may infringe the prohibition. Where an agreement had been notified, the OFT had the power to grant individual exemptions to agreements which met the appropriate criteria specified in s 9. Accordingly, parties could notify agreements for negative clearance or exemption as under, pre-Regulation 1/2003, EU law. In light of the adoption of Regulation 1/2003, the Competition Act notification and individual exemption system was removed.[165] The CMA can issue non-binding opinions in cases raising novel or unresolved questions of law and has the power to accept binding commitments in Chapter I and II, and Art 101 and 102 TFEU cases.[166] As in the EU system, block exemptions may be introduced under s 6 of the 1998 Act. Only one block exemption order has been introduced to date, the Competition Act (Public Transport Ticketing Scheme Block Exemption) Order 2001, which exempts public transport ticketing schemes which meet the Order's requirements.[167] Agreements are also exempted from the Chapter I prohibition, under s 10 of the 1998 Act, where they fall within an EU Block Exemption Regulation or an Art 10 Decision by the Commission,[168] or would do so if they had an effect on interstate trade.

Vertical agreements

This is a complex issue which was the subject of considerable debate as the Competition Bill was proceeding through Parliament. Under EU law, the European Court established in its first substantive judgment on the competition rules, that Art 101 TFEU was capable of applying to both horizontal and vertical agreements, and, furthermore, that Art 101 could apply to restrictions of intra-brand competition as well as to restrictions of inter-brand competition.[169] As a consequence, a very large number of vertical agreements were brought within the scope of Art 101(1), although they could then be eligible for exemption under Art 101(3). Given the aim of harmonisation with EU law, how would the UK deal with vertical agreements under the 1998 Act? This issue will be considered in fuller detail below, but the brief answer is that the UK approach is aligned with EU law, particularly with the Vertical Agreements Block Exemption Regulation (VABER).

Other exclusions from the prohibition

The 1998 Act excludes the application of the Chapter I prohibition from a number of other areas, some of which will be outlined here. For further detail, reference should be made to Schs 1–3 to the Act. For instance, agreements are excluded, under Sch 1, from the Chapter I

---

163 See *Gibbs Mew plc v Gemmell* [1998] EuLR 588, CA, and Odudu, O, 'Contract and Competition Law: The Euro-defence in the English Courts' in Leczykiewicz and Weatherill (ed), *The Involvement of EU Law in Private Law Relationships* (2011) Oxford: Hart, pp 395–415.
164 Competition Act 1998, s 60(6)(b).
165 See, in particular, paras 2 and 9 of Sch 1 to the Competition Act 1998 and Other Enactments (Amendment) Regulations 2004, SI 2004/1261.
166 See in particular para 18 of Sch 1 to the Competition Act 1998 and Other Enactments (Amendment) Regulations 2004, SI 2004/1261 and Sch 6A to the Competition Act 1998.
167 As amended by the Competition Act 1998 (Public Transport Ticketing Schemes Block Exemption) (Amendment) Order 2005, SI 2005/3347.
168 A finding of inapplicability in relation to the Art 101TFEU prohibition.
169 Cases 56 and 58/64 *Consten and Grundig v Commission* [1966] ECR 299.

prohibition to the extent that they give rise to a merger situation within the terms of Pt 3 of the Enterprise Act 2002.[170] The exclusion is automatic and no notification need be made. Thus, where a merger falls within the jurisdiction of the 2002 Act merger system the merger will not usually be subject to dual control under the 1998 Act. Any ancillary restriction that facilitates a merger is also excluded where it is 'directly related and necessary to the implementation of the merger'.[171] Schedule 4 to the Act originally excluded a range of designated professional rules from the application of the prohibition, but this exclusion was subsequently repealed by the Enterprise Act 2002. Furthermore, in relation to land agreements, the Land Agreements Exclusion Order has now been revoked and these agreements are now within the ambit of the Chapter 1 prohibition.[172]

Enforcement: deterrence and compliance

The enhanced investigatory and enforcement powers introduced in Chapter III of the Act make a marked difference to the impact of the new anti-cartel law, compared to the previous legislation. On various occasions it has been emphasised that dealing with cartels will be the top enforcement priority. The aim of better competition law compliance by the business community is bolstered by the deterrent effect of the wide powers of investigation under ss 26–29 of the Act and the ultimate sanction of significant fines for companies breaching the prohibitions. The deterrent impact of the legislation is enhanced by instilling a fear of being caught and subjected to significant financial penalties under the Act. The CMA is part of a network of global competition agencies and co-ordinates its enforcement policies, and employs similar enforcement tools, as other agencies. One such example is the adoption of a leniency programme for whistle-blowers in cartel cases, which seeks to destabilise existing and ongoing cartels.[173] The leniency programme openly encourages companies to confess to participation in a cartel with a view to being granted immunity from fines or receiving reduced fines. The extent of the reduction is dependent on a range of factors, primarily whether the company is first to come forward to the CMA and the extent of its involvement in the cartel. Cartel enforcement and leniency in particular are considered in greater detail in Chapter 7.

Practice and Case Law to Date

The following two sub-sections will look at the application of the Chapter I prohibition in the UK (often in parallel with Art 101 TFEU) by focusing on public enforcement of the prohibition (together with CAT judgments where relevant) and significant case-law of the civil courts in dealing with claims (or defences) related to anti-competitive agreements.

Public enforcement

There is a considerable body of decisions by the OFT in relation to what is generally regarded as the most heinous type of competition law infringement, the secret horizontal cartel. There has been a constant stream of decisions in relation to cartels under the Chapter I prohibition, virtually always kick-started by a leniency application and more recently involving early resolution/settlement. For instance, in 2009, fines totalling £129.2 million were imposed on 103 construction firms in England in relation to bid-rigging between competitors on building

---

170 This exclusion also applies to the Chapter II prohibition.
171 Competition Act 1998, Sch 1, para 1(2).
172 The Competition Act 1998 (Land Agreements Exclusion Revocation) Order 2010, SI 2010/1709.
173 See 'OFT's guidance as to the appropriate amount of a penalty', OFT 423.

contracts.[174] At the same time, total fines of £39.27 million (reduced from £173m on account of leniency) were imposed on six recruitment agencies for price-fixing and the collective boycott of another company in the supply of candidates to the construction industry.[175] Various appeals to the CAT in relation to both cartels were partially successful in having the fines reduced. Probably the most high-profile cartel infringement decision under UK law in the last ten years involved British Airways (BA) and Virgin Atlantic Airways (VAA). This was a protracted saga which involved leniency, (unsuccessful) prosecution under the cartel offence and an 'early resolution' (now called 'settlement') process.[176] The OFT found that between August 2004 and January 2006, BA and VAA co-ordinated their surcharge pricing on long-haul flights to and from the UK through the exchange of pricing and other commercially sensitive information. A fine of £58.5 million was imposed on BA, although that was considerably lower than the initial sum agreed of £121m, whereas VAA, as it was the leniency applicant, was not fined.[177]

The CAT has also had the opportunity in an early case to consider the scope of the prohibition in relation to certain types of collective dealing commercial arrangements in relation to the sale of media rights. *The Racecourse Association and BHRB and others v OFT*[178] involved two appeals against an OFT decision in April 2004 that the sale of certain media rights infringed the Chapter I prohibition and did not qualify for exemption under s 9. At the time of the dispute the RCA represented the interests of all 59 racecourses in the UK, undertaking marketing, administrative and representational functions for the courses. Each course owner owns the media rights for events at its course or courses, although historically the RCA has negotiated agreements for the exploitation of certain of those rights on behalf of its members, including those for broadcasts to off-course licensed betting offices (LBOs). The BHRB is the governing body of British racing and has a duty to ensure the proper financing of the industry. In 2001, a 'Media Rights Agreement' (the MRA), was made between various parties including Attheraces Holdings Limited (Holdings), Attheraces (ATR), the RCA and 49 of the 59 racecourses (the Courses). ATR was a wholly owned subsidiary of Holdings, a joint venture company formed by various broadcasting organisations, and was used to acquire various media rights from the Courses under the MRA, in particular 'the Non-LBO bookmaking rights', and it was their sale that the OFT held to infringe the prohibition. These were picture rights which, in combination with betting rights and data, could be used to allow interactive betting using television or the internet. ATR exploited these rights by broadcasting a basic pay-TV channel and running a website, which together allowed the provision of fixed-odds betting services and the placing of pool bets. By ATR's purported termination of the MRA, live British horseracing was no longer available on the channel or website under the arrangements set out by that agreement. The OFT decided that the MRA involved a collective sale of the Non-LBO bookmaking rights by the courses that infringed the prohibition and did not qualify for exemption as it had the effect of appreciably preventing, restricting or distorting competition in the supply in the UK by increasing the price for these rights. On appeal, the CAT considered the extent to which the collective negotiating or selling of the rights was necessary, taking into account earlier EU jurisprudence, notably in *Wouters*,[179] and held that arrangements that are necessary 'to achieve a proper commercial objective will not, or may not, constitute an anti-competitive infringement at all'.[180] The CAT concluded that 'the central negotiation in which the Courses engaged was necessary for the achievement both by them and by ATR of the legitimate commercial objective of creating the new product that ATR proposed to exploit for the

---

174 OFT Decision CA98/02/2009, Case CE/4327-04, *Bid rigging in the construction industry in England*, 21 September 2009.
175 OFT Decision CA98/01/2009, Case CE/7510-06, *Construction Recruitment Forum*, 29 September 2009.
176 See further discussion of these issues in Chapter 7.
177 OFT Decision CA98/01/2012, Case CE/7691-06, *Airline passenger fuel surcharges for long-haul flights*, 19 April 2012.
178 [2005] CAT 29.
179 Case C-309/99 *Wouters v Algemene Raad van de Nederlandse Orde van Advocaten* [2002] ECR I-1577.
180 Para 167.

benefit of itself, the punters, the racecourses and racing generally'.[181] Further, in any event, the OFT had not proved that the MRA resulted in an appreciable increase in the price that would have been paid by ATR.

Resale price maintenance

Probably the greatest publicity has been attracted by enforcement under the Chapter I prohibition in relation to resale price maintenance schemes. It is generally accepted in the EU that resale price maintenance agreements, where minimum prices are set in vertical relationships, for instance between manufacturer and retailer, are prohibited. However, the *Leegin* judgment of the US Supreme Court, outlined below, advocated a more lenient approach to RPM, which is also reflected in recent academic debate on the issue on the basis that the practice can be pro-competitive by ensuring the provision of pre-sale promotional services and an increase in the number of retail outlets.[182]

The OFT has frequently condemned RPM mechanisms. In the early case of *John Bruce (UK) Ltd, Fleet Parts Ltd and Truck and Trailer Components*, commercial-vehicle component companies were fined a total of £33,737 for price-fixing, which was in the form of resale price maintenance (RPM) agreements in respect of automatic slack-adjusters, which are devices for buses, trailers and trucks, sometimes known as 'automatic brake-adjusters'.[183] Evidence of the agreement was partly derived from a private and confidential internal memo dated 2 March 2000, one day after the entry into force of the Chapter I prohibition. The immunity for small agreements under s 39(1) of the Act was inapplicable as price-fixing agreements are excluded from its ambit. Although price-fixing was recognised as a very serious infringement that would normally attract the 10% starting point, special circumstances in this case were recognised – a new product, difficulties in penetrating the market and a small new entrant was involved – which reduced that figure to 5%. This was only a minor case and resulted in an insubstantial fine, but it did send out the message that vertical RPM arrangements were caught by the Chapter I prohibition. That message proved to be important in other, more high-profile, cases; notably *Toys and Games* and *Replica Kits* both outlined below.

In March 2003, the DGFT concluded that Lladró Comercial SA, a producer of luxury porcelain and stoneware figurines, and 155 UK retailers had infringed the Chapter I prohibition by entering into bilateral price-fixing agreements.[184] Lladró Comercial SA and the retailers concerned were required to remove the price-fixing clauses from each agreement as appropriate. No financial penalty was imposed in this case because Lladró Comercial had mistakenly relied on a comfort letter issued by DG Competition to the effect that there was no infringement of Article 101(1) TFEU as trade between Member States was not substantially affected.

In the *Toys and Games* case, Argos, Littlewoods and Hasbro were found to have been involved in price-fixing agreements in relation to games and toys and in breach of the Chapter I prohibition.[185] Argos was fined £17.28m and Littlewoods £5.37m. Hasbro's fine of £15.59m was

---

181 Para 175.
182 See Kneepens, M, 'Resale Price Maintenance: Economics Call for a More Balanced Approach' [2007] ECLR 656, and Callery, C, 'Should the European Union Embrace or Exorcise *Leegin*'s "Rule of Reason"?' [2011] ECLR 42.
183 DGFT Decision CA98/12/2002, Case CP/0717/01, 13 May 2002.
184 Decision of Director General of Fair Trading No CA98/04/2003, Case CP/0809-01 *Agreements between Lladró Comercial SA and UK retailers fixing the price of porcelain and stoneware figurines*, 31 March 2003.
185 DGFT Decision CA98/2/2003, Case CP/0480-01 *Agreements between Hasbro UK Ltd, Argos Ltd and Littlewoods Ltd Fixing the Price of Hasbro Toys and Games*, 19 February 2003. See, also, OFT Decision CA98/04/2003, Case CP/0809-01 *Agreements between Lladró Comercial SA and UK Retailers Fixing the Price of Porcelain and Stonework Figurines*, 31 March 2003.

reduced to zero under the leniency scheme.[186] Following a successful appeal by Argos and Littlewoods, the OFT issued a new Decision to the same effect, replacing its earlier Decision.[187] Prior to this a fine of £4.95m had also been imposed on Hasbro in November 2002 for participating in price-fixing agreements with a range of distributors.

In the *Replica Kits* case, on 1 August 2003, the OFT issued a finding that ten businesses had been engaging in a practice of price-fixing in the market for replica football kits, specifically those manufactured by Umbro.[188] The businesses were found to be infringing the Chapter I prohibition of the Competition Act 1998. The OFT imposed a total of £18.6m in fines, varying in size among the businesses, with some businesses qualifying for reductions under the leniency programme. The fines imposed included the following: JJB Sports – £8.373m; Umbro – £6.641m; Manchester United – £1.652m; Allsports – £1.35m; the Football Association – £198,000, reduced to £158,000 under the leniency programme; Blacks – £197,000; Sports Soccer – £123,000; JD Sports – £73,000.

Appeals were lodged by various parties to the CAT in both *Toys and Games* and *Replica Kits*, and although fines were reduced by the CAT in some cases, both the CAT, and ultimately the Court of Appeal, on hearing joined appeals by Argos, Littlewoods and JJB Sports, upheld the OFT's findings in liability.[189] In relation to *Replica Kits*, the Court of Appeal concluded that the CAT was entitled to find the following: that JJB provided confidential price information to Umbro in circumstances where it was obvious that it would or might be passed on to Sports Soccer to support Umbro's attempts to persuade Sport Soccer to raise its prices; Umbro used the information in that way; Sports Soccer agreed to raise its prices in reliance on that agreement and foreseeing that the other would be told of its agreement and act accordingly; and, that Umbro advised JJB, making it clear that they could maintain their pricing levels. In line with classic EU jurisprudence on the establishment of concerted practices, the retailers had co-ordinated their behaviour in such a way as to knowingly substitute practical co-operation for the risks of competition.[190] The facts justified a finding of a trilateral concerted practice between the manufacturer and the retailers. The Court of Appeal set out the following general test for determining the existence of a trilateral arrangement:

> if (i) retailer A discloses to supplier B its future pricing intentions in circumstances where A may be taken to intend that B will make use of that information to influence market conditions by passing that information to other retailers (of whom C is or may be one), (ii) B does, in fact, pass that information to C in circumstances where C may be taken to know the circumstances in which the information was disclosed by A to B and (iii) C does, in fact, use the information in determining its own future pricing intentions., then A, B and C are all to be regarded as parties to a concerted practice having as its object the restriction or distortion of competition. The case is all the stronger where there is reciprocity: in the sense that C discloses to supplier B its future pricing intentions in circumstances where C may be taken to intend that B will make use of that information to influence market conditions by passing that information to (amongst others) A, and B does so.[191]

---

186 See Young, G, 'Punishment for Toys and Games' [2003] Comp LJ 5.
187 OFT Decision CA98/8/2003, Case CP/0480-01 *Agreements between Hasbro UK Ltd, Argos Ltd and Littlewoods Ltd Fixing the Price of Hasbro Toys and Games*, 21 November 2003.
188 OFT Decision CA98/06/2003, Case CP/0871/01 *Price-fixing of Replica Football Kit*, 1 August 2003.
189 *Argos, Littlewoods and JJB v OFT* [2006] EWCA Civ 1318 on appeal from [2004] CAT 24, [2005] CAT 13, [2004] CAT 17, [2005] CAT 22.
190 Case 48/69 *ICI v Commission ('Dyestuffs')* [1972] ECR 619.
191 Argos, above, n 189, at para 141. See Joined Cases C-2/01 and C-3/01 *Bayer v Commission* [2000] ECR II-3383 paras 23-26.

Replica Football Kit and *Toys and Games* both involved RPM with an element of horizontal collusion.[192] Both involved the exchange of information as between retailers indirectly through the suppliers, involving the phenomenon referred to alternatively as 'A to B to C co-ordination, A-B-C information exchange and hub and spoke collusion'.[193] It appears from these cases and subsequent enforcement practice, that these types of 'trilateral' discussions involving manufacturers and retailers (whereby the retailers do not communicate directly), which results in uniform application of minimum resale prices by the retailers, is potentially rife in major UK retail markets. Nonetheless, the simple existence of independent parallel bilateral vertical agreements between A and B and B and C is not enough *per se* to establish prohibited A-B-C information exchanges. The *Tobacco* case demonstrated the ongoing difficulties in proving the horizontal element.[194] An OFT decision of 15 April 2010 found that the two main manufacturers of tobacco products in the UK, Imperial and Gallaher, had entered into a series of bilateral agreements with ten different retailers relating to the price of tobacco products in those stores. Substantial fines were imposed, including £112.3m on Imperial, and £14.1m on Asda. The OFT considered that a crucial aspect of the agreements involved the linking of horizontal competitors' retail prices through their vertical agreements, but the appeal was allowed simply on the basis that the OFT could not prove key aspects of the infringements as set out in its original Decision. The OFT issued an infringement decision under the Chapter I prohibition to various dairy producers and all the major UK supermarkets, in 2011, in relation to co-ordinated increases in the consumer prices of certain dairy products in 2002 and/or 2003, imposing fines totalling £49.51m.[195] Tesco appealed. The OFT had found *inter alia* that a number of competing undertakings had indirectly exchanged their future retail pricing intentions in respect of British-produced cheddar and territorial cheeses, via their common suppliers ("hub and spoke exchanges"). The OFT concluded that Tesco, among others, had participated in two single overall concerted practices during 2002 and 2003 which had as their object the restriction of competition, in breach of the Chapter I prohibition. The CAT upheld the findings that Tesco broke competition law three times by co-ordinating increases in the prices consumers paid for cheese in 2002, but also found that Tesco did not infringe the law with respect to other findings of exchanges of future pricing information.[196] Tesco agreed to pay a reduced fine of £6.5m to conclude the case. The continued use of multilateral resale price initiatives in UK was demonstrated in 2013 by the Chapter I decision and fines imposed on Mercedes-Benz and various dealers in relation to the distribution of Mercedes-Benz commercial vehicles, whereby M-B helped to facilitate or co-ordinate various anti-competitive arrangements amongst its dealers including price co-ordination.[197]

Court case law

There have been a number of private disputes in which the Chapter I (or Article 101) prohibition has been raised by one of the parties. For example, in *Suretrack Rail Services Ltd v Infraco JNP Ltd*,[198] it was alleged that the Chapter I prohibition was breached by an anti-competitive agreement stopping the applicant providing railway safety services. The application was dismissed by Laddie J on the basis that the three companies involved were all subsidiaries of the same parent and were not individual undertakings. Accordingly, no 'agreement between undertakings' existed.

---

192 Odudu, O 'Indirect Information Exchange: The Constituent Elements of Hub and Spoke Collusion' (2011) European Competition Journal 205–242 at p 205.

193 Odudu, ibid, at p 207.

194 *Imperial Tobacco Group plc and others v OFT* [2011] CAT 41.

195 OFT Decision CA98/03/2011, Case CE/3094-03, *Dairy retail price initiatives*, 10 August 2011.

196 *Tesco v OFT* [2012] CAT 31.

197 OFT Decision CA98/01/2013, Case CE/9161-09, *Distribution of Mercedes-Benz commercial vehicles*, 27 March 2013.

198 [2002] All ER (D) 261.

There have also been a number of follow-on court actions in the UK, in the CAT and the High Court, following various EU Commission cartel infringement decisions, notably in relation to the Vitamins cartel. As discussed in Chapter 3, follow-on actions do not consider the substantive application of the prohibition, but rely on the binding effect of the prior infringement decision and consider only issues of quantum and causation. Accordingly, stand-alone actions, in which the UK civil courts have to consider various aspects of the substantive scope of the prohibition, are of greater significance in this context, and we outline some of the more interesting case law here.

Of course the *Crehan* saga is relevant here, although that dispute focused more on the availability of remedies in respect of agreements which were caught by the Article 101(1) TFEU prohibition as discussed in Chapter 3. There is limited evidence of stand-alone actions being used in relation to hard-core cartels, but in *Secretary of State for Health and others v Norton Healthcare Ltd and others*,[199] the Secretary of State for Health and other health bodies sued over alleged participation in a Warfarin cartel, which involved elements of price fixing, supply fixing and market sharing.[200] The most significant Chapter I prohibition related claims were in *Bookmakers' Afternoon Greyhound Services Ltd v Amalgamated Racing Ltd*.[201] BAGS, a not-for-profit organisation, promoted the interests of bookmakers in licensed betting offices ('LBOs'). The other claimants were three large bookmakers. The defendants included AMRAC, which provided, to subscribing LBOs, live images and sound in respect of horseraces at various courses in Great Britain. The other defendants were operators of 30 racecourses. In *BAGS*, at first instance, the claimants had sought a declaration that collective exclusive licensing, on a closed basis, of the rights necessary for the supply to LBOs in UK and Ireland of images sound and data in respect of horseraces was prohibited. They also sought an injunction to prevent the defendants from giving effect to or providing for collective exclusive licensing of the rights on a closed basis, and damages. Since 1987 LBOs had paid a distributor, SIS, for the right to show live pictures of horseracing and payments have been made in turn to the racecourses for those LBO media rights. Over the years, racecourses became dissatisfied with the size of the payments and eventually 31 of the 60 decided to participate in a new joint venture to create a new distributor. The bookmaking industry considered that its emergence was anti-competitive and infringed Art 101 TFEU and the Chapter I prohibition. The challenge initially seemed to concern the way the racecourses went about granting exclusive rights to the venture. Following trial, in a 77-page judgment of 523 paragraphs, it was held that the relevant concerted practice between racecourses did not have the object of fixing prices, and that foreclosure was 'hypothetical'. In relation to collective selling, the claimants had not shown that the collective negotiation was likely to result in a higher price being paid, and accordingly, the claim fell and was dismissed. A subsequent appeal to the Court of Appeal was dismissed as there was no infringement of the prohibition where co-operation was the only commercially justifiable way to enter a new market or launch a new product.[202] Subsequently, the Court dismissed counterclaims relating to collusive behaviour by certain bookmakers who had allegedly formed an unlawful concerted practice to boycott Turf TV, and to withdraw sponsorship from certain racecourses which had licensed their LBO rights to AMRAC. There may have been parallel behaviour, but the evidence from all parties 'consistently explained their involvement in terms not involving any collusion of any relevant kind'.[203]

---

199 [2004] EWHC 609 (Ch). See also *Secretary of State for Health and others v Norton Healthcare Ltd and others* [2003] EWHC 1905 (Ch).
200 We are unaware of any subsequent court procedure and assume that the case must have been settled out of court.
201 [2008] EWHC 1978 (Ch) and [2008] EWHC 2688 (Ch).
202 [2009] EWCA Civ 750 (CA), at paras 101–110 in particular.
203 [2008] EWHC 2688 (Ch), at para 139.

Calor Gas Ltd v Express Fuels (Scotland) Ltd[204] is an example of how the prohibitions in Article 101/Chapter I can invalidate apparently valid contractual arrangements. In *Calor*, the market leaders in the distribution and supply of bulk and cylinder LPG in Great Britain, with circa 50% share of the cylinder LPG market, distributed its products through a network of independent dealers and retailers. The dealers' contract with Calor had two key features: for the duration of the agreement, dealers could purchase and sell only Calor cylinder LPG; and they undertook not to handle Calor cylinders after termination of the contract. The defendant terminated the agreement and entered a dealership with Flogas, but continued to handle Calor cylinders. Calor sought damages and interdict, but the action was defended on basis that the single branding obligation for five years and the post-termination restriction in the agreements were null and void in accordance with Article 101. It was held that the twin factors of market power and duration ensured that 'if a nationwide network of principal dealers is tied to the brand leader for at least five years, this will restrict competition, especially in a mature market.'[205]

Vertical Restraints

Vertical agreements are agreements made between undertakings operating at different levels of the same market. A typical example is an agreement between the producer of a product and a distributor. The contractual restrictions employed in vertical agreements, known as vertical restraints, are used, *inter alia*, to facilitate the distribution of goods and services. This part of the chapter will focus on the impact of the competition rules on distribution agreements, in particular on exclusive distribution agreements. We will also look more briefly at exclusive purchasing or 'single-branding' agreements. However, it should be noted that there are a variety of types of vertical agreement, including franchising and selective distribution systems, and often a particular vertical agreement may contain a complex mix of different vertical restraints.

The efficient distribution of goods is crucial to the success of a business and the vibrancy of the economy. It is, therefore, important that the legal framework which applies to distribution agreements, and supply chain questions more generally, is clear so that firms may operate their distribution systems efficiently. The EU's treatment, particularly by the Commission, of vertical agreements has historically been criticised for failing to create an effective framework. The Commission, aware of the criticisms of its approach, intiated a process of reform which culminated in the adoption of the first Vertical Agreements Regulation[206] in 1999 which was replaced and updated by the current Vertical Agreements BER in 2010.[207]

The effects of vertical restraints

There are various potential positive and negative effects of vertical restraints and, although much depends on the format, content and context of the specific restraint, those effects may result from all forms of vertical restraints. The following are the principal considerations which require balancing in any set of competition rules dealing with vertical restraints.[208]

---

204 [2008] CSOH 13.
205 At para 35.
206 Regulation 2790/99/EC on the application of Art 81(3) of the EC Treaty to categories of vertical agreements and concerted practices, [1999] OJ L336/21. See also the Green Paper, 'Vertical Restraints', C(96) 721 final.
207 Commission Regulation 330/2010/EU on the application of Art 101(3) of the Treaty on the Functioning of the European Union to categories of vertical agreements and concerted practices, [2010] OJ L102/1. See also Commission Guidelines on Vertical Restraints, [2010] OJ C130/1.
208 The Commission Guidelines on Vertical Restraints, [2010] OJ C130/1, should be referred to for a fuller discussion of these issues.

Restriction of intra-brand competition

The difference between inter-brand and intra-brand competition was outlined previously. The former involves competition between the varying brands of different producers, for example, Nike and Adidas sports shoes, and the latter concerns competition by retailers or distributors in the sale of a producer's particular brand, for example, between two competing retailers selling Nike sports shoes. Exclusive distribution is a good example of the potential restriction of intra-brand competition. A distributor will be appointed as the sole distributor within a particular territory. The extent of the restriction will depend upon the terms of the agreement. If absolute territorial protection is provided, then intra-brand competition will be virtually eliminated, as supplies of the product will only be available to customers from that one distributor. However, if it is possible for another distributor to make passive sales into the territory – that is, without an active marketing campaign – the restriction in intra-brand competition will be reduced. In either case, the main objection to any restriction on intra-brand competition is that it may lead to reduced consumer choice, due to the excessive concentration on brand image, and ultimately higher prices for the consumer of the particular branded product.

Foreclosure of competition

Single-branding commitments imposed upon a distributor, restricting the distributor to the purchase and resale of one particular brand, can cause foreclosure of markets by making it more difficult for other producers of competing brand products to find outlets for their particular products. Distribution agreements often contain single-branding obligations and may also, therefore, cause foreclosure of markets.

Compartmentalisation of markets

Exclusive distribution systems directly impose some form of restraint on the free flow of trade. For instance, in the most extreme case of an agreement creating an absolute territorial protection in favour of a distributor of a branded product, no possibility exists for any trade in that product, from other countries, into the restricted territory. This is particularly objectionable in the EU context given the overriding goal of market integration and competition law's role within the EU internal market. EU competition law clearly attempts to strike a balance between the procompetitive effects of vertical agreements and the limitations on cross-border trade within distribution agreements.

Efficiency gains

Distribution agreements allow a producer to manage the number of outlets that are to be supplied, which enables greater efficiency to be achieved in the overall distribution system. There may be economies of scale in particular forms of distribution, and efficiencies may be gained by the imposition of single-branding commitments.

Increase in inter-brand competition

A distributor may be unwilling to promote a producer's product unless it is granted some form of territorial exclusivity. For a product to compete effectively with other products on the market it will usually require promotion, particularly if it is a new product. Accordingly, exclusive distribution agreements may stimulate inter-brand competition by facilitating the entry of new products on to the market. This will increase inter-brand competition with existing branded products, to the ultimate benefit of the consumer.

Free-rider problems

Exclusive distribution may help to prevent one distributor from free-riding on the promotion efforts of another, particularly with new or complex products or where there are different sales channels on a market. The problem for the distributor of a product is how to encourage resellers or retailers to adopt potentially costly forms of promotion or service, which would benefit the manufacturer's brand or sales, without running the risk that others will free-ride and undercut those resellers by avoiding those costs. Obvious examples of free-riding include the 'certification free-rider issue' whereby the supplier seeks to protect the brand value of a new product by restricting its sale to quality retailers; this is common in selective distribution systems. A related factor is known as the 'hold-up problem' whereby exclusivity is required to induce a party to invest in special equipment or training where the investment is relationship specific. Another problem is where manufacturers have to manage the different, and ultimately conflicting, needs of 'expensive' bricks and mortar retailers, who offer customer service and promotional opportunities, and 'cheap' online retailers who focus more clearly on price.

Given these potential pros and cons, there has been a vigorous debate on the merits of vertical restraints, particularly in the US. Proponents of the Chicago school have based their favourable approach to distribution restraints on the free-rider rationale. This rationale suggests that intra-brand protection is necessary to allow a distributor to promote a brand effectively and thereby enhance inter-brand competition.[209] Vertical restraints would only be considered harmful under this broad approach where the parties had market power and, accordingly, inter-brand competition was weak. The late Robert Bork argued that every restraint should be completely lawful on the basis that the only reason for any form of vertical restraint is that it creates efficiencies.[210] He argued that a producer will impose restraints only where it can derive higher profits by increasing sales, and consumers will increase purchases only when the value of any additional services exceeds the additional charge imposed by the distributor. His conclusion was that vertical restraints will only lead to higher profits when customers receive a net benefit. This argument has been challenged on the basis that it fails to discriminate between existing or new consumers and established or new products. For the latter, vertical restraints may have net benefits, but, otherwise, a more hostile treatment is required.[211] In the EU context the Commission has been criticised in the past for its hostile treatment of vertical restraints and its failure to consider the free-rider rationale.[212] The Commission reviewed the position on vertical restraints and the 1999 and 2010 Vertical Agreements BERs adopted a more favourable approach to vertical restraints; focusing on market power and inter-brand competition. Interestingly, some US commentators have suggested that we should be concerned with downstream market power of distributors, and that intra-brand competition remains important.[213] Notwithstanding the increased flexibility in EU law there is a still a stark contrast between its position and that in the US. In 2007, the US Supreme Court, in *Leegin*,[214] overturned the long-established rule, set out in *Dr Miles Medical Co v John D Park & Son co*,[215] that RPM was *per se* illegal, and decided that it is now to be assessed according to the rule of reason. RPM remains a 'hard-core' restraint under the Vertical Agreement Block Exemption Regulation

209 See Telser, LG, 'Why Should Manufacturers Want Fair Trade?' (1960) 3 JL & Econ 86. See, also, Marvel, HP, 'The Resale Price Maintenance Controversy: Beyond Conventional Wisdom' (1994) 63 Antitrust LJ 59, 69–71.
210 See Bork, R, *The Antitrust Paradox: A Policy at War with Itself* (1993) Oxford: Maxwell Macmillan, Chapters 14 and 15.
211 Comanor, WS, 'Vertical Price-fixing, Vertical Market Restrictions and the New Antitrust Policy' (1984–85) 98 Harv L Rev 983.
212 See Gyselen, L, 'Vertical Restraints in the Distribution Process: Strength and Weakness of the Free Rider Rationale under EEC Competition Law' (1984) 21 CML Rev 647; Hawk, B, 'System Failure: Vertical Restraints and EC Competition Law' (1995) 32 CML Rev 973; Korah, V, 'EEC Competition Policy – Legal Form or Economic Efficiency?' (1986) 39 CLP 85; and Carlin, F, 'Vertical Restraints: Time for Change?' [1996] ECLR 283.
213 See, for example, Grimes, WS, 'Brand Marketing, Intrabrand Competition, and the Multibrand Retailer: The Antitrust Law of Vertical Restraints' (1995) 64 Antitrust LJ 83; and Comanor, WS, 'The Two Economics of Vertical Restraints' (1992) 21 Sw UL Rev 1265.
214 *Leegin Creative Leather Products Inc v PSKS Inc* 127 SCT 2705 US (2007).
215 220 US 373 (1911).

(VABER) and the debate continues as to whether the EU should follow the US lead in this regard.[216]

The European Commission approach to vertical restraints under Art 101(1)

The crucial issue under Art 101(1) TFEU is the determination of what constitutes a 'prevention, restriction or distortion of competition'. Many commentators considered that the Commission historically interpreted this requirement as being satisfied by a restriction of the economic freedom, or the freedom of action, of the contracting parties to an agreement.[217] This interpretation attracted widespread criticism, as such an approach could lead to a variety of undesirable consequences.[218] The Commission approach resulted in a wide interpretation of Art 101(1), subject to the application of the *de minimis* doctrine,[219] leaving fuller analysis to the Commission under Art 101(3). Accordingly, under Regulation 17, a considerable number of vertical agreements required notification and exemption under Art 101(3). This formalistic approach, coupled with the Commission's resources problem, meant that very few formal decisions were taken each year, leading to delays and uncertainty for businesses. As the Commission had sole power to grant exemptions, the delays hampered the ability of national courts to deal with disputes involving the purported validity of restrictions in vertical agreements. Finally, the formalistic approach may also have impeded innovative and efficient forms of distribution, as well as other forms of investment, for example, investment through technology licensing arrangements. The Commission's previous policy of issuing specific block exemptions for different types of restraints, such as exclusive distribution, alleviated the situation, although the policy also led to criticisms of 'straitjacketing' companies' commercial strategies. The Vertical Agreements BER, discussed further below, has sought to provide a more general solution, under Art 101(3), to vertical agreements. In addition, the Commission has clearly indicated, in its Guidelines on vertical restraints,[220] that its ongoing approach under Art 101(1) will be based on the economic effects of vertical agreements and will focus on agreements where market power is involved or where there is a network of similar agreements potentially foreclosing market access.

Particular types of restriction

The view of the Commission's traditional approach under Art 101(1) TFEU, outlined in the previous section, is perhaps an oversimplification, and it is of more interest to note the attitude of the EU authorities to particular types of restriction. In particular, export bans, both direct and indirect, are considered by both the Commission and Court as clear infringements of Art 101(1).[221] Similarly, resale price maintenance provisions in vertical agreements are routinely prohibited under Art 101(1).[222] Otherwise, the Court has taken a more flexible approach to the

---

216 See, for example, Callery, C, 'Should the European Union Embrace or Exorcise *Leegin*'s "Rule of Reason"?' [2011] ECLR 42.

217 See, for example, Hawk, B, 'System Failure: Vertical Restraints and EC Competition Law' (1995) 32 CML Rev 973.

218 See, also, Hawk, B, 'The American (Antitrust) Revolution: Lessons for the EEC?' [1988] ECLR 53; Bodoff, J, 'Competition Policies of the US and EEC: An Overview' [1984] ECLR 51; and Whish, R and Sufrin, B, 'Article 85 and the Rule of Reason' (1987) 7 Ox YEL 1.

219 Commission Notice on agreements of minor importance which do not appreciably restrict competition under Art 101(1) TFEU (De Minimis Notice), C (2014) 4136 final.

220 [2010] OJ C130/1.

221 For direct export bans, see Case 19/77 *Miller International Schallplatten GmbH v Commission* [1978] ECR 131. Cf Case 262/81 *Coditel II* [1982] ECR 3381. For an example of a prohibition of an indirect export ban, see Case 31/85 *ETA Fabriques d'Ebauches v DK Investments SA* [1985] ECR 3933.

222 See Case 27/87 *Louis Erauw-Jacquery v La Hesbignonne* [1988] ECR 1919. See, also, Case 161/84 *Pronuptia de Paris GmbH v Pronuptia de Paris Irmgard Schillgalis* [1986] ECR 353, in which resale price maintenance in a franchise network infringed Art 101(1) and was not capable of exemption.

consideration of when there is a 'restriction of competition' under Art 101(1). However, before considering other case law, it is necessary to look at the treatment of territorial restrictions in vertical restraints, as these territorial restrictions are very important in a wide range of vertical agreements, particularly exclusive distribution agreements.

Territorial restrictions

The starting point for any discussion of vertical restraints in the EU is the *Consten and Grundig* case.[223] It involved an agreement between Grundig, a major West German (as then was) manufacturer of electrical and electronic equipment, and Consten, a French distributor. The agreement was a sole or exclusive distributorship for France, and it included three main features:

1   it imposed an obligation on Consten, similar to that imposed on Grundig distributors in other Member States, not to export the contract goods from France;
2   Grundig undertook not to sell directly to anyone in France; and
3   Grundig assigned the rights under the trade mark attached to each piece of equipment for sale in France to Consten.

Later, a French company obtained Grundig's products in another Member State and sought to import them to and sell them in France. Consten brought an action to stop the resale of those goods. A complaint was made by the French company to the Commission, which ruled that the contracts intended that Consten be free from competition in the distribution of Grundig products in France and, therefore, the contracts restricted competition within Art 101(1). Furthermore, an exemption would not be granted under Art 101(3), as the absolute territorial protection granted was not indispensable.

On appeal to the Court, it was argued that Art 101 did not apply to vertical agreements. This was rejected by the Court, which stated that competition can also be limited by agreements which restrict competition between one of the parties and any third party. It was also argued by the parties that Art 101 should only apply to restrictions of inter-brand as opposed to intra-brand competition. This argument was also rejected by the Court, although the Court did state that unless the object of the agreement was to restrict competition, an analysis of the effects of the agreement was required. In this case, the Court considered that the object was to restrict competition, and further analysis was not required. The Court also confirmed that absolute territorial protection is prohibited under Art 101(1) and that an exemption would not be justified. However, the Court stressed that the Commission should not have prohibited the whole agreement, but merely the clauses which created the absolute territorial protection. The clauses providing for exclusive distribution were not necessarily an infringement, although the third aspect, the assignation of the trade mark, created absolute territorial protection and was, therefore, prohibited.

Consten and Grundig was a decisive case, and the Court sought to achieve a balance by prohibiting absolute territorial protection, which sought to stop any parallel imports of the contract goods, while providing that the provision of territorial exclusivity did not in itself infringe Art 101(1). Nevertheless, the line between legal territorial restrictions and illegal absolute territorial protection has become clouded in subsequent Commission decisions and Court judgments. For instance, in *Van Vliet*,[224] an undertaking, given by a producer to its Dutch distributor to prohibit its other distributors from exporting to Holland, was held to be unlawful,

223   Cases 56 and 58/64 *Etablissement Consten SA and Grundig Verkaufs-GmbH v Commission* [1966] ECR 299. While this is clearly a seminal decision, there is a good argument that it, and the line of case law it began, is very much a product of its time, and should a similar situation arise today, the Court's approach might be very different.
224   Case 25/75 *Van Vliet Kwasten & Ladderfabrieke v Fratelli Dalle Crode* [1975] ECR 1103.

as the undertaking could result in a partitioning of the market contrary to the fundamental principles of EU law. This judgment apparently signified a shift away from the more lenient approach adopted by the Court in *Consten and Grundig*. Subsequent case law confirmed a more restrictive approach to exclusive distribution agreements; the following cases took the view that the existence of export bans on the distributor constituted the infringement of Art 101(1).[225] The wide ambit of the Art 101(1) prohibition, as construed by the Commission, and also by the Court, after *Consten and Grundig*, led to repeated calls for reform towards a model based on a US-style 'rule of reason'. Nonetheless, it should be noted that, even following the adoption of the VABER, the EU's approach to territorial restrictions appears to have altered relatively little.

US rule of reason

In the US there is a dual approach to the consideration, under s 1 of the Sherman Act, of restrictions in vertical agreements.[226] Some restraints of trade are considered to be illegal *per se* and others are subject to the 'rule of reason' in order to determine whether they are reasonable or unreasonable. The major development in US antitrust law has been the dramatic reduction in restrictions which are subject to the *per se* test, which is now limited, for instance, to horizontal market division and price-fixing; as of 2007 the *per se* test no longer applies to vertical resale price maintenance. Under the *per se* rule, no further inquiry is made into the existence of anti-competitive effects, market power or intent. The rule of reason test, which requires consideration of the impact of the restraint on competitive conditions, is more complex. It now applies to all of vertical restraints and requires a detailed economic analysis of the restraint, market structure and market conditions to assess the restraint's likely pro- and anti-competitive effects. The rule of reason test, inevitably, has increased the complexity of antitrust litigation and reduced its certainty and predictability. The first major step in this direction was the US Supreme Court decision in *Continental TV Inc v GTE Sylvania*,[227] which confirmed that the rule of reason test should be applied to non-price vertical restraints to assess their legality. Sylvania had decided to limit the number of retail franchises granted, and to restrict each of its brand dealers to sales only at the particular point where it held its franchise. These territorial and customer restrictions were held to be subject to the rule of reason test. The adoption of the rule of reason acts as a significant point of contrast with EU law. After *Sylvania*, and in line with general academic opinion in the US,[228] US authorities have adopted a particularly tolerant approach to most vertical restraints based primarily on the free-rider rationale.[229] The *Sylvania* rule of reason test was extended to vertical resale price maintenance by the majority of the Supreme Court in 2007 in *Leegin Creative Leather Products Inc v PSKS Inc*.[230]

The Court of Justice and the rule of reason

There has been continued criticism of the EU authorities' treatment of vertical restraints, and calls for the adoption of a US-style rule of reason approach. Although US antitrust law has attempted to provide a more refined formulation of what actually constitutes a restraint of trade,

---

225 See, for example, Cases 100–03/80 *SA Musique Diffusion Francaise and Others v Commission (Pioneer)* [1983] ECR 1825.
226 See Hawk, Bodoff, and Whish and Sufrin, above n 218, and Callery, above n 216.
227 433 US 36 (1977).
228 Although see Grimes and Comanor, above n 213, for alternative perspectives.
229 See, for example, 'Vertical restraints guidelines of the National Association of Attorneys General' (1995) 68 *Antitrust & Trade Regulation Report* 1706. For an analysis of the complexity of the rule of reason approach in the US context, see Calvani, T, 'Some Thoughts on the Rule of Reason' [2001] 6 ECLR 201.
230 127 SCt 2705 US (2007).

the rule of reason approach can be criticised for its complexity and lack of certainty. In addition, EU law should not necessarily follow US antitrust law because EU law objectives, particularly the creation of the internal market, are different to US antitrust objectives. Finally, and most importantly, there are significant textual differences between the two sets of laws. The existence of Art 101(3) TFEU and the possibility of the prohibition being inapplicable to beneficial agreements means that there is not the same pressure under Art 101(1), compared to s 1 of the Sherman Act, to delimit what constitutes a 'restriction of competition' within the prohibition alone. Nonetheless, there have been certain important developments, within Block Exemption Regulations and the Court's jurisprudence, where some arguably anti-competitive behaviour has fallen outside the prohibition.[231] In any event, Art 101(1) refers both to agreements which have as their object the restriction of competition and agreements which have the effect of restricting competition. Accordingly, the Court has distinguished between types of vertical restraints which have the 'object' of restricting competition, which could be described as *per se*, prohibited by Art 101(1), such as export bans, and other vertical restraints which require an economic analysis of the effects of an agreement, although this is not characterised as a rule of reason approach as such.[232]

Alongside EU law's increasing focus on the market effects of potentially anti-competitive agreements, there has been more specific recognition of the need to adopt a particularly flexible attitude towards vertical restraints. For instance, there is now a body of case law that indicates that selective distribution agreements should often escape the prohibition under Art 101(1) on qualitative grounds in order to allow for the maintenance of the brand names. The Court has also decided, in a series of judgments, that restrictions, often known as 'ancillary restraints', which are necessary for the agreement to proceed may not infringe Art 101(1). For instance, in *Remia*[233] the Court ruled that a restriction on a seller not to compete with a business sold with its goodwill does not infringe Art 101(1), provided the restriction is reasonably limited in time and space. Similarly, the result of the judgment in *Pronuptia*[234] is that many provisions in franchises fall outside the Art 101(1) prohibition, where those provisions are necessary to protect intellectual property rights and the common identity of the franchise. Finally, there has been a move, led by the Court, towards a limited rule of reason approach, particularly in relation to licensing arrangements involving intellectual property rights (IPRs) and certain exclusive distribution agreements. The premise acknowledged by the Court is that the parties would not have invested in the promotion of new technology without some form of protection. For example, in *Nungesser*,[235] the Commission's finding that an exclusive licence of plant breeders' rights infringed Art 101(1) was quashed by the Court, as the Commission had failed to consider whether 'open exclusivity' was justifiable on the basis that investment was necessary to develop the product and the German market for it. Nevertheless, absolute territorial protection, or 'closed exclusivity', remains prohibited and the Commission's application of the *Nungesser* principle has been restrictive, emphasising, and thereby limiting, its applicability to the novelty of the product.[236] There has also been limited acceptance of certain territorial restrictions in exclusive distribution agreements.

---

231 See Whish and Sufrin, above n 218; Forrester, I and Norall, C, 'The Laicisation of Community Law, Self-help and the Rule of Reason: How Competition Law is and could be Applied' (1984) 21 CML Rev 11; and Callery, above n 216.
232 See Lasok, KPE, 'Assessing the Economic Consequences of Restrictive Agreements: A Comment on the *Delimitis* Case' [1991] ECLR 194.
233 Case 42/84 *Remia BV and Others v Commission* [1985] ECR 2545, [1987] 1 CMLR 1.
234 Case 161/84 *Pronuptia de Paris GmbH v Pronuptia de Paris Irmgard Schillgalis* [1986] ECR 353, [1986] 1 CMLR 414.
235 Case 258/78 *Nungesser (LC) KG and Kurt Eisele v Commission* [1982] ECR 2015, [1983] 1 CMLR 278.
236 There is, in addition, a Technology Transfer Regulation, Regulation 316/2014/EU, [2014] OJ L93/17.

The Vertical Agreements Block Exemption Regulation ('VABER')

Introduction

Regulation 330/2010[237] came into force in June 2010, replacing the original general Vertical Agreements Regulation, Regulation 2790/99.[238] Regulation 2790/99 was a radical change from previous Commission block exemption practice. The 'umbrella' exemption approach adopted ensures that every type of restraint is permitted unless it is strictly prohibited. Using only a black list of prohibited terms increases the flexibility of parties allowing them to adopt agreements that are appropriate for their commercial setting. Flexibility is also ensured by having one BER for all forms of vertical agreements as defined in the Regulation. The belief that the anti-competitive nature of vertical restraints is dependent on a degree of market power is reflected in the safe haven which is created by the Regulation where the market share held by the seller or buyer does not exceed 30%. As the Commission noted in Recital 6 of the Regulation:

> Certain types of vertical agreements can improve economic efficiency within a chain of production or distribution by facilitating better coordination between the participating undertakings. In particular, they can lead to a reduction in the transaction and distribution costs of the parties and to an optimisation of their sales and investment levels.

Regulation 330/2010 does not apply to vertical agreements falling within the scope of other block exemptions.[239] The following section will provide a brief overview of the key provisions of the VABER.

Vertical agreements

Article 1(1)(a) defines vertical agreements for the purposes of the Regulation as:

> an agreement or concerted practice entered into between two or more undertakings each of which operates, for the purposes of the agreement or the concerted practice, at a different level of the production or distribution chain, and relating to the conditions under which the parties may purchase, sell or resell certain goods or services.

Many vertical agreements will not infringe Art 101(1) in the first place, and will not require exemption under the Regulation; for instance, agreements satisfying the *Delimitis* principle outlined above. For a wide range of other vertical agreements, the above definition is certainly more expansive than under pre-1999 practice, as the definition extends to agreements in relation to intermediate goods and services. However, agreements containing provisions relating to the assignment or use, by the buyer, of IPRs are not to be exempted under Art 2(3) unless those

---

237 Commission Regulation 330/2010/EU on the application of Art 101(3) of the Treaty on the Functioning of the European Union to categories of vertical agreements and concerted practices, [2010] OJ L102/1. See De Stefano, G, 'The New EU Vertical Restraints Regulation: Navigating the Vast Seas Beyond Safe Harbours and Hardcore Restrictions' [2010] 31(12) ECLR 487.

238 Regulation 2790/99/EC on the application of Art 81(3) of the EC Treaty to categories of vertical agreements and concerted practices, [1999] OJ L336/21.

239 This currently excludes motor vehicle distribution, Commission Regulation 461/2010/EU on the application of Art 101(3) of the Treaty on the Functioning of the European Union to categories of vertical agreements and concerted practices in the motor vehicle sector, [2010] OJ L129/52, and technology transfer agreements, Regulation 316/2014/EU on the application of Art 101(3) of the Treaty to categories of technology transfer agreements, [2014] OJ L93/17.

provisions do not constitute the primary object of such agreements. Accordingly, where the agreement is, for instance, a licence of know-how, it would fall beyond the scope of the Regulation, although the agreement may be exempted under the Technology Transfer Regulation.[240] Distribution agreements containing the assignment of an IPR, such as a trademark right, would potentially be subject to exemption, where the assignation of the IPR was ancillary to the main object of the agreement; for instance, setting up an efficient distribution system. A further limitation is contained in Art 2(4), which provides that vertical agreements between competing undertakings are not exempted unless they satisfy certain conditions.

Market share threshold

Following the Commission Communication's focus on market power, Art 3 of the Regulation creates a safe haven for all vertical agreements, subject to Art 4, where:

> the market share held by the supplier does not exceed 30% of the relevant market on which it sells the contract goods or services and the market share held by the buyer does not exceed 30% of the relevant market on which it purchases the contract goods or services.

The use of market shares is a key element of the Regulation. There was some initial criticism that the use of market shares was likely to lead to uncertainty and unpredictability, but the approach is now widely accepted. The definition of the market is as set out in the Commission's 1997 Notice on market definition, considered in Chapter 4. Article 7 provides detailed rules on the calculation of market shares. The 2010 VABER altered the market share threshold to cover market power held by either the seller or the buyer.

Hard-core restraints

The 'black list' of hard-core restraints is provided in Art 4 of the Regulation. Article 4 sets out the list of provisions which are prohibited and which will render an agreement not capable of exemption under the Regulation. The following are the two most significant types of hard-core restraint in Art 4: resale price maintenance and excessive territorial protection.

Resale price maintenance

Article 4(a) provides that resale price maintenance is considered to be a hard-core restriction, whether it is imposed directly by fixing a minimum resale price or indirectly, by fixing discount levels or linking threats of delayed supplies or penalties to the observance of a recommended price level. There is no restriction on maximum pricing. This hard-core restriction was until recently largely unobjectionable, but following the US move away from RPM being considered illegal *per se* in *Leegin*,[241] the debate about the anti-competitive effect of vertical price fixing in the EU has re-opened.[242]

Territorial restrictions

Article 4(b) excludes from the scope of the exemption any 'restriction of the territory into which, or of the customers to whom, a buyer party to the agreement, without prejudice to a restriction on

---

240 Regulation 316/2014/EU on the application of Art 101(3) of the Treaty to categories of technology transfer agreements, [2014] OJ L93/17.
241 *Leegin Creative Leather Products Inc v PSKS Inc,* 551 U.S. 877 (2007) (Sup Ct (US))
242 See, for instance, Zevogolis, NE, 'Resale Price Maintenance (RPM) in European Competition Law: Legal Certainty Versus Economic Theory' [2013] ECLR 25.

its place of establishment, may sell the contract goods or services'. This exclusion is predicated upon the EU market-integration goal and the concern over the creation of compartmentalised markets within the EU. Nonetheless, even in *Consten and Grundig*, it has been recognised that some form of territorial exclusivity may be required as an incentive for a distributor to promote a product effectively, even if absolute territorial protection is not allowed. Accordingly, there are exceptions to this exclusion and the key exception allows for the restriction of 'active sales to the exclusive territory or exclusive customer group'. The Commission's Guidelines on vertical restraints highlight the distinction between active and passive sales.[243] The Commission is obviously wary of deterring the growth of e-commerce and, in general, the Commission has confirmed that the use of the internet is not considered a form of active sales as it is a reasonable way of reaching customers. As long as the website is not specifically targeted at specific customers or customers primarily inside another territory it will not constitute active sales; the language used on the website is not a crucial factor. The Commission's view of passive selling, aside from e-commerce, appears to be limited to catalogue selling and responding to unsolicited emails. The 2010 Guidelines do allow for the restriction of passive sales in very limited circumstances. Where a distributor is the first to sell a new brand, or an established brand into a new territory, there may be the need for substantial investment. Where that is the case there can be a restriction on passive sales for up to two years.[244]

Other excluded obligations

There are certain other obligations contained in vertical agreements that are not exempt. Article 5 details three types of obligations:

1   non-compete obligations;
2   post-term non-compete obligations; and
3   obligations regarding competing products in a selective distribution network.

The key difference from the hard-core restraints is that, provided these non-exempted obligations are severable, the remainder of the agreement can benefit from exemption under the Regulation.

The Guidelines

The Commission has published comprehensive Guidelines on vertical restraints.[245] The Guidelines seek to give assistance on the interpretation of the Regulation, and to outline the Commission's policy, with a view to encouraging self-assessment of agreements. The Commission has set out a four-stage approach for analysis. Firstly, parties should define their relevant market and ascertain their market share. Secondly, if market share does not exceed 30%, the agreement is covered by the Regulation, subject to the existence of hard-core restrictions. The third and fourth stages, where the agreement has a higher than 30% market share, involve an assessment of whether the agreement is caught by Art 101(1) and, thereafter, falls within the terms of Art 101(3). In formulating general rules for assessing vertical restraints the key is that agreements only raise competition concerns if there is insufficient inter-brand competition[246] and that a reduction of inter-brand competition is generally more harmful than a reduction in intra-brand competition.

---

243 Commission Notice, Guidelines on vertical restraints, SEC(2010) 411 final, para 51.
244 Ibid, para 61.
245 Commission Notice, Guidelines on vertical restraints, SEC(2010) 411 final.
246 Ibid, at para 102.

This market-power based economic approach informs the VABER and its approach to individual restraints. This approach is supported by ancillary factors, for example, a combination of restraints aggravates their negative effects, and restraints linked to relationship-specific investments are easier to justify, as are restraints in relation to opening up new product or geographic markets. The Commission notes that particular factors in the assessment of the position under Art 101(1) will be the market position of competitors, the existence of entry barriers and the maturity of the market, in that negative effects are more likely in mature markets, rather than in dynamic markets.

Examples of Vertical Agreements

Exclusive distribution

Exclusive distribution is a form of distribution whereby a producer agrees with a distributor to supply only to that distributor within a particular territory. The crucial elements in such an agreement are the allocation of a particular sales territory to the distributor and the undertaking by the producer not to appoint another distributor within that territory. It will also normally involve an undertaking by the producer not to sell directly within the territory. The producer's obligations are the key elements of the relationship, but certain obligations will also normally be imposed upon the distributor, for example:

1   to stock the complete range of a producer's goods;
2   to stock certain spare parts; and
3   to promote the producer's goods.

Reasons for adopting exclusive distribution

A producer may distribute its own goods either by in-house means or by setting up a subsidiary company. However, it may be more efficient for a producer to appoint a third party to distribute the goods. If the producer is supplying goods to a new market it would be sensible to appoint a distributor who is familiar with that market, thereby avoiding difficulties resulting from a lack of knowledge of the market or because of linguistic and legal differences. In addition, a smaller producer may lack the necessary resources for the distribution of its own goods.

Exclusive distribution may also avoid the additional cost of supplying a large number of distributors. One of the primary reasons for adopting the exclusive distribution format is to encourage a distributor to advertise the producer's goods and to provide any necessary after-sales customer service, as this would be prohibitively expensive for most distributors unless they are provided with the protection of exclusivity. Without exclusivity, other potential distributors, within the contract territory or beyond, may be able to 'free-ride' on the distributor's promotional efforts and undercut the distributor's selling price. Exclusive distribution may be particularly important for new products entering the market, as a distributor may be required to expend a considerable sum on advertisement and promotion of the product and will not want to risk such an outlay if other potential sellers of the product could free-ride on his efforts, that is, if they sought to market the product without incurring the same promotional expenditure.

Treatment of exclusive distribution agreements under Art 101 TFEU

The discussion of the pros and cons of vertical restraints outlined above is particularly relevant in this regard. The problem for EU law has been how to achieve the appropriate balance between the necessary restrictions on intra-brand competition through territorial exclusivity, which may enhance inter-brand competition, and the avoidance of the restrictions on parallel trade which are contrary to the EU goal of market integration. The most important restrictions in this context are those that create territorial restrictions.

Territorial restrictions

A distributor may only be prepared to enter into an exclusive distribution agreement that confers absolute territorial protection in order to ensure protection from 'free-riders' and safeguard investment in the promotion of the product. This will particularly be the case in respect of a new product, which will require more promotional effort than an established product, entering the market. Without adequate protection the distributor may not be prepared to distribute the product and it therefore may never reach the market. The EU authorities have recognised that territorial protection is necessary in order for certain distribution agreements to be established. For instance, in *Société La Technique Minière*,[247] the Court found that a term conferring territorial exclusivity on a distributor might not infringe Art 101(1) where the term is a vital element for the distributor to market a producer's product. Although the Commission is aware of the commercial necessity for territorial protection, it has never accepted the principle that all territorial restrictions should be permitted to facilitate pro-competitive agreements. The Commission will accept limited territorial exclusivity but will not tolerate the complete obstruction of parallel imports, even where agreements conferring absolute territorial protection may increase inter-brand competition, and therefore indirectly aid the integration of markets within the EU. *Consten and Grundig*[248] established the prohibition on the creation of an absolute territorial protection. The reason for the strict approach is that such restrictions may impede the development of the internal market by isolating national markets. The EU authorities are keen to ensure that some form of parallel trade is maintained by passive sales from outside the contract territory, except in the first years of a product's distribution within a territory where significant investment is necessary. As discussed above, the VABER places considerable restrictions on the types of territorial exclusivity which can be granted. The growth of e-commerce, and other methods of attracting trade via the internet, pose particular challenges for exclusive distribution.[249] The Guidelines on vertical restraints discuss the issues in some detail and try to strike balance between 'bricks and mortar' and internet selling, but restrict practices such as 'dual pricing', whereby products which are to be sold online are charged at a higher price.

If an exclusive distribution agreement infringes Art 101(1) and falls outside the terms of the Regulation, the parties to the agreement can seek to defend the agreement's validity under Art 101(3). However, it is extremely unlikely that Art 101(3) would be applicable in respect of an agreement conferring absolute territorial protection or providing for resale price maintenance.[250] The Guidelines now state that there is a presumption that an arrangement which contains a hard-core restraint is unlikely to fulfil the terms of Art 101(3).[251]

Exclusive purchasing or single-branding agreements

The Vertical Agreement Guidelines note that single-branding agreements involve non-compete obligations 'which have as their main element the fact that the buyer is obliged or induced to concentrate its orders for a particular type of product with one supplier'.[252] The primary competition risk concerns foreclosure of the market to competing and potential suppliers. The traditional

---

247 Case 56/65 [1996] ECR 235.
248 Cases 56 and 58/64 [1966] ECR 299.
249 See, for instance, Case C-439/09 *Pierre Fabre Dermo-Cosmétique SAS v Président de l'Autorité de la concurrence and Ministre de l'Économie, de l'Industrie et de l'Emploi* [2011] ECR I-0000.
250 In Case 161/84 *Pronuptia* [1986] ECR 353, the Court held that resale price maintenance infringed Art 101(1) and was not entitled to exemption under Art 101(3).
251 Guidelines, at para 47.
252 Guidelines, at para 129.

approach to Art 101 is reversed by considering first if an agreement falls within the block exemption 'safe harbour', where the supplier has less than 30% market share; if this is not the case, one proceeds to consider the possible application of Art 101(1) and (3). Accordingly, single-branding agreements will gain an automatic exemption where the supplier's market share does not exceed 30%[253] and the non-compete obligation[254] is limited to five years.[255] It should be noted that Art 5(1)(a) of the Regulation applies to any 'direct or indirect non-compete obligation'. This would cover indirect exclusive purchasing commitments imposed, for example, through the freezer exclusivity provisions in the Irish ice cream dispute.[256] Nonetheless, the Commission has power under the Regulation to withdraw the benefit of the Regulation where an agreement falls within Art 101(1) and does not fulfil the conditions in Art 101(3).[257] In particular, the Guidelines indicate that withdrawal may result 'when a number of major suppliers enter into single branding contracts with a significant number of buyers on the relevant market (cumulative effect situation)'.[258] Article 6 allows the Commission to exclude from the scope of the Regulation parallel networks of similar vertical agreements where the networks cover more than 50% of a relevant market.[259] Where the block exemption does not apply, the Guidelines outline a range of factors for assessing whether a single-branding agreement may be caught by Art 101; those factors include the supplier's market position, the duration of the non-compete obligations, the likelihood of 'significant foreclosure' of the market, and the existence of entry barriers.[260] Of particular relevance is the Commission's concern that with reduction in inter-brand competition 'for final products at the retail level, significant anti-competitive effects may start to arise, taking into account all other relevant factors, if a non-dominant supplier ties 30 % or more of the relevant market'.[261] The impact of a cumulative foreclosure effect is also outlined in the Guidelines.[262] In *Calor Gas Ltd v Express Fuels (Scotland) Ltd*[263] gas suppliers and distributors, Calor Gas Ltd, raised an action of damages against a dealer following their termination of a principal dealer agreement and their subsequent dealership with a rival supplier. The defence that the exclusivity arrangement for a minimum of five years rendered the agreement void under Article 101 was successful, relying, *inter alia*, on the principles set out in *Delimitis*. The Scottish court stressed the importance of market power and the duration of the single branding obligation in holding that there was a sufficient contribution to a competition restriction and an actual or potential effect on inter-State trade where a nationwide network of principal dealers is tied to the brand leader for a period of five years, especially in a mature market.

Selective distribution

Selective distribution is an important form of distribution where sales, usually of final branded products, are restricted not on the basis of the number of distributors, but on the basis of selection criteria linked to the product itself. To join the 'network' of distributors, all resellers must meet the standards set out by the manufacturer of the product. If the criteria are qualitative in nature, for example, the training of staff or the quality of service where that provision is

---

253 Article 3 of Reg 330/2010. See in particular para 131 of the Guidelines. See, also, Griffiths, M, 'A glorification of *de minimis* – the Regulation on Vertical Agreements' [2000] ECLR 241.
254 Art 1(d) of Reg 330/2010 provides that a non-compete obligation means an obligation not to manufacture, purchase, sell or resell goods or services that compete with the contract goods or services.
255 Art 5(1)(a).
256 Case T-65/98 *Van den Bergh Foods v Commission* [2003] ECR II-4653.
257 Guidelines, at paras 74–85.
258 At para 134.
259 Guidelines, at paras 74–85.
260 Paras 133–138.
261 At para 140.
262 At para 141.
263 [2008] CSOH 13. Cf *IMS v Ofcom* [2008] CAT 13.

linked to the nature of the product, there is no restriction on the number of dealers and there is little risk of an anti-competitive effect.[264] It has generally been accepted that for some products there is strong competition on factors other than price, and selective distribution allows a manufacturer to enhance competition on quality, through a selective network, without the risk of free-riders damaging the brand by lowering standards to compete on price alone.[265] Regulation 330/2010 permits both qualitative and quantitative restrictions, where there is also a restriction on the number of outlets in an area, selective restrictions are permissible as long as market share is below 30% and there are no hard-core restraints, such as restrictions on active selling by distributors to each other and to end-users.[266] Where there is no real market power, the intra-brand restrictions in selective distribution are tempered by competition from other brands. Again the exemption may be withdrawn if over 50% of the relevant market is subject to similar agreements.

The rise of internet selling and e-commerce has created interesting new issues in selective distribution. We have already discussed the issue of 'low-value' free riders taking advantage of sellers who offer a high-quality retail experience as part of a manufacturer's brand management. Web-selling offers an obvious route for low-cost retail that can compete on price with more expensive 'bricks and mortar' operations. Manufacturers have an interest in maintaining an effective high street presence to promote their high-end products and offer sales and after-sales services. How can they protect those high street retailers from web-based competition? One possible restriction is to require all members of the network to have a minimum 'bricks and mortar' operation before they gain access to the network. In that way none of the network members can free-ride on each other through their respective web-based operations. After *Pierre Fabre*,[267] it is clear that a selective distribution system cannot restrict the opportunity for its members to sell via the internet, as it is a restriction by 'object' under Art 101(1), the requirement to have a certain physical presence is the only remaining solution.

UK Competition Law and Vertical Restraints

There has never been the same level of debate in the UK as in the EU as to the relative merits of vertical restraints. This is partly due to the particular format of Art 101 TFEU and the special status accorded to market integration in the application of EU competition law. Unsurprisingly, UK law has never adopted a unified and consistent approach towards varying forms of vertical restraints. UK law has been characterised by the consideration of vertical restraints under the full range of different competition law provisions, including the common law doctrine of restraint of trade.[268] UK law has also generally adopted a fairly lenient approach, typified by the initial exclusion of vertical agreements from the Competition Act 1998 Chapter I prohibition. Nonetheless, more recently the emphasis has been on ensuring an approach to vertical restraints that is consistent with EU law, by emphasising the scope for parallel exemption from the UK Chapter I prohibition by virtue of the application of the VABER. The Competition Act 1998 (Land Agreements Exclusion and Revocation) Order 2004[269] ensures the application of the VABER to all vertical agreements, either directly, or by parallel application where, in fact, there is no effect

---

264 See Case 26/76 *Metro v Commission* [1977] ECR 1875, Guidelines, para 175.
265 See Case 107/82 *AEG-Telefunken v Commission* [1983] ECR 3151.
266 Guidelines, para 176.
267 Case C-439/09 *Pierre Fabre v Président de l'Autorité de la concurrence* [2011] ECR I-9419.
268 See Chapter 1, particularly in relation to exclusive purchasing agreements, and *Esso Petroleum Co Ltd v Harper's Garage (Stourport) Ltd* [1968] AC 269, [1967] 1 All ER 699.
269 As of 1 May 2005. See the Competition Act 1998 (Land Agreements Exclusion and Revocation) Order 2004, SI 2004/1260, and the Guideline, 'Vertical agreements', OFT 419.

on inter-state trade. In addition to the non-applicability of the VABER to hard-core restraints such as price-fixing, vertical agreements that give rise to concern could be dealt with in one of three ways. First, the CMA has the power, under Art 29(2) of Regulation 1/2003, to withdraw the benefit of the block exemption in the UK or in a part of it. Secondly, vertical agreements do not enjoy any exclusion from the Chapter II prohibition, and, consistent with the view that market power is the core concern, a vertical agreement entered into by undertakings with market power could be scrutinised under s 18 of the 1998 Act. Thirdly, where there is a competition problem in a particular sector because of the cumulative effect of the vertical agreements in operation, the CMA may undertake a market study and/or refer the market for a more in-depth inquiry under the market investigation provisions of Part IV of the Enterprise Act 2002, as discussed in Chapter 5.

Key Points

- Article 101(1) TFEU prohibits anti-competitive agreements which affect trade between Member States. The prohibition extends to anti-competitive decisions by associations and looser forms of arrangement or understanding known as concerted practices, such that even a simple exchange of commercially sensitive information between competitors can be caught by the prohibition.
- The prohibition can cover restrictions in both horizontal and vertical agreements. Certain 'hard-core' infringements such as price-fixing or market-sharing are known as 'by object' restrictions and proof of the existence of the restriction alone is sufficient for the agreement to be prohibited. In other agreements, often vertical agreements between parties at different levels of the market it has to be shown that the arrangement has an anti-competitive effect on the market for the prohibition to apply.
- As far as an agreement is caught by the prohibition in Art 101(1) it will be null and void, and unenforceable. Parties to such agreements can seek to argue that the agreement falls within the scope of the exception to the prohibition in Art 101(3) or is covered by one of the Block Exemption Regulations (such as the Vertical Agreements Block Exemption Regulation)
- The UK introduced the Chapter I prohibition, modelled on Art 101, in s 2 of the Competition Act 1998. Section 60 of the 1998 Act requires the prohibition to be interpreted in a way that is consistent with EU law. The Chapter I prohibition effectively extends the Art 101 prohibition to anti-competitive agreements on local markets which would not satisfy the effect on inter-state trade criterion.
- Vertical agreements can have both beneficial and anti-competitive effects and may thereby potentially infringe the Art 101/Chapter I prohibitions. The VABER provides a safe harbour for all vertical agreements where both parties have less than a 30% market share, provided the agreement does not contain certain restrictions which are explicitly prohibited. The VABER also provides protection to vertical agreements which do not affect inter-state trade and are potentially caught by the UK Chapter I prohibition.

Discussion

1 Why does Art 101(1) TFEU extend to concerted practices and the exchange of information, and not simply apply to agreements between competitors?
2 Explain the difference between horizontal and vertical agreements and the impact of the Art 101(1) prohibition on the two types of agreement.
3 Why is the distinction between 'by object' and 'by effect' restrictions necessary under Art 101(1)?
4 What type of justifications can be used in order to argue that an agreement falls within the Art 101(3) exception to the prohibition?

5   Given that Art 101 applies throughout the EU and can be enforced by the CMA, what scope is there for the application of the Chapter I prohibition?
6   In what circumstances might vertical agreements fall outside the scope of protection of the VABER? What is the UK approach to vertical restraints in commercial agreements?

Further Reading

Article 101 TFEU

Andreangeli, A, 'Modernising the Approach to Article 101 TFEU in respect to Horizontal Agreements: Has the Commission's Interpretation "Come of Age"?' (2011) *Competition and Regulation* 195.

Odudu, O, *The Boundaries of EC Competition Law: The Scope of Article 81* (2006) Oxford: OUP.

Odudu, O, 'Restriction of Competition by Object: What is the Beef?' (2008) 8 *Competition Law Journal* 11.

Townley, C, *Article 81 EC and Public Policy* (2009) Oxford: Hart.

Van Rompuy, B, *Economic Efficiency: The Sole Concern of Modern Antitrust Policy? Non-efficiency Considerations under Article 101 TFEU* (2012) Kluwer Law.

The Competition Act 1998: Chapter I prohibition

Riley, A, 'Outgrowing the European Administrative Model: Ten Years of British Anti-Cartel Enforcement' Chapter 10 in Rodger, B (ed), *Ten Years of UK Competition Law Reform* (2010) Dundee: DUP.

Rodger, BJ and MacCulloch, A (eds), *The UK Competition Act: A New Era for UK Competition Law* (2000) Oxford: Hart; in particular Chapter 1, Whish, R, 'The Competition Act 1998 and the Prior Debate on Reform'; and Chapter 8, Rodger, BJ and MacCulloch, A, 'The Chapter I Prohibition: Prohibiting Cartels? Or Permitting Vertical? Or Both?'

Townley, C, 'The Goals of Chapter I of the UK's Competition Act 1998' (2010) *Year book of European Law*, 29, 1, 307–360

Vertical restraints, the US rule of reason and the Vertical Agreements Block Exemption Regulation

Bork, R, *The Antitrust Paradox: A Policy at War with Itself* (1993) Oxford: Maxwell Macmillan, Chapters 14 and 15.

Callery, C, 'Should the European Union Embrace or Exorcise *Leegin*'s "Rule of Reason"?' [2011] ECLR 42.

Comanor, WS, 'Vertical Price Fixing, Vertical Market Restrictions and the New Antitrust Policy' (1985) 98 Harv L Rev 983.

De Stefano, G, 'The New EU Vertical Restraints Regulation: Navigating the Vast Seas Beyond Safe Harbours and Hardcore Restrictions' [2010] ECLR 487.

Hawk, B, 'System Failure: Vertical Restraints and EC Competition Law' (1995) 32 CML Rev 973.

Rodger, B, 'The Big Chill for National Courts: Reflections on Market Foreclosure and Freezer Exclusivity under Article 81 EC' (2004) 11(1) *Irish Journal of European Law* 77.

Zevogolis, NE, 'Resale Price Maintenance (RPM) in European Competition Law: Legal certainty Versus Economic Theory' [2013] ECLR 25.

Chapter 7

Cartels: Deterrence, Leniency and Criminalisation

Chapter Contents

Overview

- Cartels, often price-fixing conspiracies between 'competitors', which were once common across Europe, are now considered to be the most serious form of competition law violation, as there is rarely any economic justification for their existence.
- Contemporary cartel regulation is based on the principle of optimal deterrence. Cartel activity is to be discouraged by having in place suitable and adequate enforcement and penalties to remove any perceived gain from cartel activity.
- Deterrence is achieved by combining increased penalties, through corporate fines, individual sanctions and compensation payments, with enforcement enhancing tools like leniency and settlement programmes.

Introduction

The cartel is generally recognised as the most serious violation of competition law. A classic cartel is an agreement between horizontally related producers of a particular product across an industry. By being members of the cartel the producers no longer compete against each other and, effectively, gain the power of a monopolist through agreement. They will normally exploit that market power by fixing prices, reducing output, or sharing customers or markets. All of those activities will increase costs for customers, compared to the costs that would have been faced in a competitive market, and increase the profit levels for the cartel members. One of the reasons that cartels are seen as being so damaging is that there is very little economic justification for their existence; they are always detrimental and offer little or no redeeming benefit.

Not all horizontal agreements between competitors are cartels. There are some circumstances in which some horizontal agreements may be allowed to go ahead; usually through Art 101(3) TFEU. One such example would be a research and development (R&D) agreement. Under such an agreement, two competing undertakings would agree to co-operate in a research project with a view to creating a new hi-tech product. That agreement would be beneficial, as it would encourage the parties to invest in expensive, and potentially risky, research activities. The new products developed would be of benefit to their customers who would get access to new technology much more quickly than would have been possible without the agreement. The competition authorities must be alert to the possibility that the undertakings who jointly undertook the research would have decreased incentives to compete with each other on the market created by the joint activity. In the Block Exemption Regulation, which deals with R&D agreements,[1] there is tension between the desire to encourage research and the concern that horizontal co-operation could lead to cartel activity. Article 5 of the Regulation sets out the agreements that are not covered by the block exemption; these include the limitation of output or sales or the fixing of prices when selling the contract product to third parties.

A useful general description of a cartel is set out by Harding and Joshua:

> an organisation of independent enterprises from the same or similar area of economic activity, formed for the purpose of promoting common economic interests by controlling competition between them.[2]

---

1 Commission Regulation 1217/2010/EU on the application of Art 101(3) of the Treaty on the Functioning of the European Union to certain categories of research and development agreements, [2010] OJ L335/36. See also the Commission Guidelines on the applicability of Art 101 of the Treaty on the Functioning of the European Union to horizontal co-operation agreements, [2010] OJ C11/1.
2 Harding, C and Joshua, J, *Regulating Cartels in Europe*, 2nd edn (2010) Oxford: OUP, p 12.

The contemporary shorthand definition as adopted by the European Commission, is as follows:

> What is a cartel?
>
> It is an illegal secret agreement concluded between competitors to fix prices, restrict supply and/or divide up markets. The agreement may take a wide variety of forms but often relates to sales prices or increases in such prices, restrictions on sales or production capacities, sharing out of product or geographic markets or customers, and collusion on the other commercial conditions for the sale of products or services.[3]

It is therefore clear that the type of horizontal agreement that generally falls within the definition of a cartel is one that seeks to: set prices, either directly or by manipulating output; share customers by allocating them between suppliers directly or by allocating each supplier control over customers in a specific geographical area; or agree to co-ordinate other terms and conditions of sale over which customers might expect sellers to compete. One practice, which would clearly fall within the concept of a cartel, but is usually known by a more specific name, is bid-rigging. This is where a contract is to be allocated through a bidding or tendering process, which is specifically designed to ensure competing suppliers go head-to-head to win a contract, and that process is subverted by the potential suppliers getting together in advance of making their bids to decide upon a collective strategy and thereby 'rig' the bidding process. Essentially, this is simply a strategy of co-operation in order to share customers among the bidding cartel members.

The history of European cartels

The history of the European cartel in the twentieth century is a particularly interesting one.[4] At the beginning of the century the cartel was a normal feature of industry. They were so prevalent in Germany that it became known as the 'Land of Cartels',[5] with 400 operating in 1905.[6] The reasons for this high level of cartelisation are complex, but in many regards mirror the reasons that cartels form in contemporary industries. The impact of the industrial revolution, alongside the political impact of the building of the German State, had resulted in volatile markets. Many of the cartels were originally defensive in nature, in that smaller businesses grouped together for protection, but as they grew in size, and industry coverage, they became more powerful and were able to exert greater influence. The growth of cartels was generally positively received, as they were perceived as bringing stability and order to markets. It was also more closely aligned with the corporatist tradition within German society.[7] The ability of customers to access lower prices was seen as being less important than the stability of the state economy, as reflected in the health of its industrial base. Cartel-type arrangements were found in other European economies in the early part of the century, but in economies like Britain they were less formal, and businesses tended to be more independent and entrepreneurial. This began to change in the inter-war period, when multinational cartels began to form, often in industries where a national cartel had been successful. The wary toleration of cartels can be seen in the 1927 Geneva Declaration on Cartels:

3 Commission, 'Antitrust: Commission action against cartels – Questions and answers' MEMO/10/290, 30 June 2010.
4 For a full historical account see, Harding, C and Joshua, J, *Regulating Cartels in Europe*, 2nd edn (2010) Oxford: OUP, and Gerber, D, *Law and Competition in Twentieth Century Europe: Protecting Prometheus* (1998) Oxford: Clarendon Press.
5 Gerber, ibid, pp 74–75.
6 Henderson, WO, *The Industrial Revolution on the Continent 1800–1914* (1961) London: Frank Cass, p 60.
7 This can seen, in part, as a reaction to, and rejection of, the 'Manchester school' economic model; the highly unregulated laissez-faire economic development characterised by the earlier industrial expansion in the North of England. See Harding and Joshua, above, n 4, pp 69–73. It is also interesting to note that the socialist parties that sought to represent the 'worker', the closest to the contemporary conception of the consumer, supported cartels as being a step towards state control and ensuring the stability of employment (p 74).

> The Conference has recognized that the phenomenon of such agreements, arising from economic necessities, does not constitute a matter upon which any conclusion of principle be reached, but a development considered as good or bad according to the spirit which rules the constitution and the operation of the agreements, and in particular according to the measure in which those directing them are actuated by a sense of the general interest.[8]

The political turmoil in Europe that led to the 1939–45 war brought this period of development to an end. The tentative control methods first seen in the mid-1920s were overtaken by events.

The immediate post-war period saw a change in attitude towards the cartel. Part of that attitude shift probably relates back to the use of cartels by the totalitarian governments in Germany, Italy and Japan in the lead-up to the 1939–45 war. That association, and the influence of the United States in European politics,[9] led to increased suspicion of previously accepted organisations. Notwithstanding that change in attitude, there was no rush to follow the US prohibition model. The first European-level control was seen in the European Coal and Steel Community (ECSC) in 1951. It is interesting to note that the ECSC regime did not challenge cartels *per se* – it promoted the public use of cartel-like organisations in industry, but certainly challenged the operation of private cartels. It did have a prohibition, in Art 65, of anti-competitive cartel practices, but also had a system of exemptions, decided by the High Authority. The new model was a blend of European and American experience.

Before going on to examine the EU prohibitions, which will be the focus of much of this chapter, it is interesting to spend a few moments looking at the UK's relationship with cartels before the UK joined the EEC in 1973. The changing relationship is indicative of the wider European view. The common law always had a tolerant attitude towards cartel arrangements.[10] In *Jones v North* in 1875 a, no-doubt secret, bid rigging arrangement was described as 'perfectly lawful'.[11] In later cases, such as *North Western Salt Co v Electrolytic Alkali Co Ltd*[12] and *Rawlings v General Trading Co*,[13] attitudes had hardened somewhat, but cartel agreements were still not unlawful, unless there were aggravating features such as fraud, misrepresentation, or intimidation, although they may have been considered to be a restraint on trade and held to be void and unenforceable. The first statutory controls in the UK, the Restrictive Practices (Inquiry and Control) Act 1948, allowed the Secretary of State to refer cartels to the Monopolies Commission to establish whether they operated contrary to the public interest. The next legislative attempt to control cartel activity was the Restrictive Trade Practices Act 1956. This introduced compulsory registration of cartel agreements on the basis of a rebuttable presumption that such agreements were contrary to the public interest. Parties could seek to justify their agreements before the Restrictive Practices Court. It therefore appeared that the UK had a relatively strong control regime; however, studies of the registration requirements indicated that while formal legal agreements had been abandoned, with some increase in competition, there was a move towards less formal restrictions which could have had a similar result.[14]

---

8 Adopted 24 May 1927, by the Economic Conference.
9 The decartelisation of German industry ran alongside the de-nazification process in occupied Germany; see Harding and Joshua, above, n 4, p 87.
10 In *Norris v Govt of the United States* [2008] UKHL 16 the House of Lords set out an interesting history of the common law in relation to cartels.
11 *Jones v North* (1875) LR 19 Eq 426, at 430.
12 [1913] 3 KB 422.
13 [1921] 1 KB 635.
14 See Allen, GC, *Monopoly and Restrictive Practices* (1968) London: George Allen & Unwin.

The early history of the EU provisions

The introduction of the competition law provisions in the Treaty of Rome was a significant step forward in European cartel control. The prohibition-based administrative enforcement model, that retained the possibility of notification for the purpose of approval, followed the developing European norm, but the move to supranational control was a decisive step away from political interference by national governments. One of the key features of the prohibition was its place within the common market programme set out in the Treaty: such agreements were deemed 'incompatible with the common market'. There was relatively little enforcement of the new rules in the early stages of the EU's development, certainly before the Commission was granted formal enforcement powers in Regulation 17/62. But even after the Commission was empowered to enforce the rules there was a significant gap before those powers were exercised against cartels. Early Art 101 TFEU cases seemed to focus on specific types of vertical agreements, typified by *Consten & Grundig*,[15] which contained explicit, Member State-centred, territorial market-sharing clauses. It was not until the early 1970s that the Commission brought its enforcement resources to bear on cartels. The first Decisions, in the late 1960s and early 1970s, were in relation to the Noorwijks Cement Accord,[16] but as this was an 'old' agreement which pre-dated the Treaty, there was immunity from the imposition of a fine. The first examples of the Commission challenging 'underground' cartels, of the type more likely to be encountered in the current climate, were in *Quinine*[17] and *Dyestuffs*.[18] These were particularly significant cases, in that they highlighted industry's attempts to adapt to the changing regulatory climate and the Commission's new willingness to challenge less formal, better concealed, arrangements. Co-operation in the quinine industry dated back to 1913 with a defensive cartel being formed in the late 1950s. The existence of this cartel was not notified to the Commission, unlike the *Cement* cases. The cartel was formally discontinued – due to changing market conditions – in 1965, but investigations in both the EU and US were launched in 1967, leading to the Decision adopted in 1969. At the same time the Commission was investigating the *Dyestuffs* cartel, which proved to be a much more complicated case, based largely on economic and circumstantial evidence. It also heralded the beginning of a long battle between the Commission and the chemicals industry in Europe.

Cartel wars: the cartel strikes back

Emboldened by its early successes, the Commission increased its activity against cartels leading to an increasing number of cartel prosecutions through the 1970s into the 1980s. In the first half of this period a number of cases came from traditional arrangements in the Low Countries, but towards the end of the period the most significant cases came from large pan-European cartels supplying bulk industrial commodities.[19] By the late 1980s it was apparent that those accused of being involved in cartel activity were more willing to challenge the Commission's imposition of increasingly sizeable fines. The Commission was embroiled in a number of complex legal challenges before the EU Courts in relation to, for instance, *Wood Pulp*,[20] *Polypropylene*[21]

---

15 Cases 56 and 58/64 *Consten & Grundig v Commission* [1966] ECR 299.
16 See Cases 8–11/66 *Cimenteries v Commission* [1967] ECR 75 and Case 8/72 *Vereeninging van Cementhandelaren v Commission* [1972] ECR 977.
17 Cases 41, 44–45/69 *ACF Chemiefarma v Commission* [1970] ECR 661.
18 See, for example, Case 48/69 *ICI v Commission* [1972] ECR 704.
19 While the Commission's attitude had definitely hardened, it was still willing to occasionally sanction 'crisis cartels' when an industry was in significant difficulties. See, for example, Commission Decision 84/380/EEC *Synthetic Fibres* [1984] OJ L207/17.
20 Cases C-89/85 etc. *Ahlström Oy & Others v Commission* [1993] ECR I-1307.
21 Cases T-1/89 etc. *Rhône-Poulenc v Commission* [1991] ECR II-867, on appeal Case C-51/92P *Hercules Chemicals v Commission* [1999] ECR I-4235.

and *PVC*.[22] The Commission's decisions were upheld in the majority of cases, but they also suffered some major defeats. It became abundantly clear that the Commission would have to invest significant resources in order to find good evidence to support their cartel findings, and then support those decisions against the judicial review that would inevitably follow. It is interesting to note that the challenges to the Commission's decisions were largely on procedural and due process grounds, rather than on the basis of the substantive findings. Another growing complexity stemmed from the increasingly broad scope of large cartel cases. An increasing number of cases were not only pan-European, but global in nature. This necessitated greater co-operation with other enforcement agencies, particularly the Department of Justice in the United States, who were running parallel investigations within their jurisdictions. As the fight against cartels moved into the 1990s, it was clear that the Commission was keen to focus its efforts on fighting international cartels, and that it would need to develop new tools and make better use of its resources to be more effective. It is the development of those tools that the rest of this chapter will focus upon.

The Contemporary View of Cartels

It is a truism to suggest that cartels are generally seen as being the most heinous and damaging form of competition law violation. They are the only form of anti-competitive conduct that is almost universally condemned. A great many forms of anti-competitive behaviour are treated differently, for cultural and political reasons, in different jurisdictions, but in virtually all industrial economies, cartels are seen as being highly damaging and are therefore treated harshly. The high level of co-ordination in cartel control is demonstrated by the depth of international co-operation into best practice published by bodies such as the OECD[23] or ICN.[24]

The problem facing the competition authorities is somewhat different in cartel control compared to other areas of competition law and merger control. The problem is not identifying which conduct is anti-competitive and inefficient, and therefore should be prohibited. All cartel behaviour is clearly damaging and should therefore be unlawful. The 'cartel problem' is identifying when such behaviour occurs, and gathering enough evidence of the unlawful behaviour to bring the behaviour to an end and successfully prosecute cartel members. Much of the debate is therefore about designing an enforcement regime that will be successful at catching cartelists and dissuading undertakings from entering cartel arrangements. It is clearly better that cartels are not formed, and therefore the economy does not suffer the economic harm that would follow. Accordingly, the contemporary focus is on the regulatory successes and failures of the key competition regimes, largely in the US, Europe, Canada and Australia. The key issues in the debate are not always clearly stated but, in essence, the driving force behind much of the contemporary thinking is the concept of deterrence. This is the idea that the regulatory regime should seek to deter potential cartelists from entering into cartel arrangements. The usual method of deterring such behaviour is through some form of punishment or consequence should an undertaking violate the rules. The basic concept of deterrence is very simple, but the difficulty stems from attempts to design a system of deterrence that works to produce the right level of deterrence, optimal deterrence, which discourages unlawful behaviour, but does not discourage any lawful, and therefore legitimate, business activity.

---

22 Cases T-79/89 etc *BASF & Others v Commission* [1992] ECR II-315.
23 See OECD, 'Recommendation of the Council concerning effective action against hard core cartels', 1998; OECD, 'Hard Core Cartels', 2000; and, OECD, 'Hard Core Cartels: Third Report on the Implementation of the 1998 Recommendation', 2005.
24 See the work of the ICN Cartel Working Group as set out in the 'ICN Statement of Achievements 2001–2013', April 2013, available at www.internationalcompetitionnetwork.org.

Optimal deterrence

When a regulator seeks to design a regulatory system to deter violations of a set of legal rules they have to balance various elements within that system in order to try and create the appropriate level of deterrence.[25] If the system fails to sufficiently deter, producing under-deterrence, it will not discourage potential violators from embarking on unlawful behaviour. If the system deters too much, producing over-deterrence, the system will discourage businesses from adopting legitimate business models near the edge of legitimate conduct. Businesses will be discouraged as they will be concerned about the potentially high levels of punishment which they may face if they have misread the rules as to what is permissible; the rules may therefore have a 'chilling' effect on legitimate competition. The process of finding the right level of deterrence follows a utilitarian calculus. To effectively discourage the behaviour the system must ensure that there is no incentive for the potential violator to embark on the unlawful conduct. One clear way to ensure there is no benefit is to ensure that the punishment imposed removes all the benefit the potential violator would expect to gain from the unlawful acts. In the context of cartels this would mean that the increased profit that a cartelist would expect to gain from the operation of the cartel is removed when the cartelist is caught. If that were the case, there would be no incentive for them to enter into a cartel. That is only one side of the calculus; the expected gain/punishment equation alone is not sufficient to devise a policy. No matter how effective the enforcement system is, it is unrealistic to expect the regulators to catch all violations of the rules. If the regulator only catches one in every three violations there will still be an incentive to act unlawfully. The cartelist will expect to keep the gain from two cartels, even if the gain from the third cartel is stripped away. The chances of being caught and punished must therefore be factored into the equation. As one of the key punishments in competition law is an administrative fine, Wils explains the optimal deterrent punishment in the following way:

> The minimum fine for deterrence to work thus equals the expected gain from the violation multiplied by the inverse of the probability of a fine being effectively imposed.[26]

An example of this approach would be the following. A cartelist expects to gain an increase in profits of approximately £200,000 by being a member of a cartel. They also have reason to believe that there is only a one in four chance of being caught and a fine being imposed. In such a situation the optimal fine to deter that behaviour would be:

$$gain \times \left(\frac{inverse}{probability} \right) = fine \qquad £200,000 \times \left(\frac{4}{1} \right) = £800,000$$

It is obviously impossible to try to calculate accurately what a potential cartelist's expected gain might be: the calculation will have been made at a point in time when they considered the course of action, and it is possible that they decided to act without making a proper calculation, or one based on limited information.[27] Deterrence theory may not offer a perfect model, but it does form a useful structure in which to consider the likely success of a particular enforcement regime and

---

25 For discussion of deterrence see, for example: Motta, M, 'On Cartel Deterrence and Fines in the European Union' [2008] ECLR 209; Wils, WPJ, 'Optimal Antitrust Fines: Theory and Practice' (2006) 29(2) World Comp 183; Landes, WM, 'Optimal Sanctions for Antitrust Violations' (1983) 50 Uni Chicago LRev 652; and Becker, GS, 'Crime and Punishment: An Economic Approach' (1968) 76 J of Political Economy 169.

26 Wils, WPJ, 'Optimal Antitrust Fines: Theory and Practice' (2006) 29(2) World Comp 183, 191.

27 The limited ability of a cartelist to calculate the real gains or chance of being caught is often described as 'bounded rationality'.

gives a useful methodology to assess any attempt to improve the regulation of hard-core cartels. Deterrence is a model used in many areas of law,[28] but it is particularly suited to cartel regulation as it might be expected that business people, whose main aim is profit maximisation, can be expected to act as 'amoral calculators' in that they will calculate the expected costs and benefits of any behaviour before acting.

It is clear that in many recent reforms the aim of increasing the deterrent effect of the law has been an important factor. While the competition authorities can do little to reduce the profit that can be gained from being a member of a successful cartel, they can use enforcement tools to try and put in place effective and deterrent punishments to strip away the expected gains and increase the chances of the cartelist being caught and punished.

Punishment

One of the key features of any attempt to regulate hard-core cartels is effective punishment or sanctions. Most regimes use fines as their main sanction, but there is increasing resort to other forms of sanction to bolster the effect of traditional fines. Before going on to look at the range of new sanctions being used to control cartels, and other anti-competitive behaviour, we shall first examine the way in which corporate fines are calculated in the EU and the UK.

Administrative corporate fines in the EU

The level of fines imposed for cartel infringement under EU competition law has increased dramatically since the 1990s.[29] The then largest fine for a single competition law infringement, of €992.3m, was imposed against the *Elevators and Escalators* cartel in 2007. The level of fines imposed in cartel cases in the recent past is as follows:[30]

Year	Fines imposed	No. of undertakings	Average fine
2004	€390,209,100	30	€13,006,970
2005	€683,029,000	41	€16,659,244
2006	€1,846,385,500	47	€39,284,798
2007	€3,333,802,700	45	€74,084,504
2008	€2,271,232,900	37	€61,384,673
2009	€1,540,651,400	40	€38,516,285
2010	€2,868,459,674	69	€41,571,879
2011	€614,053,000	14	€43,860,929
2012	€1,875,694,000	37	€50,694,432

The increase in fines in 2006 can largely be ascribed to a combination of the severity of the cartel conduct, the size of the markets affected, and the Commission's hardening attitude. The

---

28 Criminal law is an obvious example, but regulatory theory is employed in many areas. Notable examples, as they share many commonalities with competition law, are consumer law and environmental law.
29 For an analysis of fines across this period, see Motta, M, 'On Cartel Deterrence and Fines in the European Union' [2008] ECLR 209 and Connor, JM, 'Cartel Fine Severity and the European Commission: 2007–2011' [2013] ECLR 58.
30 All figures from 'Cartel Statistics', 10 July 2013, available at ec.europa.eu/competition/cartels/statistics/statistics.pdf and 'Cartels – Questions and answers', available at ec.europa.eu/competition/cartels/overview/faqs_en.html.

rise in the level of fines subsequent to 2006 can be attributed to the Commission beginning to operate on the basis of the 2006 'Guidelines on the method of setting fines'.[31] Connor suggests that the mean fines increased by 25% under the 2006 Guidelines, when compared to fines under the 1998 Guidelines,[32] but much of that can be accounted for by inflation.[33] He also suggests that the majority of the 'starting points' for Commission fines are at the lower end of the scale set out in the Guidelines and the fines are less severe than those imposed in the same period in the US by the DoJ.

The Guidelines explain the process that the Commission uses to calculate fines. It is important that the Commission is able to justify the fines it imposes, as they will invariably be subject to review by the GC.[34] In many cases the Court of Justice has been critical of the fines imposed by the Commission. While the Guidelines set out the process, the Commission still retains a significant amount of discretion, which can make it difficult to predict, in advance, what fine might be imposed. The Commission's approach has a two-step methodology: first, it sets the basic amount of the fine; and, second, it may adjust that amount either upwards or downwards.

The basic amount

The first step in calculating the fine for a single undertaking is to calculate the value of the goods or services that relate, directly or indirectly, to the infringement within the EEA within the last business year.[35] Adjustment may be made to the figures if, because the cartel extends beyond the EEA, the EEA value does not properly represent the relevant weight of each undertaking within the infringement.[36] The basic amount is a proportion of the value of sales, multiplied by the duration of the infringement. The proportion of the value of sales will be set at a level up to 30%. Because of the nature of secret hard-core cartels, it might be thought that fines would generally be at the top end of that scale; however, while some fines are around the 25% mark, most are much lower – the average being 17%.[37] The use of low starting points means that the Commission still has considerable leeway under the current Guidelines to increase fines even further. The duration, in years, acts as a multiplier, with the multiplier being calculated in six-month increments.[38] To reflect the damage caused by mere entry into a cartel the Commission will also impose an additional 'entry penalty' of between 15 and 25% of the value of sales.[39] While the basic amount is calculated from actual figures it will always be rounded out to produce a final amount.

Adjustment to the basic amount

Once the basic amount has been calculated, the Commission can then take into account a number of other factors that may then increase or decrease the applicable fine. A number of aggravating

---

31 Commission Guidelines on the method of setting fines imposed pursuant to Art 23(2)(a) of Regulation No 1/2003, [2006] OJ C210/02. For discussion of the Guidelines see, Volcker, SB, 'Rough Justice? An Analysis of the European Commission's new Fining Guidelines' (2007) 44(5) CMLRev 1285.

32 Commission Guidelines on the method of setting fines imposed pursuant to Art 15(2) of Regulation No 17 and Art 65(5) of the ECSC Treaty, [1998] OJ C9/3.

33 Connor, JM, 'Cartel Fine Severity and the European Commission: 2007–2011' [2013] ECLR 58.

34 For instance, all the Commission's cartel decisions in 2005 and 2006 were subject to review. See, also, Motta, M, 'On Cartel Deterrence and Fines in the European Union' [2008] ECLR 209.

35 Commission Guidelines on the method of setting fines imposed pursuant to Art 23(2)(a) of Regulation No 1/2003, [2006] OJ C210/02, para 13.

36 Ibid, para 18.

37 Connor calculates that *Marine Hose* had a starting point of 25%, see Commission Press Release IP/09/137, 28 January 2009, but the mean value was much lower. See Connor, JM, 'Cartel Fine Severity and the European Commission: 2007–2011' [2013] ECLR 58.

38 Cartel duration of two years would result in a multiplier of 2. Duration of two years and three months would result in a multiplier of 2.5. Duration of two years and nine months would result in a multiplier of 3.

39 Commission Guidelines on the method of setting fines imposed pursuant to Art 23(2)(a) of Regulation No 1/2003, [2006] OJ, C210/02, para 25.

circumstances may result in an increase in the level of fine. These include: where an undertaking continues or repeats the same or similar infringement; refusal to co-operate; or being a leader or instigator of the infringement, or coercing others to participate.[40] Mitigating factors that may result in a decrease of the fine include: evidence of limited involvement or the adoption of competitive behaviour during the infringement; co-operation with the Commission; or where the anti-competitive conduct has been authorised or encouraged by public authorities or legislation.[41] Provision is also made for a specific increase for deterrence purposes.[42] This would be applied where a fine is being imposed against an undertaking that has a large turnover outside the market affected. In that situation the fine may look relatively small compared to the overall financial resources of the undertaking. The Commission may also increase the fine, to ensure its deterrent effect, when the gains made by the cartelists are large compared to the value of relevant sales. In practice the most significant aggravating factor is recidivism, where an undertaking is found to have been the subject of a previous cartel finding in the past. The Guidelines allow for a fine uplift for a recidivist of up to 100%, but, again, in practice the Commission has been more conservative. Analysis suggests that a single previous finding leads to a fine uplift of around 30%, with a further 30% being added for each additional previous finding.[43]

Once this calculation has been made, there are two final caveats that the Commission must consider. The power of the Commission to impose fines under Regulation 1/2003 is limited. It cannot impose a fine that exceeds 10% of an undertaking's total turnover in the preceding business year.[44] In the majority of cases this has not proved to be a practical limitation, as the fine is calculated based on a percentage of sales affected by the infringement rather than total sales, but it may prove to be an issue if a single product undertaking is involved in a cartel, given that the basic amount in cartel cases is likely to start at approximately 20% of sales value. Connor calculates that 8% of cartelists had their fines reduced by the cap between 2007 and 2011.[45] Finally, upon application by an undertaking, the Commission may consider reducing a fine on account of an undertaking's inability to pay.[46] Such reductions are rare, but SGL's fines in *Speciality Graphite* and *Carbon & Graphite* were reduced, due to financial constraints.[47]

Administrative corporate fines in the UK

The methodology through which administrative fines are calculated in cartel cases is set out in the 'OFT's guidance as to the appropriate amount of a penalty'.[48] The two main objectives of the policy are to impose penalties that reflect the serious nature of the infringement and to deter undertakings from engaging in anti-competitive practices. The Guidance stresses that cartels are one of the most serious infringements of competition law.[49] The UK's approach was amended in 2012 largely to mirror that of the Commission in its 2006 Guideline. The CMA now adopts a six-step approach.

---

40 Ibid, para 28.
41 Ibid, para 29.
42 Ibid, paras 30–31.
43 See Connor, above, n 37, p 63.
44 Regulation 1/2003, [2003] OJ L1/1, Art 23(2).
45 See Connor, above, n 37, p 65.
46 Commission Guidelines on the method of setting fines imposed pursuant to Art 23(2)(a) of Regulation No 1/2003, [2006] OJ C210/02, para 35.
47 Commission Decision 2006/460/EC *Specialty Graphite*, [2006] OJ L180/20, and Commission Decision 2004/420/EC *Carbon & Graphite*, [2004] OJ L125/45, para 360. See Stephan, A, 'The Bankruptcy Wildcard in Cartel Cases' [2006] JBL 511.
48 OFT's guidance as to the appropriate amount of a penalty, OFT 423, September 2012.
49 Ibid, para 1.4.

Step 1 – the starting point

The level of the starting point for the fine is calculated on the basis of the seriousness of the infringement and the relevant turnover of the undertaking.[50] The seriousness of the infringement will be based on consideration, *inter alia*, of the following: the nature of the product, the structure of the market, the market shares of the undertakings involved, and the effect on competitors and third parties. The starting point can be up to 30% of the relevant turnover. Cartel activities are seen as being among the most serious violations and the CMA indicates it will use a starting point towards the top of the scale. The relevant turnover is the turnover of the undertaking in the relevant product market in the preceding business year. When enforcing the EU prohibitions the CMA may take into account turnover outside the UK, in another EU Member State, if the market is wider than the UK.

Steps 2 to 6 – adjustment for duration and other factors

The starting point may be increased, in step two, to take into account the duration of the infringement. Infringements that last for more than one year may be multiplied by the number of years of the infringement.[51] Part years may be treated as full years. During the third step there is an adjustment for aggravating or mitigating factors.[52] Step four allows for explicit adjustments to may be made to ensure the deterrent effect and proportionality of a penalty, because of the financial benefit made from the infringement or the size and financial position of the undertaking.[53] Step five adjusts any penalty to ensure that it does not exceed the maximum penalty of 10% of the worldwide turnover of the undertaking in the preceding business year and to avoid double jeopardy.[54] In the final step the CMA will apply any fine reductions necessary under their leniency or settlement programmes, or, exceptionally, on the basis of financial hardship.[55]

The problem with corporate fines

The clear problem with deterring cartelists through corporate fines, in both the EU and UK, is that the current fining levels are simply too low. While, in absolute terms, the amounts of money involved may appear to be large, they are unlikely to strip away all the benefits of being involved in a cartel. That is particularly true if one considers that it is highly unlikely that the competition authorities are able to discover and successfully fine all the participants in all cartel arrangements. It is obviously difficult to estimate the gains that a cartelist can expect from taking part in an infringement, but a number of academic studies have sought to calculate the overcharge caused by discovered cartels.[56] By looking at those figures it is estimated that the median overcharge from a cartel is about 25%. There appears to be some variation, depending on the type of cartel and its geographic extent. A cartel within a single European country has a median overcharge of 17%, but a Europe-wide cartel has a median overcharge of 43%. These figures tend to suggest that cartel fines in Europe tend towards under-deterrence. EU and UK fines, if at the top end of the range in the Guidance, are close to the overcharge which cartels may be able to

---

50 Ibid, paras 2.3–2.11.
51 Ibid, para 2.12.
52 Ibid, paras 2.13–2.15.
53 Ibid, paras 2.16–2.20.
54 Ibid, paras 2.21–2.24.
55 Ibid, paras 2.25–2.27.
56 See, in particular, Connor, JM and Lande, RH, 'The size of cartel overcharges: Implications for US and EU fining policies' (2006) 51(4) *Antitrust Bulletin* 983. Connor has updated his cartel dataset and released a second edition of his study, Connor, JM, 'Price-Fixing Overcharges: Revised 2nd Edition', 27 April 2010, ssrn.com/abstract=1610262. In the updated data the median overcharge had declined to 23.3%. The median overcharge for international cartels also fell to 30% overall, in the 1990-2005 period it was 24.4%. EU-wide cartels were still the most successful, but the median overcharge dropped back to just under 40%.

impose; however, the figures indicate that, historically at least, pan-European cartels are among the most profitable for the participants. If the authorities wish to impose fines with real deterrent effect it therefore appears that they should not be discouraged from using the full extent of their powers.

Even if the EU and UK authorities begin to impose fines at the top end of their Guidance, there are still two issues that mean that fines alone are unlikely to be of deterrent effect. Both EU and UK fining powers are limited by a 10% global turnover cap. While this has not proved to be an issue in a large proportion of cases, it does not sit well with a policy aimed at deterrence. This limitation, combined with the limitation based on ability to pay, is usually justified on the basis that a corporate fine should not result in the social costs associated with corporate insolvency.[57] The fines imposed must punish, but should not in effect be a 'corporate death sentence', which substantially damages shareholders, employees and suppliers who had no part to play in the infringement itself. The second, and probably most important, issue is the cartels that 'get away'. As it is unlikely that the authorities will be able to impose fines on all infringements, we would expect to see some form of multiplier to ensure that optimal deterrence is achieved. At present it appears that corporate fines in the EU and UK do not strip away the full benefits of being a member of a cartel; they will therefore not deter when there is always a chance to escape detection and retain all the profit. One way of enhancing deterrence would be to dramatically increase the level of fines, but as noted above, the existence of the 10% global turnover cap means that such a policy is impossible in the current European legislative context. It has therefore become important to find ways of increasing deterrence by means other than ever-larger corporate fines.

Increasing financial penalties: damages

One area that offers the potential for increasing deterrence in cartel cases is compensation claims as discussed in Chapter 3 on Private Enforcement. These would be private claims for compensation brought by those who have suffered loss at the hands of the cartel. If cartelists were required to pay large sums in compensation this would constitute an additional 'penalty' faced by them for acting unlawfully. The private enforcement of competition law has been a topical issue of some controversy in both the US and EU in the 2000s, and is likely to remain so for some time. There is little history of successful private actions in Europe, but this can be contrasted with a strong plaintiff-led history of compensation claims in the US. The reasons for this disparity are both legal and cultural, but the European authorities are seeking to learn from the US experience and encourage a more active role for compensation claims in Europe. In developing this area there are a number of difficulties that need to be addressed. One issue is the balance between EU law and national procedure. The other is the balance between the, sometimes competing, goals of compensating loss and increasing deterrence.

The seminal ruling in *Courage v Crehan*,[58] and the Court's subsequent judgment in *Manfredi*,[59] set out the position of compensation claims in relation to EU competition law. It is now clear that, as a matter of law, 'any individual' who has suffered loss through a breach of EU competition law can bring a claim. Domestic procedure is also restricted through EU law, in that it cannot make such a claim 'excessively difficult'. While Mr Crehan's claim was eventually unsuccessful,[60] it was crucial in setting the scene for future developments in the area. What

57 For discussion of the insolvency concern, see Stephan, A, 'The Bankruptcy Wildcard in Cartel Cases' [2006] JBL 511, and Motta, M, 'On Cartel Deterrence and Fines in the European Union' [2008] ECLR 209.
58 Case C-453/99 *Courage v Crehan* [2001] ECR I-6297.
59 Cases C-295-298/04 *Manfredi* [2006] ECR I-6619.
60 *Inntrepreneur Pub Company (CPC) and others v Crehan* [2006] UKHL 38.

became clear in the *Crehan* and *Manfredi* litigation was that the procedural rules in place in the Member States can make it very difficult to bring compensation claims in competition cases. The particular problems in cartel cases were highlighted by the circumstances in *Manfredi*, where hundreds of small claims were brought by Italian consumers who had been affected by an insurance cartel. This means that in competition cases there is a mix of EU and domestic law operating together. As the number of cases increase, it is likely that the Court of Justice, through the Art 267 TFEU procedure, will be involved in an increasing number of disputes, and may begin to develop a framework of procedural rules that apply across Europe. This would be relatively novel as the Court has always been at pains to respect the 'procedural autonomy' of Member States' domestic legal systems.

The other main source of development in EU law is the Directive on Antitrust Damage Actions.[61] The Directive is designed to optimise the relationship between public and private enforcement and ensure that victims of infringements of EU competition rules can effectively obtain compensation.[62] The Directive seeks to give EU citizens consistent access to competition law evidence from public law authorities, and standardise the response to some difficult issues in relation to private actions such as limitation periods, indirect purchasers and 'passing-on'.

When one looks at the substantive problems in bringing claims, it is clear why the use of private actions across Europe was described as being in a state of 'astonishing diversity and total underdevelopment' in 2004.[63] The main problem with bringing such claims in cartel cases can be explained by looking at the nature of the loss suffered. The cartelist will charge an inflated price to its customers and therefore they will apparently suffer a loss. But in a great many cartel cases the direct purchaser is a manufacturer, as many cartelised industries are in bulk products used as industrial inputs, and therefore may be in a position to pass on the cartel overcharge, in whole or in part, to its customers when it places its product into the retail chain. The eventual harm may well be suffered by the final consumer, who cannot pass the loss any further down the supply chain. The direct purchaser is probably in the best position to claim against the cartel, but in reality they may have not suffered much, or any, loss. The final consumer will definitely have suffered loss, but their loss is very remote from the unlawful act and may, in each individual case, be relatively small; will they be able to effectively bring a claim and be incentivised to undertake the cost, and risk, associated with legal action?

Standing and procedure

All jurisdictions that allow individuals to make compensation claims in relation to cartel activity must decide on who should be allowed to claim. By deciding who can claim, and how, a system will generally favour the award of compensation or be designed to encourage deterrence. All compensation claims will obviously further both goals, but a balance must be struck between them. In the EU it seems likely that the indirect purchaser will be given standing to claim. This stems from the Court's ruling in *Crehan v Courage*, where it held that 'any individual' can make a compensation claim under EU law. Domestic procedure that makes such claims 'excessively difficult' must be disapplied. That choice means that the EU focus will necessarily be on compensation, but that has consequences for the deterrent effect of private actions. The main problem that follows from allowing indirect purchaser standing is that, in a compensation-focused system, you cannot allow both indirect and direct purchasers to claim

---

61 See the Proposal for a Directive of the European Parliament and of The Council on certain rules governing actions for damages under national law for infringements of the competition law provisions of the Member States and of the European Union, COM(2013) 404 final. The Directive was adopted by the European Parliament in April 2014.

62 The detail of the Directive and its impact on private enforcement is discussed in more detail in Chapter 3.

63 Ashurst, 'Study on the conditions of claims for damages in case of infringement of EC competition rules', August 2004.

for the same loss; if both were able to claim for the whole sum, one would make a 'windfall' recovery greater than their actual loss. Either only one class is given standing, or a potentially complex apportionment task must be undertaken. If the indirect purchaser only is given standing, the problem is that they have a limited incentive to bring a claim. They are comparatively distant from the unlawful activity and their individual loss is usually quite small. If they are unlikely to receive a significant sum of compensation, they are unlikely to begin the costly process of litigation. Under federal law in the US, only the direct purchaser is given standing.[64] As the direct purchaser is closer to the unlawful activity they will find it easier to calculate their loss. They are also more likely to have suffered a significant individual loss which would incentivise them to bring a claim.

When indirect purchasers have been given standing the direct purchaser's ability to claim is limited, as they will face the passing-on defence, that they have passed on their loss to their customers. The indirect purchaser will be less incentivised to sue. The question then becomes: how do we make it easier for them to bring a claim, and therefore more likely that they will? Much of the current debate focuses on this issue. The European Commission began a consultation in 2005 with its Green Paper.[65] That was followed, in the UK, in 2007, by the OFT's Discussion Paper and Recommendations.[66] In 2008, the Commission published a White Paper[67] which, after much delay, led to the Proposal for a Directive in 2012.[68] Many of the issues in this debate concern procedural mechanisms to make it easier for the final consumer, who clearly will have suffered loss, to bring a successful claim.

The EU Antitrust Damages Directive suggests a number of measures that should be enacted by all EU Member States to make it easier for claimants to bring private actions in competition cases. It requires: enhanced disclosure of evidence; decisions of NCAs to be considered as proof of infringement before Member States' courts; clear rules on limitation periods; full compensation, including lost profits; acceptance of the passing-on defence for defendants, but a bar on that defence when indirect purchasers are legally barred from claiming; a presumption that an indirect purchaser has suffered loss, a court deciding on the estimated share of pass on; a rebuttable presumption that cartels cause harm; and that cartelists should have joint and several responsibility for harm, unless they are leniency applicants. Some of these issues have already been addressed at Member State level, but the Directive will ensure that all Member States have similar provisions to facilitate claims.

Another popular option to facilitate compensation claims is representative actions, where a representative body brings an action on behalf of a wide class of purchasers.[69] Such an action would spread the cost, and the risk, within a wide class. The representative body would also be incentivised to bring an action, as it would enhance its standing and legitimacy with the consumers it represents. Such actions are already available under s 47B of the 1998 Act,

---

64 See *Hanover Shoe v United States Shoe Machinery Corp* 392 US 481 (1968) and *Illinois Brick Co v Illinois* 431 US 720 (1977). It is interesting that while this is the position in federal law, many state legislatures have overturned the federal position to give back standing to indirect purchasers.

65 Green Paper on damage actions for breach of the EC antitrust rules, COM(2005) 672 final. For discussion, see Pheasant, J, 'Damages Actions for Breach of the EC antitrust Rules: the European Commission's Green Paper' [2006] ECLR 365; and Eilmansberger, T, 'The Green Paper on Damages Actions for Breach of the EC Antitrust Rules and Beyond: Reflections on the Utility and Feasibility of Stimulating Private Enforcement through Legislation' (2007) 44(2) CMLRev 431.

66 OFT Discussion Paper, Private actions in competition law: effective redress for consumers and business, OFT 916, April 2007, and OFT Recommendations, Private actions in competition law: effective redress for consumers and business, OFT 916resp, November 2007.

67 White Paper on Damages actions for breach of the EC antitrust rules, COM(2008) 165 final.

68 Proposal for a Directive of the European Parliament and of the Council on certain rules governing actions for damages under national law for infringements of the competition law provisions of the Member States and of the European Union, COM(2013) 404. The Directive was adopted by the European Parliament in April 2014.

69 On representative actions, see Dayagi-Epstein, O, 'Representation of Consumer Interests by Consumer Associations – Salvation for the Masses' (2006) 3(2) CompLRev 209.

but have so far been of limited use. The only major representative action is *The Consumers Association v JJB Sports PLC*, which settled in January 2008.[70] While the action did recover compensation, and the Consumers Association recovered its costs, the action highlighted the limitations of representative actions in their current form. Further procedural modifications will be needed to facilitate other actions in the future. The UK Consumer Rights Bill, when enacted, will facilitate collective redress by the introduction of an opt-out representative mechanism for claim by consumers in competition infringements. The Commission has also adopted a 'lowest common denominator' EU-wide position on representative actions for breaches of EU provisions in its Recommendation on Collective Redress.[71] Under the Recommendation the Commission envisages opt-in actions by designated bodies, much like the underused UK provision.

In the ongoing debate it will be important for DG Comp and the NCAs to balance the needs of compensation – ensuring that those who have suffered loss can seek compensation – with the needs of deterrence, maximising the number and value of claims to increase the 'penalty' faced by cartelists.[72] Those who are best placed to bring a claim may not be those who suffered a loss, and those who have suffered the clearest loss may be the least able to bring a claim. Any increase in private actions from the current low base will improve the current situation and the risks of a US-style 'litigation culture' are probably overstated.[73] Even if there is individual overcompensation, in that the total amount of compensation exceeds the losses suffered by that claimant, it is unlikely that the compensation awarded will, in reality, exceed the amount of gain made by the cartelist. This is because, even in opt-out actions, some of those who have suffered loss will not be in the class making the claim and the gains made by a cartel do not always equate to direct losses attributable to their customers.[74]

Individual penalties: criminalisation and disqualification

The penalties discussed so far have been imposed on undertakings, usually against companies. One of the reasons that it is not possible simply to increase corporate fines to a deterrent level is that it may result in insolvency for the company, thereby causing undesirable social costs.[75] The cost of insolvency would fall upon the shareholders, employees and suppliers of the company. The shareholders may have benefited from the cartel, via increased profitability, but they would not have been aware of, or responsible for, the unlawful behaviour. The company's suppliers and the majority of the employees, barring those directly involved,[76] would also suffer when they were not responsible for the harm caused. Accordingly, we should seek to focus penalties more specifically on those directly responsible. If the only penalties are imposed on the undertaking there is a risk that individual decision-makers will decide to risk a future penalty being imposed

---

70 CAT Case 1078/7/9/07. For information on the settlement see, Consumers Association, 'JJB to pay fans over football shirt rip-off', 9 January 2008.
71 Commission Recommendation on common principles for injunctive and compensatory collective redress mechanisms in the Member States concerning violations of rights granted under Union Law, C(2013) 3539/3.
72 See, Nebbia, P, 'Damages Actions for the Infringement of EC Competition Law: Compensation or Deterrence?' (2008) 33(1) ELRev 23. See also the acceptance of 'umbrella' damages claims in Case C-557/12 *Kone* [2014] ECR I-0000.
73 See Martin, JS, 'Private Antitrust Litigation in Europe: What Fence is High Enough to Keep Out the US Litigation Cowboy?' [2007] ECLR 2.
74 It is interesting that the award of restitutionary damages – those based on the gain made through the unlawful conduct – were rejected in the Vitamins litigation; see, *Devenish Nutrition Ltd v Sanofi-Aventis SA* [2007] EWHC 2394 (Ch).
75 For a sceptical analysis of social cost concerns, see comments in Motta, M, 'On Cartel Deterrence and Fines in the European Union' [2008] 4 ECLR 209–220.
76 It is often the case that by the time a corporate fine is imposed, those individuals who were directly responsible may have left the company and will not be directly affected by the penalty. This can be justified, as it is the company which must take responsibility for ensuring that its officers and employees comply with the law.

on the undertaking as its impact will be diffused across the company, whereas they would be more circumspect if a penalty would be directly imposed upon them. On the basis of this rationale the UK introduced a number of individual penalties in relation to competition law. The most severe penalty, the cartel offence, is only available in cartel cases.

The cartel offence

When the original cartel offence was introduced in ss 188 and 189 of the Enterprise Act 2002, the rationale put forward was largely based on the deterrence of cartel conduct.[77] The offence itself criminalised an individual who 'dishonestly agrees' to 'make or implement' a horizontal cartel arrangement within the UK.[78] The scope of the offence was limited to the most serious, so-called 'hard-core', cartel restrictions, namely, price-fixing, preventing supply or production, dividing supply or customers, or bid-rigging.[79] The cartel offence has subsequently been amended, but before we turn to the amended offence it is important to understand why the use of a criminal sanction, in itself, is important. It is generally believed that individual financial penalties are of limited effectiveness. There is nothing to stop the undertaking concerned from compensating an executive who has been held personally liable and, in effect, paying the fine. This would simply increase the corporate fine imposed to a minimal extent. For that reason it is believed that the possibility of a real chance of imprisonment is an important aspect of deterrence. Under the cartel offence the maximum sanction is one of up to five years' imprisonment.[80] While a fine can be reimbursed by a company, it cannot go to jail on behalf of an offender. The likelihood of spending time in jail should focus the minds of those company representatives who are actively involved in a cartel. Even if the company is willing to risk the chance of being caught, and having a corporate fine imposed, an individual may not be willing to risk their liberty in order that the company may inflate its profits.[81] This seeks to drive a wedge between the incentives for the company to involve itself in a cartel, and the individual incentives of those who have to implement the day-to-day cartel activity. The first successful UK prosecutions, in the *Marine Hose* cartel, resulted in three cartelists initially being sentenced to jail time of between two-and a half and three years.[82] If there was no real prospect of jail time, the cartel offence would have limited deterrent effect.

The most controversial aspect of the cartel offence as introduced in the 2002 Act was the concept of dishonesty. The dishonesty test, in English criminal law, is that developed under the Theft Act 1968 as set out in *Ghosh*:[83] behaviour is dishonest according to the 'ordinary standards of reasonable and honest people'. It is arguable that there was no need to introduce this difficult concept into the cartel offence at all.[84] The challenge for the OFT to prove the dishonesty of cartel behaviour was highlighted by the House of Lords in *Norris*, which held that, in the period before the adoption of the cartel offence, the collusive fixing of prices was not, in itself, dishonest under

---

77 See MacCulloch, A, 'The Cartel Offence and the Criminalisation of UK Competition Law' [2003] JBL 615.
78 Enterprise Act 2002, s 188(1) as enacted in 2002.
79 Ibid, s 188(2).
80 Ibid, s 190. An unlimited fine is also available, but, for the reasons given, even large fines would have limited impact.
81 In US cases there is some evidence that some individuals are willing to risk imprisonment for a personal gain through promotion and financial reward. They are sometimes dubbed the 'Vice President in Charge of Going to Jail'.
82 OFT Press Release 72/08, 'Three imprisoned in first OFT criminal prosecution for bid rigging', 11 June 2008. This case was a result of guilty pleas based on a US plea bargain. The sentences were reduced on appeal, *R v Whittle, Allison & Brammar* [2008] EWCA Crim 2560.
83 *R v Ghosh* [1982] 2 All ER 689.
84 See, in particular, Fisse, B, 'The Australian Cartel Criminalisation Proposals: An Overview and Critique' (2007) 4(1) CompLRev 51 and MacCulloch, A, 'The Cartel Offence: Is Honesty the Best Policy?', pp 283–307, in Rodger, BJ (ed), *Ten Years of UK Competition Law Reform* (2010) Dundee: DUP. The US has brought a large number of criminal prosecutions without having such a mechanism.

English law.[85] In practice the dishonesty test was also said to create problems for prosecutors as it forced them to directly address the morality of cartel conduct.[86] The dishonesty test is essentially a question of morality for the jury to decide, according to their 'ordinary' standards of honesty. This poses questions as to whether the public at large consider cartel activity to be dishonest or immoral. The best evidence in relation to the UK suggested that while the public saw price-fixing as wrong, and deserving of punishment, they did not, as yet, equate it with serious crimes where one would necessarily expect imprisonment as a sanction.[87] Notwithstanding the convictions in the *Marine Hose* case the cartel offence was not widely considered to be a success. The only other prosecution that reached trial, the 'BA Four' case, resulted in the trial collapsing after it was revealed that the OFT had failed to disclose a considerable amount of potentially exculpatory evidence to the defence.[88] Subsequently, the UK Government published a consultation paper in 2011 which, *inter alia*, included significant reform to the cartel offence.[89] The option that was eventually enacted in the Enterprise and Regulatory Reform Act 2013 was the removal of the dishonesty element from the offence and, as a result, the introduction of a number of new defences.

Section 188 of the Enterprise Act 2002 was amended, by s 47 of the ERR Act 2013, to omit the word 'dishonestly'. Accordingly, for the offence to apply now, an individual must only 'agree' to 'make or implement' a cartel arrangement. The need to prove dishonesty was seen as being overly complex and difficult to prove. It is interesting to note that when Australia adopted a criminal offence in relation to cartel behaviour in 2010, after observing the UK experience, they too decided not to adopt a formulation including a dishonesty element as was originally proposed.[90] One of the functions of the dishonesty element in the original UK cartel offence was to distinguish the limited number of cartel-type situations that are lawful from 'criminal' cartels. The new defences, found in ss 188A and 188B of the 2002 Act, now take on that role.[91] Section 188A provides that an individual does not commit an offence if 'customers would be given relevant information about the arrangements before they enter into agreements for the supply to them of the product or service', or if 'relevant information' about the arrangements was 'published' before the arrangements are implemented in the manner specified by the Secretary of State. The existence of this defence is reminiscent of the old registration regime for restrictive trade practices under the RTPA 1976. If the parties to the agreement are 'open' about the existence of the cartel, they will not commit an offence, but their customers would be able to take action under UK or EU law and could report the agreement to the CMA. Unless the arrangements had been approved, they would presumably be short-lived. The defences in s 188B are more controversial, and are likely to be much more difficult to deal with in practice. Under s 188B(1) and (2) a defence is available if an individual can show, at the time of the making of the agreement that they did not intend that the nature of the arrangements would be concealed from customers or the CMA. This provision will presumably capture arrangements that have been made but not yet implemented, but where the provision of 'relevant information', under s 188A, has not yet occurred. By far the most controversial of the new

---

85 *Norris v Government of the United States of America* [2008] UKHL 16.
86 See MacCulloch, A, 'Honesty, Morality and the Cartel Offence' [2007] ECLR 355, and Stucke, ME, 'Morality and Antitrust' [2006] Colum Bus LRev 443.
87 See Stephan, A, 'Survey of Public Attitudes to Price-fixing and Cartel Enforcement in Britain' (2008) 5(1) CompLRev 123.
88 See Stephan, A, 'Collapse of BA Trial Risks Undermining Cartel Enforcement' CCP Competition Policy Blog, 12 May 2010, and Joshua, J, 'Shooting the Messenger: Does the UK Cartel Offence have a Future?', *The Antitrust Source*, August 2010. Several other prosecutions are ongoing in relation to the *Galvanized Steel Tanks* cartel. One conviction has been secured, and two others have been charged. See CMA Press Release, 'Two men face charges in on going criminal cartel investigation', 11 July 2014.
89 BIS, 'A Competition Regime for Growth: A Consultation on Options for Reform', March 2011. See also Wardhaugh, B, 'Closing the Deterrence Gap: Individual Liability, the Cartel Offence, and the BIS Consultation' [2011] Comp Law 175.
90 See Beaton-Wells, C, 'Cartel Criminalisation and the Australian Competition and Consumer Commission: Opportunities and Challenges', pp 183-199, in Beaton-Wells, C, and Ezrachi, A (eds), *Criminalising Cartels* (2011) Oxford: Hart.
91 For Guidance on how the CMA will approach the defences, see CMA9, 'Cartel Offence Prosecution Guidance', March 2014.

defences is the provision in s 188B(3), which was added to the Act very late in its passage through Parliament, and received little scrutiny. A defence is available where an individual can show that:

> before the making of the agreement, he or she took reasonable steps to ensure that the nature of the arrangements would be disclosed to professional legal advisers for the purposes of obtaining advice about them before their making or (as the case may be) their implementation.

This provision can only be described as bizarre. It appears that any individual can now seek to escape the criminal cartel sanctions in the UK by simply consulting a lawyer. There is no requirement that the advice of those legal professionals is heeded, or behaviour altered as a result of any advice received. This appears to render the criminalisation of cartels in the UK completely nugatory if a file note from a local solicitor can be produced once the cartel is discovered. Only the most cynical and organised cartelists may be able to avail themselves of this defence but it does seem to be entirely contrary to the purpose of the criminalisation project.[92]

Competition Disqualification Orders

The Enterprise Act also introduced another form of individual penalty, the Competition Disqualification Order (CDO). The Company Directors Disqualification Act 1986 was amended – adding s 9A – to allow for a court to disqualify an individual from being a director as 'unfit' where they were a director of a company that has breached competition law.[93] This would include any breach of Arts 101 or 102 TFEU, or the 1998 Act prohibitions. The director's conduct must have contributed to the breach, they should have suspected, or ought to have known of, the breach. A disqualification under this provision can be for up to 15 years. This gives the CMA the opportunity to seek an individual sanction against a company director in relation to their involvement in wide range of anti-competitive conduct. It is possible to seek such an order where a prosecution under the cartel offence would be unlikely to succeed.

Increasing punishment

The level of punishment associated with cartels has increased dramatically as the attitude towards cartels has hardened. That trend will continue as the authorities appear to be more willing to adopt ever-larger fines and more legal systems consider the imposition of individual penalties to bolster the 'standard' corporate penalties. This inexorable increase is not without costs. As penalties increase the likelihood that undertakings will challenge infringement decisions also increases. A legal challenge to the imposition of a fine is now the norm under EU law. The cost and complexity of bringing both a criminal prosecution and an administrative infringement procedure in relation to the same conduct will be considerable. Nonetheless, an examination of the deterrent effect of the current regimes in the EU and UK indicates that underdeterrence is a distinct possibility. While penalties are now increasing it is unlikely that an increase in penalties alone will sufficiently deter cartels.

Increasing the Likelihood of Catching Cartels

European competition authorities have a number of tools at their disposal to investigate possible cartel activity in European markets, but those investigative powers are only really useful when

---

92 Hansard suggests that the Government had a particular narrow class of agreements in mind, after representations from industry, but the defence is drafted very broadly. See HL Deb, 26 February 2013, Cols 1055–1059.
93 See OFT Guidance, 'Competition Disqualification Orders', OFT 510, June 2010.

the enforcer has a clear indication that something is amiss within a particular industry. As the authorities have limited resources, they have to focus their regulatory efforts on situations where there is a realistic chance of discovering an infringement. One potential source of information for the authorities is complaints from customers of a cartel; however, there are many reasons why customers are unlikely to have a good indication that their supplier's behaviour is a result of a cartel agreement, or they may simply be wary of complaining about an important trading partner. Given the clearly unlawful nature of cartels, they can only be truly effective if they are organised in secret. A cartel that acted openly would face challenge very quickly. It is therefore likely that cartelists will take steps to disguise their activity from both the authorities and their customers. Even if a customer had suspicions, that something was going on, it is unlikely that they would have much in the way of useful evidence that they could pass on to an enforcement agency. When a customer is suspicious about their suppliers, there are reasons they may not want to press the issue and make a formal complaint. A successful cartel is likely to include the vast majority of suppliers in a market. If that is the case, a potential complainant may be wary of harming its relationship with all the potential suppliers of an important input product. It is not unheard of for cartels to protect themselves by disciplining customers who act against the cartel's interests.

It is vital that enforcement authorities develop tools to break open secretive cartel arrangements and gather enough evidence to initiate a formal investigation. There are a number of ways that information from inside a cartel has found its way to the attention of the authorities. Information may leak from the cartel and find its way into the media.[94] Information may come from disgruntled former employees of cartelists. In recent years an interesting new route for the discovery of cartels has emerged: due diligence in mergers and takeovers. When companies are in merger discussions there will be a process of diligence whereby the parties will attempt to ensure all potential legal liabilities are taken into account. If one party discovers the other may have been involved in a cartel in the past, they will require that that liability be minimised before the deal can go ahead. The cartel will often then come out into the open.

The problem with relying on these sources of information is that they will occur relatively rarely. The authorities need to find a way to get good information out of the cartel itself, as the participants will obviously be able to provide the best evidence of what has gone on and be able to point the authorities in the right direction when they want to undertake an investigation. The most viable option for the authorities to facilitate the break-up of cartels is by encouraging some of the participants to inform the authorities of what has gone on. Accordingly, the main tool that is used to put pressure on cartels and encourage parties to become 'whistle-blowers' is a leniency policy, which offers some form of immunity in return for information.

Leniency policies

Leniency policies have proved to be the most significant feature in the ongoing battle between competition law enforcers and cartels. The potential reward of immunity for information to assist in the investigation of an infringement is not a new feature of enforcement regimes, but the way in which leniency policies operate has now been fine-tuned, through a greater understanding of cartels, to make them increasingly effective. To understand how a leniency policy works it is important to understand the pressures that a cartel faces and the mechanisms that are used to keep cartels together.

Cartelisation is not the natural state of an industry. In order for a cartel to operate successfully there must be some form of structure and management to maintain it. If one accepts that the

---

94 See, for instance, OFT Decision CA98/05/2006 *Exchange of information on future fees by certain independent fee-paying schools*, 20 November 2006.

natural state is competition, in the sense that it serves self-interest and profit maximisation, in order for a cartel to form there must be a concerted effort to reshape a market. Even in situations where an industry can get together and come to some form of arrangement as to future conduct there will still be strong individual incentives to 'cheat' on that arrangement. The best way for a cartel member to maximise its short-term profits is to agree the cartel price with other cartel members and then cheat by selling larger quantities at a slightly lower price. This is sometimes known as 'chiselling', and is beneficial in the short term, as the cheat will gain extra customers, as it has undercut the cartel, but will make a supra-competitive profit on each sale, as the price will be above the 'competitive' price, even though it is below the inflated cartel price. This incentive to cheat suggests that cartels may be inherently unstable and are only likely to succeed if the cartel is able to hold its members together. Although there are short-term benefits in cheating, it does jeopardise the future prospects of the cartel, as a price war may break out, which would return the market to competitive pricing levels. The long-term benefit of a cartel comes from all cartel members keeping to the deal and staying true to the commonly adopted policy.

For a cartel to be successful there must be some mechanism to ensure that all the members of the cartel are keeping to the agreement. The most obvious way of doing so is through a formal, and legally enforceable, cartel agreement; the cartelists would all know that if any member stepped out of line there would be a legal sanction for non-compliance. The first step in the early days of cartel control was to deny the enforceability of such agreements and other legal mechanisms, such as trust companies in the US, which were used to support cartels. As cartels are driven underground, with increasing levels of secrecy, it becomes more difficult for them to successfully build and maintain long-term cartel organisations. The secret of a cartel's success is building trust within the group.[95] The problem for cartelists is that most of the trust-building mechanisms which they might employ would increase the risk that the cartel's activities will be noticed by the authorities, thereby increasing the risk of prosecution. Many such mechanisms, such as direct communication, information sharing or auditing, leave a paper trail, which, if discovered, would provide good evidence of the cartel's activity. By reducing the ability to use such trust-building mechanisms, competition law decreases the chance of cartels successfully forming and increases the likelihood that a cartel will collapse through chiselling and the reprisals which would no doubt follow.

Leniency policy has been particularly effective as a regulatory tool when deployed against contemporary cartels, as it accentuates the inherent instability and distrust within them. A leniency policy is designed to give members of an ongoing cartel further reason to distrust their co-conspirators. If there is an active leniency policy, they not only have to worry about cheating, but also that a member of the cartel who wishes to exit and resume competition, may seek to protect its future position by going to the authorities and blowing the whistle on the cartel in return for immunity. By gaining immunity they protect themselves, but by informing on the cartel they also place their former friends, but future competitors, at a competitive disadvantage. When a cartel does not have strong trust relationships within it the existence of such a policy can generate a level of fear and distrust, that someone might conceivably go to the authorities, such that it might encourage one member to 'get their retaliation in first'. For a leniency policy to be successful it only needs to encourage one cartelist to leave and inform. This is sometimes known as the 'race to the courthouse door', where former cartelists compete to be the first to inform and get the benefit of immunity. A successful leniency policy will play on these fears to maximise the chances of two things happening: (i) the cartel breaking up, and (ii) one of the cartel members providing good evidence, in return for immunity, which will allow the authorities to begin infringement proceedings.

---

95 The important nature of trust in the formation and maintenance of cartels is comprehensively discussed in Leslie, CR, 'Trust, Distrust, and Antitrust' (2004) 82(3) Texas LRev 515.

Leniency in the EU

The leniency policy operational within the EU is set out in the Commission's 2006 'Notice on Immunity from fines and reduction of fines in cartel cases'.[96] This Notice follows on from the earlier 2002 and 1996 Notices.[97] The 2002 Notice was generally perceived as being a success, particularly as a great many cartelists sought immunity or fine reductions under the Notice, but the 2006 Notice sought to refine the earlier practice and make the leniency option more enticing by increasing the transparency and predictability of the scheme. Some form of leniency has been seen in the majority of recent cartel cases. In *Elevators and Escalators*,[98] KONE received immunity in relation to the cartel's activity in Belgium and Luxembourg (€74.5m), and Otis received immunity in relation to its activities in the Netherlands (€108m). In *TV and Computer Monitor Tubes*, the imposition of a cartel fine of €1.4bn, Chungwa received 100% leniency, avoiding a fine of €17m, and Samsung received a 40% reduction in its fine, reducing it to €150m.[99] UBS escaped a €2.5bn fine in relation to the *YIRO* cartel through immunity.[100] The 2006 Notice offers immunity to the first undertaking to come forward disclosing its participation in a cartel and offering information and evidence to allow the Commission to: (a) carry out a targeted inspection, or (b) find an infringement of Article 101 TFEU.[101] In order to be able to carry out a targeted inspection, the Commission will need a corporate statement, which includes: a detailed description of the alleged cartel arrangement; the names and addresses of all the other undertakings that participated in the alleged cartel; the names, positions and locations of all individuals who, to the applicant's knowledge, are or have been involved in the alleged cartel; information on which other competition authorities have been approached in relation to the alleged cartel; and other evidence relating to the alleged cartel in the possession of the applicant or available to it.[102] The applicant must also continue to co-operate with the Commission's investigation.[103] The introduction of a 'marker' system in the 2006 Notice was designed to enhance confidence in the system. An applicant may now go to the Commission and provide information concerning its name and address, the parties to the alleged cartel, the affected products and territory, the estimated duration of the alleged cartel, and the nature of the alleged cartel conduct.[104] On the basis of that limited information the Commission will grant a marker, essentially holding a place in the leniency queue, and allow the applicant to provide the rest of the information, and 'perfect' its marker, within a particular time frame. Only the first undertaking to provide such information can be granted immunity. To benefit from the leniency policy, undertakings must provide information the Commission is not already aware of through its own efforts,[105] or immunity may be denied if the undertaking concerned took steps to coerce other undertakings to join the cartel or to remain in it.[106] If an undertaking is not the first to come forward, it will not

---

96 Commission Notice on Immunity from fines and reduction of fines in cartel cases, [2006] OJ C298/17. On the operation of the 2006 Notice, see Sandhu, JS, 'The European Commission's Leniency Policy: A Success?' [2007] ECLR 148.

97 [2002] OJ C45/3 and [1996] OJ C207/4. The offer of immunity was introduced by the 2002 Notice, with only fine reductions being available under the 1996 Notice. For discussion of the earlier Notices see Riley, A, 'Cartel Whistle-blowing: Towards an American Model?' (2002) 9 Maastricht J 67, and Arp, DJ and Swaak, RAA, 'A Tempting Offer: Immunity from Fines for Cartel Conduct under the European Commission's Leniency Notice' [2003] ECLR 9.

98 Commission Press Release IP/07/209, 'Commission fines members of lifts and escalators cartels over €990 million', 21 February 2007, and Commission Decision, *Elevators and Escalators*, C(2005) 512 final.

99 See Commission Press Release, 'Antitrust: Commission fines producers of TV and computer monitor tubes € 1.47 billion for two decade-long cartels' IP/12/1317, 5 December 2012.

100 Commission Press Release, 'Antitrust Commission fines banks €1.71 bn for participating in cartels in the interest rate derivatives industring, IP/13/1208, 4 December 2013.

101 2006 Notice, OJ 2006, C298/17, para 8.

102 Ibid, para 9.

103 Ibid, para 12.

104 Ibid, para 15.

105 Ibid, para 10.

106 Ibid, para 13.

be able to seek immunity, but it may still be able to be rewarded for information it provides through a reduction in fine. In order to be eligible for a fine reduction it must provide evidence of the alleged infringement, which represents significant added value with respect to the evidence already in the Commission's possession, and co-operate fully.[107] Information of added value does not need to be completely new, as long as it strengthens the Commission's ability to prove its allegations. An undertaking that provides the first information of added value can expect a reduction in fine of between 30% and 50%; the second between 20% and 30%; and, subsequent applicants up to 20%.[108] The availability of fine reductions is somewhat controversial. There are no such reductions formally available under the Department of Justice's (DoJ) Corporate Leniency Policy (CLP) in the US.[109] It only offers immunity to the first applicant; there is no prize for second place. The DoJ's CLP is generally regarded as being highly effective, and therefore the starkness of the incentive to be first could be one of the reasons for its success. In practice, the difference between the EU policy and its counterpart in the US is less stark. Although there is no leniency for second place set out in the policy, the DoJ is often willing to enter into a plea bargain if a cartelist is willing to admit involvement and co-operate with its investigation; a fine reduction will usually be the reward for accepting a plea bargain.

The EU's leniency policy, particularly since 2002, has proved to be very successful. The increasing decentralisation of competition law enforcement does, however, create some problems for a centralised approach to leniency. An undertaking that is granted leniency by the Commission, protecting it in relation to the application of Art 101 TFEU, is not necessarily protected from the application of domestic competition law within one or more Member States. The Commission has sought to address this by adopting an EU Model Leniency Programme in 2006,[110] and updating it in 2012.[111] The model sets out the treatment that a leniency applicant should expect from any NCA within the ECN. This creates a minimum leniency standard across the EU, although each Member State can operate a more generous policy if it desires. It is designed to reduce the chance that an undertaking will decide not to seek leniency because of the fear that it will be subject to fines in one Member State.

The final area of concern in relation to leniency policy is its interaction with the developments seeking to increase the impact of private actions for damages in cartel cases. There is an inherent contradiction between the desire to increase deterrence by increasing compensation awards, and the policy of rewarding cartelists who 'blow the whistle' by informing on a cartel. Although a cartelist will avoid administrative penalties through leniency, they may still have to pay considerable compensation to their customers if compensation claims are made easier. Could the fear of compensation claims discourage potential lenience applicants? The policy developments in relationship to compensation claims are discussed above,[112] but in relation to leniency policy we can note that the EU Antitrust Damages Directive would give a leniency applicant some, limited, benefits in relation to any 'follow-on' claims.[113] Leniency documents will not be accessible by claimants and those who have been granted immunity (noting that this only applies to the first applicant), will only be liable to their own direct or indirect purchasers, unless others who have suffered loss from other cartelists are unable to obtain compensation elsewhere. This

---

107 Ibid, paras 24–25.
108 Ibid, para 26.
109 Department of Justice, Corporate Leniency Policy, August 1993. For a discussion of the CLP see, Harding, C, and Joshua, J, *Regulating Cartels in Europe – A Study of Legal Control of Corporate Delinquency* (2000) Oxford: OUP, Chapter VIII.
110 DG Comp, ECN Model Leniency Programme, 29 September 2006.
111 DG Comp, ECN Model Leniency Programme, November 2012.
112 And in Chapter 3.
113 Proposal for a Directive of the European Parliament and of the Council on certain rules governing actions for damages under national law for infringements of the competition law provisions of the Member States and of the European Union, COM(2013) 404, Art 11. The Directive was adopted by the European Parliament in April 2014.

effectively limits the principle of joint and several liability for cartel harm that operates in relation to cartelists not granted immunity, but also seeks to protect the principle that all EU citizens must be able to access compensation.

Leniency in the UK

The CMA has adopted a full leniency policy. As there is a wider range of sanctions for cartel conduct in the UK, there is a corresponding range of leniency policies which give protection against all those sanctions. Immunity is available from administrative fines under Art 101 TFEU and the Chapter I prohibition under the 1998 Act, the Cartel Office under the Enterprise Act 2002, and Competition Disqualification Orders under the Company Directors Disqualification Act 1986.[114]

The CMA's leniency policy for all aspects of cartel cases is set out in a single Guidance, which must also be read alongside its Guidance on Fines.[115] In order to be guaranteed immunity an undertaking must: (a) accept the undertaking participated in cartel activity; (b) provide the CMA with all non-legally privileged information available; (c) maintain continuous and complete cooperation; (d) refrain from further participation, except as directed by the CMA; and (e) the applicant must not have taken steps to coerce another undertaking to take part in cartel activity.[116] Various types of immunity are available: Types A, B and C immunity. Type A immunity is the most valuable and is available to the first applicant to report and provide evidence of a cartel where there is no pre-existing investigation. This form of immunity gives guaranteed corporate immunity for fines under the 1998 Act, and guaranteed 'blanket' immunity from criminal prosecution for all current and formers employees, and protection from director disqualification. Type B immunity is less valuable, and is available to the first applicant to report and provide evidence of a cartel when the CMA is conducting a pre-existing investigation. It provides for discretionary corporate immunity from penalties, up to 100%, discretionary criminal immunity for co-operating current and former employees which can be granted on a 'blanket' or more limited basis, and protection from director disqualification proceedings. The discretion excisable in relation to both corporate and criminal immunity is assessed on the basis of the public interest in the particular case by weighing up the benefits of the additional evidence and what information the CMA have already gathered.[117] The discretion in relation to corporate and criminal evidence is exercised separately. The final form of leniency, Type C immunity, is available where another undertaking has already reported the cartel activity. The grant of Type C immunity is always discretionary. The information provided must 'add significant value' to the CMA investigation.[118] A successful applicant is eligible for discretionary reductions in corporate penalties up to 50%, discretionary criminal immunity to specific individuals, and protection from director disqualification proceedings. 'Blanket' criminal immunity is not available under Type C. The CMA will not accept immunity applications after a Statement of Objections has been issued or criminal charges against individuals have been brought.[119]

The discretionary nature of the reductions in Type B and C immunity may be seen as 'fair', but there is an argument that they may be counterproductive. The key factor in encouraging a leniency applicant to come forward is, as discussed above, a balance between the fear of betrayal, and its associated costs, against the rewards of leniency. If the rewards of the leniency policy are not clear to a potential applicant, because they cannot predict whether they will get immunity or

---

114 See OFT, 'Applications for Leniency and No-Action in Cartel Cases', OFT 1495, July 2013.
115 Ibid, and OFT's guidance as to the appropriate amount of a penalty, OFT 423, September 2012.
116 Ibid, para 2.7.
117 Ibid, para 2.18.
118 Ibid, para 2.26.
119 Ibid, para 2.41.

a much lower reduction, it may discourage them from coming forward, particularly in Type B cases where there have been no previous immunity applications. In this area there is much to be said for offering potentially 'unfair' rewards in order to ensure that cartels are much more likely to break down. The case for the removal of discretion is much less powerful in Type C cases where it can be argued the cartel has already been revealed by the first immunity applicant and subsequent applications are by their nature far less valuable. The OFT has successfully operated its leniency policy on many occasions. One of the most notable cases was *Long-Haul Passenger Fuel Surcharges*[120] where Virgin Atlantic was awarded full immunity for bringing the cartel to the OFT's attention.

The CMA has adopted a number of innovative developments to bolster its leniency policy. One is the provision of confidential guidance. Discussions can take place on a 'hypothetical' and 'no-names' basis to gain comfort on an issue while considering the making of an application. The CMA will be bound by reassurances given in those discussions if an application is made, and they give assurance that if an application is not made the CMA will not attempt to establish the undertaking's identity through 'reverse engineering'.[121] These discussions are presumably to help increase an undertaking's confidence that they are eligible for the grant of immunity without having to reveal themselves to the authorities. Another innovation is known as 'Leniency Plus', named after 'Amnesty Plus' its US counterpart. If an undertaking is not able to be awarded full immunity in relation to a cartel, perhaps because it was not the first applicant, it may be awarded an increased fine reduction in that case if it can provide information on another, separate, cartel of which the CMA is not aware.[122] Of course, by being the first to come forward in relation to the second cartel, the undertaking may also be entitled to full immunity in regard to that case. They can therefore be described as getting 'leniency' in the second cartel 'plus' an additional fine reduction in the first. Such a policy is potentially very powerful as practice tells us that if an undertaking has been a member of a successful cartel in one market it is more likely to be involved in cartels in related markets.[123] Another innovation adopted by the CMA is the offer of direct financial incentives for information about cartels. In February 2008 the OFT introduced a policy, which sits alongside its leniency policy, which offers a financial reward to anyone who can provide useful information about cartel activity.[124] The discretionary financial reward offered can be up to £100,000, depending on the nature and usefulness of the information. This will not usually be available to anyone directly involved in the cartel, who will be expected to seek leniency, but will be for others, of a more peripheral nature, who have 'inside' information on a cartel's activity.

The impact of individual leniency for the cartel offence and CDOs

The CMA, as noted above, offers both corporate and individual leniency. The individual leniency policies offer the same incentives as the corporate policies, discussed above, but they also offer another dimension to the effectiveness of leniency as a whole. Corporate leniency seeks to heighten distrust between the corporate members of a cartel, to encourage undertakings to defect and inform. An individual leniency programme not only heightens inter-corporate distrust, but also encourages distrust within an undertaking. Not all the individuals within an undertaking will be as willing to risk

---

120 See OFT Press Release 113/07, 'British Airways to pay record £121.5m penalty in price fixing investigation', 1 August 2007.
121 Leniency Guidance, OFT 1495, July 2013, paras 3.3–3.7.
122 Ibid, paras 9.1–9.4.
123 The complex series of cartels across the chemicals industry is a clear example of this sort of behaviour. The US also operates a 'Penalty Plus' policy, whereby a company or individual under investigation for cartel activity, which decides not to take 'Amnesty Plus', and inform the DoJ of another ongoing offence, will be treated very harshly should a second offence be discovered later.
124 OFT, Rewards for information about cartels, 29 February 2008.

their liberty or career to generate an increased corporate profit. For a leniency policy to be successful, it does not need to encourage the undertaking as a corporate entity to seek leniency, although that would be beneficial in terms of gathering evidence. All that is required is that one individual, who has limited personal incentive to stay in the cartel, informs the CMA about the cartel activity. An undertaking that is involved in a cartel will therefore have to be very careful about which personnel become involved, as they are all potential leniency applicants. This further level of internal distrust, and increased complexity in managing a cartel, makes it more likely that the cartel will collapse.

Direct settlement

The most recent development in the fight to increase competition authorities' effectiveness against cartels is the adoption of a form of 'settlement procedure' in cartel cases. Such a procedure allows the authority to negotiate a settlement with the members of a cartel and bring the case to a successful conclusion more quickly. If the authority has to devote less resource to an individual case that settles, it will be in a position to handle more cases and take action against a greater number of cartels. If the authorities are seen as being more active, and are seen to be catching more cartels, this will obviously have a positive impact on deterrence.

The availability of direct settlement in the US, through its plea bargaining system, is an acclaimed feature of its regime, with the majority of cases settling in this way following leniency applications. A settlement procedure is attractive to cartelists as, after a leniency application has triggered an investigation, their continued co-operation in an investigation is rewarded through a fine reduction. The model adopted in the EU is not as flexible, or as attractive to cartelists, as a US plea bargain.[125] The settlement discussions between DG Comp and the members of the cartel would take place before the Statement of Objections is issued. Discussions would seek to reach a 'common understanding' on the following: the facts alleged, the gravity and duration of the infringement, and an estimation of the range of the fines. At the end of the discussions the parties should formally request to settle in a settlement submission acknowledging their liability, indicating a maximum amount of fine they foresee being imposed, confirming they have had the opportunity to make their views known, and that they do not envisage requesting access to the file or requesting an oral hearing. The last of these elements indicates the benefit for the Commission of settling such a case. It will be able to proceed to adopt an infringement decision, on the basis of the settlement submission, without having to give full access to the file or conducting a hearing. To avoid going through these steps, it is important that as many parties as possible agree to settle. Five cases have been settled to date, with only one being a 'hybrid' settlement, where one party dropped out of the settlement procedure and was handled under the standard procedure.[126] The reward for the parties will be a fine reduction of 10%. It is questionable whether the 10% fine reduction alone will be enough to offer sufficient encouragement to settle; but there are other procedural and cost benefits which parties will weigh up before deciding to enter into negotiations.

One key difference between a US plea bargain and the EU settlement procedure is the ability of the parties to appeal following a settlement. In the US there is a fuller form of negotiation, resulting in a full agreement over the fine levied and the information that becomes public. As a

---

125 Commission Regulation 622/2008/EC amending Regulation (EC) No 773/2004, as regards the conduct of settlement procedures in cartel cases, OJ 2008, L171/3. See also Commission Notice on the conduct of settlement procedures in cartel cases, [2008] OJ C167/1.

126 See Commission Press Release IP/10/985, 'Antitrust: European Commission fines animal feed phosphates producers €175,647,000 for price-fixing and market-sharing in first "hybrid" cartel settlement case', 20 July 2010, and Ortega Gonzalez, A, 'The Cartel Settlement Procedure in Practice' [2011] 4 ECLR 170–177.

result, the party who 'pleas out' will generally waive its right to appeal. The EU system does not have such a broad negotiation. The Commission had stated that it 'would neither negotiate nor bargain the use of evidence or the appropriate sanction, but could reward the parties' co-operation'.[127] The final fine will still be set by the Commission, although the parties will have an opportunity to put forward their views on their potential liability, and a short form Statement of Objections will still be published. The parties will also retain their right to seek a review of the Commission decision before the GC. It is hoped that as the parties have accepted their liability the chances of a legal challenge are reduced. However, most challenges do not concern liability, but the calculation of the fine. Accordingly, the potential for challenge would still exist; but this would strip away many of the cost benefits for both the Commission and the parties that encouraged them to engage with the settlement procedure. One of the main benefits of settlement for the parties is to bring the process to an end more quickly and reduce the legal costs they would face in a prolonged contested procedure in which a great deal of information could be published which may be of benefit to potential compensation claimants.

The CMA also operates a settlement process. One of the most striking examples was the OFT's innovative settlement in the *Independent Schools* case.[128] As the schools involved in the price-fixing arrangement were charitable institutions it was not seen as appropriate to set anything more than a nominal fine of £10,000 on each institution. The OFT reached a settlement with the schools that they should make an 'ex-gratia' payment of £3m into an educational charitable trust to benefit the pupils who attended the schools during the affected period. More typical settlements, referred to by the OFT as 'early resolution agreements', can be seen in cases like *Long-Haul Passenger Fuel Surcharges*,[129] in which British Airways agreed to pay a penalty of £121.5m, thereby allowing the OFT to close its case, and *Dairy Products*,[130] in which Asda, Dairy Crest, Safeway, Sainsbury's, the Cheese Company and Wiseman admitted liability in relation to certain activities in an 'early resolution agreement' and agreed to pay reduced penalties of £116m. *Dairy Products* highlighted one of the potential difficulties in 'hybrid' settlements, where not all the parties are involved. In that case two supermarkets did not settle, and the investigation continued. Eventually the investigation against one of the 'hold-outs' was dropped and the findings against Tesco were limited,[131] and reduced further on appeal.[132] Given the limited evidence that the OFT had, it is interesting to speculate why so many parties settled and agreed to pay substantial fines. Was there a strong commercial incentive to resolve the case as soon as possible; even in a situation where the evidence was weak and contestable? The settlement process has been formalised by the adoption of a specific Procedural Rule and inclusion of details of the settlement process in the CMA's Procedural Guidance.[133] The CMA may consider settlement for any case, provided the evidential standard for giving notice of its proposed infringement decision is met, and the reward for a business which settles is a settlement discount which will be capped at 20% for settlement pre-Statement of Objections and 10% for settlement post-Statement of Objections.

---

127 Commission Press Release IP/07/1608, 'Antitrust: Commission calls for comments on a draft legislative package to introduce settlement procedure for cartels', 26 October 2007.

128 See OFT Press Release 88/06, 'Independent schools agree settlement. Competition investigation resolved', 19 May 2006, and OFT Decision CA98/05/2006 *Exchange of information on future fees by certain independent fee-paying schools*, 20 November 2006.

129 See OFT Press Release 113/07, 'British Airways to pay record £121.5m penalty in price fixing investigation', 1 August 2007.

130 OFT Press Release 170/07, 'OFT welcomes early resolution agreements and agrees over £116m penalties', 7 December 2007. See also OFT Press Release 82/08, 11 July 2008, on the tobacco cartel.

131 Decision of the Office of Fair Trading, CA98/03/2011, *Dairy retail price initiatives*, 26 July 2011. See Stephan, A, 'OFT Dairy Price-fixing Case Leaves Sour Taste for Cooperating Parties in Settlements' [2010] ECLR 432.

132 *Tesco v OFT* [2012] CAT 31.

133 See CMA8, 'Guidance on the CMA's investigation procedures in Competition Act 1998 cases', March 2014, at paras 14.1–14.33.

The Future of Cartel Regulation

The fight against cartels, the 'supreme evil of antitrust',[134] has been stepped up remarkably in the early years of the twenty-first century. It is also notable that there appears to be a broad consensus within the global competition law enforcement community that cartels pose a serious threat that must be addressed through co-ordinated action. The 'spiritual' leader of competition policy in this sphere is the United States, as its long history of criminal enforcement is seen as a useful model for other jurisdictions. Other competition regimes are now learning from that experience and moving to increase the effectiveness of their regulatory efforts. The rapid development of cartel control mechanisms, typified by the increase in penalties and the development of leniency, which went in hand-in-hand with the European Commission's modernisation, through Regulation 1/2003, highlights the renewed ambition in Brussels to take real steps to seek out and deal with cartels in Europe. The number of cases dealt with by the Commission indicates two things. Firstly, the policy is having some success. The possibility of immunity from sanctions following the introduction of a leniency policy appears to have been successful in bringing cartels to the attention of the Commission. There is, however, evidence that the policy does not disrupt successful cartels; rather, it encourages members of a failing cartel to seek protection from potential liability.[135] Secondly, it appears that while we may have had some success, there are a significant number of cartels still operating. That indicates that still more needs to be done.

The introduction of individual criminal offences in relation to some cartel activity in the UK, Ireland, and Australia also indicates the increasing seriousness with which the cartel problem is being treated.[136] It is interesting that the debate surrounding the criminalisation of cartels, as typified by that surrounding the UK's cartel offence, is not about whether the use of criminal law is appropriate, but rather that the form of offence used is suitable to ensure that successful prosecutions can be brought.[137]

While there is a consensus that strenuous efforts must be taken to control cartels, there are also potential areas of concern that should be addressed. There are fears that while the competition law enforcement community shares a consensus that cartels are highly damaging and deserve serious punishment, that feeling is not necessarily shared by the wider public,[138] politicians or the business community.[139] It is important that the authorities take steps to ensure that the public are educated as to the problems that cartels cause in markets. Another important issue for competition enforcement agencies is to seek a balance between the various elements of any successful anti-cartel regime. In this chapter we have outlined a number of policies that operate to increase the regulatory pressure on cartels. While they all have a role to play, it is also true that some of the individual elements 'pull' in opposing directions. For example, increasing compensation awards in private actions increase the effective 'penalty' for involvement in a cartel and therefore overall deterrence; however, an increase in compensation claims can reduce the impact of leniency policy, by limiting the reward for leniency, as a leniency applicant can only be given immunity from administrative fines and will continue to face potentially large compensation payments.

---

134 *Verizon Communications v Law Offices of Curtis V Trinko*, 540 US 398, 408 (2004).
135 See, for example, Stephan, A, 'An Empirical Assessment of the 1996 Leniency Notice' CCP Working Paper 05–10, September 2005.
136 There are also long standing criminal sanctions for cartel activity in Canada and Germany.
137 See, for example, MacCulloch, A, 'The Cartel Offence and the Criminalisation of UK Competition Law' [2003] JBL 615; Beaton-Wells, C, 'The Politics of Cartel Criminalisation: A Pessimistic View from Australia' [2008] ECLR 185; MacCulloch, A, 'The Cartel Offence: Defining an Appropriate "Moral Space"' (2012) 8(1) *European Competition Journal* 73; Stephan, A, 'How Dishonesty Killed the Cartel Offence' [2011] *Criminal Law Review* 446 and Stephan, A, 'Four Key Challenges to the Successful Criminalization of Cartel Laws' (2014) *J of Antitrust Enforcement* 1–30.
138 See Stephan, A, 'Survey of Public Attitudes to Price-fixing and Cartel Enforcement in Britain' (2008) 5(1) CompLRev 123.
139 See Yeung, K, 'Does the Australian Competition and Consumer Commission Engage in "Trial by Media"?' (2006) 27 Law & Policy 549.

Similarly, a move towards direct settlement will mean that a competition authority is able to better utilise its resources against other cartels, but it will also mean that the overall level of fines is reduced and the limited information published by an authority in a case that settles may hinder 'follow-on' compensation claims. If the EU and UK competition authorities want to use all these enforcement tools fully, they must be aware of these overlaps and seek to ensure that they are coordinated, where possible, to ensure that overall policy is as effective as it can be. The debate on the future of private compensation actions in Europe gives a clear indication that the effective coexistence of compensation actions and leniency policy is one of the key issues being considered.[140]

The control of cartels has seen rapid development in Europe since the 1980s. The change of legal attitude is even more remarkable when you consider that the 'cartel problem' is almost as old as European industry itself. Many changes in the EU and UK have been put in place to increase the deterrent effect of the law. As these policies develop, it will be interesting to see how effective they are at breaking up existing cartels and deterring others from coming together.

Key Points

- Cartels are horizontal agreements which set prices, either directly or by manipulating output; share customers by allocating them between suppliers directly or by allocating each supplier control over customers in a specific geographical area; or agree to co-ordinate other terms and conditions of sale.
- Cartels in Europe were tolerated or even encouraged until the second half of the twentieth century. Attitudes have since hardened considerably, and cartels are now seen as the worst form of competition law violation.
- The orthodoxy which underlies contemporary cartel enforcement is the concept of optimal deterrence. This is the idea that penalties will only deter cartel activity if they strip away the gains that a cartelist can expect from engaging in unlawful activity.
- Cartel punishments can take many forms including: corporate fines, compensatory damages, individual criminal sanctions, and director disqualification. Finding the right balance between the various sanctions available is also important.
- One of the most important features of optimal deterrence is increasing the chance of cartels being detected. The key tool to improve cartel detection is an effective leniency policy, where cartel members are encouraged to defect and 'blow the whistle' on a cartel by providing evidence to the relevant authorities.

Discussion

1   Are the financial penalties imposed on cartels sufficient to discourage cartelists from entering into potentially lucrative arrangements? Would there be negative implications if financial penalties were increased ever higher?
2   What do individual penalties, particularly criminal penalties, add to competition law enforcement that cannot be provided by corporate penalties alone?
3   An effective leniency policy is one of the key tools in the fight against cartels, but is it appropriate to waive sanctions, and reward an undertaking which has entered into a clearly unlawful agreement and profited from it?

---

140 See Proposal for a Directive of the European Parliament and of the Council on certain rules governing actions for damages under national law for infringements of the competition law provisions of the Member States and of the European Union, COM(2013) 404. The Antitrust Damages Directive was adopted by the European Parliament in April 2014.

Further Reading

General

Harding, C and Joshua, J, *Regulating Cartels in Europe: A Study of Legal Control of Corporate Delinquency*, 2nd edn (2010) Oxford: OUP.

Leslie, CR, 'Trust, Distrust, and Antitrust' (2004) 82(3) Texas LRev 515.

Leslie, CR, 'Cartels, Agency Costs, and Finding Virtue in Faithless Agents' (2008) 49 William & Mary LRev 1621.

Fines

Connor, JM and Lande, RH, 'The Size of Cartel Overcharges: Implications for US and EU fining policies' (2006) 51(4) *Antitrust Bulletin* 983.

Motta, M, 'On Cartel Deterrence and Fines in the European Union' [2008] ECLR 209.

Wils, WPJ, 'Optimal Antitrust Fines: Theory and Practice' (2006) 29(2) World Comp 183.

Private actions

Dayagi-Epstein, O, 'Representation of Consumer Interests by Consumer Associations – Salvation for the Masses' (2006) 3(2) CompLRev 209.

Komninos, AP, 'Private Enforcement in the EU with Emphasis on Damages Actions', Chapter 4 in Lianos, I and Geradin, D (eds), *Handbook on European Competition Law* (Vol 2) (2012) Cheltenham: Edward Elgar.

Nebbia, P, 'Damages Actions for the Infringement of EC Competition Law: Compensation or Deterrence?' (2008) 33(1) ELRev 23.

Criminalisation

MacCulloch, A, 'The Cartel Offence: Defining an Appropriate "Moral Space" (2012) 8(1) *European Competition Journal* 73.

Stephan, A, 'How Dishonesty Killed the Cartel Offence' [2011] *Criminal Law Review* 446.

Stephan, A, 'Four Key Challenges to the Successful Criminalization of Cartel Laws' [2014] *J of Antitrust Enforcement* 1–30.

Leniency and settlement

Ortega Gonzalez, A, 'The Cartel Settlement Procedure in Practice' [2011] 4 ECLR 170–177.

Stephan, A, 'An Empirical Assessment of the European Leniency Notice' (2009) 5(3) J of CompL & Econ 537–561.

Chapter 8

Control of Mergers

Overview

- The principal focus of merger control concerns the potential competitive consequences that may arise as a result of the increased concentration in a market caused by a merger.
- The EU Merger Regulation was originally designed to reduce the confusion and bureaucracy arising from large-scale mergers across the EU, by offering a 'one-stop-shop' for qualifying mergers.
- The EU Merger Regulation covers any 'concentration', whereby an undertaking acquires control over another, which has a 'Community dimension'. A merger has a Community dimension when it meets one of the relevant turnover thresholds. A case allocation system involving the European Commission, the NCAs, and the parties themselves is employed to avoid the duplication of efforts in as many merger cases as possible.
- Mergers that fall under the EU Merger Regulation must be notified to the Commission, and notification triggers mandatory suspension until clearance.
- The Commission assesses whether mergers are compatible with the internal market, according to the 'significant impediment to effective competition' test. Most mergers are cleared during a short Phase 1 investigation. Mergers that raise serious doubts as to their compatibility with the internal market go through a longer investigation in Phase 2.
- In order to gain approval for a merger, parties will often offer 'remedies' to remove the competition concerns identified by the Commission. The Commission prefers structural solutions, as opposed to behavioural remedies.
- The UK merger control system is in Part 3 of the Enterprise Act 2002, as amended by the Enterprise and Regulatory Reform Act 2013. The CMA is now the unitary authority which oversees UK merger control.
- A 'relevant merger situation' under the Enterprise Act requires two or more enterprises to have ceased to be distinct, and, either that: the UK turnover of the enterprise being taken over exceeds £70m; or the 25% market share supply test is satisfied. There is no mandatory notification in the UK system.
- The CMA must decide in Phase 1 of their investigation whether to refer a relevant merger for a full investigation in Phase 2 if the merger would bring about a 'substantial lessening of competition'. The CMA may accept undertakings in lieu of a reference.
- Following a reference a CMA inquiry group will prepare a full report on a merger and set out any possible remedies, to mitigate or prevent the substantial lessening of competition and any adverse effects on competition that stem from it.

Introduction

Merger control is a particularly political area, principally due to divergent beliefs as to the merits of mergers and the contrasting analyses of the likely economic outcomes of proposed individual merger arrangements. In this context the term 'merger' connotes a welcome, uncontested, union, but it applies equally to a hostile takeover. The intricacies of both EU and UK merger control ensure that the respective controls also apply to wider situations than the commonly understood full legal merger. The principal focus of merger control concerns the potential competitive consequences that may arise as a result of the increased concentration in a market caused by a merger. However, other policies and interests may also have a role to play, such as industrial and employment policy or national ownership of industry.

The general consensus in a free-market economy is that shareholders of a company are entitled to act as they wish in the pursuit of a more profitable return on their property. This right can be viewed as an incentive, or threat, to the management of the company to maintain a high degree of efficiency and profitability. The interests of the shareholders can consequently be viewed as a stimulant for a vibrant economy and, hence, any takeovers or mergers acceptable to shareholders should be welcomed. However, it is also generally recognised that mergers may have implications that extend beyond the shareholders' interests, requiring some form of control due to their possible wide-ranging effects on the economy. There are two general schools of thought concerning the appropriate degree of control of merger activity. The first would advocate intervention only if the proposed merger is likely to have an adverse effect on competition in a market, otherwise merger decisions should be left in the capable hands of entrepreneurs and, ultimately, shareholders. The second approach believes that a more interventionist stance is required because mergers have often not yielded the benefits anticipated by their advocates and have wide-ranging potential societal repercussions.

The primary benefit which a merger can bring is to improve the efficiency of the companies involved, particularly when there are economies of scale that can only be achieved by a merger. Efficiency can also be enhanced by better management or easier access to capital, both of which can result from a merger. Other benefits include the possibility of the takeover of a firm facing closure, thereby extending its life and reducing concerns regarding unemployment.

Of all the arguments raised against mergers, the most significant argument concerns the potential reduction in competition which may result. However, there are also wider concerns raised by mergers which may justify intervention by national and supra-national competition authorities. These concerns include objections as to the size and power of the merged firm, the possible detrimental effect of the merger on the balance of payments, and the transfer of control of a company into 'foreign' ownership. It may, in appropriate circumstances, be considered that these disadvantages reduce or negate any purported economic advantages which are raised in justification of a particular merger. There is also empirical evidence that suggests merger objectives are not always achieved.[1]

The three generic types of merger which may be affected are horizontal mergers, vertical mergers and conglomerate mergers. One can identify different objections to each type of merger based on their purported benefits and detriments. Horizontal mergers are generally of greatest concern for competition law. They are effected by parties at the same level of the market, such as a merger between two producers, and the concern is that the increased concentration in the market may result in a reduction in inter-brand competition. This will particularly be the case where there are already few market participants, competition is limited, and the merged entity will have significant market share and market power, all of which is seen as being contrary to the central competition policy objectives outlined in Chapter 1. A vertical merger may result between a producer and a distributor of its products. Such mergers may have competitive consequences if they foreclose competitive opportunities to other market participants at either level of the market; for instance, if another producer can no longer find an outlet for its products as a result of the merger. On the other hand, as with vertical restraints, and as considered in Chapter 6, a vertical merger may enhance inter-brand competition by increasing the efficiency of distribution of that particular brand. Finally, although conglomerate mergers may not be directly associated with any competition gains or losses, it has been suggested, according to the 'deep-pocket theory', that conglomerates may cross-subsidise across products, thereby facilitating predatory pricing to defeat competition illegitimately, and that their wide 'portfolio' of products across a whole range may give them other advantages, perhaps through bundling or improving

---

1   Cowling, K et al, *Mergers and Economic Performance* (1980) Cambridge: CUP. See, also, Schenk, H, 'The Performance of Banking Mergers: Propositions and Policy Implications', in *The Impact of Mergers and Acquisitions in France on Workers, Consumers and Shareholders* (2000) Uni Europa.

interoperability.[2] However, the most interesting issue concerns the extent to which conglomerate mergers, and indeed also vertical and horizontal mergers, may be controlled on the basis of policies unconnected with the traditional competition policy objectives. This has been of particular interest in the UK context, although there has also been some discussion of this issue at the EU level. Finally, the trend towards 'global' mergers has an impact on merger control, requiring closer international co-operation between competition authorities.

This chapter will look at the approach to merger control undertaken by the EU and UK authorities, respectively. In the EU context, the Merger Regulation will be addressed.[3] Thereafter, we will focus on the UK merger control system contained within Pt 3 of the Enterprise Act 2002.

Historical Background to the EU Controls

There was no explicit provision for the control of mergers in the Treaty of Rome,[4] and the lack of a regulatory mechanism was recognised as being a problem. In a report in 1966 the Commission suggested that Art 102 TFEU would cover mergers where the merger amounted to an abuse of a dominant position.[5] This view was controversial although it was supported by the Court of Justice in *Continental Can*.[6] Continental Can, a US company with a dominant position in the market for metal containers, attempted to obtain control of a Dutch undertaking operating in the same market. The Commission argued that the acquisition of the target company would constitute an abuse of Continental Can's dominant position as it would eliminate future competition between the two undertakings. On appeal, the Court overturned the Commission's Decision but upheld its reasoning in relation to the possibility of Art 102 applying to the extension of a dominant position through a merger.

The control of mergers by the use of Art 102 raised a number of problems. Article 102 would only apply to the extension of an existing dominant position, not to the creation of a dominant position through a merger. Article 102 would, therefore, not be useful in the regulation of a hostile takeover of a dominant undertaking by a non-dominant undertaking, a conglomerate merger,[7] or a vertical merger. Article 102 would also be limited in that there is no provision for defences or exemptions where a merger may prove to be beneficial. Beneficial mergers would only be permitted if they could be objectively justified and, therefore, not considered to be abusive within the terms of Art 102 itself. Furthermore, a major procedural difficulty in the use of Art 102 is that it would only be possible to control mergers after they had been completed. Once a merger is complete, and the appeal process is exhausted, a number of years may have passed and it would then be difficult to return the market to its original position.

The use of Art 101 TFEU to control mergers was not envisaged in the aforementioned 1966 report; however, in the *Philip Morris* case,[8] Art 101 was held to be applicable to some mergers. Philip Morris was to purchase a 50% share of Rothmans Holdings, another cigarette manufacturer. After receiving complaints from competitors, the Commission intervened and Philip Morris agreed to change the nature of the purchase to lessen its competition concerns. Philip Morris

---

2   See Scherer, FM and Ross, D, *Industrial Market Structure and Economic Performance*, 3rd edn (1990) Boston: Houghton Mifflin. See, also, Bork, R, *The Antitrust Paradox: A Policy at War with Itself* (1993) Oxford: Maxwell Macmillan.
3   Regulation 139/2004/EC on the control of concentrations between undertakings (the EC Merger Regulation), [2004] OJ L24/1.
4   There were merger provisions in the European Coal and Steel Community Treaty (the Treaty of Paris). See Newton, C, 'Do Predators Need to be Dominant?' [1999] ECLR 127.
5   'Le problème de la concentration dans le marché commun' (1966) 3 Etudes CEE, série concurrence.
6   Case 6/72 *Continental Can v Commission* [1973] ECR 215.
7   As there would be no extension of market power in any one market.
8   Cases 142 and 156/84 *BAT v Commission* [1987] ECR 4487.

reduced the size of its holding to 30.8% of the shares, with only 24.9% of the voting rights, and gave the Commission undertakings as to its influence on the Rothmans board. The Commission was happy with this arrangement, but the original complainants challenged the Commission's Decision before the Court. The Court stated that Art 101 was applicable to the acquisition of shares in a competitor where the acquisition leads to an ability to influence the conduct of the target undertaking. The Court was careful to emphasise that it was discussing the acquisition of a minority shareholding in undertakings which remained independent after the purchase, but the Commission took a much wider view of the judgment, arguing that the judgment also meant that Art 101 would be applicable where a majority interest was acquired.[9] Nonetheless, the use of Art 101 to control acquisitions has a number of problems. The sanction of nullity under Art 101(2) is not suitable to the purchase of a controlling interest in an undertaking, and an Art 101(3) exemption can only be granted on the basis of the narrow grounds set out in the Treaty. The concerns raised by mergers are much broader than those mentioned in Art 101(3). There would appear to be limited scope for important social and political concerns to be taken into account. Exemptions granted must also be of limited duration. It is very difficult to undo a merger after a period of time, and it would be better practice to give the parties a firm decision after the initial consideration.

Alongside the development of potential merger controls under Arts 101 and 102 TFEU, the Commission attempted to persuade the Council to adopt a separate system for the control of mergers within the EU. The Commission put forward its first proposal for a Merger Regulation in 1973 but the Council did not give the introduction of specific merger controls a high priority. The low political priority accorded to merger control meant that the Commission proposals were not acted on for 15 years. Several of the larger Member States wished to maintain their own controls over mergers while the smaller Member States, who did not have their own controls, wanted the EU to assume responsibility. One of the major impediments to reaching agreement was the setting of an appropriate demarcation between any EU and the remaining Member State merger control systems. The eventual change in the Council's priorities resulted from two factors. Firstly, the increasing number of large-scale and cross-border mergers within the EU, which resulted from preparation for the 1992 Single Market programme, raised awareness of the need for a unitary EU system. An EU system was viewed as being better placed to deal with large multi-State mergers, as there would be one set of controls applicable, rather than a number of separate national regimes. In addition, common EU criteria could be used rather than criteria that focused on national interests. Secondly, the Commission argued that a specific merger control system would be more satisfactory than increasing resort to the existing, and deficient, set of rules under Arts 101 and 102 TFEU. Finally, the Regulation may have been advocated as a means of promoting EU-scale mergers which would make European industry more competitive in the global market, particularly in relation to the leading industrialised economies of the time in Japan and the US.

The EU's first Merger Regulation was adopted by Council in December 1989 and came into force in September 1990.[10] The new system operated well in practice; however, the debate continued over the thresholds which brought a merger within the EU system. In 1996 the Commission issued a Green Paper outlining the issues which would be addressed in the review of the Merger Regulation.[11] The main concern was the level of the thresholds. They were initially fixed at a very high level in order to obtain support from Member States that wished to retain control over 'national' mergers. The Commission proposed that the thresholds be lowered. Political agreement was reached on the reform of the merger control system along the lines of a

---

9 A wide interpretation of the applicability of Art 101 appeared to be used in *Smalbach-Lubeca v Carnaud*, IP/88/14; [1988] 4 CMLR 262.
10 Regulation 4064/89/EEC on the control of concentrations between undertakings, [1990] OJ L257/13.
11 Community Merger Control Green Paper on the review of the Merger Regulation, C(96) 19 final.

'multiple filing' proposal, whereby a merger which would otherwise have to be filed in several Member States would go to the Commission, and an amending Regulation was adopted by Council in June 1997.[12] The Commission process of review continued and a Commission report on the application of the Merger Regulation thresholds was published in 2000.[13] Following that report, the Commission proceeded to investigate a number of issues and published a Green Paper on the review of the Merger Regulation in 2001.[14] Following consultation, a draft proposal was published in late 2002[15] but was not adopted immediately and was subject to some important revisions, outlined below. The new Regulation was eventually approved in early 2004 and came into force on 1 May 2004.[16]

The Merger Regulation

The Merger Regulation was originally designed to reduce the confusion and bureaucracy arising from large-scale mergers across the EU. Cross-border mergers, and mergers affecting different national markets, often required notification under several different systems, each with different filing requirements. This duplication was costly and time-consuming. A single system at the EU level would reduce the administrative burden, the single system being a 'one-stop shop'. Control at the EU level was also seen to be important to allow European undertakings to compete with global competitors. Mergers between successful European undertakings were perceived as being one way in which EU-based industries could compete effectively in global markets. National controls were considered to be more likely to prevent important mergers on national, rather than competition, grounds. In addition, national merger controls were more likely to consider the competitive effects on the national market alone, even if the merger made competitive sense in a global industry. The adoption of the Regulation also led to a reorganisation of the Directorate General for Competition. A special unit, the Mergers Task Force, was set up to deal with all the cases stemming from the new system.[17]

The scope of the Regulation

Although the Regulation is known as the Merger Regulation, it does not use the term 'merger' but refers rather to the 'control of concentrations'. The Regulation covers not only full mergers, as used in the normal commercial sense, but all concentrations, whether through the acquisition of shares or assets, where an undertaking acquires control over another undertaking. Some joint ventures are also considered to be concentrations. Article 3 of the Regulation defines concentrations as:

(a) the merger of two or more previously independent undertakings or parts of undertakings; or

(b) the acquisition, by one or more persons already controlling at least one undertaking, or by one or more undertakings, whether by purchase of securities or assets, by contract or by any other means, of direct or indirect control of the whole or parts of one or more other undertakings.[18]

---

12 Regulation 1310/97/EEC amending Regulation 4064/89 on the control of concentrations between undertakings, [1997] OJ, L180/1.
13 Report from the Commission to the Council on the application of the Merger Regulation thresholds, C(2000) 399 final.
14 Green Paper on the review of Council Regulation 4064/89, C(2001) 745/6 final.
15 Proposal for a Council Regulation on the control of concentrations between undertakings, C(2002) 711 final, [2003] OJ C20/06.
16 Regulation 139/2004/EC on the control of concentrations between undertakings (the EC Merger Regulation), [2004] OJ L24/1.
17 See Krause, H, 'EC Merger Control: an Outside View from Inside the Merger Task Force' [1995] JBL 627.
18 Regulation 139/2004/EC, [2004] OJ L24/1, Art 3(1).

Article 3 of the Regulation gives a fairly detailed definition of the term 'concentration' and the Commission has published a Notice giving more detailed guidance as to how it will be applied.[19]

An obvious form of concentration is where previously independent undertakings merge and where one or both original undertakings cease to exist. Less obvious concentrations occur where a transaction results in a change of control over an undertaking. In these cases the central concern is whether the rights gained by one undertaking in another confer on the undertaking that gains the rights 'the possibility of exercising decisive influence'.[20] It is possible to gain such influence over another undertaking by acquiring a majority of voting shares in that undertaking, or by having the right to appoint half of the members of the controlling board. In *St Gobain/Poliet*, a 4.7% interest in Poliet was enough to give sole control when the majority shareholder agreed that St Gobain would appoint the majority of the supervisory board.[21] It is possible to be seen as having 'decisive influence' even where the undertaking concerned has a minority holding in the target. In *Arjomari/Wiggins Teape Appleton*,[22] Arjomari acquired a 39% share of Wiggins Teape, and this was seen as being capable of giving sole control. No other shareholder had more than a 4% holding and only three shareholders owned over 3% of the issued share capital. As Arjomari had such a comparatively large holding, Arjomari was considered to be, in effect, gaining control of Wiggins Teape. When examining whether the acquisition of a minority holding establishes decisive influence, it is important to explore the practical implications of such a level of control. It may be the case that shareholder participation is historically low in that undertaking. If it is, a relatively low shareholding may give de facto control over its decision-making. The key issue concerning the point at which control is achieved was examined in *Ryanair/Aer Lingus*.[23] Ryanair's initial acquisition of a 19.16% share in Aer Lingus was not notified to the Commission. However, Ryanair's attempt to gain full control was the subject of a prohibition Decision in 2007. Subsequently, Aer Lingus challenged the Commission's failure to require Ryanair to divest an additional 6.01% holding it had acquired during its bid, taking the overall holding to 25.17%, but the GC confirmed that the Commission did not have the power to do so, as at that point there was no overall change of control.[24]

The discussion above concerns sole control of an undertaking, but it is also possible for two or more undertakings to acquire joint control of another. The utilisation of such joint ventures or strategic alliances is becoming increasingly common. This situation normally occurs where two undertakings transfer part of their respective businesses to a joint venture. Both the parent undertakings will have joint control over the joint venture. Even where one of the parents has a majority shareholding, for example, 60% of the voting shares, the minority party may well be in a position to cast a blocking vote over certain strategic decisions. Where the undertakings are forced to co-operate to avoid a minority veto, they are considered to have joint control.[25] Where one of the parent undertakings has a much smaller shareholding, for example, 20%, it will not normally have a blocking veto; however, there may still be joint control where a shareholders' agreement provides for co-operation.[26] There is a distinction between concentrative and co-operative joint ventures in Community law. The distinction between the two types of joint venture and the difficulties surrounding them will be discussed in more detail in a later section.

---

19 Commission Consolidated Notice under Council Regulation (EC) No 139/2004 on the control of concentrations between undertakings, 10 July 2007.
20 Regulation 139/2004/EC, [2004] OJ L24/1, Art 3(2).
21 Case IV/M764, [1996] OJ C225/08.
22 Case IV/M025, [1990] OJ C321/16.
23 Case Comp/M4439. On appeal Case T-411/07 *Aer Lingus Group v Commission* [2010] ECR II-3691.
24 Ryanair were eventually forced to reduce their holding to below 5% following a CC investigation in the UK; Competition Commission Report, *Ryanair Holdings plc and Aer Lingus Group plc*, 28 August 2013. The *Aer Lingus* case has prompted the Commission to re-examine how it handles minority shareholdings.
25 Case IV/M010 *Conagra/Idea*, [1991] OJ C175/18.
26 Case IV/M229 *Thomas Cook/LTU/West LB*, [1992] OJ C199/16.

The 'Community dimension' and case allocation

The concept of the Community dimension is crucial to the creation of what is known as the 'one-stop shop' in EU merger control.[27] Once the existence of a concentration has been established, the next step is to decide whether a concentration will be considered at the EU level or by the relevant national authorities. One of the key benefits of the EU system is the creation of a 'one stop shop', whereby the parties to a concentration are only subject to one set of administrative controls. This avoids potential conflicts between different administrative systems. The Regulation sets out the thresholds for the application of the EU system, where the thresholds are based on the concept of 'concentrations with a Community dimension'.[28] Furthermore, Art 21(1) of the Regulation provides that only the Commission shall take action in respect of Community dimension mergers. This provision is supported by Art 21(3), which provides that no national law will apply to such mergers. Due to the importance of the thresholds, they have proved to be one of the most controversial, and most revised, elements of the Regulation.

The main threshold for the existence of a Community dimension in a concentration, in Art 1(2) of the Regulation, is where:

(a) the combined aggregate worldwide turnover of the undertakings concerned is more than €5,000m; and

(b) the aggregate Community-wide turnover of at least two of the undertakings concerned is €250m, *unless* each of the undertakings concerned achieves more than two-thirds of its aggregate Community-wide turnover within one Member State.[29]

The main threshold test for identifying a Community dimension merger is, therefore, based entirely on the turnover of the undertakings concerned. There is no qualitative assessment at this stage. For those involved, this approach has the benefit of certainty, which will only be apparent where the figures on worldwide, EU and Member State turnover are available. As undertakings may not keep accounts in this fashion, the certainty may be more apparent than real. Other difficulties arise in relation to the calculation of the relevant figures for turnover. To aid the undertakings involved, there is more detailed guidance in Art 5 of the Regulation, as well as in the Commission Consolidated Jurisdictional Notice.[30]

The 1997 amendment of the regime introduced a second way in which concentrations are deemed to have a Community dimension. A concentration will also have a Community dimension, under Art 1(3), where:

(a) the combined aggregate worldwide turnover of all the undertakings concerned is more than €2,500m;

(b) in each of at least three Member States the combined aggregate turnover of all the undertakings concerned is more than €100m;

(c) in each of at least three Member States included for the purpose of point (b), the aggregate turnover of at least two of the undertakings concerned is more than €25m; and

(d) the aggregate Community-wide turnover of each of at least two of the undertakings concerned is more than €100m, *unless* each of the undertakings concerned achieves more than two-thirds of its aggregate Community-wide turnover within one Member State.[31]

---

27 This is the last remaining area of EU competition law where the use of 'Community', as opposed to 'EU' or 'Union', is retained. Perhaps a shift to EU is inevitable in a post-Lisbon world.
28 Regulation 139/2004/EC, [2004] OJ L24/1, Art 1.
29 Regulation 139/2004/EC, [2004] OJ L24/1, Art 1(2) (emphasis added).
30 10 July 2007.
31 Regulation 139/2004/EC, [2004] OJ L24/1, Art 1(3) (emphasis added).

It is important to note that if this final proviso applies, the concentration will not have a Community dimension even if the other four criteria are satisfied.

The Art 1(3) criteria are designed to catch concentrations that fall below the original, and principal, threshold test but which would normally qualify for consideration under more than one Member State's national controls. Following the 1996 review, the addition of Art 1(5) was preferred to a simple reduction of the thresholds contained in Art 1(2). The outcome is probably best understood in the context of subsidiarity. The Member States were unwilling to extend further power to the Commission unless it was in circumstances where the duplication of national merger controls was imminent. That was likely to be the case where the concentration was significant in several Member States and, therefore, the Commission would be best placed to consider the concentration. The retention of the two-thirds rule, and the requirement that the turnover of the relevant undertakings reaches €25m in at least three Member States, will exclude from the Commission's competence concentrations that are likely to have their principal effects in one Member State.

This option made sense as a political compromise but has several practical difficulties. One of the original benefits of the EU regime was the 'one-stop shop' principle, and the certainty produced by this may have been reduced by the introduction of the alternative threshold criteria, although the subsequent changes in Arts 4(4), 4(5), 9 and 22 suggest that, increasingly, flexibility is preferred to certainty. The question whether a concentration between undertakings with a combined turnover of between €2,500m and €5,000m falls under the EU regime will depend on a complex breakdown of the turnover spread between Member States. Each undertaking will need to examine its turnover in each Member State to assess whether the various thresholds have been reached. In the 2000 review of the Merger Regulation, the Commission noted that 9% of notifications came through the Art 1(3) route and most of those notifications had a clear Community dimension.[32] In the Commission's view, the new threshold had been successful. Notwithstanding that success, the Commission report suggested that a large number of mergers still do not fall within Art 1(3) and require notification in several Member States. To resolve that concern the 2004 reforms added a further 'multiple filing' route through the procedure for pre-notification referral in Art 4(5) of Regulation 139/2004. Under that provision, undertakings whose concentration may be reviewed under the national competition laws of at least three Member States may, before notifying those Member States, inform the Commission, by reasoned submission, that the concentration should be reviewed by the Commission. The Member States are then informed of such a submission, but if there is no disagreement by any Member State within 15 days of being referred the concentration will be deemed to have a Community dimension.[33] This procedure should minimise the potential for wasteful multiple filings in cases where the normal thresholds have not been met, without extending the scope of the Merger Regulation to a large number of smaller concentrations which do not have a significant multi-state dimension. While the procedure has been welcomed, there are concerns that the administrative requirements that go with making a reasoned submission, in Form RS, are very burdensome for the parties, and that the process could be improved.[34]

Case allocation and referral

As can be seen from the reference to the 'multiple filing' procedure under Art 4(5) of the Regulation, there is a move away from a simple reliance on the 'Community dimension' thresholds in Art 1. There are various case allocation mechanisms, in Arts 4, 9 and 22 of the Regulation,

---

32 Report from the Commission to the Council on the application of the Merger Regulation thresholds, C(2000) 399 final.
33 See Commission Notice on case referral in respect of concentrations, [2005] OJ, C56/2.
34 See J Connolly *et al*, 'Pre-notification Referral under the EC Merger Regulation: Simplifying the Route to the One-stop Shop' [2007] ECLR 167. The same administrative burden applies to the procedure under Art 4(4) of the Regulation.

which allow cases to be referred to authorities other than those that are suggested by the normal thresholds. These case allocation mechanisms work to fine-tune case allocation between the Commission and the National Competition Authorities (NCAs). The Commission has also produced a Commission Notice on case referral.[35] The Notice states that the intention of the system is to create a 'jurisdictional mechanism which is flexible, but which at the same time ensures effective protection of competition'.[36] Cases should be allocated to the authority most appropriate for dealing with the merger, bearing in mind the characteristics of the case and the tools and expertise available to the agency.[37] In the following paragraphs the various case allocation mechanisms will be examined; first, where concentrations without a Community dimension are brought within the Regulation, and secondly, where concentrations which would normally fall within the standard thresholds can be referred back to the Member States.

Article 22 of the Regulation allows a Member State or Member States to seek to refer a concentration which does not have a Community dimension, according to the thresholds, to the Commission.[38] The NCAs can only make such a request where the concentration 'affects trade between Member States and threatens to significantly affect competition within the territory of the Member State or States making the request'. The request can only be made within fifteen days of the concentration being notified or made known to the Member States concerned. The Commission then has ten working days to decide if the criteria have been fulfilled and if it will take on the case. The referral test in Regulation 139/2004 is less strict than the previous test under Regulation 4064/89. The increased co-operation of NCAs under the European Competition Network (ECN) should also facilitate such referrals. The case referral Notice foresees the use of Art 22 only where there are serious concerns in markets which are wider than national, or where there are a series of concerns in a number of sub-national markets across the Community.[39] The *Sara Lee* merger cases in 2009 are clear examples of cases in which the Art 22 procedure is useful, but not perfect. The well-known US company Sara Lee decided in 2009 to dispose of a number of its non-food brands. It decided to sell its bodycare and detergents businesses to Unilever,[40] its air freshener business to Procter and Gamble,[41] and its insecticide business to SC Johnson.[42] The bodycare merger was referred to the EU Commission as it met the thresholds in Reg 139/2004, but the others did not. The air freshener merger was sufficiently large to be notified in Germany and a number of other Member States. The authorities in Germany, Belgium, Spain, Portugal, Hungary and the UK all made requests for referral under Art 22. The Commission requested that the merger be notified to them, but by the time the Commission took the case the merger had already been cleared by the Cypriot NCA. In the case of insecticides, the transaction only required notification in Spain and Portugal, and therefore would even have fallen outside the scope of Art 4, but Spain, Belgium, Greece, France, the Czech Republic and Italy submitted referral requests. Those requests were accepted, but the Portuguese NCA did not join with the Spanish request and continued to carry on its own parallel investigation.[43]

---

35 Ibid. See also, Krajewska, T, 'Referrals under the New EC Merger Regulation Regime: A UK Perspective' [2008] ECLR 279.
36 Commission Notice on case referral, para 7. See, also, Regulation 139/2004/EC, [2004] OJ L24/1, Recital 11.
37 Commission Notice on case referral, para 9.
38 This Article is sometimes known as the 'Dutch clause', as one of the reasons for its inclusion was at the behest of the Dutch authorities who did not, at the time, have a system of domestic merger control; however, while most Member States now have domestic controls, there are still a stream of cases referred upwards.
39 Commission Notice on case referral in respect of contributions, at para 45. See also OFT press release 29/05, 16 February 2005, confirming the OFT's decision not to request the Commission to examine the proposed bids for the Stock Exchange.
40 Case COMP/M.5658, *Unilever/Sara Lee Body Care.*
41 Case COMP/M.5828, *Procter & Gamble/Sara Lee Air Care.*
42 Case COMP/M.5969, *SCJ/Sara Lee.*
43 See Commission Press Release IP/10/1770, 'Mergers: Commission opens in-depth investigation into SC Johnson's acquisition of Sara Lee's household insect control business', 22 December 2010.

The 'back referral' procedure in Art 9 of the Regulation is designed to allow concentrations with a Community dimension to be referred back to the NCAs for consideration under domestic merger control.[44] Article 9 allows a Member State to request that consideration of a concentration be referred back to its competent authority if:

(a)   a concentration threatens to affect significantly competition in a market within that Member State, which presents all the characteristics of a distinct market; or

(b)   a concentration affects competition in a market within that Member State, which presents all the characteristics of a distinct market and which does not constitute a substantial part of the Common Market.[45]

The Member State must seek a referral within 15 working days of it receiving the copy notification from the Commission. The Commission may invite a Member State to seek a back referral but the Member State is not required to act following such an invitation. The Commission should, as a general rule, make a decision whether to refer all or part of the concentration to the competent authority within the 25 working day period set out in Art 10(1) of the Regulation, where proceedings are not initiated, or within 65 working days, where proceedings have been initiated, but no preparatory steps to adopt measures under Art 8 have been taken.[46] If the Commission does not take a decision within the relevant time period, or has not taken the preparatory steps towards a decision, the concentration is deemed to have been referred back to the competent national authority.[47] Once the concentration is referred back, the competent authority should report on its findings under national law within 45 working days after referral.[48] The Member State may only take measures which are strictly necessary to safeguard or restore effective competition on the market.[49] Examples of the operation of the Art 9 procedure include: the OFT's request to have the joint venture between Deutsche Telecom, owners of T-Mobile, and France Telecom, owners of Orange, referred back to them because of its concerns over the impact of the joint venture on retails markets in the UK;[50] and, the *Thomas Cook/Travel business of Co-operative Group/Travel business of Midlands Co-operative Society* merger where the market effected was UK-wide.[51] One particular draw-back of the Art 9 procedure is the extra delay it causes. The parties will already have gone through all the time and cost of notifying the Commission before the Member State even begins the Art 9 process, which still has to be followed by the domestic merger review process

While the NCAs may seek a 'back referral' under Art 9, the parties to a concentration may seek to initiate back referral, pre-notification, via Art 4(4). The parties may submit a reasoned request to the Commission setting out why they consider the concentration to significantly affect competition in a market that presents all the characteristics of a distinct market and should, therefore, be considered by that Member State. After receiving such a submission the Commission must transmit it to the Member State without delay. The Member State then has 15 working days to agree or disagree with the referral. If there is no disagreement from the Member State the Commission then has 25 working days to decide whether it will refer the case back to an NCA to

---

44 The exception is sometimes known as the 'German clause', as it was inserted at the behest of the German authorities.
45 Regulation 139/2004/EC, [2004] OJ L24/1, Art 9(2).
46 Ibid, Art 9(4).
47 Under Art 9(5).
48 Under Art 9(6).
49 Under Art 9(8).
50 Case COMP/M.5549, *T-Mobile/Orange*.
51 Case COMP/M.5996.

be considered under its domestic merger control, if the criteria have been fulfilled and the NCA is the most appropriate authority.[52]

Another exception to the 'one-stop shop' principle is provided for in Art 21(4) of the Regulation which allows for the protection of legitimate interests. This exception is designed to allow Member States to protect three named interests: public security, plurality of the media, and prudential rules. If the Member State wants to invoke a 'legitimate interest', it must notify the Commission of its intention prior to the adoption of the measure, and the Commission will consider its applicability with the general principles of EU law before the adoption of the measure. The Commission has 25 working days to undertake this task. The exception in Art 21(4) allows a Member State to adopt measures based on existing national law on the basis of non-competition grounds. Those measures must comply with general EU law principles, such as non-discrimination and proportionality. The exception does not allow a Member State to permit a prohibited concentration to go ahead, but it does allow a Member State to impose restrictions on a concentration which has been cleared by the Commission.

In addition to the exceptions provided for in the Merger Regulation, there are additional challenges to the concept of the 'one-stop shop' within the Treaties. Article 346 TFEU provides that Member States are not precluded from taking measures necessary to protect national security. This is most likely to arise in the context of takeovers and mergers related to the defence industry. Also, the Merger Regulation, as secondary EU legislation, does not prevent the continued applicability, as discussed above, of Arts 101 and 102 TFEU. Accordingly, for mergers without a Community dimension, as defined in Art 1 of the Regulation, Arts 101 and 102 may have continued effect. While it is unlikely that the Commission would take any such action, Arts 101 and, particularly, 102 are directly enforceable in the national courts which might seek to provide remedies, for instance, interim relief, in the context of merger.

All of the above provisions, and the co-operation mechanisms in the ECN, are designed to avoid jurisdictional conflict between the Commission and the NCAs in merger cases, but a number of high-profile disputes have shown the sensitivity of these issues. In the *Gas Natural/Endesa*[53] and *E.ON/Endesa*[54] dispute the Commission took action under Art 21 of the Merger Regulation regarding several conditions imposed by the Spanish Energy Regulator (CNE) following E.ON's successful bid for Endesa. The Commission had previously cleared the merger without remedies. The conditions were eventually modified. In *Abertis/Autostrade*[55] the Commission cleared the merger but it was blocked by ANAS, the Italian body responsible for granting motorway concessions, as they were concerned that the merged entity might not be able to properly carry out the investment required to maintain and improve the motorway network. The Commission opened proceedings and the Italian measure was withdrawn.[56] While there are obviously still shortcomings in the system of cooperation between the Commission and the NCAs, and between different NCAs, there are ongoing attempts to improve cooperation within the ECN. In 2011 the Commission published the final guidance from an EU Working Group on mergers: 'Best Practices on cooperation between EU National Competition Authorities in Merger Review'.[57] It is designed to 'foster cooperation and sharing of information between NCAs

---

52 See the Commission Notice on case referral in respect of concentrations, paras 19–23.
53 Case COMP/M.3986, 15 November 2005. In this case it was decided that there was no Community dimension.
54 Case COMP/M.4110, 25 April 2006, and Case COMP/M.4197, 20 December 2006.
55 Case COMP/M.4249, 22 September 2006, and Commission Press Release IP/06/1418, 18 October 2006.
56 The balance between merger control and national industrial policy is discussed in Galloway, J, 'The Pursuit of National Champions: The Intersection of Competition Law and Industrial Policy' [2007] ECLR 172.
57 EU Merger Working Group, 'Best Practices on cooperation between EU National Competition Authorities in Merger Review', November 2011.

in the European Union, for mergers that do not qualify for review by the Commission itself (the one-stop shop review) but require clearance in several Member States'.[58]

Mandatory notification and suspension

Concentrations that have a Community dimension must be notified, under Art 4(1), to the Commission 'prior to their implementation and following the conclusion of the agreement, the announcement of the public bid, or the acquisition of a controlling interest'. The 2004 reforms introduced into Art 4(1) the possibility of undertakings notifying a merger where they can demonstrate 'a good faith intention to conclude an agreement'.[59] It is obviously important that the Commission is informed of a proposed concentration as soon as possible, but it is also vital that sufficient finalised detail is available in order that there can be a full consideration of the relevant facts. As a quick resolution of the procedure is vital in commercial situations, a timely notification is beneficial to the parties involved. If the undertakings fail to notify the Commission of a concentration, a fine not exceeding 10% of aggregate turnover may be imposed.[60] On receipt of a notification the Commission publishes the fact of the notification, along with the names of the parties and the nature of the concentration.[61] The publication of the notification is designed to elicit third party observations. These will have to reach the Commission within a tight time limit, which is specified in the published Notice. The notification must contain a considerable amount of detailed information about the relevant undertakings and the market concerned. The Commission must be in a position to decide whether the concentration has a Community dimension and to make an initial appraisal based on the facts provided. Due to the complexity of the information required, it is often advisable for parties to approach the Commission informally before the official notification is made.[62] Consultation will assist the undertakings concerned in compiling the relevant information.

According to Art 7, a concentration cannot be put into effect until the concentration has been declared compatible with the Common Market by the Commission. Suspension of a concentration is the key to the success of the merger control system; as concentrations are very difficult to undo once they have gone ahead, it is important that the appraisal of any concentration takes place during the period of suspension. The Commission can, if it considers it necessary, waive the suspension period and allow the concentration to be implemented.[63] Before granting a derogation, the Commission must take into account the potential effects of implementation on other parties and competition.

Appraisal procedure

Once notification has taken place, the Commission will begin the examination of the concentration. Because of the sensitive commercial nature of most concentrations, it is considered vital that the Commission examination is completed without delay. To that end very strict time limits are imposed by the Regulation. The timetable was reformed in 2004 to introduce increased flexibility, but it remains highly focused. The initial decision must be taken within 25 working days,

---

58 Commission Press Release IP/11/1326, 'Mergers: competition authorities agree best practices to handle cross-border mergers that do not benefit from EU one-stop shop review', 9 November 2011.
59 See Berg, W and Ostendorf, P, 'The Reform of EC Merger Control: Substance and Impact of the Proposed New Procedural Rules' [2003] ECLR 594.
60 Regulation 139/2004/EC, [2004] OJ L24/1, Art 14(2)(a).
61 Ibid, Art 4(3).
62 In October 2006, [2006] OJ C251/2, the submission rules were altered to require one signed original, five paper copies and 30 copies on CD or DVD-ROM format. This will facilitate electronic transmission of files.
63 Regulation 139/2004/EC, [2004] OJ L24/1, Art 7(3).

that period starting on the day following receipt of the notification.[64] The Commission has been very successful in adhering to the Regulation's time limits. Increasing merger activity and the strict deadlines have placed great pressure on the Mergers Task Force. The Commission has sought relief from that pressure from two sources. Firstly, the Commission has been given increased resources[65] and, secondly, a simplified procedure for the treatment of certain concentrations[66] has been introduced. The detail of the simplified procedure will be discussed shortly.

The Commission has been given various investigative powers to assist in its appraisal. Article 11(1) gives the Commission the power to request information from undertakings. Information will usually be sought from the undertakings involved in the merger and the Commission is required to detail the information requested, to set a time limit for the provision of the information and to set out the penalties for noncompliance. It must also provide the relevant competent authority with a copy of the request. The Commission may, alternatively, make a formal decision requiring the provision of information.[67] Fines for failing to provide information or for providing incomplete information were increased in the revised Regulation to a figure not exceeding 1% of aggregate turnover and a periodic penalty payment not exceeding 5% of average aggregate daily turnover is possible for each day of delay.[68] The Commission may also, under Art 11(7), interview, with the purpose of collecting information, any person who consents to be interviewed. These powers are not restricted to the undertakings who are the subjects of the investigation.

The Commission may also conduct on the spot investigations[69] or ask the competent authorities of the Member States to conduct investigations on its behalf.[70] The Commission can enter the undertaking's premises to examine books and business records, take copies and ask for explanations. The Commission may also seal premises or records, if necessary. The Commission is required to co-operate closely with the competent authorities of the relevant Member States while planning and conducting investigations. Requests for information and investigations will often take a considerable amount of time. This will cause the Commission difficulties in meeting the strict time limits imposed by the Regulation. Consequently, in situations where one of the relevant undertakings is responsible for the circumstances leading to the request or investigation, the time periods will be suspended.[71] Details of the procedure followed by the Commission during an investigation are set out in the implementing Regulation[72] and the Commission's guidance on 'best practices'.[73]

A simplified procedure for dealing with certain concentrations was introduced in 2000 and reformed in 2004. It allows uncontroversial concentrations to be declared, with minimal investigation, as compatible with the Common Market. The Commission Notice[74] sets out a number of categories of concentration which will benefit from this procedure:

---

64 Ibid, Art 10(1). If the information supplied with the notification is incomplete, the period does not start running until the necessary information is provided. The period may be extended to 35 working days if the Commission receives a 'German' clause request from a Member State under Art 9. Under Regulation 4064/89 the period was one calendar month.
65 *XXXth Report on Competition Policy*, 2000, Point 238.
66 Commission Notice on a simplified procedure for the treatment of certain concentrations under Council Regulation 4064/89, [2000] OJ C217/32.
67 Regulation 139/2004/EC, [2004] OJ L24/1, Art 11(3).
68 Ibid, Arts 14(1) and 15(1).
69 Ibid, Art 13.
70 Ibid, Art 12.
71 Ibid, Art 10(4).
72 Regulation 802/2004/EC implementing Council Regulation (EC) No 139/2004 on the control of concentrations between undertakings, [2004] OJ L133/1.
73 Directorate General for Competition, 'Best Practices on the conduct of EC merger control proceedings', Directorate General for Competition website: http://europa.int/comm/competition/index_en.html.
74 Commission Notice on a simplified procedure for the treatment of certain concentrations under Council Regulation (EC) No 139/2004.

1   where undertakings acquire joint control over a joint venture and where that joint venture
     has no, or negligible, activities in the European Economic Area (EEA); or
2   where none of the parties are engaged in business activities in the same product and
     geographic market (horizontal relationships), or in a product market which is upstream or
     downstream of a product market in which any other party is engaged; or
3   where two or more of the parties are engaged in the same product and geographic market
     or upstream or downstream market, provided that their combined market share is not 15%
     or more for horizontal relationships or 25% or more for vertical relationships; or
4   where a party is to acquire sole control of an undertaking over which it already has joint
     control.

Commission practice has shown that these types of concentration rarely give rise to competition
concerns. If a concentration falls within any of these categories, a short form decision will be
published within one month of the notification. The Commission may intervene at any point
before the publication of the decision and revert back to the normal procedure. The simplified
procedure reduces the administrative burden for both the parties and the Commission, making
the system more efficient and allowing the Commission to focus its resources in other, more
problematic, areas.

After the initial examination the Commission may deal with the case in a number of ways. It
may conclude that the concentration does not fall within the scope of the Regulation,[75] and will
close the case. If the concentration does fall within the Regulation, the Commission may declare,
under Art 6(1)(b), that the concentration does not raise serious doubts as to its compatibility with
the Common Market, and allow it to go ahead. In 2006 there was an interesting development, in
Impala v Commission, as the CFI upheld an appeal against a clearance Decision in a merger
case.[76] The CFI made clear that when the Commission is adopting a clearance Decision it must
provide the same level of clarity and completeness as it would in a prohibition Decision. The
Commission went on to reassess the merger and it was approved again in October 2007.[77]

During the initial investigation the Commission may be concerned that a concentration may
raise serious concerns for the Common Market, but, through negotiation with the parties, may be
able to agree changes to the proposed concentration that would alleviate those concerns. If the
undertakings concerned agree to modify the proposed concentration, the modified concentration
can be declared compatible, under Art 6(2). The Commission can also attach conditions and obligations to the decision that a modified concentration is compatible with the Common Market in
order to ensure that the undertakings concerned comply with the commitments they have entered
into. Negotiated modifications of this nature are known as 'remedies' in the Commission's
parlance. In order to assist parties who are planning a merger, and to encourage them to consider
potential remedies and bring them to the Commission as soon as possible, the Commission
published a Notice on Remedies.[78] In *Vodafone/Airtouch*,[79] a merger between UK and US mobile
communications operators, the Commission was concerned as the merged company would have
control over two of the four major mobile communication operators in Germany. In order to allay

---

75 Regulation 139/2004/EC, [2004] OJ L24/1, Art 6(1)(a).
76 Case T-464/04 *Impala v Commission* [2006] ECR II-2289. On appeal, Case C-413/06P *Bertelsmann and Sony v Impala*,
    [2008] ECR I-4951, the ECJ allowed the appeal on various grounds and referred the case back to the CFI. It did, however,
    confirm that the same standards apply to approval and prohibition Decisions.
77 See Commission Press Release IP/07/1437, 'Mergers: Commission confirms approval of recorded music joint venture
    between Sony and Bertelsmann after re-assessment subsequent to Court decision', 3 October 2007.
78 Commission notice on remedies acceptable under Council Regulation (EC) No 139/2004 and under Commission Regulation
    (EC) No 802/2004, [2008] OJ C267/1. See, also, Went, D, 'The Acceptability of Remedies under the EC Merger Regulation:
    structural versus behavioural' [2006] ECLR 455.
79 Case IV/M1430, [1999] OJ C295/2.

its concerns, a divestment remedy in which Vodafone agreed to sell its stake in one of those operators was submitted to the Commission by Vodafone. The sale eliminated the overlap in the German market for mobile telecommunications between Vodafone and Airtouch. If the conditions attached to a decision are not fulfilled, the Commission may revoke its decision and initiate the second stage. Where an undertaking offers remedies the time limit for the initial stage of the investigation is extended to 35 working days.[80] Another example of an Art 6(2) decision was seen in *Air France/KLM,* where the Commission approved the creation of Europe's largest airline group.[81]

The Commission's final option is to decide to initiate proceedings – the second phase of the examination – if it believes the concentration raises serious doubts as to its compatibility with the Common Market. The second-phase investigation is more detailed, and operates in accordance with longer time limits. After the decision has been made to go into the second stage the Commission must notify the undertakings concerned and the relevant Member States. Where the Commission fails to make a decision within the time period, the concentration will automatically be deemed to be compatible with the Common Market under Art 10(6).

The second-stage proceedings involve a more detailed investigation and have a time limit of 90 working days from the initiation of second-stage proceedings.[82] An example of the rationale behind a second-stage investigation can be seen in the *Sony/Bertelsmann* case.[83] The Commission was concerned that the concentration might create a dominant position in the market for recorded music, but also that it might have an impact on other vertically integrated markets, such as television, downloadable music, and portable music players.[84] At the end of the investigation the Commission may declare the concentration to be compatible, under Art 8(1), or incompatible, under Art 8(3), with the Common Market. Where a concentration has been implemented and is then declared to be incompatible with the Common Market, the Commission can order the separation of the assets and/or the cessation of joint control.[85] The Commission may impose a fine on the undertakings concerned. The fine can be up to 10% of aggregate turnover and, in addition, a periodic penalty (increased in 2004) of up to 5% of average aggregate daily turnover per day until the assets are separated or control is relinquished.[86] The final options for the Commission are therefore very simple, but in practice the procedure can be quite complex. When making a Decision the Commission must provide sufficient justification. Following the CFI's judgment in *Schneider II*[87] it is clear that if the Commission makes a 'manifest error', it will be liable to pay compensation to the parties to the merger, under Art 340(2) TFEU; however, the Commission retains a margin of discretion in complex economic analysis. During the investigation it may well become apparent that the concentration is unlikely to be compatible with the Common Market, and if that is the case a process of negotiation may begin in an attempt to find some form of compromise with a view to allowing a modified concentration to proceed. The Commission has the power to clear a concentration, under Art 8(2), if the concentration has been modified in such a way that it is compatible with the Common Market. The use of remedies is the norm if a clearance is granted after an investigation advances into the second stage. Where the parties involved offer commitments after day 54 of the proceedings, the time limit for the investigation is extended to 105 working days. The extension of the time limits, where remedies are offered late, should

80 Regulation 139/2004/EC, [2004] OJ L24/1, Art 10(1).
81 Case IV/M3280, [2004] OJ C60/5, Commission Press Release, IP/04/194.
82 The time period under Regulation 4064/89 was four calendar months.
83 Case IV/M3333 (4064).
84 See Commission Press Release, IP/04/200.
85 Under Art 8(4).
86 Regulation 139/2004/EC, [2004] OJ L24/1, Arts 14(2) and 15(2).
87 Case T-351/03 *Schneider Electric SA v Commission* [2007] ECR II-2237. On appeal Case C-440/07 P *Commission v Schneider Electric*, [2009] ECR I-6413.

encourage the parties to offer commitments within the first 54 days. In order to assist the transparency of negotiations, the Commission's Remedies Notice sets out the underlying principles upon which Commission practice is based, but it must be noted that each case is very different and the Commission retains a large degree of flexibility.[88] It is for the parties to show that the commitments they suggest remove the competition concerns highlighted by the Commission. The Commission prefers structural solutions, as opposed to behavioural remedies, to competition concerns as they are more likely to solve the problem and do not require medium- to long-term monitoring.[89] It is also clear that an authorisation cannot be granted where suggested remedies are so complex that the Commission cannot determine whether competition will be effectively restored.[90] An incompatibility decision under Art 8(3) is required to avoid automatic clearance under Art 10 at the end of the investigation period. As the Commission must consult the Member States and the Advisory Committee on Concentrations before granting a clearance, the Commission needs to finalise the modifications in advance of the deadline. In a number of cases, late commitments have been rejected as it would have been impossible for the Commission to undertake sufficient 'market testing'.[91] The automatic extension of the time limit for late commitments should mitigate this problem to some extent. If the parties do not fulfil the conditions contained within a clearance, the Commission may impose a fine of up to 10% of aggregate turnover and, in addition, impose a period penalty payment of up to 5% of average aggregate daily turnover per day until the situation is rectified.[92]

An example of a negotiated clearance was *Kimberly-Clark/Scott Paper*.[93] The deal would have combined the Andrex, owned by Scott Paper, and the Kleenex, owned by Kimberly-Clark, brands of paper products in the UK and Ireland. The post-merger undertaking would have had a combined market share of 20–45% of branded products, that is, Kleenex and Andrex, and 40–60% of branded and private label products, products made by the companies for others. The Commission discovered that the concentration raised particular concerns as the vast majority of relevant retailers stocked the branded products, and that the merger would result in the creation of the leading supplier of private branded products. Before the Commission cleared the concentration, the Commission required the divestiture of a major UK production facility and the licence of the use of the Kleenex brand for ten years to a third party. In other geographical markets the competition concerns were different. To address those concerns, other conditions were attached by the Commission in relation to those markets: the continued use of the Kleenex brand was allowed, while the Andrex brand was not to be used for an indefinite period. It is interesting to note that the merger was also the subject of investigation, and eventual approval, in the US.

In *AOL/Time Warner*,[94] another large-scale international merger, the Commission approved the merger after the parties agreed to sever all links with the German media group Bertelsmann. The merger between AOL, the leading internet access provider in the US and the only access provider across Europe, and Time Warner, one of the world's biggest publishing and media companies, created the first vertically integrated internet content provider with access to Time Warner's content library. AOL operated in Europe through several joint ventures with Bertelsmann whose operations include a large music publishing interest and, therefore, a large musical library. The Commission was concerned that AOL would have had a dominant position on the market for

---

88 Commission notice on remedies acceptable under Council Regulation (EC) No 139/2004 and under Commission Regulation (EC) No 802/2004, [2008] OJ C267/1.
89 At paras 9–13.
90 At para 14.
91 See, for example, Case IV/M1524, Commission Decision 2000/276/EC *Airtours/First Choice*, [2000] OJ L93/1.
92 Regulation 139/2004/EC, [2004] OJ L24/1, Arts 14(2) and 15(2).
93 Case IV/M623, Commission Decision 96/435/EC, [1996] OJ L183/01.
94 Case IV/M1845, Commission Decision 2001/718/EC, [2001] OJ L268/28.

online delivery of music, as it could utilise both Time Warner's and Bertelsmann's content. There was also concern that AOL would have been in a position to format its music libraries to work only with their own music player potentially allowing that player to become dominant. By severing all links between AOL and Bertelsmann the concerns were removed.

Basis of the appraisal

The Commission's decisions under Arts 6 and 8 are based on the concept of 'compatibility with the Common Market', and that concept is explained in Art 2 of the Regulation. The basic prohibition is against concentrations that:

> would significantly impede effective competition, in the common market or in a substantial part of it, in particular as a result of the creation or strengthening of a dominant position.[95]

The 'Significant Impediment to Effective Competition' (SIEC) test was introduced by Regulation 139/2004 and replaced the 'dominance' test in Regulation 4064/89. The original 'dominance' test focused on concentrations that created or strengthened a dominant position as a result of which competition would be significantly impeded in the Common Market.[96] Although similar words are used in the Regulation 139/2004 test and in Regulation 4064/89, the change in emphasis of the new test, emphasising the impediment of competition rather than dominance, focuses the Merger Regulation on wider competition concerns rather than a narrow focus on 'dominance', as in Art 102 TFEU. In other words, the revised test allows for the Commission to intervene in mergers which raise unilateral effects absent dominance, for instance where a fringe market player, which imposes competitive constraints on the larger competitors, is taken over by one of those competitors, but without it gaining a dominant position in the process. The impact of the change in focus, and one of the main reasons for it, is set out in Recitals 24–26 of the Regulation which centre on the consequences of concentrations in 'oligopolistic market structures'. The particular problems of oligopolistic markets will be discussed more fully below. The retention of the dominance criteria within the new SIEC test means that previous Commission practice under Regulation 4064 is still, however, of relevance.[97] The Commission is also required to take into account the need to maintain and develop competition within the Common Market, the market position of the undertakings, and the development of technical and economic progress that is to the consumers' advantage.[98] Practice since the coming into force of the new Regulation has indicated that the Commission has refocused its decision-making, and the language used concentrates on 'unilateral effects' or 'coordinated effects' on competition rather than dominance or collective dominance. A good example is the January 2013 Commission Decision prohibiting the proposed acquisition in *UPS/TNT Express* in relation to the small package delivery market.[99]

The appraisal of a particular concentration will, therefore, require detailed market analysis to establish if there is a significant impediment to competition. The Commission Notice on the definition of the market[100] is largely based on the Commission's practice in merger control. In the context of some joint ventures the Regulation provides, in Art 2(4), that any

---

95 Regulation 139/2004/EC, [2004] OJ L24/1, Art 2(3).
96 Regulation 4064/89/EEC, [1990] OJ L257/13, Art 2(3).
97 Regulation 139/2004/EC, [2004] OJ L24/1, Recital 26.
98 Regulation 139/2004/EC, [2004] OJ L24/1, Art 2(1).
99 Case M.6570, 30 January 2013. See Commission Press Release IP/13/68, 'Mergers: Commission blocks proposed acquisition of TNT Express by UPS', 30 January 2013.
100 [1997] OJ C372/5. See the discussion in Chapter 4.

co-ordination between the competitive behaviour of independent undertakings is to be appraised within the merger investigation and in accordance with the criteria in Art 101 TFEU.

To enhance transparency in the appraisal of horizontal concentrations under the Regulation, the Commission has published an important Guideline.[101] The Guideline stresses that while it sets out the analytical approach of the Commission, the Guideline cannot detail all possible applications, and each case will be handled according to its own particular facts.[102] The Guideline also makes clear that most prohibition decisions will still be based on a finding of dominance,[103] although its subsequent decisional practice indicates that it does not rely heavily on the dominance concept in its Decisions, preferring to rely directly on the SIEC test.[104] Following the perceived success of the Horizontal Guideline the Commission went on to publish a Guideline on Non-Horizontal Mergers, which gives similar guidance on the assessment of vertical and conglomerate mergers.[105] The Commission's assessment is split into two main elements: the definition of the market and the competitive assessment of the merger. Market definition follows the same process as under Art 102 TFEU, as discussed in Chapter 4. A fascinating recent example of the definition of the relevant product market involving an assessment of the interchangeability of products arose in the *Kraft/Cadbury* Decision of 2010,[106] where the distinctive markets for tablet, countline and praline chocolates were deemed to be separate product markets within the overall 'chocolate market' for the purposes of the assessment.

Once the market is defined the Commission uses a number of tools to appraise the impact of the concentration. Market shares can be used to calculate the overall level of concentration in the market. A combined market share of less than 25% rarely leads to the creation of a dominant position and is unlikely to impede competition significantly.[107] Another useful tool is the Herfindahl-Hirschman Index (HHI). The HHI is calculated by adding the squares of the individual market shares of all the firms in the market.[108] The difference between the pre-merger HHI and post-merger HHI, the 'delta', is useful to show the impact of the merger.[109] If the post-merger HHI is less than 1,000 the merger is unlikely to raise concerns. Mergers with a post-merger HHI of between 1,000 and 2,000 and with a 'delta' of less than 250 are also unlikely to raise concerns[110] unless there are special factors present, for example, if one of the merging parties is an important market innovator or a maverick firm with a likelihood of disrupting co-ordinated conduct.[111]

If a concentration is above the 'safe harbour' outlined in the Horizontal Notice, there are two main competitive concerns which the Commission will examine: the merger may eliminate

---

101 Commission Notice, Guidelines on the assessment of horizontal mergers under the Council regulation on the control of concentrations between undertakings, [2004] OJ C31/3. On the draft Notice, see Bishop, S and Ridyard, D, 'Prometheus Unbound: Increasing the Scope for Intervention in EC Merger Control' [2003] ECLR 357.

102 At para 5.

103 At para 4.

104 See, for example, Case COMP/M.3916 *T-Mobile Austria/Tele.ring*, C (2006) 1695 final, 26 April 2006, where there were unilateral effects, but it would have been difficult to conceive of the Decision being made in the context of a single dominant position.

105 Commission Notice, Guidelines on the assessment of non-horizontal mergers under the Council Regulation on the control of concentrations between undertakings, 28 November 2007.

106 Case COMP/M.5644, 6 January 2010. See Commission Press Release IP/10/3, 'Commission clears proposed acquisition of Cadbury by Kraft Foods, subject to conditions', 6 January 2010.

107 At para 18.

108 The Commission Notice uses, as an example, a market containing five firms with market shares of 40%, 20%, 15%, 15% and 10%, respectively, which has an HHI of 2,550 ($40^2 + 20^2 + 15^2 + 15^2 + 10^2 = 2,550$). The HHI ranges from close to zero (in an atomistic market) to 10,000 (in the case of a pure monopoly).

109 The increase in concentration can be calculated independently of the overall market concentration by doubling the product of the market shares of the merging firms. For example, a merger of two firms with market shares of 30% and 15%, respectively, would increase the HHI by 900 ($30 \times 15 \times 2 = 900$).

110 Or mergers with a post-merger HHI above 2,000 with a delta below 150.

111 Commission Notice, at paras 19–21.

important competitive constraints on one or more firms which would have increased market power; or the merger may change the nature of competition in such a way that firms would be significantly more likely to co-ordinate and raise prices or otherwise harm effective competition.[112] The first concern corresponds more closely with the Commission's previous practice under the dominance test in Regulation 4064. In the Horizontal Guideline the Commission set out a number of factors which might be taken into account, if they are appropriate for the individual concentration: the merging firms have large market shares; the merging firms are close competitors; the customers have limited possibilities of switching supplier; the competitors are unlikely to increase supply if prices increase; the merged entity is able to hinder expansion by competitors; and/or the merger eliminates an important competitive force.[113] The Guideline also sets out several distinct issues that the Commission will examine: whether the merger might involve a potential competitor; whether the merger might create or strengthen buyer power in upstream markets; whether there is countervailing buyer power on the market which could control the post-merger undertaking; or whether entry into the market is sufficiently easy to ensure sufficient competitive constraint on the post-merger undertaking. The concern regarding co-ordinated effects is more likely to be of importance in cases where there is not a clear problem with the creation or strengthening of single firm dominance. The problem arises where the concentration of the market makes future tacit collusion or co-ordination more likely in an oligopolistic market. Mergers in oligopolistic markets are considered in more detail below.

A number of 'defences' are also discussed by the Commission in the Guideline. These are factors which tend to reduce the impediment to competition which may be threatened by the concentration. One of the most important 'defences' available to merging undertakings is to indicate that the merger would result in a level of efficiency which would outweigh the competition concerns.[114] The possibility of an efficiency defence was partially recognised under Regulation 4064/89 in *Mercedes Benz/Kassbohrer*[115] where the improvements in research and development, and savings in production and administration, were recognised. The existence of efficiencies giving rise to consumer benefit was also considered in *St Gobain/Wacker-Chemie/NOM*.[116] The proposed joint venture was prohibited even though the concentration would have improved efficiencies in Wacker-Chemie's troubled operations. The Commission was of the opinion that consumers would receive more benefit through the cessation of Wacker-Chemie's operation than through the concentration.[117] The Guideline sets out that '[i]t is possible that efficiencies brought about by a merger counteract the effects on competition and in particular the potential harm to consumers that it might otherwise have'.[118] For an efficiency defence to be successful, 'the efficiencies have to benefit consumers, be merger-specific and be verifiable'.[119] All of these conditions must be met. As only the merging undertakings will have sufficient evidence to verify the efficiencies created by their merger the responsibility is on the parties to the merger to provide all the necessary information to the Commission. The other major defence discussed in the Guideline is the 'failing firm' defence.[120] To qualify for the merging, undertakings must show that one of the undertakings is a failing firm and that, therefore, the merger itself does not bring about any

---

112 Commission Notice, at paras 22–23 et seq.
113 Commission Notice, at paras 24–38.
114 See, for example, Luescher, C, 'Efficiency Considerations in European Merger Control – Just Another Battle Ground for the European Commission, Economists and Competition Lawyers?' [2004] ECLR 72.
115 Case IV/M477, Commission Decision 95/354/EC, [1995] OJ L211/1.
116 Case IV/M774, Commission Decision 97/610/EC, [1996] OJ L247/1.
117 See Camesasca, PD, 'The Explicit Efficiency Defence in Merger Control: Does it Make the Difference?' [1999] ECLR 14, and Halliday, J, 'The Recognition, Status and Form of the Efficiency Defence to a Merger' (1999) 22 World Comp 91.
118 Commission Notice, Guidelines on the assessment of horizontal mergers under the Council regulation on the control of concentrations between undertakings, [2004] OJ C31/3, para 76.
119 At para 78.
120 See, for example, Baccaro, V, 'Failing Firm Defence and Lack of Causality: Doctrine and Practice in Europe of Two Closely Related Concepts' [2004] ECLR 11.

anti-competitive effects. The logic in the defence is that the deterioration in the competitive structure of the market would have occurred even in the absence of the merger through the exit of the
failing firm. There are three criteria for the defence:

1   the allegedly failing firm would, in the near future, be forced out of the market;
2   there is no less anti-competitive alternative purchase than the merger; and
3   in the absence of a merger, the assets of the failing firm would inevitably exit the market.[121]

Other broader goals within the EU may also have an impact on merger control. Recital 19 of the
Regulation states that consideration should be given to the objectives set out in the EU Treaties.[122]
The Court of First Instance (CFI) was asked to rule on non-competition factors under Regulation
4064/89 in *Comité Central d'Entreprise de la Société Anonyme Vittel v Commission*.[123] The CFI
was of the opinion that the primary considerations should be competition-related, though in some
circumstances social goals could be taken into account where the concentration was likely to have
adverse effects on the objectives set out in Art 2 of the EC Treaty. The extent to which the Merger
Regulation can be used as a tool of EU industrial policy by the promotion of 'European champions'
is also of interest. As noted earlier, one of the considerations in introducing the Regulation was the
intention to ease the formation of European alliances which could go on to compete on the global
market. Nonetheless, the Commission prohibited a merger in *Aerospatiale/Alenia/de Havilland*,[124]
where the objective was to create such a 'European champion' in the aircraft manufacturing
industry. The role of EU industrial policy in merger control remains uncertain.[125]

Concentrations in oligopolistic markets

The substantive appraisal test in Regulation 4064/89 referred only to the 'creation or strengthening
of a dominant position' and made no direct reference to the control of 'collective' or 'joint' dominance in oligopolistic markets. As the definition of dominance under Art 102 TFEU was extended
to cover collective dominance the Commission also sought to extend the scope of Regulation
4064/89 to similar situations. In *Nestlé/Perrier*,[126] the Commission attached conditions to its clearance that certain parts of the business were to be sold to third parties to avoid the strengthening of
a collective dominant position. In *Kali and Salz/MdK/Treuhand*,[127] the Commission again cleared
a concentration on the basis of conditions attached to the Decision to avoid the creation of a duopo-
listic dominant position. The Commission was of the opinion that the concentration would create
a duopoly controlling 60% of the market for potash. As outside operators were fragmented, they
would provide little competition, and competition between the duopolists would probably be
limited because of the structure of the potash market and close economic links between the duopolists. The Decision was challenged before the Court in *France v Commission*[128] on the basis that
Regulation 4064/89 had no application to the creation or strengthening of collective dominance.
The Court rejected that argument, confirming that collective dominance did come within the terms
of the Regulation. Although the Court upheld the principle, it annulled the Commission Decision

121 At para 90.
122 It is interesting to note that Regulation 139/2004 removed the reference to Art 158 EC on economic and social cohesion in
     Regulation 4064/89, but replaced it with reference to, the then, Art 2 EU which had a somewhat broader ambit.
123 Case T-12/93 [1995] ECR II-1247.
124 Case IV/M53, Commission Decision 91/619/EEC, [1991] OJ L334/42.
125 See Banks, D, 'Non-competition Factors and Their Future Relevance under European Merger Law' [1997] 3 ECLR 182 and
     Galloway, J, 'The Pursuit of National Champions: The Intersection of Competition Law and Industrial Policy' [2007] ECLR
     172. See, also, Case IV/M315, Commission Decision 94/208/EC *Mannesmann/Valourec/Ilva*, [1994] OJ L102/15.
126 Case IV/M190, Commission Decision 92/553/EEC, [1992] OJ L356/1.
127 Case IV/M308, Commission Decision 94/449/EC, [1994] OJ L186/38.
128 Cases C-68/94 and C-30/95, [1998] ECR I-1375.

on the basis that the Decision had not established, to the necessary legal standard, that the concentration would give rise to a collective dominant position.

The most comprehensive examination of the handling of collective dominance under Regulation 4064/89 was seen in the litigation which followed the Commission Decision in *Airtours/First Choice*.[129] The Commission was of the view that a merger between Airtours and First Choice would result in a collective dominant position between the post-merger undertaking and the two remaining leading tour operators, Thomson and Thomas Cook, on the short haul package holiday market in the UK. The Commission therefore prohibited the merger. The Commission's Decision was eventually overturned on appeal but the CFI set out important guidance on the standard and type of proof that was required under Regulation 4064/89 to support a finding of the creation of or strengthening of a collective dominant position.[130] The quashing of the Commission's Decision was seen as being a serious setback and the evidential requirements set out by the CFI seemed to be a very difficult hurdle for the Commission to cross. The CFI made it clear that if the Commission wanted to support a finding of collective dominance it must be able to show that the post-merger undertaking and the other undertakings remaining on the market would be able to adopt a common policy without having to enter into an agreement or a concerted practice.[131] The CFI set out three conditions which must be met before a potentially dominant oligopoly would be shown to be possible. First, the dominant oligopoly must be transparent in order that each of the members is aware of the others' market conduct. Secondly, the co-ordination must be sustainable with the members of oligopoly able to deter others from departing from the common policy. Thirdly, the reactions of current and future competitors and customers should not be able to end the benefits of the common policy.

The new test, in *Airtours*, for a finding of collective dominance was, arguably, one of the reasons for the Commission's volte-face with regard to the substantive test in Regulation 139/2004.[132] Recitals 24–26 of the Regulation make it clear that to improve 'legal certainty' it was necessary to bring oligopolistic markets clearly within the Merger Regulation. The shift away from dominance, and therefore collective dominance, as the only test, towards the consideration of collective dominance as an aspect of what significantly impedes effective competition means that the dicta in *Airtours* will be less crucial, but still important, in such decisions. Recital 25 makes it clear that the new test extends:

> beyond the concept of dominance, only to the anti-competitive effects of a concentration resulting from the non-coordinated behaviour of undertakings which would not have a dominant position on the market concerned.

In the horizontal merger Guideline the Commission relies heavily on the judgment in *Airtours* but does seem to depart from it in some instances.[133] The section of the Guideline that examines the 'co-ordinated effects' of a merger sets out that it may be possible, post-merger, for undertakings to co-ordinate their behaviour, 'even without entering into an agreement or resorting to a concerted practice within the meaning of Article 81 [101 TFEU] of the Treaty'.[134] Paragraph 41 of the

---

129 Case IV/M1524, Commission Decision 2000/276/EC *Airtours/First Choice*, [2000] OJ L93/1.
130 Case T-342/99 *Airtours v Commission* [2002] ECR II-2585. See, also, Haupt, H, 'Collective Dominance under Article 82 EC and EC Merger Control in the Light of the *Airtours* Judgment' [2002] ECLR 434, and Stroux, S, 'Collective Dominance under the Merger Regulation: A Serious Evidentiary Reprimand for the Commission' (2002) 27 EL Rev 736.
131 At para 61.
132 The Commission strongly rejected the 'substantial lessening of competition' test in early reform discussions and the new substantive test was not introduced until after the final draft Regulation was published in December 2002.
133 See Black, O, 'Collusion and Co-ordination in EC Merger Control' [2003] ECLR 408.
134 Commission Notice, Guidelines on the assessment of horizontal mergers under the Council Regulation on the control of concentrations between undertakings, [2004] OJ C31/3, para 39.

Guideline, in effect, replicates the three conditions in *Airtours*. It would, therefore, appear that while the substantive test has been widened by Regulation 139/2004 the Commission still accepts the need to utilise the conditions in *Airtours*, even though the conditions are no longer the only issues which may be taken into account. Interestingly the Commission decided not to oppose the Sony/BMG merger after a Phase II investigation which resulted in four major record companies[135] holding 80% of the recording market.[136]

Vertical and conglomerate mergers

Three years after publishing its Guideline on Horizontal Mergers, the Commission began consultation on Guidelines setting out its approach to non-horizontal cases.[137] A vertical merger is a merger between a manufacturer of a product and a supplier, an upstream firm, or a customer, a downstream firm. In a conglomerate merger the relationship is neither vertical nor horizontal, but the firms supply products that can be described as complementary. The consultation and subsequent Notice must also be viewed in light of the criticism of the Commission's approach to such mergers by the Community courts in cases such as *Tetra Laval/Sidel* and *GE/Honeywell*.[138] As vertical and conglomerate mergers do not result in the direct elimination of a competitor, they are less likely to result in a significant impediment to effective competition. There are, however, some situations in which such a merger may allow the post-merger entity to damage future competition by using power in one market to foreclose competition in the related market.[139] It is this foreclosure question that the Guidelines seek to address.[140] The Guidelines first stress the generally benign nature of such mergers and that they may lead to enhanced efficiencies.[141] It also notes that a vertical or conglomerate merger may be able to 'change the ability and incentive to compete on the part of the merging companies and their competitors in ways that cause harm to consumers'.[142] Foreclosure is only likely to occur when the merged entity has significant market power, but not necessarily dominance. It is therefore unlikely that the Commission will find concern in mergers where the post-merger market share is below 30% and the post-merger HHI is below 2,000.[143]

In vertical mergers, two potential harms are foreseen: input and customer foreclosure. In input foreclosure the post-merger entity can make it more difficult for a downstream rival (who was merely a customer in the pre-merger situation) by supplying at less advantageous prices or conditions, allowing the post-merger entity to raise prices. In order to do this, the vertically integrated firm must have market power in the upstream market.[144] Customer foreclosure occurs when a supplier merges with a downstream customer holding market power. Such a merger may make it difficult for upstream rivals to find outlets for their output, effectively reducing competition in the upstream market.[145] The Guideline also indicates the Commission's concern that a

---

135 Universal, SonyBMG, Warner and EMI.

136 Case IV/M3333 (4064), [2004] OJ C13/15, Commission Press Release, IP/04/200 and IP/04/959; there were also concerns about Sony and BMG's vertically integrated structure.

137 Draft Commission Notice, Guidelines on the assessment of non-horizontal mergers under the Council Regulation on the control of concentrations between undertakings, 13 February 2007.

138 Case T-5/02 *Tetra Laval v Commission* [2002] ECR II-4381, Case C-12/03P *Commission v Tetra Laval* [2005] ECR I-987, and Case T-210/01 *GE v Commission* [2005] ECR II-5575. See Killick, J, 'The GE/Honeywell Judgment – in Reality Another Merger Defeat for the Commission' [2007] ECLR 52.

139 See Bishop, S, et al, 'Turning the Tables: Why Vertical and Conglomerate Mergers are Different' [2006] ECLR 403.

140 Commission Notice, Guidelines on the assessment of non-horizontal mergers under the Council Regulation on the control of concentrations between undertakings, November 2007. For a critique of the Guidelines see, Bishop, S, '(Fore)closing the Gap: The Commission's Draft Non-horizontal Merger Guidelines' [2008] ECLR 1, and Alese, F, '(Fore)closing the Gap: The Commission's Draft Non-horizontal Merger Guidelines – a "Response" to Simon Bishop' [2008] ECLR 196.

141 Ibid, paras 11–14.

142 Ibid, para 15.

143 Ibid, paras 23–27. The introduction of the HHI test is criticised by Simon Bishop as being more relevant in horizontal mergers, Bishop, above n 140.

144 Ibid, paras 31 et seq.

145 Ibid, paras 58 et seq.

vertical merger may make it more likely that co-ordinated effects, tacit collusion within an oligopolistic market, would be sustainable, as the market becomes easier to monitor, increasing the effectiveness of punishment mechanisms, or reducing the scope for external destabilisation by removing a 'maverick' firm.[146]

The main concern with conglomerate mergers is the ability of the post-merger entity to leverage market power from one market and foreclose another, largely through the tying and bundling of products. In 2012, the *Microsoft/Skype* deal was approved without conditions following the rejection of possible conglomerate concerns regarding commercial bundling.[147] Pure bundling occurs when the products are only sold jointly, in a fixed proportion, whereas mixed bundling occurs when the products are available separately but at a higher price than the bundled product. Tying occurs when the sale of the tying product is linked to the sale of the tied product. The tie can be 'technical', when the tying product only functions when used with the tied product,[148] or 'contractual', when the products are tied through a contractual agreement between the parties.

Joint ventures

The control of joint ventures, also known as strategic alliances, has presented challenges to EU competition law for many years. Joint ventures involve the setting up of a company by two or more parent companies. The main difficulty for merger control when dealing with joint ventures is that in practice the formation of the joint venture, and the roles undertaken by the various parties, can vary to such a great extent that a unified approach is difficult. Under the original form of the Merger Regulation, if two independent undertakings transferred their activities in one area to a joint venture and then withdrew permanently from that area the joint venture would be considered to be a concentration, a concentrative joint venture, falling within the Merger Regulation and its procedures. If, on the other hand, two independent undertakings set up a joint venture to control their sales, for instance, through a joint sales agency, this would have been seen as part of a strategy to operate a cartel and would have fallen under Art 101 TFEU as a co-operative joint venture. These are fairly polarised examples of what are termed concentrative and co-operative joint ventures, respectively. It was often difficult to decide whether a proposed joint venture would be concentrative or co-operative and, consequently, under which procedure it should be considered. In most circumstances, joint ventures are encouraged by the EU authorities on policy grounds. It is considered that European industry will enhance its competitiveness on the global market by the formation of alliances between companies which are able to pool their resources and respective specialisations. The Merger Regulation's speedy procedures allow such beneficial concentrative joint ventures to proceed with minimal disruption to the parties' competitive strategy. However, many businesses complained that co-operative joint ventures – those that fell under the Art 101TFEU procedure but were not anti-competitive – were disadvantaged because of the uncertainty and delays in the then Art 101(3) exemption procedure. Many advisers suggested that undertakings should structure their joint ventures so that the joint ventures fell within the definition of a concentrative joint venture and, as such, would be considered within the Merger Regulations time limits. In an attempt to deal with many of these criticisms the Commission sought to both clarify the distinction between concentrative and co-operative joint ventures and reduce the scope of co-operative joint ventures to situations where there was likely

---

146 Ibid, paras 79–90.
147 Case COMP/M.2681, 7 October 2011, see Commission Press Release IP/11/1164, 'Mergers: Commission approves acquisition of Skype by Microsoft', 7 October 2011.
148 An example would be a laser printer, which will only function when using the 'tied' proprietary toner cartridges.

to be co-operation between the parents. The distinction between concentrative and co-operative joint ventures still exists but the balance has shifted with many more joint ventures now being considered as concentrative.

Every 'full function' joint venture, that is, a 'joint venture performing on a lasting basis all the functions of an autonomous economic entity',[149] will be considered to be a concentrative or a structural joint venture to be dealt with under the Merger Regulation. A joint venture that is not full function will be considered under Art 101 TFEU. Before a joint venture is considered to be full function, it must have all the characteristics of an independent, self-contained, business unit. It must not be reliant on its parents for survival. It should, therefore, have its own human and material resources to allow it to carry on business, and not rely on others' staff or assets. The Commission has also considered the research and development capacity, ownership of intellectual property rights, and access to distribution networks as being relevant to the status of a joint venture.[150] Even if it has limited staff and financial resources, a joint venture may not be considered full function if those resources would not enable it to operate on a lasting basis.[151] In many cases the joint venture will continue to deal, in some capacity, with its parent companies. This will obviously bring into question the joint venture's status of independence on the market.[152] The Commission must be sure that the joint venture is not simply a disguised sales agency.[153] An example of the way in which the Commission determines the existence of a joint venture was in *Texaco/Norsk Hydro*.[154] The joint venture was established to distribute refined oil products to consumers in Denmark, Norway and Iceland. The parent oil companies withdrew from the market but would still be active in the upstream market, supplying products to the joint venture. Although the parent companies would have supplied the joint venture with up to 50% of its requirements in some areas the Commission ensured that the sales by the parent company would be at arm's length and the joint venture would be able to purchase substantial supplies from the parents' competitors. The Commission was, therefore, of the opinion that the joint venture was sufficiently independent to be concentrative. In *BT/AT&T*,[155] the parties gave various divesture undertakings to allay Commission fears over parental co-ordination.

There are still, however, concerns that full function concentrations may give rise to the threat of co-ordination of competitive behaviour between the parties forming the joint venture, or between them and the joint venture. This might be the case where both parents retained significant activities in the same market as the joint venture. The concern is primarily about the co-ordination of competition between the parents rather than co-ordination between one or both of the parents and the joint venture.[156]

These situations are considered in the same way as other concentrative joint ventures; however, where the Commission believes that the concentration has 'as its object or effect the co-ordination of the competitive behaviour of undertakings that remain independent', that co-ordination shall be appraised 'in accordance with the criteria of Article 81(1) and (3) [now Art 101 TFEU] of the Treaty, with a view to establishing whether or not the operation is

---

149 Regulation 139/2004, [2004] OJ L24/1, Art 3(4). See, also, relating to the position under Reg 4064/89, the Commission Notice on the concept of full function joint ventures, [1998] OJ C66/1. For criticism of the Commission's handling of the 'full function' test, see Radicati di Brozolo, LG and Gustafsson, M, 'Full-function Joint Ventures under the Merger Regulation: the Need for Clarification' [2003] ECLR 574.

150 See Case IV/M160 *Elf Atochem/Rohm and Haas* [1992] OJ C201/27.

151 See, for example, Case IV/M722 *Téneo/Merrill Lynch/Bankers Trust* [1996] OJ C159/4.

152 See Case IV/M3003 *Electrabel/Energia Italiana/Interpower* [2003] OJ C25/2.

153 See Commission Notice, [1998] OJ C66/1, para 14.

154 Case IV/M511, [1995] OJ C23/3.

155 Case IV/JV15, Commission Decision 30 March 1999; Commission Press Release, IP/99/209.

156 The guidance for the old system was found in the Commission Notice on the distinction between concentrative and co-operative joint ventures, [1994] OJ C385/1.

compatible with the common market'.[157] This means that the Commission will carry out its normal appraisal alongside an assessment based on Art 101. The dual appraisal must take place within the time limits set out in the Regulation. The Commission is required to take two factors into account:

1   whether two or more parent companies retain, to a significant extent, activities in the same market as the joint venture, or in a market which is downstream or upstream from that of the joint venture, or in a neighbouring market closely related to this market; and

2   whether the co-ordination which is the direct consequence of the creation of the joint venture affords the undertakings concerned the possibility of eliminating competition in respect of a substantial part of the products or services in question.

These two factors give the Commission an opportunity, within the merger system, to examine the potential for co-ordination following the creation of a joint venture, while giving the parties to a concentration the benefits of the time limits contained in the Regulation.

International mergers

The increasing globalisation of markets demands a response from the competition authorities, and given the spate of high-profile worldwide mergers which has taken place in recent years this is most evident in relation to merger control. The most dramatic solution would be to institute some form of global authority to deal with mergers which affect a range of markets and territories. The introduction of a global authority is unlikely to occur, at least in the foreseeable future, and any developments are likely to be procedural, such as ensuring similar filing requirements under different merger control systems. In the meantime the EU has entered a number of bilateral enforcement co-operation agreements, most notably with the US, as discussed in Chapter 2. It is clear that the co-operation practice under the agreement has focused on merger activity, as exemplified by the mergers involving *Boeing/McDonnell Douglas*[158] and *AOL/Time Warner*[159] which were dealt with under both EU and US competition law systems. Notwithstanding these examples of co-operation it is clear that disputes between the Commission and the US authorities will still arise. A clear example of such a conflict was seen in *GE/Honeywell*.[160] GE and Honeywell are both very large US-based companies with large EU turnovers; therefore, their proposed merger fell to be considered under both the US and EU merger regimes. The US authorities cleared the merger shortly after the Commission went into its Phase II investigation. The Commission eventually prohibited this high-profile 'US' merger when remedies could not be agreed, as the Commission was concerned with, *inter alia*, potential links between GE's aircraft engines, Honeywell's avionics, and GE's aircraft leasing businesses. More generally, the possibility for surveillance of international mergers is linked to the issue of extra-territoriality (discussed in Chapter 2) evidenced by the dispute regarding the Commission's intervention in the *Gencor/Lonrho*[161] merger, which involved two mining companies based in South Africa.[162]

---

157 Regulation 139/2004/EC, [2004] OJ L24/1, Art 2(4).
158 Case IV/M877, Commission Decision 97/816/EC, [1997] OJ L336/16.
159 Case IV/M1845, [2000] OJ C73/4; Commission Press Release, IP/00/1145.
160 Case IV/M2220, Commission Decision 2004/134/EC, [2004] OJ L48/1, and Case T-210/01 *GE v Commission* [2005] ECR II-5575. See, also, Burnside, A, 'GE, Honey, I Sunk the Merger' [2002] ECLR 107.
161 Case IV/M619, Commission Decision 97/26/EC, [1997] OJ L11/30.
162 See Fox, EM, 'The Merger Regulation and its Territorial Reach' [1999] ECLR 334.

Review of Commission Decision-making

In relation to any decisions taken by the Commission during the merger control process, there exists the possibility of an Article 263 TFEU action for annulment before the EU's General Court. That provision gives *locus standi* to any party for whom a decision has 'direct and individual concern'. This obviously includes parties subject to a prohibition decision, but more commonly will include parties who are dissatisfied with the remedies accepted to assuage the Commission, or third parties (often competitors) affected by a decision to allow a merger to proceed. The grounds for review are as discussed in Chapter 2, and in this context the most frequent argument is that that there has been a 'manifest' error of assessment giving rise to an infringement of a rule of law relating to application of the Treaties. Given that the merger control process inherently involves predictive and complex economic analysis, it is accepted that the Commission has a margin of discretion in undertaking its assessments. Case law has emphasised the high standard of proof ('convincing') required of the Commission in making its factual assessments.[163] Given the time-sensitive nature of corporate mergers, there is the possibility of requesting an expedited procedure at the General Court. There is also a further level of review on a point of law before the Court of Justice (CJEU).

Background to UK Merger Control

It was only in 1948, through the Monopolies and Restrictive Practices (Inquiry and Control) Act 1948, that any form of merger control was introduced into the UK. However, the procedures were sterile, because the authorities could not prevent a merger from taking place, nor was there the possibility of remedial action through divestiture. Partly due to the inadequacy of the procedures available under these provisions, and also partly due to the impact of the Restrictive Trade Practices Act 1956, the Monopolies and Mergers Act was introduced in 1965 in order to provide effective merger controls in the UK. The 1956 Act had led to a 'merger boom' as companies sought alternatives to collusive activities which were caught by the Act's provisions. The form of control instituted in 1965 was a benign investigative system, applicable to monopoly references since 1948, reflecting the predisposition on the part of the authorities to favour mergers taking place.[164] The merger control provisions were subsequently contained in Pt V of the Fair Trading Act 1973, which maintained the same basic format as under the previous legislation.[165] In 2001 the Department of Trade and Industry (DTI) proposed radical reform of UK competition law.[166] Subsequently the Enterprise Act 2002 was enacted and it replaced the main merger control provisions of the 1973 Act with new provisions for merger investigations, set out in Pt 3 of the 2002 Act. The institutional structure and other aspects of the merger control system under the 2002 Act were revised by the Enterprise and Regulatory Reform Act 2013.

Statutory Developments

Over the years there were a number of criticisms of the Fair Trading Act 1973 and its merger control system. The system of referral, based on the exclusive power of the Secretary of State to

---

163 See, for instance, Cases C-12 and 13/03 P *Commission of the European Communities v. Tetra Laval BV* [2005] ECR I-987 and 1113.
164 Exemplified by a speech by the then President of the Board of Trade, Anthony Crosland, at a launch of the British Association of the Chambers of Commerce on 25 June 1969.
165 The market share criterion for referral was reduced from a figure of 33% to 25%.
166 White Paper, *Productivity and Enterprise: A World Class Competition Regime*, Cm 5233, 31 July 2001.

refer mergers, was criticised as being political. The broad scope of the public interest test, under s 84, was also criticised together with the length of time taken by and the inconvenience of Commission public interest inquiries. There were a number of reports which considered possible reforms of the merger control provisions. The Competition Act 1998 contained no provisions directly relating to merger control, the traditional public interest investigation system being retained under the 1973 Act. However, the DTI issued a consultation document on proposals for reform, in August 1999,[167] and this was followed by the DTI's October 2000 document, *The Response to the Consultation on Proposals for Reform*, which endorsed the main proposals in the earlier document.[168] The 1999 document noted the key objectives of reform as being threefold:

1   to enhance clarity, transparency and consistency;
2   to be more responsive to the needs of business and impose only the minimum necessary burdens; and
3   to ensure effective and proportionate control of mergers with harmful effects.

The October 2000 document noted that response had been favourable on the two fundamental proposals in the 1999 consultation document: 'that Ministerial involvement in mergers decisions should be minimised and that the current public interest test should be replaced by a competition-based test.'[169]

In July 2001 the Government set out its legislative plans in its White Paper, Productivity and Enterprise: A World Class Competition Regime.[170] One of the key objectives of the White Paper was based on the populist support for 'politicians to be taken out of merger decisions'.[171] The Government favoured the retention of a system involving a fuller investigation of a merger by the Competition Commission (CC), and a clearer role for the Office of Fair Trading (OFT) to make an initial assessment of mergers and to refer mergers, in appropriate cases, to the CC. Following the barrage of criticism the public interest test received over the years, the key proposal in August 1999 was to replace the public interest test with a competition-based test with a view to increasing certainty and predictability. The October 2000 document confirmed a competition-based test as appropriate and proposed a test based on the 'substantial lessening of competition' (SLC). The experience of the Merger Regulation dominance test when dealing with problems of collective dominance suggested that this more flexible test was suitable. In addition, it was noted that the competition analysis would consider efficiency gains and consumer benefits. The 2001 White Paper confirmed the SLC test but added that mergers may be allowed where the merger brings overall benefits to UK consumers. It was recognised that there may be exceptional circumstances where the competition test will not be appropriate and where mergers should be determined on exceptional public interest grounds, which would be determined by the Secretary of State.[172] The 2000 document confirmed, uncontroversially, that criteria based on national security, covering defence interests and other public security concerns, would be introduced and defined in the legislation. In addition, the White Paper considered a number of ancillary issues, including the retention of the voluntary notification scheme and the important extension of the CC's powers to allow it to decide on remedies following a critical report. These were based largely on the drive

---

167 DTI, *Mergers: A Consultation Document on Proposals for Reform*, URN 99/1028, 6 August 1999.
168 DTI, *Mergers: The Response to the Consultation on Proposals for Reform*, URN 00/805, 26 October 2000. These proposals were subsequently confirmed in the Government's strategy document for the next Parliament; HM Treasury Document, 'Productivity in the UK: enterprise and the productivity challenge', June 2001 and *Productivity and Enterprise: A World Class Competition Regime*, Cm 5233, 31 July 2001.
169 Executive Summary, p 3.
170 Cm 5233, 31 July 2001.
171 DTI Press Release, P/99/690, 6 August 1999.
172 *Mergers: A Consultation Document on Proposals for Reform*, URN 99/1028, n 167, para 4.12.

for greater certainty and predictability in the law and the desire to take politics out of the merger control process.[173] The new approach reflected the shift to a pure competition objective, also identified with the introduction of the Competition Act 1998. These proposals were enacted by Pt 3 of the Enterprise Act 2002, and its key provisions will be outlined in this chapter. The Enterprise and Regulatory Reform Act 2013 maintained the same set of substantive rules for merger investigations, but introduced some revisions to the Enterprise Act provisions for merger investigations, notably in relation to the institutions involved. As discussed in Chapter 1, ERRA13 introduced the unitary competition authority in the UK, the CMA, which as of 1 April 2014 assumed the tasks undertaken by both the OFT and the Competition Commission. This was driven primarily by arguments based on resources and efficiency, on the basis of criticisms that the prior regime was too slow and involved duplication of tasks between the OFT and the CC, whereas the CMA could avoid duplication in evidence-gathering while maintaining separation between the two stages of decision-making. The tasks of the OFT and CC will be undertaken by the Markets and Mergers Directorate of the CMA Board and CMA panel groups respectively. The CMA has published a central Guidance document: Guidance on the CMA's jurisdiction and procedure,[174] and this has superseded the prior procedural guidelines published by the OFT and Competition Commission.[175] However, given the limited changes in substance, and to ensure a smooth transition to the new regime, the CMA has adopted the existing main substantive guidance documents by the OFT and CC in relation to merger investigations, notably the Merger Assessment[176] and Merger Remedies: Competition Commission Guidelines.[177] There has obviously been minimal practice to date under the new provisions, but we will look at merger investigation practice under the Enterprise Act 2002 provisions, albeit in a different institutional context, and also review practice under the 1973 Act to illustrate the types of issue that remain a concern under Pt 3 of the 2002 Act.

Miscellaneous issues

Under the Enterprise Act there are three types of 'public interest' mergers in which the Secretary of State has a continuing role. Section 58 of the Act specifies, as public interest consideration mergers, those involving:

1   national security (including public security);
2   plurality and other considerations relating to newspaper and other media mergers; and
3   the stability of the UK financial system.

A brief appraisal of each of these will be provided, as there is a complex set of mechanisms in the legislation, following intervention by the Secretary of State in those mergers with a Public Interest Intervention Notice (PINN). Despite the proclaimed depoliticisation of merger control heralded by the 2002 Act, the first category of public interest mergers are self-explanatory in terms of the justification for continued government involvement.

Regarding the second category, it should be noted that the Fair Trading Act 1973 contained a distinctive set of provisions for newspaper mergers, which ensured that mergers qualifying as 'newspaper mergers' could only be effected with the approval of the Secretary of State. In the past the Commission has, for instance, been asked to take into account, in its public interest

173 For a fuller critique, see Rodger, BJ, 'UK Merger Control: Politics, the Public Interest and Reform' [2000] ECLR 24.
174 CMA2. See also CMA18, 'A Quick Guide to UK Merger Assessment', March 2014.
175 OFT 517 and CC18.
176 OFT1524/CC2, save for Appendix A which is replaced by the guidance in CMA2.
177 CC8, save for Appendix A which is replaced by the guidance in CMA2.

assessment, the need for accurate presentation of news and the free expression of opinion.[178] Chapter 2 of the Communications Act 2003 repealed the 1973 Act newspaper merger regime and adapted the main merger regime introduced in the 2002 Act to apply to media mergers generally, including newspaper mergers. The provisions in ss 375–388 of the 2003 Act include media mergers within the special public interest category in which the Secretary of State still has a key role, and these provisions place emphasis on the need for a plurality of media within the UK, 'the media public interest considerations' as specified in s 582A of the 2002 Act. An example of the application of these provisions is the inquiry, during 2007, into the acquisition of a 17.9% shareholding by BSkyB in ITV, referred by the Secretary of State. The Commission concluded that the acquisition would not be expected to affect adversely the plurality of media public interest consideration. Nonetheless, the Commission's finding was that the acquisition would result in a substantial lessening of competition, with a consequent reduction in quality and innovation and increase in prices, due to the loss of rivalry in the all-TV market.[179] The Secretary of State subsequently ordered BSkyB to reduce its stake in ITV to below 7.5%.[180]

Following the financial crisis of 2008, and in the midst of the proposed takeover of HBOS by LloydsTSB, a further public interest consideration was added, in s 58(2D) of the Enterprise Act 2002, namely the interest of maintaining the stability of the UK financial system. Consequently, despite the test for a merger reference being satisfied on the basis of a SLC in relation to certain banking services, notably personal current accounts, the Secretary of State decided that a reference was not necessary taking into account the public interest, and the merger was thereby effectively cleared. An application for judicial review, discussed below, was subsequently unsuccessful.

It should also be noted that, for reasons of space, the particular issues involved in the regulation of utilities will not be dealt with in any detail in this book, although, for instance, by virtue of Sch 4ZA to the Water Industry Act 1991, the Enterprise Act provisions apply to mergers involving water and sewerage undertakings, subject to certain modifications.

Agreements are excluded, under Sch 1 to the 2002 Act, from the Competition Act 1998 Chapter I prohibition to the extent that the agreements result in any two enterprises ceasing to be distinct enterprises within the terms of Pt 3 of the 2002 Act.[181] Thus, where a merger falls within the jurisdiction of the 2002 Act merger system it will not usually be subject to dual control of both the 2002 Act and the 1998 Act. Any ancillary restriction that facilitates a merger is also excluded from the 2002 Act where the restriction is 'directly related and necessary to the implementation of the merger'.[182]

Before assessing the merger controls in further detail, one should also be aware of the necessity to differentiate between competition-based merger control provisions and the protection of investors. The latter is a matter of company law and the additional protection afforded by the City Code on Takeovers and Mergers if a quoted company is involved.

---

178 See MMC Press Release 183; *Newsquest Media Group Ltd/Westminster Press* [1996] 7 ECLR R-183. In *Daily Mail/General Trust and Bailey Forman Ltd*, Cm 2693, 1994, the MMC advised that some benefit would accrue to readers as a result of the takeover but this would be outweighed by the adverse consequences which would arise from the significant increase in the concentration of local newspapers in the region, including reduced choice for advertisers. The Secretary of State advised that unless satisfactory undertakings were negotiated consent would be refused: (1994) DTI Press Notice, 31 October; [1995] ECLR R-26.

179 Competition Commission, *Acquisition By British Sky Broadcasting Group plc of 17.9 per cent of the shares in ITV plc*, Report sent to Secretary of State (BERR), 14 December 2007.

180 See BERR Press Release, 'Final decision on BSkyB's stake in ITV', 29 January 2008. See also subsequent unsuccessful judicial review application in *BskyB v Competition Commission and Secretary of State for BERR* [2008] CAT 25. At the Court of Appeal, the appeal on the competition points was dismissed, and although the appeal on the media plurality issue was allowed, this did not affect the outcome – [2010] EWCA Civ 2.

181 Para 1(1) of Sch 1.

182 Competition Act 1998, Sch 1, para 1(2).

Part 3 of the Enterprise Act 2002

UK merger control is undertaken by the CMA. There are now two main stages involved under the merger control provisions of the 2002 Act. Those stages will be considered in this section as follows:

1   Phase 1 and merger references;
2   Phase 2 – investigation and report, including remedial action.

The 1973 Act allocated the Secretary of State the formal statutory role in relation to references and subsequent enforcement. The DGFT's duty, through the OFT, was merely to advise and support the Secretary of State in those tasks.[183] The CC was exclusively involved in reporting on the public interest implications arising out of merger situations.

Under the 2002 Act, following the replacement of the OFT and the Competition Commission, the CMA Mergers Unit case team will initially make a Phase 1 assessment as to whether the competition issues in a merger are serious enough to merit a merger investigation reference for a Phase II investigation. If this is the case, the merger will be referred to a CMA panel inquiry group, an independent group of experts selected from a panel appointed by the Secretary of State, which will undertake the in-depth Phase II investigation and compile a report. The CMA inquiry group has a duty to take action to remedy any adverse effects on competition which it identified in its report. An important change from the pre-2002 practice is the enhanced role of the CMA inquiry group. It will decide how best to devise and implement remedies, effectively merging the second and third stages of the previous process. The CMA Board has the key role in referring mergers for further investigation as the Secretary of State's role has been removed subject to possible involvement in public interest cases. Public interest cases are set out in Chapters II and III of Pt 3 of the Act and are restricted to matters involving national security, newspaper and other media mergers, and mergers impacting on the stability of the UK financial system. As noted above, for reasons of space, this complicated set of provisions will not be considered in detail in this chapter. Overall, despite considerable change in the statutory language used, the basic purpose of merger investigations under the 2002 Act remains broadly similar, in most cases, to the purpose under the 1973 Act. Despite the developing practice under the 2002 Act, many references in the following sections will be to reports completed under the earlier statute by the Monopolies and Mergers Commission (MMC) (pre-1 April 1999) and CC. Nonetheless, there are certain important differences. The first is the specific provision, in s 120 of the 2002 Act, for review of decisions taken under Pt 3 of the Act; a number of important review cases will be considered later in the chapter. The second is the confirmation, by both the Competition Appeal Tribunal (CAT) and the Court of Appeal in *IBA Health Ltd v OFT*,[184] that the duty to refer under Pt 3 of the 2002 Act and the role afforded the CMA thereunder differs considerably from the discretionary 1973 Act scheme. Finally, the repeal of the public interest test removed the possibility for certain mergers potentially raising non-competition concerns, such as significant employment loss or regional policy, to be considered under the UK merger control process. In any event, the application of the Tebbit doctrine, by successive Secretaries of State, effectively precluded the referral of such mergers under the 1973 Act.

Phase 1 and merger references

This is the initial assessment stage at which it will be decided whether to escalate the investigation of the merger to a full Phase II inquiry by making a merger reference to a CMA inquiry

---

183   Section 76 of the Fair Trading Act 1973.
184   [2003] CAT 28; on appeal *OFT v IBA Health Ltd* [2004] EWCA Civ 142.

group. The CMA is under a duty to refer mergers which satisfy the statutory threshold. It should be noted that there are almost identical provisions in ss 22 and 33 regarding, respectively, the duty to refer completed and anticipated mergers. The CMA's activities under merger control are co-ordinated by the Mergers Unit, which is part of the Markets and Mergers Directorate. The CMA is normally required to make a decision within forty days of either a Merger Notice notification by parties or confirmation by the CMA that it has sufficient information to enable it to begin its investigation.[185] Decisions as to which mergers are to be referred involve a number of separate sub-stages where the following questions are to be addressed:

a   Does EU competition law preclude the exercise of UK merger control?
b   Is a 'relevant merger situation' established?
c   Is the SLC test satisfied?
d   Can and should undertakings be sought in lieu of a reference?
e   Is notification possible?

The CMA is under statutory duties to notify and publish all of its phase I decisions.[186]

EU merger control

As noted earlier in relation to EU merger control, the Merger Regulation, Regulation 139/2004, provides a set of merger controls at the EU level. The central idea is that mergers with a Community dimension are investigated only by the Commission. Article 21(1) provides that only the Commission is to deal with Community dimension mergers, and this is reaffirmed by Art 21(3), which states that no national legislation may be applied to such mergers. Accordingly, the first stage for the CMA is to assess whether the particular merger situation qualifies as a Community dimension merger and should, therefore, be considered solely under the Merger Regulation. This assessment involves consideration of the thresholds under Art 1 of the Merger Regulation, which were discussed in the EU merger control section of this chapter. There are certain limited exceptions to the exclusive competence of the Commission, under Arts 4, 9 and 21(4) of the Regulation and Art 346 TFEU. For instance, in relation to the anticipated *Boots/Unichem* merger,[187] the proposed merger was referred to the OFT by the Commission following a request from the parties under Art 4(4) of the Merger Regulation, in which case, the OFT was required, within forty-five working days of the Commission Decision, to decide whether to make a reference to the Competition Commission.

Establishing the creation of a 'relevant merger situation'

The provisions for determining which mergers may qualify for investigation, primarily in s 23 of the Enterprise Act requires two or more enterprises to have ceased to be distinct enterprises. In addition, the merger must satisfy one of two alternative tests, either that:

a   the value of the turnover in the UK of the enterprise being taken over exceeds £70m; or
b   the 25% market share supply test is satisfied.

Ceased to be distinct enterprises

Section 129(1) of the Enterprise Act defines a merger situation as arising where two or more enterprises, of which at least one was carried on in the UK, or carried on by or under a body

---

185   See further discussion below. Note that as a result of the 2013 reforms, a fee is now payable to the CMA by merging businesses whether the merger is notified or reviewed by the CMA on its own initiative.
186   See s 34ZA(1)(b) and s 107 of the 2002 Act.
187   See *Celesio v OFT* [2006] CAT 9.

corporate incorporated in the UK, have ceased to be distinct enterprises. An enterprise is defined by s 129(1) of the Act as comprising the activities, or part of the activities, of a business. Accordingly, UK merger control under the Enterprise Act, as previously under the Fair Trading Act, applies to mergers and takeovers of companies, but it can equally apply to the purchase of particular assets that form a business, for example, where a bus company acquired a depot and some buses from a rival company.[188] The crucial issue under this provision is identifying when the enterprises have ceased to be distinct.

Section 26(1) is similar to the equivalent provision under the 1973 Act and provides that enterprises cease to be distinct when they are brought under common ownership or control. However, full mergers are relatively rare. The most common practice is for the acquisition of some extent of control in another enterprise, normally via the acquisition of shares. The Act envisages, under s 25(2)–(4), three possibilities in the consideration of whether or not common ownership or control has been brought about, namely where the same person has:

a   actual control of the enterprise;

b   the ability, directly or indirectly, to control policy; or

c   the ability, directly or indirectly, to materially influence policy.

The first possibility is the most straightforward, and would cover a situation where a parent company acquired a 100% stockholding in a subsidiary company, or any other shareholding, which conferred a majority in voting terms. However, the legislation acknowledges that control may be achieved even where the majority of shares and voting rights are not acquired, particularly in cases where the remaining shareholding is dispersed widely. The relationship with other institutional investors may also be important. In one example, under the equivalent provisions of the Fair Trading Act, a 29% shareholding was considered sufficient for control and a 20% holding gave a position from which the company could materially influence policy.[189] In the *BSkyB/ITV* inquiry the CC considered that the acquisition of 17.9% of the shares in ITV was sufficient for BSkyB to materially influence policy, partly by allowing it effectively to block special resolutions proposed by ITV's management.[190] Shareholdings of over 15% will often be considered to allow for 'material influence', although whether the material influence threshold is satisfied is dependent on a range of other circumstances, notably the spread of shares, the voting rights attached to particular shareholdings and the board representation. The difference in approach between EU and UK merger control has been exemplified by the *Ryanair/Aer Lingus* saga, whereby the proposed full takeover was considered and blocked by the European Commission, and thereafter the minority shareholding by Ryanair in Aer Lingus (which did not fall within the scope of the EU Merger Regulation) was required to be reduced following a UK merger control inquiry. A merger situation may also arise where the acquisition of a further interest triggers a change in the level of control of the other enterprise. For example, in *Amalgamated Industries/Herbert Morris*,[191] a merger reference was not made at the stage when the ability to materially influence policy was acquired, but rather was made later when the ability to influence policy was extended to allow actual control. The thresholds for establishing a merger situation are not easily identifiable on an objective basis, and it is difficult to ascertain exactly when any threshold has been triggered. Accordingly, if a transfer of common ownership or control takes place by a series of

---

188 *Stagecoach Holdings plc/Lancaster City Transport Ltd*, Cm 2423, 1993. The MMC considered that, in effect, the business had been acquired as the purchaser could provide all the services previously offered by the vendor. For a more recent consideration of the issue, see *Groupe Eurotunnel SA v Competition Commission*, [2013] CAT 30.

189 *Eurocanadian Shipholdings/Furness Withy/Manchester Liners* (1975–76) HCP 639.

190 Competition Commission, *Acquisition By British Sky Broadcasting Group plc of 17.9 per cent of the shares in ITV plc*, Report sent to Secretary of State (BERR), 14 December 2007.

191 (1975/76) HCP 434.

share transactions over a period of time, there may be uncertainty as to when a merger situation is established, as the thresholds are only triggered when there is a change in the level of control from one threshold to another. In order to clarify this problem and prevent any attempted avoidance of the merger control provisions, s 29 of the Act provides that, where a series of transactions over a two-year period has the aggregate effect of bringing two or more enterprises under common ownership or control, that series of transactions may be treated, for the purposes of referral under the Act's provisions, as having occurred simultaneously on the date on which the latest transaction occurred.

Value of turnover test

The Enterprise Act replaced an assets value test with a test which states that the turnover in the UK of the enterprise being taken over must exceed £70m in value before the takeover qualifies for referral. The primary reason for the change was that many 'new economy' businesses would not qualify for investigation under an assets value test. Also, turnover is generally considered to be a better indicator of the real size of an undertaking. There are developing concerns that turnover thresholds may still fail to capture some important technology mergers where one of more undertakings involved may have limited turnover, but very high market valuations.

Market share test

This alternative test, set out in s 23(3) and (4) of the 2002 Act, will be satisfied where, as a result of the merger in question, at least 25% of the goods or services of any description are supplied by, or to, the same person in the UK or in a substantial part of the UK. The test can be easily satisfied due to the use of the fairly flexible criterion of goods or services of any description and the possible resort to a wide range of criteria, including value, quantity, and/or number of workers employed. The test will also be satisfied where one enterprise already supplies or consumes 25% of goods or services of the description, and this figure is increased as a result of the merger.[192] Case law has considered the extent to which the market share test is satisfied in a substantial part of the UK. In the *South Yorkshire Transport* case,[193] under the equivalent provision in the Fair Trading Act, the House of Lords (now the Supreme Court) considered that, although the term 'substantial part' could not be defined by arithmetical criteria based on area of coverage or population, 'the reference area must be of such size, character and importance as to make it worth consideration for the purposes of the Act'.[194] In *Stagecoach Holdings plc v Secretary of State for Trade and Industry*,[195] the market share test was applied and satisfied where the Commission had considered a designated area which represented 1.4% of the UK population and 1.8% of the UK geographical area. In *Lloyds Pharmacy/Pharmacy Care Centres*,[196] this test was considered to be satisfied in relation to five primary care trusts, which represented around 2% of the total UK population.

Is the substantial lessening of competition (SLC) test satisfied?

The new competition-based test was one of the most important UK merger control innovations introduced under the 2002 Act. The Act sets out a duty to refer merger situations, but only where 'the creation of that situation has resulted, or may be expected to result, in a SLC within any market or markets in the United Kingdom for goods or services'.[197] The Act introduced a

---

192 As a result of the provision in s 23(2)(5) that the conditions in subss (3) and (4) prevail 'to a greater extent'.
193 *R v Monopolies and Mergers Commission ex p South Yorkshire Transport Ltd* [1993] 1 All ER 289. See, also, *South Yorkshire Transport Ltd Acquisitions*, Cm 1166, 1990.
194 *R v Monopolies and Mergers Commission* [1993] 1 All ER 289, 296.
195 1997 SLT 940 (OH).
196 OFT Decision, 18 January 2007.
197 Section 22(1). Section 33(1), in relation to anticipated mergers, is in almost identical terms.

substantial lessening of competition ('SLC') test, and this determines whether a reference is to be made by the CMA, and the test will also determine the outcome of the CMA group inquiry. To understand the fundamental reform of the UK merger control process by the introduction of a competition test for referral purposes and the imposition of a duty, we will first consider in outline the merger referral process under the 1973 Act.

Policy on referrals under the 1973 Act

Under the 1973 Act, where a merger situation existed there were no further formal tests to determine which mergers could be referred. Only the Secretary of State could make a merger reference to the CC, and, given the small number of qualifying mergers that were referred, inevitably government trade and industry policy was reflected in the choice of mergers referred for further consideration. The exclusive merger referral power of the Secretary of State reflected the political nature of the UK merger control system. Furthermore, there was nothing in the Act that required references to be made in accordance with the public interest test in s 84. The key policy development in UK merger control, under the 1973 Act, was known as the Tebbit doctrine. In July 1984, the then Secretary of State for Trade and Industry, Norman Tebbit, stated that his 'policy has been, and will continue to be to make references primarily on competition grounds'.[198] As merger policy was, to a great extent, made at the referral stage, the Tebbit doctrine ensured that other public interest issues in s 84, such as consideration of regional policy and employment issues, would have no practical impact on UK merger control. The practical limitations of the public interest test were exemplified by the decision not to refer the final takeover bid by Guinness for United Distillers in 1982, despite concerns over the likely effect of the takeover on the Scottish economy.[199] The continued application of the Tebbit doctrine at the referral stage was confirmed by subsequent Secretaries of State. Nonetheless, in addition to the focus on competition concerns, other relevant policy factors were discernible at the referral stage in the past. These policy factors demonstrated the breadth of possible public interest issues and the diversity of approach adopted in different periods. For instance, employment and regional policy issues were often considered to be important prior to the introduction of the Tebbit doctrine.[200] On the other hand, Michael Heseltine stressed the international competitiveness of UK companies, and, in 1995, in order to encourage higher sales of UK board games abroad, he refused to make a merger reference of Hasbro UK Ltd's takeover of Waddington Games.[201]

Substantial lessening of competition (SLC)

A duty to refer under s 22 of the 2002 Act arises where the creation of the merger situation:

> has resulted, or may be expected to result, in a substantial lessening of competition within any market or markets within the United Kingdom for goods and services.

In determining whether this test is satisfied, the CMA will undertake a market definition analysis which is required to provide a proper understanding of the competitive constraints faced by the merged undertaking. The SLC test focuses on the extent to which competitive rivalry is likely to be diminished as a result of a merger, and to the detriment of consumers by increasing prices or

---

198 DTI Press Notice, 5 July 1984. A policy also confirmed subsequently in the Government's Blue Paper on *Mergers Policy*, 1988.
199 See Rodger, BJ, 'Reinforcing the Scottish "Ring-fence": A Critique of UK Mergers Policy vis à vis the Scottish Economy' [1996] ECLR 104.
200 Ibid.
201 In this context the approval by the Secretary of State of the Post Office's acquisition of German Parcel in January 1999 is notable as representing a major step towards becoming a global communications organisation. See DTI Press Release, P/99/018, 11 January 1999.

reducing customer choice. The CMA is required to undertake a comparative exercise on the extent of competitive rivalry pre- and post-merger. This exercise may be required in the context of the three types of merger identified at the start of this chapter: horizontal, vertical and conglomerate mergers. Competition concerns are most likely, but not necessarily, to arise as a result of horizontal mergers due to the loss of a rival or the greater likelihood of co-ordination between remaining market rivals. Vertical mergers may be problematic where either party has market power, and conglomerate mergers may reduce competition by, for instance, the exercise of portfolio power, as considered by the European Commission in *GE/Honeywell*.[202] Generally, when ascertaining the likelihood of the SLC, the CMA will be guided by a range of possible indicators, including market shares, concentration ratios measuring the aggregate share of a small number of leading market firms, and the use of HHIs as favoured in America. The CMA will consider the likelihood of either non co-ordinated, or unilateral, anti-competitive effects arising directly from the merger or the possibility of co-ordinated effects; it will apply the test set out in *Airtours*[203] to determine whether tacit co-ordination in oligopolistic markets is feasible and/or likely. A number of other factors may also be relevant in the CMA's competition assessment, including entry and expansion by new or existing competitors, countervailing buyer power, efficiencies which are likely to increase rivalry and the possibility of a failing firm defence.[204] As an example, the proposed acquisition by FirstGroup plc of the ScotRail franchise was referred on the basis that the acquisition might be expected to result in a SLC in the supply of passenger transport services and thereby reduce consumer choice.[205]

The duty to refer

The CMA is under a duty to refer any merger which satisfies the SLC test for a Phase II inquiry. The mechanics of the referral process were considered by both the CAT and the Court of Appeal in review proceedings following the Decision by the OFT not to refer a proposed merger between Isoft plc and Torex plc, direct competitors in the supply of software applications to hospitals. A rival company, IBA Health Company Ltd, sought, under s 120 of the Act, review of that OFT Decision before the CAT,[206] which was required to construe the requirements placed upon the OFT.[207] The CAT considered, first, that the OFT faced a real question as to whether the merger might be expected to lead to a SLC. In that context, the CAT sought to construe the words of the statutory provision, which requires a reference when the OFT believes 'that it is or may be the case' that the competition test would be satisfied. The CAT concluded that these words implied a two-part test, requiring not only the OFT's belief that there was no significant prospect of a SLC, but also no significant prospect of an alternative view being taken, given the OFT's role merely as 'a first screen', after a fuller investigation by the CC. The statutory framework reinforced the view that complex cases raising real issues as to SLC should be referred. The CAT subsequently granted leave to appeal as the case raised 'legal and constitutional issues as to the respective roles of the OFT, the Competition Commission and the Tribunal under the legislation'.[208] There were concerns, following the CAT judgment, that the merger control provisions

---

202 Case IV/M2220, Commission Decision 2004/134/EC *GE/Honeywell*, [2004] OJ L48/1, and Case T-210/01 *GE v Commission* [2005] ECR II-5575.

203 Case T-342/99 *Airtours v Commission* [2002] ECR II-2585; [2002] 5 CMLR 7. See, for instance, the reference by the OFT in *Weinerberger Finance Service/Baggeridge Brick*, 11 December 2006, although the Commission report concluded that the transaction would not give rise to co-ordinated effects.

204 The failing firm defence was rejected by the OFT in *Flybe Group/BA Connect*, OFT Decision of 7 February 2007. See OFT Press Release 16/07.

205 See OFT Press Release, 13 January 2004.

206 *IBA Health Ltd v OFT* [2003] CAT 28.

207 It should be noted that the dispute concerned a proposed merger and the construction of s 33 of the Act in relation thereto, although the same issues arise, under s 22 of the Act, in relation to completed mergers.

208 [2003] CAT 28, at para 6.

would become a complainant's charter and that the OFT would be required to refer considerably more mergers than in the past, increasing the workload of both of the competition authorities and delaying more merger transactions to the detriment of the business community. However, the Court of Appeal did not follow the CAT's interpretation of the relevant provision, s 33, which involved a two-stage test, and considered that the use of the words 'may be the case' clearly excluded the 'purely fanciful'. Between the purely fanciful and a degree of likelihood 'less than 50%' of a significant lessening of competition, the OFT would have a wide margin in which to exercise its judgment as to whether a reference was necessary.[209] Nonetheless, on the facts, the appeal failed as the OFT had failed to adequately explain or justify its conclusion in accordance with the test. The Merger Assessment Guidance, 'Mergers – substantive assessment',[210] was subsequently revised to reflect the substance of the Court of Appeal's judgment. Instead of a 'significant prospect' of a merger resulting in a SLC, the revised guidance requires a 'realistic prospect' of SLC, identified as 'not only a prospect that has more than a 50 per cent chance of occurring, but also a prospect that is not fanciful but has less than a 50 per cent chance of occurring'. While the statutory provisions remain the same, the underlying potential tensions between two distinctive competition authorities in the merger control process have been limited by the ERRA 2013, albeit that the two phases of merger control will be undertaken by separate parts of the CMA.

A considerable body of decisional practice involving unconditional clearance decisions has developed under the 2002 Act, even in mergers involving high market shares.[211] An excellent example was the proposed acquisition of Umbro plc by Nike Inc, which was cleared. There were overlaps in relation to sports footwear and equipment where the parties' shares were low, and although their combined market shares in replica kits were over 45%, bidding data demonstrated that they had not been competing bidders, and the considerable strength of football clubs in negotiating deals, lead to the conclusion that there were no competition concerns regarding tacit or explicit collusion between rivals post-merger.[212]

Exceptions to the duty to refer

There are three exceptions to the duty to refer a merger where the referral criteria appear to be satisfied. The first is where the merger, either in progress or in contemplation, is insufficiently advanced to warrant a reference, for instance, where parties have sought informal advice at an early stage from the CMA. The second is a *de minimis* provision, introduced by s 22(2)(a) of the Act, where the market in question is of insufficient importance to warrant fuller investigation. The *de minimis* exception applies to markets where the aggregate turnover of the parties is £10 million or less – for instance, two rail franchise mergers were cleared where the overlap markets between the bus company acquirer and the franchise were under £1 million and just over £1 million, respectively.[213] Finally, the CMA may decide not to make a reference where any 'relevant customer benefits' outweigh the adverse competitive consequences of the merger.[214] Relevant customer benefits are defined by s 30 as benefits in the form of, *inter alia*, lower prices, higher quality or greater choice of goods or services and greater innovation. These benefits must be

209 *IBA Health Ltd v OFT* [2004] EWCA Civ 142, V-C at para 48. See, also, *Celesio v OFT* [2006] CAT 9, discussed further below.
210 OFT 1254.
211 As discussed in greater detail by Went, D, 'Recent Developments in UK Merger Control – Establishment of Solid Foundations for the New Regime' [2007] ECLR 627, 634–637.
212 OFT Press Release 8/08, 16 January 2008.
213 OFT Press Release 180/07, 20 December 2007, re awards of the Intercity East Coast Rail Franchise (ICEC) to National Express Group and the Cross Country Rail Franchise to Arriva plc. See, also, OFT Press Release 16/08, 4 February 2008 regarding the non-referral of the award of the East Midland Rail franchise to Stagecoach plc.
214 Section 22(2)(a). There is an identical provision in relation to anticipated mergers in s 33(2)(c).

quantifiable and have accrued or be likely to accrue within a 'reasonable period' of the merger and be unlikely to have arisen without the merger. This is a difficult balancing exercise for the CMA. Although efficiencies may be relevant at this stage, customers need to be better off as a result of the merger to satisfy this test, and, ordinarily, lower prices, higher quality and choice are more likely to result from a more competitive market.

Making a merger reference

In the vast majority of cases, where no serious competition issues are raised, the CMA Mergers Unit will decide to clear the merger, the case team will prepare a clearance decision which will be adopted by the CMA, then related to parties or their advisers and announced publicly.[215] In cases raising more complex issues or more serious competition issues, a more formal process will be undertaken. A 'state of play' discussion with parties will be followed by the distribution of an 'issues' letter to the parties and an issues meeting with officials, prior to a final published decision. A reference will often lead to the abandonment of an acquisition or merger due to the time-consuming and costly inquiry that follows. In that event the inquiry will be cancelled.[216] Accordingly, parties may seek to avoid a lengthy inquiry by meeting the CMA's competition concerns by offering what are known as 'undertakings in lieu of a reference'.

Undertakings in lieu of reference ('UILs')

Section 73 of the Enterprise Act provides for undertakings in lieu where the CMA considers that it is under a duty to refer a merger. Accordingly, a merger reference can be avoided if the CMA's concerns about the merger, or proposed merger, can be alleviated in some way by the parties offering appropriate undertakings. 'Undertakings' is the technical term for legally binding commitments, offered by parties involved in the merger, to modify their behaviour and/or the structure of the combined enterprises in the future in order to meet the competition concerns identified by the CMA. The possibility of giving 'structural undertakings' was first provided for by the Companies Act 1989, which added ss 75G–75K to the Fair Trading Act 1973.[217] However, the undertakings in lieu of a reference introduced by the Companies Act 1989 were limited to undertakings relating to the sale or divestiture of assets or the splitting up of the merged enterprises. The power to accept undertakings was subsequently extended to provide for undertakings in lieu of a reference on any issue.[218] Structural and behavioural undertakings can be accepted in lieu of a reference under the 2002 Act. For example, in relation to the takeover by Stagecoach Holdings plc of Cambus Holdings Ltd in 1996, undertakings were accepted which provided for the divestment of two other companies and a depot in Huntingdon, in addition to a number of behavioural undertakings regarding fares, service levels, tenders, responses to competition and the provision of information.[219] Examples of undertakings in lieu include: divestment undertakings by William Hill plc following the acquisition of the licensed betting office business of Stanley plc, where there was concern about the significant lessening of competition in around 80 local areas, which would have led to a reduced choice for punters,[220] and undertakings to

---

215 The text of the decision will be published at www.gov.uk/cma.
216 See, for example, Competition Commission Press Release 70/05, 4 November 2005, notifying the cancellation of an inquiry into the proposed acquisition by Robert Wiseman Dairies of the fresh milk business of Scottish Milk Dairies, where the acquisition had been abandoned following the OFT referral.
217 For example, the first case in which an undertaking was accepted was in 1990 and concerned the commitment by the Rank Organisation to dispose of ten of Mecca's bingo clubs in Greater London in order to alleviate concerns over the effects on competition of the proposed merger: DTI Press Release, P/90/576.
218 Section 39, Sch 11, para 2 of the Deregulation and Contracting Out Act 1994.
219 DTI Press Release, P/96/408. See, also, the undertakings received from Scottish and Newcastle plc in relation to its acquisition of the pubs, restaurants and lodges business of Greenalls plc; DTI Press Release, P/99/1054, 22 December 1999.
220 See OFT Press Release 144/05, 2 August 2005.

license IP rights to an upfront buyer by the Tetra Laval group, to protect the cheddar cheese-making equipment sector from reduced competition, innovation, and service levels, and increased prices, in order to avoid a reference of a proposed acquisition.[221] It has become clear that the preferred approach in determining appropriate remedies is to seek structural rather than behavioural remedies.

Section 73 of the 2002 Act permits the CMA to have regard to any relevant customer benefits when deciding whether particular undertakings in lieu are appropriate. Where undertakings in lieu are considered to be a suitable remedy, the OFT will normally make a public announcement and consult on the proposed undertakings in order to give interested third parties an opportunity to comment. The normal statutory timetable for making a reference may be extended to allow time for the negotiation process. Section 73 is supported by s 75, which provides the CMA with the power to make appropriate orders where undertakings in lieu have not been fulfilled. Any decisions by the CMA in this context are subject to review.

Informing the CMA

The provisions of the Enterprise Act allow for references after a qualifying merger has taken place. In the case of a proposed merger,[222] there is no system of compulsory notification under the Act. However, parties are encouraged to contact the CMA in order to discuss and assess the likely application of the Act to their merger situation. In this way they can avoid the risk of a completed merger transaction later being investigated and ordered to be undone. There is a range of ways in which the CMA may give advice: informal advice, pre-notification discussions and statutory voluntary written notification (a 'Merger Notice'). These possible options indicate that the procedures under the Act are generally preventative rather than curative. Moreover, in respect of completed mergers, the CMA has powers to ensure that an inquiry will not be prejudiced, by maintaining the separation of the parties' businesses.

Informal advice/pre-notification discussions

Informal advice may be given in order to assist on the planning by companies and their advisers of possible mergers. This preliminary form of advice is confidential, based on the assumed accuracy of the information provided, and does not bind the CMA. At a slightly more advanced stage in the merger process, and where parties may seek to gauge whether undertakings in lieu (UILs) may be acceptable, the parties can seek pre-notification discussions as to whether a proposed transaction was likely to be referred for a Phase II investigation.

Statutory pre-notification: submitting a merger notice

Formal pre-notification procedures are contained in ss 96 and 97 of the Enterprise Act 2002. Full details of the merger, including market shares, financial information, and the intended timescale of the merger, must be given in a formal merger notice. Section 97(1) provides that the period for consideration of a merger notice is 40 days after receipt by the CMA. If this period expires without a reference being made, no subsequent reference can be made. The obvious advantage to the parties of proceeding with a merger notice under the statutory pre-notification procedure is that a final, formal decision should be guaranteed within 40 days. The procedure is only available if the merger proposals have been made public.

---

221 See OFT Press Release 162/06, 20 November 2006.
222 Section 33 provides for references of anticipated mergers.

The Phase 2 inquiry and report

Introduction

As of 1 April 1999 the Competition Commission replaced the MMC. Until the ERRA 13 it investigated and reported on references made to it under the merger provisions of the Enterprise Act 2002. In addition, the Act gave the Commission the authority to make and implement decisions with regard to most competition questions arising out of merger inquiries in the UK. As a result of the institutional changes introduced by the ERRA 2013, the Competition Commission's tasks in this context are now undertaken by CMA Panel Inquiry groups. In effect, the way of working in inquiry groups made up of independent experts has continued, but within the same overall organisation, the CMA, that also decides on whether a Phase 2 inquiry and report is necessary. The CMA's panel members come from a variety of professional and business backgrounds and reflect a mix of expertise and industry experience. For a Phase 2 inquiry a group will comprise at least three, and normally no more than five, members.

The Phase 2 inquiry

If a reference is made for a phase 2 inquiry, a CMA Inquiry group it is required to conduct an investigation and determine:

a   whether there is a qualifying merger situation; and
b   whether that merger situation has resulted, or may be expected to result, in a SLC.[223]

The Inquiry group is required to conduct its investigation and prepare and produce its report within twenty-four weeks of the reference, although this may be extended by no more than eight weeks. A merger reference may be laid aside if the merger has been abandoned following the reference.[224] Upon receiving a reference, four or five members, with a minimum of three, are appointed to form an inquiry group and one of the group is selected as Chairman. Each inquiry group has the ability to decide upon its own procedures; however, decisions must be made and published within statutory time limits. The main stages of inquiries are as follows:

a   gathering information, including the issue of questionnaires;
b   hearing witnesses;
c   verifying information;
d   providing an issues statement;
e   considering responses to the issues statement;
f   notifying parties of and publishing provisional findings, including notice of possible remedies;
g   considering exclusions from disclosure; and
h   publishing reports.

The CMA inquiry group will publish information on the CMA website explaining the purpose of the inquiry and inviting submissions of evidence. The inquiry group will specifically ask all interested parties including the main parties to the inquiry and third parties, such as competitors and consumer organisations about their views on the merger. The CMA will gain information by a variety of means including: letters and questionnaires; press notices; advertisements; surveys; and, visits to the principal parties. Unlike the merger laws of many countries there is no

---

223 Sections 35(1) and 36(1) in relation to completed and anticipated mergers, respectively.
224 Section 75(5).

requirement for mergers to be pre-notified to the CMA and there are separate provisions in the legislation to deal with completed mergers. Pending completion of any inquiry, and in order to prevent the outcome of a reference being frustrated by the parties' actions, the inquiry group may accept interim undertakings, under s 80, or adopt interim orders, under s 81.[225] This includes taking action to prevent pre-emptive steps that might prejudice the reference. It will normally consider the appointment of a Hold Separate Manager (HSM) and/or a monitoring trustee at the outset of an inquiry where a merger has already been completed in order to prevent the separate businesses being merged. A series of oral hearings, normally in private with the parties, may be held in order to confirm factual evidence obtained and to clarify issues arising in relation to the inquiry.

If there is no SLC finding in the CMA's final report, this is the culmination of the Stage II process. Otherwise, the CMA is required to consult on its provisional decisions and possible remedies. After the consultation process the Commission will publish its final report, following which the CMA will implement its remedies, as discussed further below.

The inquiry group is required to verify that the merger meets the statutory criteria for referral. The most contentious issue in most cases will involve the assessment of whether the merger satisfies the SLC test. In contrast with the 'realistic prospect' of an SLC at phase 1, the CMA decides at phase 2 whether the merger is more likely than not to lead to a SLC (on the 'balance of probabilities'). Before we proceed to consider this test, it is still relevant to review the merger investigation practice under the 1973 Act as, despite the different statutory framework, it still gives an idea of the types of competition issues, competition authority approaches and remedies to resolve them likely to be adopted in UK merger investigations.

Competition-related inquiries under the 1973 Act

The Fair Trading Act 1973 required the Competition Commission to report on whether the merger situation was expected to operate against the public interest. Section 84 of that Act provided a variety of factors which it should be taken into account in its evaluation of the public interest test. Notably, the promotion of competition was not the only factor to be considered and was not given pre-eminence over the other factors. Nonetheless, due to the overriding importance of the referral stage and the Tebbit doctrine, the Commission was inevitably constrained in the public interest issues upon which it could consider and report. The focus of the latter merger inquiries under the 1973 Act was on the potential anti-competitive consequences of referred mergers. Accordingly, despite the clear formulation of the new substantial lessening of competition test, it is still instructive to look at some examples under the 1973 Act for the types of market competition problems that are likely to arise, given the prominence afforded the 'competition' aspect of the public interest test in the latter years of its application.[226]

Many reports were about the takeover of bus services, particularly involving Stagecoach Holdings plc. For instance, in one report there was concern that the company would engage in predatory conduct and that in the long term, the company might raise prices or cut services.[227] The merger controls were also involved in the long running saga of the takeover of Strathclyde Buses Holdings Ltd (SB Holdings Ltd), based in Glasgow. The proposed takeover by FirstBus plc of SB Holdings Ltd was referred. The Commission noted that SB Holdings Ltd was the largest operator

---

225 There are similar powers available to the CMA under ss 71 and 72 of the Act.
226 For a fuller discussion, see Goodman, S, 'Steady as She Goes: The Enterprise Act 2002 Charts a Familiar Course for UK Merger Control Law' [2003] ECLR 331.
227 *Stagecoach/Ayrshire Bus (A1 Service)*, Cm 3032, 1995. See, also, [1996] ECLR R28; DTI P/95/772; and [1997] ECLR R104; DTI Press Release, P/97/293, confirming that undertakings had been accepted which remedied the Commission concerns. The Commission reported that, following the merger, there would be a modest loss of actual competition and a significant loss in potential competition between the two in commercial bus services and schools transport.

in Glasgow with over two-thirds of the market in certain districts. The merger was found to be contrary to the public interest because of the loss of actual and potential competition between the two bus companies. It was recommended that FirstBus should divest itself of another bus company, Midland Bluebird, and some of the operations of SB Holdings Ltd in order to allow the merger to proceed.[228] A proposed takeover by Robert Wiseman Dairies plc of Scottish Pride Holdings Ltd was also considered as likely to operate against the public interest, due to the proposed takeover's likely effect on competition in the supply of processed fresh milk to customers in Scotland, other than national supermarket group customers. The parties were found to have 80% of the wholesale market and, although national supermarket groups could prevent exploitation, other customers could not; therefore, the merger could lead to higher wholesale prices and possibly also increased retail prices.[229] Other examples include the report in connection with the *Bass/Carlsberg-Tetley* merger. In that report it was considered that the merger was likely to be anti-competitive by strengthening the companies' combined brand portfolios, and lead to a significant increase in market power, a conclusion similar to the conclusion in the high-profile *Ladbroke/Coral* merger. Ladbroke was required to divest Coral as the merger would damage competition and disadvantage punters.[230]

Probably the most high-profile merger investigation in the last 20 years involved the proposed acquisition of Manchester United by BSkyB.[231] The merger was blocked following the report which concluded that the proposed merger would reduce competition for the broadcast rights of Premier League matches.[232] In addition, the merger would adversely affect football in two ways: first, by reinforcing the trend towards greater inequality between football clubs; and secondly, by giving BSkyB influence which might not be in the long-term interest of football.

Another well-documented merger investigation arose in March 2003 when four supermarket operators (Asda Group Ltd, Wm Morrison Supermarkets plc, J Sainsbury plc and Tesco plc) competed to acquire Safeway plc. The report concluded that the acquisition by any of Asda, Sainsbury or Tesco would be anti-competitive and operate against the public interest, as such an acquisition would substantially reduce consumer choice.[233] A takeover by any of those three companies was expected to operate against the public interest at both a national and local level which, it was decided, could not be remedied by divestiture. Morrisons, however, could overcome local level competition concerns provided it could successfully negotiate undertakings relating to the divestment of 52 stores as recommended by the CC.

The substantial lessening of competition (SLC) test and CC practice

Following considerable debate over reform of the 1973 Act's public interest test an American-style SLC test was adopted in preference to the, then, EU dominance-based test. Although, in most cases, the application of both tests would lead to the same result, the SLC test should avoid the difficulties evidenced by the application of the collective dominance model under the 1989 Merger Regulation.[234] The Merger Assessment Guidelines require an assessment of the counterfactual: the competitive constraints on firms after the merger compared to the situation which would have been expected to prevail without the merger occurring. Clearly, the focus is on the

---

228 *FirstBus plc/SB Holdings Ltd*, Cm 3531, 1997. The Secretary of State granted FirstBus nine months to seek a buyer or divest its full interest in SB Holdings.
229 Cm 3504, 1996.
230 *Bass/Carlsberg-Tetley*, Cm 3662, 1997; [1997] ECLR R-132, *Ladbroke plc/Coral*, Cm 4030, 1998; DTI Press Release, P/98/713, 23 September 1998.
231 Cm 4305, 1999.
232 DTI Press Release, P/99/309, 9 April 1999.
233 *Safeway plc and Asda Group Ltd (owned by Wal-Mart Stores Inc); Wm Morrison Supermarkets plc; J Sainsbury plc; and Tesco plc – A Report on the Mergers in Contemplation*, Cm 5950, 2003.
234 See, for example, Case T-342/99 *Airtours v Commission* [2002] ECR II-2585; and Motta, M, 'EC Merger Policy and the *Airtours* Case' [2000] ECLR 199.

effects on competition likely to be produced by the merger in question. The CMA's approach in applying the text involves two stages: identification of the relevant market, and assessment of whether the merger would increase the market power of firms in the market. It will generally apply the hypothetical monopolist test to market definition. When assessing the competitive effects of a merger, the CMA will consider market shares and levels of market concentration in addition to looking at other structural factors, such as network effects. With particular reference to horizontal mergers, the CMA will concentrate on the likely impact of the merger on competitive rivalry. An example is the report in *Stena/P & O*,[235] which was the first report published under the 2002 Act provisions. The report blocked the transfer of the Liverpool–Dublin route to Stena, as the transfer would lead to a substantial lessening of competition in the central Irish Sea corridor and give Stena the scope to increase prices. However, the CMA will also seek to ascertain if there are any efficiency gains resulting from a merger, although these gains will: be required to happen within a short period of time; be a direct consequence of the merger; and increase rivalry between the remaining firms. As at the Phase 1 stage, the CMA will consider the likelihood of non-co-ordinated and co-ordinated effects of a merger, the latter being possible due to the greater interdependence between remaining competitors in an oligopolistic market. Finally, the CMA will consider a range of other potential competitive constraints, such as the possibility for entry and expansion on the market, or countervailing buyer/supplier power, which may offset the initial view that a merger will result in an SLC. In addition, the CMA may be required to examine a 'failing firm' justification for a merger, which would mean that the firm would be unable to meet its financial obligations in the near future and it would not be feasible for it to restructure itself successfully.

It is clear that not all Phase 2 inquiries lead to a finding that there is, or is likely to be a substantial lessening of competition.[236] For instance, in March 2006, the CC formally cleared the completed acquisition of HP Foods Group by Heinz, concluding that it was not expected to lead to a substantial lessening of competition within the markets for the supply of tomato ketchup, brown sauce, barbecue sauce, tinned baked beans and tinned pasta products in the UK, despite the referral based on concerns about higher prices for consumers as a result of the combination of the two largest branded sauce suppliers in the UK.[237] In relation to the market for tomato ketchup, it was found that the Daddies brand, owned by HP, did not provide any competitive constraint on the leading Heinz brand prior to the merger, and accordingly the merger would not alter the competitive situation. Again, in March 2006, the acquisition of the Greater Western Rail franchise by FirstGroup was cleared as only a few routes where buses and trains were in competition and therefore the profit incentive to shift passengers from bus to rail by raising fares or revising services was minimal.[238] In May 2006, the Waterstones/Ottakars merger was cleared on the basis that it would not lead to a substantial lessening of competition in the sale of new books to consumers in any part of the UK. There had been a vociferous campaign in Scotland to protect the independence of Ottakars, based on its role in supporting Scottish literature and culture, but these arguments were irrelevant in the context of the SLC test. Similarly, the proposed acquisition by AG Barr plc of Britvic plc was formally cleared in 2013 on the basis that the two companies'

---

235 *Stena AB and The Peninsular and Oriental Steam Navigation Company: A Report on the Proposed Acquisition of Certain Assets Relating to the Supply of Ferry Services on the Irish Sea between Liverpool–Dublin and Fleetwood–Larne*, 5 February 2004. See, also, the CC report on *FirstGroup plc and Scottish Rail Franchise*, 28 June 2004, which concluded that the merger might be expected to result in a SLC and adverse effects such as higher bus fares, poorer services and a loss of choice to passengers, mainly in the Glasgow and Edinburgh areas.
236 See PWC report for the OFT 'Ex Post Evaluation of Mergers', assessing ten merger clearance decisions by the CC, at www.competition-commission.org.uk/our_role/evaluation/ex_post_evaluation_of_mergers.pdf.
237 See Competition Commission, Final Report, *HJ Heinz and HP Foods*, 24 March 2006.
238 See Competition Commission, Final Report, *FirstGroup plc and the Greater Western Passenger Rail franchise*, 8 March 2006.

brands were not close competitors, notwithstanding both were active in a range of carbonated and non-carbonated soft drink brands.[239] However, the parties did not proceed with the merger, which would have brought Barr's Irn Bru and Orangina brands together with Britvic's J2O, Fruit Shoot, Tango and Pepsi.[240]

There have been a number of inquiries, in addition to Stena/P & O, under the Enterprise Act provisions, which have necessitated remedial action. In relation to the acquisition by Somerfield of 115 stores from Morrison supermarkets, the fifth and fourth largest supermarkets, respectively in the UK at that time, a September 2005 Report considered that the acquisition would lead to a substantial lessening of competition in 12 local grocery markets in Great Britain, and ordered Somerfield to divest 12 of its stores to suitable retailers approved by the Commission.[241] The starting point was that Somerfield should divest itself of the disputed acquired stores, or satisfactory alternatives. This demonstrates that the UK merger control process often concerned with competitive effects in localised markets. Another example is the report in February 2006 into the acquisition of six multiplex cinemas in the UK by Vue Entertainment Holdings (Ltd) ('Vue'). It was concluded that Vue would be required to sell one of two cinemas in Basingstoke, one it already owned and one it had acquired, to avoid the higher prices and reduced choice for consumers in that area as a result of the merger.[242] Similar issues have arisen in relation to subsequent proposed takeovers of smaller cinema chains; for instance, Cineworld and City Screen where the competitive consequences were focused in Aberdeen, Bury St Edmunds and Cambridge.[243] In October 2006, the joint venture between Stagecoach, with its Megabus brand, and Scottish Citylink, was considered to be likely to lead to a substantial lessening of competition on the 'Saltire Cross' routes (Glasgow–Aberdeen and Edinburgh–Inverness routes, which cross at Perth). The removal of competition between Megabus and Scottish Citylink could have led to higher fares and reduced service levels, and the sale of certain services was required.[244] A later inquiry, in 2009, which subsequently became very contentious, concluded that the takeover by Stagecoach of Preston Bus Ltd would reduce competition and potentially harm passenger interests, and required Stagecoach to sell the business.[245] In another transport services inquiry, it was concluded in 2013 that by adding ferry services to its Channel Tunnel business Eurotunnel would increase its market share to over 50% and prices would rise. Accordingly, the acquisition of ferries and assets from a former ferry operator would lead to a SLC.[246] Also in 2013, it was considered that Ryanair's minority shareholding of 29.8% in Aer Lingus would lead to a SLC, primarily because of the tension inherent in Ryanair's dual position as a competitor with and largest shareholder in Aer Lingus.[247]

Remedial action

If the inquiry group decides that there is an anti-competitive outcome from a merger, the CMA has to decide what action should be taken. The CMA may exercise its order-making powers

239 See Competition Commission, Final Report, *AG BARR plc/Britvic plc*, 9 July 2013.
240 See also for instance, other clearances, for example: Competition Commission, Final Report, *Kerry Foods Ltd/Headland Foods Ltd merger inquiry*, 2 December 2011; and, Competition Commission, Final Report, *Brightsolid Group Ltd and Friends Reunited Holdings Ltd*, 18 March 2010.
241 Competition Commission, Acceptance of Final Undertakings, *Somerfield plc/Wm Morrison*, 9 March 2006.
242 Competition Commission, Final Report, *Vue Entertainment Holdings (UK) Ltd and A3 Cinema Ltd*, 24 February 2006.
243 See Competition Commission, Final Report, *Cineworld Group plc and City Screen Ltd*, 8 October 2013.
244 Competition Commission, Final Report, *Stagecoach and Scottish Citylink*, 23 October 2006.
245 See Competition Commission, Final Report, Stagecoach Group Plc/Preston Bus Ltd Merger Inquiry, 11 November 2009.
246 See Competition Commission, Final Report, *Groupe Eurotunnel SA and SeaFrance SA merger inquiry*, 6 June 2013. It should be noted that following a CAT judgment in December 2013 (*Groupe Eurotunnel SA v Competition Commission*, [2013] CAT 30), the issue was remitted to the Competition Commission.
247 See Competition Commission, Final Report, *Ryanair Holdings plc and Aer Lingus Group plc*, 28 August 2013.

or accept undertakings from parties, under ss 82 and 84 of the 2002 Act, respectively. These possibilities are broadly similar to the twin remedies available originally under the 1973 Act although under that legislation, the power to make remedies lay with the Secretary of State and he could ignore the findings of a merger investigation report.[248] Under the 2002 Act the CMA has the primary role for taking remedial action following a market investigation. It has a duty, under s 41, to take such action as is reasonable and practicable under ss 82 and 84 to remedy, mitigate or prevent the substantial lessening of competition concerned and any adverse effects resulting therefrom.[249] In doing so, the CMA is required to 'have regard to the need to achieve as comprehensive a solution as is reasonable and practicable'.[250] Schedule 8 to the 2002 Act specifies what may be included in an order, although there are no statutory limits on the CMA's power to obtain undertakings. The types of remedy which may generally be available include: divestiture of a business or assets; removal of entry barriers by requiring know-how licensing; either the discontinuance or the adoption of specific behaviour; or the imposition of a price cap, or monitoring of prices and profits. The Act allows the CMA to take into account, when deciding on appropriate remedial action, any customer benefits derived from the market feature, such as lower prices, higher quality or choice of goods and greater innovation.[251] The CMA has adopted the Guidance on Merger Remedies introduced by the Competition Commission, which provides detailed guidance and information on the remedies available and their appropriateness in the event of a SLC finding.[252] The starting point is that the CMA would prefer a structural remedy to behavioural solutions, as they are more direct than behavioural remedies in seeking to restore effective rivalry and impacting on the SLC, and they normally do not require monitoring and enforcement once implemented.

In the first two full inquiries under the Enterprise Act 2002 provisions, *Stena/P & O* and *FirstGroup/Scottish Rail Franchise*, the new remedial powers were exercised by clearing the mergers, subject to undertakings being given to meet the competition concerns in each situation. Following the *Vue cinema* report, Vue gave undertakings to ensure the effective sale of one of the two Basingstoke cinemas it owned, including the appointment of a divestiture trustee to oversee the process. Similar undertakings were given following the Stagecoach/Scottish Citylink joint venture to divest either the 'Scottish Citylink' or 'Megabus'-branded operations on the Saltire Cross route group. Following the *Preston Bus* inquiry, Stagecoach completed the sale of Preston Bus Ltd to a third party in accordance with undertakings given by it following the CC Report.[253] In 2013, Ryanair was forced to reduce its shareholding in Aer Lingus down to 5% from its 29.8% stake. It should be noted that for any remedial action to follow, a decision that there is an anti-competitive outcome must be taken by at least two-thirds of the members of the CMA inquiry group. This is the same requirement as under the Fair Trading Act 1973.[254] The CMA is required to monitor undertakings and orders following a merger investigation report.

---

248 For instance, following the Commission's majority report on *Charter Consolidated/Anderson Strathclyde*, Cmnd 8711, 1982, the Secretary of State decided to allow the bid to go ahead. This refusal to accept the Commission's findings was challenged by judicial review. However, the challenge was rejected by the Court, which confirmed that the final decision in a merger case rested with the Minister: *R v Secretary of State for Trade and Industry ex p Anderson Strathclyde plc* [1983] 2 All ER 233, DC.

249 Section 41(2).

250 Section 41(4).

251 Section 134(7)–(8).

252 CC8, 'Merger Remedies: Competition Commission Guidelines', November 2008.

253 See, Competition Commission, Final Undertakings, *Completed Acquisition By Stagecoach Group plc of Preston Bus Limited*, 1 February 2010. However, see below regarding subsequent judicial review of the Competition Commission's decision-making process.

254 *Scottish Milk: A Report on the Supply of Fresh Processed Milk to Middle Ground Retailers in Scotland*, Cm 5002, 2000. DTI Press Release, P/2000/863, 22 December 2000.

Review

Any decision by the CMA (or Secretary of State) at any stage under Pt 3 of the 2002 Act is subject to judicial review by the CAT and thereafter on appeal to the Court of Appeal in England and Wales and the Court of Session in Scotland.[255] The first application for judicial review took place in *IBA Health Ltd v OFT*,[256] outlined in the section above, on the duty to refer. The next two challenges also involved mergers in the pharmaceutical industry. First, in *Unichem Ltd v OFT*, Unichem sought review of the decision not to refer the proposed acquisition by Phoenix of East Anglian Pharmaceuticals Ltd ('EAP') in relation to the supply of prescription-only medicines.[257] Referral of an earlier proposed merger involving AAH and EAP had led to its abandonment, and confidential guidance subsequently provided to Unichem was to the effect that any acquisition by it of EAP would result in a reference. Overall, despite acknowledging the margin of judgment or evaluation available on the facts in the decision whether to make a reference, the CAT could not be satisfied that all material considerations had been taken into account in taking the decision not to refer. It accordingly quashed that decision and the issue was referred back for reconsideration.[258] In *Celesio v OFT*,[259] a third party sought review of the OFT's decision to negotiate undertakings with the parties in the proposed Boots/Unichem merger rather than make a reference, where the OFT considered that there was a realistic prospect of a substantial lessening of competition. This application was unanimously rejected by the CAT, confirming the approach set out by the Court of Appeal in *IBA Health Ltd v OFT*. The first challenge to an OFT decision by a merging party was unsuccessful in *Co-operative Group (CWS) Ltd v OFT*.[260] The OFT had earlier accepted an undertaking in lieu of reference, but refused purchaser approval on the basis that it would not satisfy the undertakings' requirement for a proposed purchaser to be independent and unconnected to the acquiring party. The CAT held that the OFT's decision was reasonable and supported the OFT's approach that remedies should restore competition to the pre-merger levels. The first challenge to an inquiry group decision followed the September 2005 Report in relation to the acquisition by Somerfield of 115 stores from Morrison supermarkets, which concluded that the acquisition would lead to a substantial lessening of competition in 12 local grocery markets in Great Britain. Somerfield was required to divest itself of the disputed acquired stores or alternatives satisfactory to the inquiry group. In *Somerfield plc v Competition Commission*,[261] the CAT considered this to be a reasonable approach and rejected the applicant's submission that they should be free to choose which stores to divest. In *Stericycle International LLC and others v Competition Commission*,[262] the applicants sought review of an inquiry group decision contained in an interim order. In this case, the inquiry group required the appointment of a hold separate manager (HSM), on the basis of concerns regarding the substantial integration of the two businesses and the strong incentives for management to operate the acquired business on behalf of the acquirer, and the potential ensuing difficulties if divestiture was to be required. The CAT dismissed the application as the inquiry group had taken its decision that an HSM was necessary in the public interest and within its margin of appreciation. In *Stagecoach v Competition Commission*,

---

255 For an example of the (unsuccessful) use of the provisions for judicial review, see the legal saga in Ryanair/Aer Lingus at *Ryanair Holdings v Competition Commission* [2012] CAT 21, and *Ryanair Holdings v Competition Commission* [2012] EWCA Civ 1632, involving two unsuccessful judicial review applications before the CAT and the Court of Appeal in relation to two distinct phases of the inquiry process.

256 [2003] CAT 27; on appeal *OFT v IBA Health Ltd* [2004] EWCA Civ 142, 19 February.

257 [2005] CAT 8.

258 The OFT reassessed the issue and subsequently decided again that the merger would not be expected to result in a SLC and that it would not be referred to the Commission; see OFT, *Anticipated acquisition by Phoenix Healthcare Distribution Limited of East Anglian Pharmaceuticals Ltd*, 29 June 2005.

259 [2006] CAT 9.

260 [2007] CAT 24.

261 [2006] CAT 4.

262 [2006] CAT 21.

in relation to the *Preston Bus* inquiry, the CAT held that the there was no evidence to support certain factual conclusions in the report and consequently that the remedy required was not proportionate.[263] The CAT can deal with a successful judicial review application in a number of ways. In *Groupe Eurotunnel SA v Competition Commission*,[264] the CAT remitted the question whether there was a qualifying merger to the Competition Commission on the basis that two enterprises had in fact ceased to be distinct. In *CTS Eventim AG v Competition Commission*, the applicant, a provider of ticketing services, ticket agent and promoter of live music events sought review of a decision to give unconditional clearance to the merger between two of its competitors, Ticketmaster Entertainment Inc and Live Nation, Inc. On the basis that the applicant had been denied the right to a fair hearing and, in particular, the right to comment on the provisional findings. The CAT quashed the report and referred the matter back to the Competition Commission.[265]

Decisions by the Secretary of State under the statutory scheme for special public interest mergers are also subject to potential judicial review by the CAT.[266] This was demonstrated in relation to the *LloydsTSB/HBOS* merger in *Merger Action Group v Secretary of State for BERR*,[267] which was approved by the Secretary of State. That case was interesting as the CAT considered that the scope of 'aggrieved persons' who could seek judicial review extended to the group of applicants on the basis that there were all resident in Scotland, some of whom (or their business or families) had bank accounts or received banking services in Scotland, and all had a generalised consumer interest in UK banking. The limits of judicial review were clear as the application was ultimately dismissed on the basis that the Secretary of State had not fettered his discretion in taking the decision.

Key Points

- Mergers can have both beneficial and anti-competitive effects. A merger between two companies competing in a market may be anti-competitive as it will reduce the number of competitors and lead to an increase in prices or reduced choice for consumers. Horizontal mergers are particularly problematic in markets where there are already few competitors, but vertical and conglomerate mergers may also raise competition concerns.
- The EU merger control rules are found in Regulation 139/2004. Any merger (termed a 'concentration') with a 'Community dimension' (based on turnover thresholds) must be notified to the European Commission for approval. The Regulation creates a 'one-stop shop' whereby Community dimension mergers only have to be notified and approved by the European Commission rather than by various Member State NCAs. This simplifies the process of merger approval, but retains some flexibility for mergers to be referred to and dealt with by Member State NCAs.
- Mergers have to be suspended when notified. The substantive test is whether there is likely to be a significant impediment to effective competition ('SIEC test'). Commission merger investigations are in two possible phases. Most mergers are cleared after the short Phase 1. If a merger passes to Phase 2, the parties will often have to offer remedies to the Commission to approve the merger.

---

263 [2010] CAT 14.
264 [2013] CAT 30.
265 [2010] CAT 7.
266 See also subsequent unsuccessful judicial review application in *BSkyB v Competition Commission and Secretary of State for BERR* [2008] CAT 25. At the Court of Appeal, the appeal on the competition points was dismissed, and although the appeal on the media plurality issue was allowed, this did not affect the outcome – [2010] EWCA Civ 2.
267 [2008] CAT 36; see Rodger, B, '*Merger Action Group v. Secretary of State for BERR*: External Control of the Scottish Economy, Merger Control and the Scottish "Ring-fence": The LloydsTSB/HBOS Merger' [2009] *Competition Policy International* 2–7.

- Where a merger raises serious competition concerns, parties will usually make structural commitments, such as divestment or sale of part of a business to allow the deal to proceed. Very few mergers lead to a final prohibition decision. The Commission decision-making process is subject to review by the European Courts.
- UK merger control is set out in Part III of the Enterprise Act 2002. The Competition and Markets Authority can deal with any qualifying merger although notification is not mandatory. The substantive test for assessment of mergers in the UK is whether a merger will lead to a substantial lessening of competition (the 'SLC test'). There are special provisions for public interest mergers.
- UK merger control also has two phases, and if the CMA Mergers Unit considers a merger raises serious competition concerns, and undertakings in lieu of reference are not offered or accepted, it will refer the merger to an inquiry group which will undertake a full merger investigation, and publish a report on its outcomes including, where appropriate, any necessary remedies. Normally, these will be structural remedies to ensure competition in the market for the longer term. All aspects of the UK merger control process are subject to judicial review by the Competition Appeal Tribunal.

Discussion

1   There are no grounds for interfering with the market for corporate control except where a serious risk to competition is likely to arise from any merger. Discuss.
2   How has the Merger Regulation proved to be a useful additional tool in the Commission's competition law armoury?
3   Does the 'fine-tuning' of case allocation under Arts 4, 9 and 22 of the Merger Regulation fundamentally damage the 'one-stop shop'?
4   Outline the distinction between a dominance based-test and a SIEC test under EU merger control.
5   The mantra 'removing politics from UK merger control' is unachievable. Discuss.
6   To what extent have the Enterprise Act 2002 and the Enterprise and Regulatory Reform Act 2013 radically reformed the institutions involved in and substance of UK merger control?

Further Reading

General

Davies, S and Lyons, B, *Mergers and Merger Remedies in the EU* (2008) Edward Elgar.
Kokkoris, I and Shelanski, H, *EU Merger Control: A Legal and Economic Analysis* (2014) Oxford: OUP.
Parker, J and Majumdar, A *UK Merger Control* (2011) Oxford: Hart Publishing.

EU Merger Regulation

Burnley, R, 'Who's afraid of Conglomerate Mergers? A Comparison of the US and EC Approaches' (2005) 28(1) World Comp 43.
Connolly, J, Rab, S and McElwee, M, 'Pre-Notification Referral under the EC Merger Regulation: Simplifying the Route to the One-stop Shop' [2007] ECLR 167.
Fountoukakos, K and Ryan, S, 'A New Substantive Test for EU Merger Control' [2005] ECLR 277.
Iversen, H, 'The Efficiency Defence in EC Merger Control' [2010] ECLR 370–376.
Maudhuit, S and Soames, T, 'Changes in EU Merger Control' 3 parts: Part 1 [2005] ECLR 57; Part 2 [2005] ECLR 75; Part 3 [2005] ECLR 144.
Nikpay, A and Houwen, F, 'Tour de Force or a Little Local Turbulence? A Heretical View on the Airtours Judgment' [2003] ECLR 193.
Schmidt, J, 'The New ECMR: "Significant Impediment" or "Significant Improvement"?' (2004) 41(6) CMLRev 1555.

UK merger control

Goodman, S, 'Steady as She Goes: The Enterprise Act Charts a Familiar Course for UK Merger Control' [2003] ECLR 331.

Parr, N, 'The Competition Commission, Merger Control and the SLC Test' Chapter 8 in Rodger, B (ed), *Ten Years of UK Competition Law Reform* (2010) Dundee: DUP.

Rodger, BJ, 'UK Merger Control: Politics, the Public Interest and Reform' [2000] ECLR 24.

Todorovic, T, 'The Reform of the UK Merger Regime in the Enterprise and Regulatory Reform Act 2013 – Not Much to Shout About?' (2013) Comp LJ 12(3) 338–352.

Went, D, 'Recent Developments in UK Merger Control – Establishment of Solid Foundations for the New Regime' [2007] ECLR 627.

Glossary of Key Competition-related Terms

allocative efficiency A distribution of resources whereby the resources are put into the production of goods that customers want most, in the quantities they require. Through the most efficient allocation of resources, goods will be produced to meet demand at the lowest possible price.

anti-competitive Behaviour that is considered to be contrary to the prevailing competition rules. For instance, under EU law, note the possibility of anti-competitive agreements or anti-competitive abusive conduct. The term anti-competitive has no fixed meaning and depends largely on the rules of the relevant legal system.

antitrust US competition law is usually known as antitrust law. The name is taken from the trust companies that were prevalent at the time of the adoption of the Sherman Act in 1890. Trust companies formalised large cartels which antitrust law was designed to prevent. In the EU, antitrust is used to refer to the practice surrounding the Art 101 and 102 TFEU prohibitions.

barrier to entry A cost or obstacle that falls upon entrants to a market but which does not fall on existing market operators. There is a debate whether a barrier to entry is restricted to a cost that was not borne by existing operators when they entered the market, or is simply a cost that must be borne by new entrants before they can enter a market

cartel A group of undertakings which, usually through agreement or understanding, act together in a market. By acting together they can, in effect, act as a monopoly and fix prices or allocate markets.

Chicago school A school of antitrust economics that developed at the University of Chicago and came to prominence in the 1960s. Its proponents believe that free markets are the most effective way to decide upon the allocation of resources. They also take a non-interventionist stance over the regulation of 'free' markets through the law.

collective dominance An alternative term, adopted under EU competition law, to denote the collective power of oligopolists. Collective dominance by a group of undertakings may, where there is abusive conduct, be dealt with under Art 102 TFEU.

collusion A generic term for any form of agreement or understanding reached between competitors.

compartmentalisation of markets A concept related to the market integration goal within EU competition law. The concern is that certain types of agreement, for example, networks of distribution agreements, will be organised along national boundaries, in effect separating national markets from each other, thereby defeating the aim of the internal market.

concentration The generic term adopted under EU law to cover mergers, takeovers and joint ventures. What constitutes a concentration is determined under the Merger Regulation.

consumer welfare The description given to the economic goal of much contemporary antitrust law. Its exact meaning is a matter of controversy and debate, but in the European conception it is usually taken to mean all forms of efficiency in markets that generate benefits for customers and final consumers in the medium term.

cross-elasticity of demand The degree of influence the price of one good has on the demand for another. If cross-elasticity between goods is high, a reduction in price of good X will cause a drop in demand for good Y. The fall in price of good X encourages customers to use it at the expense of good Y. A high cross-elasticity of demand indicates that goods are substitutable.

demand-side substitutability The extent to which the consumer will regard different products as substitutes for each other. The legal test adopted on the basis of this economic test is referred to as interchangeability.

direct effect This doctrine means that certain EU law provisions give rise to rights and obligations that may be enforced by individuals before their national courts.

dominant position The classic definition is that it is a position of economic strength enjoyed by an undertaking, which enables the undertaking to prevent effective competition being maintained on the relevant market by affording the undertaking the power to behave, to an appreciable extent, independently of its competitors, customers and ultimately of its consumers.

economic entity doctrine This doctrine may require legally distinct companies to be considered as one undertaking, for the purposes of EU law, where they are not independent from each other, for example, in a parent/subsidiary situation. The doctrine requires an examination of the managerial and economic independence of the undertakings in question.

effects doctrine This doctrine provides that a legal system's competition laws are applicable where the action or behaviour takes place outside the jurisdiction but produces economic effects on markets within the jurisdiction. It is unclear whether or not the doctrine applies under EU competition law. It is inapplicable under UK competition law.

essential facility This concept is relevant under EU competition law in the context of refusals to supply, which may be deemed abusive under Art 102 TFEU. Certain types of infrastructure, such as a national electricity grid or computer reservation systems, may be considered to constitute an essential facility, such that access is essential for competition to develop, and the refusal to allow access to the facility may amount to abusive behaviour.

exclusive distribution This is a form of distribution whereby a producer agrees with a distributor to supply only to that distributor within a particular territory. This is a type of agreement involving vertical restraints.

exclusive purchasing This is a type of agreement requiring an exclusive commitment by the purchaser to purchase goods of that type only from the vendor. It is often known as a 'single-branding' agreement. Such commitments are frequently associated with exclusive distribution agreements

free-rider The free-rider rationale is associated with the debate on the merits of vertical restraints and the rationale suggests that some form of intra-brand protection is necessary to allow a distributor to promote a brand effectively and thereby enhance inter-brand competition. The basic idea is that, without a degree of exclusivity, competitors of the distributor would take a free-ride on the distributor's advertising and promotional outlays and be able to sell the product at a cheaper price.

game theory A mathematical or economic analysis of decision-making, which attempts to predict the results of a situation as if it were a game of strategy. For each event, a prediction can be made based on the state of knowledge of the players at the time of the decision and their knowledge of earlier events.

Harvard school This school of antitrust analysis had its origins in the 1930s and it placed emphasis on market structure as the root of market failure, by exploring the link between market structure, conduct and performance, stressing that excessive concentration of market power resulted in undeservedly high profits.

intellectual property rights These are types of property rights, normally granted by national legal systems, which give the holder or owner the exclusive power to exploit the property. Examples are patents, trade marks and copyright. These exclusive property rights may come into conflict with the application of competition law.

inter-brand competition The competition between different brands of competing goods.

intra-brand competition Competition, normally between market operators at the same level of the market, for example, between two distributors, in relation to one brand of product.

joint ventures (concentrative and co-operative) These involve the setting up of a company by two or more separate parent companies. The formation of the joint venture and the roles undertaken by the various parties can vary greatly. The distinction between concentrative and co-operative joint ventures, made by the Commission under the Merger Regulation, is now less significant. A concentrative joint venture is a full function joint venture performing, on a lasting basis, all the functions of an autonomous economic entity, and will be assessed by the Commission under the Merger Regulation. All other joint ventures are co-operative as they give rise to the threat of the co-ordination of competitive behaviour between the parent companies or between the parent companies and the joint venture and are considered under Art 101 TFEU.

margin squeeze Anti-competitive behaviour where a vertically integrated dominant firm controls the input to a downstream market, and also directly operates downstream. As the main supplier to its own downstream competitors, it can raise the price it charges for the input product to near the retail price its charges its own customers. It can thereby squeeze out the potential profit margin of its competitors.

market integration One of the key goals of EU competition policy to create an integrated Internal Market across all the Member States. The desire to create such a market shapes the EU's definition of, and response to, anti-competitive conduct.

merger (horizontal, vertical, conglomerate) The term connotes both a welcome uncontested union between two or more parties and, equally, a hostile takeover. In addition, merger control will normally also cover differing degrees and forms of transfer of control of an undertaking, normally via the transfer of shares or assets. A horizontal merger involves parties at the same level of the market, such as two producers. Vertical mergers involve parties at different levels of the market, such as a producer and a distributor. Conglomerate mergers bring together unassociated types of business, often in a portfolio of company purchases by a holding company.

monopoly A market structure where, in theoretical terms, one producer controls 100% of production or the supply of services (monopsony exists where one purchaser takes 100% of the goods produced or services supplied). Such a level of control is unlikely to exist in practice without governmental involvement, and the term is more generally used to refer to producers or service providers who have achieved a high level of control of a market.

multiple filing A situation in which a business is forced to go through a number of similar administrative procedures for a single transaction in more than one national or supranational jurisdiction, for instance, in several Member States regarding the same merger. The requirement to file similar notifications in more than one jurisdiction is seen as wasteful and likely to encourage divergent results. Its avoidance is one of the benefits of the 'one-stop shop'.

oligopolistic interdependence The theory of oligopolistic interdependence asserts that, due to the limited number of parties involved in an oligopolistic market, the parties will each be able to derive a monopolist's excess profit without having to conspire together or form a prohibited cartel, as a result of the combination of the profit-maximising motive and their mutual self-awareness on the market.

oligopoly A type of market where the majority of production is by a group of a few suppliers, none of which is dominant, but all of which are relatively large (oligopsony involves a limited number of purchasers, and duopoly exists where there are only two producers). A market that is characterised by the existence of an oligopoly is known as an oligopolistic market. Although oligopolistic markets will be different, they will tend to have similar features. There will usually be a small number of sizeable undertakings operating in a market with homogeneous products. The market may also be characterised by limited price competition and parallel behaviour.

one-stop shop A single agency that deals with all the regulatory matters in an area. The term is usually connected with EU merger control where the Commission took over responsibility for large scale mergers from the Member States' national authorities, creating a single regulatory system.

passing off A common law action in the UK providing a remedy where the public are confused into thinking that the goods marketed are, in fact, produced by someone else, thereby unfairly benefiting the party marketing the goods, which profits from the goodwill of someone else.

per se A Latin phrase meaning 'by or in itself or themselves'. In a competition law context this phrase normally suggests that a particular type of market activity or agreement will be illegal without any further requirement to investigate and assess its economic impact.

perfect competition The theoretical neoclassical model of competition, which results in optimum allocative and productive efficiency. The model has certain prerequisites. It must be in relation to a homogeneous product, there must exist an infinite number of buyers and sellers, there must be free entry to and free exit from the market, and there must be full information available to consumers, allowing them to make rational decisions. Because real markets rarely meet the prerequisites, the model is virtually unknown in practice.

predatory pricing A pricing strategy whereby a powerful operator reduces its prices to near or below cost, to drive a competitor out of the market.

relevant market In order to determine an undertaking's market strength, one must define exactly which market the undertaking is competing in; that market is known as the relevant market. This is normally the first stage in any competition inquiry into dominance, particularly under EU law. It is also relevant for merger inquiries and under Art 101 TFEU. The relevant market is itself divided into three parts: product market, geographical market and temporal market.

restrictive trade practices legislation In the UK the area of law dealing with the problems associated with cartels and other anti-competitive agreements has traditionally been known as restrictive trade practices legislation. This legislation has been repealed by the Competition Act 1998.

rule of reason A term derived from US antitrust law, the rule of reason approach runs counter to the *per se* approach. It requires a detailed economic analysis of an agreement, the market structure and market conditions in order to assess the likely pro- and anti-competitive effects. It increases the complexity of antitrust/competition law enforcement and reduces certainty and predictability. It has been partially adopted by the EU authorities.

selective distribution A type of distribution system whereby a manufacturer chooses its authorised distributors according to qualitative criteria. If a potential distributor meets the criteria, the potential distributor should be allowed to distribute the product.

state aid There are specific EU rules in the Treaty on state aid. It is defined as aid, normally financial, to companies by public authorities of Member States. The aid can vary from state subsidies and capital injections to exemptions from taxation and loan guarantees. State aid can jeopardise the level competitive playing field in the EU.

supply-side substitutability Otherwise referred to as supply-side interchangeability. This involves consideration by the competition authorities of the extent to which other suppliers, currently manufacturing other products, can quickly, and without major expenditure, begin producing a product which is substitutable. This possible alternative supply is known as potential competition and is relevant in assessing the likely competitive pressures on the supplier under consideration.

tacit collusion A phenomenon found in oligopolistic markets whereby the undertakings involved act in a parallel manner through enlightened self-interest after they become aware that they are highly interdependent. There is no need for communication between the undertakings for tacit collusion to occur.

tie-ins Transactions where a seller insists on selling additional products, tied products, to buyers of another product, tying products. Such a transaction forces the buyer to accept products that it did not want or could have acquired at a lower price elsewhere.

vertical integration Where a producer has control over many stages of the production and/or marketing of a product. For instance, the producer may control the supply of raw materials, processing, manufacture, transport and distribution, rather than operating at only one level of the market.

vertical restraints These are the contractual restrictions employed in vertical agreements, made between undertakings operating at different levels of the market, to facilitate the distribution of goods and services. An example would be an exclusive distributorship requirement in a distribution agreement.

workable competition A level of competition that falls short of 'perfect competition', but which produces a reasonable level of allocative efficiency. The prerequisites of perfect competition do not have to be present, but an efficient scale of production will be reached with genuine alternatives for consumers and without overcapacity for producers. The concept is difficult to define in detailed terms, but is an obtainable policy goal somewhere between perfect competition and monopoly.

Index

A

Aberdeen Journalists Ltd v DGFT 132
abuse of dominance 92
    abusive conduct 107–8
    collective dominance 104–7, 261–3
    dominant position 95–104
    exclusionary abuse 110–25
    exploitative abuse 108–10
    TFEU Article 102 92–3, 125–7
    TFEU Article 106(2) 127
    undertakings and effect on interstate trade
        93–5
    see also Chapter II prohibition
access to file, European Commission
        enforcement 50–1
Albion Water Ltd v Water Services Regulation Authority
        134–5
allocative efficiency 9
anti-competition agreements
    1976 legislation and reform 183–4
    block exemptions 180–2
    vertical agreements block exemption
        regulation (VABER) 201–3
    vertical restraints 194–200
    see also Chapter I prohibition
    TFEU Article 101

B

barriers to entry 101–3
    conduct 103
    economies of scale 102
    financial resources 102
    legal provisions 102
    product differentiation 103
    technological advantage 102
    vertical integration 103
barriers to trade, prevention of 17
behavioural economics 20
BetterCare II 132–3
BIS and draft Consumer Rights Bill 87–8

block exemptions (anti-competition
        agreements) 180–2
    see also vertical agreements block exemption
        regulation (VABER)
Bork, Robert 13–14
bundling, tying and 118–19
Burgess v OFT 133–4

C

cartel offence 226–8, 234–5
cartels 3, 5–7, 212–13
    administrative corporate fines 218–21
    Competition Disqualification Orders (CDO)
        228, 234–5
    contemporary view 216
    damages 222–5
    definitions 212–13
    direct settlement 235–6
    disqualification 64–5, 225–8
    early EU provisions 215
    enforcement: deterrence and compliance
        188
    future of regulation 237–8
    history in Europe 213–14
    increasing likelihood of catching 228–9
    increasing punishment 288
    individual penalties 225–8
    investigations 64–5
    legal challenges 215–16
    leniency policies 42, 60–1, 229–35
    optimal deterrence 217–18
    punishment 218–28
    secret horizontal 188–9
case law
    abuse of dominance 130–8
    anti-competition agreements 188–94
    private enforcement 86
Chapter I prohibition (anti-competition
        agreements) 184–8
    agreements and concerted practices 185–6